W9-DJB-735

Making the European Monetary Union

Making the European Monetary Union

The Role of the Committee of Central Bank Governors and the Origins of the European Central Bank

Harold James

With a Foreword by Mario Draghi and Jaime Caruana

THE BELKNAP PRESS OF
HARVARD UNIVERSITY PRESS
Cambridge, Massachusetts
London, England
2012

EMMA S. CLARK MEMORIAL LIBRARY
Setauket, L.I., New York 11733

Copyright © 2012 by the Bank for International Settlements
All rights reserved
Printed in the United States of America

The Bank for International Settlements and the European Central Bank do
not warrant or guarantee the accuracy, completeness, or fitness for purpose
of any of the material reproduced in this publication, and shall in no
circumstances be liable for any loss, damage, liability, or expense suffered by
any person in connection with reliance by that person on such material.

Library of Congress Cataloging-in-Publication Data

James, Harold, 1956–
    Making the European monetary union / Harold James.
      p. cm.
    Includes bibliographical references and index.
    ISBN 978-0-674-06683-0 (alk. paper)
    1. Economic and Monetary Union.   2. Monetary unions—European
Union countries.   3. Monetary policy—European Union countries.
4. Europe—Economic integration.   I. Title.

HG3894.J36 2012
332.4'94—dc23   2012015210

Contents

Figures

Foreword

European monetary union came to fruition with the creation of the European Central Bank on June 1, 1998, followed by the introduction of the Euro on January 1, 1999. Euro banknotes and coins were issued on January 1, 2002. Behind this achievement lay a unique process of monetary cooperation and unification that was set in motion by the 1957 Treaty of Rome. As this initiative was driven primarily by the political will to give the Common Market a stable monetary anchor and to set Europe on course toward an ever closer integration, it was only natural that the political decisionmakers were the key players. These included the heads of states and governments acting through the European Council; the European Commission and the EU Monetary Committee working from Brussels; and the European Parliament and the national parliaments. A very important role was also played by the central banks of the European Economic Community (later European Union) member states and particularly by the central bank governors. As guardians of monetary and financial stability at the national level, the central banks were directly affected by the European monetary cooperation and unification process. However, their specific contribution since the late 1950s is neither widely known nor well understood, either in academic circles or by the broader public.

In order to fill this gap, in 2008 the European Central Bank (ECB) and the Bank for International Settlements (BIS) commissioned the present historical study by a renowned expert, Professor Harold James. The forum in which EU governors cooperated and prepared for monetary union was the Committee of Governors of the Central Banks of the Member States of the European Economic Community (Committee of Governors for short), created in 1964 by a European Council decision. As the Committee of Governors played such an important role in the European monetary unification process over three decades (1964–1993), it was felt it deserved a history of its own. Somewhat surprisingly, the Committee of Governors held its regular meetings at the BIS in Basel,

Switzerland, that is to say outside the European Union, until its successor—the European Monetary Institute (EMI)—moved to Frankfurt in 1994. In that way, the governors not only underlined their independence from the EU's political center in Brussels, but also were able to draw on the secretariat services provided by the BIS to the central bank community.

The cutoff date for this study is the end of 1993. This date marks the formal end of the Committee of Governors as it had existed since 1964, and its replacement by the newly created EMI. It can therefore be considered an important milestone on the road to European monetary unification. Following the three-stage process toward European Economic and Monetary Union outlined in the 1992 Maastricht Treaty, the EMI would itself be superseded by the creation of the ECB on June 1, 1998, and the introduction of the Euro shortly afterward. These latter events, however, are not the subject of this book. Ending the story in 1993 has allowed enough time to pass to permit a sober historical assessment of a crucial transitional period. Yet the events are still sufficiently recent that many of the protagonists could be interviewed or otherwise consulted for this project.

Because this history was commissioned jointly by the ECB and the BIS, both institutions exceptionally waived the thirty-year restriction on access to their archives, including the historical records of the Committee of Governors (held by the ECB in Frankfurt). In exchange, Professor James agreed to use the more recent archival materials solely for the writing of this history. Under the same conditions, certain other central banks likewise agreed to open their archives up to 1993.

A panel of distinguished experts on European monetary history and on the monetary unification process was invited to review the manuscript. Its members—Barry Eichengreen, Marc Flandreau, Gert Jan Hogeweg, Hanspeter Scheller, Niels Thygesen, Gianni Toniolo, and Jürgen von Hagen—have provided helpful feedback and further input, for which they rightly deserve our gratitude.

Finally, although the BIS and the ECB have commissioned and given their full support to this research project, it should be clear that this book does not in any way present an official BIS or ECB view. What is offered here for the benefit of a wider audience is Professor James's own analysis and interpretation, based on the original source material, of the role played by the central banks in this important episode of European integration. We hope that readers will agree that this is a story well worth the telling, and that Harold James has done it justice.

Mario Draghi, *President, European*
Central Bank, Frankfurt am Main
Jaime Caruana, *General Manager, Bank*
for International Settlements, Basel

Abbreviations Used in Text

BCCI   Bank of Credit and Commerce International

BIS   Bank for International Settlements

CoG   Committee of Governors of the Central Banks of the Member States of the European Economic Community

EC   European Communities

ECB   European Central Bank

ECOFIN Council of Ministers of European Communities (economy and finance ministers)

ECU   European Currency Unit

EEC   European Economic Community

EMCF   European Monetary Cooperation Fund

EMF   European Monetary Fund (proposed)

EMI   European Monetary Institute

EMS   European Monetary System

EMU   Economic and Monetary Union

ERM   exchange rate mechanism

ESCB   European System of Central Banks

EU   European Union

GDP   gross domestic product

G-7   Group of Seven (heads of state and government plus finance ministers of Canada, France, Germany, Italy, Japan, United Kingdom, and United States)

G-10   Group of Ten (central banks of Belgium, Canada, France, Germany, Italy, Japan, the Netherlands, Sweden, United Kingdom, and United States, plus Switzerland as associated member)

IGC   Intergovernmental Conference (European Union)

IMF	International Monetary Fund
MC	Monetary Committee of the European Community
OECD	Organization for Economic Cooperation and Development
SDR	Special Drawing Right
VSTF	Very-Short-Term Facility

Making the European Monetary Union

The Making of a Non-National Currency

This book examines the whys, whens, hows, whos, and what-ifs of the process of making the European monetary union. Why was this innovative, daring, and risk-filled experiment undertaken? How was the process designed, and who did the designing? What were the risks, and were they calculated correctly?

First, why? The major theme of this book is that the quest for European monetary coordination and then for union was a response to genuine (and still-existing) problems of currency instability and misalignment at the international level. It was not simply—as it has often been represented—a fundamentally political project "to make a future European war impossible, and to set the stage for a federal United States of Europe."[1] Such an endeavor would have been rather strange, as there is no evidence that common money prevents wars (think of the U.S. Civil War or, more recently, Yugoslavia). Nevertheless, the idea has been endlessly repeated by high-minded European politicians with a rhetorical bent, from Roy Jenkins to Hans-Dietrich Genscher. The rhetoric derives from the very beginning of the effort at European integration, when German Chancellor Konrad Adenauer in 1950 told parliament that "the importance of this project is above all political and not economic."[2] That a currency union can be driven by an urgent political concern, overriding economic logic, was demonstrated in a costly way by the case of the 1990 German-German currency union that preceded political unification; but it will be clear in the subsequent account that there was a clear economic as well as a political logic behind the creation of a single European currency.

The erroneous political interpretation of the move to a European money spawned a flurry of conspiracy theories, seeing the Euro as a plot by central bankers, technocrats at the European Commission (especially Jacques Delors, the highly influential president of the Commission from 1985 to 1994), or Germans seeking to preserve unfair advantages for their powerful export-driven economy and thus to achieve some sinister new mastery over Europe.

Second, when? The push to devise a European solution was particularly intense when global imbalances (also reflected in the emergence of large German current account surpluses) threatened the international system in the late 1960s, the late 1970s, and the late 1980s.

Third, by whom? In the late 1970s, politicians took charge of the process of finding solutions, and launched high-profile initiatives (the European Monetary System, EMS). But the results were disappointing, and in another series of initiatives, in the late 1980s and early 1990s, whose result was Monetary Union (but not really Economic and Monetary Union) as laid down in the Maastricht Treaty, the detailed planning of how to move was left to experts, and in particular central bankers. They designed both the road map for how to get to monetary union (in the work of the Delors Committee) and the actual operationalization through the statutes of the new European Monetary Institute, the future European Central Bank, and the European System of Central Banks.

Fourth, the problems and risks. EMU, as discussed in the 1970s and 1980s, stood for economic and monetary union. But the technical plans went ahead of the political initiatives on European integration, with the result that there was imperfect agreement on crucial aspects of the monetary union, in particular fiscal rules and banking supervision and regulation. Both these issue areas raised political concerns about loss of national sovereignty and about the redistributional consequences of Europeanizing a fundamental part of economic policy-making. As a result, the makers of the settlement looked back on a task that was only half accomplished. As former EU Commission President Jacques Delors put it, "the finance ministers did not want to see anything disagreeable which they would be forced to deal with."[3]

The Quest for Stability

Jean-Claude Trichet, president of the European Central Bank from 2003 to 2011, liked to claim that money was like poetry, before adding that both give a sense of stability.[4] This unusual but accurate formulation is reminiscent of the famous answer of the Prussian general August von Gneisenau, whose patriotic concerns in the early nineteenth century were dismissed by the Prussian king as "nothing more than poetry." Gneisenau replied: "Religion, prayer, love of one's ruler, love of the fatherland, what are these but poetry? Upon poetry is founded the security of the throne."[5] The idea of stability is profoundly appealing because of European experiences of past disorder. Monetary instability decisively helped to threaten or even to blow apart fragile political systems. The monetary authority never agrees simply to convert every outstanding obligation into money. Instead, it will decide that some industries, or some banks, or some political authorities need to be kept going for the good of the general community, and that their debts should as a consequence be monetized. Those industries, banks, and political authorities that are not so privileged inevitably see the central bank's actions as an abuse of power. In federal systems, in particular, businesses and political authorities far removed from the center of the federation are most likely to be excluded from the monetary stimulus and hence inclined to be resentful.

Hyperinflation in early 1920s Germany fanned separatism in Bavaria, the Rhineland, and Saxony, because these remote areas thought that the German central bank and the central government in Berlin were discriminating against them and privileging the capital city and its interests. The separatists were radical: on the left in Saxony, on the far right in Bavaria and the Rhineland. The scar created by the memory of inflation is particularly acute in Germany, but it is by no means a purely German phenomenon. There are also more recent cases of federations eroded by inflation. In late 1980s Yugoslavia, as the socialist regime disintegrated, the monetary authorities in Belgrade were closest to Serbian politicians such as Slobodan Milošević and to Serbian business interests. The Croats and Slovenes wanted to get away. In the Soviet Union, inflation appeared as an instrument of the central Moscow bureaucrats, and more remote areas wanted to break away. Hyperinflation thus fueled the national tensions that broke up federal systems in the Soviet Union and Yugoslavia.

In the 1970s inflation became a general concern for all industrial countries. Previous views about how higher inflation might produce greater growth (as suggested in the Phillips curve literature) proved to be empirically unsustainable.[6] At the same time there was considerable evidence that short-term political pressures on central banks led to higher levels of inflation—often, for instance, before elections. Given a general preference for price stability, there seemed to be an excellent case for democratically validated decisions on the delegating of monetary policy-making to central banks whose autonomy was legally guaranteed.

In consequence, the institutional framework for the single European currency was designed by central bankers, who tried to isolate themselves from political pressures. They gave a great deal of attention to central bank design, but other elements that would have been needed for the successful and enduring operation of a durable monetary union were neglected. In the draft of the European Central Bank statute produced by the central bankers, Article 2 on the objectives of the European System of Central Banks stated that it should "support the general economic policy of the Community." But on the grounds that there was a multiplicity of national economic policies, at a late stage in the Intergovernmental Conference that culminated in the Treaty of Maastricht, the Dutch presidency substituted the phrase "support the general economic policies in the Community." In other words, there was to be no mechanism for making an economic policy to go alongside the new monetary regime.[7]

The decisive debates about how monetary policy could respond to the challenges of global instability took place in a committee of central bankers established by the European Economic Community in 1964, and generally referred to as the Committee of Governors (or CoG). Writing the history of the CoG is in some ways an odd exercise. Why does this committee matter more than any other of a number of international forums that developed in the 1960s as a response to increasing strains in the international monetary order—for instance, the Group of Ten that managed the IMF's General Arrangements to Borrow (1962), or the OECD's Working Party Three (after 1966); or from subsequent institutions, many of which had a much higher initial profile, the G-5 (1974) and then G-7 finance ministers (1986–1987), or the G-20 (1999) that had evolved out of a G-22 and then a G-33?[8] All enjoyed great vigor from the 1970s on, prompting political scientists Robert Keohane and Joseph Nye to see the "extensive and deep network of relationships" as building a new level of "transgovernmental coordination."[9] Committees are the core mechanism in the networked world analyzed by Anne-Marie

Slaughter.[10] This particular committee decisively pushed history along. Without the Committee of Governors, one of the most momentous (and, in the view of many commentators, especially after 2010, disastrous) events in modern financial history, the decision to create the European single currency, would not have taken place.

In choosing a "pure" money in the 1990s, free of any possibility of political interference and simply designed to meet the objective of price stability, Europeans flew in the face of the dominant tradition of thinking about money. The creation of money is usually thought to be the domain of the state: this was the widely prevalent doctrine of the nineteenth century, which reached its apogee in Georg Friedrich Knapp's highly influential *State Theory of Money*.[11] Money could be issued by the state because of the government's ability to define the unit of account in which taxes should be paid. In the *Nicomachean Ethics,* Aristotle explained that money owes its name to its property of not existing by nature but as a product of convention or law.[12] Greek coins usually carried depictions of gods and goddesses, but the Romans changed the practice and put their (presumed divine) emperors on their coins. In the New Testament, Christ famously answers a question about obedience to civil authorities by examining a coin and telling the Pharisees, "Render unto Caesar the things which are Caesar's."[13] Unlike most banknotes and coins, there is no picture of the state or its symbols—no Caesar—on the money issued and managed by the European Central Bank. This feature sharply distinguished the new money from the banknotes that had circulated before the common currency and that were carefully designed to depict national symbols. Especially in the nineteenth century, the formation of new nation-states was associated with the establishment of national moneys, which gave the new polities a policy area in which they could exercise themselves.[14]

For many centuries, it is true, a metallic money circulated, but the task of defining units of account—livres tournois, marks, gulden, florins, or dollars—remained a task of the state, in other words an outcome of a political process. Since the value of money fluctuated on the exchanges, there was continual and costly uncertainty about business transactions. As world trade expanded in the mid-nineteenth century, some economists and politicians began to think about the possibility of creating a global currency in just the same way as there was an enthusiasm for unifying weights and other measures. In 1866 a U.S. Congressional

Coinage Committee expressed exactly this sentiment when it concluded that "the only interest of any nation that could possibly be injuriously affected by the establishment of this uniformity is that of the money-changers—an interest which contributes little to the public welfare." John Stuart Mill in his *Principles of Political Economy* asked readers to "suppose that all countries had the same currency, as in the progress of political improvement they one day will have: and, as the most familiar to the reader, though not the best, let us suppose this currency to be the English. . . . So much of barbarism, however, still remains in the transactions of the most civilized nations that almost all independent countries choose to assert their nationality by having to their own inconvenience and that of their neighbors, a peculiar currency of their own."[15] Ultimately, however, as Mill feared, initiatives that aimed at world money got nowhere, though there were some nineteenth-century regional monetary unions (the Latin Monetary Union, the Scandinavian Monetary Union).[16] In smaller European states, but also in the United States until the mid-nineteenth century, a multiplicity of small coins circulated in different denominations, requiring heroic acts of arithmetic sophistication in order to carry out even quite simple daily commercial transactions. Then money became nationalized, with such a simplifying effect that by the twentieth century many people assumed that money had simply been national forever. English people began to assert, quite wrongly, that the monarch's head had been on banknotes for time immemorial.

The European Central Bank was designed as a nonstate actor whose primary purpose was to issue money—the kind of institution that had basically only been imagined before the 1990s by antistatist liberal economist and philosopher Friedrich Hayek and some of his wilder disciples. By the time of the monetary union, some influential interpreters saw Hayek as one of the inspirations. As Otmar Issing, the first chief economist of the European Central Bank, put it, "many strands in Hayek's thinking . . . may have influenced the course of the events leading to Monetary Union in subtle ways. What has happened with the introduction of the euro has indeed achieved the denationalisation of money, as advocated by Hayek."[17] Hayek's answer, competitive moneys produced by "free banking" in which numerous private authorities would issue their own money, was substantially more radical than the solution adopted by Europeans in the 1990s. But the Hayekian element of a money-issuing authority that was extensively protected against political pressures, and consequently against political opprobrium, was a key part of the Maastricht Treaty. Niels Thygesen, a Danish monetary economist who as an independent expert was one of three non-central-bank members of the Delors Committee that provided the first extensive blueprint for monetary union, referred approvingly to the Hayekian concept as a way of "reducing the scope for the kind of lax and divergent monetary policies" that characterized Europe in the 1970s.[18]

John Maynard Keynes too, in planning for the postwar order, had proposed a synthetic international currency that he named *bancor* that would guarantee stability and the avoidance of deflation, on a global level.[19] In this way, the two most influential economists who combined technical economics with a vision of political order, Keynes and Hayek, were advocates of an alternative to unstable and politically abused state-issued money.

Twentieth-century European history would certainly suggest the dangers of money creation by the state. As the Italian liberal economist, central bank governor, finance minister, and president of the republic, Luigi Einaudi, put it in the immediate aftermath of the Second World War, in a plea to take away the right of individual states to print their own money: "The [interwar] devaluation of the Italian lira and the German Mark, which broke the middle classes and increased working-class discontent, was one of the causes which produced the band of troublemakers and unemployed intellectuals who gave power to the dictators. If the European federation takes away from the individual states the power of running public works through the printing press, and limits them to expenses that are financed solely by taxes and by voluntary loans, it will by that act alone have accomplished a great work."[20] Above all, the legacy of the German hyperinflation of the early 1920s has had a profound impact on the attitudes of Germans to their central bank and to the goal of monetary stability.

True, there were alternative traditions, which emphasized either a natural-law origin of money or a hypothetical contractual origin for monetary arrangements. In natural-law theory, money represented an intrinsic good or value, and the theory dealt well with the problem of the interrelationship of different monetary standards in varying political structures.[21] Alternately, it is possible to conceive of money's arising out of conventional agreements about the exchange of goods, between parties that are not necessarily in the same political unit. Aristotle in the *Politics* set out a theory of money as arising out of exchange, a theory that seems at odds with the account in the *Nicomachean Ethics* in that the state and its authority play no role in establishing monetary values in such a version.[22]

One aspect of these alternative theories is superior to the state theory of money in explaining what happened in the creation of the institutional framework for a European money. In particular, it is striking that in discussions of monetary union, there was a focus not on who was to issue a new currency, but on what its characteristics should be: above all, on how monetary stability could be achieved. The supranational character of a new money was often perceived as a valuable instrument in a fight against the scourge of inflation, since national moneys were too easily manipulated in accordance with national political preferences, especially in weaker or more insecure political systems. Supranational money was impossible as long as different countries had very different levels of inflation—in short, as long as there was no consensus about the desirability of anti-inflationary policy. The process of monetary integration was thus accompanied by intensive reflection about what money is and what money should do, but also by little worry about who should issue it. Some commentators have in consequence suggested that "money becomes the operative hinge-concept for European identity."[23]

The decisive and radical measure that made European monetary unification possible was that, in the institutional framework as established by European politicians in the 1990s, money was divorced from the fiscal activities of the state. There was no obvious Europe-wide fiscal counterpart to the monetary authority (the European Central Bank), and fiscal policy remained in the hands of the member states. That division of policy responsibilities between the member states and the Eurozone institution (the ECB) was inherently fragile. One of the most creative thinkers behind the move to the Euro, the Italian economist Tommaso Padoa-Schioppa, commented appropriately that "Neither the U.S. Fed nor any other central bank in the world is, like the Eurosystem, confronted with the challenge of not being the expression of a political union. This is indeed a challenge, because normally the soundness of a currency does not rest exclusively on the central bank."[24] Italian Prime Minister Silvio Berlusconi was making a similar point in a much cruder way when he called the Euro a "strange currency" that "has convinced nobody."[25] From the 1990s on, the makers of the Euro had seen that the single currency did not conform to the criteria for an optimum currency area (OCA), as set out in the 1960s by Robert Mundell, Ron McKinnon, and Peter Kenen.[26] Some commentators, mostly from the United States, tried to revive OCA type arguments about the need for automatic fiscal stabilizers in a monetary union, but they were largely ignored.[27] Indeed the concept of an OCA was conspicuous by its absence in the more recent phase of European monetary integration, when a single currency was seen as a harmonization and coordination exercise outside the boundaries of nation-states. In the wake of the financial crisis, and especially dramatically in 2011–2012, the idea that the state is ultimately the issuer of money, backstop of the financial system, creator of value, and guarantor of value has returned in a powerful form.

European monetary union is a unique process, and the subject of great fascination in other parts of the world: in the Gulf region, where there are periodic discussions of monetary unification; in Turkey, where the government is thinking about institutional ways of linking countries in the eastern Mediterranean and Middle East; in the former Soviet Union, where Vladimir Putin holds up the European path of currency integration as a blueprint for closer economic and political ties; as well as in Asia and Latin America, where movements toward greater monetary integration also have some support but encounter a plethora of difficulties and obstacles.

Global Problems and European Solutions

The debate in the late twentieth century about an institutionalization of European monetary arrangements always took place in a wider context of discussions of the global monetary system and its problems. Debates about new institutional mechanisms (such as a basket currency) that took place on the global level were also replicated with respect to European affairs. The first discussions of monetary union occurred in the late 1960s and culminated in the Werner Plan, as a way of managing a European response to the crisis of the dollar and the breakdown of the fixed exchange (par value) system that had been devised in 1944 at Bretton Woods. The next two surges of European monetary institutionalization followed crises in the international system. The creation of the European Monetary System in 1979 was a self-conscious response to the rapid decline of the dollar in 1977–1978, the perceived crisis in American leadership under Jimmy Carter, and the consequent search for a new international mechanism to replace the dollar standard. The core of the new approach was originally intended to be a basket currency as a unit of account, the European Currency Unit (or ECU, which conveniently echoed the name of an ancient French coin). A new European money would possibly be a replacement for the dollar, and thus take some of the strains out of the international monetary system. There were also parallels in thinking about how an international currency could operate between attempts to redesign or reform the IMF's artificial currency (the "Special Drawing Right") on the one hand and ideas of making the ECU into a currency on the other.

In the 1980s the dollar again caused worldwide chaos as its value soared until 1985, and then declined rapidly. Europeans felt that they were especially vulnerable because they did not control an international reserve currency that could stand up to the dollar. Europe's response to that international uncertainty began with the report of the Delors Committee in 1989 and continued through the negotiation and approval of the Treaty of Maastricht to the legal realization of the Euro in 1999. The establishment of the physical currency had its origins in an attempt to devise mechanisms that would generate a more stable global exchange rate regime. The critical policy innovators, in particular French Finance Minister Edouard Balladur, took an international answer and started to advocate its realization on the European level.

By the 1960s West Germany had emerged as the strongest European economy, with a dynamism built on a powerful export performance. German current account surpluses, driven primarily by trade surpluses, which appeared briefly in the 1950s, were corrected after a currency revaluation in 1961, but emerged again in surges in the late 1960s, in the late 1970s, a more powerful burst in the late 1980s as capital movements were liberalized, and in the 2000s. They disappeared in the 1990s, when the costs of German unification pushed the German external account into deficit, and Germany's relations with its European partners were consequently more harmonious. The counterpart of the current account surplus was a high level of savings that was in part channeled abroad to finance deficits that appeared elsewhere (see Figure I.1).

The German surpluses provided a focus of attention on both a global and a European scale. Could the imbalances be financed and sustained? If not, there was a need for adjustment. At each stage, the extent of the imbalance measured as a share of gross domestic product (GDP) increased, mostly because international capital markets were deeper and thus allowed bigger imbalances to be financed for longer periods. One way of thinking about these imbalances is as a reflection of changes in relative competitiveness. Thus a German surplus was a reflection of a favorable development of productivity gains, and of wage costs contained by a collaborative and collective approach to wage setting that came to be the hallmark of late-twentieth-century German-style capitalism. By contrast, deficits in Germany's trade partners reflected either lower innovation or (especially in late-1960s France and Italy) a less disciplined approach to wages in an era of full employment and increased social radicalism. At the beginning, in the Bretton Woods era of fixed exchange rates and controlled capital markets, even relatively small deficits could not be financed, and produced immediate pressure on the exchange markets. The deficit countries then had to apply fiscal brakes in a stop-go cycle. Germany's partners, notably France, were faced by the prospect of austerity and deflation in order to correct deficits. This alternative was unattractive to the French political elite because it constrained growth and guaranteed electoral unpopularity. Their

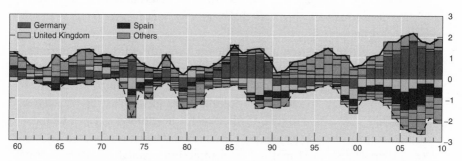

Figure I.1. Sum of current account imbalances of deficit and surplus countries, 1960–2010, as a percentage of GDP. *Note:* Figures for balance of payments for Germany from 1991 include the external transactions of the former German Democratic Republic. "Others" includes Belgium, Denmark, France, Greece, Ireland, Italy, Luxembourg, Netherlands, and Portugal. *Sources:* OECD, *Economic Outlook;* European Commission, Annual Macro Economic database.

preferred policy alternative was thus German expansion, but this course was unpopular with a German public worried about the legacy of inflation and was opposed by the powerful and independent central bank, the Deutsche Bundesbank. Solving the challenge posed by German current accounts in the European setting at first appeared to require some sophisticated and ingenious political mechanism that would force French politicians to take on more austerity than they would have liked, and Germans to accept less price orthodoxy than they thought they needed. A political mechanism, however, requires continual negotiation and public deliberation, which would have been painful given the policy preferences in the two countries (and in those countries that lined up with each of the Big Two). The increased attraction of monetary union was that it required no such political process, and that the operation of an entirely automatic device would constrain political debate, initiative, and policy choice. The monetary union occurred in the aftermath of an era of capital market liberalization, in which current account imbalances were sustainable for much longer periods. The effects of movements of capital in allowing current account imbalances to build up to a much greater extent, and ensuring that corrections, when they occurred, would be much more dramatic, were already noticeable in the late 1980s and early 1990s, before the move to monetary union. Indeed, the large cumulative imbalances were what convinced Europe's policymakers that a monetary union was the only way of avoiding the risk of periodic crises with currency realignments whose trade policy consequences threatened the survival of an integrated internal European market.

The "German question" figured in analyses of both global and European economic challenges. The reform proposals that led to initiatives for European integration in 1970, in 1978, and again after 1988 all were conceived as ways of addressing imbalances among European states. These dates were also moments of crisis in the global system. The most radical approach to Europe's problem was monetary union, which had the intrinsic appeal of making current account imbalances apparently vanish, as well as of providing a mechanism for non-Germans to constrain or limit the Bundesbank. In the often-proffered example of the United States, there is no concern about imbalances among states, and the federal economy is seen as self-correcting (but largely because of flows of labor, and of transfer payments in a federal fiscal system). It was thus a shock to financial markets when the sustainability of current account imbalances reemerged as a major challenge to the Eurozone after 2010, even though there had previously been official warnings about the problem of fiscal deficits.

At each stage, monetary planners in Europe needed to consider some parallel fiscal commitments. In particular, how much of the financing of deficits would need to be channeled through the public sector? From the beginnings of discussions on the possibility of European monetary union in the 1960s, it was clear to many participants that some support mechanism—regional funds or short-term lending facilities—would be required to function alongside the new monetary mechanisms. And such transfers would be likely to involve governments if they were to be more than short-term revolving credits. The relationship between a monetary institution and the fiscal authorities that would be involved if severe strains appeared in the monetary arrangements was consistently problematic.

The international monetary system established in 1944 had as a crucial component the International Monetary Fund, in part designed as the enforcer of the system's rules about currency valuation, but in part intended as a support mechanism. Originally the conception was analogous to a credit union, but in its practical operations after the 1950s the IMF relied increasingly on ever more complex (and controversial) conditionality: in other words, external support would depend on the adoption of possibly harsh austerity programs, imposed by the multilateral institution.[28] Europeans found it hard to evolve a European analogue to the IMF, because the cooperative and interstate character of the integration process and the demand for unanimity in European Community decision-making made it easy to play games with conditionality and water down its rigor. The IMF was much more at arm's length, much less vulnerable to the application of political pressure to relax conditionality (although such pressure was also exerted, and was sometimes successful). What would have been impossible for most IMF members encountering balance-of-payments or other problems was thus extraordinarily tempting for European states. Consequently the likely creditors, above all Germany, adamantly resisted such institutional innovation.

In the 1970 Werner Plan (whose major proposal of monetary union was not realized), a new institution, the European Monetary Cooperation Fund (EMCF), initially envisaged as a potential Federal Reserve

System for Europe, was supposed to be at the heart of monetary reform. Some countries wanted such a fund to make major transfers between members; others (notably Germany) were heavily resistant. The major difficulty lay in the actual implementation, which in fact severely circumscribed the operations of the EMCF. The EMCF began with very high ambitions, but in practice remained a rather subsidiary and shadowy institution and became simply the agent for the administration of medium-term financial assistance provided by EC loans. The "director" of the institution, which was housed in the Bank for International Settlements (BIS) building in Basel and had a staff of just six, Jean-Claude Dagassan, was described rather satirically in the early 1990s in the following terms: "He is monetary Europe. More exactly, the living part, the bud of the European Central Bank."[29] The EMCF in practice was managed by the BIS, and Dagassan was not in any sense a director but was a BIS staff member who simply headed the section of the BIS that acted as agent for the EMCF. This body would not be a powerful driver of European monetary integration.

Similar considerations would later prevent the emergence of a European Monetary Fund, which was intended as part of the 1978 reform that established a European Monetary System, but never materialized because of intense hostility from Germany and from the German central bank, which feared that this would be the beginning of large transfers to weaker and poorer states. This part of the architecture was conspicuously absent in the new debates in the late 1980s and the early 1990s, as it was assumed that markets alone could bear the responsibility of funding government debt, and that there would be no conceivable situation in which a dramatic combination of market and government failure would lead to a need for official financing. After all, no European government had needed to use the IMF after 1976. The defect was rectified only in July 2011 with a proposed extension of the functions of the European Financial Stability Facility.

Unlike the Werner Plan or the Franco-German initiative of 1978, the discussions of the committee chaired by European Commission President Jacques Delors in 1988–1989 produced a major institutional outcome, the design of a stage approach to European monetary union that was then embodied in the Maastricht Treaty (negotiated in December 1991 and ratified over the next two years). The technical details for this operation were produced not by politicians but by central bankers. The

Delors Committee could not have produced the blueprint for Maastricht and for monetary union if it had not been preeminently a committee of central bankers. The statutes of the European Monetary Institute (EMI) and the European Central Bank (ECB)/European System of Central Banks (ESCB) could not have been productively hammered out by anyone other than central bankers.

Twenty-five years of policy debate and of high-level tensions and clashes had highlighted the exchange rate and monetary policy as issues that were essential to the working of European policy. Bad management of currencies had tremendous political force, enough to shatter the fragile framework of cooperation. The idea of the reform was a fundamentally simple one: since exchange rates and the possibility of their alteration produced so much tension between European states, they should simply be abolished. Instead of looking to exchange rates (an external goal), Europeans would pursue an internal goal, namely price stability. That objective was at the heart of the deliberations of the Delors Committee and dominated the preparations for implementing the Maastricht Treaty.

Before the acute stage of the financial crisis in 2008, there was a worldwide, not simply European, consensus that central banks were concerned primarily with price stability and with monetary policy. The dominant view was the product of an intellectual revolution in central banking that emphasized the desirability of central bank independence. The ECB was indeed conceived as the model of a new type of central bank, which should be concerned only with the operation of monetary policy so as to ensure a low level of inflation (usually thought of as less than 2 percent).

The intellectual shift toward central bank independence, which characterized the late twentieth century, and which brought a considerable degree of price stability, was possible only on the assumption that there was a clear rule or principle that the central bank should follow. When that rule or principle became muddied, and discretion in policy-making returned in the aftermath of the financial crisis, the case for central bank independence began to look more problematic. Thus the historical pendulum is now swinging back, toward a politically controlled Bank of England or a more accountable Federal Reserve. The ECB is likely to face analogous pressures and demands, from politicians and from the public, often running in contradictory directions in their policy demands. The new postcrisis vision of the central bank is often of a very different sort of institution from the 1990s vision of a mechanism for guaranteeing price stability.

Flaws in the Institutional Framework

The monetary union as conceived in the Maastricht Treaty was intended to be accompanied by a political union. The fact that the broader political framework was not realized produced two fundamental flaws: the mechanisms for enforcing fiscal discipline were inadequate, and there was no Europe-wide banking supervision and regulation.

In public, the most rigorous intellectual criticisms of the Euro project came from American academic economists as well as from some within the Federal Reserve System and some American private-sector figures (bankers). Their criticism—often expressed in a very dramatic form, such as Martin Feldstein's prediction that a monetary union would bring Europe to civil war as states fought about secession from an economically costly union—were widely cited by European critics, especially by Germans who feared the loss of their enviably stable currency, the Deutsche Mark, and by British "Euro-skeptics." Milton Friedman in press statements predicted the collapse of the Euro within five to fifteen years.[30] There is plenty of historical evidence of currency regimes that are designed fundamentally as a policy corset working well for a period of ten or so years, and then succumbing to strains. The Bretton Woods currency regime really lasted only from 1958 to 1971, and was already quite crippled after 1968. The so-called Snake arrangements of the Europeans in the 1970s involved an increasingly narrow group of countries polarized around Germany. The European Monetary System of 1979 exploded after 1992. The Euro, launched in 1999, came under heavy fire just over a decade later in the aftermath of a combination of banking and sovereign debt problems.

But the fact that this criticism came from the United States, and especially from people who might be regarded as being in some sort of competition with Europe, devalued the criticism, as it could be simply presented as a defense of waning U.S. hegemony. The same issues, however, were seen just as clearly in Europe by the original makers of the monetary project. Both the fiscal and the financial stability problems were accurately diagnosed and analyzed by the technocrats in the Committee of Governors and the BIS. Alexandre Lamfalussy, then the General

Manager of the BIS, for instance, put the case with admirable clarity during the debates of the Delors Committee in December 1988, when he asked whether "the idea, not shared by him, that market discipline was sufficient to bring about fiscal convergence should be considered in the report."[31] In retrospect, the Delors Committee pinned too many of its hopes on the ability of market forces to deliver warnings to states before they entered fiscally dangerous areas.

It was clear at the time of Maastricht that the shift to monetary union should impose new limits on fiscal policy. There is a more or less unchanging language in this regard from beginning to end of the European saga. The central bankers meeting in Basel regularly worried about inadequate fiscal discipline. Baron Jean Snoy, the Belgian finance minister, for instance, made that point in the following way in 1970: "In a system of a currency union the position of finance ministers would be stronger in their efforts to achieve budget balance, because they could point to 'European necessities.'"[32]

The fiscal pressure played a powerful role in the 1990s as countries tried to prepare themselves for EMU. But the commitment to "European necessities" was not deep enough for members of the monetary union really to anchor the requirements in watertight domestic legislation. History indicates clearly that monetary unions require some measure of fiscal union, but that was not what was agreed in the treaty commitments of the early 1990s. Instead, as a substitute, governments agreed to a system of fiscal rules that ultimately proved unenforceable, and that were even ridiculed by figures such as the president of the EU Commission, Romano Prodi. The mechanism softened in part because of political pressures in the respective national frameworks that led to fiscal destabilization; as well as because of a buildup of private (above all banking-sector) debt that created potential implicit but unmeasured fiscal liabilities. It turned out that market pressure did not actually constrain the room for policy maneuver, but that in a strange paradox the commitment to monetary union actually *reduced* any market constraints.

In the original Maastricht Treaty, convergence criteria were set out that specified a limit for government deficits at 3 percent of GDP and for public-sector debt levels at 60 percent. In the 1990s governments made a major effort to bring down deficits, though the entering debt level of Belgium was still 130 percent in 1997, and it was unthinkable that the project could go ahead without Belgium. But Belgian membership also meant letting in Italy, with a debt of 120 percent. These criteria were maintained in the Stability and Growth Pact (the word "Growth" had originally been inserted at French insistence to balance the German obsession with "Stability").

A major blow came when France and Germany ignored the Stability and Growth Pact and had it suspended in November 2003 as a counter to a—as it proved spurious—threat of recession. Romano Prodi called the pact "stupid."[33] The European Council agreed not to apply the deficit procedure against France and Germany, though later the European Court of Justice ruled that this step contravened EU law. In 2005 the disciplinary mechanism was softened, many processes became merely discretionary, and new procedural provisions made it harder to take action against noncompliant states.[34] Smaller EU countries were outraged by France and Germany's initiative. But the behavior of the Big Two had a corrosive effect on other countries. While there had been a great deal of fiscal convergence in the 1990s on the Maastricht criteria, in the 2000s (even before the financial crisis) fiscal discipline in Europe deteriorated. Was this just a European phenomenon? The same trajectory occurred in the United States, from fiscal responsibility in the 1990s (under President Clinton) to persistent and high deficits in the 2000s under George W. Bush. So other explanations posit that the United States also provided a bad example, or (more plausibly) that the markets were apparently willing to finance almost limitless amounts of government debt, as they perceived the debt of industrial countries to be an entirely risk-free asset.

The second flaw was the failure to provide for Europe-wide banking supervision and regulation. The focus in the Maastricht Treaty on price stability ignored financial stability, which became a major issue as a result of the explosive growth of financial markets in the 1990s and 2000s, a development that is in part itself the product of increased confidence about monetary stability ("the great moderation"). Many critics would also argue that the focus on monetary integration and on the role of the experts who shaped it created a Europe that was too technocratic and too removed from the concerns of ordinary citizens. At the time of Maastricht, there was extensive discussion about the need to accompany the creation of a single market and a single capital market—and then a single money—with a Europe-wide system of banking supervision and regulation. This outcome was resisted by some national regulators, but especially by the banks (which did not want to be controlled or disciplined). The argument against a Europe-wide system also had a certain logic, in that any large failure of regulation would require a bailout that could occur only with taxpayers' money, but (in the absence of a fiscal union) this could only be done on a national level. The problems of the future were foreshadowed in 1991, when the large cross-national Bank of Credit and Commerce International (BCCI) collapsed, but everyone wanted to present the BCCI as an exceptional case. Furthermore, the BCCI failure damaged the regulatory credibility of the Bank of England, whose officials had been at the forefront of the push for European-wide supervision and regulation.

There were few really cross-national banks in the early 1990s. After that, European banks went on an acquisitive spree. In part this was driven by a quest for greater size; in part also by the opportunity to move into less regulated jurisdictions, so that for instance German banks worked through Irish and Luxembourg subsidiaries. But it was the introduction of the single currency that really set off a surge of lending by European banks. Like banks elsewhere—notably in the United States—the European institutions reduced their capital relative to the rapidly expanding balance sheets; they also engaged in an aggressive search for yield through off-balance-sheet affiliates. The 1998 Asia crisis was already a warning of sorts, in that many European banks had become badly exposed as a result of their demand for high-yield assets; that lesson was brought home in a much more dramatic way less than a decade later when losses began to appear in the U.S. subprime market. Europe-wide banking produced self-sustaining and self-propelling credit booms and bubbles, without any built-in corrective mechanism. If capital flowed into a deficit country, the result was the creation of debt instruments—at no penalty price—that could be the basis of even more lending. Such capital inflows, and their inherently inflationary effects, thus fueled a divergence of labor costs that made southern European economies, the principal beneficiaries of the inflows, increasingly uncompetitive.[35]

Like U.S. banks, European banks required recapitalization after losses on security holdings and the drying up of the interbank market following the financial crisis of 2007–2008. The European regulators, however, were less keen to enforce such a recapitalization than their U.S. counterparts. Then there was a second wave of strain: European banks were especially exposed to the sovereign debt of southern European borrowers, which had promised slightly higher yields, and which had been treated by regulators as highly secure. Both banks and their regulators were slow in recognizing the potential damage that such an exposure could bring. The governments of the host countries (notably France and Germany) were unwilling to take measures that might expose the banks (and taxpayers) to large losses. The Europeanization of debt finance created a vicious cycle of interaction between the problems of European banks and the debt problems of governments.

The banking issue was all the more important because the move to monetary union had removed a policy tool that had been a cushion against adverse shocks. In theory, before the union and the permanent fixing of exchange rates, higher interest rates and currency appreciation might curtail a credit boom, and lower rates and depreciation could be employed to combat a downturn. In the aftermath of the loss of monetary independence, some new instrument would have been required as a countercyclical steering instrument. That might have been fiscal policy, but it could also be conceived as the application of so-called macroprudential regulation. After 2008, and in particular with the establishment in 2011 of the European Systemic Risk Board, there was intensive policy innovation in this area.

Committees and Crises

A central focus of debates about central bank action and about the role of central bank cooperation in building European integration was the cumbersomely named Committee of Governors of the Central Banks of the Member States of the European Economic Community (CoG), established in 1964 by the European Economic Community (later the European Communities, and eventually, after the Treaty of Maastricht, the European Union; see Figure I.2). Throughout its existence it met mostly in Basel, outside the territory of the EEC's member states. Its activities concluded at the end of 1993, when its staff provided the basis for a new institution, the EMI, set up to supervise the transition to monetary union. The EMI was a sort of embryo ECB.

The CoG was based in Basel because of the location there of the Bank for International Settlements, a cooperative forum for central banks worldwide that had been in existence since 1930. The BIS already hosted,

Figure I.2. Committees and comitology

European/EEC system	World/United Nations system
Political structure of the EC/EU	*Political*
European Council (since 1975): heads of state or government defines general political direction and priorities of EC/EU	**G-7** (from 1975–1976): heads of government or state **G-5** (from 1974), **G-7** (from 1987): finance ministers
Council of Ministers: regular gatherings at EC/EU level of national ministers on topics within their specific responsibilities ECOFIN: council of finance and economics ministers	
European Commission: executive body ("government") of the EC/EU ("ministers" of the different departments are called "commissioners")	
European Parliament (directly elected since 1979): legislative body of the EC/EU	
European Court of Justice: judiciary body of the EC/EU	
Economic and monetary committees/bodies	*Financial/monetary policy*
EC Monetary Committee Alternates	**International Monetary Fund** (IMF; global)
Committee of Governors (CoG) Alternates Foreign exchange experts' group (Théron) (from 1971) Monetary policy experts' group (Bastiaanse) (from 1971) Banking supervision experts' group (from 1991)	**Organisation for Economic Cooperation and Development** (OECD; developed economies) OECD Working Party 3 (financial and monetary policy)
European Monetary Cooperation Fund (from 1973): same membership as CoG	**G-10 Deputies** (representatives of the ministries of finance of the G-10 countries)
	Bank for International Settlements G-10 Governors (governors of the G-10 central banks meeting regularly at the BIS in Basel)

since the 1960s, the regular G-10 meetings of central bank governors. It now also provided (for a fee) the staffing for the CoG's initially very modest secretariat (though in the early 1990s the secretariat expanded rapidly). From the beginning, the location meant that the new body would play with the geometry of power, or engineer what later came to be called variable geometry. All the member countries were represented in the CoG (with the exception of Luxembourg, which was already in a de facto monetary union with Belgium), but as the CoG began to devise new monetary arrangements in the 1970s (in particular, the so-called Snake arrangements), some member countries excluded themselves from the new forms of monetary cooperation, as they found the discipline too constraining. At the same time the CoG devised association arrangements to work with non-EC members, notably Norway, Sweden, and Switzerland (the Swiss agreement was never implemented). This development was welcomed by the EEC Commission as a contribution to an enhanced integration process: Denmark, Ireland, and the United Kingdom all participated in the CoG well before they joined the EEC. The repercussions of the locational peculiarity and consequent flexibility and openness were felt for a long time. The Treaty of Maastricht, which laid down the timetable for monetary union, did not end this separation of European monetary institutions from European Community or Union constitutionalization. It found an end only in the provisions of the Lisbon Treaty, which came into force in December 2009 and which amended Article 9 of the EEC treaty to include the European Central Bank as an "institution" of the European Union.

The CoG was not established as part of the original architecture of the EEC. Nor was it envisaged as the embryo of a future European Central Bank, although that paradoxically is what it would become. It was created to provide a specifically European mechanism and voice in the discussion and resolution of global monetary issues. Indeed, at the beginning, the global and the regional were closely linked. And that linkage continued to be a constant feature.

Committees in the popular imagination are either boring or sinister, especially when they deal with financial or monetary matters. Conspiracy theories abound when it comes to central banks and their origins. The 1910 meeting of New York bankers in Jekyll Island, South Carolina, which prepared the way for the creation of the Federal Reserve System, has spawned a richly paranoid literature.[36] When politicians want to attack or even abolish central banks, as U.S. Congressman Ron Paul has demanded for some time with respect to the Federal Reserve, they like to refer to the stories of the illegitimate and conspiratorial origins of those institutions. In the wake of the financial crisis, diatribes against central banks have gained a new momentum.

The European Central Bank too has a penumbra of conspiracy theories attached to it, often couched in terms of how one country or group of countries has outwitted and outmaneuvered the rest. Non-Germans, especially in southern Europe, like to see a conspiracy to lock in German competitive advantages as other societies increasingly priced themselves out of the market. Populist-minded Germans on the other hand see attempts to extract resources from Germany, and to place limits on German drive and innovation. There is a deep paradox in the way in which Europe ended up with a central bank that looked and behaved very much like the German Bundesbank, even though the Bundesbank was more or less consistently critical of ideas about Europeanizing its model.

How could a committee of central bankers, mostly meeting outside the territory of the European Community in Switzerland, transform itself step by step into the European Central Bank? Do secretive committees naturally and inevitably and always try to expand their influence and authority?

The group of central bankers underwent a dramatic transformation as it prepared monetary union. Institutionally, it suddenly looked completely different, but the basic DNA remained the same. This reflection prompts an analogy with natural history. What follows in this book might be seen as the story of the central bankers' committee as a caterpillar that turned into the chrysalis of the European Monetary Institute and then eventually became a beautifully winged but fragile butterfly (the European Central Bank). It is conceivable that, if there were ever to be a world currency as occasionally proposed by economists such as Richard Cooper or Robert Mundell, some of the other committees or clubs might be seen in a similar way, as protomechanisms of a new dynamic of institutionalized cooperation and integration. Such a development would inevitably also spawn its own conspiracy theories. This history will discuss the evolving anatomy of the caterpillar as it tried to respond to the challenges posed by the environment in which it functioned.

The central bankers who constituted the CoG quite properly never saw it as their task to make large-scale political decisions about the structure of the European Community or the political framework needed to support a monetary union. So it is natural to look for metaphors that do not involve too much agency. The political scientist David Andrews in a series of biological metaphors sees the CoG as the "primary incubator of EMU" and also argues that "the basic organizational elements of EMU bear the genetic imprint of the Committee of Governors."[37] Yet in fact the "economic" dimensions of EMU (which were supposed to include some measure of economic governance) were quietly neglected until the Euro crisis after 2010 shed a fierce light on governance inadequacies in the Eurozone.

The environment that produced the CoG's adaptive process included a clash between different national political interests, formulated as a conflict of visions; and also increasingly the tensions that arose as politicians sought to control or influence increasingly dynamic and powerful market forces.

Crises play a particular role in this story. They are moments of uncertainty, when politicians are bewildered and public sentiment is mobilized; but experts—in this case the central bankers—have a unique leverage because of the perception that they can provide more reliable guidance. A great deal of the literature on technocratic rule by "epistemic communities" of experts makes the point that a source of power or legitimacy for such bodies lies in the ability to offer a road map through uncertainty.[38] The complexity of issues seems to imply that democratic mechanisms are too simple or crude. As one political scientist points out, the epistemic communities are "more successful when confronting problems that used recognized quantitative data." Democracy finds it hard to deal with the complexities of money supply, risk provision, bank supervision, and so on.[39] And although crises often lead to an intense politicization, they also produce a conviction that matters cannot be solved by a process of politics as usual, and political factors can thus be effectively ignored or circumvented.

A history of the broad institutional evolution of monetary integration inevitably requires discussion of how at particular moments of crisis, often corresponding to problems of the global financial order that strained European politics and required institutional innovation, politicians produced new and increasingly sophisticated responses: in the early 1970s, at the time of the Werner Report; in the late 1970s, with the establishment of the European Monetary System; and above all, in the late 1980s and early 1990s. Crises proved to be points at which basic conflicts about policy adjustment were played out.

The book is also a study of the story of the formation of an intellectual consensus about appropriate monetary policy and about adjustment. For much of the period, while there was some feeling that a common European approach was desirable, there were also acute national differences about how coordination should be achieved. That is because the debate focused for a long time on exchange rates, and an exchange rate system was at the heart of the European Monetary System designed in 1978 as a successor to the less than completely convincing and much narrower exchange rate system around the Deutsche Mark, the so-called Snake. Because the EMS looked so much like a larger version of the Snake, it inevitably had the same problems. In particular, differences were focused on the question of who should do adjustment; and in this way the Europeans echoed global debates about monetary order. The countries with surpluses saw surplus as a virtue and their partners as having strayed from the path, so that an asymmetric adjustment primarily on the part of the deficit countries was needed. The countries with deficits preferred to see the external position as neither intrinsically virtuous or vicious, and hence believed that there was a symmetrical obligation to adjust (in other words, to correct surpluses as well as deficits). The longevity of this debate ensured that politicians were saying almost the same things in the 1960s as in the 1970s and the 1990s. Germany must take "energetic measures for speedier growth and the stimulation of imports," as Raymond Barre of the EEC Commission put it in 1968.[40] One of the striking features of post-2008 financial crisis debates is that the old language came back.

The way out of the asymmetry/symmetry polarization was to choose an internal approach to currency stability rather than an external one: price or inflation stability rather than an exchange rate target. A great deal of constructive thought on this issue occurred, and evolved, within the framework of the CoG. Throughout the 1970s and more in the 1980s there was increased discussion in the CoG about the need for the harmonization of monetary policy. But it was only in 1992–1993, when a dramatic series of really violent exchange rate crises hit Europe, that the intellectual center of gravity shifted entirely to the priority of an internal rather than an external anchor. Exchange rate stability had simply become too problematic. The view of the importance of an internal rather than an external definition of monetary stability, institutionally guaranteed by legal safeguards of the autonomy of the central bank, was essentially a Europeanization of a position that had been long held by the Deutsche Bundesbank. Germans had seen this from the beginning: Karl Schiller, for instance, the powerful German economics minister at the time of the Werner Report, noted in 1970: "The independence of the Bundesbank must be maintained if possible to the final stage of economic and monetary union. [Germany] intends to present the autonomous central bank as a model for the European central bank."[41]

In addition, the whole debate about monetary integration would occur in a political (and perhaps a broader moral) framework. As France's President Georges Pompidou put the point in 1971: "For France it is important that the Germans understand that it is not a simple economic problem, but a question of Community morality."[42]

The almost endless debate about the same fundamental policy problems that seems to characterize the history of the CoG is deceptive. The course of the development needs to be charted very carefully, as what sometimes appeared as futile or pointless policy proposals later suddenly acquired an institutional reality. In his judicious account of the early phase of that history, Gianni Toniolo sensibly quotes a major EEC figure on the disappointment that not only was monetary union a nontopic, but also that no progress was made on "the less ambitious goal of monetary policy harmonisation."[43] The latter verdict could indeed be extended to the work of the CoG right up to 1992. The contribution of the CoG was more mundane: "to stimulate exchanges of view" on the differing policy and outcome stances of the various countries, to "encourage consultations" between economic and financial leaders, and to improve the comparability and timeliness of statistical collection. In retrospect it is clear that such work was essential to a realistic formulation of an approach based on targeting price stability.[44] Other accounts make a similar point. Gunter Baer, for instance, who as rapporteur for the Delors Committee worked closely with the CoG (and later became its secretary-general), acknowledges that "for those who expect monetary cooperation to result in a strategic interaction in policy making . . . the record of the Committee's achievements may be disappointing." But the CoG did contribute to the establishment of economic and financial stability, and "the process of mutual information and consultation and the intensive discussions in the Committee certainly enhanced the understanding of, and promoted a convergence of views on, important questions of principle," in particular the recognition that "the attainment of price stability is the primary objective of monetary policy."[45]

The CoG formed a critical element in the debate about European monetary management. Was it an instrument of European cooperation, designed to produce European answers as an alternative to the institutions of global governance; or was it part of a process of making the global monetary order more stable? What was its precise relation to the EEC, as it evolved in part deliberately outside the carefully planned institutional framework of the Community? The institutional indeterminacy of the CoG makes its development a striking contrast to that of the European Economic Community, whose future was laid down by the founding document, the 1957 Treaty of Rome, in a built-in teleology.

There is another aspect of the long-standing European discourse about the objective of monetary union. Particularly at the political level, the debate was driven not just by technical concern with adjustment in the international monetary system, but also by a large-scale political vision. Politicians developed the habit of attaching grand geopolitical ambitions to a currency. In the 1960s European statesmen—and in particular French policymakers—criticized the political benefits that the United States allegedly drew from the fixed exchange rate regime of the Bretton Woods order. Finance Minister Valéry Giscard d'Estaing termed this the "exorbitant privilege" in 1965; President Charles de Gaulle explained to Alain Peyrefitte that "no domain escapes from American imperialism. It takes all forms. The most insidious is that of the dollar."[46] De Gaulle's successor, Georges Pompidou, saw European monetary union as a "card" that Europeans could play in an international power game. And later, as president of the French Republic, Giscard, together with German Chancellor Helmut Schmidt, saw politics as the major reason why Europeans needed to act in the monetary sphere. As Schmidt told Giscard: "The Americans need to stop believing that if they whistle, we will obey."[47] The politicians who took this approach consistently believed that money was much too important to be left to technocrats and central bankers; and Schmidt at the highpoint of the debate on the establishment of the European Monetary System, on

November 30, 1978, went to the Bundesbank to lecture the conservative bankers about the primacy of politics. If European power politics
prevailed, the creation of a European order looked like a challenge to
the U.S.-based global system. As British Prime Minister James Callaghan,
a veteran of many British struggles with the IMF, put it: "I think there
comes a clear question—do we try to build a world monetary system or
are we going to have a European one?" The European Commission president, Roy Jenkins, replying to Callaghan, stated: "I think we might move
to a substantially more coordinated European monetary position which
could help to create a better world monetary position."[48]

It was the constant and inevitable clash between the two logics—the
one political, seeing European money as an instrument of power politics, and the other technocratic, in which European monetary integration was simply a more feasible version of a desirable international
cooperation—that resulted in the peculiar dynamic that created Europe's money. To work effectively, the European monetary order had to
be insulated from political pressures and from the grand vision; but
that process of insulation itself produced a substantial vulnerability as
national politicians would set themselves at odds with European money.

The often-concealed underpinnings of the struggle for a European
money—above all the idea that money was all about politics—bubbled
up at moments of trouble and distress. Such beliefs nourished all manner of paranoid interpretation. And this is a history with which Europeans are still living.

1

A Napoleonic Prelude

The sixties were a wild decade. Communications improved, fiery musicians drove a culture revolution, reformers wanted to clear away odd relics of the past, the United States was involved in a bloody war of ideologies, and Europeans wanted a new money and began to negotiate over new institutional ways of providing it. Which century? Both the 1860s and 1960s were revolutionary.

History repeats itself. But in odd ways. In the middle of the nineteenth century, the world was galvanized by the transatlantic cable and the ubiquitous railroad, by Verdi's and Wagner's music, by the reforms of Bismarck, Cavour, Gladstone, and Lincoln. Questions of European monetary unification and a simplification of the world's money were intimately linked, and Emperor Napoleon III provided a solution. He and his advisers had already pushed through the Latin Monetary Union, by which the coinage systems of France, Belgium, Switzerland, and Italy were homogenized, with a standard franc or lira coin of a standard weight and purity of silver that would circulate freely in the member countries of the currency union. The 1867 World Monetary Conference, held in Paris, went substantially further in its ambitions. Only a very slight alteration of parities would be required to bring into line France and Great Britain, as well as the United States, which was just recovering from the massively costly and destructive Civil War. France was on a bimetallic standard, its coinage set in terms of both gold and silver weights; Britain was on a pure gold standard; and the United States was considering a return to a stable currency based on metal.[1]

It would be relatively easy to change the weights of coins so as to create an equivalent of five francs to one dollar, and of five dollars or twenty-five francs to a British pound. The new gold coin would contain 112.008 grains of gold, while the existing British sovereign contained 113.001. Britain would thus need to undertake a slight devaluation in order to make the British coinage fit into the new system. Predictably, after some debate, Parliament was unwilling to take this step, which critics would have interpreted as a (small-scale) robbery of the holders of debt denominated in pounds.

The leading British monetary commentator, the editor of *The Economist*, Walter Bagehot, wrote enthusiastically about the new proposals. In his view, monetary unification would require France to give up a theoretically unsustainable bimetallic base, while Britain would have to give up the odd coinage of twenty shillings to a pound and twelve pence to the shilling. Decimalization would have provided a rational answer to Britain's monetary arithmetic. Readers of Anthony Trollope's Palliser novels encountered a political hero, Plantagenet Palliser, whose major political obsession was currency decimalization.

Bagehot gave another perspective on monetary simplification. Money, he argued, should not be seen as the creation of the state:

> We commonly think, I believe, that the coining of money is an economic function of government; that the Government verifies the quality and quantity of metal in the coin out of regard to the good of its subjects, and that Government is admirably suited to this task—that it is a very reliable verifier. But in truth, if we look at the real motives of governments, and the real action of governments, we may come to think otherwise. The prevalent notion about coinage is not an economic but a mystic notion. It is thought to be an inalienable part of sovereignty; people fancy that no one but a government can coin— that it is nearly a contradiction that anyone else should coin. A superstition follows the act. Coining is called a "natural" function of government, as if nature would not permit a government without it.[2]

Bagehot thought it much better to conceive of money as serving the needs of commerce (and of the people more generally) rather than the interests of the state and its rulers.

Furthermore, American currency instability in the wake of the Civil War gave the world the chance of having a currency based on a British-German vision of stability. Bagehot was sympathetic to the view that a small change in the value of the pound would be costly, unnecessary, and undesirable. But Britain could take the opportunity to harness a newly powerful Germany into its monetary orbit, and then associate the United States with the new project of a strong currency. As Bagehot put it: "In that case, there would be one Teutonic money and one Latin money; the latter mostly confined to the West of Europe, and the former circulating through the world. Such a monetary state would be an immense improvement on the present. Yearly one nation after another would drop into the union which best suited it; and looking to the commercial activity of the Teutonic races, and the comparative torpor of the Latin races, no doubt the Teutonic money would be most frequently preferred."[3]

Bagehot also reckoned with the possibility that some people would have to make complicated arithmetic adjustments before they could calculate in the new currency. Since he considered the northern Germans to be the best-educated people in Europe, it would be easier, he believed, for them rather than the arithmetically more lethargic Britons to make the calculations that would be needed for a new currency.

Nothing came of these bold proposals, in either the Napoleonic or the Bagehotian version, though the Latin Monetary Union remained in existence until it was broken up as a result of wildly different national inflation rates during the First World War. But the ambition was always there. In the nineteenth-century debates, there was no obvious reason why a monetary union should just be European. Indeed the logic that Napoleon and his advisers applied would just as obviously point to world monetary union. The economic and commercial calculation was compelling. At the height of the nineteenth-century wave of globalization, Carl Menger in his work *The Origin of Money* argued that the advantage of using the same medium of exchange as one's potential trading partners leads a network of merchants to accept a common medium of exchange and unit of account.

In the twentieth century, an alternate tradition of national money, first really developed in the nineteenth century, reached an apogee. According to this vision, a strong link tied money to political authority. That link—and the capacity of states to manipulate value—was intensified as a result of the attractions of paper or fiat money. The German economist and politician Karl Helfferich argued that the dependence of a monetary standard on metallic metal produced price fluctuations that in theory might be eliminated by the adoption of fiat money; but he also added the rider that that fiat money would be subject to unbearably intense political pressures. He concluded that "pure paper money represents the logical culmination of the history of the development of money." At the same time he soberly presented the political disadvantages of this quite logical development. The capacity of the state and of public policy to shape value would, he predicted, encourage a mobilization and a polarization of interests, on the one hand of those who might benefit from monetary depreciation, and on the other of recipients of fixed incomes, whether as wages or interest payments, who wanted an increase in the value of money. The capacity to manipulate value would lead to a new sort of class war, in which groups would form and mobilize in order to seize the levers of power that would give them the capacity of determining value. The conflict had the capacity to lead to a "complete demoralization of economic and social life," he wrote quite prophetically (in fact as Germany's finance minister during the First World War he became the major architect of the great German inflation). Helfferich's remarks were not just a speculation about the future. He was thinking of the example of agrarian populists' campaign at the end of the nineteenth century, both in America and in Europe, to inflate the currency in order to reduce the oppressive load of farm debt.[4]

The ideas on monetary unification were taken up again in the later twentieth century. In building Europe, the tie between money and political authority needed to be undone. Monetary populism and its inflationary aftermath discredited the approach of national money. One hundred years after Bagehot, the British decimalized their currency, and Europeans, prompted by a new war-induced episode of American currency disorder, again began to reflect seriously on the possibility of a European monetary union.

In February 1991 the Spanish Finance and Economics Ministry concluded its note on the preparations for the Maastricht Treaty and for European monetary union by citing Bagehot's work:

> The new system must be one which will do no violence to national jealousies. It will not do for one nation to say to any other, still less to all others—"My coinage is better than yours; my trade is larger, and my coinage better known than yours; therefore do you adopt my coinage and give up your own." Most nations—all great nations perhaps— are too sensitive and too proud to bear such language. The desire for an international coinage is not an imperious desire. The advantages it

promises are substantial and real, but they do not at once strike mankind. The mass of residents in every country will say—"We do not trade abroad; we do not travel abroad; we can use our native currency very well; why should we change it? Why should we learn a new system? We do not care about foreign currencies." There is a great mass of stagnant selfishness in all nations which will oppose this improvement, as well as all others. We must not reinforce that selfishness by wounded national pride; if we ask the mass of English people to take the French coinage, or the mass of French to take the English, we shall not prevail; the French will say—"We will not yield to England"; the English will say—"We will not yield to France." Any plan must be based on mutual concession. Everyone may hope to gain much, but everyone must sacrifice something.[5]

But negotiating the mutual concessions can be very hard. Most subsequent European discussions in consequence avoided Napoleon III's idea that a national money could be a general or universal currency, and thought that they needed to devise an entirely fresh store of value. When most national moneys were discredited by the aftermath of war finance and inflation, it looked easier to invent a completely new currency. In the late 1920s, during the negotiations that preceded the establishment of the Bank for International Settlements in Basel, the brilliant French economist Pierre Quesnay suggested an artificial currency unit (*grammor*) based on a specific weight of gold in order to avoid choosing any particular national money as the basis of a world standard. The great German statesman Gustav Stresemann in a speech before the League of Nations in 1929 deplored the new customs barriers and Europe's fragmentation, and casually asked, "Where is the European money, where is the European postage stamp?"[6] In the summer of 1932, Hans Fürstenberg, the head of the Berliner Handelsgesellschaft, the only big German bank to have survived the financial crisis of 1931 without state support, called for a European currency union, with a European central bank. Fürstenberg worried about the "confusion" of price levels at the beginning of the transition to new monetary units, but thought that there would be a quick resumption of economic activity on a basis of stable prices. A new money might have provided a stabilization of expectations in the middle of the world depression and at the beginning of a period of intense currency wars and competitive devaluations. But this was not a time when anyone was prepared to sacrifice anything.

Exactly one century after Napoleon III's conference, in 1967, Sir John Hicks concluded an analysis of the instability of credit with the claim that international credit, like international money, required to be managed. Today, credit transcends national frontiers to a much greater extent than it did when Hicks wrote his prescient warning:

> We do not need, on the international plane, to feel the Keynesian fear, that purely monetary management will be unable to fight depression; on the international plane it is not Depression, in the old sense, that is the danger. National governments, taught by Keynes, however indirectly, can see to that. What is liable to happen, if there is a failure of international credit, is that nations will turn in upon themselves, becoming more autarkic or more protectionist, impoverishing themselves and each other by refusing to trade with each other. (And this means, we can already see, refusing to *aid* each other.) That is the danger with which we are confronted; we can already see that it is no imaginary danger at this present time. The remedy, my old nineteenth-century experience would tell us, would be an International Central Bank, an International Bank which would underpin the credit structure, but in order to underpin it must have some control over it.[7]

Dealing with internationally connected flows of credit requires a great deal of coordination, and the sacrifice of particular national interests.

Even more powerfully but problematically, the coordination of international money involves giving up national ideas about money. National differences in regard to monetary practice are not just formulated as clashes of interests, but usually also appear as different and contrasting philosophies. As a consequence, negotiating commonalities between national positions involves some compromise of theoretical astringency. To take the examples that will be at the center of the story set out in the following pages: throughout the whole of the postwar era, a key French demand was for a mechanism of political control over the economy, and extension of the principle of some kind of planning, or, as it was frequently termed, economic governance. By contrast, Germany was for historical reasons deeply attached to an anti-inflationary policy anchored in the strong institutional autonomy of the central bank. How could these positions be reformulated to be brought into harmony with each other? Obviously, both could be translated to a European level, even though each country feared that translation might mean dilution: that the central bank would be under more pressure, or that the economic governance might simply take the form of budgetary rules. But there might also be conflict as a result of the Europeanization of the national policy preferences, and governance and autonomy might clash.

Academic commentators are often inclined to extremes, to be either Cassandras or Dr. Panglosses. Economists are very often Cassandras, in that they are irritated by the intellectual imperfections and flaws that often accompany the compromises implied by any big project: such as European monetary integration. Many economists, particularly Americans, warned that there was in the end no strict symmetry in the progress, and some reforms got ahead of other areas of policy in which there was insufficient advance: the removal of capital controls in 1990 was not accompanied by an equivalent move in monetary and exchange rate arrangements; and the move to monetary union was not accompanied by adequate reflection on the implications of a single money and capital market on the need for banking supervision and regulation that went beyond the national level, on the need for structural flexibility and for preserving competitiveness, and perhaps also on the fiscal concomitants of monetary union. Europeans largely ignored such warnings, which they put down to a one-sided American view of the European project summed up in the flippant catch-phrase: "It can't happen, It's a bad idea, It won't last."[8]

By contrast, political scientists are more easygoing characters and tend to the Panglossian. The intense study of how and what actually happens inclines them to slip into the easy assumption that that is the best, perhaps the only possible outcome. Even grotesquely unjust and dysfunctional systems such as Soviet rule were uncritically justified in this way; but so too is dysfunctionality in the governance of Europe.[9]

Of these dangers, the greatest by far is the lulling effect that Panglossianism brings—or, to use another metaphor, the blurring of the focus that means that real problems become indistinct and incapable of being defined or solved; in this view they are merely the necessary outcome of complex political maneuvering and interest bargaining. Historical accounts present the narrative of big international developments and advances; but they need to be sensitive to the historically conditioned flaws and compromises that are often deeply embedded in a process of institutional development. And these flaws have a tendency to be exposed at precisely the least propitious moment. Such exposure is precisely what constitutes a crisis.

2

The Origins of the Committee
of Governors

In the 1960s, European economies were growing very quickly, in what proved to be the last phase of the postwar economic miracle. As in the 1860s, the world was transformed by what might be called a globalization boom. In both cases global integration of capital, goods, and labor markets was driven by new technologies of communication and transport. In the 1860s the drivers were the transatlantic telegraph cable and the steamship; in the 1960s, information technology and new approaches to the bulk shipping of commodities. In both cases, the rapid pace of economic change called for institutional adaptation and innovation.

What was later celebrated as the postwar miracle, the *Wirtschaftswunder,* or the golden era, or the *trentes glorieuses,* may just have been a naturally occurring period of catch-up.[1] After years of destructive nationalism and wrongheaded and counterproductive economic and financial and monetary policies, European business could at last realize the potential inherent in newly developed technologies. But Europe's politicians inevitably wanted to take credit for the surprising rate of growth, and tried also to harness it for their purposes.

The impressive growth performance in Europe seemed to reflect favorably on the integration mechanism adopted by the six countries—Belgium, France, Germany, Italy, Luxembourg, and the Netherlands—that in 1957 had signed the Treaty of Rome and launched the European Economic Community. This treaty should be seen as part of the great and successful global postwar effort at trade liberalization. The initial effect of the EEC was to promote trade within the EEC, although there was also some diversion of non-EEC trade. Globalization surges almost always provoke some kind of backlash.[2] Initially the formation of the EEC provoked a series of transatlantic trade spats, especially over agricultural issues, with a "chicken war" in 1962–1963, when the United States imposed retaliatory tariffs in response to European tariffs on imported chicken. Some European countries also began to fear or resent the intrusion of U.S.-based multinational corporations, a feeling powerfully expressed in Jean-Jacques Servan-Schreiber's *Le défi américain* (The American Challenge), published in 1967.[3] The early years of the EEC were also dominated by the political rhetoric of France's wartime leader, Charles de Gaulle, who had returned to power in 1958 as the republic's prime minister and then as its president. De Gaulle explained that "the purpose of Europe is to avoid domination by the Americans or Russians. . . . Europe is the means by which France can once again become what she has not been since Waterloo, first in the world."[4]

The feature of the world economy that was obviously dominated by the United States was the international monetary order. Though forty-five countries had been represented at the Bretton Woods conference of 1944, which established the rules of the monetary system, the negotiations had taken place largely on a bilateral, Anglo-American basis; and in practice the power of the United States was so great that the settlement largely reflected American interests. The major reserve currencies were the dollar and the pound, which still played a significant role not just for Britain's overseas empire but also for many Latin American countries. The Bretton Woods settlement required current account convertibility, in line with the requirements of Article VIII of the International Monetary Fund's Articles of Agreement. But in practice the European countries were so weak that they could not afford such a move until 1958. Yet almost as soon as the Bretton Woods regime started to operate, it seemed to face serious problems.

The prevailing view of modern economists is that the 1960s collapse of Bretton Woods was inevitable, and was staved off only by able and sophisticated management of the system through the 1960s, in particular through the action of the BIS and the creation of the swap system, and through the IMF's General Arrangements to Borrow. Two views are usually presented to explain the ineluctability of breakdown. In the first, following the analysis given by Robert Triffin, the growth of other countries' dollar reserves (or claims on the United States) would lead to an increasing probability of crises of confidence, as reserve holders might realize that their assets were not liquid in the sense that they might not be convertible into gold. Alternatively, if reserve accumulation did not occur, the world would face liquidity shortages.[5] For part of the 1960s, more attention focused on the latter part of the dilemma, and the construction of a new reserve currency, the IMF's Special Drawing Right (SDR), was intended to relieve liquidity constraints. Yet by the time the SDR came to be issued, the world was perhaps suffering more from the first element of the Triffin dilemma, namely that of excessive reserve creation leading to crises of confidence. The dollar appeared to be like the infamous Chevrolet Corvair, which the burgeoning consumer movement in the United States had condemned as being "unsafe at any speed": threatening world deflation if too slow, or inflation and crises of confidence if too fast.

The second interpretation sees the problem in terms of the inconsistent trinity—fixed exchange rates, capital mobility, and independent monetary policies—that became well known in Europe from debates about whether a new version of Bretton Woods could be applied in the regional setting of the European Monetary System after 1979.[6] Capital mobility in a fixed-rate regime makes it impossible for countries to set their own monetary policies or determine their own monetary preferences. As applied to Bretton Woods, this interpretation emphasizes the frustration of some of the growing export economies about rising levels of inflation that were interpreted as being imported from the United States.

Neither of these widely shared interpretations is completely watertight, either factually or logically. The problems of the 1960s look much more easily soluble in retrospect, when compared with the challenges posed by global imbalances in the new millennium. In order to understand why the 1960s problems looked so bad, the political dimension, in particular the growing suspicion of the role of the United States, needs to be taken into account.

The consequence of the increasingly precarious U.S. position in the international monetary order was that European countries were inclined to negotiate their problems not in a European context, but bilaterally with Washington. Money—as represented by the U.S. dollar— was thus the worm in the European apple.

At the time the EEC was established as a consequence of the 1957 treaty, there was no effectively operating international monetary system. The European Payments Union, whose fiscal agent was the BIS, had been established in 1950 and played a major role in facilitating Europe's transition to convertibility by evolving a mechanism for multilateraliz- ing a complex web of bilateral arrangements that represented the out- growth or logical extension of 1930s protectionism. From the outset, the European Community also contributed to the improvement of na- tional monetary and fiscal policy by making its assistance dependent on policy reform in a manner that anticipated the later development of IMF conditionality. The German balance of payments crisis of 1950– 1951 avoided the imposition of trade restrictions—as was advocated by many influential commentators such as Thomas Balogh—and ensured a continuation of a German liberalization strategy.[7] Barry Eichengreen concludes in consequence that as early as 1950–1951 "it was clear that the EPU was working to solve the coordination problems that had pre- vented European countries from moving down the road of trade liber- alization. Export-led growth would not have proceeded as quickly or continued as successfully in its absence."[8]

Once the move to convertibility and a global monetary order had oc- curred, a series of questions was raised that seemed to require a Euro- pean response if the logic of the integration process foreseen in the Treaty of Rome was to be followed. As it was, instead, questions such as exchange rates and financial support packages were discussed within the framework of a transatlantic dialogue rather than as an issue of the European family. The debate about monetary rapprochement was a way of shifting from the international or global to the European setting, and in that way regaining the sense that Europeans could be masters of their own destiny.

The European Economic Community began to operate on January 1, 1958. The Treaty of Rome opened with a bold and inspirational pream- ble that referred to "the foundations of an ever closer union among the European peoples" and a decision to "ensure the economic and social progress of their countries by common action in eliminating the barriers which divide Europe." Economic harmonization was to drive a much broader process of reconciliation and pacification. The makers of Europe were building on an old and profound liberal insight that went back to Montesquieu, namely that increased commerce reduces tensions and removes the causes of war.

The treaty more particularly provided for the eventual liberalization of markets for services and for labor, as well as providing for an eventual free movement of capital. Article 67 stipulated:

> 1. Member States shall, in the course of the transitional period and to the extent necessary for the proper functioning of the Common Market, progressively abolish as between themselves restrictions on the movement of capital belonging to persons resident in Member States and also any discriminatory treatment based on the nationality or place of residence of the parties or on the place in which such capital is invested.
>
> 2. Current payments connected with movements of capital between Member States shall be freed from all restrictions not later than at the end of the first stage.

In addition, Article 68 required authorizations for exchange transactions to be granted "in the most liberal manner possible." In part in consequence of the treaty stipulations, the member countries of the EEC moved quickly to fulfill the international obligations of the Bretton Woods Agreement (Article VIII), after a long period in which it had seemed that most countries would find it impossible to move to current account convertibility. Between 1958 and 1961 the EEC member states adopted current account convertibility according to IMF criteria. In addition the EEC Commission continually pressed for the lifting of capital controls, with little appreciation of how such a move would limit the scope for monetary policy—perhaps because the intellectual climate of the time gave little attention or priority to monetary policy.

A basic economic policy framework was provided in Article 104:

> Each Member State shall pursue the economic policy necessary to ensure the equilibrium of its overall balance of payments and to maintain confidence in its currency, while ensuring a high level of employment and the stability of the level of prices.

In order to make coherent economic policy across the EEC, some degree of harmonization was required, with obligations on member countries and responsibilities of the newly established EEC Commission. The Monetary Committee of the European Community, composed of representatives of finance ministries and central banks, was established under Article 105(2) of the Treaty of Rome. Its function as laid down in the treaty was to observe the monetary and financial policies and general payments systems of the member states and, more generally, to "promote the co-ordination of the policies of Member States in monetary matters to the full extent necessary for the functioning of the Common Market." It was given the following tasks: "to keep under review the monetary and financial situation of Member States and of the Community and also the general payments system of Member States and to report regularly thereon to the Council and to the Commission" and "to formulate opinions, at the request of the Council or of the Commission or on its own initiative, for submission to the said institutions."

Section 1 of the same article spoke of an obligation by governments to "coordinate economic policies." Exchange rate policies were a common interest of the EEC, and Article 107(2) specified:

> If a Member State alters its exchange rate in a manner which is incompatible with the objectives laid down in Article 104 and which seriously distorts the conditions of competition, the Commission may, after consulting the Monetary Committee, authorise other Member States to take for a strictly limited period the necessary measures, of which it shall determine the conditions and particulars, in order to deal with the consequences of such alteration.

These sections seemed to echo another document that had been ratified as a treaty, the Articles of Agreement creating the International Monetary Fund. This is yet another of the cases in which the regional and the global stages of integration marched in parallel. Article IV, Section 4, of the Articles of Agreement required members to collaborate with the IMF in promoting exchange rate stability, and Section 5 laid down the conditions under which members might adjust exchange rates (the IMF's agreement was required for a change that moved more than 10 percent from the original parity).

The Treaty of Rome was to play another important role in subsequent discussion about monetary institutions and their reform. The EEC Council of Ministers (the highest decision-making body) and the

EEC Commission (in effect a combination of civil service and think tank) had extensive power to make institutional innovations as long as they were covered by the original terms of the treaty under Article 235 and thus constituted a "necessary" part of the operation of a common market.

> If any action by the Community appears necessary to achieve, in the functioning of the Common Market, one of the aims of the Community in cases where this Treaty has not provided for the requisite powers of action, the Council, acting by means of a unanimous vote on a proposal of the Commission and after the Assembly has been consulted, shall enact the appropriate provisions.

In the late 1980s some politicians and also academics would try to make the logical case that a really integrated market would require a monetary union. But the argument that a single currency was "necessary" for a market was always something of a stretch. Any action that went beyond being "necessary" for the functioning of the Common Market would require a treaty alteration. Such a maneuver was obviously complex and directly political, requiring positive votes in every national legislative assembly. Thus the European Monetary System established in 1978 required no treaty alteration in order to operate, and in fact was legally an agreement between central banks; but it was generally recognized that the establishment of a European Central Bank did require a treaty revision (as occurred in the Maastricht Treaty). The original text of Article 236 specified:

> The Government of any Member State or the Commission may submit to the Council proposals for the revision of this Treaty. If the Council, after consulting the Assembly and, where appropriate, the Commission, expresses an opinion in favour of the calling of a conference of representatives of the Governments of Member States, such conference shall be convened by the President of the Council for the purpose of determining in common agreement the amendments to be made to this Treaty. Such amendments shall enter into force after being ratified by all Member States in accordance with their respective constitutional rules.

Article 236 thus provided the legal reason why the establishment of a monetary union required a treaty (which was to be the Maastricht Treaty). It ensured that such a union was democratically legitimate in the sense that it was authorized in member states by parliamentary votes (and in one case also by referendum).

In the 1960s, such discussions about the legitimacy of a common currency would have seemed very remote. There was no obvious demand for such a currency. Since the values of European currencies were globally fixed under the terms of the 1944 Bretton Woods Agreement, and the beginning of the EEC coincided with a major and successful attempt to stabilize the French franc, exchange rate issues played only a minor role in the initial years of the EEC. Regulation of exchange rates took place on a global, not a European, level, and it was the IMF rather than the EEC that provided the primary forum for negotiation. That displacement posed a problem for European politicians, who resented what some saw as transatlantic meddling. In the later stages of the Bretton Woods system, in the 1960s, as currencies became more and more political, policymakers, especially in France, loved to quote a prophetic remark by the French poet Paul Valéry, who in 1931 had written that "Europe visibly aspires to be governed by an American committee."[9] The IMF, which supervised exchange rate arrangements in the post–Bretton Woods world, looked to Europeans like a perfectly American committee.

Central banks did not play a large part in the IMF, which was conceived of as a vehicle of finance ministries to manage international monetary cooperation and displace the central bankers who had made so many mistakes and attracted so much opprobrium in the 1930s. European central banks could act within the framework of the Bank for International Settlements (whose dissolution had been provided for in the Bretton Woods agreement but was never carried out). By a series of coincidences, notably U.S. suspicions of the IMF in the aftermath of revelations about the activities of its cofounder Harry Dexter White as a Soviet spy, the BIS rather than the IMF was chosen as the financial agent of the European Recovery Plan. In particular, the BIS administered the European Payments Union that began operating in 1950 as a means of multilateralizing European settlements. There was thus already some European central bank cooperation, even though at this time the central banks were for the most part politically controlled and there existed no well-developed conceptual framework as to why or how central banks could be independent. Later, as central bank cooperation intensified, their leaders were often regarded as a "brotherhood," or in

political science parlance as an "epistemic community," but at the outset they were firmly integrated into quite different national political
and institutional settings.

The EEC, however, also immediately had an institutional setting in
which central banks were represented. The Monetary Committee (MC)
started functioning in 1958, with representatives of both central banks
and finance ministries, and the latter definitely had the upper hand.
Some central bankers felt that they should establish their own institutionalized form of cooperation, as had been provided for in Article 105
of the Rome Treaty on the coordination of policy in monetary matters
(which may not be the same as coordination of monetary policy). An
early indication of a new approach came from the Netherlands. In a
1957 speech at the Alpbach Economic Forum in Austria, the governor
of the Nederlandsche Bank, Marius Holtrop, had gone further and
asked whether a common central bank policy was necessary in a unified
Europe, and then went on to answer the question in the affirmative.[10]

On November 10, 1957, Holtrop circulated a note in which he suggested that the five central banks of the EEC countries (Luxembourg
had none, as it was in a monetary union with Belgium) should send
identical letters to the finance ministers proposing enhanced cooperation between central banks. The Belgian, French, and German governors responded skeptically, arguing that such a move would look like a
concerted effort and raise national suspicions. In a subsequent discussion in Basel in January 1958, on the fringes of the monthly BIS board
meeting, the five men raised many of the issues that would be central to
the future debates of the Committee of Governors. The German governor, Karl Blessing, stated emphatically that the activities of the MC
should not be seen as central bank cooperation; the Italian, Donato
Menichella, argued that the governors should not be bound by decisions of the EEC (and still less by the opinions, or *avis*, of the MC). But
the outcome of the meeting produced no institutional innovation: the
five simply agreed to meet again in February or March to determine
whether they should hold regular meetings, and that they should tell
the Council of Ministers that central bank cooperation was "well assured."[11] So long as capital markets were not connected with each other
and exchange rate policies were not problematical, the case for greater
monetary cooperation was pretty weak.

One country in particular was skeptical. In the late 1950s, German
current account surpluses started to increase, setting off a pattern of

discussion that was echoed in the 1960s, the late 1970s, the late 1980s, but also in the late 2000s after the establishment of a monetary union. From the perspective of the Bundesbank, central bank cooperation might involve the demand for some German support operations, and thus involve pressure to follow policies that might be costly or inflationary in their impact on Germany. Blessing consequently spoke out to German Chancellor Konrad Adenauer against any plan for a fund of EEC countries.[12]

The 1957 statement of the five EEC central banks that everything was well and that no innovation was needed seems to have been accepted until an event occurred which showed that there was really not too much central bank cooperation between Europeans. In March 1961 the Deutsche Mark and the Netherlands guilder were revalued, after a long period of tensions in the markets, and after a great deal of discussion within the IMF about the appropriate response to the buildup of German surpluses, but after no particular consultation with Germany's fellow EEC members. All the negotiation was done in Washington. The Deutsche Mark revaluation came at a sensitive time for European politics because relative prices were at the forefront of policymakers' minds as they focused on negotiating agreements on agricultural prices. A change in parity upset very carefully negotiated results, and laid bare the whole fragile mechanism of the Common Agricultural Policy. The upset produced the first EEC-level response to the issue of monetary policy in member countries. The Van Campen report to the European Parliament (April 7, 1962) argued that monetary policy needed to be coordinated with other aspects of economic policy. It made the point that policy coordination alone would not be enough, and envisaged a federal system of monetary management analogous to the structure of the Bundesbank or the Federal Reserve System.

There was an acute European concern about imbalances among the member countries of the EEC, as well as within the broader international system. Trading imbalances obviously raised the existential question of whether the European customs union was operating sustainably and adequately. Holtrop was very worried about U.S. pressure on European surplus countries—in particular the Netherlands and Germany—to expand in order to correct the surpluses. He objected to American economists' lecturing the Europeans on the need for expansion or what he called advice "to follow a policy of hardly disguised inflation. I must object . . . to being told that surplus countries at the top of the boom should follow an expansionist policy." Instead, the United States should reject its "cheap money" bias.[13]

The EEC Commission published its Action Programme for the Second Phase of the Community on October 24, 1962, of which Part 8, inspired mostly by Robert Marjolin, the vice-president of the EEC Commission, who also held the economic portfolio, focused on monetary relations and called for the establishment of a council or committee of the EEC's central bank governors. The Commission's call was preceded by a sharp reminder that monetary policy was by no means a central concern of the EEC and the people who directed its fortunes at this stage: "Even though monetary policy no longer plays the almost exclusive directive role that it assumed in various epochs of the past, it still plays an essential role in the general equilibrium, even if it is only as the brake that slows down an economy threatened by inflation."[14] The brake would form the "stop" part of a stop-go cycle driven by domestic demand, but some central bankers were also worrying about inflation transmitted externally through the exchange rate system.

The monetary policy section of the Action Programme also spoke of the desirability of a general liberalization of capital accounts, in accordance with the provisions of the Treaty of Rome. It concluded in a visionary way that made explicit the logical link between monetary union and fiscal union. That linkage, which also figured in the lead-up to the Maastricht Treaty, was actually stated with greater clarity and force than it would be in the 1990s discussions. There would be parallel councils or committees to coordinate or determine fiscal policy as well as monetary policy, because both were seen as part of the management of demand. The central bank governors' committee would have its counterpart in a budget committee staffed by senior finance ministry officials. In this way the monetary and fiscal sides of union would advance in parallel: "The creation of a monetary union could become the objective of the third phase of the Common Market. The Finance or Economics Ministers of the Community, assembled in Council, would decide on conditions that should be fixed at an opportune time: the overall size of national budgets, and of the Community budget, and the general conditions of financing of these budgets. The Council of Central Bank Governors would become the central organ of the banking system of a federal type."[15] It would begin to resemble what was later sometimes called a Eurofed. This passage might be thought of as prophetic, in that the latter part of this suggestion was followed fairly precisely in the 1990s; but there was a major difference in that by the end of the twentieth century, central banks placed a very substantial premium on devising legal guarantees of their institutional and operational independence.

For the moment, however, economic theory was deeply unsympathetic to any idea of independent central banks. Monetary policy was a low priority. The 1960s consensus view of central banks as a fundamental nuisance, posing a threat to growth through their interest-rate policy, and requiring subordination in a general framework of economic policy direction, did not however meet with a great deal of enthusiasm in the central banking community—even at that time. Central bankers in consequence devoted some imagination to how to neutralize this political initiative of Marjolin, which would greatly extend the power of the Commission.

What was it that 1960s central banks actually did? They were rather like the House of Lords in Gilbert and Sullivan's *Iolanthe,* doing nothing in particular and doing it very well. They did not really even bother to act, and the economies of the European countries grew spectacularly, while the rate of inflation was for the most part tolerably and acceptably low. There was nothing to worry about and nothing to do. They rarely did monetary policy in the sense of an earlier or a later age. The basic tools of monetary policy for most European central banks at this time were thought to consist of discount policy and the alteration of the reserve ratios that banks were required to hold with the central bank. There was not a sufficiently deep market in government securities outside Britain or the United States for open market operations to play a significant role. But in practice, central banks did not like to change their headline policy tools at all. Any change of interest rates or alteration of bank reserve ratios would alter income and wealth distributions and create political waves. Italy's first postwar central bank governor, the eminent economist and liberal thinker Luigi Einaudi, put it this way in 1960, at the height of Italy's postwar economic miracle: central banks did not like "noise" *(rumore).* "Noise" would produce public comment and political pressure: "Newspapers blow up the news, stir up public opinion: financial commentators come close to prophesying chaos, crisis. Predictions are made of falls on the stock exchange, of its being impossible to obtain advances or discount bills." Einaudi went on to give a perceptive description of an informal, whispered system of management and control. Instead of being loud and political, the central bank governor would "receive the managers of the banks, friends of his or persons devoted to him, the heads of firms large and small in his study. . . . In the Governor's study orders are not given, there is discussion, the situation is examined, the intricate knots are disentangled, and advice is given. Instead of raising the discount rate, why not politely reduce some overdraft limits, why not increase the interest rates on facilities whose restriction is desired?"[16]

The informal pattern of control, characteristic of all European countries, would be threatened by any central European direction of monetary policy. On November 12, 1962, the EEC central bank governors met in Basel to prepare a response to the Marjolin initiative. They eventually concocted a statement that marks the real beginning of the Committee of Governors, but the document was inevitably controversial and seemed to rock the boat of quietly whispered policy. In a note agreed by all the EEC central bank governors on December 12, 1962, they stated their wish for periodic meetings in Basel, which would "prepare" for meetings of the ministers and governors in the framework of the EEC Council. They would also consider public finance issues. The memorandum, however, also pointed out that many policy aspects could not be tackled at this level but required either a treaty modification or some interstate negotiation that could not be undertaken by central banks. Such issues included reform of the international monetary system, mutual financial support, and the creation of a monetary union among the Six (the founding states of the EEC).[17] Decades later, this point about the logic of interstate cooperation may seem obvious, but at that time it posed a clear challenge to strongly held concepts of national sovereignty. The idea that central banks might undertake some sort of political initiative clashed with a vision in which central bankers were more a silent part of the operation of a government, which inevitably had fundamentally domestic political objectives and priorities.

Such feeling ran particularly strong in France. The day after the first Basel meeting in November, an interministerial committee in France laid down some fundamental principles: that "France has long insisted that free exchange be accompanied by a harmonization of conditions of competition." The French officials were also worried about the likely consequences of the enlargement of the EEC to include the United

Kingdom, and noted that "experience shows that national imperatives are very strong in this respect."[18] Corresponding with other central bankers, the governor of the Banque de France, Jacques Brunet, consequently insisted that "the role of governments in monetary policy be emphasized."[19]

Governor Brunet was then so worried by the potential ramifications of the governors' note that he insisted that it not be communicated to anyone apart from the governors and the ministers. In particular, the note was not to be presented to Marjolin, although the latter explicitly asked for it in the course of a long lunch meeting with the governors. A Banque de France minute recorded that Marjolin's exposition had indicated that he emphatically wanted to pursue other propositions that belonged to the sphere of competence of governments and not of central bankers. Marjolin had also proposed to hold two "symbolic" meetings in Brussels to emphasize the link with the EEC, a suggestion backed by the Belgian central bank governor, Hubert Ansiaux. The Banque de France was also basically hostile to the idea of the note, which it considered "in a bad style, because the discussion was often delicate and some of the governors either have an imperfect knowledge of French, or no French at all."[20]

The critics did not just set out their views behind closed doors. There was also a hostile public response from the Bundesbank, whose president, Karl Blessing, argued that monetary integration was not possible without prior economic integration and that anyway monetary policies needed to be dealt with at the transatlantic level rather than in a European context.[21] By contrast with the French government's restrictive view of central bank action, Blessing had a rather more expansive view. A veteran of the prewar predecessor of the Bundesbank, the Reichsbank, he had been dismissed in 1939 by Hitler after the bank criticized government spending policy in the last phase of the 1930s Nazi rearmament drive.

Marjolin's frustrations with the governors increased as a consequence of their uncommunicative reaction to his initiative. In July 1963 he set out his new plans publicly. He suggested that the strengthening of economic integration should involve the creation of a Committee of Central Bank Governors, as well as the enlargement of the competence of the MC, so as to include consultations before any important decision affecting international monetary relations, including drawings on the

IMF. In particular, and most importantly, EEC members should be consulted before any parity alteration. An EEC Budgetary Policy Committee should be established to coordinate fiscal policies of member countries, and special meetings of the Council should be convened to examine the entirety of member country policies. The CoG, Marjolin hoped, would form the "embryo of a Community Federal Reserve Board."[22]

The urgency of a European mechanism for discussing monetary policy increased because of heightened tension within the Community in the aftermath of Italy's large public-sector deficit in 1963 and the resulting balance-of-payments problems. In March 1964 a major speculative attack occurred, with the Italian treasury losing $82 million in reserves on March 12 and 13. The Italian government imposed austerity measures without consulting other European governments, and negotiated exclusively in Washington with the U.S. Treasury and the IMF. Italy, a deficit country, was doing what Germany, a surplus country, had done in 1961; and the Italians found the atmosphere in Washington agreeable and congenial. They may have thought that the importance of the Italian peninsula to U.S. strategic security thinking would give them greater leverage than they had in Brussels. Undersecretary George Ball said he was sympathetic because "the lira is an important currency." The Italian record of the Washington conversations shows that Treasury and State Department officials wanted to help, in view of "Italy's generous cooperation in assisting the United States in recent years."[23] The governor of the Banca d'Italia, Guido Carli, concluded a swap arrangement of $100 million with the U.S. Treasury and a $250 million swap with the Federal Reserve, as well as an Export-Import Bank standby credit of $200 million, $250 million for the financing of U.S. commodity exports to Italy from the Commodity Credit Corporation, and $300 million in credits for the Cassa del Mezzogiorno (a fund for the development of southern Italy) from the World Bank. The IMF increased its lira holdings to the maximum of the gold tranche within the fund ($225 million), and the World Bank repurchased Italian government bonds. In all, Carli managed to obtain $1,000 million in support in the United States. Soon afterward the Italian treasury minister wrote to the prime minister that Italy's EEC partners judged Italy's situation "in less cordial terms."[24] Washington was not only more understanding than Brussels (or Paris or Frankfurt); it had so much more cash to offer!

European fingers quickly wagged at the excessively Atlanticist stance of Rome. It seemed particularly offensive that Carli had traveled straight from Basel, where he had been vague about his worries, to Washington.[25] Carli was asked by the Monetary Committee to explain the Italian position, which seemed to be at odds with the ideals of the EEC and the explicit provisions for mutual economic assistance in Article 108 of the Treaty of Rome. The president of the MC, Dutch Treasurer-General Emile Van Lennep, started the discussion with an expression of regret about the "failed organization" of contacts between the Banca d'Italia and other European central banks. There had in fact been parallel agreements with the Bank of England (a swap of $100 million) and with the Bundesbank ($150 million). But Carli replied to Van Lennep's attack by observing that Brussels institutions were not suitable for "emergency action" because of their complex procedures. The U.S. arrangements by contrast had been quick and flexible. Other Europeans took the opportunity to give lectures to Italy. André de Lattre from the French treasury suggested that Italy should adopt a wage control policy, while the vice-governor of the Banque de France, Bernard Clappier, called for an examination of the Italian program, and finance ministry officials from other countries wanted assurances that monetary support would not be used to support the impoverished south via the Cassa del Mezzogiorno.[26] Thus while Washington opened its pocketbook, Brussels read out its sermons.

There was inevitably an anti-American edge to the European reform debate at this moment. At the same meeting of the EEC Monetary Committee, Van Lennep also proposed a European scheme to deal with the liquidity issues of the international monetary system. Since the influential articles of Robert Triffin in the late 1950s, policymakers had worried about a dilemma in which, on one side, there might be insufficient liquidity and a deflationary drag in the world, and on the other the United States might oversupply liquidity so that dollar claims might be far greater than the gold and other liquid assets the United States had to cover them. Triffin's approach had always involved a call to European action. Van Lennep was acting in the spirit of Triffin when he proposed that the EEC Six should evolve their own reserve system as an alternative to the further creation of dollars in the international system "in case the dollar can no longer fulfill its functions or if there is deflationary pressure." But the suggestion divided the MC. De Lattre spoke very emphatically in favor of European rather than U.S. reserve creation, which "must not depend on the needs of an individual country but must be agreed collectively." Otmar Emminger from the Bundesbank and Rinaldo Ossola from the Banca d'Italia were quite critical of the French suggestion, and Emminger reasoned that there was no need to replace the dollar with another reserve unit, and that if assistance was required, an expansion of the General Arrangements to Borrow was the most appropriate mechanism.[27] That arrangement had been established by ten major countries in 1961, with the objective of providing credit of up to $6 billion, additional to the resources of the IMF. The fundamental eventuality that the G-10 might have to cope with lay in the increasing strains facing the major reserve centers: the United States and the United Kingdom. Switzerland joined this group in October 1963, although it continued to be known as the Group of Ten.

A proposal for a collective reserve unit had already been made in a broader international context in 1963 by the former head of the IMF's Research Department, Edward Bernstein, and in October 1963 a G-10 Deputies' Study Group began work on "the functioning of the international monetary system and its probable future needs for liquidity." But it was only in July 1965, when the U.S. Treasury secretary came around to an appreciation of the Triffin concerns and called for a major new international monetary conference, that the intense negotiations began that eventually produced a very circumscribed possible new reserve asset, the Special Drawing Right.

In contrast, the April 1964 discussion about Italian stabilization, occurring at a sensitive moment in international monetary negotiations over alternatives to the dollar as a reserve currency, showed how deep the divisions were within Europe. In particular, the debate underlined how much some European countries—especially Italy and Germany—looked to Atlantic rather than European solutions. The divisions appeared greatest in the positions of the different central banks; and those divisions seemed most appropriately dealt with by an exclusive committee of central bankers, in which finance ministries played no role.

The Committee of Governors of the Central Banks of the Member States of the European Economic Community was created one month later by an EEC Council decision of May 8, 1964. Article 2 of the decision stated: "The Committee shall be composed of the Governors of the

Central Banks of the Member States. If they are unable to attend, they may be represented by another member of the directing body of their institution. The Commission shall, as a general rule, be invited to send one of its members as a representative to the meetings of the Committee." Article 3 specified that the tasks of the Committee would be:

- to hold consultations concerning the general principles and the broad lines of policy of the Central Banks, in particular as regards credit and the money and foreign exchange markets;
- to exchange information at regular intervals about the most important measures that fall within the competence of the Central Banks, and to examine those measures. This examination shall take place before the measures concerned are adopted where circumstances, and in particular the time limit for their adoption, allow. In carrying out its task, the Committee shall keep under review the trend of the monetary situation both inside and outside the Community.[28]

The 1964 decision inevitably played a crucial role in subsequent debates among the governors about the status of their committee. In particular, it was of great significance that though this was not an EEC (later European Community, and finally European Union) institution, ultimately the Council of Ministers had made a decision to establish the committee. Some German central bankers, who were particularly sensitive to the issue of the instruction of central banks by political authorities, consequently saw 1964 as "original sin" (*Sündenfall*).[29]

The vice-president of the EEC Commission, Robert Marjolin, who had largely been behind the initiative of creating the CoG, set out at the outset a bold project for its future work. Later Marjolin was profoundly disappointed. He left Brussels in 1967, convinced that the "dynamic period" in the life of the EEC had ended, and that it would henceforth simply be concerned with management ("une période de gestion").[30]

The first meeting of the CoG occurred on July 6, 1964. Five governors from the central banks of Belgium (also representing Luxembourg), France, Germany, Italy, and the Netherlands sat around a table in Basel, along with their deputies (known as alternates). The governors appointed the secretary-general of the BIS, the Italian Antonio d'Aroma, as secretary-general of the committee.[31] The Dutch central banker Marius Holtrop, who because of his 1958 proposals might have been thought of as the real originator of the CoG, was elected chairman. He continued in this position for the next three years (until he retired from the central bank) although the term of the chairmanship was nominally only one year. The EEC commissioner with responsibility for economic and monetary affairs, Robert Marjolin, also attended the meeting. Indeed, at the first session he seemed to play a dominant role.

In October 1964 the CoG agreed the definitive version of the rules of procedure initially discussed at the first meeting, which provided for an annual election of the chairman; and the governors concluded an agreement with the BIS on the establishment of a secretariat, staffed by the BIS but paid by the member central banks. The BIS consequently provided the rapporteur, who compiled quite detailed minutes of the monthly meetings, which were usually held in Basel.[32]

At the initial meeting of the CoG, Marjolin explained that "the Commission has rather ambitious views on the future of the committee, because it believes that the Europe of the Six can also be realized in the monetary field."[33] He mentioned three particular areas of work: action to stop fluctuation in agricultural prices arising from the value of the unit of account; anti-inflationary action, since too often this was left to central banks, which tightened interest rates, restricted credit, and thus confined the possibilities of investment; and determining the usefulness of capital controls, used in particular by Germany to block inflows.

Responding to Marjolin, the chairman of the CoG, Holtrop, emphasized the composition of Europe by sovereign states, and also argued that there was a fundamental difference between the Monetary Committee and the new committee: "The former was formed by representatives of governments and experts from central banks, and is called on to advise the EEC, while the latter must above all give the possibility to the governors of exchanging views on specific topics, for instance on the nature of measures adopted by a central bank and the influence that such measures might have on other central banks." Otmar Emminger, the vice-president of the Bundesbank, spoke of a natural division of labor between the MC, whose principal task was promoting coordination of the policies of member countries in international monetary affairs, while the CoG had the major mission of "coordinating the main lines of future policies of central banks."[34] In practice, this meant that the CoG was never concerned with the most political and sensitive issue affecting central banks and their interrelationship: the sustainability of the exchange rate.

In the initial agenda-setting meetings, the governors expressed considerable skepticism about Marjolin's ambitious schemes. In October Brunet politely opined that the monetary union could advance at the same time as an economic union, but that would demand a "reasonable wait." Blessing was more candid: there could be monetary union only in the case of political union and with the transfer of national sovereignties. "Monetary union in substance represents the conclusion of the unification process and is not conceivable without a European parliament. A pooling of reserves appears premature." Carli fully supported the stance that monetary union needed to coincide with political union, and thus that the task was to focus much more on the practical problems of the present. Only Ansiaux seemed to wish to go further in Marjolin's direction: a monetary union before a political union was not unthinkable, but the organ that would run such a union would be analogous to a central bank and "have such great powers that the governments would hesitate to surrender to it powers that they currently wielded with regard to their own central banks."[35]

In practice a close relationship existed between the CoG and the MC. The governors' alternates in the CoG (the deputy governors), who by the 1970s would hold their own regular preparatory meetings, were also generally the representatives of the central banks on the Monetary Committee, sitting alongside senior officials from the finance ministries. The surviving records of the two bodies, however, look rather different. The MC prepared material for meetings of the finance ministers in the European Council, and did not maintain extensive verbal minutes; as a result, reconstruction of what happened in the MC depends on the informal reports prepared by central bank and finance ministry representatives. By contrast, the CoG secretariat in Basel made extensive minutes that preserve the basic outlines of the argumentation presented by members.

In the event, the high hopes of the EEC and of Marjolin of finding a way of dealing with inflation without high interest rates or stop-go monetary policies were disappointed. Political interruption also limited the scope for effective policy discussion. The work of the MC was also damaged by French nonparticipation from July 1965 to March 1966, as a part of France's "empty chair" strategy at the EEC level (when France refused to accept an agricultural policy reform that would have limited its ability to influence subsequent policy); but Chairman Holtrop made sure that Brunet was kept informed of the central bankers' discussions.[36]

The CoG developed in a different direction, as a forum for the provision of short-term financial facilities in the form of central bank swaps (reciprocal lines of credit between central banks to establish additional resources to be used if needed in exchange market interventions). It became a European appendage to the swap network that the Federal Reserve had created in 1962, as a potential source of support for the dollar as well as for European currencies in difficulties.[37] The CoG, because it met in Basel at the same time as the BIS and G-10 meetings, could thus evolve mostly into an instrument for formulating a common European response to the international financial and monetary problems of the day: the threats of a crisis emanating from the overstrained position of the British pound, and later from the U.S. dollar; and the discussion of a new reserve unit that might supplement or replace the dollar and provide a stable supply of international liquidity. This was also the background to the CoG's first financial support package, which—rather extraordinarily—did not involve mutual support, or lending to a member country of the EEC. Because of the logistics of coordinating a series of meetings in Basel with U.S., Canadian, and Japanese representatives, the G-10 meetings generally were timed to precede those of the CoG. Thus the Europeans could not really be accused of precooking the outcome—a suspicion that American financial diplomats often raised. But the sessions were opportunities to work out the details of a European reaction.

On September 13, 1965, the CoG considered the discussions that had been unfolding with the Bank of England about a support operation through the General Arrangements to Borrow. For most of the 1960s, the weakest institutional link in the international monetary chain was the United Kingdom. Support for the United Kingdom lay in the interest of the whole international community and of the system as a whole, with the consequence that the United Kingdom was generally able to extract support.[38] The problems of sterling as a major reserve currency potentially foreshadowed those of the dollar.

From August 29 to September 5, 1965, a representative of the Bank of England had visited Basel to ask for assistance from the G-10.[39] The EEC central banks, which saw themselves increasingly as a coherent caucus within the G-10, agreed to contribute $350 million as a three-month credit, but the Banque de France withdrew from the scheme, reducing the amount to $260 million. Was support of the United Kingdom a proper task for the EEC central banks? The Belgian central bank governor, Hubert Ansiaux, began by explaining that it did not seem likely that the United Kingdom would be able to repay promptly; and in fact much larger amounts were needed ($4–5 billion), and Ansiaux suggested replicating something like the big stabilization loans of the 1920s, the Dawes and Young Plan bond issues, which had been used to prop up the fragile Weimar Republic, and which had (in the end) failed rather miserably. The group then discussed the British situation with U.S. Treasury Secretary Henry Fowler, who expressed his confidence in the pound sterling ("in a manner more or less nuanced," the minutes record).[40] France withdrew from the planned rescue, leaving the Bundesbank to support sterling with a three-month credit line of $120 million and the Federal Reserve with $400 million. The French purse was as empty as the French chair. The European support briefly buoyed the pound, in that it allowed the Bank of England to conduct what was described at the time as "the most massive bear squeeze in the history of foreign exchanges"; but the long-term effect was less dramatic, and British authorities began highly secret discussions about a possible devaluation.[41]

The issue of sterling support credit was discussed again by the CoG in May 1966. Again Ansiaux was deeply critical: "the United Kingdom has apparently undertaken no effective or serious measures, and in this way the Europeans might be obliged to support sterling indefinitely."[42] In general, a sense that Europe was managing its currencies in a better way than the Anglo-Saxon reserve centers was an important undercurrent of the discussions on financial assistance. Governor Guido Carli of the Banca d'Italia argued that the IMF should intervene to criticize the U.S. balance-of-payments deficits, and believed that such action might have a big impact on U.S. public opinion.[43]

The problems of the pound and the dollar required more than central banks' short-term support operations; a real solution would depend on rethinking the issue of international reserves. That discussion occurred mostly on the international level, with France engaged in a rather unequal bilateral negotiation with the United States. The program that French Finance Minister Valéry Giscard d'Estaing proposed in 1965 involved a collective reserve unit linked to gold, with the aim of restoring external discipline on the United States. President Charles de Gaulle saw the plan as a tool against "American inflation." Instead of providing unconditional reserves, there would be a possibility of drawing conditional credit. In 1967 France set about convincing the other members of the EEC of the merits of Giscard's plan, and proposed to link it at the same time with a reform of the voting system at the IMF so as to give the six EEC members a veto on IMF decisions. As a result of French pressure, the name of the proposed new reserve unit was not to include "reserve" but looked more like a credit instrument: the Special Drawing Right.[44]

The European position was hammered out in the CoG. In the first discussion, in May 1967, Emminger of the Bundesbank rightly presented the demand for a European veto right on SDR issues as a political demand.[45] But France and Belgium pushed hard on this issue and secured a common European position. Brunet and Ansiaux made the case that agreement on the SDR should be dependent on greater European influence in the IMF, and should also involve general discussion of global monetary reform issues.[46] In short, the CoG at this time was acting mostly as a regional caucus or pressure group pushing for global adjustments.

The CoG also discussed capital controls, with the National Bank of Belgium and the Banca d'Italia supporting the EEC Commission's arguments about the desirability of lifting capital controls, while the Bundesbank, the Nederlandsche Bank, and to some extent the Banque de France argued for the desirability of maintaining them. At this point it was the weaker and poorer economies, which hoped that external inflows of capital might provide a powerful locomotive for development, that were most enthusiastic about liberalization; whereas the richer countries were worried about reversals and outflows. Emminger explained that Germany needed capital controls in order to prevent flows of capital from undermining monetary policy-making and the maintenance of monetary stability.[47] Guido Carli replied, speaking with great pride about the first six months of 1966, when Italy had largely liberalized its capital account. The Franco-German core of the EEC was highly resistant to change on this issue; but the Franco-German relationship became vulnerable when the French exchange rate—the subject of an obsessive national pride—came under threat. In particular, French deficits and German surpluses raised a problem of adjustment. Did France need to adopt austerity and contract, or could Germany be pushed to be more expansive? In some ways, France and the United

States, as increasingly vulnerable deficit countries, should have held a common position vis-à-vis the big new surplus countries, Germany and Japan; but that commonality was impossible because of transatlantic political strains.

A dramatic move by the CoG to an active lending policy occurred in July 1968. It was now the French turn to proffer the begging bowl. Given the harsh anti-American tone in the aftermath of de Gaulle's press conference of February 4, 1965, and the persistent French criticisms of the American "exorbitant privilege" of imposing the dollar as the world's leading currency, it is not surprising that French policymakers did not want to crawl to Washington for additional credit. The governor of the Banque de France, Jacques Brunet, explained that French reserve losses had required a drawing of $745 million from the IMF, as well as gold sales to the Federal Reserve, the Swiss National Bank, and EEC central banks. By the beginning of July, the French reserves were nevertheless exhausted, and the Banque de France embarked on swaps of $600 million with the Federal Reserve and with the EEC central banks. In Basel the central bank governors resolved that the French situation met the mutual assistance conditions stipulated by Article 108 of the EEC treaty. They agreed on a three-month $600 million credit, with half coming from the Bundesbank, $200 million from the Banca d'Italia, and the remainder shared by the National Bank of Belgium and the Nederlandsche Bank.[48] The deal was linked with an agreement by the Banque de France to sell $300 million in gold to the participating central banks.[49] At the next meeting the Bundesbank explained that it was prepared to extend further credit lines to the Banque de France, in order to deal with speculative pressure against the franc, and in expectation of a Deutsche Mark revaluation.[50] These negotiations took place, in the European setting, in parallel with global (G-10) discussions of an analogous arrangement of up to $2,000 million in support of Britain. The big move of the CoG into financial support operations came not because the IMF was unable to provide a greater amount of resources, but because France was worried about the political implications of drawing further on the IMF.

Pressure on the franc also raised the much more difficult issue, which could not be addressed by the CoG, of the sustainability of European exchange rates. At the MC, where the politicians clearly held the upper hand, there had been a consensus that a parity alteration of the

French franc should be avoided. But then the European political confusion with respect to monetary arrangements was demonstrated very vividly at the Bonn G-10 summit of November 1968, when Europe's political consensus on exchange rates dramatically fell apart. The meeting took place largely at the insistence of the U.S. administration, and was exceptionally badly prepared. It took place in the very bleak modern building in Bonn occupied by the German Economics Ministry, with large quantities of beer and sparkling wine on offer, but nothing to eat but meager canapés. The corridors were filled with bored officials who had been expelled from the high-level political discussions. Outside the building, demonstrators held up placards with the slogan "Save the Mark." In the course of the negotiations the German hosts presented a package that had been the subject of intense bargaining within the German coalition government, in which Social Democratic economics minister Karl Schiller sought an alteration of the Mark parity but was in a minority. Finance Minister Franz Josef Strauss, of the Bavarian Christian Democrats, passionately opposed a revaluation of the Deutsche Mark because it would be harmful to German export interests.

When it was clear in the meeting that Germany would not act on the currency, the pressure shifted to France. After a telephone conversation with President de Gaulle, French Finance Minister François-Xavier Ortoli agreed to an 11.1 percent devaluation of the French franc, but one day after the summit de Gaulle announced that France would maintain the parity of the franc. It was very obvious that the G-10 mechanism was incapable of dealing with the European money muddle. In consequence, the desirability of evolving a European response mechanism became much more evident.

On February 12, 1969, the EEC Commission produced a new memorandum on monetary cooperation, largely at the instigation of the French economist Raymond Barre, Marjolin's successor as economics commissioner. The governors were much happier to deal with this renewed effort than with the Marjolin proposals of the early 1960s. In part, this was simply a chance outcome of the impact of different personalities. Barre was a technocrat, whom Giscard later described as "the best economist of France."[51] He was chubby and friendly, with a low-key manner that contrasted with the self-conscious intellectual superiority of Marjolin. But the proposals were not that different. Barre proposed to establish a close link between economic policy and monetary cooperation;

and he also liked to discuss the possibility of coordinating cyclical fiscal policies. Monetary support would be linked with the convergence of medium-term economic objectives and coordination of short-term policies. Essentially, he proposed systematizing the support mechanism established to deal with the French case in July 1968.[52]

It was a matter not just of contrasting personalities, but of a different international environment for the discussion of possible European reforms. It is striking that the European discussion after Barre's initiative did not really focus on monetary policy adjustments; this neglect was largely the consequence of the fixed-exchange-rate regime, in which monetary policy tagged along. But the fixed-exchange-rate regime was increasingly vulnerable.

European monetary coordination had its origins not in a failure of global financial mechanisms to offer via the IMF quick and responsive balance-of-payments support, but in political worries about the Washington-based institution. That was the backdrop to the French support operation of July 1968. That operation demanded a logic of regularizing a mechanism for short-term financial support. It was only after this that a much more fundamental problem emerged—the IMF's failure in its role as steward of the international monetary order, namely its inability to address the increasingly severe exchange rate tensions that developed between 1968 and 1971. As a consequence of the limitations of the international institution, there was a real need at the end of the 1960s for a new European approach to the general question of monetary relations.

3

The Response to Global
Monetary Turbulence

Global monetary turbulence centered upon the role of the dollar in the fixed-exchange-rate regime. From 1968, when the London gold pool stopped operating and the private gold market was disconnected from an official market at which transactions still occurred at the fixed parities, to 1971, when President Nixon finally "closed the gold window," the system was in crisis. The dollar was predicted to lose its role in the international system, and France in particular engaged in constant criticism of the dollar order. The older reserve currency, the pound sterling, which still played a significant role (though mostly for countries in the British Commonwealth), was in deeper trouble than the dollar throughout the 1960s. The aftermath of the British devaluation of 1967 threatened wider monetary instability. There was increased concern about rising inflation. Such concerns raised the question of whether there could be an alternative store of value to the dollar, which was at the heart of the Bretton Woods regime. A more stable monetary measure might be desirable, and in the wake of the creation of the IMF's (heavily circumscribed) Special Drawing Rights there was increased interest in the institutional creation of liquidity and also in artificial units of account. In addition, the Europeans wanted a monetary unit that reflected their interests, rather than those of the United States. In consequence, two issues began to be prominent that would remain central to the pursuit of European monetary integration: the possibility of establishing a European unit of account, and the interrelationship of monetary with more general economic policy.

American policymakers did not see themselves as the source of the world's trouble. On the contrary, they saw the current account surpluses that were building up in West Germany (and also in Japan) as an indication of a currency manipulation in which the surplus countries were forcing exports on the rest of the world. The surpluses of Germany also raised a question about whether there could really be an effectively coordinated European response. Should new exchange rates be negotiated? Or was there a need for a short- or medium-term support mechanism to finance imbalances within Europe?

In the late 1960s, the first of the major sustained political initiatives aiming at the creation of a monetary union was launched by the EEC Commission. The result, usually referred to as the Werner Plan (after the prime minister of Luxembourg, Pierre Werner, who chaired the committee that produced the document), is frequently regarded as a failure. It was characteristic of many of the phases of European monetary integration in that the approach depended excessively on an unlikely simultaneity of multifarious aspects of the integration process. But in fact the suggestions made at this time (including an extended role for the CoG) were not that dissimilar to those made in more apparently auspicious circumstances at the end of the 1980s and the beginning of the 1990s. As a result Amy Verdun characterizes the Werner Plan as a "remarkably similar blueprint" to that of Jacques Delors and the committee he chaired in 1988–1989, which provided a basic draft of the mechanism required for European monetary union.[1] Institutional innovation, in the form of the European Monetary Cooperation Fund, initially envisaged as a potential Federal Reserve System for Europe, was at the heart of the proposals. The major difficulty lay in the actual implementation, which proved to circumscribe severely the operations of the EMCF (similar considerations would later prevent the emergence of a European Monetary Fund). In consequence, it is not surprising that in 1988 Delors's initiative started with a reflection on the lessons of the Werner Plan, and on the reasons why the Werner proposals had been only very partially and ineffectively implemented.[2] The Werner Plan would have brought monetary institutionalization closer to the heart of Europe. It produced, for instance, a proposal to shift the headquarters of the new fund and the regular meetings of the fund and the CoG to Luxembourg, as well as to link the work of the CoG with that of the Monetary Committee.

The issue of monetary reform gained additional urgency because of Europe's exchange rate crises, in particular the August 1969 French devaluation and the October revaluation of the Deutsche Mark. The currency moves created chaos in the Common Agricultural Policy (CAP), and Germany's new foreign minister, Walter Scheel, irritated French policymakers by saying that the CAP was practically finished as a consequence.[3] France in particular worried about the inflationary effect of increases in food prices and postponed changes in the so-called Green Franc, the exchange rate used to calculate agricultural subsidies and payments. Keeping the agricultural price at the old level gave French exporters an advantage, and other countries then imposed retaliatory taxes on French exports and paid subsidies on their exports to France. But exchange rates generated a very politicized debate, and such parity discussions never occurred within the CoG.

Raymond Barre

The MC was extensively concerned with discussion of the reserve issue. At the same time that France's official policy since 1965 had been to convert its dollar reserves to gold, Germany had embarked on a very different path. As a concession that was regarded as part of the deal to secure a continued U.S. defense commitment to central Europe, and as a response to a threat by Treasury Secretary Henry Fowler that the United States would take dramatic steps if foreign central banks were not more cooperative, the Bundesbank pledged itself not to convert its dollar reserves. The text of the letter that Bundesbank President Karl Blessing wrote to Federal Reserve Chairman William McChesney Martin stated that so far the Bundesbank had refrained from converting dollars to gold and that the United States "may be assured that also in the future the Bundesbank intends to continue this policy and to play its full part in contributing to international monetary cooperation." The words "intends to" were calculatedly less of a commitment than the "will" that the U.S. negotiators would have preferred. Blessing nevertheless soon regretted the letter and in an interview in 1970 stated that "we simply should aggressively have converted the dollars into gold until they [the Americans] were driven to despair."[4]

The divergence between the French and German treatments of the dollar-reserve issue helped to spur the demand for a more effective and coordinated European policy. In February 1968, without much publicity, the Commission of the European Communities submitted to the conference of finance ministers in Rome a "Memorandum on Community action in the monetary field." The Commission suggested that the CoG and the MC might take up the following questions:

(i) The possibility of Member States undertaking to make no change in their currency parities, except by common accord; parity changes would not be ruled out completely, but as they are a matter of common interest under the Treaty of Rome, this would involve first considering the possible impact on the Community and seeking alternative solutions if necessary;

(ii) The elimination, for the currencies of the Member States, of day-to-day fluctuations around the parities, and the adoption of identical ranges of fluctuation in respect of non-member countries, not only to facilitate commercial and financial relations within the Community, but also to make possible a common position for the Member States should non-member countries adopt floating exchange rates;

(iii) The setting up, as part of the Community, of mutual assistance machinery under Articles 108 and 109 of the Treaty, for example in the form of a multilateral network of mutual credit rights which the institutions concerned could use when needed;

(iv) The definition of a European unit of account which would be used in all fields of Community action requiring a common denominator.[5]

At the finance ministers' conference in Rotterdam on September 9 and 10, 1968, the MC was given a mandate to continue its work, in cooperation with the CoG, on identifying and recommending progress to be made in the field of monetary relations in the European Communities.

Initially the major figure at the European level in drawing up the new approach was the vice-president of the EC Commission, Raymond Barre. The background was provided by imbalances not only in the transatlantic relationship, but also within Europe, with German surpluses surging in 1967 and 1968 as France ran into deficits. In 1967 the German current account surplus amounted to DM 10 billion, or 2 percent of GDP, and in 1968 to DM 11.8 billion (2.2 percent). The first real attempt to produce a closer European monetary union was thus a direct attempt to solve the problem of the German surpluses. Barre had taken the line at the Bonn G-10 meeting that neither a German revaluation nor a French devaluation was needed, and that they were indeed politically "undesirable." Instead, Germany should take "energetic measures for speedier growth and the stimulation of imports," as well as "special action to inhibit the flow of speculative capital into Germany."[6] In other words, there should be some way of applying pressure to push German economic policy in the direction of more expansion.

Barre met regularly with the CoG, and in December 1968 sketched out a response to the failures of the G-10 meeting. On December 7, 1968, he told the governors that for several months the Commission had wanted a "discrete discussion of several themes (fluctuating rates, enlargement of the bands of fluctuation) to arrive at a common attitude." But at the same time, he denied that the Commission had any bigger agenda that might include proposals for a European money, a common reserve fund, or the merging of the IMF quotas of the Six. The Belgian governor, Hubert Ansiaux, was quite skeptical; he acknowledged the need for a better balance of economic policy and improved coordination, but argued against measures such as floating, wider bands, or automatic credits that would "solve the wrong problems and allow the maintenance of permanent disequilibria." In other words, Germany should not continue to allow its export surplus to mount. His alternate, Cecil de Strycker, seemed to go further when he suggested that the Six might contemplate a short-term mutual support mechanism; but he also argued that the shocks posed by short-term capital movements could not be solved at the level of the Six.[7]

Barre subsequently drew up a report that focused on the failure of mutual assistance mechanisms in the Italian crisis of 1964 and in the French difficulties of 1968. Specifically, the report analyzed the way in which Community objectives could be frustrated by the action of large member states. It constituted one of the first expressions of the fear that Germany and its anti-inflationary policy priorities might dominate and distort European discussions.

Barre intended to establish a close link between economic policy and monetary cooperation, and he also discussed the possibility of coordinating cyclical fiscal policies. Monetary support would be linked with the convergence of medium-term economic objectives and coordination of short-term policies. Essentially, he proposed systematizing the support mechanism established to deal with the French case in July 1968, thus creating "the first multilateral instance to deal with the problems of a member state and offer assistance on specified conditions: composed of short-term monetary support and medium-term financial assistance." In the new proposal, the short-term assistance would be entirely automatic and hence would avoid a politicization of the issue of European transfers. The thought ran in parallel lines to John Maynard Keynes's plans for automaticity in IMF lending in the negotiations leading up to the Bretton Woods settlement, an approach that the United States, as the largest and most powerful creditor, had rejected in the 1940s. Barre's initiative was a response to the debacle of the Bonn G-10 meeting and its intense political maneuvering. "It was clearly necessary to change often dilatory procedures."[8] The dilatoriness had been the inevitable consequence of political intrusions.

The Barre report was presented on February 12, 1969.[9] It started with some quite specific lessons from the November 1968 debacle. "Tax measures adopted by Federal Germany and France in November 1968 also show clearly that there can be no lasting harmonization of indirect taxation unless economic policies are better co-ordinated to reduce imbalances." There was thus some need to devise a high-level process for reconciling differing national preferences.

But the report also set out a more general examination of how the activity of a new age of large government was shaping the world:

> The free movement of goods and services in a customs union in the twentieth century has only very little in common with the regional free trade of the second half of the nineteenth century. The developed economies, which now form a customs union, are strongly influenced and guided by the economic policies of the individual States and by the action of large units, which develop their own strategy; there is a danger that incompatibility between these policies and between these strategies will become a threat to the existence of the customs union. . . . There is a need, therefore, to increase the co-ordination of current economic and financial policies to forestall short-term imbalances early enough and under the most favourable conditions for all the Member States, and to combat them as effectively as possible should the need arise.

The best mechanism for dealing with EEC-wide problems was to extend financial assistance within the Community, and to operate the same sort of credit cooperative that Keynes and his associates had envisaged at the international level in 1944 at Bretton Woods. As Barre put it:

> The Treaty makes specific provision in Article 108 for "mutual assistance" between Member States. No use was made of this facility when

a balance of payments crisis affected a member country a few years ago. It was applied more recently after clumsy and complex procedures; but its main aspect was not monetary or financial; and it was not able to prevent the application of safeguard measures. . . . There is a particular need for the States' draft budgets to be discussed in future not merely in the Budget Policy Committee—as at present—but at a meeting between ministers responsible for economic policy and financial policy.

As specific remedial measures, Barre suggested not only improved coordination of short- and medium-term policies, developing the initiatives of the May 8, 1964, decision that had originally established the CoG, but also the creation of specific mechanisms for short-term monetary support and for medium-term financial arrangements.

In the EEC Monetary Committee, France, Belgium, and Italy viewed the "monetary mechanism" positively, while Germany and the Netherlands were restrained. No participant wanted an entirely automatic mechanism. Clappier suggested recreating a purely European mechanism analogous to the Federal Reserve's swap system, instituted in 1962, wherein reciprocal lines of credit could be used if needed for interventions; and additionally recommended that there be regular "multilateral surveillance" from Basel. The German representative, on the other hand, argued that deficit countries should use credits rather than central bank assistance to deal with their problems.[10]

In the CoG, the governors were more comfortable in dealing with Barre's subtle approach than with the cruder and more politicized Marjolin proposals of the mid-1960s. Replying for the Bundesbank, Vice-President Otmar Emminger spoke also as the deputy president of the Monetary Committee, and explained that the MC had considered the proposals on February 27 and 28, and had fundamentally agreed on the general issue of a better convergence of medium-term policy targets in economic policy. But he also emphasized the problems concerning coordination of business cycle strategy, and specifically argued that Germany was suffering from inflationary pressure, and that a more expansive policy might be justified from the EEC viewpoint but not from that of Germany. On monetary coordination, there had been many reservations, but Emminger recommended that the CoG give a general view on the desirability or necessity of creating a short-term support mechanism. The governor of the Banque de France, Jacques Brunet, seemed to display an étatist orientation, claiming that the contribution of central banks should simply involve ensuring the "operationalization of the decisions and orientations undertaken by the Council."[11] There was extensive discussion of possible short- and medium-term support mechanisms in three meetings, in September, November, and December 1969.[12] The central bankers proposed that it would be appropriate to refuse to support the central bank of a country that did not respect Community procedures regarding the use of the funds. When explaining these debates to the Bundesbank Council, Otmar Emminger stated that the proposal was a step on the road to creating a common European reserve fund in line with the proposals of Barre's report.[13] But the initiative was really only taken up at a political level over the course of the next year.

A critical issue, which had already been raised by the 1964 Italian case, was that of the relationship of possible EEC support to IMF programs. Barre began the discussion in the CoG by saying that it was curious that a country needing short-term support should turn more easily to the United States than to its European neighbors; and Brunet noted that the medium-term resources of the IMF did not correspond to the short-term needs of a country and might be insufficient. In consequence, it would be desirable to organize "spontaneous help" through the EEC. On response, Brunet, Emminger, and the Banca d'Italia's Paolo Baffi all made the point that the problem was not really one of capital movements within the EEC, but that the major flows had been to the United States, the United Kingdom, and Switzerland. In such cases, purely EEC solutions would be inadequate. Jelle Zijlstra of the Nederlandsche Bank thought that the combination of IMF help and the swap network was sufficient to deal with the question of short-term support.

As the central bankers envisaged it, a short-term support mechanism would be largely apolitical, and would not depend on government decision-making. The Banque de France also insisted that there should not be a stricter conditionality than was applied by the IMF to non-member countries of the EC (such as the United Kingdom).[14]

It is striking that this discussion did not really focus on monetary policy adjustment. This neglect was largely the consequence of the fixed-exchange-rate regime, in which monetary policy was required to respond to exchange rate signals. But the fixed-exchange-rate regime was increasingly vulnerable.

Political Shifts

Europe's political landscape changed with the more or less simultaneous end of the German Great Coalition (a coalition of Social Democrats and Christian Democrats) and the sputtering collapse of de Gaulle's presidency. The accident of these changes at both ends of the Franco-German axis allowed a much more radical approach to currency issues. A unilateral and quite personal high-level initiative from the German chancellor, Willy Brandt, now contributed to a new momentum over European monetary integration. Brandt had been persuaded by an eloquent memorandum from one of the principal architects of the original European project, Jean Monnet, which laid out a path for a new Europeanization of German politics. Monnet had stated that "Germany could take a peaceful, constructive, and generous initiative which would overlay—I might even say efface—the memories of the past." In the wake of this document, which greatly impressed Brandt, the two men had an extended conversation on November 7, 1969. Monnet also tried to convince Brandt that "It is not natural for men to unite. It is necessity that pushes them." Monnet consistently saw European integration as a response to crisis. Brandt was aware that his advisers viewed a bold European initiative on monetary integration with great skepticism. In particular, the German Foreign Office had been critical of the idea of producing economic convergence through monetary policy. He thought that only a high political initiative could break through the chicken-and-egg problem created by alternate emphases on the primacy of monetary or economic integration.[15] There were some exceptions to the German bureaucratic critique, and in the German Economics Ministry the Europe department, under the young Hans Tietmeyer, had produced at the end of October a memorandum including a "Plan by Stages" (*Stufenplan*) for European Economic and Monetary Union. Tietmeyer's document (which bears resemblances to the 1990s discussions of the Stability Pact) envisaged that a "code of rules on cyclical good behavior" could achieve coherent economic policy; it also envisaged a Business Cycle Advisory Council and a European Central Banking council.[16]

Brandt's room for maneuver in monetary diplomacy was further extended by the resignation of de Gaulle and the election of Georges Pompidou as French president on June 15, 1969. Pompidou appointed Valéry Giscard d'Estaing as finance minister, and Giscard immediately signaled to Bonn that he hoped for closer monetary cooperation across the Rhine.[17] Raymond Barre was skeptical of these proposals, and wrote to the Commission on October 21, 1969, that the moment was not favorable.[18]

Brandt sprung his proposals as a surprise in December 1969, when the heads of government of the EEC met at The Hague for a first summit conference. He secured the adoption of a text in which Europe's leaders agreed to "affirm their faith in the political objectives which give to the whole Community its whole meaning and significance." The meeting was heavily influenced by Barre's proposals, and it agreed both to a plan "by stages," to be elaborated in 1970, "with a view to the creation of an economic and monetary union," and to an examination of the feasibility of a European reserve fund. The communiqué explicitly included the German view of the priorities of monetary union: "The development of monetary cooperation should be based on harmonization of economic policies."[19]

Various plans taking up Barre's suggestions were presented to the finance and economics ministers on January 16, 1970, and to the same group, with the addition of the central bank governors, on February 23 and 24, 1970. The German economics minister, Karl Schiller, had worried that other EC member countries would be "quick in forcing inflation" on Germany.[20] He submitted proposals on February 12, 1970, to impose more discipline, with a four-stage mechanism, which would begin with the harmonization of economic and monetary policies. There would be a short-term monetary support mechanism as well as medium-term financial assistance. There would be "concerted" representation of the EEC countries in international monetary forums, and strengthened consultation of "national interest and credit policies" in the CoG. "Fixed and guaranteed" exchange rates would come only after a substantial convergence of economic performance, and each subsequent stage would depend on the achievements of the previous phase. But eventually the scheme would lead to a "sort of Federal Reserve System." At the outset, Schiller's proposal emphasized that there should be a single legal framework to prevent distortions of competition. "The harmonization of tax policy is just as important to a successful economic and monetary union as an economic policy framework that is open to the world."[21] The views set out in the Schiller paper remained a central part of the German approach for two decades: Germany insisted on the importance of prior progress in the convergence of economic policy and outcomes as a prerequisite for successful monetary progress.

Under the direction of Tietmeyer, a group in the German Economics Ministry, drew up more detailed proposals that were later presented in a paper signed by State Secretary Johann Baptist Schöllhorn. Currency agreements "should only be accepted if the necessary harmonization or communalization of economic policy is secured." There should be general and compatible European national targets for the magic quadrilateral of growth, full employment, stability, and external (balance of payments) balance. The program would require the liberalization of capital markets and the guarantee of effective competition. National budgets should be coordinated and harmonized, and tax policy also required harmonization. National sovereignty would be "considerably reduced" with regard to economic policy; and central banks needed a "central autonomous organ." The Tietmeyer and Schöllhorn papers laid down a German policy that would be consistently advocated over the next twenty years.[22]

Barre disliked Schiller's skepticism about the idea of a reserve fund, which would be needed for the operation of a short-term support mechanism: that was the skepticism of the creditor akin to the U.S. hesitation over Keynes's monetary plans in the 1940s. The French government also found Schiller's proposals on tax and more general economic harmonization contrary to the logic of political Gaullism, which emphasized national sovereignty.[23]

Another set of options came from Belgium and was concerned primarily with the logic of institutional coordination. There were three stages in the Belgian plan, put forward on January 23, 1970. In the first, the EC Council of Ministers would issue recommendations to national governments; in the second stage, directives. By the third stage, EC institutions would pursue a single economic policy. Belgian Governor Hubert Ansiaux wrote a supplementary study of how a European reserve fund would operate, and how fluctuation mechanisms could be reduced and then eliminated. Luxembourg also presented a seven-stage proposal, which included a final statement by its prime minister, Pierre Werner, on how British accession would strengthen EC monetary coherence.

In December 1969, in addition, the Belgian economist Robert Triffin provided a report on how Europe might move to a common pooling of reserves through the creation of a reserve fund; and on February 26,

1970, Hubert Ansiaux prepared a similar note.[24] Triffin was a close collaborator with Jean Monnet, and the important memoranda on Europe's monetary future that he produced between 1968 and 1970 were closely coordinated with Monnet's Action Committee for the United States of Europe. Monnet's committee had been pushing the desirability of a European reserve fund since 1959, in other words from the moment that European countries had gone over to current account convertibility; and for Triffin and Monnet the pooling of reserves lay at the heart of monetary reform.[25]

In discussing these proposals in the CoG, the central bankers treated as a serious possibility a general international movement to slightly greater exchange rate flexibility, which had been held out as a possibility in an IMF paper prepared for the G-10. The IMF position paper had laid out as one alternative "somewhat wider margins," such as a doubling of the one-percent move permitted on either side of the central dollar parity.[26] There was also a parallel discussion of enhanced economic flexibility in the context of the OECD's Working Party Three, at that time a major forum for the discussion of exchange rate issues among industrial countries. In the CoG, suggestions such as those of the IMF paper met with some skepticism. The Germans were clearly worried that a general loosening of discipline in the international system would impose strains on the EEC. In addition, the governor of the Banca d'Italia, Guido Carli, wondered whether proposals for a European fund devoted to exchange equalization could really serve as an instrument of monetary integration, and he warned against the creation of a "new bureaucracy." Bundesbank president Karl Klasen and President Jelle Zijlstra of the Nederlandsche Bank wanted to wait for the results of the new committee established by the Council (which would be known as the Werner Committee), while the other central bankers held that this topic was of central concern to the CoG. Carli and Otmar Emminger, the highly influential vice-president of the Bundesbank, also wanted an examination of the unification or harmonization of European banking legislation. In discussions in Monnet's Action Committee, Carli had also made the case for greater currency flexibility, a plea that had earned him a telegraphic rebuke from the veteran visionary himself, to the effect that even a temporary flexibility of exchange rates would be a "considerable regression."[27]

The French central banker Olivier Wormser began by outlining two alternative approaches: what he thought to be the more limited view that a European reserve fund might be "the coronation" (or final stage) of efforts at monetary collaboration, or a more ambitious version in which it might be an instrument for building closer relations.[28] Most members of the CoG supported the first of these interpretations, which was that of the German Bundesbank, and also held that the coronation view was reflected in the communiqué of the Hague summit. Barre suggested that implementation should be progressive, with at first a modest pooling of a certain fraction of reserves, perhaps of the newly created Special Drawing Rights, before eventually moving to a complete unification of reserves. Emminger suggested that a fund could develop out of a network of short-term support mechanisms.[29] The instrumental view was held only in Paris and Rome, and there only incompletely. As Governor Carli put it later, "In accepting the fact that monetary unification precedes economic unification one must bear in mind that the former cannot last unless it is followed by the latter in a fairly short space of time. Monetary unification is thus instrumental."[30]

In response to the German critique, Barre began by stating that the interest of the EEC was not to allow "stratagems or artificial means" in the international monetary system, and appealed for a closer convergence of EEC policies so that the EEC countries could follow a common policy vis-à-vis the dollar. Emminger also argued that in six or seven years, if U.S. inflation persisted, the EEC countries would have to contemplate the possibility of a collective change of parities relative to the dollar.[31]

Pierre Werner

On March 6, 1970, the Council created a Committee of Committee Presidents, chaired by Pierre Werner, in which the MC, the CoG, the EEC Committee on Medium Term Economic Policy, the Committee on Business Cycle Policy, and the Budgetary Committee, as well as the Commission were represented. The Werner committee was charged with identifying "the basic issues for a realization by stages of economic and monetary union in the Community." Two of the seven members were central bankers (Ansiaux and Bernard Clappier, the deputy governor of the Banque de France), and Ansiaux regularly reported to the CoG on its meetings. The committee was divided between those who wanted to accelerate monetary integration (France, Luxembourg, Belgium, Italy, and the Commission) and Germany, supported by the Netherlands, which argued the case, powerfully made by the group around Tietmeyer, that greater economic coherence was a prerequisite for closer monetary coordination. From the beginning, the members found that they could come together only around the notion of "parallel" development of economic and monetary integration.

Indeed, it is striking how little prominence was at first attached to the big theme of monetary union. At the Werner committee's first meeting, on March 20, 1970, the Luxembourg premier had started off by arguing that a common reserve fund was more important than a common currency; and he also emphasized the need for convergence, in particular with respect to the harmonization of fiscal policies. Governor Clappier emphasized the desirability of implementation in small steps.[32]

The CoG was divided as it followed the work of the Werner committee, and many of the central bankers were highly skeptical of the new initiative and its likely outcome. Guido Carli thought that "parallelism" was not acceptable in the current state of the Community, and that it was important to establish priorities.[33] In his view (which was shared by the Bundesbank) the most important result of the discussions would be to achieve a coordinated response to the problems of the American dollar, in other words to resolve the global debate about liquidity. A harmonization of legislation on banking and on the control of capital movements would also be desirable. On the other hand, as a member of the Werner Committee, Ansiaux consistently defended the outlines of the report, and especially the idea of an exchange stabilization fund.[34]

The CoG held a special meeting, in Venice, to consider the Werner ideas immediately before the Venice meeting of EEC finance ministers. Barre emphasized that a "division into stages according to the terminology of coordination, harmonization, and decision or directive represented a juridical approach that had not been helpful in the past in the Community and risked failure." Zijlstra pleaded for a practical approach, in which "the definition of principle and grand lines of action are no less important in monetary matters . . . but it is also important to harmonize the instruments of monetary policy." He proposed that study groups working in the central banks should concern themselves with this issue.[35]

At the subsequent finance ministers' meeting, there seemed to be a political deadlock. Werner started out by observing that the EEC should develop a "personality" with regard to debates on global monetary policy, reflecting a common European standpoint rather than the clashing views of individual national governments. Barre assured the ministers that the end goal of currency union "could be achieved in a decade, if there was permanent political support by governments." French Finance Minister Valéry Giscard d'Estaing and Belgian Finance Minister Baron Jean Snoy d'Oppuers argued in the early stages of European integration for a reduction of European fluctuation bands (the extent to which currencies could move either way from a central fixed dollar rate). Giscard claimed that "current currency bands could not be used as an instrument of balance-of-payments adjustment or as a way of dealing with business cycle issues. A moderate reduction in fluctuation margins would be a good exercise in preparing for a further reduction of margins or for their complete elimination." He also noted that when he had recently been to the United States, he had been confronted with demands that the Europeans begin a series of small currency adjustments to accustom markets to the notion of a gradual European revaluation in relation to the dollar. That revaluation should be a collective exercise. By contrast, Schiller demanded much greater flexibility (the "time was not yet ripe" for a reduction of fluctuation margins), and he emphasized the long-term issue that EMU would require a "central institution with responsibility for general business cycle policy." (In the Bundesbank Council, Otmar Emminger made a similar point, explaining that currency coordination required a control of the net positions of public-sector budgets, and that a harmonization of business cycle and balance-of-payments developments would be needed before the band widths for currency fluctuations could be reduced.) In the CoG, Nederlandsche Bank Governor Zijlstra made the same argument when he stated that coordination of fiscal policy was the major issue in a currency union. And Snoy thought that such an imperative would require a collective strengthening of the position of finance ministers: "in a system of a currency union the position of finance ministers would be stronger in their efforts to achieve budget balance, because they could point to 'European necessities.' "[36]

In the last stages of the drafting of the Werner Plan, Schöllhorn tried, unsuccessfully, to press for the German vision with regard to the autonomy of the "currency and monetary organ."[37] The German-Dutch axis that was so important in the later stages of discussions on monetary coordination, in the 1970s and 1980s, had already emerged, with Emminger and Zijlstra corresponding about the need for more domestic coordination: on central bank instruments, and in particular on actions by central banks to influence the development of what was then the most common monetary indicator, the domestic credit expansion introduced in IMF analyses.[38]

The final version of the Werner Report was presented on October 27, 1970.[39] It came at a moment when the G-10 was debating whether bands of fluctuation in the Bretton Woods system should be widened. Such a challenge required some European response. "The increasing interpenetration of the economies has entailed a weakening of autonomy for national economic policies. The control of economic policy has become all the more difficult because the loss of autonomy at the national level has not been compensated by the inauguration of Community policies. The inadequacies and disequilibrium that have occurred in the process of realization of the Common Market are thus thrown into relief." The report's most striking feature was the sharp delineation of a final objective of monetary union. "Economic and monetary union will make it possible to realize an area within which goods and services, people and capital will circulate freely and without competitive distortions, without thereby giving rise to structural, or regional disequilibrium. . . . The implementation of such a union will effect a lasting improvement in welfare in the Community and will reinforce the contribution of the Community to economic and monetary equilibrium in the world."[40] Werner did not reflect on historical precedents for disequilibrium in the aftermath of monetary union, the most striking and immediately relevant of which was the story of north-south relations in Italy, where monetary union had heightened rather than minimized regional differences.

Neither did the report really establish a clear road map of how to achieve that union. Instead, it offered quite specific details of a first stage, in which there would be enhanced monetary cooperation and institutional innovation in the shape of a European Monetary Cooperation Fund. The Werner committee reflected profoundly on how differences in growth could undermine monetary union, and proposed as a consequence a wide-ranging program of fiscal transfers.

The realization of global economic equilibrium may be dangerously threatened by differences of structure. Cooperation between the partners in the Community in the matter of *structural and regional policies* will help to surmount these difficulties, just as it will make it possible to eliminate the distortions of competition. The solution of the big problems in this field will be facilitated by financial measures of compensation. Economic and monetary union implies the following principal consequences:

- the Community currencies will be assured of total and irreversible mutual convertibility free from fluctuations in rates and with immutable parity rates, or preferably they will be replaced by a sole Community currency;
- the creation of liquidity throughout the area and monetary and credit policy will be centralized;
- monetary policy in relation to the outside world will be within the jurisdiction of the Community;
- the policies of the Member States as regards the capital market will be unified;
- the essential features of the whole of the public budgets, and in particular variations in their volume, the size of balances and the methods of financing or utilizing them, will be decided at the Community level;
- regional and structural policies will no longer be exclusively within the jurisdiction of the member countries;
- a systematic and continuous consultation between the social partners will be ensured at the Community level.

A result of this is that on the plane of *institutional reforms* the realization of economic and monetary union demands the creation or the transformation of a certain number of Community organs to which powers until then exercised by the national authorities will have to be transferred.[41]

In the first stage, "regular examinations will make it possible to proceed to a permanent surveillance of the situation." A system of indicators would be developed to deal with potential dangers. "The coordination of economic policies during the first stage will depend on increased activity by the Community organs, in particular the Council and the Commission as well as the Committee of Governors of the Central Banks." The CoG would be responsible for preparing Council meetings, and the governors would attend those meetings. Fluctuation margins would be reduced and the intra-Community capital market liberalized. Central bankers would have to meet more frequently in order to allow the Council to "define the general guidelines of monetary and credit policy within the Community." The first stage would last for three years and might begin in 1971.[42]

In the second stage, "Progress in the convergence of economic and monetary policies should be such . . . that the Member States no longer have to resort on an autonomous basis to the instrument of parity adjustment. In any case, it will be necessary further to reinforce the consultation procedures." This stage involved an institutional innovation: "In order to prepare the final stage in good time, it will be necessary to set up as soon as possible a 'European Fund for monetary cooperation' under the control of the Governors of the central banks."[43]

The CoG was to play a central role, but Werner also believed that central banks required political supervision, and that that should be done by a parliamentary body. "On the institutional plane, in the final stage, two Community organs are indispensable: a centre of decision for economic policy and a Community system for the central banks. These institutions, while safeguarding their own responsibilities, must be furnished with effective powers of decision and must work together for the realization of the same objectives. The centre of economic decision will be politically responsible to a European Parliament."[44]

One crucial lesson that later policymakers learned from the Werner experience concerned the question of a timetable. Ambitious in other areas, the report avoided imposing a specific time line, and thus allowed its recommendations to slide into the wings when new crises demanded urgent action. "At this stage the laying down of a precise and rigid timetable for the whole of the plan by stages does not seem feasible. It is necessary in fact to maintain a measure of flexibility to permit any adaptations that the experience acquired during the first stage may suggest: Particular emphasis should therefore be placed on the first stage, for which a package of concrete measures is presented."[45]

The issue of currency fluctuations within the EEC was more than simply technical, and lay at the heart of the challenge of finding a response to the increasing disorder of the international monetary system. At the Venice meeting of May 1970, Barre had been concerned that the EEC countries should not enlarge their margins if there was a general global move in this direction, and that the EEC countries should establish a common position. Ossola explained that he wanted a more flexible position that would allow the EEC countries to reduce their dependence on the dollar.

Werner then charged Ansiaux with forming a committee of experts to consider the reduction of margins of fluctuation, and that group met repeatedly, on June 25 and July 1, 2, 9, 16, 23, 24, and 30. Ansiaux's group eventually suggested three alternative routes: a concerted action by central banks to limit exchange rate movements, but no official reduction of margin; an official reduction; or an enlargement of margins relative to the dollar with the EEC margins being maintained. The last course seemed to lead to a greater monetary room for maneuver. In an initial discussion, Ansiaux emphatically stated that "the Community must not accept more flexibility in exchange rates and in particular one member state must not unilaterally enlarge its margin relative to the dollar." Emminger noted at the same time that only Germany was receiving a massive inflow of dollars, and that the Bundesbank and the government "were not disposed to apply the controls to the nonbanking sector that some Germans wanted."[46]

The Ansiaux group generated a mechanism that assumed more significance in the longer run for the discussion of technical aspects of foreign exchange issues. One of the major figures in moving discussion in the Ansiaux group had been Marcel Théron of the Banque de France, and on October 30 he chaired a meeting of a new group of experts to consider the timing and hours of foreign exchange market activity, and the mechanisms for central bank interventions. Some of the particular or technical steps that were to be an element of the Werner process were then gradually implemented. In particular, in November 1970 the CoG considered proposals for the creation of a telephonic network between EEC central banks. From March 17, 1971, Théron supervised a system of "concertation" in which there was a thrice-daily discussion among the central banks, and which laid down the practical basis for coordination among central bank activities in the foreign exchange markets.

Looking at the range of options offered in the Ansiaux paper, Carli in September 1970 suggested widening the dollar margin from 0.75 percent to 1 percent, which was possible without any major negotiation at the IMF. Klasen preferred a reduction of the intra-EEC margin.[47] By

March 1971 there was consensus on a maintenance of the 0.75 margin with the dollar and a reduction of the intra-Community margin to 1.20 percent.[48] In April there was agreement that the new regime should start on June 15. The Carli suggestions were widely welcomed as a way of bringing new members into the EEC. A newspaper article by the British economist John Williamson used Carli's crawling peg arguments to explain how Britain could manage the accession process.[49]

The Werner Report also considered the coordination of monetary and credit instruments within the EEC. Ansiaux and Clappier had prepared a paper on that topic, which envisaged a gradual process of rapprochement. Klasen thought that a coordination of activities would "reinforce the authority of Community central banks," and added: "Just as the Central Bank Council of the Bundesbank has a great authority in Germany and does not hesitate to criticize orientations and measures taken in economic policy, so the Committee of Governors at the Community level could become a comparable instance, which would reinforce the authority of central banks."[50] The Bundesbank, in short, could serve as an indispensable model for central banking on a European level.

Finally, in September 1970 the CoG also reflected on how to build closer relations between European institutions and the CoG. The Dutch alternate explained that the EC Commission might do much of the preparatory work, but Klasen snapped back that this task would be better handled by the central banks. Ansiaux complained that the meetings of the CoG were held too late, on a Monday afternoon, after a heavily burdened weekend at the BIS, and suggested that central banks might send high officials as permanent emissaries to Brussels. In November 1970 Ansiaux also recommended regular whole-day meetings of the CoG in Brussels, at the offices of the Commission, followed by dinner at the Belgian National Bank. There was no outright opposition, but Klasen did not want to make the change for a year, and Baffi appealed for half of the meetings to be held also in Basel, which was obviously a more convenient location because the regular BIS and G-10 governors' meetings were held there.[51] Later Barre proposed that the CoG should attend three meetings of the Council of Ministers each year.[52] None of these proposals to bind the central bank governors more closely into political Europe ever materialized.

At the political level, the Werner Plan had a mixed reception. On the whole, Bonn was enthusiastic. On October 22, 1970, the German cabinet accepted a plan to embark on the initial steps toward EMU in the "next weeks." On November 6 the government told parliament that the Werner Plan should not be "watered down." The Bundesbank was more hesitant, and the Central Bank Council argued that the CoG as an early precursor of a Central Bank Council should be responsible for monetary and credit policy, but that it should be independent of the council and only be required to consider guidelines produced by the Council for Economic Policy.[53] At a meeting in the Federal Economics Ministry, the Bundesbank representative expressed skepticism about the whole process.[54] In private, Emminger was much more scathing. In a letter to the president of the German Banking Association he described the French position as "pseudo-monetarist": "The French do not begin with a common centrally managed monetary or credit policy. They are fundamentally interested in using the EEC currency bloc as a ram against the dollar, and in centralizing currency reserves in order to reduce pressure on their balance of payments." In another letter, to State Secretary Schöllhorn, he wrote that France wanted to stop Germany from making use of a flexible exchange rate policy and intended the "monetarist harmonization of inflation."[55]

Economics Minister Karl Schiller told the Bundesbank Council that in his view there should not be an automatic transition from stage one to stage two of economic and monetary union, and that an intergovernmental conference was required to agree on the treaty alterations that would be needed for such a move to occur. He added that Bonn insisted that "the independence of the Bundesbank must be maintained if possible to the final stage of economic and monetary union. It intended to present the autonomous central bank as a model for the European central bank."[56]

By contrast with the cautious but positive German welcome, the French reaction was rather flat. Giscard, the French politician who might have been most likely to approve, thought that Werner had offered a "too centralized conception," and urged a course that did not require the abandonment of essential elements of sovereignty but still had some elements of "confederation." Pompidou critically wanted to emphasize the cooperation of central banks and the coordination of fiscal policy, but believed that there should be no longer-term institutional integration. He also let slip that he believed that German support for EMU stemmed from a "desire to be the strongest." The idea of central bank autonomy was particular anathema to him, and he recalled the legacy of Léon Blum and the Popular Front in the 1930s, when the French left believed that the Banque de France was at the center of an antidemocratic conspiracy to bring down reformist governments.[57] In the subsequent French-German bilateral consultation meeting in January 1971, France made it clear that it was interested only in the proposed first phase of integration.

Other voices, prophetically, saw the Werner Plan as incomplete in that it failed to deal with the fiscal issues raised by monetary union. The British economist Eric Roll wrote: "Whether this daring conception can be realized, remains to be seen. If it is, it must go all the way, for it is impossible to see how a system of rigid or even semi-rigid parities can be maintained without virtually automatic and possibly massive balance-of-payments support where this should become necessary. This, in turn, would require much more automatic domestic adjustments of fiscal, monetary and perhaps other economic policies than is practicable in the case of sovereign countries."[58]

The EEC Commission accepted the Werner Report and produced its own policy road map on October 30, 1970. It noted that some aspects of the process of monetary unification required a treaty alteration, and also pointed out that the Werner committee had not defined a "precise and rigid" calendar for action. The Commission proposed to the EC Council of Ministers a resolution requiring a move to monetary union in the present decade and a program of action to be established between 1971 and 1973. The realization of economic and monetary union would require first a coordination of short-term economic policy, including the harmonization of fiscal policy; and second, intensified central bank cooperation. A system of central banks would eventually supervise the elimination of short-term fluctuations and proceed to an "irrevocable" fixing of exchange rates. The governors of the central banks should twice yearly define the orientation of monetary policy "within the framework of the directing lines determined by the Council in questions of economic and monetary policy and within the limits of central bank cooperation." Central banks that deviated from such an orientation would be obliged to report on the infraction to other central banks and to the Commission. The Commission's paper thus proposed a very radical extension of its powers in monetary policy.[59]

When the CoG discussed the final version of the Werner Plan in November and December 1970, the overwhelming tone was skeptical, especially concerning the Commission's more ambitious interpretation of

Werner in its own paper of October 30, 1970. Zijlstra reflected the consensus of all the governors (with the exception of Wormser) that it was the governors and not ministers who should elaborate the procedures for improving central bank cooperation. Deputy Governor Paolo Baffi from the Banca d'Italia explained that "the report has too much of a tendency of defining constitutive elements of a common strategy, while achieving collectively decided objectives would be better done by national authorities using their own instruments freely." Baffi complained that there was a lopsided concentration on the coordination of monetary policy. He argued that a currency fund or an agent was not needed. The Commission's representative Ugo Mosca (Barre was absent) tried to defend the idea that both Werner and the Commission attached a high priority to monetary stability, but concluded by emphasizing that the Commission wanted an irreversible move in the direction of monetary union. Klasen then added that he supported the Werner Plan "fully," but not the proposals of the Commission.[60] The Bundesbank report on the CoG meeting focused on the overwhelmingly critical tone of the discussion.[61]

In response to these criticisms, the Council of Finance Ministers asked the permanent representatives to reformulate the Commission's position. A particularly sensitive point, in which the precise nuances of phraseology were vital, concerned the position of central banks. Emminger stated that the German and Dutch delegations were prepared to include only the phrase "taking account" (compte tenu) of the Council's orientation on general economic policy rather than "respecting" (dans le respect). Ansiaux seemed to support the German and Dutch position when he added that "respect" "implied a certain notion of constraint."[62]

The pressure for political control came above all from France, and emanated from the highest level. President Pompidou was deeply involved with monetary issues: he had corrected the draft speeches for the IMF meetings of Finance Minister Valéry Giscard d'Estaing in order to emphasize an anti-American tone; and he repeatedly took up the same theme in bilateral discussions with the German government. In January 1971 he told Chancellor Brandt that he was happy that the central bankers should meet more regularly, but proposed that they transfer power to a president of the CoG who would hold the position only for a short rotation ("so as not to hold authority for too long"). In practice, the CoG chairmanship did indeed rotate on an annual basis after

1971. Above all, the central bankers needed to report to the Council. "In a crisis, governments need to meet and take decisions. Such decisions cannot be left to a Community organization of central banks. He [Pompidou] knew by the way that the English were particularly disturbed about this aspect of an economic and monetary union."[63]

At the Council of Ministers meeting of February 8 and 9, 1971, when it appeared that France was not willing to accept a strict parallelism between monetary and economic integration, Germany obtained what it referred to as a "terminal date": monetary integration measures should be limited to five years and then lapse if there was no equivalent progress on the harmonization of economic policy.[64]

On March 3, 1971, the Monetary Committee created two groups of experts that would work with both committees, but the MC agreed that the experts should primarily reflect a central bank viewpoint. Bernard Clappier, the chair of the MC, suggested that the CoG alternates should act as the liaison with the Monetary Committee.[65] The first group, on the harmonization of monetary policy, would begin work straightaway; the second group, working on the fund, would begin in September 1971 and would report by June 1972. In practice these groups did not immediately play a significant role in increased European monetary cooperation, but they were eventually reorganized within the framework of the CoG and provided the basis of an infrastructure that developed into the subcommittees of the 1990s and then into departments of the European Monetary Institute and of the European Central Bank.

The Exchange Rate Regime

In retrospect, the discussions around the Werner Plan seem to have been rapidly overtaken by events. It took over a year to achieve a consensus on reducing the intra-Community marginal band from 1.50 to 1.20 percent. The date on which the new system would take effect (June 15, 1971) was agreed on April 19, 1971: but before the system could be inaugurated, the Bundesbank's response to exchange turbulence blew up the whole system.

Germany had faced a massive inflow of dollars, with capital flows from January 1970 to May 1971 amounting to DM 35.3 billion ($9.6 billion). The German strategies of looking for international solutions— either a wider European fluctuation band or international pressure on the United States to tighten its loose monetary policy—had achieved no results. In March 1971 the Bundesbank cut its discount rate to try to stop the dollar inflow, but the measure seemed only to produce still more lending and greater inflationary pressure in Germany. Germany had been trapped in the fixed-exchange-rate system, and its monetary policymakers had been helpless. At the end of April 1971 the Bundesbank and the German government discussed possible strategies with the managing director of the IMF, Pierre-Paul Schweitzer, who attempted to plead for the maintenance of the par value system and for respecting its rules. Vice-President Emminger strongly supported a floating of the Deutsche Mark, while President Klasen was opposed; the economics minister, Karl Schiller, was also sympathetic to floating.[66] The same issues were debated in the Monetary Committee on May 6, with Emminger appealing for a temporary widening of bands, and France opposing a revaluation or a floating of exchange rates, which would merely provide future incentives for speculation. The Belgian representative agreed that widening bands would not be an effective way of countering speculation. Italy argued that the EEC currencies, including the Deutsche Mark, were not undervalued. Only the Netherlands sided with Germany, making the case that the possibility of concerted floating should be held out as a way of forcing the United States to devalue the dollar. Other strategies might include massive conversions of dollars or temporary restrictions on capital imports.[67] Schiller also tried to persuade other EEC governments of the virtues of a joint float, but failed, and on May 10, 1971, Germany embarked on a unilateral float, even though both the Bundesbank president and the majority of the Central Bank Council were still opposed to such a move.

On May 9, 1971, the CoG held an emergency meeting to suspend the old exchange rate regime. It looked as if there were major differences not only in the policies followed by the European states, but also in their range of policy instruments. In particular, France pointed out that French controls allowed a quite effective limitation of foreign exchange pressure, while Germany was incapable of controlling the bank and nonbank borrowing, which had accounted for a major part of the inflows into the Deutsche Mark in May. In a postmortem on the German events in June, Vice-Governor Clappier of the Banque de France noted that the Bundesbank alone did not have the legal means to control directly the net external position of commercial banks, and that the Germans thus had very few options with which to fight the influx of dollars.[68]

The unilateral German move inevitably produced major tensions in German relations with every EEC country except the Netherlands. At the next meeting of the Monetary Committee, Italy stated that it did not want to be drawn into a common float with Germany and the Netherlands, while the Belgian representative prophetically noted that a general dollar crisis was imminent.[69]

The Franco-German debate took place at the highest political level. Meeting Chancellor Brandt near Koblenz in July 1971, President Pompidou issued a lengthy rebuke to the Germans. Unstable exchange rates, he said, threatened the agricultural pricing structure that was at the heart of the EC; the German move had inflationary consequences for France; and the German proposal to ask the United States for wider margins of movement was tantamount to giving the Americans a present. He thought that Germany had introduced floating only as a way of securing a new revaluation. Pompidou finished by saying: "For France it is important that the Germans understand that it is not a simple economic problem, but a question of Community morality."[70] He later told Finance Ministers Schiller and Giscard d'Estaing that it would be impossible for ten currencies within the EC to move within narrow margins with a wider fluctuation externally (that is, against the dollar) without constantly requiring financial assistance from the IMF.[71]

Klasen reported to the CoG on the discussions between Brandt and Pompidou, and on the French government's insistence that there was to be no discussion of wider fluctuation margins before the EEC had announced a return to fixed exchange rates. He also noted that the French delegation "did not have in monetary matters a completely defined, fixed and immutable position," and that it might be possible to get an agreement with Germany on wider bands of fluctuation in the dollar rate (even though Pompidou was hostile to such a position). The Bundesbank had some mechanism of control, and was proposing to impose a tax on foreign credits obtained by nonbanking institutions. If the Six agreed on wider fluctuation margins with the dollar, it would be possible to bring the Deutsche Mark back to a fixed parity with a slight revaluation.[72]

But these debates quickly seemed irrelevant, after the United States in effect left the fixed-exchange-rate regime on August 15, 1971. President Nixon's decision was entirely unilateral—he and his officials had not consulted the IMF or the G-10—and was presented in a dramatic televised address in which he also announced tax cuts and a temporary 10 percent surcharge on imports in order "to ensure that American products will not be at a disadvantage because of unfair exchange rates." There was a strong element of mixed xenophobia and paranoia prevailing in Washington, and Treasury Secretary John Connally had been sending dire warnings to Nixon of the motives behind all the European initiatives. "I believe we must realize that there is a strong element of thinking within Europe that would take advantage of weakness or clumsiness on our part to promote the Common Market not as a partner but as a rival economic bloc, competing vigorously with the dollar and reducing or shutting out, as best it can, U.S. economic influence from a considerable portion of the world."[73]

Klasen was now in favor of simple solutions, such as returning to fixed parities with a "reasonable realignment," and stated that he believed that the G-10 would be the most suitable forum for resolving the debacle.[74] This was also the position taken by the few internationalist voices in Washington, in particular by Treasury Undersecretary Paul Volcker. Carli added the interesting reflection that if the G-10 did not produce a solution, there would be a need to look for a Community answer, and that this would be more difficult to find with six rather than with ten or eleven countries. Italy could hope that an enlargement might bring more allies to counterbalance the strength of the Paris-Bonn axis. But more importantly, the terms of the debate would change as the emphasis reverted to global—rather than EEC-wide—monetary reform.

Europeans would no longer simply work on their own proposals for monetary reform. They believed that they should suspend their deliberations until an answer was found to the pressing global problem. But negotiating a global-level solution would almost certainly take a long time. Only when there was a recognition that global reform—at least on the lines that the Europeans contemplated—was a hopeless exercise would they be willing to resume the discussion of the alternative schemes that had first been elaborated in the late 1960s.

The Snake and Other Animals

We often judge institutional arrangements by their measurable outcomes: some crude figure such as higher growth rates, or lower inflation rates. By these criteria, the 1970s were a decade of failure and of unsolved problems. Growth collapsed, and inflation soared. Budgets came under strain. Such problems also produced a vigorous institutional activity, a search for solutions. Judged by results, then, the 1970s mark a low point of international cooperation. But the failures were so apparent that a plethora of schemes and plans on monetary and financial issues, on both a global and a European level, were formulated.

It is appropriate that the major symbol of the fraught business of European monetary cooperation in the 1970s should have been the Snake. Most people do not like snakes, and do not think of them as productive; they are associated with duplicity ("forked tongues"), with evil in the Garden of Eden, and with the Fall of Man. At the time, some European policymakers paid a great deal of attention to the idiosyncratic nomenclature of the new mechanisms for coordinating Europe's money and currencies. The Dutch treasury secretary, Conrad Oort, made a jocular habit of commenting on the way exchange rate bands within bands were described as the worm in the snake in the tunnel. In 1974 he suggested in a speech during the annual IMF meeting that "The snake has become the favorite animal of the Eurocrats. It resides on an empty floor in Luxembourg, called the European Monetary Cooperation Fund. So far, its most distinctive virtue is that it has created a whole new serpentine folklore and a Eurolingo exclusively devoted to the life and habits of the snake." And in 1976 he thought the joke so good that he went further: "If ever we shall have a common European currency, I am sure it will carry the symbol of the serpent. For a new religion has invaded Europe: the cult of the Snake. Its mystic origins are in the canyons of Luxembourg, its most faithful followers live across the Rhine and in the Rhine delta, but its most ardent prophets, recently turned heretics, were to be found in Gallia. A religious war is on: beware Britannia!"[1] In reality, by this time the Snake as a currency mechanism was confined to an increasingly small group of countries, and it seemed a symbol of failure rather than success. A member of the CoG's secretariat, André Bascoul, in reviewing a book on European monetary unification by the Italian central banker Giovanni Magnifico, produced a glorious string of mixed metaphors: "In the event, the snake refused the slimming cure and indeed after a few serious rejection crises, its very existence is constantly threatened in spite of several kisses of life. Many believe, or hope, that it is already writhing in the throes of death."[2]

The 1970s represent a crucial watershed not just of monetary history, but also more generally of European social and economic history.[3] Certainties and optimism about growth disappeared, to be replaced by worries about the sustainability of fiscal positions, about inflation, and about economic openness. There were major divergences over monetary policy as countries disinflated at very different speeds. All the new developments posed substantial challenges to the European ideal, whose attractions had largely rested in practice on the capacity of trade to open in order to deliver high rates of growth while protecting vulnerable groups. What would happen when growth faltered and social discontent surged?

The threats and challenges produced a great deal of debate and also many reform suggestions. Though there was a perplexing and polyphonic plethora of suggestions and semideveloped realizations, in the short term these were largely unproductive. In consequence, most analysts have concluded that the 1970s were a lost decade, in which the European momentum toward integration stalled. A much-cited verdict of Robert Marjolin in 1975 stated that "if there has been any movement it has been backwards."[4] A longer-term view, however, suggests that all the failures, the dead ends in the reform discussions, and the aborted initiatives eventually led to a refined sensibility about how institutional change could be accomplished in a highly complex system.[5]

The collapse of the Bretton Woods system of fixed exchange rates necessarily prompted a fundamental rethinking of European monetary issues. Originally the CoG had been concerned with monetary policy coordination in a world in which monetary policy was not thought to be particularly important. The European political establishment now wanted to add new potential tasks: the management of support mechanisms, the design of an exchange rate regime, and possibly even also a joint approach to reserve management.[6] The CoG emerged as an important forum for planning the response of European central banks to international problems, but also for debating a range of regional initiatives. The European and global discussions were deeply intertwined: there was a new discussion of monetary policy in the wake of the collapse of the par value system, as well as deep-seated worries about the preeminence of any national currency in the international order. French policymakers in particular thought it imperative to "banaliser le dollar." There was intensified interest in ways of ensuring exchange rate stability, with varying amounts of fluctuation permitted. The problems of the gold market in the later 1960s drove the discussion of new types of artificial or synthetic currencies, and the debate over the role of the Special Drawing Right (SDR) in the international order spilled over into a consideration of a new European unit of account. The Europeans attempted to duplicate something in between the IMF and the Federal Reserve System on a European level. Finally, in institutional terms, the emergence of alternates (deputy governors of central banks, but also deputy finance ministers) as key drivers of international reform discussions within the framework of the IMF's Committee of Twenty also drove the CoG to upgrade the role of their alternates, as well as to give greater prominence to ad hoc groups of experts.

The very active (though largely unproductive) reform debates also changed the dynamic in Europe, and pushed the Commission into a more exposed role in launching policy initiatives. By and large, the central bank governors of the 1970s were rather conservative men, who thought of themselves very firmly as practitioners, not as theoreticians and certainly not as visionaries. They increasingly came to be seen—especially from the point of view of the Commission—as obstacles to far-reaching reform initiatives.

These initiatives are discussed in the following pages. The Commission started to push not only for stronger exchange rate arrangements but for coordination of monetary targets and of monetary policy-making, and in consequence of economic policy. This discussion ultimately led nowhere in this period, but it was accompanied by initiatives concerned with financing, the provision of credit for exchange rate intervention and for balance-of-payments support, and the broad issue of the design of the exchange rate regime. Among the institutions produced as a result of the reform initiatives, the European Monetary Cooperation Fund became a largely automatic mechanism for accounting for the central bank swap operations needed for the management of the Snake.

There were also initiatives concerning the exchange rate from national policymakers, above all from France and the Netherlands. But the proposals were confronted by equally strong objections. Germany, and especially the Bundesbank, was hostile to many of the ideas set out in the 1970s, not necessarily because the Bundesbank was especially hidebound and conservative, but because it remained committed to a global vision.

The CoG at this stage provided a forum where European and global institutions came together. The major central bank governors who met in the CoG had just come from a dinner and a meeting with U.S., Canadian, and Japanese counterparts in the framework of the G-10. The content of the discussion was inevitably more broadly focused than it would have been in the more introspectively European climate of Brussels.

Another development was crucial for the future: a number of relatively young policymakers emerged, none of them at the time in central banks, who would later play a vital role in implementing the European project in the central banks. Jacques de Larosière became director of the treasury—in other words the official in charge of the French Finance Ministry—in May 1974 at the age of forty-four, after having already played an important part on the EEC Monetary Committee in handling the exchange rate implications of the end of Bretton Woods. His German equivalent, Karl Otto Pöhl, a former journalist who was close to Helmut Schmidt, became state secretary in the Finance Ministry in 1972. Born in 1929 within a month of each other, these two men would be the key poles of European (and to some extent also global) monetary policy-making for two decades. Two other figures played a central part at this time as mediators in monetary politics, and resumed this role in the central banking world of the 1980s and 1990s: Wim

Duisenberg, the Netherlands finance minister in the center-left Joop den Uyl government from 1973 to 1977, produced one of the most important proposals for moving on to European monetary union in 1976 via target zones for EEC member countries. The Belgian, with Hungarian roots, Alexandre Lamfalussy was the chief economist of the BIS from 1976 to 1985, when he became its general manager, and showed a strong interest in the work of the CoG and in particular in attempting to bring the global and European concerns into alignment.

The Language of Reform

The language of the debates of the 1970s continued to affect the way European institutions handled monetary integration in the 1980s and even in the 1990s. It is worth examining the key concepts that were evolved at this time.

1. *Monetarists and economists.* These terms have a specifically European usage, one that is completely detached from the application of "monetarism" as a label for the theories of Milton Friedman and the Chicago School. European "monetarists" believed that the establishment of a series of monetary rules might create the framework for general economic convergence, whereas "economists" stressed that convergence needed to precede the imposition of a single monetary framework. The former saw institutions as working a sort of magic; the latter held that the magic required would lie in the fundamentally political hard choices needed in order to produce mutually consistent policy outcomes. The former philosophy prevailed in France, the latter in Germany. During the 1970s the term *coronation* was frequently used, especially by the Bundesbank, to emphasize that monetary union could come only as the final symbolic act of an integration that had been prepared by solid policy work. The problem during much of the decade was that national financial and economic policies were diverging rather than converging: an easy and obvious indicator was the increased diversity of inflation performance.

2. *Parallelism.* The key concept of the Werner Report was that monetary integration should not take place without a parallel coordination of fiscal and economic policy. Monetary union without a closer fiscal

and economic convergence would impose intolerable strains on the politics of monetary policy formulation. A high degree of economic convergence, however, required the absence of monetary fluctuations that brought chaos to the highly politicized price regime in agricultural support, and that also threatened to produce worries about competitive devaluation and currency manipulation. For some interpreters, "parallelism" was nothing more than a euphemism for deadlock and incoherence. The positions of "economists" and "monetarists" could not be synthesized, as they stood for two radically incompatible approaches. In consequence, "parallelism" was no more than a "temporary expedient" that was "acceptable precisely because it was vague enough to mean whatever the user intended."[7]

3. *Parallel currency.*   In the Bretton Woods system, the key currency had been the dollar. In a new monetary system, it might be desirable to have a new currency that could be used as a reference point. The first mechanisms for providing a new synthetic currency had evolved out of private initiatives. In 1954 the Belgian airline Sabena had issued bonds with a "currency option clause" under which they might be repaid in the lender's choice of currency; and from 1962 the Luxembourg Kredietbank SA, inspired by Robert Triffin, issued bonds in a European currency unit (*unité de compte européen*), which seemed to challenge central banks as monopoly issuers of currency. In 1974 the bank launched a bond denominated in the IMF's SDRs. In 1973 the European Investment Bank, an official EEC institution, developed the Eurco (European composite unit).[8] The most prominent 1970s political statement of the need for a new currency appeared in an article (known as the All Saints' Day Manifesto) by nine economists from eight EC countries published in *The Economist* on November 1, 1975, calling for the EC central banks to issue a new currency, the "Europa." A few months later most of the All Saints' group, reorganized into an independent commission under the auspices of the EC Commission, suggested instead a currency with the same standard as the currency with the lowest inflation rate, justifying this choice on "political" grounds. This idea remained an important, but ultimately irrelevant, part of European thinking until the early 1990s, when Britain produced a suggestion for a "hard ECU" in parallel to existing Community currencies; but that proposal was widely interpreted as a diversionary move to stymie other mechanisms for establishing monetary integration.

4. *European Currency Unit.*   Since 1950, when it had been needed for the monetary arithmetic of the European Payments Union, there had been a calculation of a European Unit of Account, but it became a problematic concept only after the depreciation of the U.S. dollar on August 15, 1971. The EUA was defined in terms of gold, at the old value of the dollar (0.088867088 gram of fine gold). But with the advent of floating exchange rates, a debate started about whether this was the best way of basing calculations about EEC financing, about the Common Agricultural Policy, or about exchange rate behavior. The term *European Currency Unit* appears to have been coined in official usage by EC Commission President François-Xavier Ortoli, who told a New York audience in September 1974 that he wanted "a new monetary unit, which we could call ECU, as the Latin countries would quickly be familiar with this now defunct continental currency, while the Anglo-Saxons would be happy to see the English initials of the 'European Common Unit' for the common European currency."[9]

5. *Monetarism (again).*   When the fixed-exchange-rate system broke down, the most obvious external source of monetary discipline disappeared. This was the most obvious explanation of the increasing policy divergence. Some central banks (in particular the Bundesbank) began to consider monetary targeting as an alternative to provide a policy anchor. There always remained some ambiguity as to whether (as in the view of academic monetarists) changes in the quantity of money directly determined price developments, or whether (in a softer European version of monetarism) the setting of targets might affect the behavior of trade unions and business, lead to lower wages and costs, and thus bring down an inflation that had been driven fundamentally by rising costs. The CoG was a forum for this debate, but none of the central bank governors ever wanted to adopt an explicitly monetarist approach; intriguingly, the chief source of the new doctrine was the Commission, and particularly the powerful personality of Raymond Barre, who talked explicitly about monetary targets and about what measures of money should most appropriately be used, more than two years before the Bundesbank introduced its policy innovation of a public monetary target.

6. *Globalization.*   The term *globalization*, which became a widely popular concept in the 1990s, had a much earlier usage in which central banks

and governments wanted to multilateralize their relationship, and also to link conceptually different kinds of operation. It meant in effect "issue linkage." Thus in 1972 the CoG discussed the fact that "bilateral financing operations and the narrowing of margins did not permit cooperation and globalization."[10]

7. *Asymmetry.* A central European complaint about the fixed but adjustable exchange rate system (or Bretton Woods system) had been the "exorbitant position" of the United States, in that other countries were obliged to accumulate dollar reserves, but the United States had no corresponding accumulations of liabilities in a foreign currency. The task of adjustment thus fell mostly on the other countries. In the exchange regime of the 1960s the American problem spilled into Europe to the extent that Germany had made a political commitment not to convert its dollar reserves, which it saw as a justifiable price to pay for U.S. security protection. By the 1970s Germany started to take on some of the attributes of American hegemony in the European system, with adjustment again being required primarily of Germany's partners, but not of Germany. Deficit countries intervening to defend their currencies needed to borrow reserves, while surplus countries could simply issue more of their own currencies to finance interventions. Consequently other countries, especially France, began to fear that the power dynamics of the global system were being replayed in Europe with Germany as the new hegemon. They interpreted Germany's more rapid adoption of an anti-inflationary course, with lower monetary growth and lower wage settlements producing competitive advantages for German exporters in a fixed-exchange-rate system, as a power play, in which economic and political benefits were mixed in the same way as they had been in the making of U.S. policy in the 1960s.

The discussions of the multiple initiatives for financial support mechanisms, as well as for a broad variety of experts' groups with differing but overlapping remits, all took place in the context of a new political setting as well as a new political and economic vocabulary.

The Smithsonian and Its Aftermath

After August 15, 1971, there was no immediate general European agreement on proposals for a joint float against the dollar. An EEC Council of

Ministers meeting of August 19 was unproductive, with France refusing to contemplate any suspension of parity alterations or general realignment.[11] Germany continued to let the Deutsche Mark float independently; France had a two-tier arrangement, with separate rates for capital account transactions and the old dollar rate for current account dealings. The Netherlands agreed, however, on a common float with Belgium and Luxembourg, in which their exchange movements were limited to ±1.5 percent.

The EEC Monetary Committee discussed a response on September 2, when it considered two parallel position papers, one by the Italian Rinaldo Ossola and the other written by Otmar Emminger of the Bundesbank. Both suggested a narrow zone of fluctuations for European currencies of ± 1.5 percent; the papers differed simply in that Ossola wanted to think about a fixed relationship with the dollar while Emminger did not, and suggested that EEC countries should refrain from interventions in third currencies (that is, the dollar). In large part, this difference reflected the divergence of European experiences after August 15: the dollar/Deutsche Mark rate had swung wildly, as Emminger pointed out in the meeting, while other currencies had been fundamentally stable. De Larosière had a policy explanation, and noted that France had been able to stabilize French exchange rates through the introduction of separate official and private markets.[12] By contrast, Germany was gripped by the realization of how difficult it would be to stabilize its currency, which had emerged (with the Japanese yen) as the major alternative to the dollar.

On the international stage, France acted as the spokesman for Europe, even though its position in many of the internal European debates appeared to be that of an outlier. A general international agreement was prepared by a preliminary meeting between Presidents Nixon and Pompidou in the Azores (December 13–14, 1971). There was an agreement on a general alignment, in which Nixon would accept a devaluation of the dollar from $35 to $38 an ounce. The terms of a general agreement were worked out at the Smithsonian meeting of the G-10 finance ministers and central bank governors (December 17–18). The German economics minister, Karl Schiller, described this meeting as "carpet trading." The managing director of the IMF, Pierre-Paul Schweitzer, jotted down figures in pencil on a yellow pad (faithfully preserved in the IMF archives) as the ministers haggled. The French finance minister, Valéry Giscard d'Estaing, believed that more time was needed to produce a really sustainable new exchange rate system, and would have preferred a discussion at the end of January. But Schiller broke the ice by agreeing to a revaluation of the Deutsche Mark by 13.57 percent. The very forceful U.S. Treasury secretary, John Connally, then turned his attention to pressing Japan for a greater revaluation. He originally wanted 20 percent, but eventually (after frequent calls to Tokyo) Finance Minister Mikio Mizuta agreed to 16.9 percent. Thereafter other European rates were established relatively quickly. France and the United Kingdom did not change their gold rate, and thus appreciated by 8.6 percent against the devalued dollar, while Italy and Sweden devalued by 1 percent. There was more than simply a change of parities, however: the bands of fluctuation in relation to the dollar were widened from 2.0 to 4.5 percent, so that nondollar currencies, including the European ones, might vary by as much as 9 percent against one another. The new system itself was a shock to Europeans, but worse was to come.

In a pattern that was repeated in many subsequent "crises" of the international monetary order, the United States then embarked on a monetary policy that was inconsistent with a European or global notion of stability. In particular, Nixon—driven by worries about the presidential election of 1972 and memories of the 1960 election, which he thought he had lost to John F. Kennedy because of excessively tight policy by the Federal Reserve—pressed for an expansive monetary policy. The U.S. trade balance deteriorated sharply.

In September 1971 Pompidou had called for an institutionalization of the European response to the exchange rate crisis. He told a press conference on September 23 that there was a new opportunity for Europe on the international stage: "Once the international system is reestablished, Europe will be able to play the card of economic and monetary union, and she already needs to prepare herself." There would also be increased coordination of economic policy. The CoG would play a central role. "What we need is to organize a common defense against the flows of floating capital, and at the same time, a concerted management of reserves, under the control of the governments and through the intermediary of the Committee of Central Bank Governors. If in order to do this we need to give the committee supplementary means, in other words an executive organ, France is prepared to accept and even welcome this."[13] Following up on the presidential suggestion, Giscard d'Estaing on January 27, 1972, told the French Financial Commission that the committee should be endowed with a permanent secretariat.[14]

The BIS, and especially its dynamic French general manager, René Larre, saw an institutional opportunity. Larre undertook a round of visits in Paris, as well as writing a personal letter to Giscard d'Estaing. His major argument was that the BIS ("a body that normally acts as the organization for concerted action and cooperation among the European central banks"), which had in the past acted as the agent of the European Payments Union and as the "depository" (that is, fiscal agent) for the European Coal and Steel Community, offered an already existing depth of experience in monetary operations and in the exchange market.[15]

Immediately after the Smithsonian meeting, on December 15, 1971, the CoG asked a group of experts under the chairmanship of Marcel Théron, the Banque de France's director-general of foreign services, to examine the operation of a system of narrower margins among the European currencies. Such a system was required by the working of the price support mechanism of the Common Agricultural Policy, by the needs of intra-European trade, and by the overall goal of European Monetary Union. The decisive push for action came from the Commission: in February 1972 Raymond Barre explained at the CoG meeting that the forthcoming Council meeting would require a broad-ranging reform agenda, including the reduction of intra-Community margins in exchange rates, a system of intervention, a European Monetary Cooperation Fund, and concerted policy regarding capital movements.

The Bank of England began to participate as an observer in the CoG in November 1971, just before the Smithsonian meeting, even though the details of Britain's membership in the EEC had not been finally settled. The most obvious rationale was that Britain was still the provider of the world's second most important reserve currency (after the dollar), and that a critical issue in the reform discussion was the replacement of inadequate reserve currencies. The pound very clearly looked overburdened by its reserve role; in 1971 the dollar was apparently going down the path of decline already taken by sterling. In legal terms, the participation of a non-EEC central bank looked peculiar, however, and the rationale for British participation became the idea that Britain was soon to become a member. That argument opened the door to the participation of other countries. From March 1972, the Danish and Irish central bank governors also participated; and from April 1972 an "enlarged Committee" also included Austria, Sweden, and Switzerland, countries whose neutrality seemed to preclude EC membership. The CoG was thus well ahead of the EEC in terms of an extension of its membership, a universalization of its embrace.

Britain was a major international player, with very different interests and traditions from those of the continental Europeans. In particular, it was among the European countries least disposed to want a fixed-rate system that would constrain its domestic room for maneuver; and Britain had been politically traumatized by the long and fraught debates about sterling devaluation in the 1960s. The British immediately took the position of outliers in the exchange rate debate. The governor of the Bank of England, Sir Leslie O'Brien, did not think that he should just sit quietly on the sidelines as an observer.

In the CoG, O'Brien, together with the president of the Nederlandsche Bank, Jelle Zijlstra, set out the view that a wider fluctuation band of ±3 percent was desirable, would reflect more accurately the differences in the performance of various currencies, and would reduce the possibility of new speculative crises leading to exchange rate alterations. At the other end of the scale of possibilities, the Belgian economist and central banker Robert Vandeputte argued for ±1.5 percent, while the French and Italians opted for ±2.25 percent, and Otmar Emminger of the Bundesbank was prepared to accept either that or the wider margin. Barre explained that because of the price definition problems of the Common Agricultural Policy, the Commission had a preference for ±2 percent, and that ±2.25 percent was the furthest that the Commission would be prepared to move.[16] O'Brien was also concerned about the possibility of imposing an "onerous" mechanism for the settlement of balances.[17]

French policymakers were worried that a transition to generalized floating would result in the emergence of regional exchange rate blocs and an extension of German power and influence in the EEC. There was thus systematic French opposition to the German idea of a collective European float. As a French Finance Ministry official put it, "inside the Community, the relative weight of the most powerful countries, and notably that of the Federal Republic of Germany, will be increased."[18] France consequently pushed for a new European initiative. But the

CoG was at the center of European attempts to create some regional stability.

There were some signs of policy convergence. On a very modest and small scale, the Benelux agreement limiting movements between the franc and the guilder to 1.5 percent (in other words, a narrower range than was permitted under the Bretton Woods regime) had survived all the currency chaos. More importantly, Germany, dominated by a classically liberal approach while Schiller was the "super" finance and economics minister (in a combined portfolio), now seemed willing to accept a measure of capital controls and thus convergence with the French policy framework. On December 12, 1971, the Bundestag passed a law requiring banks to make a cash deposit (*Bardepot*) corresponding to foreign borrowing, in order to penalize inflows.

There were also signs that the governors were willing to accept some variant of the new initiatives for enhanced European currency discipline. A group of experts chaired by Marcel Théron under the auspices of the CoG (see below), in a preliminary report of January 8, 1972, noted that some of the most influential governors, Karl Klasen, Olivier Wormser, and Robert Vandeputte, were opposed to an idea of any escape clause in a new currency mechanism.[19]

In these difficult circumstances, the EEC Commission pressed for a relaunching of the project of economic and monetary union, with proposals on January 12, 1972, for a maximum 2 percent deviation from parity, and for the realization of the monetary fund as a way of administering short- and medium-term support within the EEC. On March 21, 1972, the ECOFIN (the Council of Finance Ministers, acting as the executive of the EC), reflecting the consensus that had emerged at the CoG, asked the central banks to reduce fluctuation margins to ±2.25 percent, or half the amount allowed under the terms of the Smithsonian agreement, "as a first step toward the creation of a[n EEC] monetary zone within the framework of the international system."[20] The mandate explicitly took up again the concept of parallelism. The CoG had moved in its March meeting in the direction of short-term support, which would be designated in a European unit of account defined as 0.088867088 of a gram of fine gold. The Théron Group was also asked to draw up a proposal for a European Fund.

This new system of a reduced fluctuation band was generally referred to as "the EEC snake in the Smithsonian tunnel." Within this system, the Netherlands and Belgium-Luxembourg continued to have the smaller room for maneuver (1.5 percent), which was sometimes called "the worm." The United Kingdom and Denmark joined the Snake on May 1, 1972, although their membership in the EC only began in January 1973. Norway, which was also expected to join the EEC, became an associate member on May 23 and remained within the exchange mechanism, although in a referendum on September 26, 1972, Norwegian voters rejected EEC membership. Sweden also applied to join the mechanism in May 1972, but the application was deferred because of a British exchange rate crisis, and the membership did not take effect until March 19, 1973. In 1975 there were also intensive negotiations about a formal association of Switzerland with the narrow exchange rate system for the most stable EC currencies, though in the last resort these discussions were unproductive.[21] The Commission's representative, Ugo Mosca, the head of the Economic and Financial Directorate, explained that Brussels was pleased with the idea of an extension of the newly evolving European monetary order.[22]

In what became known as the Basel Accord, the central banks on April 10, 1972, set out the operational details of the new system, which began to function on April 24.[23] New "very-short-term" facilities were established to finance interventions, which was supposed to be symmetrical, with the central bank of a strong currency buying a weak currency, and vice versa. The credits had no initial ceiling, and a limited part could generally be renewed for up to three months with the creditors' consent (a stipulation that was dropped in 1975); the arrangement corresponded with the presumption of unlimited intervention at the margins of the exchange rate commitments. Settlement was to be made in gold, dollars or other foreign exchange, or SDRs, between the central banks involved (after April 1973 the process was multilateralized through the EMCF, as discussed below). There might also be interventions before the limiting bands were reached (intramarginal interventions), but these needed to be agreed between the central banks involved in a process called "concertation."

The new provisions supplemented an existing scheme, created on February 9, 1970, for short-term support for three-month periods that could be extended for a further three months (Agreement Setting Up a System of Short-Term Monetary Support). This support applied to all members of the European Community, not just members of the Snake system. Unlike the 1972 scheme, there was in the older mechanism a definitive limit set by quotas, with the total quotas initially amounting to $1 billion and a provision that double that amount might be provided through extensions (*rallonges*). The quotas were subsequently raised, in 1974 and again in 1977. The quotas under the short-term scheme were used to set the limits for the renewals of the very-short-term intervention credits.[24] Britain regarded the financing arrangements of the Snake as inadequate, and this view played a role in the British decision to leave the mechanism. By contrast, German policymakers constantly pressed to limit the financing that would be made available. The short-term support mechanism was used by Italy on two occasions, in June 1973 (for 1.5625 billion EUA, or $1.885 billion) and in May 1976 (for 400 million EUA or $482.5 million). It was associated with a mild policy conditionality: in 1973 the Banca d'Italia increased its rate penalties for lending to banks, and also increased reserve requirements for banks.[25] In the late 1970s the CoG tried to examine why other countries, notably France, which had massive reserve losses in January 1974 and again in March 1976, or Denmark, which also sustained major speculative attacks, did not use this scheme.[26]

In a third credit option, in line with the original provisions of the Rome Treaty (Article 108) for balance-of-payments support, the Council of Ministers agreed in March 1971 to the provision of medium-term (three to five years) balance-of-payments support, with a quota system and a link to policy conditionality. The decision included the provision that implementation "shall be closely linked with the standing arrangements for consultation and coordination of economic policy among the member states." Such support could be granted by the Council of Ministers on the recommendation of the Commission and after consultation with the Monetary Committee. An initial 2 billion EUA quota was created, with 600 million each from France and Germany, 400 million from Italy, and 200 million each from Belgium and the Netherlands.[27] The mechanism was only ever used by Italy, when it used 1.1592 billion EUA in December 1974 to convert part of a large outstanding very-short-term credit into a three-and-a-half-year credit.

A fourth mechanism was created in response to the oil shock, at the same time as the IMF was also creating a new facility. The ECOFIN established a "balance-of-payments mechanism" on February 17, 1975, to respond to situations in which there was need for support at a time when the majority of member countries were in a payments deficit. It was used in March 1976, with $1.3 billion divided between Italy and Ireland, and again in May 1977, with $500 million for Italy.

The longer-term financing never became a routine, and it always represented something of an embarrassment for the country obliged to take it. Governor Guido Carli consistently argued that the need for financing came not from inappropriate fiscal and monetary policies for regulating aggregate demand but rather from "disequilibria that are due to the varying degree of cost inflation, to the intensification of such inflation as a result precisely of economic integration between countries with different standards of living, and to the impossibility of correcting the effects of such inflation by recourse to monetary policy without their having repercussions on the level of employment, even when the labor force is sufficiently mobile. In my opinion, this type of tension is destined to increase inside our Community in the years to come."[28] Carli was right, but there was no real solution to the demand for support that went beyond short-term operations.

On the other hand, technical cooperation went quite well. The central banks agreed on "concertation" procedures: the coordination of standard times for interventions, as well as the establishment of a telephone network. There were three rounds of telephone discussions on each trading day between the EEC central banks, the Sveriges Riksbank, and the Norges Bank at 10:00 and 11:30 A.M., and then at 4:05 P.M., after the close of European business. In 1975 the Federal Reserve, the Bank of Canada, and the Swiss National Bank joined the network. In the 1970s the technical quality was still quite poor, and participants claimed that important exchanges of information were not fully audible.

A major part of the work of the Théron Group involved the elaboration of the intervention techniques, with strong pressure from the governments to undertake these interventions as far as possible in EEC currencies and not in dollars.[29] At this stage the governors emphasized that to accept dollar interventions as a rule would be to undermine the exchange rate mechanism proposed by the Council of Ministers.

The agreement required substantial modification within two months of its initiation. In practice, Britain was always an uneasy member of the system. The chancellor of the Exchequer, Anthony Barber, had explained in his annual budget speech that "It is neither necessary nor desirable to distort domestic economies to an unacceptable extent in order to retain unrealistic exchange rates, whether they are too high, or too low." A highly expansionist budget added 2 percent of GDP to demand, and by April there were signs of an incipient balance-of-payments crisis. By the middle of June, a major speculative attack developed. Between June 16 and 22, 1972, $2.6 billion moved out of the United Kingdom, two-thirds of it into Deutsche Marks, and on June 23 the government announced that sterling would be put on a temporary float, with the result that it left the Snake mechanism less than two months after joining. Ireland, which was in a currency union with the United Kingdom, left at the same time; Denmark, which had extensive trade links with the United Kingdom, announced its departure on June 27, but kept the krona within the Snake limits and actually rejoined on October 10. In assessing the problems in European money at this time, the Bank of England emphasized a purely technical aspect: the EEC members had a "rigid rule" under which they stopped interventions on exchange markets at 4:00 P.M. Central European Time, when the British and U.S. markets were still trading, so that exchange rates showed little movement in the European day and then suddenly moved. As a result the Bank of England had to make its interventions in dollars, which the European central banks in turn complained about.[30] The British experience highlighted the limits of European cooperation, in that the continental central banks had bought pounds but only as agents of the Bank of England, which at the end of the subsequent month was obliged to pay these sterling balances at the official rate, and thus to bear any exchange loss. There was also no EEC financial assistance to the United Kingdom.

The sterling crisis also highlighted the fact that a speculative attack on one country would pose problems for the whole of the European bloc. The new support mechanism kept up the pound/dollar exchange rate while pushing down the rates of other European countries, so that there was a substantial inflow into the hard European moneys, notably into the Deutsche Mark.[31] At the end of June, a new wave of doubt about the dollar set in, and there were major inflows to Germany as well as to other European countries. The different levels of inflows inevitably increased tensions in the exchange rates (see Figure 4.1).

The other increasingly problematical European country, Italy, was dealt with in a different way. The British exit from the Snake had increased the pressure on Italy. On June 26, 1972, in the Accord de Luxembourg, Italy was given a derogation to remain in the Snake, but was allowed to use dollars for intervention in the domestic market. The United Kingdom tried to avoid any attempt at the European level to establish a link between the Italian derogation and an attempt to bring the United Kingdom back into a fixed-rate regime.[32] The continued Italian membership required the operation of the new very-short-term financing facility that had been designed as part of a reordering of European monetary arrangements. Thus the Banque de France bought 4.6 billion lira as soon as the market reopened, and the Nederlandsche Bank 340 million lira. Relieving the pressure on the Italian lira required in all some $1.5 billion in interventions in June and July. At the same time the Banca d'Italia was intervening heavily to buy dollars borrowed by Italian banks in the Euromarkets. In the Théron Group there was substantial unease about the Italian derogation, and the non-Italian members pressed Italy to move back to settlements in currencies that were linked to gold. This suggestion was resisted both by the Italian expert in the group and by Governor Carli in the CoG.[33]

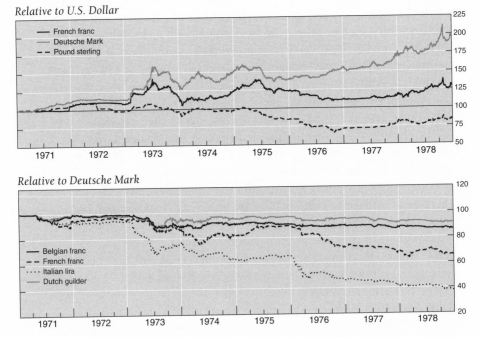

Figure 4.1. Exchange rates, 1971–1979. Beginning of period = 100. *Source:* National data.

By this stage, credit operations for exchange rate interventions had become highly politicized because they were often interpreted as constituting some sort of subsidy. The concertation, originally envisaged as being at a technical level, became more and more a concern for governors and ministers. At the highest political level, the goals of European economic and monetary union were reasserted, and the October 1972 Paris summit even specified that the beginning of the transition to stage two of the Werner Plan process would begin in January 1974. In their meeting of July 16–17, 1972, the EEC finance ministers asked the central bank governors to provide a position on the measurement of value in currencies. The central bankers finally reported on March 12, 1973, just at the moment when the fixed-exchange-rate regime was finally disintegrating. The report simply went through a series of options for restoring currency stability and explained why they might be implausible: an increase in the gold price would lead to speculation about future changes in the gold price, and anyway it was unlikely that the United States would agree to such a move. Using the SDR to define currencies without an alteration of the gold price would simply produce a dollar standard under some other name, and that outcome was not acceptable. A joint system based on both the SDR and gold was impossible because "history shows that the parallel existence of two measures of value by itself creates problems." The report raised the possibility of regional arrangements under which a gold price could be set, then concluded that "no world monetary system, however technically perfect, could last for long if in one or more major economies too lax a domestic economic policy were conducted."[34] The same meeting of the CoG also discussed a report by a group of experts on foreign exchange issues (discussed below), which sketched out more fully an idea of a European money.

The Definitive End of Global Fixed Exchange Rates

After the ending of U.S. wage and price controls on January 11, 1973, major capital movements out of the dollar resumed. The flow into Deutsche Marks immediately hit the weaker European currencies, which experienced their own form of capital flight, obliging the Bundesbank to intervene along the lines of the Basel Accord. On January 20 Italy imposed measures to halt capital flight. On February 9 the Bank of Japan closed the foreign exchange market, and a float of the yen began; the European markets were closed on February 10. American policymakers were trying to negotiate new parities, and on February 12 they announced a 10 percent devaluation of the dollar. But at the same time, Treasury Secretary George Shultz, who was sympathetic to Milton Friedman's view on the superiority of flexible exchange rates, stated that the United States had "undertaken no obligations to intervene in foreign exchange markets," and that capital controls were being scrapped.[35]

The smaller European countries were dissatisfied by their exclusion from the diplomacy over exchange rates. At the Monetary Committee on February 14, 1973, representatives of Belgium, Italy, and the Netherlands complained that they had not been consulted during the crisis; while the German representative tried to argue that the main negotiations did not concern EEC countries. Ugo Mosca, from the EEC Commission, suggested that joint European action was needed, and proposed accelerated European integration as a possible response to the crisis.[36] But Germany saw itself as bearing the main brunt of the currency storm, and German policymakers in consequence inclined again, as in 1971, to unilateral action.

In early March the storm on the currency markets was renewed, with the Bundesbank issuing DM 8 billion on March 1, an equivalent of 16 percent of the value of currency in circulation. Of the total of around $10 billion of foreign exchange purchased, three-quarters was bought by Germany, and an eighth by the Netherlands.[37] Bundesbank Vice-President Otmar Emminger, also a long-term proponent of greater exchange rate flexibility in the international system, concluded that the markets had sounded "the death knell of the Bretton Woods parity system." On March 2 the Bundesbank announced that it would no longer intervene to support the dollar rates. On March 4 the EEC finance ministers discussed a joint float, and on March 9 and 16 G-10 meetings were expanded to include the smaller EEC states. On March 11–12, at the EEC Council of Ministers, France agreed to join a German float, with a 3 percent revaluation of the Deutsche Mark relative to the franc and other currencies, and a future fluctuation margin of 2.25 percent among the currencies. France and Benelux also retained a dual foreign exchange rate system. The United Kingdom, Ireland, and Italy remained outside this new system.

The March 1973 crisis lent itself to conflicting interpretations. On the one hand, the Snake survived the currency chaos that seemed to have been produced primarily by the mismanagement of monetary policy in the United States; but on the other hand, the Snake was not a complete monetary embodiment of the EEC. Some analysts in consequence concluded that the Snake "ceased to be a visible means of working towards economic and monetary union because it was no longer an instrument for promoting the integration of the *Community*."[38]

The Snake was now free from its Smithsonian tunnel. It started to wriggle wildly as the dollar fell sharply. By the beginning of July the American currency had fallen to a discount of 14.7 percent relative to its Smithsonian parity. But the inflows affected only some of the members, and placed immense strains on the European system, requiring very substantial interventions (1.19 billion EUA in July), with most of the interventions taking place in EEC currencies (whereas before March 1973 most foreign exchange operations had been in dollars). First, predictably, the major flows went into Deutsche Marks, with the Bundesbank undertaking DM 5 billion in interventions, until on June 29 the Deutsche Mark was revalued by 5.5 percent. Then the flows switched to the smaller northern European currencies, the Danish krone, the Netherlands guilder, and the Norwegian krone. Denmark followed closely the terms of the Basel Accord and intervened only in EEC currencies, buying currencies worth 186 million EUA. At the CoG meeting on July 9, Bundesbank President Klasen defended the German move and added that many prominent economists and the major institutes in Germany were calling for the Deutsche Mark to leave the Snake. Emminger, who was much more outspoken than Klasen, liked to comment on how membership in the Snake limited the capacity of the Bundesbank to defend its external stability because of the obligation to intervene in defense of the Snake parities.[39] The July meeting, however, produced an agreement to extend coordinated interventions, and also a proposal to engage with the Federal Reserve in a stabilization of the dollar.

In the next major wave of speculative attacks in September, even more interventions were required: 2.45 billion EUA. Again, the only solution seemed to be a parity change, and the other non-German currencies subjected to big inflows were also revalued, the guilder by 5 percent on September 17 and the Norwegian krone by 5 percent on November 26. On the other hand, the French franc remained perpetually weak in relation to the other currencies, and required support intervention. Between September 17 and 21 France required 1.538 billion EUA in support interventions, with 645 million EUA on one day, September 20, 1973.[40]

Turbulence increased with the Yom Kippur War, the imposition of the Arab oil embargo on October 16, and the onset of the first oil price crisis. It was clear that all European countries would face a major current account shock. Exchange rate issues were directly bound up with international diplomacy. The dollar started to rise again relative to the European currencies, and by early January 1974 the discount on the Smithsonian parities had fallen to 2 percent; in the middle of February the Snake was back in its old tunnel.

The improvement of the dollar did not reduce the problems for the weaker European currencies. The German real exchange rate (which had been forced up by the revaluations of the late Bretton Woods period) now depreciated significantly (see Figure 4.2), generating advantages for German exporters and increasing the competitive pressures on Germany's neighbors. France suffered from a considerable loss of reserves, and instituted measures to attract capital inflows; the Banque de France was also obliged to undertake large-scale interventions. None of the measures was successful, and with the reserves vanishing, on January 19, 1974, France temporarily withdrew from the Snake. In the

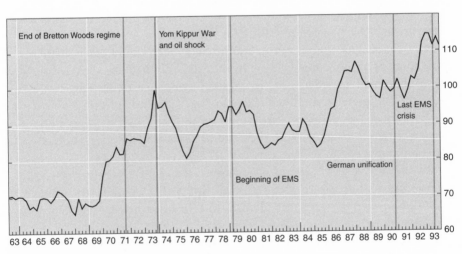

Figure 4.2. Real effective exchange rate for Deutsche Mark, 1963–1993, based on unit labor cost. 1990 = 100. *Sources:* OECD database; IMF, *IFS.*

Monetary Committee, the French Finance Ministry representative, Yves Haberer, explained that the French action was a preventive measure, that it was needed in order to take account of social demands (Giscard d'Estaing had appeared on television to say that in the past French authorities had given precedence to exchange rate issues over employment issues), that it was experimental and was limited to a six-month period. Dutch Treasury Secretary Oort criticized the isolated and uncoordinated character of the French action and stated that "social demands" should be ignored; the coordination of economic policy was more important than "currency political games."[41]

In its report on the crises, concluded in early January and thus just before the drama of the French departure, the Théron Group concluded that "The absence of the 'tunnel' made the maintenance of the 'Snake' more difficult and expensive." The Danish experience of crises in September 1972, which the Danmarks Nationalbank dealt with by dollar interventions, and in June–July 1973, when very large interventions were required, showed that European currency interventions could be more costly. The experts also noted that since interventions occurred almost entirely when the margins of the system were reached, the markets had a degree of certainty and could embark on one-way bets against target currencies. The logical conclusion was that more intramarginal intervention was required, but such a step might be costly. The experts also tried to signal that greater coordination of economic and monetary policy was needed.[42]

The currency turbulence thus prompted widespread rethinking of the European management of currencies, and considerable skepticism about the more ambitious goals. In December 1973 the chairman of the CoG, Bundesbank President Karl Klasen, stated that "for essentially practical reasons" the CoG was not sympathetic to Commission proposals for a permanent mechanism at the EMCF for the coordination of monetary policies in member countries. But, he added, this objection did not preclude intensified collaboration within the framework of the CoG.[43]

The Proliferation of "Groups"

In the early 1970s, in order to deal with the new complexities of the international financial order, new forms of cooperation emerged. From

May 1974, prior meetings of the governors' deputies or alternates were instituted on a regular basis, as a response to Article 8 of the February 18, 1974, decision of the EC Council on the achievement of a high degree of convergence of economic policies pursued by member states.[44] The alternates' mandate involved preparing the CoG meetings. Like other high-level groups that emerged at this time, notably the G-5 (later G-7) finance ministers, a great deal of the agenda setting and preparatory work was done in the preliminary meetings of the number-two officials.

The CoG was also augmented by a number of more technical experts' groups, which laid a potential basis for an enhanced policy role. But initially—and indeed for a very long time in two of the five groupings—they did not even have real names describing their functions, but were simply known under the names of the chairmen.

- Foreign exchange issues were dealt with by the Théron Group, established at the CoG meeting of September 12–13, 1971, but which was in many senses a continuation of a group of experts discussing technical aspects of concertation in the aftermath of the August 1970 Ansiaux report. As such, experts from central banks under the chairmanship of Théron produced two detailed reports, on October 30, 1970, and April 7, 1971. The meetings were attended by representatives of the European Commission. At first the group was known as the "Groupe d'experts sur les problèmes techniques soulevés par la concertation," but it became customary to refer simply to the name of the first chairman, Marcel Théron. In a different configuration, these experts also met with non-EEC central bank representatives as the "concertation group."
- Monetary policy was dealt with by two groups, one on "the harmonization of monetary policy instruments" (Groupe d'experts sur l'harmonisation des instruments de la politique monétaire) under Adraan Bastiaanse of the Nederlandsche Bank, established at the CoG meeting of April 19, 1971, and by the EC Monetary Committee on April 20, 1971. The group was composed of both central bank and finance ministry officials, and its reports were sent to both the CoG and the Monetary Committee.
- At the same CoG meeting of April 19, 1971, a parallel group, also under Bastiaanse, was established with the goal of "coordination

of the monetary policy of the Community central banks"
(Coordination de la politique monétaire suivie par les banques
centrales de la Communauté).

- Following the resolution of the European Council of March 22,
  1971, an experts' group under the Belgian lawyer Josse Mertens
  de Wilmars prepared the establishment of a European Monetary
  Cooperation Fund (Groupe d'experts sur le Fond européen de
  coopération monétaire).

- A further informal group (Groupe de Contact, or Contact Group)
  was concerned with banking supervision. The origins of this
  group lay not with the member countries, the Commission, or
  the CoG, but with an initiative by Herman Baeyens, the deputy
  director of the Belgian Banking and Finance Commission, and
  Huib Muller, from the banking supervisory department of the
  Nederlandsche Bank. It discussed the explosion of liquidity in the
  Euromarkets, solvency and capital requirements, and limitations
  on large exposures of individual banks; but it was primarily
  conceived as a way of handling in a coordinated way the regulatory
  challenges posed by foreign bank offices and subsidiaries. It was
  not primarily a central bank institution, in that officials from only
  two EEC central banks, the Nederlandsche Bank and the Banca
  d'Italia, participated; in the other four EEC countries, banking
  supervision and regulation were handled outside the central
  bank, by separate institutions. The first meeting took place in
  Amsterdam on June 29–30, 1972.[45]

As in the CoG, there was a long debate within the Contact Group
about how relations with the European Commission should be handled. Participation of EEC representatives in the banking group would
make for more formality and might inhibit the discussion of individual
bank cases. On the other hand, this was a discussion that evolved in the
context of the EEC, and if there was to be a policy implementation, it
would need to come in the form of EEC directives. So Commission participation looked even more crucial for the work of the Contact Group
than was the case for the CoG. The initial meetings of this group, which
moved in rotation from one central bank to another, were quite informal, and the Commission was simply invited to send an observer.

This arrangement changed, with fateful consequences, when really
serious banking problems emerged in many countries in 1974, and some

observers began to fear a general or global banking crisis.[46] A specific problem arose in the aftermath of the failure on June 26 of a small (and old) German bank, Herstatt. The foreign exchange transactions of the bank occurred in two legs, so that the institutions dealing with Herstatt paid in Deutsche Marks during the German working day, but the dollar payments were made during U.S. business hours, when the German markets were closed. The result of the failure was that the German receiver blocked the bank's payments to the U.S. counterparties; the technical term for this sort of risk subsequently became *Herstatt risk.*

The Herstatt crisis and the perception that the Euromarkets were dangerous transformed the nature of discussions occurring in the Contact Group. Banking questions were not ones that should sensibly be discussed or solved in a purely European context, and European institutions consequently lost touch with banking supervision and regulation issues. When Huib Muller and Albert Dondelinger, the Luxembourg bank supervisor (a great deal of Herstatt's business had run through Luxembourg), were in Washington for the annual IMF meetings, they talked to Federal Reserve officials. The G-10 governors, rather than the CoG, now seemed the correct interlocutors for bank regulation and supervision issues.[47]

At the G-10 meeting in September 1974, banking supervision was a major topic of discussion. The G-10 communiqué of September 10, 1974, stated:

> At their regular meeting in Basle on 9th September, the Central-Bank Governors from the countries of the Group of Ten and Switzerland discussed the working of the international banking system. They took stock of the existing mechanisms for supervision and regulation and noted recent improvements made in these fields in a number of major countries. They agreed to intensify the exchange of information between central banks on the activities of banks operating in international markets and, where appropriate, to tighten further the regulations governing foreign exchange positions. The Governors also had an exchange of views on the problem of the lender of last resort in the Euro-markets. They recognized that it would not be practical to lay down in advance detailed rules and procedures for the provision of temporary liquidity. But they were satisfied that means are available for that purpose and will be used if and when necessary.[48]

In December 1974 the G-10 governors decided to create a Committee on Banking Regulations and Supervisory Practices (subsequently known as the Basel Committee on Banking Supervision, or BCBS), to be chaired by George Blunden from the Bank of England. Soon afterward the European Commission established an EEC Liaison Committee to deal with bank regulation issues and to attempt a coordination of legislative and regulatory approaches to the establishment of credit-giving institutions. A majority on the Monetary Committee was, however, skeptical that a liaison committee of this kind would fulfill a "real function."[49] The BIS also became intensely involved in the apparently simple but in practice enormously problematical task of gathering statistics on banks' international exposure.

The result of the global (G-10) initiative was that banking supervision issues failed to appear as central to the European discussion until the 1990s. But even in the early 1990s, when the CoG attempted to move into this area and to provide a specifically European mechanism for ensuring financial stability, the institutional basis was too thin, and the initiative failed.

The European Monetary Cooperation Fund

Exchange rate issues rather than financial stability seemed to be at the center of the European debate. The overall political drive of policymakers in the EEC countries was to think of an alternative, on a global level, to the dollar as a reserve currency. In this sense the debate after August 15, 1971, merely took up, with much greater urgency, the topics of the monetary discussions of the 1960s. The EEC Monetary Committee took charge of preparing documentation for the IMF Committee of Twenty that would produce reform suggestions for the international monetary system and the IMF itself. The major European demand was an end to the hegemonic role of the dollar, which in the eyes of the Europeans had been the key weakness of the 1960s order. A May 1973 paper on reserve assets and convertibility put the European position on the lessons of recent history very clearly:

> In order to eliminate the asymmetry and to prevent the instability, caused by delayed adjustment action and by an excessive build-up of currency reserves, reserve centres should not finance their balance of payments deficits by incurring liquid liabilities in their own currency. Conversely the system should ensure that reserve centres earn reserve

assets when in surplus. . . . Reserve creation in the future system should take place only on the basis of international decisions, based on the criterion of global need for additional reserves.[50]

In the late 1970s this thinking led de Larosière (as managing director of the IMF) to champion a "Substitution Account" that would change dollars into international reserves so as to free the world from its dependence on a national currency.

The EMCF was a logical part of the new apparatus, in that a stable exchange rate regime would require interventions, and these might be financed by short-term borrowing through the fund. The CoG was anxious that the new mechanism should be controlled by the central banks (unlike the IMF, which was fundamentally owned by finance ministries and had been conceived in 1944 as a way of breaking the power of central banks). A report of August 1, 1970, from a commission chaired by the governor of the National Bank of Belgium, Hubert Ansiaux, on the consequences of a narrowing of fluctuation margins had also argued that the new institution's role would be parallel to that of the Federal Reserve System in the United States. The original draft of the EMCF statute was finalized in late 1972 by Barre along with Wormser and Emminger, and more or less fully reflected the viewpoint of the central banks: in particular the governors believed that it was of paramount importance that they manage the operations of the EMCF.[51]

A substantial amount of the initial drafting work was carried out in the Banque de France. The new mechanism would replace bilateral interventions and consequently remove the strains that they had imposed on European currency markets. It would offer longer-term finance than the short-term swap network that had developed in the 1960s. Its operation would require a unit of account, defined in an autonomous way (that is, not in relation to any existing currency), which would be issued by the EMCF and guaranteed by gold or assets linked to gold. The fund would also manage an increasing share of EEC reserves.[52] It would progressively extend its operations, and would be folded into a juridical system in which the CoG's competences would be essentially enlarged. The central bank governors would form a sovereign body, analogous to the IMF's Board of Governors. Senior officials of the central banks would make up an Executive Board, which would supervise the day-to-day tasks of the agent who ran the system.[53]

The statute was redrafted by the group of experts presided over by the Belgian lawyer Josse Mertens de Wilmars, and then referred to both the Monetary Committee and the CoG for opinions; but it was also expected that there would be active engagement by the Commission. In June 1972 Wilmars presented to the CoG a draft statute, whose major features were a more readily accessible form of short-term support, a unit of account, multilateralization of financing within the EEC, and a sharing of reserves. The debate began with the Bundesbank president, Karl Klasen, saying that the EMCF should be an "organ of assistance" to the CoG, and not a new authority that would have reporting responsibilities to the Council and the Commission as well as to the CoG. O'Brien then stated that the task of concertation could be as well managed by the BIS as by the new institution; and Guido Carli complained about the asymmetry that would remain if some countries were committed to the accumulation of unconvertible dollars.[54] At the next meeting the discussion continued, and Vice-President Otmar Emminger from the Bundesbank warned that it was important not to replicate global problems in the Community and allow the accumulation of permanent imbalances. The problem of the Bretton Woods system had lain in the building up of current account problems; Europe should not be devising ways of financing substantial deficits in the framework of European institutions.[55] In addition, Britain and the other two prospective new member countries of the EEC, Denmark and Ireland, argued with the continental countries whether gold-based assets, such as the high British SDR quota, should be included in the calculation of quotas in the EMCF.[56]

The inauguration of a short-term support mechanism provoked the question of which countries would become the long-term beneficiaries of the new mechanism. France in particular was deeply worried that the scheme was intrinsically linked with the imminent accession of the United Kingdom in the EEC, and that the Community would now have to "swallow the bitter pill" of committing itself to endless sterling support. President Pompidou's economic adviser, Jean-René Bernard, also pointed out that in such an event it would be the Bundesbank that would have the major task of propping up the British pound, and that the result would be a "German hegemony over Europe that would revive in a more spectacular manner the initiative taken by the German chancellor at The Hague" in December 1969.[57]

A definition of the mission of the EMCF regarding the larger objectives of the EEC came from the CoG: that the EMCF should contribute to the realization of economic and monetary union, either by moving to convertibility at irrevocably fixed exchange rates or by introducing a common currency.[58] But the Commission also contributed to the drafting process, and one addition (which provoked a fierce response in the CoG from Emminger and Zijlstra) supplemented Article 2 with a provision that the EMCF should report biannually and that it should act in conformity with the directives of the Council. Emminger commented that the Commission's formulation would risk being interpreted as "precise instructions on particular problems" and that it raised the issue of relations between governments and central banks, "which are different in the member countries and whose particularism should be preserved." But the text was supported as "reasonable" by the governor of the Bank of England, Sir Leslie O'Brien, who added that "he had the impression that the British Treasury had wanted more, and that further editing might produce an outcome even less favorable to the cause of the governors." The U.K. Treasury had indeed worried about the extension of control by the European Parliament over the EMCF. The CoG chairman, Olivier Wormser, immediately endorsed the Bank of England view and concluded that "the Committee might trust the diplomacy of the Commission."[59]

This drafting alteration—accepted by the CoG largely in deference to a powerfully asserted British viewpoint—proved crippling to the EMCF. Emminger had quite faithfully presented the position of the Bundesbank, which in view of its fiercely guarded independence would never accept a major role for a European central banking institution that had to obey directives from governments or from the Commission. The Bundesbank tried to refer back to the communiqué of the EEC foreign ministers in Rome in September 1972, in which the politicians seemed to accept a much more limited role, with the fund's administrative council simply operating in "the framework of the general orientation of the Council." Germany was also skeptical about whether the EMCF should have a legal personality, and argued that such an innovation was not in conformity with Article 235 of the EEC Treaty; a constitutional or treaty change would be required.[60]

But the preparations for launching a major new institution went on regardless. A group was established by the CoG under the chairmanship of a member of the board of the Bundesbank, Hans Georg Emde, to draft a personnel statute for the new institution; it took until 1976 to finish its work.[61] The CoG, especially through the Théron Group, also devoted a great deal of attention to the critical issue of the choice of a *numéraire*, an anchor or reference currency.

The European unit of account was at the heart of the tenth report of the Théron Group, drawn up as the governors finalized their rather confusing presentation of proposals for the creation of an international store or measure of value.[62] It was intended not only to facilitate the initial tasks of the EMCF but also to "prefigure the future European money." But the experts could not decide on whether the unit of account should be fixed in terms of gold or reflect a composite currency based on EEC currencies. The Théron Group laid out as alternative options, first, a gold-based unit (so that it might also be used for the IMF's SDR), which would be only indirectly linked to the value of EEC currencies. This path was problematical, since the role of gold in the international monetary system had not yet been defined. Second, Europe might adopt a basket currency, which would potentially require a cumbersome and continuous series of adjustments. Within the basket approach, there were several alternatives in terms of choices of weight, and the experts warned about the "complexity" of that approach. The question of a definition of money was debated in terms of principles: either "stability," which was supported by the Commission, and would correspond to a worldview in which there should be little movement of exchange rates; or "representativity," tracking the developments of the various separate currencies.[63] At one point in the governors' discussion, Sir Leslie O'Brien had argued (rather unrealistically) that the SDR would replace gold as the international standard; but he was promptly contradicted by Karl Klasen, who pointed out that the SDR did not conform to an idea of stability, and that the intense debate fostered in particular by representatives of poorer countries about a "link" of the SDR with development showed that the synthetic international money would very likely become highly politicized.[64] But some governors still thought that the European and international processes of creating a new *numéraire* could go in tandem. The Danish governor, Erik Hoffmeyer, for instance, argued that "a real gold standard (implying an official price of gold somewhat higher than the free market price) is not feasible. The committee therefore pointed at the SDR as the numéraire of the system."[65]

There were obvious objections to the simplest option, that of basing European currency developments upon an existing currency. Wormser in January 1973 as chairman of the CoG had laid down very clearly the principle that the *numéraire* of a new international monetary order should not be any national money.[66] This was a comment directly aimed at the global position of the dollar, but it could be equally interpreted as a challenge to any claims that the Deutsche Mark should serve as a new European anchor currency. The discussion also foundered on the problem of how intervention obligations should be distributed between the countries and central banks. Thus there was no immediate solution; not until 1978 was a basket solution adopted. For the time being the EUA remained a relic of the days of gold and the Bretton Woods order.

The EMCF was established by the EEC Council by a decision (*réglement*) of April 3, 1973.[67] It was technically responsible for decisions on short-term financing. But there was no regrouping of intra-Community financing, and instead the rules for financing and credit mechanisms continued to be thrashed out in the CoG. The EMCF's initial activity was overshadowed by disputes surrounding a three-month support credit to Italy of 1.5625 billion EUA (June 28, 1973) under the 1970 Short-Term Support Agreement. Under that agreement, a one-time credit renewal was allowed, and further renewals required unanimity among the creditors. Both France and the United Kingdom were hostile to the repeated renewal, in part because of increasing strain on their own resources.[68] At the second renewal, a group chaired by the Belgian central banker Cecil de Strycker delivered a brief report on the Italian economy, in which it urged a reduction in growth in order to correct the balance-of-payments deficit. The EMCF was thus essentially replicating at the European level the conditionality procedures of the IMF, and de Strycker's group concluded that Italy needed to remain within the limits of its pledges in the letter of intent submitted to the IMF. The Germans took a tough line: Emminger stated that the extreme seriousness of the situation of a loss of a billion dollars a month had been "masked by the ease with which Italy had obtained credit"; he also doubted whether the current exchange rate was adequately competitive.[69] In October 1974 the CoG produced a formal opinion (*avis*), in which "it recorded the necessity of imposing precise conditions of an economic character on borrowing countries that would permit an adjustment of their situation. Periodic and penetrating controls should be envisaged."[70]

In March 1974 France suggested that the EMCF might become a channel for European borrowing in global markets from the new surplus countries, the Arab oil producers, or that it might issue bonds; but neither of these proposals was taken seriously enough in Frankfurt or London for the idea to appear on the agenda of the CoG. The Bank of England simply noted that "the Governor should stress that the eurobond market is not an EEC phenomenon and therefore no useful purpose would be served by attempting any kind of monitoring in an EEC framework."[71]

The high hopes of the Commission remained: in December 1973 Mosca was still explaining that the EMCF would be a European version of the Federal Reserve System. But by this stage, such a view seemed to be whistling in the dark.

In February 1974 the CoG met in Luxembourg, where the government of the Grand Duchy hoped that the EMCF would be sited. Many of the participants felt that this exercise in committee locomotion was a waste of time. The Bank of England's rapporteur penned an acidic note in which he talked about the very limited discussion of substantive issues. "Apart from travelling to Luxembourg, the day had previously been spent inspecting the imposing but empty premises set aside by the Luxembourg Government for the EMCF and progressing in limousines, with police escort, to various rendezvous."[72] The Luxembourg initiative was doomed: a year earlier, Emminger had argued that additional Luxembourg meetings would be an insupportable burden for the central bankers, and that any meetings of the EMCF could be much more conveniently arranged in Basel.[73]

In the winter of 1974–75 the Commission relaunched its offensive for a wider role for the EMCF. It suggested that the EMCF should be made a permanent organization, headed by a director-general, and that it should provide a setting for "permanent and preliminary" negotiations on monetary, banking, and credit policies, collecting information on international currency developments, and recommending measures to avoid monetary disturbances. Above all, the EMCF was conceived as a tool of the European institutions: it should "address the Commission with opinions on domestic and foreign monetary strategy in order to assist the Commission with proposals for the Council." The Commission's proposals were put to a meeting of the Monetary Committee on January 6 and 7, 1975, where they found little favor. The CoG debate was even more negative; the governors strongly objected to this mission creep of the Commission. In its response, it noted that the role of the EMCF in relation to the Snake was in decline, with no intervention in November and December 1974, and that the EMCF had no capital and was entrusted with no European reserves.[74] In a formal opinion of February 11, 1975, delivered to the ECOFIN and the Commission, the CoG stated that a redistribution of functions between committees would not produce substantial improvements in national monetary policies or make for better European coordination.

One solution from the Brussels perspective was to create a longer-term borrowing mechanism. In February 1975 the Community launched a $3 billion bond issue in order to meet particular needs in the aftermath of the oil crisis. In practice, in the 1970s the credits financed in this way went exclusively to Italy and Ireland (the mechanism was later used in 1983 to support France, and in 1985 for Greece).[75] The Italian support operation in 1975 created some difficulty, as the United Kingdom also ran into balance-of-payments difficulties and argued that it could no longer participate in the Italian credit.[76]

In the European Parliament all the major political groupings endorsed a 1975 report by the Committee on Economic and Monetary Affairs that was bitterly critical of the CoG for its restrictive stance over the EMCF. That committee's rapporteur, the German Social Democrat Erwin Lange, complained that the "representatives of governments in the Council were not prepared to allow the Fund to act as a European organ." He called on both the Council and the CoG to renounce their "national ideas and their somewhat antiquated concepts of sovereignty in this field," and instead to accept solutions that were genuinely postnational or *communautaire* in spirit. Wilhelm Haferkamp, the commissioner for economics, finance, credit, and investments, responded by emphasizing that the fund should be independent and work independently, but he also set out the big Commission agenda, which included coordination of interest rates and the need for a "well-founded and solid European unit of account."[77]

The discussion of the operation of European currencies and the relationship between a monetary mechanism and financial support became highly political as a result of the current account problems that threatened to engulf Italy. The Italian economy grew at an unsustainably high rate of growth in the early 1970s (with 5.4 percent real GDP growth in 1974), but the country was then plunged into a balance-of-payments crisis in the wake of the oil price shock. The government concluded a program with the IMF in 1974 to finance the oil-related part of the Italian deficit, and tried to tighten interest rates and reduce domestic credit growth, but then confronted a sharp recession in 1975. The Christian Democratic minority government had an unstable parliamentary basis, became increasingly worried, and in August 1975 reversed course with a big surge in public spending and also of monetary growth. The director-general of the treasury is said to have advised the governor of the Banca d'Italia to open his window and "throw out bundles of 10,000 lira notes."[78] As a new foreign exchange crisis broke out in January 1976, Italy began simultaneous negotiations with the IMF and the EEC, with a $1 billion five-year credit concluded in March.

On April 26, 1976, in Luxembourg the EEC foreign ministers discussed the possibility of instituting additional medium-term financial assistance in order to allow the Banca d'Italia to reconstitute its foreign exchange reserves. Italy's currency stood at risk during a tense and polarized election campaign in which Italy's European partners feared that the Communist Party might hold the balance of power. In parallel, Italy requested 400 million EUA in short-term support as well as a $600 million BIS facility.[79] The short-term support was renewed for a further two months in July.[80] In a new crisis of the lira, in September the Italian authorities, instead of drawing on short-term monetary support, imposed new restrictions on the outflow of capital and imposed a corset on bank lending. But the CoG continued to agree to the extension of the short-term support.[81] The Italian economist Marcello de Cecco wrote about the problem in a contemporary analysis: "The stock of Italian debt is so high that creditors just cannot afford to see Italy go bankrupt. Like Samson, Italy would go down together with all the Philistines. While it remained virtuous, Italy had no power to ignite the powder keg. Now it does have."[82]

The simultaneous track of EEC-level and IMF negotiations made it clear that the European credits were associated with much laxer conditionality than the IMF would have allowed. By late 1976 the German government had lost patience and started to urge Italy to work with the IMF, and the Italian government reciprocated by accusing Germany of

"ganging up" with the United States and the IMF.[83] Governor Paolo
Baffi complained to the IMF that Italians were being treated more harshly
by the IMF than the British had been in their equivalent IMF negotiations in 1976.[84] When the IMF program was finally agreed it solved the
long-standing problem of exchange intervention by limiting such intervention to smoothing disruptive short-term fluctuations of the exchange
rate. The Italian government deficit, domestic credit, and wage indexation were all subject to control. With a more competitive exchange rate
position, Italy's current account rapidly improved, with the odd consequence that in the end there was no need to draw on the credit line provided in the controversial standby agreement. But it was clear that the
IMF, not Europe, had solved the Italian problem.

In July 1977 the Council asked the CoG to study the existing credit
mechanisms and to respond to Belgian proposals for an extension of
the EEC's resources. After this possibility was considered by the alternates (September 12) and the governors (September 13) it was clear that
there was fundamental opposition from the central banks of Germany
and the Netherlands. Karl Otto Pöhl, the new vice-president of the
Bundesbank, who had come from the German Finance Ministry and
had close connections with Chancellor Helmut Schmidt, explained that
the Monetary Committee favored an increase in medium-term support
rather than in the short-term facilities, which were under the supervision of the CoG. Governor Baffi pointed out that in one day during the
crisis of October 1976, Italy had lost more foreign exchange reserves
than its EEC short-term quota; and argued that if the amounts were
raised (as they eventually were in December 1977, to 3.0 billion EUA),
such operations would make sense only if they were accompanied by
IMF-style conditionality.[85] He thereby explicitly endorsed the IMF-style
solution. Such an admission looked like a major flaw in the notion of
European solidarity and of the *esprit communautaire*. The Bundesbank
explained bilaterally to the Banca d'Italia that "the financing potential of
the Community would be overtaxed if the original orientation of the
short-term supports were to be changed in such a way that they would
be destined to finance lasting deficits in current and basic balances."[86]

Monetary Aggregates

The 1964 decision creating the CoG had made monetary policy one of
its central concerns. But what did that mean? A potential replacement

for the exchange rate discipline of the Bretton Woods system lay in the analysis of monetary aggregates and monetary targeting. Before August 15, 1971, there had been some concern with monetary policy coordination, but it was a rather esoteric and peripheral concern. On September 12–13, 1970, the CoG had entrusted a group of experts with a study of the coordination of monetary policy as a supplement to the work of the Ansiaux committee on the narrowing of exchange rate margins. On March 22, 1971, the ECOFIN asked the Monetary Committee and the CoG to harmonize monetary policy aggregates.

The operationalization of monetary targeting came initially from national central banks, in particular the Bundesbank. The Bundesbank started monetary targeting in mid-1974 as inflation surged in the wake of the oil-price shock set off by the Yom Kippur War; but some German policymakers—notably Bundesbank Vice-President Otmar Emminger— had been pressing this point in international discussions at a much earlier stage. Emminger in particular used his role as chairman of the EEC Monetary Committee as a bully pulpit. He repeatedly "stressed the need to avoid the expectation of inflation becoming ingrained. This had required shock therapy in the U.S. What Europe needed was joint therapy—concrete objectives the success of which could be reviewed after 6–9 months."[87] In October 1972 the U.K. Treasury reported on the "hard line" taken by the Germans in the EEC Monetary Committee, and its representative (F. Cassell) wrote a highly skeptical commentary on quantitative targeting:

> The Germans were very keen on this. Almost everyone else was opposed to it, though all accepted the general objective of slowing down the growth of money from its recent rates. . . . Since "money supply" means such different things in different countries, common targeting in this field is ridiculous. . . . Even the Germans, when pressed, admitted that if the growth of the money supply had been slower it did not necessarily follow that the rate of inflation would have been less: unemployment might have been higher. The difference was that they were less concerned about that than the rest of us.[88]

At the CoG meeting in Paris in October 1972, Raymond Barre, the vice-president of the EEC Commission, set out a series of ideas that he would present to the Council of Ministers at the end of the month on how to tackle the problem of increasing levels of inflation (6 percent in 1972, with a projection of 7 percent for 1973). The Commission believed that the primary responsibility in fighting inflation rested with national measures, but that "it was clear that the expansion of the monetary mass was too great, and that the member states should attempt to bring this rate down to that of the level of economic growth." There were in some cases external reasons for rapid monetary growth (as a consequence of capital movements), but in most cases, domestic monetary expansion was the preponderant cause of inflation. It was consequently necessary to examine the monetary aggregates M1 (notes, coins, and demand deposits) and M2 (M1 plus savings deposits), and Barre set out a much clearer formulation of the importance of following a quantitative approach to monetary policy than had any of the national central bankers (including the Bundesbank president). The EEC could support an anti-inflationary stance by pressing for lower tariff rates, by reducing the rate of growth of agricultural prices set under the Common Agricultural Policy, and by implementing a more aggressive competition policy in cases in which prices were excessive (he specifically singled out the case of pharmaceuticals).[89]

In the CoG, Emminger and Zijlstra were highly sympathetic to Barre's approach, while the Belgian governor, Robert Vandeputte, was equally emphatic in his criticism. This division remained a characteristic through the 1970s of the CoG's discussions about improving monetary policy coordination. After a roundtable discussion, the chairman summed up what he held to be the CoG's consensus view that monetary policy "could not bear the sole responsibility in the fight against inflation."[90]

The initiative to formalize a monetary approach came again from Brussels. The ECOFIN meeting on October 30–31, 1972, focused on the fight against inflation and proposed setting a target under which consumer prices should rise by no more than 4 percent during 1973. (This figure came at the insistence of France, which found the 3.5 percent that the Commission had originally proposed to be too rigorous, and Finance Minister Giscard d'Estaing had stated that such a target could be achieved only through direct wage and price controls, which were intellectually unacceptable to the Germans.) The meeting then proposed limiting money growth to the real growth of GDP plus the normative price increase; and the adoption of a fiscal rule, restricting budget growth to the growth rate of GDP.[91] ECOFIN resolutions of December 5, 1972, and September 14, 1973, on "actions against inflation" required member states to reduce rates of monetary growth to GDP growth plus a normative increase planned in line with overall economic policy. The CoG was asked to carry out a quarterly review of trends in the money supply of member states. The first meeting of the experts' group charged with that task took place in May 1973 under the chairmanship of Bastiaanse.

Much of the debate on monetary policy had been limited to the discussion of disturbances emanating from short-term capital movements. The July 1972 meeting of European finance ministers in London called for an investigation of ways to limit such disruptive movements. In parallel to the monetary group, the EEC Monetary Committee thus also established in November 1972 a group tasked with analyzing short-term capital movements. Its report to the Monetary Committee on October 9, 1973, was, however, essentially negative: it could recommend no way of harmonizing instruments of control of capital movements in the member countries.

In Germany, discussions of the role of monetary targeting within the Bundesbank were controversial. Emminger was opposed to the announcement of a specific target because he believed that there existed no precise relationship between monetary growth and GDP.[92] In February 1974, at the Luxembourg meeting of the CoG, Emminger circulated a draft resolution drawn up in the Bundesbank with a view to giving effect to the Council decision of February 18 to pursue a high degree of convergence of economic policies. It produced some irritation, as the draft had apparently been prepared without the knowledge of Bundesbank president Klasen, and the discussion was left until dinner, when the task of reformulating the resolution was entrusted to a bilateral process between the Bundesbank and the Bank of England.[93] That resolution was eventually adopted at the CoG meeting of May 14, 1974, and asked the alternates' committee to "supervise the evolution of monetary policy in the member countries and to draw attention to any conflicts of interest that monetary policy might produce and to propose solutions to such conflicts."[94] At the June 9 meeting the governors called for quarterly reports on recent monetary developments in member countries, which would deal with credit policy and the development of bank credit as well as with monetary policy.

The result of the Barre initiatives (the Council decision of March 22, 1971, on stages in economic and monetary union, and the decision of December 5, 1972, on measures to combat inflation) was the creation of not one but two groups, both chaired by Bastiaanse, one on the harmonization of monetary instruments and one on recent monetary evolution. Section III, paragraph 5 of the 1971 decision had required the CoG and the Monetary Committee to undertake studies on the harmonization of monetary policy instruments. The Bank of England summed up the conceptual difference between the two groups: the harmonization group was "concerned with the kind of house we live in," while the monetary group dealt with "how we behave in it."[95] But the British central bankers also noted that the Bastiaanse group was "an analytic, interpretative and mildly normative body whose membership rightly consists of professional economists and statistical experts," and that there was little real work on the coordination of monetary policy-making. There was "no parallel dialogue except between Governors and then rather sparingly, between the actual executants (in part the makers) of monetary policy."[96] The Bundesbank noted equally critically that the monetary volume group had no real raison d'être after the end of 1973, while the policy harmonization group had some justification in that it had been established as a result of a Council decision.[97] In May 1974 the CoG discussed whether the Bastiaanse meetings still made sense, and in September it agreed that the group should examine the development of GDP and of M2.[98]

The issue of the coordination of monetary targets became much more acute after the German (and Swiss) adoption of monetary targeting in 1974, and as inflation took off at very different rates in the member countries. The bigger differentials in inflation rates produced an obvious challenge to exchange rate stability. But the German position was not an obvious answer for other countries. In May 1975, for instance, the Bank of England noted with regard to an EEC Working Group on the Harmonisation of Monetary Policy that discussion of monetary theory was "inclined to be non-productive, particularly for those like the UK who hold no clear ideas about the way in which the monetary sector integrates with the rest of the economy."[99]

In February 1976 the Bastiaanse group on monetary mass reported for the first time on the development of monetary aggregates in the EEC.[100] Bastiaanse noted that only Germany provided normative guidelines for the development of a monetary indicator, and that the indicators presented by the other central banks rested on a broad variety of methodologies applied by the different central banks. The initiative to systematize national approaches to monetary aggregates was strongly supported by the Commission. Commissioner Haferkamp noted that the other group of experts chaired by Bastiaanse was considering the harmonization of intermediate objectives as well as of the instruments of monetary policy. "The establishment of normative projections of monetary growth as in Germany had a positive effect on the behavior of economic actors and represented a useful concept that should be adopted on the Community level" as a means to promote "better cooperation between the social partners and the government." The governor of the Banque de France, Bernard Clappier, also supported this vision and added that it was a way of "arriving in small steps at a harmonization of domestic monetary policies." Bundesbank President Karl Klasen gave a lesson in the German approach that sounded skeptical and hesitant: "on the one hand, monetary policy has in large part a psychological effect, and on the other hand the central bank needs above all to ensure that it contributes to the realization of fundamental objectives (employment, stability, etc.). Nothing is more damaging than negative and plausible official projections, because the public has a tendency to regard them as too optimistic." De Strycker added an even more cautious note: "one should not hesitate in modifying projections and objectives in order to stay quite close to reality." It became clear that there was no fundamental consensus about adopting the German policy approach as a model, not least because it was articulated in such a fuzzy way. The Bundesbank was unenthusiastic about the general applicability, and was unwilling to cast its policy in terms of a hard rule. In November 1976 the EC Monetary Committee resolved that the rapprochement of national monetary targets should be used in "a pragmatic way" and "without affecting national competences and responsibilities." Four days later the Commission accepted such a formulation as the basis of a European approach.[101]

One year later the governors reflected on the experience of dealing with monetary aggregates. Bastiaanse asked whether monetary aggregates or some measure of credit should be used more appropriately as a guide to monetary policy. The chairman of the CoG, the governor of the Bank of England, Gordon Richardson, noted that British authorities were mostly concerned with the IMF's measure of domestic credit expansion, because this was regarded as being most closely linked to Britain's balance-of-payments problem. Emminger suggested that domestic credit expansion was appropriate for countries with an adverse balance of payments, but that surplus countries such as Germany would do better to work with the monetary mass aggregate. Commission President Ortoli again proposed a fixing of quantitative objectives, but there was a considerable amount of hostility to this suggestion. In particular, de Strycker was very direct in his condemnation of convergence along monetarist lines. "The experience of the last twelve months shows that the monetary authorities have not let themselves be blinded by the radical theses of monetarism and locked into rigid targets . . . it is important to be more realistic than the monetarist professors who consider that the fixation of mathematical targets is the indispensable condition for the convergence of monetary policy." The Bank of England's account of the discussion added that de Strycker "drew the conclusion (aimed at Ortoli) that his country should not be pressured into adopting targets that it did not want." The Dutch central banker, Zijlstra, however, said that "one should acknowledge that the monetarists have played a useful role and that negligence in this issue could lead to damaging consequences for external and domestic stability."[102]

The battle was fought out on a number of fronts—perhaps in this regard the CoG was not as significant as the academic arena, in which "monetarist professors" increasingly prevailed. An academic turning point, or at least a very public humiliation for the eclectic Belgian approach, came in September 1977, when the Société Universitaire Européenne des Recherches Financières held a meeting in Wiesbaden, where both central bankers and academics participated. The National Bank of Belgium boldly presented a paper with the title "The Setting of Targets for Monetary Aggregates: A Non-Monetarist View." The Bank of England's representative commented on the intellectual reorientation of monetary economics and even seemed eager to join the new consensus: "Many of the participants," he wrote, "seemed to cast us on what they saw as the side of the angels—along with the Germans and the Swiss, for example. In contrast, the Belgians . . . did not come across well."[103]

When the Belgian economist Alexandre Lamfalussy became chief economist of the BIS in 1976, he started to present economic data in a new and much more policy-relevant way at the meetings of the CoG and provided a level of analysis and expertise that the CoG had until then lacked. His initial presentation focused on the development of inflationary expectations and included a speculation on whether—given the persistence of inflation in the wake of the oil-price shocks—there should not be some form of indexation of financial assets. Most of the governors were highly unsympathetic to such a view. Klasen and Zijlstra considered indexation a way of accepting the inevitability of inflation, while Baffi described inflation as "redistribution to the disadvantage of the bourgeois class, and unjust because the beneficiaries usually had a substantially higher income than that of the classes hit by inflation."[104]

Lamfalussy also dedicated one session to the question of whether rises in interest rates could deter currency speculation. He presented the case of the United Kingdom in 1976 as one in which "extreme" speculation made the interest rate tool ineffective (because the speculators believed that the rise was politically unsustainable). Pöhl presented in contrast the more orthodox view that interest rate changes were generally effective.[105]

In 1977 the Commission wanted to issue quantitative guidelines for monetary policy, as well as to include all EEC countries in the Snake. The German Finance Ministry and the Bundesbank agreed that this proposal should not be implemented, "as further progress in coordination in this area is not foreseeable and it would be dangerous to awake unfounded hopes."[106] Germany was prepared to agree to a thrice-yearly examination of whether budgetary and monetary policy was compatible with internal and external currency stability, though the Bundesbank rejected the idea of a specific questionnaire.[107] Opposition from Frankfurt was not a deterrent, and at the end of the year the Commission put the suggestion forward again. Within the CoG, Commissioner François-Xavier Ortoli pressed hard on the issue. In March 1978 he explained to a skeptical audience in Basel that it would be good to have a preliminary discussion with the governors on an appropriate way of fixing monetary targets, and on what targets should be used; at an earlier meeting he had pressed for the governors to "develop the theoretical foundations" of the Bastiaanse group. There was an immediate barrage of doubt: Zijlstra tried to explain that the development of money stock was a consequence of a broad diversity of causes, not all of which could be controlled by central banks: private credit, public finance, and the balance of payments. De Strycker argued that the Committee had no common view. Lamfalussy made the obvious point that some countries did not have quantitative targets, and that the interpretation of quantitative targets was different in different countries. But probably the most resolute opposition came from Emminger, in other words from the person most associated publicly with "monetarism": "A monetary objective is an instrument of monetary policy only in the sense that it constitutes a discipline that leads monetary authorities to examine the causes of monetary growth, and also an obligation to justify policy to the public, even though this sometimes has inconveniences."[108]

Monetary policy had also become in many discussions a euphemism for the provision of inflationary stimulus. When the Bastiaanse group produced a report that was permeated by skepticism about the use of monetary expansion to provide economic stimulus, Lamfalussy complained about its "defeatist" tone.[109] In March 1978 a report by the CoG on improving policy coordination concluded that "the value of quantitative monetary guidelines has been a matter of keen discussion among the EEC central banks, but no consensus of opinion exists."[110] The problem was that this discussion was taking place at the moment when the Bundesbank was having the greatest difficulty with its monetary targeting. In an earlier meeting, Lamfalussy had explained that the Bundesbank was confronted by a simultaneous high rate of monetary growth and economic stagnation. He suggested that the experts' discussions were based on the philosophy that fiscal policy should look to short-term objectives and monetary policy to medium-term objectives.[111]

Could central bankers produce some consensus on a disciplinary method that would ensure monetary and fiscal rectitude? For some months it appeared that the exchange rate regime might do precisely that, as it had under the Bretton Woods regime for every country except the United States. At the December 1977 meeting, Baffi had stated that "the role of superexperts does not fit the Committee of Governors, who are men of experience who could pronounce on the political viability of actions suggested by theoretical analysis." At the same time, he called for a deeper theoretical discussion of the relation between the choice of instruments and the exchange rate regime.[112] In fact the alternative to the adoption of the monetary aggregates approach was often seen as lying in a more formally defined exchange rate system.

Attempts to Redefine the Exchange Rate System

Attempts to design a new exchange rate system began almost immediately after it had become apparent that the Snake was a rather limited construct. In late 1974 France started to work on a new initiative that might circumvent the stymied discussion of the EMCF and its functioning. Jacques de Larosière, the director of the treasury, introduced his initial memorandum on the subject with a harsh verdict: "The results achieved in regard to European monetary unification up to this day constitute the most mediocre aspect of the Community's achievements." The Snake was ill suited to deal with international monetary problems; and the generalization of floating made European monetary relations more difficult. He also criticized slow EEC decision-making, and pointed out how heterogeneous was the situation of the different European countries. "Europeans have the tendency to give in to the temptation to compensate their insufficient dynamism through formalism and procedural perfectionism."[113]

De Larosière was the central figure in elaborating what became known as the Fourcade plan, which was launched at a European Council of Ministers meeting on September 16, 1974.[114] The finance minister of the Chirac government, Jean-Pierre Fourcade, proposed a Community credit mechanism, a European unit of account, an exchange rate system with wider fluctuation margins, and coordinated action on the Euromarkets. The most innovative part of the proposal was that intra-Community fluctuations should be fixed relative to a new European Unit of Account, based on a basket of currencies. The EEC could then have its own collectively determined policy toward the U.S. dollar. Shortly after the French initiative, the Commission presented its own proposals for a transition to "concerted floating"; this involved fundamentally an extension of the Snake, with "full, frequent and effective coordination of all aspects of macroeconomic policy between the participating countries." Policy objectives for balance of payments and a trade-off between inflation and unemployment would be internationally negotiated. Such a process would allow the non-Snake currencies to return to a regime of narrow margins.[115] The president of the Council then instituted a European monetary relaunch that would examine a common bond issue, the unit of account, coordinated action on the Euromarkets, and a mechanism for floating.[116]

The discussion on an ECU or EUA was strangely parallel to the debate about redefining the SDR on the international stage. In 1969 the SDR had originally been defined in relation to a gold value; in June 1974 it was redesigned as a basket currency, based on sixteen currencies, selected because they had an average share of world trade in goods and services of over 1 percent in the five-year period 1968–1972; that definition included most EC countries, including Denmark, which was later eliminated from the SDR basket. Not until 1981 was the SDR simplified to include only the G-5 countries.[117] Should there not be a purely European equivalent to the new international yardstick? If the European Community were to take a syndicated loan on the newly active financial markets, should it not borrow in a composite currency that would reflect the shares of liabilities of all its members?[118] The impulse to innovate received additional momentum from the fact that the SDR valuation in the post-1973 floating regime created considerable difficulties for Europeans, who had to make intra-European settlements in SDRs in which the par value of the dollar amounted to an overpayment.[119] In the mid-1970s the Europeans, too, needed to move their unit of account away from gold, and they would have a long debate over composition and weighting of a basket, with the result that the European step to a basket currency occurred almost a year after the redefinition of the SDR.

The reception of the Fourcade proposals in the CoG and in the EEC Monetary Committee was rather skeptical. The CoG meeting was held in Washington during the annual IMF meetings. The major initial critic in the framework of the CoG was the Banque de France official Pierre Barre, who had become the chair of the group of experts on foreign exchange issues (still known as the Théron Group rather than by any formal title). The group opposed the idea of a coordinated dollar policy.[120] The inspector-general of the Belgian treasury, Jacques van Ypersele, later described the French proposals as setting up a "kind of boa [constrictor] around the Snake."[121] The Bundesbank argued that the Snake should not be "softened," and that a new definition of the unit of account was "not urgent." Its report concluded that the idea of a coordinated European dollar policy was "unrealistic."[122]

In the Monetary Committee on December 3–4, 1974, the German representative stated that "the hour of progress in monetary cooperation has not yet struck."[123] On December 4, 1974, the Monetary Committee's "Report on Joint Floating" delivered a killing verdict on plans that would be "dangerous and unfeasible" in the absence of much greater economic cohesion:

> The committee believes that it is premature to take a stand on the definition of the following phases, which it might be appropriate to contemplate at a later stage. The majority of the committee doubts the advisability of taking definitive steps at the present time with regard to concerted floating. . . . Among countries likely to be in a position to extend credit, some consider present facilities to be adequate and that any increase in their size would not be justified. . . . A move to moderate day-to-day fluctuations in dollar rates and to control excessive movements of individual EEC currencies represented a useful, if modest, move toward promoting closer cooperation in the monetary field.[124]

The report emphasized its close adherence to the position of the CoG.

In the framework of the CoG, the experts' groups were no more encouraging. The Heyvaert group (François Heyvaert of the National Bank of Belgium had succeeded Barre in the chair of the foreign exchange group in 1975) compiled a hesitant report on the varieties of a possible unit of account, and in the discussion at the CoG Heyvaert reported that the French experts had "failed" to show that a basket approach would strengthen the EMCF.[125]

At the December 1974 meeting, the CoG reached an agreement to introduce an experimental system of limiting currency movements on EEC markets to a daily limit of 1 percent (although this limit might be "relaxed" in cases of very strong upward or downward movements).[126] Even the modest proposal for a mechanism to limit international disorder and extreme movements of European rates against the dollar did not fare well. Meeting in Washington in January 1975, the European governors in discussions with the Federal Reserve had suggested placing a daily limit on exchange rate movements. But in February they heard that the United States was "reluctant."[127] The Europeans had practiced this kind of intervention to support the dollar in the weak phase at the beginning of 1973, though their interventions were lopsided in that they were prepared to allow greater dollar rises than 1 percent at moments of dollar strength. Despite the ineffectiveness of the practice, and the hesitations of Washington, European central bankers discussed interventions and concertation mechanisms with their American counterparts in Washington on March 3 and 4, 1975. The U.S. central bankers were worried about the possibility that European operations in dollars to support their own currencies might end up weakening the dollar.[128] A formal discussion on limiting exchange rate movements took place in March in Basel, where the most European-minded governor of the Federal Reserve, Henry Wallich, was present. Wallich suggested using the New York closing rate of the dollar as a guide for the next day's movements. In the discussion, Emminger appealed to the United States to intervene more in European currencies other than the Deutsche Mark (in practice only the Netherlands guilder was a realistic candidate), and also to end the policy of "benign neglect" of the dollar.[129] But such a decision or commitment could hardly be made by Wallich alone. In March 1975 the EEC central banks announced an agreement in which they renounced "aggressive intervention," and according to which they were supposed to limit daily fluctuations of their currencies against the dollar to 1 percent. But the agreement quickly proved unworkable in the light of continued exchange volatility, and in December 1975 it was modified so as to allow the rule to be broken in the interest of coherence of the Snake. In practice the March 1975 agreement was never really enforced, and as early as June 1975 the Snake ministers and governors concluded that "at present it is impossible to introduce firm rules for supporting dollar intervention."[130]

There were plenty of grounds for gloom. In March 1975 the long-retired commissioner Robert Marjolin submitted a report to the Commission on "Economic and Monetary Union 1980." Looking at the efforts to deal with the aftermath of the Werner Plan, Marjolin concluded that "Europe is no nearer to EMU than in 1969. In fact if there has been any movement it has been backwards." Initiatives had failed because of "unfavorable events, a lack of political will and insufficient understanding in the past of the meaning of an EMU." The main message of the report was the emphasis on political will; and the Marjolin report listed an extensive range of policy areas in which coordination was needed in order to make EMU work: industrial policy, energy policy, capital market policy, fiscal policy, and Community unemployment policy. But it also emphasized some technical improvements, which might be implemented more quickly. A "short-term programme" would involve better coordination of domestic monetary policies, an Exchange Stabilization Fund to develop the work of the EMCF, and the introduction of a new unit of account (European Currency Unit).[131]

France returned to the Snake on May 9, 1975, at the insistence of French President Giscard d'Estaing, and despite warnings from de Larosière, who considered the step "premature and likely to fail quickly." Monetary solidarity would not be possible between two countries that did not have an economic convergence. And in any case, the Snake had stopped being a Community mechanism, and had become instead a club of strong currencies.[132] The imminence of French reaccession was the principal reason given by the French and Belgian governors for a mild but effective resistance to Swiss participation in the Snake mechanism.[133] The Bundesbank and the Heyvaert group, which had been favorable to the Swiss feelers on participation in the Snake, were frustrated.[134] On the other side, Germany tried to block a Belgian proposal to lengthen the limit of credit terms to five months and to allow a maximum credit of three times the EMCF quota.[135] The Basel Accord was amended in July 1975 so as to allow debtor central banks to ask for a three-month renewal of the initial finance operation when it matured at the end of the month subsequent to the intervention.

The move had been preceded by renewed French insistence on institutional innovation. In April 1975 there was an agreement at the European Council to establish the European Unit of Account, and Fourcade claimed that within five years the EUA would be, along with the SDR, the major means of international payments. The new currency, like the SDR, was based on a standard basket, and that basket included all nine EEC members; in other words, it was not confined to Snake participants.[136]

Following the return to the Snake, France pressed to change the operating conditions of the exchange rate system: there should be more systematic and coordinated interventions against the dollar, with central banks of currencies at both the upper and lower limits of the margin bands intervening; and extended financing of interventions.[137] France also pressed for fluctuation margins against the dollar to be halved. In the Monetary Committee, Yves Haberer of the French treasury presented a paper on the exchange rate system laying out a step-by-step plan to reintroduce a fixed-exchange-rate regime via "stability zones," first at the European and then on the global level. The representatives of Great Britain, Italy, and Germany all opposed such a move; Italy warned against discrediting the floating rate system, and Chairman Oort concluded that the French proposal was not a good basis for discussion among the finance ministers.[138] Not surprisingly, the ambitious French ideas found little support from the Bundesbank. The CoG concluded that "a return to mandatory support for the dollar was not sustainable."[139] The Council did, however, agree to allow more possibilities for the extension of financing support.[140]

Although the Bundesbank was nervous about the operation of the Snake, it also saw the discipline involved as establishing the only viable path to monetary integration. In May 1974 the Bundesbank Council recorded a consensus that the Snake should be "the core of a future economic and monetary union."[141]

The operation and discipline of the Snake undoubtedly exercised some influence on countries outside the arrangement as well as on members. The governor of the Banque de France, Bernard Clappier, was forthright and critical of the French government's fiscal policy. In the CoG meeting of November 1975 he explained that France was "deliberately financing its large public deficit in an inflationary manner." He added that he was "concerned about the effects on the Snake, and this was one of the reasons he rather regretted the rapid reentry of the French franc."[142] Bastiaanse's group had again presented their position that "it was important that the monetary authorities of member countries follow a neutral monetary and credit policy," but that "the variable size of public deficits risks producing new divergences in the monetary policies of member countries."[143]

The debates about fiscal sustainability of the mid-1970s rarely erupted in public. But there were in fact substantial disagreements between finance ministers and central bankers. At the ministerial level, notably at the finance ministers' meeting in Venice on August 24, 1975, there was substantial pressure from Denis Healey (the British chancellor of the Exchequer) and Netherlands Finance Minister Wim Duisenberg for greater expansion in France and Germany. Healey explained that he was convinced that "the Community needs more reflation than is actually anticipated."[144]

Sometimes the discussion of fiscal stability spilled out in a more general debate, but for the moment it did not occur at the highest political level. The discussions of the EMU proposals were delegated by the EC

Council in September 1974 to the Monetary Committee and the CoG. But the Council was quite impatient: in October it demanded that the committees "accelerate the work requested of them."[145] It looked as if the technical level was not providing adequate solutions. Hence there was a push from the EC Commission for a much more dramatic and radical approach. In June 1975 in its *Report on Monetary Union,* the Commission advocated the "transformation of the whole complex of the relations of Member States into a European Union." Monetary policy would become an exclusively Community policy domain, in the same way as trade policy and the common external tariff. There would be a European central bank or system of central banks with a "fairly high degree of independence." A new parallel currency would be established, to be managed by the EMCF.[146]

Any hopes of monetary and economic convergence were dashed by French domestic politics. The Gaullist Jacques Chirac had supported Giscard d'Estaing in the 1974 presidential campaign, and had been rewarded with the premiership; but he was increasingly worried about an electoral challenge from the left, which he saw as gaining ground because of the government's austerity policies. In consequence, in September 1974 he embarked on a *"relance,"* an economic stimulus program with public infrastructure investment and increased social transfers to families, the elderly, and the disabled.

The Chirac stimulus intensified the concern of the French Finance Ministry about the operation of the Snake, and de Larosière continued to point to the very different inflation experiences of the EC member countries. Predictably, in March 1976 the French franc was forced out of the Snake for the second time, after France had spent some $5 billion on currency intervention. Giscard in April 1976 relayed to the European Council in Luxembourg the long-standing complaints of the French treasury about the working of the system: interventions demanded an asymmetrical sacrifice by the weaker countries, and the system was insufficiently flexible. Helmut Schmidt replied by saying that it "was astonishing that some people could believe that budgetary errors could be corrected by monetary mechanisms." He could also use a momentary German superiority after the French humiliation to sink Giscard's idea of having the European Council adopt a text affirming the goal of EMU. And when Giscard talked about improving the mechanisms of the Snake, Schmidt snapped back: "It doesn't help to manipulate a thermometer."[147] The primacy of the domestic focus and the divergence of national policies ruled out high-level discussion of closer monetary union. In particular German Chancellor Helmut Schmidt continued to take a hard line on the fiscal side of the discussion. In November 1976 at the European Council at The Hague he told the other leaders that "we are not living in the time of Keynes," and that "with such disparities Economic and Monetary Union is nothing but a diplomats' dream."[148] Nevertheless, the Commission continued to produce proposals for intensified monetary cooperation. It had prepared for the Luxembourg meeting a document on "Action économique et monétaire," in which EMU was reaffirmed as a "fundamental objective," and in which the Commission restated its goal of reinforcing economic and monetary coordination. It talked about establishing economic policy norms.[149]

The analysis of the Snake divided Europeans. The outsiders saw the mechanism as nothing more than a Deutsche Mark zone. In November 1976 the French chairman of the CoG, Governor Clappier, began the discussion of a range of currency proposals by stating firmly that the Snake was "not an instrument of community integration." It had started as a project for fostering economic and monetary integration, but had waned into a monetary mechanism. The non-Snake members did not have sufficient financial resources to be able to contemplate joining; and all of them had serious macroeconomic disequilibria that ruled out the prospect of a return to the Snake. On the other hand, the president of the Bundesbank, Karl Klasen, argued that "in order to progress toward economic and monetary union, members will need to use empirical methods, like that of the Snake, which was conceived as an experimental approach." In contrast with France, the smaller members of the EC could see the Deutsche Mark link of the Snake as offering a solid path to stability, as the governor of the Swedish Riksbank, Krister Wickman, noted in the same discussion. The CoG commissioned the Heyvaert group to study the enlargement of the March 24, 1974, agreement on intramarginal intervention in European currencies, as well as the question of market interventions by the floating currencies in Snake moneys.[150]

It is not surprising that at this stage the boldest proposals came from the smaller states, from the Netherlands and Belgium, since they bore a great deal of the brunt of tensions between the major players. Dutch

Finance Minister Wim Duisenberg in the summer of 1976 had proposed a greater degree of policy coordination of economic policies: "the medium-term economic policy programme of the Community should be made to play a central role in a periodic review of national programmes." The non-Snake members at present had no obligations on exchange rate policy: they should, Duisenberg believed, be involved in a "general Community framework for consultation and surveillance of exchange rate policies." This process could be used to establish target zones. In turn, "periodic review of the target zones, and Community surveillance on the basis of such guidelines, could provide the start of an effective framework for Community action in that area."[151] The Duisenberg plan was developed by the Finance Council on July 26, 1976. At the Monetary Committee in September 1976, the Dutch proposals were greeted with some skepticism. De Larosière thought that it was premature to take on additional exchange rate commitments prior to economic stabilization, and commented that the target zone proposal would make it easier for currency speculators to bet against the official exchange rates. Pöhl also said that it was preferable to fight against inflation and reinforce the coherence of EEC economic policies.[152]

There were other initiatives from the outside. On November 1, 1975, *The Economist* published the "All Saints' Day Manifesto" of nine economists proposing the creation of a new currency with a constant purchasing power, the Europa. It would be guaranteed by the EEC, and would compete with existing national currencies (this aspect was an anticipation of the hard ECU proposal of the early 1990s).[153] Reports by another group of economists, the OPTICA group, in 1976 and 1977 interpreted exchange rate movements as a source of economic instability within the EEC, and proposed a purchasing power parity rule as a guide to the management of nominal exchange rates, so that rates should not be allowed to move faster than inflation differentials indicated.[154]

One month after the controversial discussion of monetary targeting, the CoG discussed Dutch Finance Minister Wim Duisenberg's plan for a target zone system for all European Community currencies. At first the suggestion was that the zones should simply be "triggers for consultations on general economic policy" rather than requiring a specific intervention commitment in defense of the adopted parities.[155] The alternates had already discussed (and largely rejected) the proposal on November 8, 1976, in the immediate aftermath of a turbulent re-alignment within the Snake. The only differences among the alternates arose about the terms in which the proposal should be rejected. Some thought that a too-curt refusal would push ministers to demand further studies. Zijlstra, unsurprisingly, wanted a conciliatory tone so as not to provoke his finance minister, though he added that he "did not particularly agree" with Duisenberg's scheme. Clappier considered the alternates' report "a decent burial." Ortoli pleaded for greater exchange rate stability, but added that stabilization might be better achieved on a "bilateral or international level than at the European Community level."[156] On March 14, 1977, the CoG reported to the European Council that it could not recommend the introduction of target zones, but as a substitute proposed thrice-yearly consultations examining the public-sector borrowing requirement and its impact on interest and credit and the possible effects on exchange rates and the balance of payments.[157] The effect in the CoG's view was to provide an extended mandate for the Bastiaanse group on monetary policy harmonization. On the same day the EEC Monetary Committee agreed that it was not feasible to introduce a coherent exchange rate policy system at this time. In practice, it seemed to the Commission that the independently floating countries, France, Italy, and the United Kingdom, had been "quietly operating a system of target zones (albeit with the dollar as the numéraire, rather than the effective exchange rate, as proposed by the Netherlands authorities)."[158]

A further set of initiatives came from Belgium. In March 1978 Jacques van Ypersele, the inspector-general of the Belgian treasury, who was then chair of the EC Monetary Committee, suggested a system in which non-Snake members should fix their currencies in reference to the U.S. dollar as well as to the Snake. The proportional weights of the peg would initially be 50:50, but the ratio would gradually decrease in favor of the Snake. He also proposed the creation of a fund to issue EUAs, which would take on a role analogous to that of the IMF's SDRs. In April 1978 the Belgian governor de Strycker provided a modification of this plan, which would use only the dollar and the Deutsche Mark as reference currencies, rather than the whole Snake group. The Bundesbank reacted positively to the proposal, in particular to the variant suggested by Van Ypersele; but the reform initiative was overtaken by the high-level political moves of 1978 that produced a new European Monetary System.

Problems of the Snake

In the meantime the idea of a wider Snake fell apart when the Snake lost its Scandinavian component. Higher levels of inflation and very large current account deficits in the wake of the oil-price shocks made the Scandinavians seem closer to the United Kingdom or Italy than to Germany. In 1977 consumer price inflation in Denmark ran at 11.1 percent, in Sweden at 11.5 percent, and in Norway at 9.0 percent, while the German figure was 9.0 percent.[159] Sweden undertook two realignments within the Snake mechanism, the first on October 18, 1976, with a relatively small 1 percent depreciation against the Deutsche Mark, as part of the "Frankfurt realignment," when the Danish krone was also devalued by 4 percent and the Deutsche Mark was revalued against all the Snake currencies by 2 percent. This looked like a model realignment, in that with a small devaluation the band around the new rate overlapped with the band around the old rate, and market expectations could remain in place. Thus the change in the market rate was substantially less than the change in the parity rate.

But the pressure on exchange rates soon resumed. Sweden undertook a further 6 percent devaluation on April 4, 1977, when there was another realignment, with a 3 percent Danish and Norwegian devaluation. Sweden had originally pressed for a larger downward move, but in mid-April the governor of the Sveriges Riksbank said he was retrospectively convinced that it was the "right choice."[160] The Scandinavian currencies briefly strengthened, pushing the Deutsche Mark down to the lower end of the Snake, and Germany did not undertake any dollar interventions in support of the Deutsche Mark. But the Scandinavian devaluation soon proved to be insufficient, the speculative flows resumed, and on August 29, 1977, there was a 10 percent Swedish devaluation, and Sweden left the Snake mechanism. The result was generally thought to be highly successful, in that Swedish competitiveness increased as wage costs were held steady.[161]

Norway had followed the first of these moves, but on a smaller scale, with a 3 percent devaluation against the Deutsche Mark on October 18,

1976, 3 percent on April 4, 1977, and 5 percent on August 29, 1977. The governors of the Norwegian and Swedish national banks were invited to attend the first meeting of the CoG after the August 1977 devaluations. Nordlander from the Sveriges Riksbank declined, although he expressed hope for a return to the Snake in "a near future." At the CoG meeting Getz Wold of the Norges Bank described Norway's high balance-of-payments deficit as the "second greatest in the world," and explained that in his view the Snake continued to be a very useful mechanism. (In fact on 1977 Sweden had the third-largest overall balance-of-payments deficit in the world, at $1.075 billion, behind Australia at $1.154 billion and the United States at $35.039 billion, but Norway's at $121 million was relatively modest.)[162] Norway indeed stayed in, but only for just over a year. Another, this time more substantial, devaluation of 8 percent was required on February 13, 1978. On December 12, 1978, as the EEC members were agreeing on a new currency mechanism, Norway left and pegged instead to a basket of currencies. From the Scandinavian perspective, the Snake was essentially an exercise in pegging to the Deutsche Mark, and because of the volatility of the dollar/Deutsche Mark rate the peg gave no real protection against dramatic swings in foreign exchange rates and in the international competitiveness of the country. Hence a basket float appeared a more attractive option for generating more certainty about price expectations.

By 1977–1978 it looked as if every approach to reform had failed. In particular, European-level integration was faltering. The EMCF had neither become a European IMF nor a European Federal Reserve System; there was no mechanism for it to borrow on the increasingly active international capital markets; discussions about a European Currency Unit had stalled; the Snake had collapsed into a small Deutsche Mark bloc; monetarism as a source of monetary discipline had been clearly rejected by politicians and central bankers. Global solutions—through the IMF or through the newly initiated G-5/G-7 summit process—had prevailed. But in these global solutions, Europeans felt that they were vulnerable to pressures from the United States, and to the vagaries of the domestic policies of a (at that time) visibly declining hegemon. The rapid decline of the dollar in 1977–1978, when Europeans began to detect a policy of "malign neglect" in which the dollar was artificially depreciated, put new strains on the European order. Dollar weakness prompted inflows into the Deutsche Mark and pushed it up relative to neighboring currencies. The impetus to relaunching the reform discussion in Europe came inevitably from heightened concerns about the U.S. role and about U.S. vulnerability. The Europeans soon complained about U.S. indifference to continuing short-term capital outflows and the deteriorating trade balance. The dramatic weakness of the U.S. dollar not only provided the background to one of the most conflictual G-7 summits (in 1978 in Bonn) but also stimulated a new European approach to the question of monetary integration.

5

Negotiating the European
Monetary System

Can European integration be simply a creation of political will, or are
there bureaucratic or technocratic conditions that dictate the trajectory
of development? The year 1978 was one of high-level decisions, but the
long-term results were rather meager. The new settlement extended the
limited cooperation mechanism of the Snake, and was originally intended to be accompanied by much more far-reaching institutional
reform, including a European Monetary Fund. The reform debate was
accompanied by an intensive discussion of fiscal issues, and in particular of the extent to which the membership of poorer countries (notably
Ireland and Italy) would necessitate long-term fiscal transfers.

In 1978 the European monetary regime was remade, but the CoG did
not play a central role in the reform. The major initiative came from
politics, and in particular from President Giscard d'Estaing and Chancellor Schmidt. Those high-level debates were charged with lofty geopolitical ideas, and the new monetary arrangements were frequently seen
as a challenge to the preponderant role of the dollar in the international
monetary system. U.S. policymakers were skeptical or hostile. The CoG's
involvement was largely confined to an elaboration of the so-called
Belgian compromise, which reconciled divergent French and German
conceptions of how to institutionalize fixed-exchange-rate agreements.
In the end, however, despite an enormous amount of political energy
expended on the project, not very much changed. The agreement on a
new basket currency could potentially have been a basis for monetary
unification, but in practice it was not. There was no EMF, and the outcome was difficult to distinguish from a strengthened or revitalized

Snake. The experience of 1978 shows that reform could not come from a political initiative alone, however great the eloquence and passion of the political leaders.

By 1978 a number of diverse plans for European monetary reform were in the air, or at least in the filing cabinet—the Fourcade proposals, the Duisenberg plan, the Van Ypersele plan, the All Saints' Day Manifesto, the plans of the OPTICA group of economists for rules on devaluation, the initiative of Belgian Finance Minister Gaston Geens to increase financial support in the Community and reinforce budgetary and monetary policy discipline and coordination, or the scheme of The Times Group.[1] Europe was under great economic stress, with wildly varying rates of inflation, and a sharp dollar depreciation against the Deutsche Mark that exacerbated the strains on the other European currencies. The Snake was confined to a very small group of countries and had become basically a Deutsche Mark zone, while the other large EC currencies, the franc, the lira, and the pound, floated. There were simply both too many ideas and too many problems. When multiple problems breed a destructive proliferation of possible answers, the result will be confusion unless the issue is tackled at a very high level of political authority.

There was a great deal of policy innovation in 1978, but the CoG stood on the sidelines. Often its role was more one of erecting obstacles than of cheering on the process. In this respect, the innovations of 1978 were strikingly different from those of the late 1980s, when the role of the CoG was central to the process of policy reform and innovation. One important difference in the late 1970s was that central bank governors did not yet have the credibility or prestige that they acquired by the later years of the twentieth century. The European central banks presided over different monetary regimes and different inflation performances. Monetary performance was a source of divergence, not of convergence. As a result, there was little that might convince politicians or a broader public that a committee of central bank governors *should* play a vital role in the process of European monetary integration.

The eventual outcome of the intensive negotiations of 1978, the European Monetary System (EMS) is often regarded as a transformative step on a progressive path to monetary integration. But was it? Or was it nothing more than an elegant repackaging of the Snake arrangements, a "swimming trunk" coverup of the bare essentials, as Helmut Schmidt contemptuously put it when addressing the German Bundesbank, to soothe French susceptibilities about having been twice ejected ignominiously from that arrangement?[2] How much did the new European currency order derive from initiatives of the political leaders, in particular of German Chancellor Helmut Schmidt, and how far did it represent rather a continuation of an already-existing institutionalization of monetary coordination?

In 1978 a fundamental bilateralization of monetary discussions occurred. The Franco-German relationship was always at the core of debates about reshaping the monetary order, but in 1978 a series of personal initiatives was launched by Schmidt and President Valéry Giscard d'Estaing. One outcome was that the role of the Bundesbank, as a possible obstacle to the new initiatives, assumed a new importance, and it appeared as if the Bundesbank held a veto position. Schmidt often seemed to regard the German central bank as his primary adversary. The centrality of the Bundesbank to policy initiatives is also clear from the timing of debates. On a number of occasions in 1978, meetings of the Bundesbank Council immediately preceded discussions of monetary reforms in the CoG. The Banque de France also held some policy meetings just before the CoG (on January 10, September 7, and October 5, 1978). The political initiative of 1978 produced a widespread recognition that the power of the Bundesbank was central in any future discussion of European monetary arrangements.

The enhanced power of the Bundesbank and its ability to wield a de facto veto did not simply follow from the strong legal status of the Bundesbank. The bank's practical power also stemmed from its central role in the management of the major inflows of money that followed from the problems of the international system and the weakness of the dollar. Inflows into the Deutsche Mark could not effectively be sterilized through central bank sales of securities offsetting the liquidity effect of purchases of dollars. Thus German price stability, which the Bundesbank saw as its major and overriding objective, was compromised. The Bundesbank believed that its role as the most effective anti-inflationary central bank in Europe or indeed in the world was under challenge in the 1978 negotiations.

The new proposals appeared to have political origins, in particular in the European Commission. The relatively new commission president, Roy Jenkins, tried to reignite the currency discussion with a grand and visionary proposal that he launched at the European University Institute in Florence in October 1977.[3] In December 1977 the European Council at its Brussels meeting stated that it "reaffirmed its attachment to the objective of Economic and Monetary Union." But it admitted that though such a union was "an integral part of the process leading to European Union . . . since 1972, this great endeavour has been stagnating." Jenkins' activism was not universally applauded, even in Brussels, where the Bank of England reported with relish that he was becoming known as "Roi Jean-Quinze."[4]

Jenkins addressed the issue of Europe's currency arrangements as primarily a response to the faltering of American monetary hegemony and the strains that were consequently imposed on Europeans. In April 1978 Jenkins prepared a new version of his proposal for the European Council in which he set out his concerns about sluggish European growth and the currency disorder that followed from the pervasive and excessive weight of the dollar. "There is a fundamental asymmetry about the United States having withdrawn from the responsibilities of Bretton Woods, while dollars, like legions without a central command, continue to dominate the currency transactions of the world."[5] The governor of the Banque de France, Bernard Clappier, who emerged as a central figure in the elaboration of the EMS proposals, talked of "common reflection on means to solve the problem of the dollar."[6]

The focus on the external problems of the dollar as the central driver of closer monetary cooperation was not shared by all Europeans. The British government in particular was worried that Jenkins and Helmut Schmidt, who seemed sympathetic to the Jenkins initiative, were brewing up an anti-American concoction. At the beginning of April a British Treasury official noted that Schmidt was treating the dollar as a "lost cause," and observed a national difference that divided the European Community: "The German emotional reaction to the state of the dollar is to turn away from it and withdraw into Europe; the British reaction is to go and see our American friends." In a conversation with Jenkins, Prime Minister James Callaghan stated: "I would be very much against us moving on the European front on currency because it might give the impression to the Americans that we weren't really interested in them. . . . I think there comes a clear question—do we try to build a world monetary system or are we going to have a European one?" Jenkins replied: "I don't think the two are necessarily contradictory. I think we ought to play a larger part. I mean we aren't going to create a European single currency. . . . But I think we might move to a substantially more coordinated European monetary position which could help to create a better world monetary position."[7]

At the beginning of 1978, former Commission president François-Xavier Ortoli, who had stayed on as vice-president and retained responsibility for monetary affairs, set out before the CoG a new Commission version of the eventual European goal of a common monetary policy with a pooling of reserves. In response, Clappier recalled earlier fits of enthusiasm about economic and monetary union:

> It is now ten or so years since M. Marjolin, who then occupied the functions that M. Ortoli currently exercises, noted the relatively strong convergence of the six economies that were at that time members of the EEC. M. Marjolin concluded that it was necessary to seize the moment and to definitively harmonize the economic and financial policies of member countries. Everyone knows the result of that initiative. For that reason, it is perhaps not desirable to start a process of coordination of lips; if one continues to speak of coordination, it is necessary to take different and more efficacious routes whatever the skepticism that may be entertained on that account.[8]

Clappier's skeptical reply had a special irony in that he was about to become the spokesman for his president's relaunching of the monetary integration project.

Alexandre Lamfalussy in his January 1978 response to the Ortoli proposal had been rather dry: he wanted to focus attention away from the insoluble high political issues and onto the analytical issues involved in the international economy, and thought that the CoG should regularly study a general economic overview, analogous to the IMF's World Economic Outlook, as well as a series of issues papers. In February 1978 Ortoli recommended the creation of a group of economists who might advise the Bastiaanse experts' group on monetary policy harmonization and "deepen its theoretical foundation."[9] He also wanted these discussions to go beyond the nine member countries, and suggested that the Commission could participate in such work. He repeatedly noted the difficulty of institutionalizing quantitative monetary objectives at the EC level. Cecil de Strycker, the Belgian governor, and by the rotation principle chairman of the CoG, replied that there existed no common view on how monetary policy should support economic policy:

> Some central banks believe that it is necessary to maintain a certain rigor in monetary policy in order to avoid inflationary threats; while others have underlined that in the present circumstances it was above all important to restart economic activity and that monetary policy should not be rigorous and should not undermine the efforts at expansion made in other areas, notably budgetary policy. If this divergence of view persists, it is scarcely possible to hope for a coordination of monetary policy.[10]

The meeting took on something of the air of an academic seminar, in that Emminger then went on to set out the Bundesbank's approach to monetary targeting, and was immediately followed by a presentation by Jelle Zijlstra of the alternative Dutch approach.

The specific but very modest outcome of the EC's attempt to prod for more action was that the CoG gave an enhanced mandate to the Bastiaanse experts' group to prepare a biannual report on the consistency of national monetary policies in the EC, which in a second part would provide an analysis of their mutual compatibility. The subdued response looked like a disappointment to the European politicians.

At the high political level geopolitical considerations mattered as much as technical monetary affairs. The fundamental problem for currency management lay not in European but in transatlantic incompatibilities and clashes. The major difficulties followed from the weakness of the dollar, which followed from lax fiscal policy in the aftermath of the oil shock, but also, many Europeans felt, from a deliberate U.S. strategy that amounted to a competitive currency devaluation of the type that had been so disastrous in the 1930s. Treasury Secretary Michael Blumenthal was "talking down the dollar," the Europeans believed. The German newspapers carried titles such as "Crazy Blumenthal," and Helmut Schmidt called the Blumenthal strategy "suicidal." The American policymakers, by contrast, were pressing Germany to engage in more expansion and act as a "locomotive" for the world economy. Their German counterparts reacted allergically. In Paris, at the OECD the leader of the German delegation, Hans Tietmeyer, explained that there would be no German stimulus measures, and ridiculed the locomotive theory. At the political level, Chancellor Schmidt explained that "the United States has neither accepted nor even understood its leadership role in the economic field."[11] Dollar depreciation increased European coordination problems because it strengthened the Deutsche Mark (which was taking on a role as a reserve currency), while the other European currencies correspondingly weakened. The phenomenon was later termed dollar/Deutsche Mark polarization.[12]

The April 7–8, 1978, Copenhagen summit meeting of the European Council changed the terms of the debate. The outcome reflected a highly personal and originally quite secret initiative of President Giscard d'Estaing and Chancellor Helmut Schmidt. Some observers, including the British Foreign Office, believed that Giscard had initiated the discussion that led to Schmidt's dramatic move at Copenhagen, since they thought that "Chancellor Schmidt has never been a European idealist." The British also noted that both leaders wanted to act "in spite of their own bureaucracies."[13] Schmidt in particular was highly skeptical about experts and central bankers, and felt that economic diplomacy, whether on the world or the European level, needed to be personalized. In the lead-up to Copenhagen, he had been urged by his principal economic adviser, Horst Schulmann, to consult with Bundesbank President Emminger and Finance Minister Hans Matthöfer, but he had clearly preferred to restrict discussion of his new initiative as much as possible. In fact Karl Otto Pöhl, Schmidt's former press adviser and then economic Sherpa, and now vice-president of the Bundesbank, had written to Schmidt to inform him that the Bundesbank's directorate had discussed the question of a "European contribution to solve the problem of the dollar," but that "the views of my colleagues are known to you. They continue to be skeptical and critical of such an initiative."[14] In addition, Emminger wrote to Schmidt after a telephone conversation with Clappier on March 29, 1978, that Clappier was thinking of proposals that included bringing non-Snake currencies into the system via a looser target zone system around the Snake, pooling European reserves, and developing the EUA.[15] Emminger had no idea that Schmidt was elaborating a much more political version of the same proposal.

The preparations for two bilateral meetings with Giscard d'Estaing, on February 28 and April 2, were thus kept secret from the German ministries and the central bank, although just before the first of these meetings Schmidt informed the executive committee of the Social Democratic Party that he was "preparing in foreseeable time a European response to the catastrophic consequences of the collapse of the dollar."[16] The Franco-German approach relied on a deliberate exclusion of EEC institutions, including the CoG. According to a strategy paper that Schmidt drew up at this time, he was intending to operate "not on a national or autonomous level, but in the framework of the European community and the [NATO] alliance."[17] The CoG needed to be avoided, from Schmidt's perspective, in part because a close involvement would have meant that he would have had to channel his schemes through the deeply skeptical Bundesbank; and he preferred to present the Bundesbank with a *fait accompli.* In Schmidt's thinking, the best approach for the government was to make an end run around the technocrats.

Schmidt did not really talk *with* the Bundesbank (later he did talk to or at the Bundesbank), but he did tip off the British prime minister on March 12 about what he quaintly called an "exotic idea" for European currency moves:

> The idea was to create another European snake, but of a different kind. He would not be going as far as Roy Jenkins wished to in terms of EMU, but what he would propose was that the FRG [Federal Republic of Germany] and certain other members of the Community should each put half of their reserves into a new currency pool, the currencies of which would be fixed against a European Unit of Account. This Unit of Account would be the currency which operated vis-à-vis the dollar, and would be the sole unit of intervention. The pool would be managed by Finance Ministers. Countries in difficulties could borrow from this pool, and repay in one of three periods: over eight weeks; over six to twelve months; or over two years. He would not want this pool to be tied to the dollar because the U.S. economy was too large and uncontrollable: the captain was not in charge, even though he was well meaning.[18]

The political urgency of a European stance against the dollar became much more evident over the next few weeks. Schmidt became very angry on April 4, when the *New York Times* announced that without even informing Schmidt President Carter had just abandoned the neutron bomb and thus left Schmidt domestically isolated in his party, since he had spent a great deal of political capital trying to persuade the SPD to accept the necessity of a new American defense initiative. His frustrations appeared when he told Giscard that "The Americans need to stop believing that if they whistle, we will obey."[19]

During the Copenhagen summit, in the late afternoon of April 7, the government leaders were separated from their advisers and from the foreign ministers and driven out of the city to a dinner in Marienborg castle for a "fireside chat." Schmidt began with a plea for a wider use of the European Unit of Account. At the dinner, Giscard spoke of the dilemma of the non-Snake countries: they could either try to rejoin the Snake or work on a different and new project. Schmidt proposed that a European Monetary Fund be created, as a regional version of the IMF and as a revival of some of the 1940s idealism that had driven the Bretton Woods conference. There was also to be a revival of some of the aspirations that had originally surrounded the EMCF. The details of his plan show the extent to which he was mesmerized by the Bretton Woods construction. Countries should pool 15–20 percent of their reserves, they should increasingly use EC currencies rather than dollars in foreign exchange intervention, and there should be an enhanced use of the EUA.[20] In Schmidt's view, these proposals would move the world away from reliance on the dollar as the sole reserve currency; he even held out the prospect that OPEC members might invest a part of their surplus in the EUA, and that the EMF might issue EUA-denominated Special Drawing Rights. "To the extent that the EUA became an alternative reserve instrument it would take the pressure off the dollar. . . . there is absolutely nothing anti-American in the scheme although it might lead to the EC becoming a little bit more inward-looking than in the past."[21]

An initial response was to see Schmidt's proposal as a harmless expansion of the Snake concept. As Ken Couzens of the British Treasury noted: "The proposal *was* basically for a new European snake, the intention *was* that the European unit of account should be used for settlements between central banks only. It was however intended that the EUA should develop into a new currency in the longer term."[22]

Despite Schmidt's assurances that there was nothing anti-American about the plan, British Prime Minister James Callaghan called President Carter ten days after the meeting to denounce Schmidt's intentions:

> my understanding of his thoughts is that he believes the dollar is going to get into serious trouble, and we ought to try to insulate ourselves from it as much as possible. Now I don't know whether that thinking has got across to you, but with the strength of the German economy it could be extremely serious and I don't know, Jimmy, how

to obviate it. . . . You see he knows about international finance, he understands it, he was a Minister of Finance himself, he cares about it and he believes American policy is all wrong. Now as long as that persists there's going to be trouble.[23]

Carter himself does not appear to have been very worried by the British indiscretions about Europe's money, but Assistant Treasury Secretary Fred Bergsten pushed his boss into interpreting the European initiative as a threat to American interests.

Whitehall was much more worried than Washington, fearing marginalization. On the eve of the Copenhagen summit the Cabinet secretary, John Hunt, noted: "Some of the disadvantages to us are fairly clear. This could however be a move towards a two-tier community. The Prime Minister will obviously bear in mind the political and other implications if this happened and we were not in the top tier. Thus there is a case for ensuring either that this is a scheme that we can live with or that it founders."[24] The Treasury suspected the plan as a German exercise in power projection, and sketched out a plausible interpretation of German motives:

> If other EEC countries stick with the mark more and with the dollar less, that helps intra-EEC German trade and also helps Germany in competition with its EEC partners in other markets. . . . The Germans have been much preoccupied with maintaining the competitiveness of their exchange rate and the German Government has been under strong pressure from industry on this; although that has not stopped the Germans from suggesting that any preoccupation by deficit countries with the competitiveness of their exchange rate was misguided inflationary Keynesianism.[25]

Indeed later in the year German Finance Minister Manfred Lahnstein allegedly told the British chancellor of the Exchequer, Denis Healey, that Germany expected to get a competitive edge by limiting the scope for other currencies to depreciate.[26] Commentary of this kind, surfacing particularly during the 1978 negotiations, gave rise to the widely held concept that the EMS (as well as later the monetary union) were strategic political devices on the part of the German authorities to lock in competitive advantages for German exporters.

The task of working out the details was entrusted by Giscard, Schmidt, and Callaghan to a troika of experts: the governor of the Banque de

France, Bernard Clappier; Horst Schulmann from the German chancellor's office; and the second permanent secretary of the U.K. Treasury, Ken Couzens. Clappier was well known as a civil servant highly sympathetic to the European cause, who had worked very closely with Jean Monnet. Some French policymakers, including Raymond Barre and former governor of the Banque de France Renaud de la Genière, tried to press Giscard to use a less committed Europhile.[27] Like Clappier, Schulmann was a Europeanist, sympathetic to Schmidt's vision of the need for European cooperation as a response to U.S. weakness. By contrast, Couzens was not an integration enthusiast, and was suspicious of his continental colleagues. Clappier and Schulmann had already been working on a (secret) joint position paper since the spring of 1978. The existence of this group remained a secret until it was revealed in an article in *The Economist* on May 26, and Emminger and other central bank governors were profoundly shocked to hear of the work of the troika. Emminger in particular was deeply irritated that the Bundesbank had been conspicuously and humiliatingly sidelined.[28] In fact, in a telephone call of March 29, Clappier had tried to tip off Emminger about the likely French initiative, but Emminger does not seem to have been prepared to hear that message, and he simply naïvely relayed the French message to the German chancellor without understanding its implications as a challenge to the work of the central bankers.[29]

There were three meetings between all members of the troika, on May 12, May 26, and June 14, 1978. On May 26 Clappier had set out a sketch for what he called the European Monetary System, which would be run by a European Central Monetary Authority. At the third meeting, Clappier produced a draft of the operational details of the system, and Schulmann elaborated an intellectual justification of the move. Clappier argued about the need to replace the constraints of the Snake: "It would be an object of the exercise to make the new system as unlike the Snake as possible. This would have important political advantages both in France and in the United Kingdom, as well as dissociating the new system from earlier failures with the Snake."[30] By contrast, Schulmann's summary of the rationale behind the new EMS intentionally looked much more like the Snake: "A system of closer monetary cooperation will be established in the Community. In terms of exchange rate management it will be at least as strict as the so-called snake. In the initial stages of its operation, however, member countries currently not participating in the snake may opt for somewhat wider margins around central rates. Changes in central rates will be subject to mutual consent. The European Unit of Account will be the *numéraire* [anchor currency] of the system."[31]

Couzens found working with Schulmann particularly hard, and eventually dropped out of the process. On June 23, when Giscard and Schmidt met in Hamburg to discuss the draft produced by Schulmann and Clappier, Couzens was no longer present. He had not made a substantive contribution, and appeared increasingly as a skeptical and disengaged observer.[32] At his first meeting with Schulmann, Couzens had worried that "if we entered 'a snake' with the DM we must expect to have to devalue at intervals, as Denmark and Norway have had to do in the present snake." Schulmann had replied brusquely that "devaluation was 'almost entirely a monetary phenomenon' and suggested that our concern with competitiveness through the exchange rate was a reflection of our addiction to Keynesian economics, which found very little support in Germany."[33]

At the same time, the EC committees were working on monetary proposals. The Belgian chairman of the Monetary Committee, Jacques van Ypersele, produced three papers, setting out a series of options for floaters to work out a new target zone based half on the Snake and half on the dollar, and holding out the prospect of using very-short-term funds in order to support these target zones. In June a report by the MC laid out the following options: an extension of the Snake, with an improved mechanism for linking a modification of central rates with policy adjustment; a weighted index as the basis for a new system; and the Duisenberg proposal of target zones.[34] The Belgian chairman of the CoG, de Strycker, presented a parallel paper on the convergence of exchange rate policy. In line with previous Belgian initiatives, it suggested two snakes: in addition to the existing arrangement, a second snake in which there would be a 50 percent orientation to the Deutsche Mark and 50 percent to the dollar. There would be increased interventions, financed through the EMCF, and the long-term goal would be to create a single currency in stages. The German response was that such reforms would push the Deutsche Mark into a dominant position in the Community that would be increasingly problematic. As a key currency, the Deutsche Mark would be regularly used in exchange interventions, and would become "overburdened."[35]

Within the Bundesbank, Vice-President Karl Otto Pöhl circulated a memorandum on European currency integration, summarizing the current state of play. According to this account, the coordination of central banks did not correspond with the Council decision of March 22, 1971, and the CoG did not provide monetary and credit policy guidelines. The new initiatives being discussed were aimed at making the existing EUA a reserve medium (and renaming it the ECU, or European Currency Unit), as well as at providing financing for currency interventions by non-Snake members. The Bundesbank paper argued that these suggestions were not "well thought out," because there were no existing attractive instruments for the holding of EUAs; but that an attractive ECU would provide competition for the dollar and might embarrass Europeans by producing a further decline in the dollar exchange rate; and, if another scenario should materialize, a weak ECU would necessarily focus even more unwelcome attention on the Deutsche Mark as an investment currency.[36]

The CoG had no detailed information about what had been discussed at the Copenhagen meeting, or about the negotiations between Clappier and Schulmann. When in April the CoG began discussing the question of a new European monetary regime, the governors referred to the Commission statement about economic and monetary union of November 17, 1977, and to the action program of February 15, 1978, rather than to the Giscard-Schmidt proposals. They seemed to be self-consciously ignoring the high-profile political initiatives. Emminger proposed that the CoG should not wait for the heads of state, but rather work out its own program, picking up the Van Ypersele initiative and involving some rule of association between the floating currencies and the members of the Snake. All that he was prepared to offer was some debate on how the European policy toward the dollar should be "defined." The most skeptical reaction came from the Banca d'Italia governor, Paolo Baffi, who stated that there was no economic basis for a second "snake" involving the British, French, and Italian currencies, because of their substantial divergence in inflation rates.[37] In fact in 1979 inflation rates were rising in all European countries, but there were clearly big differences in national performance. At the one extreme, Germany moved from 2.7 percent in 1978 to 4.1 percent in 1979, while France went from 9.1 percent to 10.8 percent, the United Kingdom from 8.2 percent to 13.5 percent, and Italy from 12.1 to 14.8 percent.[38] Lamfalussy pleaded for a global perspective, since European initiatives had regularly been destroyed by Atlantic tensions: "if one looks at the history of attempts at monetary integration in the Community, it is possible to see that the weakness of the dollar has always played a destructive role." Dollar weakness had different effects on different European countries. Clappier had already set out in the April CoG meeting how the French franc had tried to steer a middle course between the dollar and the Deutsche Mark, and how this strategy had left it open to periodic speculative attacks. Emminger responded to Lamfalussy by saying that even in optimistic circumstances, it was difficult to imagine concerted European intervention in respect to the dollar.[39]

On May 9, 1978, the CoG alternates presented a note in which they argued that exchange rates in the Community did not make for stability in intra-Community transactions; that greater monetary cohesion depended on the reestablishment of fundamental economic equilibrium; that a Community-level improvement of exchange rate arrangements was desirable; and finally that intra-Community rates were being negatively affected by the volatility of the dollar. If fundamental economic convergence was required, a technical fix could offer only rather limited possibilities. The note then set out a series of questions about bringing in countries outside the Snake and about intervention obligations, which served as a basis for debate in the next meetings of the CoG. In the ensuing discussion, Emminger resolutely tried to avoid the question of coordinated intervention, a strategy that had already been tried unsuccessfully in 1975. Zijlstra noted that replacing the Snake was fundamentally a political choice. Clappier said that the Snake was a useful mechanism but was not well adapted to the interests of the non-Snake countries. Ortoli endorsed this interpretation and argued for a target zone proposal. Christopher McMahon of the Bank of England supported Clappier's position but added that Britain was skeptical about target zones and felt that more discipline was required, as target zones were vulnerable to speculative attacks.[40]

Immediately after the May CoG meeting, the Monetary Committee presented a negative response to the possibility of improving monetary arrangements: "The discussions have not permitted a registration of any appreciable rapprochement of the positions expressed by the different countries." The German representatives made some concessions in that they were willing to agree to a Snake with wider fluctuation margins.[41]

A subsequent meeting presented the alternatives, including fixed parities and reference zones.[42] A similar tone characterized the MC report of June 9 on improved exchange rate stability: "As a point of departure of its report, the Committee has assumed that the Council wishes to see progress toward exchange rate stability even before Member States have entirely solved the problem of differences in inflation rates and balance-of-payments performance; such progress on exchange rates could politically, psychologically, and technically contribute to improving the convergence of economic trends and policies of the Member States." The report, however, ended with no recommendations but rather with a series of questions:

1. Does the scheme include a formal obligation to intervene?
2. Is the intervention band defined in relation to Community currencies only or to trading currencies at large?
3. How wide is the band?
4. Is the scheme to be publicly announced?
5. By what procedure could a country's reference rate be changed (including arrangements for temporary leave of absence)?
6. What degree of prior Community consultation and subsequent surveillance of domestic policies is involved?
7. What amount of credit facilities are available and what would be their terms and conditions?
8. Would all member countries participate?[43]

The CoG alternates initially took an even more distanced look at the new political initiatives. Their paper at the end of May, "Efforts to Ensure Greater Exchange Rate Stability among EEC Member Countries' Currencies," started out by observing that the fundamental problem was a global one, driven by the fluctuations of the dollar; hence "efforts to achieve greater exchange rate stability must be made on a world scale." They then considered target zone proposals, on the lines originally suggested by the Netherlands; as a complement, the paper then also considered the adoption of dollar policies by the non-Snake members that would provide a complex mechanism to bring them gradually nearer to the Snake. The key to this progressive convergence would be a "reference axis," in which policy would target a basket including the Snake currencies (and with a greater weight over time given to the Snake currencies). If adopted, either of these alternative policies would require "an enlargement of available resources." That requirement pointed to the conclusion. At the end of the document, the alternates simply stated that they could at present not back either scheme.[44]

In June the CoG alternates presented a report on exchange rate stability to be submitted to the Council, but it was basically cool and skeptical—in other words, corresponding perfectly to the May discussion of the governors, as well as to the indecisive conclusion of the June 9 report of the Monetary Committee. The chairman of the alternates, Georges Janson, summed up the tone of the alternates' draft report in the following way: "in current circumstances, it seems scarcely possible to take on more formal and more constraining engagements."[45] Most sentences in the report felt like a cold shower intended to cool off the enthusiasm that was emanating from Brussels and Bonn. After a discussion of the alternatives of target zones and an adjustment of the rates of the floating countries "with a view to mutual convergence," the report stated: "the Community central banks do not all feel ready to recommend joint commitments devolving from either of the arrangements described above." In consequence, the alternates suggested the following formulation:

> The Governors wish to underline that in the final analysis any implementation of joint arrangements going beyond the non-obligatory mutual national interventions mentioned above, just as any choice between these arrangements, could only result from decisions of a political nature taken at Community level. Some of them feel that any such decision should in the first place concentrate on ways and means of ensuring effective co-ordination of national policies; in their view, the effectiveness of technical arrangements concerning exchange rates depends on parallel progress towards the convergence of member countries' economies.[46]

The draft report of the alternates was largely endorsed by the governors, who presented the final CoG report on "Efforts to Ensure Greater Exchange Rate Stability among EEC Member Countries' Currencies" on June 12, 1978. It raised alternative possibilities: a target-zone system for the four major EEC currencies, with the Snake continuing in its existing form; and a dollar policy for the Snake, with "certain fixed-exchange-rate objectives" for non-Snake members. These looked like a working out of the Van Ypersele proposals. The CoG report presented the global framework as central to establishing an effective European currency reform: "efforts to achieve greater exchange rate stability must be made on a world scale." The dollar relationship was thus seen as crucial to improving coordination within the EEC. It concluded, rather ambivalently: "the Community central banks do not all feel ready to recommend joint commitments devolving from either of the arrangements described above." Some countries might adopt the policies on "a pragmatic and individual basis." But to go further would require decisions at a political level.[47]

And that is what happened. On June 19, 1978, the EC finance ministers agreed on a system that would include all EEC currencies and possibly be open to other currencies (such as the Swiss franc and the Scandinavian currencies), would involve intervention commitments, and might give a more active role to the EMCF. The finance ministers concluded their meeting with the statement that "the Council wishes to see progress towards exchange rate stability even before Member States have entirely solved the problem of differences in inflation rates and balance of payments."[48]

The European Council meeting at Bremen on July 6–7, 1978, spelled out a much more detailed version of the Giscard-Schmidt proposals. The central institution would be the new European Monetary Fund, which would be established within two years, though the Snake would continue to exist; and "concurrent studies" would examine ways of improving the situation of poorer member countries so as to make their membership in a coordinated monetary system an economic and political feasibility. The "Bremen Annex," which contained the detailed proposals, specified that the ECU would be at "the center of the system." It began with the observation: "In terms of exchange rate management the European monetary system (EMS) will be at least as strict as the 'snake.'" The annex closed with an appeal for monetary stability: "A system of closer monetary cooperation will be successful only if participating countries pursue policies conducive to greater stability at home and abroad; this applies to deficit and surplus countries alike."[49] An initial supply of ECUs would be created against deposits of gold and dollars, at a level corresponding to 20 percent of the existing stocks of member central banks. This initial stock amounted to 3.9 percent of the value of European merchandise trade, roughly in the same range as the 3.4 percent of world trade that the initial SDR creation of 1969 had provided. There was thus a considerable resemblance between the two attempts—first global, then European—to provide a new synthetic currency.

At Bremen, both British Prime Minister James Callaghan and his Dutch counterpart, Dries van Agt, expressed irritation about the way that the package had been precooked. Schulmann indeed had warned Schmidt that he needed to avoid giving the appearance that the decisions of the European Council had been anticipated by a "Direktorium," but the procedure followed clearly from Schmidt's strategy of forging ahead in the narrowest and least bureaucratic setting.[50] Callaghan responded to Giscard's presentation of the Clappier-Schulmann proposals in a very hostile way. When Danish Prime Minister Anker Jørgensen commented that this was "a very exciting prospect," Callaghan curtly replied that "it was equally exciting if you drove over a cliff except that you hurt yourself at the bottom."[51]

The European initiative was followed almost immediately by the Bonn G-7 summit meeting, at which Germany (together with Japan) found itself the subject of very heavy-handed American pressures to expand demand by adopting looser monetary and fiscal policies. The United States seemed to be aligned with France and the United Kingdom in exerting pressure on the surplus countries to undertake the heavy lifting in adjustment. In parallel with the pressure from Washington, the European finance ministers had already called for Germany to commit to expansion in order to produce faster growth.[52] One of the public justifications for a new exchange rate agreement became that large and irrational currency fluctuations were acting as a brake on growth.[53] At Bonn, Giscard argued that the European negotiations simply involved reintroducing the Bretton Woods principles at the European level. That step would involve not just the stabilization of currencies but also a commitment to adjust, which would bind the key currency of the system.[54]

On July 11 at the regular CoG meeting, Clappier began by giving an overview of the Bremen initiatives, while stressing that he had not attended the Bremen meeting in his capacity as governor of the Banque de France but rather as a technical expert. He added that he thought it desirable that the "governors not yield to the easy temptation of making criticisms in principle of the various proposals." Ortoli tried to calm fears about the "durability of a system whose elements will be necessarily monetary" by adding reassurances about the strengthening of the positions of poorer member countries, presumably by increased transfer payments. But the substance of the Bremen initiative was discussed only briefly.[55]

Emminger talked about the need for more extended study of the issues involved, while Zijlstra posed a series of more precisely targeted questions: about the basis of participation in the EMF, about the composition of the ECU basket; about mechanisms for modification of the central rates; about the practice of currency intervention in the new system; and about the role of the Snake in the transition period.

The Bremen initiative was also at the center of discussion two days later in the Bundesbank Council meeting of July 13, when Emminger reported on his participation in the previous day's German cabinet discussion. Emminger stated that—like the political leaders—he wanted a durable solution that would not produce new crises every few years. He worried about the risk that some members would maintain unrealistic and damaging exchange rates that would set off speculative movements and might also pose an inflationary danger; about the quantity of international credit that would be required to make the scheme work; and about a possible undermining of the Bundesbank's monetary policy through commitments to interventions. The German finance minister, Hans Matthöfer, who was present as a "guest" at the Bundesbank discussion, conveyed Chancellor Schmidt's promise that there would be no additional creation of international liquidity; he also argued that France was showing signs of wanting to accept more stability. In the subsequent discussion, the Council's members complained that they had been inadequately informed about the Federal Republic's intentions, and recalled the bad experiences during the collapse of the Bretton Woods system. The "wrong" stable exchange rates could pose a burden on economic growth in the industrialized world. Karl Otto Pöhl was critical of the implications posed by a system based on exchange rates fixed against a unit of account. In the final summary, Emminger reasserted that "the final responsibility in currency issues lies with the Federal government, but the law gives the Bundesbank the duty to advise in the determination of policy."[56]

The Bundesbank technicians now set to work with the Finance Ministry to produce an alternative to ECU-based exchange rates. The key to the exchange rate system would be a parity grid. While the Bretton

Woods regime had fixed exchange rates relative to the dollar, and the French proposals saw a similar fixing of central rates against a basket currency, the Bundesbank had no central reference rates. Under such an exchange rate system—essentially derived from the practice of the Snake—a series of bilateral rates would be calculated and fluctuations of 2.25 percent either way of those rates permitted. In such a system, if one country is at the bottom of its rate, another is at the top, and it is unclear which country should perform the adjustment.[57] By contrast, the Banque de France elaborated proposals for something much closer to the Bretton Woods concept, namely a central ECU base with permitted margins of fluctuation suggested at 1 percent.[58] In that case it would be clear which country had the obligation to adopt corrective measures; and it was assumed by both French and German policymakers that in practice the Deutsche Mark would be divergent, and that the result would lead to Bundesbank interventions and pressures on domestic policy to be more expansive. The Bundesbank emphasized the need for inflation reduction as a basis for the new regime, rather than a harmonization of inflation rates around a mean, which it dismissively termed an "inflation community" (*Inflationsgemeinschaft*).[59] Many in the Bundesbank regarded any ECU-based basket as representing a "perfect inflation machine" at a time when three major EC countries had inflation rates of more than 10 percent.[60]

On July 18 there was a clash in the Monetary Committee, when the German representatives Manfred Lahnstein (state secretary in the Finance Ministry) and Karl Otto Pöhl (Bundesbank vice-president) opposed the French idea of expressing central rates in ECUs. The conflict escalated at the political level at the finance ministers' meeting of July 24, when Germany expressed preference for a parity grid, and Britain and Italy for ECU-based central rates. Defining central rates via a basket mechanism in ECUs would raise arithmetical but also political problems if a member country were to withdraw from the scheme. There would also be a difficulty in deciding what currencies should be used for intervention (for instance, if the Deutsche Mark was too strong, the Bundesbank would need to sell Deutsche Marks and buy some other currency, but doing so would then strengthen that particular currency, even though it might not be at the bottom of the band). By contrast, the use of a grid in which each currency's rates were set against those of all others did not pose a problem in regard to the central rate, but raised the question of who should undertake interventions, the weaker or the stronger currency, even more acutely. The non-Germans feared a German *diktat* in which the weaker currency would be assumed to have the greater obligation to take corrective measures. Denis Healey fanned the flames of conflict by insistently referring to the monetary policy document as "the Franco-German annex." His fears seemed to be realized when the French bargaining position changed. Surprisingly, though France had been the major proponent of the ECU-based approach, the French representatives did not present a viewpoint. Emminger devoted most of his energy to arguing that coordination with regard to the dollar should be "applied flexibly" and the formulation of any intervention strategy left to the CoG.[61]

The reconciliation of the clashing views took place in both the Monetary Committee and the CoG. The MC discussed the options on August 11 and 12, and on August 21 the CoG Heyvaert experts' group came up with a "compromise between the basket and grid variants."[62] That compromise was heavily weighted in favor of the Bundesbank-favored parity grid approach. The Heyvaert report emphasized the disadvantages of the basket, in particular that it "complicates the choice of intervention currency or currencies and raises controversial issues regarding the application of the rules for the settlement of debts arising out of interventions." The parity grid offered the advantage that it was "impossible for one currency to reach its upper or lower limit without [another's] simultaneously reaching its opposite limit." Above all the advantage was that parity changes in one currency vis-à-vis the *numéraire* did not require parity changes in other currencies. There would be none of the definitional questions associated with nonparticipation or opting out that the basket approach would pose. The compromise involved establishing a grid based on the ECU. As in the case of the Snake, the need for bilateral interventions could be derived from central rates. The ECU base, however, would allow identification of a divergent currency by treating movement against the ECU as an objective indicator of divergence.

The Heyvaert report laid out the details of other aspects of the new system. Changes in rates would be possible and indeed desirable, but would be subject to mutual consent. The Snake could continue. Bands of fluctuation would be "sufficiently wide to be respected without unduly frequent recourse to intervention of adjustment of central rates and sufficiently narrow to impose some measure of discipline and make the system effective." It would be possible to consider adopting different margins for different currencies, and one possibility presented (as a minority option) included graduated margins, with the width of margin being in inverse proportion to the weight of each currency in the basket. The large currencies, especially the franc and the Deutsche Mark, would thus be more closely bound together.[63]

The report also considered the problem of heavy-weight countries' (namely Germany) intervening in light-weight currencies, and thus inducing substantial movements in the latter. It might thus be necessary to specify that only heavy-weight currencies on the other side of the central rate should be used, so that the Bundesbank would preferably buy French francs rather than Belgian francs or Danish kroner; and dollars could be used whenever exchange rate interventions in European currencies might prove inappropriate or inadequate.

The treatment of the European Monetary Fund was rather skeptical in the Heyvaert report. It was presented as having the objective of demonstrating "that the new European monetary system is a step towards European monetary union." Two possible routes were laid out: in the first, it would be essentially an accounting entity and would not coordinate policies of member countries or act in its own right (in this way it would be simply an extension of the EMCF); in the second, it would have its own assets and would lay down guidelines or policy conditionality for the central banks using its resources. The issue of the transfer of national reserves was unlikely to be resolved by the beginning of 1979, and in consequence it was felt to be "more realistic to concentrate initially on the possibility of expanding the role not only of the EMCF in its present form but also of the agent of the EMCF [namely the CoG]." In essence, the process of burying the EMF proposal had already begun.[64]

The final element of convergence among the varied reform plans came with a Belgian suggestion in the Monetary Committee meeting of September 20, 1978, of a divergence indicator. According to what became known as the "Belgian compromise," maximum fluctuation bands on either side of the prescribed parities would be supplemented by a presumption that if a country reached 75 percent of the maximum divergence its government and central bank should contemplate corrective action, including interventions but also changes in domestic policy and in interest rate.

The German central bank appeared to take a tough position. In a public declaration the Bundesbank explained that the plan established not an obligation to intervene, but rather "a presumption to take action." In the Bundesbank Council discussion, Karl Otto Pöhl criticized the basket system as a means of forcing the Bundesbank to make large-scale interventions. The Council voted a resolution emphasizing the risk of including high-inflation countries in any new scheme; criticizing the basket system as reflecting average inflation rates and hence increasing Community expectations of inflation; and emphasizing the danger that the Bundesbank would lose monetary control.[65]

There was also a considerable amount of skepticism in Britain. Callaghan told the House of Commons on July 10: "A number of heads of government, including myself, wished to see the details fully worked out before entering into any commitments by our respective governments."[66] Despite these statements and the remarkably intimate character of the British-American dialogue, British Treasury officials worried that Callaghan was too enthusiastic about Schmidt's plans, and they tried to dissuade the prime minister from continental European commitments and entanglements. Callaghan's chief negotiator, Couzens, noted: "I am clear that it would have been better for the UK in every event if this plan had never come forward," and laid out his view of how Britain could live outside the EMS.[67]

By contrast, in Italy the prospect of joining a new European project generated considerable political enthusiasm. On August 31 Finance Minister Filippo Pandolfi justified his new austerity budget program in terms of moves toward Europe. But in Rome as well as in London the technicians of the central banks were skeptical. On November 1 Schmidt met Prime Minister Giulio Andreotti in Siena and won over Italian support for his plan, but at the cost of EEC support for the reorganization and restructuring of the Italian economy in the framework of the Pandolfi plan. The central hope was that the "concurrent studies" that had been accepted in Bremen as part of the monetary reform package would produce major financial assistance to Ireland and Italy as the two poorest EEC countries. Italy envisaged budget transfers rising from 0.76 percent of the EEC GDP to around 2 percent.[68] Discussion of something approaching a "transfer union" was thus a necessary part of thinking about monetary union. When at Siena the Italian delegation argued that the government was under pressure from the Socialists and Communists to obtain certain objectives, Schmidt exploded: "What do they know about money?" Similarly, when Andreotti presented the Italian demand in Brussels in December, asking for an annual subsidy of 800 million EUA, Giscard was outraged and tried to block the deal.[69]

The Italian central bank was on the side of the skeptics of this high-level political bargain. Governor Baffi had thought that Italian participation was unsustainable in the absence of the United Kingdom, the other EC country with really high inflation levels. He emphasized the desirability of a regime with wider fluctuation margins, of 6 to 8 percent, or what Horst Schulmann called a "snake with two skins."[70] The solution of a wide band—eventually accepted by the other European leaders—indeed provided the only possible foundation for Italian engagement in the new monetary project. The Banca d'Italia was at this time quite vulnerable. A few months later its political position was threatened by a scandal that had erupted with the arrest on March 28, 1979, of Baffi and Deputy Governor Mario Sarcinelli for allegedly concealing an investigation of loans by a Sardinian bank. Sarcinelli was imprisoned, and Baffi was spared that humiliation only because of his age. Eventually, in 1981, the two central bankers were completely exonerated, and it is likely that the arrest was a preemptive action by politicians who themselves feared exposure.[71] The scandal was a dramatic illustration of the divide between the Banca d'Italia and the government.

The CoG discussed the EMS proposals, as well as the Heyvaert group's report on the possibilities of fixed and adjustable baskets, and on reciprocal credit arrangements, on September 12, 1978, a few days before the Council of Ministers' meeting on September 18. Bank of England Governor Gordon Richardson stated initially that it was not possible to obtain a consensus of the governors on the basis of the technical reports of the Heyvaert group. In particular, there was a pronounced clash about the fundamental mechanism of the EMS. Emminger argued that although the goal might be to include all Community members, there might well be a case in which one or two members were either temporary or permanent nonparticipants. If these were major currencies, "the orientation of interventions by reference to a basket that would be codetermined by absent moneys would lead to a curious and unsupportable situation." This problem would not appear if the Bundesbank's suggestion of a parity grid were to be adopted. Clappier by contrast claimed that the goals of the Bremen project would not be realized if some countries were not to participate. The new system was not intended to be a continuation of the Snake, but was a "political project." For this reason it needed to be based on the ECU rather than on a parity grid, and a firm standard was preferable to an adjustable basket. The struggle between basket and parity grid became the key issue in Franco-German relations in drawing up the monetary proposal. France was backed consistently by another high-inflation country, Italy; and Germany was equally consistently supported by the Netherlands, which had fundamentally committed to following Bundesbank policy. In the CoG, the BIS chief economist Alexandre Lamfalussy drew attention to the fact that there might be periods when a currency "took leave" from the exchange mechanism, and this possibility would make the adjustable basket the more appropriate instrument of policy.[72]

The problem of the composition of the basket was raised when EC Commissioner François-Xavier Ortoli said that a European monetary system "should include and continue to include" all the moneys of the EC, and that in consequence the system should be precisely designed to avoid exits and reentrances. The CoG chairman, the Belgian central bank governor de Strycker, tried to conclude that there was a "relatively general" preference for an adjustable basket, but immediately encountered opposition from the Irish and Dutch governors, as well as from Emminger. De Strycker then tried to paper over the divisions by adding in his final summing-up that the new system should allow members of the Snake to continue their arrangements (in which there was no unit of account or basket currency).[73]

Clappier produced a proposal for the 25 billion ECU medium-term facility mentioned in the Bremen communiqué, but Emminger explained that he could not give a verdict on the size and characteristics of the credit mechanism as long as there was no agreement on the monetary standard. Clappier then went on to talk about the final stage in which a European Monetary Fund would be launched, with a pooling of reserves; and Emminger warned against including too many details of the second phase.

After the September 12 CoG meeting, Giscard telephoned Schmidt to say (rather misleadingly) that the governors were very close to agreement, and that a new round of bilateral Franco-German negotiations could seal the deal.[74] By the time of the symbolically highly charged meeting of Giscard and Schmidt in Aachen on September 14–15, 1978,

France had already abandoned the simple notion of a currency basket that had been at the center of Clappier's original scheme. The Aachen agreement was based on the German preference for a parity grid, but following the lines of the Heyvaert report included the "Belgian compromise" of a divergence indicator based on the ECU to signal the need for action if exchange rates were indicating the existence of a threat to sustainability. At Aachen the definition of the role of the European Monetary Fund was left until after the meeting of the European Council in December, although it was suggested that "there is a presumption that it should be modeled after the International Monetary Fund"; in the meanwhile the BIS might serve as the agent for the system on an interim basis. Credits were subject to conditionality. And the membership was still very uncertain: "Since it is difficult to discuss many details of the EMF as long as its membership is uncertain, it will not be possible to address these questions in a meaningful way before the next European summit (and perhaps not even by that date)." The Aachen meeting seemed to many outsiders to be an expression of an exclusive Franco-German bilateralism, and in a draft paragraph that was eventually deleted from the agreement, there was a provision that "a joint Franco-German working group will be established at high level immediately after the annual meeting of the IMF in order to work out the details for a common position on these matters in the Council meeting(s) before the next European Council." Another deleted provision stated that "in extreme situations a participating country might be compelled to opt out of the intervention system for an indefinite period." The deleted points referred explicitly to ways in which the Franco-German group might "enable Italy and the United Kingdom to participate in the EMS even if these countries chose not to become full members from the outset."[75]

Shortly after the Franco-German agreement at Aachen, British Chancellor of the Exchequer Denis Healey made it clear at the Brussels meeting of the ECOFIN that Britain would be unlikely to join the new mechanism. Soon afterward Emminger launched a very public critique of the monetary proposals in a speech to a meeting of German employers in Baden-Baden when he pointed out that even the very small Snake interventions had led to an inflow to Germany of DM 10 billion over a short period; and that keeping little Denmark in the mechanism had required four parity adjustments in eighteen months, and large amounts of currency intervention. How much harder would it be to have a single exchange rate mechanism that would include France and the United Kingdom! Jenkins was outraged by the obstructionism emanating from Frankfurt and noted in his diary that "Emminger is, I fear, anxious if he can to block the EMS and, if he cannot, to be dragged into it only by his hair, screaming, and with as puny a scheme as possible."[76] A British comment on the Monetary Committee debate noted in a similar vein that "The Germans . . . especially when they get onto their persecution theme, 'You are sacrificing German internal stability on the altar of external monetary stability,' rightly get little sympathy."[77]

When the CoG discussion resumed in October on the basis of a new Heyvaert report, the issue of the basket had been settled. But the Bundesbank now trained its artillery on a new target: What response would be required as a result of the establishment of indicators as a guide to policy? The day before the CoG meeting, the Bundesbank Council had unanimously rejected automatic intramarginal intervention requirements, while voting for an intervention system in the EMS based on a parity grid, with eleven votes in favor, one opposed, and four abstentions; and Emminger at the CoG correspondingly argued vigorously against automatic intervention requirements based on a divergence indicator. The terms of the international negotiation were thus fundamentally set by the Bundesbank Council. The French record of the subsequent discussion in the Monetary Committee noted sarcastically that "the Bundesbank president with his customary rigidity claimed that he was not defending an extreme position."[78]

In the CoG Clappier said that an indicator that served only to launch discussions would not represent any significant advance. He appealed for a careful definition of intramarginal intervention obligations. De Strycker tried to moderate the difference again with the suggestion that a divergence indicator should require intramarginal intervention, "except if the participants agreed that this was not indicated and other measures were preferable." Sarcinelli of the Banca d'Italia warned against a new failure of the discussion and restated the Latin view that the burden of adjustment should not fall asymmetrically on the weaker countries. An important new element was introduced into the discussion by Lamfalussy, who argued for a "factor time" in establishing intervention commitments: intramarginal interventions should occur only when a currency had diverged from its central rate for a "durable period."[79]

At the end of October 1978 at a CoG meeting in Brussels de Strycker presented the Belgian compromise on the credit issue, which seemed to go back to some 1973 proposals, and would multilateralize the use of the ECU in the EMCF. Emminger saw this as a way out in that a new ECU system, which would require central banks to accept ECUs in intra-Community transactions, could not be created under Article 235 of the Treaty of Rome but required Article 236 (that is, agreement on the negotiation of a new treaty). The Bundesbank's reluctance to accept a total credit figure remained a feature of the discussions in November.[80] Zijlstra supported Emminger in objecting to keeping a 25 billion ECU figure, and the Dutch-German faction demanded a reduction to 15 billion. He also wanted to insert a concertation exercise before intramarginal intervention, even though de Strycker warned that this process would make intramarginal interventions slower and less effective.[81]

The Brussels CoG meeting also agreed to a report suggesting an adjustable basket, which could be revised every five years in accordance with economic criteria, and it avoided any reference to the concept of a "leave" from the EMS. The draft report took the divergence indicator as the major difference from the Snake regime. But it also carefully spelled out, in accordance with the concerns of the Bundesbank, that if the divergent country was the weak one, and when "the divergent country was clearly exercising a 'pull' on the whole of the Community band, interventions in third currencies would have to be undertaken by the central bank whose currency was divergent, as a rule in the same proportion at least as interventions in other Community currencies."[82]

The report also specified that credit facilities should be available for a longer period, since "For as long as significant disparities persist, the system must be sufficiently flexible to accommodate imbalances. It will therefore be necessary to reconcile the need for intra-Community credit facilities on a scale which allows economic and monetary policies time to take effect with the aim of maintaining a satisfactory degree of strictness in order to achieve greater stability." The short- and very-short-term facilities should consequently be made available for fourteen to fifteen months rather than ten to eleven months.[83]

In line with his stance during the high-level negotiations with Schmidt at Siena, Baffi made a strong plea for wide (6–8 percent) bands around the parities, on the grounds that Italy had seen a 22 percent depreciation over two years, and would have been forced to make continual parity adjustments with a narrower band. But the governors' version instead specified wider bands set at only 4 percent.

The major outstanding issues were settled at an ECOFIN meeting on November 20. Germany accepted the 25 billion ECU credit figure. The width of the margin of fluctuation would be 2.25 percent, but the current floaters could have a wider margin up to 6 percent (in other words, in line with the preferences of the Banca d'Italia rather than with the lines set in the CoG negotiations). It was envisaged that this margin could subsequently be narrowed but not enlarged.

Was this just a new version of the Snake? British Foreign Secretary David Owen had already commented in October that "What is emerging is conspicuously like the Snake writ a little larger. But the Snake was unable to keep all Community currencies inside, even when inflation differentials and the sums of money available for speculation were both smaller than they are today. We do not therefore see how the pound, the franc and the lira could safely join a system which would operate essentially like the existing snake since the result could be the opposite of the stability sought at Bremen."[84] Jenkins was asked this question directly by Prime Minister Callaghan, and replied that "on any examination the EMS was very much more than the snake. It had great potentialities, in particular the use of large reserves."[85]

In a historic appearance before the Bundesbank Council on November 30, 1978, Chancellor Schmidt tried to persuade the council to accept the new monetary regime. He explained that the currency basket was only a "façon de parler, a swimming trunk, or makeup to cover up the fact that the French are joining for the third time a European currency association that they twice left."[86] The core of the message was that he had accepted the critical Bundesbank demand, made in a November 16 summary of key elements of the EMS agreement, that the Bundesbank should be released from the obligation to unlimited intervention if such a measure would pose a threat to the goal of German price stability. Emminger had written that the central bank council had agreed "under the precondition that the government and central bank agree on the legal basis and also on the future possibility of opting out in specific circumstances."[87] Schmidt checked the memorandum with the letter r, for *richtig*, "correct," and returned it to the Bundesbank. Germany agreed to a currency mechanism, but only to one that had a readily usable escape hatch.

At the Bundesbank meeting, the chancellor explained the nature of his compromise with the anti-inflation proclivities of the central bank, and why he did not want to make it public, for such a declaration would have ended any chances of an agreement on the European level:

> What interests me here is a part of the third point of your letter. I must say to you openly that I have quite severe misgivings about a written specification of this sort, a written specification of the possibility of an at least temporary release from the intervention. Let us first of all assume that it appeared tomorrow in a French or Italian newspaper. What accusations would the newspapers then make in editorials against their own Government who got themselves mixed up with such a dodgy promise with the Germans. A Government which promised them to intervene in the framework of certain rules of the game, but internally put in writing its intention to be able to do otherwise if need be? . . . In the matter itself I agree with you, gentlemen, but I deem it out of the question to write that down. . . . there has been a beautiful saying in the world for two thousand years: *ultra posse nemo obligatur.* And where the *ultra posse* lies one decides for oneself. My suspicion is that, if it came to a real crisis, it would then run according to historical experience, as it has run previously: that the debtor countries clear out first and not the creditor countries. But it could perfectly well be that case that the creditor Federal Republic might one day have to clear out; it is all thinkable, only one cannot write such a thing down. One can also not write down, to give you a relevant example, something else that likewise has to shy away from the light of publicity: what we would do, if need be, if the association, if the new membership of Greece, Spain, and Turkey led to our having at the end of the transition period, instead of four million foreigners in Germany, five or six million.[88]

The Bundesbank's immediate problem lay in the need to deal with the vast accumulations of reserves that piled up as a result of interventions. In his speech Schmidt predictably paid a great deal of attention to the problems of the dollar:

> If I see it correctly, you [the Bundesbank] have spent something in the region of $35 billions in support of the American dollar since 1970. I do not know how many Deutsche Marks that is at the present point in time, at any rate, far fewer Deutsche Marks latterly than you put in at that time. The sum resulting from interventions in the "Snake" is

incomparably smaller. All the same, when France and Italy come in, this amount will possibly rise, at least theoretically. I think, where the European Monetary System is concerned, it has already triggered in America a quite strong psychological signalling effect. It has become very burdensome, thank God, for the American Government to get told by its own banking community, also by its own industrial community, by its own published opinion: the dollar cannot carry on like this. But after they now also have to read in the newspapers that these Europeans are possibly ready to achieve something like a zone of stable currencies in their area, that is naturally a very strong additional psychological pressure on the American politicians to give up the policy of "benign neglect" on their side.[89]

But Schmidt cast his message in a very broad historical context. He said: "There are bad exaggerations around when each views it through national spectacles. One side prattles about an inflationary community, the others, English and Italians in particular, prattle about a deflationary community that would be accomplished there and would disrupt their whole national economy." He also referred to the more fundamental dilemmas of German foreign policy:

> We are doubly vulnerable and will remain so far into the next century. Vulnerable on account of Berlin and also on account of the open flank to the East, on account of the partition of the nation, symbolized by the insular position of Berlin, and secondly we remain vulnerable on account of Auschwitz. The more successful we are in the areas of foreign policy, economic policy, socioeconomic matters, and military matters, the longer it will be until Auschwitz sinks into history. So much the more we remain reliant on these two pillars, of which I spoke, one of which is the Common Market. A European Community without an efficiently functioning common economic market will decay.[90]

Schmidt used a grand political vision as a way of relativizing the technical objections of the central bankers. But in the course of the debate, the Bundesbankers also forcefully expressed their view of some of the reform proposals. In particular, it was clear that the Bundesbank vision held the basket indicator to be, in the words of one member of the Council, "a perfect inflation machine." In the end, Schmidt was prepared to accept the core of the Bundesbank case.[91]

The Emminger letter and Schmidt's secret acceptance of the Bundesbank demand leaked out to the public when on December 6, 1978, in the course of a Bundestag debate, Economics Minister Otto Graf Lambsdorff explicitly referred to the possibility of suspending the intervention requirement. But the government disliked any reference to it by the Bundesbank. In April 1979 Finance Minister Hans Matthöfer explained in a letter to Emminger that a temporary absolution from its obligations had not been explicitly mentioned in the EMS agreements, but that it had been discussed bilaterally, including at the critical Aachen meeting of September 1978. Such action would require "cooperation" between the Bundesbank and the German government in what Matthöfer described as a "covert relationship," since the government had the ultimate say in the choice of exchange rates and the Bundesbank in interventions *within* the EMS bands.[92]

The United Kingdom, like the United States at the Bonn summit, was worried about the "persistent German surplus" and the "difficulties of achieving substantial German capital exports to match it." In mid-November State Secretary Manfred Lahnstein from the German Finance Ministry visited the British chancellor of the Exchequer, who was still maintaining that there was "a good chance (but no certainty yet) that the UK would participate fully in other aspects of the EMS," presumably in the proposed monetary fund.[93] On November 30, the same day as the historic Bundesbank meeting, the British Cabinet decided on a half-way house: the United Kingdom would not join the exchange rate mechanism of the EMS but would keep the door open for later participation. Thus the United Kingdom was said to be engaged in the EMS without following the exchange rate rule.

The United States took a position that seemed closely aligned to that of London. Leading figures in the U.S. Treasury such as Fred Bergsten argued that there were flaws in the EMS that would have a negative impact on the world economy, presumably because the German obsession with austerity that he had often criticized in public, but also in face-to-face meetings with Schmidt, would force the whole of Europe into suboptimal growth. Secretary Blumenthal believed that the proposed EMF would weaken the IMF, and was incompatible with its Articles of Agreement. The most nuanced verdict was given by Undersecretary of State for Economic Affairs Richard Cooper, who recommended holding a balance between long-term support for European integration, and "legitimate prudence" with respect to American financial and economic interests.[94] Like London, Washington was worried.

In a December 5, 1978, meeting at Brussels, the European Council agreed to the establishment of a European Monetary System, but it included only six member states. The United Kingdom remained outside the system, while Ireland and Italy demanded time for reflection. Ireland was in a particularly difficult position, as it had a monetary union with the United Kingdom, which indeed continued during the initial weeks of its EMS membership. The political godfathers of the deal did not want to include Italy, whose participation would almost inevitably in their view constitute a constant strain. Giscard put pressure on Italy not to participate, and Schmidt also told Jenkins that "in his view the only thing to do now was to push the Italians out of the EMS."[95] Prime Minister Andreotti looked "helpless," while Irish Prime Minister Jack Lynch was "almost on the verge of tears."[96] But in the event Schmidt agreed to the provision of extra borrowing facilities, with 1 billion EUA being provided, of which one-third was to be made available to Ireland and two-thirds to Italy. Italy agreed to the wider (6 percent) bands. Members of the new system were obliged to intervene without limits at the 2.25 percent fluctuation margins either side of a central parity calculated bilaterally on the basis of an ECU central rate. The ECU was to be "at the centre of the EMS." Central rates could be adjusted "subject to mutual agreement by a common procedure which will comprise all countries participating in the exchange-rate mechanism and the Commission." A divergence indicator of 75 percent of the maximum spread of each currency would, when attained, allow the identification of the country that was diverging, and then trigger corrective action. Such action would include "diversified intervention [in a range of currencies]," the adjustment of domestic monetary policy and of central [interest] rates, as well as "other measures." The Very-Short-Term Facility (VSTF) with an unlimited amount was needed to finance the unlimited interventions, and would need to be settled forty-five days after the end of the month in which the intervention occurred. In the "final stage" of the EMS, the VSTF would be consolidated with the other credit facilities. Twenty percent of gold and reserves were to be deposited at the EMCF in exchange for ECUs that could be used to settle intervention balances (but not to make interventions, which would have to be made in conventional currencies).[97]

The core of the system became an "Agreement between the Central Banks of the Member States of the European Economic Community

Laying Down the Operating Procedures for the European Monetary System."[98] On December 12 at Basel, the CoG agreed to recommend to the Council of Ministers to use the existing central parities of the Snake, and to derive central rates for the new EMS members from the rates in effect at 2:30 on December 29, 1978. The ECU was to be the center of the system, as a *numéraire,* as a basis for calculating divergence, as the denomination of claims and liabilities arising from central bank interventions, and as the means of settlement among the EEC monetary authorities. The system was to be reexamined every five years, or whenever there was a serious change (defined as more than 25 percent) in the weight of any currency. EMS central banks were limited in their reserve policy, and could have only "small working holdings" of other EMS currencies unless they had the approval of the issuing bank.[99]

A great deal of the immediate response and analysis was political rather than technical. Especially in France, the new mechanism was heavily criticized from both the left and the nationalist and Gaullist right. *Le Monde* termed it a German triumph that presaged the "Empire of the Mark," and a brake on European growth. In practice the exchange rate agreement provided a way for Germans to improve their national competitiveness relative to countries with higher levels of inflation. It also gave Germany the "right to intervene in the policies of its partners." In short, France was replacing an "American master" with a "second master, in practice an accomplice of the former master."[100]

The entry into force of the system was delayed by France, which put a reserve on the activation until there was an agreement on proposals for eliminating the Monetary Compensation Amounts used in calculating the adjustments and subsidies of farm prices in the EEC. The complex negotiations on the arrangements that followed from the interaction of monetary agreements and agricultural price support meant that it was March 13, 1979, before the EMS began to operate.

In many aspects, the EMS was a profoundly truncated system. First, despite the language of the agreement, and as the French critics suspected, the ECU was in reality not at the center of the system; such a role would have required an institution capable of issuing or creating ECUs. Schmidt had told Andreotti at Siena that "he could not understand Giscard's idea of putting the ECU at the centre of the system but had had to include a reference in the Bremen communiqué to please the French."[101] In the same way as the 1960s vision of an IMF as a world central bank that might create SDRs was doomed to failure, the European monetary mechanism of the late 1970s did not fulfill the aspirations of its most enthusiastic proponents. Second, the divergence indicator was of little practical use, and it did not remove the asymmetric burden of adjustment by deficit countries. By the time it showed a divergence, that divergence would also become clear to speculators, who could mount an attack on the exchange rate. In other words, the indicator sent a signal not as an early warning but when there was already an obvious and imminent crisis—and in the early years, the result was usually a parity adjustment. In this aspect, the mechanism shared a conceptual flaw common in many attempts to establish official early warning systems: the signals of a potential crisis become self-fulfilling. In addition, in practice countries tended to cluster in groups within the bands, and so it was difficult to single out individual cases. Furthermore, an increased emphasis on convergence and on fighting inflation meant that in reality the pressure to adjust continued to fall on the weaker countries, those with deficits. Within a few years everyone recognized that the divergence indicator had been discarded, or, as it was put in officialese, turned into "a useful but not a privileged indicator."[102] Third, the agreement provided for a further stage, the establishment of the European Monetary Fund after two years. In practice there was no attempt to implement this goal.

The result of these failures was that the CoG moved ever closer to the "economist" position and avoided any suggestion that integration could be forced through monetary action. Instead, responding to dramatic changes in U.S. policy after Paul Volcker's radical tightening of Federal Reserve policy in October 1979, the focus of interest shifted once more to the general international situation. Europe could not simply manage its money on its own. That was the problem that constantly and necessarily beset the new EMS.

6

The Malaise of the 1980s

The first half of the 1980s appears as a monetary interlude or a period of transition. In some countries, notably the United States, Germany, and Switzerland, better monetary policy resolved the inflationary problems of the previous decade. There were thus good examples for European countries to follow, but there was little cooperation. Summit meetings at both the world and the European level were fractious and largely unproductive. International policy in specific national settings was generally improving, but international coordination was just marking time. Countries with a good policy regime inevitably feared that better cooperation might lead to an erosion of their strong policy framework. Such a view, entirely intelligible and even creditable, meant that institutions such as the IMF or the potential European Monetary Fund were regarded with great skepticism in strong countries. Meanwhile capital markets globally were transformed by the long-drawn-out debt crisis of 1982 that followed the collapse of the explosive lending to Latin American and eastern Europe.

Thus the early working of the new EMS was unpromising. The reform seemed at the time to be even more of a recipe for instability and tension than the Snake had been. Samuel Brittan in the *Financial Times* dismissed the regime as "a mere crawling peg."[1] If the objective was held to be European currency stability, it appeared that the new mechanism was a failure.

Volatile exchange rates not merely generated heightened economic uncertainty, but also threatened the political process on which the EC depended. Article 107 of the Treaty of Rome had defined exchange rate policy as a "matter of common interest," and apparently authorized retaliation by member states in the case of aberrant behavior. It was easy to see how an escalation of protective responses to perceived exchange rate misalignments might even include trade measures that would threaten the entire logic of European integration.

There was a general lowering of inflation rates in industrial countries, which can plausibly be interpreted as part of a move to a new anti-inflation consensus; but there was still little stabilization of exchange rates. Indeed the major hallmark of the currency history of this era is the dramatic rise of the U.S. dollar until early 1985, and its decline after September 1985 (see Figure 7.2, p. 217). Such global currency movements strained the EMS.

Only in retrospect was another and contrasting interpretation of the EMS formulated that found virtue in a flexible peg. The desirable objective was not currency stability, but the avoidance of substantial misalignments. The Italian economist Curzio Giannini argued that the first years of the EMS were its most successful time, as parity alterations could be achieved smoothly and without great drama; in his interpretation, the systemic difficulties came only with attempts to harden the EMS, in other words to reduce the frequency of exchange rate realignments.[2] There were in this period no large German current account surpluses: on the contrary, Germany was in deficit from 1979 to 1981. Thus the problem that had in the past led to so many attempts to solve a European monetary problem appeared to have been ended by the advent of the EMS. Exchange rate crises were handled in emergency meetings of the Monetary Committee, whose relative significance consequently increased relative to that of the CoG.

Those exchange rate changes arose out of fundamental divergences in national policies. What could be done to remove the source of instability? In December 1981 the CoG prepared a verbal note for the ECOFIN on the future of the EMS, in which it stressed that "the success of the EMS depended ineluctably on the success of internal stabilization"—in other words, the absence of substantial misalignments—but also observed that "there had been no discernible progress in domestic economic stability." As a consequence, "any initiative to accelerate institutional change risked compromising rather than consolidating the work already achieved."[3]

The only way to explain the need for realignments and hence of rescuing the idea of the EMS and the political process that underlay it was to think of its problems as essentially externally generated. This was the path taken by some of the most skillful monetary technocrats. The dollar was an easy whipping boy, as it looked as if it was misbehaving in a spectacular way as a consequence of the Reagan administration's combination of tight monetary policy and loose fiscal policy. By 1982, in the face of substantial disenchantment with the functioning of the EMS, Alexandre Lamfalussy described the majority of problems as emanating from the general international situation rather than from the workings of the Community mechanism. He thought that the problem lay in the global character and significance of the dollar, and that a solution might be found only in an international extension of the role of the ECU. Bundesbank President Karl Otto Pöhl was much more critical: he did not think that "a change in technical modalities could contribute to the solution of real problems."[4]

There were fundamental flaws in the European order, as well as in the management of the dollar. Instead of converging, levels of inflation in different European countries were moving further apart. One large country, the United Kingdom, remained outside the EMS. Another, Italy, was now inside, but with a special regime of wider (6 percent) fluctuation margins. But the fact that both currencies were part of the calculation of the ECU basket made the operation of the divergence indicator additionally complicated, requiring the periodic use of a "correction mechanism," and in practice led to its marginalization. Gordon Richardson, the governor of the Bank of England, agreed that technical changes would not solve "fundamental deficiencies." Banque de France Governor Renaud de la Genière agreed that there could be no immediate prospect of a transition to the second, institutional, phase of the EMS, but he continued to press for an "examination" of the EMF, an extension of the role of the ECU, and a definition of the ECU to replace the currency basket.[5]

The Dublin meeting of EC heads of state in November 1979 had confirmed the time frame for the establishment of an EMF as a cornerstone of the new EMS, and many of the governors viewed this as a vital component, in that the operation of the fixed-exchange-rate system implied a constant need for external support. Two variants existed: in one, the

EMF would become a genuine central bank; in the other, it would be a regional version of the IMF that would apply policy conditionality in its lending to governments. For Frankfurt, however, a role of the EMF as a constant and consistent provider of external support was anathema; and the Bundesbankers could use the instability of the international system to force home their point.

The tensions in the new system were much greater than had been expected, because of the very substantial volatility of the international system, in particular the dramatic depreciation and appreciation of the dollar, as well as because of the international recession that followed the second oil price shock. In September 1979 a realignment occurred after the German government threatened that it would otherwise authorize the Bundesbank to suspend interventions (as provided for in the 1978 Emminger letter), and the Deutsche Mark was revalued by 2 percent against the Belgian, French, Irish, Italian, and Netherlands currencies and by 5 percent against the Danish krone.[6] But very quickly, in October 1979, with a new Federal Reserve chairman, Paul Volcker, there came a major change in U.S. monetary policy, leading to a strengthening of the dollar and a weakening of the Deutsche Mark not only against the dollar but also against other European currencies.

Thus at different times both the international key currencies, the dollar and the Deutsche Mark, were under pressure. In 1979–1981 the Deutsche Mark was weak because of large current account deficits and initially traded at the bottom of its EMS range. The deficits followed in some part from deliberate policy measures by the German authorities to respond to the heavy international pressures in 1978 to reflate, with budget deficits rising; as well as from the development of labor costs, with the real exchange rate appreciating heavily in 1979 and 1980.

The result of the dollar and Deutsche Mark difficulties was a high level of activity in the foreign exchange markets by central banks. Heavy interventions by the Bundesbank (as well as some much smaller-scale interventions by the United States) were almost entirely in dollars, but nevertheless at the beginning of April 1980 the Deutsche Mark was at the bottom of its EMS band. As the dollar began to rise in early 1980, the Bundesbank regularly intervened to sell dollars. German interventions in other European currencies were much rarer, since the Bundesbank did not hold them as reserves, and consequently the burden of intervention in the European system fell mostly on the non–Deutsche

Mark currencies. But as the Deutsche Mark fell, the Bundesbank engaged in the European currency markets as well. From October 1980 to March 1981, the Bundesbank drew substantially on the EMCF's very-short-term financing, and was with Belgium the largest debtor, while France had a substantial surplus position (see Figure 6.1). France was financing the system at the outset of the EMS, and in consequence briefly appeared to be in a hegemonic position beyond challenge.

During the first half of the 1980s—and indeed for the whole history of the EMS with the exception of the last cataclysmic year—the overwhelming bulk of exchange rate interventions occurred intramarginally, rather than when currencies had reached the band limits. They were thus voluntary and deliberate policy choices; and they were thought to be much more effective in altering market expectations than the compulsory interventions specified by the EMS agreement when currencies had reached their band limits. Indeed such interventions were generally read by market participants as an unambiguous sign of imminent crisis, implying that currencies were ready to be pushed out of the EMS bands. Between 1979 and 1983, intervention at the EMS limits constituted only one-fifth of the total of EMS-related interventions. In most cases of intramarginal intervention, there was no need to use the EMCF's Very-Short-Term Facility (VSTF), which was indeed drawn on only once for this purpose in this early period (in 1979).[7] These intervention data are not altogether simple to assemble and assess, as it is hard to distinguish between operations designed specifically as interventions with the purpose of altering market rates from

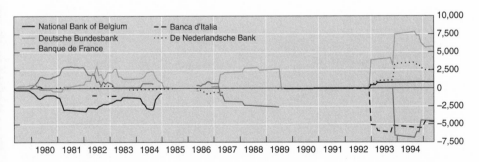

Figure 6.1. Net positions in EMCF, 1979–1995 (millions of ECU). *Source:* CoG files, ECB, Frankfurt am Main.

other exchange operations conducted by central banks—for instance in their function as fiscal agents for their governments.[8] We can be sure, however, that all movements financed through the EMCF were genuine exchange market interventions (see Figure 6.2). Movements in EMCF positions were promptly and efficiently unwound, indicating that the system of short-term support functioned quite well and was not being used to finance the buildup of persistent deficits.

Most of the intensive discussion of exchange rate issues occurred in the alternates' meetings and in the experts' groups, rather than in the full meetings of the CoG; as well as in the Monetary Committee. In the MC in October 1979, France had argued for an increase in coordination: Michel Camdessus of the French treasury had stated that the agreements of March and December 1975 to restrict dollar movements to a daily limit of 1 percent had not been adequate, and that it was time to formulate a general view on what an acceptable dollar rate should be, based on "objective indicators." The Bundesbank representative, Wolfgang

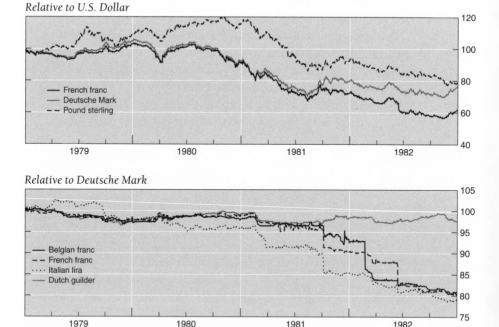

Figure 6.2. Exchange rates, 1979–1983. Beginning of period = 100. *Source:* National data.

Rieke, hit back with the observation that such a decision would not be compatible with Germany's domestic monetary objectives, and that agreements on an appropriate dollar level would look "merely academic."[9] In an internal paper, the Bundesbank argued cogently that it would be impossible for EC countries to agree on a dollar rate, and that individual countries would be forced into an exchange rate that did not correspond with their interests. In addition, dollar policy was really made by the United States and not by Europe, and Germany was better than its European partners at dealing with the United States.[10]

At the beginning of 1980 Germany was still in a surplus position in the EMCF. At that time the alternates discussed the establishment of the EMF and elaborated an "evolutionary" approach to the establishment of what in practice would amount to a European central bank. Their central constraint lay in the Bundesbank's insistence that "the fund must be an independent central banking system," that reserves could not be transferred until that independence was guaranteed, and that the fund must be instituted in such a way as not "to affect negatively" national central banks in their credit or monetary policy. In other words, central banks should not be forced into inflationary adjustment.[11]

The EC Commission called for a common policy with regard to the U.S. dollar—in other words, a realization of the expectations of Giscard and Schmidt—and pointed out the risks to the internal stability of the EMS, and also the trade risks that might be posed by a supercompetitive dollar.[12] The Banque de France reported on a December 1979 meeting of the experts' group chaired by Heyvaert (working on foreign exchange issues) that it had been a demonstration of the "firmness of the German opposition to any attempt at the construction of genuinely common policy." The Bundesbank in particular had blocked the formulation of any general intervention principles, and even seemed to the French to have gone back on the agreements of March 1975, according to which the European central bankers would refrain from dollar interventions if these risked provoking compulsory (that is, marginal) interventions in EMS currencies. The other central banks were willing to agree not to sell the dollar if it appeared undervalued and the strong EMS currencies were buying dollars to support the weaker currencies (with conversely, in the case of a strong dollar, weak EMS currencies selling dollars and strong currencies refraining from intervention). The Bundesbank also tried to block attempts to reach an agreement with the Federal Reserve to multilateralize interventions, so that there would be a substantial U.S. use of currencies other than the Deutsche Mark. The other central banks wanted to see a greater use of intramarginal interventions; the Bundesbank was opposed.[13]

French frustration with the Bundesbank mounted. According to the Banque de France, the preliminary draft of the CoG secretariat paper on the development of the EMS was "not as balanced as was desirable," but rather reflected the Bundesbank's skepticism about a "qualitative leap" in creating the EMF. The French saw that the Bundesbank would accept a central bank only if it reflected Dutch or German styles of independence, and that it was trying to frustrate the development of an ECU market. By contrast, the Bundesbank stated that the "report accurately reproduces the views of the Bundesbank, if only as a minority opinion."[14]

In January 1980 Karl Otto Pöhl participated for the first time in the CoG in his new role as president of the Bundesbank. He immediately took a much more critical and confrontational tone than was customary in the conventionally rather polite climate of the central bankers' meetings. He was, for instance, quite impatient about the discussion of the "evolutionary" development of an EMF, and suggested that the current EMS system was working adequately, and that the best way of improving it was to secure the participation of the countries that were presently outside the EMS. He also emphatically reasserted the German position that any legal framework that permitted the EC Council to give instructions to the EMF would be incompatible with German law and would require a revision of the Bundesbank law. Pöhl also made very clear his belief that it would be impossible to submit all monetary policy decisions to preliminary discussion by the CoG. In the case of the Bundesbank, he emphasized that the president could not commit the Central Bank Council to a specific course of action.[15] In his view the EMF in particular would require German parliamentary approval, a point that Emminger had already made to the Bundesbank Council in November 1979. For Pöhl, there were three possibilities: what he termed a "minimal solution" of keeping existing institutions and simply renaming the EMCF the EMF; creating a regional fund as a governmental institution that would control medium-term financial resources within the EC; and developing the EMCF into a common central banking system. Pöhl sometimes expressed a preference for the third and most radical of these solutions, as he claimed it corresponded most precisely with the Bremen and Brussels European Council decisions. But this seemed more of an academic argument than a policy proposal. It was not the first or last time a theoretically convincing case for an ambitious program was put forward as a way of blocking practical and realizable small-scale steps. After discussion in the Bundesbank Council, Pöhl concluded that the functioning of the system did not really require the invention of a special new fund.[16]

As a result of the sharp divergence of views, the CoG found it impossible to produce a joint statement on the EMF, and in February it agreed only to present a short and noncommittal verbal report to the March ECOFIN meeting that would consider the question of the EMF.[17] By December 1980 the EMF had been abandoned.

Pöhl explained to the EC Commission that the objections of the Bundesbank to an EMF were nothing more than an expression of its unease with the international monetary order: "The IMF as a model for an EMF frankly contains some attractive, but also some very unattractive, characteristics. In its politicized methods of liquidity creation through SDR allocation, of quota review processes, as well as in the practical application of its conditionality, the IMF can hardly be a model for the EMF."[18]

The clash of interpretations within the CoG became more extreme in April 1980 as a result of very violent currency fluctuations. The dollar had substantially strengthened since October 1979, but fell very abruptly in April at a time when the European markets were closed for Easter. Heyvaert reported on exchange rate movements and concluded that more intervention was needed to ease tensions within the EMS. For the majority of the CoG, this point seemed self-evident. Not so for Pöhl. He explained that the markets had worked rather well, and that there had been a "valuable lesson" for speculators who were making a one-way bet on the appreciation of the dollar. "The market was capable of adapting to exaggerated moves in one or the other direction." There was no need for major currency interventions. Cecil de Strycker immediately replied that the divergence of views in the CoG was "astonishing," as there had previously been a "general conviction" about the desirability of more stable exchange rates, and hence about the desirability of regular foreign exchange intervention.[19]

One answer was that the problem might lie with the one-sided character of interventions. Lamfalussy pointed out the asymmetry in the practice of the Federal Reserve, which intervened only when the dollar was falling (and the Europeans mostly also intervened only when their own currencies were falling).

But the more fundamental problem of the early 1980s lay in the increasing divergence of monetary policies, both globally and in Europe. At the beginning of 1981, with persistent Deutsche Mark weakness, the Bundesbank had concluded that interventions alone could not deal with the problem and that monetary policy action was needed, and in February it imposed a dramatic 3 percent increase in interest rates. The Deutsche Mark then suddenly strengthened and attracted capital inflows from other European countries. With the interest-rate hike, the full extent of policy divergence in the EMS became apparent, especially since it was followed by political turmoil in Italy and France.

The Heyvaert group's report No. 48 noted the "divergences, which remain disappointing, in the fundamental areas of domestic prices and costs, public-sector budgets, and current-account balances of payments."[20] The United States and the United Kingdom undertook a radical disinflation, but in both cases the results initially looked very precarious and the strategy highly costly. For continental Europeans, by contrast, relatively high levels of inflation seemed acceptable even for a long period, and they rejected radical projects of disinflation. The governor of the Banca d'Italia, Carlo Ciampi, hailed the reduction of inflation by one percentage point (from 20 percent) as a great success. The French governor, Renaud de la Genière, argued that "it was probably not possible to envisage rates of inflation below 5 percent as in the 1960s." Reflecting on a report on British counterinflationary measures, the CoG concluded that little progress had been made in harmonizing the instruments of monetary policy. The governor of the National Bank of Belgium, de Strycker, who had always made dislike of academic monetarism his intellectual calling card, argued that attempts at monetary control such as the one adopted by the United Kingdom entailed substantial and volatile exchange rate movements that were harmful to the working of a system such as the EMS. De Strycker also attacked the U.S. authorities as following a "dogmatic" policy of thinking that "the struggle against inflation could only be fought with the monetary instrument."[21]

The German position was isolated. In contrast to his colleagues in the CoG, Pöhl vigorously and consistently defended the U.S. approach, arguing that Europe would benefit from lower U.S. inflation and that "it would be erroneous to recommend to the American authorities any other monetary policy."[22] It would be a grotesque illusion to think that any European démarche could lead to a change in U.S. policy. The non-German members saw a problem not only in U.S. policy, but also in the German actions. Inevitably, de la Genière criticized German as well as U.S. high-interest policy, and argued that if monetary policy were used as the principal instrument it would need to be applied with "great brutality" and would produce major disturbance and discontent.[23] Only later in the year was Pöhl willing to signal through intervention policy a desire that the Federal Reserve abandon its "benign neglect" (benign because the dollar was rising, in contrast to the "malign neglect" of the late 1970s).[24] In October he told a meeting of finance ministers and governors in London that in the first nine months of 1981, the G-10 (with Switzerland and Norway) had spent a net $25 billion in dollar sales, of which Germany had sold $10 billion, while the Federal Reserve had not intervened at all.[25]

While dollar strength was a theme of global debates, there were also big strains in the European system. On March 23, 1981, an Italian devaluation of 6 percent was carried out without any prior consultation with the EMS countries. Italy, with its regime of wider margins, had always looked like a special case; but then the problems of the system appeared to become more general. Soon a parallel crisis enveloped France as a consequence of the presidential elections of April 13 and May 11, 1981, which produced a narrow victory for the candidate of the left, François Mitterrand. In the two weeks after May 11, the Banque de France needed to use $3 billion of its reserves in defense of the franc, and on May 22 France introduced exchange controls. From May, France also had to borrow substantial amounts through the VSTF. The position of 1980, in which France had been the major creditor of the system, was dramatically reversed. The Deutsche Mark shot up to the top of its band. Germany and the Netherlands became the major creditors. Pöhl began to speculate about whether the developments in France were even compatible with membership in a fixed-exchange-rate system.[26]

On October 5, 1981, a general exchange rate realignment took place, with an appreciation of the Deutsche Mark and the guilder by 5.5 percent and a devaluation of the French franc and the Italian lira by 3 percent. In the aftermath the Deutsche Mark fell to the lower end of its new higher band. In the next meeting of the CoG, there was general satisfaction that the issue had been well handled, although some governors thought that there should have been more informal negotiation before the formal realignment meeting in Brussels; and the director-general of economic and financial affairs at the Commission, Tommaso Padoa-Schioppa, argued that the realignment showed that the EMS was still "quite fragile" and needed to be reinforced.[27]

At this point the Banque de France had very strained relations with the government to which it was legally subordinate. In October 1981 it bluntly refused to quadruple the advances on treasury securities requested by the government, and for the next two years the central bank was persistently critical, and made arguments about European necessities arising out of exchange rate commitments a key part of its case for more government fiscal restraint.[28]

The EC Commission and Padoa-Schioppa now saw France as a potential threat to the EMS. They thought that Mitterrand viewed the EMS as the intellectual construct of his rival and predecessor as president, Giscard d'Estaing, and worried that the French left might now reject the EMS. Something needed to be done to appeal to French Socialists. As a result the Commission developed a series of initiatives for strengthening the system, involving in particular a greater use of the ECU, but also a new surveillance process that would use "a set of comparative indicators" and would determine objectives by "common agreement."[29] The technical changes were designed in part as a political maneuver to win over the new French government, though there had been some Commission discussion of ways of making the ECU into a regional version of the SDR even before the French elections.[30] The proposals for greater use of the ECU inevitably attracted criticism from the Bundesbank, which together with the Nederlandsche Bank and the Central Bank of Ireland argued that a greater use of the ECU would depend on its full convertibility. In the Bundesbank Council, critics of the 1978–1979 agreements took a much tougher line, arguing that the aims of the EMS had not been achieved and were endangering the stability policy of the Bundesbank, and that the European system was plagued by a fundamental lack of consensus on basic assumptions and priorities.[31] In consequence, in the lead-up to the ECOFIN meeting at which the EMS was to be discussed, Pöhl wrote to Chancellor Schmidt to argue that the Commission's proposals would weaken discipline in the system.[32]

In the wake of the debate between the Commission and the Bundesbank, a surprising idea was floated. When Padoa-Schioppa visited Pöhl in his Frankfurt office on March 1, 1982, the Bundesbank president explained his opposition to further institutionalization of the EMS, but also laid out his position (which he had also explained to the Bundesbank Council) that the better solution intellectually would be a complete monetary union. Already before that, Padoa-Schioppa had explained in a letter to Pöhl: "To couple the defense of monetary orthodoxy with that of the institutional status quo may lead to defeat in terms of both monetary stability and independence. Your 'monetary constitution' has been too successful on the fight for stability. It will now either become the monetary constitution for Europe or be contaminated by the sins of the others. That is, by the way, a very 'deutsches Schicksal.'"[33] The germ of the idea of a new push for monetary union thus lay in the very unsatisfactory early experience of the EMS.

The apparent fragility of the EMS was highlighted by further repeated waves of parity changes. On February 20–21, 1982, the Belgian franc was devalued by 8.5 percent and the Danish krone by 3 percent. Belgium had originally wanted a 12 percent change and Denmark 7 percent. There were no discussions by the CoG, and the countries undertaking the changes did not signal their intention in advance. Everything was handled at the political level. German policymakers were worried about the trade effects of such large currency moves by Germany's major trading partners. It was the German government, and not the Bundesbank, that pressed Belgium for a smaller realignment by threatening to suspend support interventions on the currency markets.[34] In addition to the sidelining of the central banks, there was some leaking of the likely changes. Pöhl contrasted the current confusion with the smoother operation of the 1970s Snake, when adjustments had been "well prepared and confidential." A realignment should not, he said, be seen as "a unilateral act."[35] The Belgian and Danish moves were followed by expectations of further alterations that might affect the French franc and the Italian lira. Pöhl in the Bundesbank Council warned that parity changes were being used by other European countries as a substitute for internal discipline.[36]

But in practice, the 1982 Belgian parity alteration marked a turning point in the attitude of small countries to the EMS, and in retrospect it was judged much more favorably than at the moment of the exchange rate crisis. This was the moment when smaller EMS members began to take a more "German" view of monetary matters. Pöhl could be agreeably surprised. The parity alteration had been less than the Belgian government had wanted, and in dealing with the aftermath of a smaller devaluation it was required to impose a harsher adjustment policy. Taking more adjustment and looking to increasing fixity of exchange rates became the optimal policy path for smaller EC members. There was still major uncertainty about the positions of the large countries. By March 1982 France needed to draw very large amounts under the EMCF's Very-Short-Term Facility.

The alternates in the CoG emphasized the importance of budgetary stabilization, but they also accepted the logic of accompanying austerity with some technical changes that might make the system appear more attractive. In particular, they proposed the following measures: the extension of the length of European swaps from three to six months; an agreement of other central banks to make currencies available for support of one country once it crossed the 75 percent divergence threshold; and an increase in remuneration of the ECU (which had been set as the weighted average of the various official discount rates), in order to make the holding of accounts in ECUs more attractive to the surplus countries.[37] However, it proved to take a frustratingly long time before even these minor piecemeal improvements to the operation of the system could be made. A more fundamental improvement, the regularization of intramarginal intervention, came only five years later, in 1987.

In a new report for the ECOFIN, the CoG repeated the view, strongly articulated from Frankfurt, that technical improvements "could not be considered as a viable alternative to economic convergence." Overfrequent and large realignments risked increasing rather than reducing economic divergence.[38] They did not see the frequency and magnitude of realignments as a sign of the success of the EMS as a monetary framework.

Cooperation at the global level was also increasingly problematic. The Versailles G-7 summit (June 4–6, 1982) was overshadowed by a Franco-American clash on monetary policy. It is usually described as the "first failed summit." The sense of crisis was highlighted by the weakness of the French franc. At the summit, the French prime minister, Pierre Mauroy, ran through the palatial corridors of Versailles chasing President Mitterrand and shouting "I can't hold it, I can't hold it."[39] On

June 12 the franc was devalued by 5.75 percent and the lira by 2.75 percent, while the Deutsche Mark and the Netherlands florin were revalued by 4.25 percent. There were few substantial outcomes of the Versailles summit. The G-7 agreed to a study on the effectiveness of exchange market intervention. But Americans interpreted the rather ambiguous report, which was generally known as the Jurgensen report, as showing intervention to be ineffective, while Europeans reached exactly the opposite conclusion.[40]

At the CoG in November, the new chair of the alternates, the Italian Lamberto Dini, suggested that a system of European multilateral surveillance might reinforce the process of domestic adjustment.[41] This was a revival of a term from the debates of the late 1960s and early 1970s: by the middle of the 1980s, the call for "surveillance" became a central feature of international monetary discussions. Eventually surveillance came to be associated with an identification of objective indicators that would require policy responses; but in the early 1980s it was still unclear which indicators should best be used to assess a country's monetary stance.

How little fundamental consensus there existed was illustrated by the CoG's response to a February 1983 report by the Raymond group (Robert Raymond, an official of the Banque de France, was the successor to Bastiaanse) on intermediate quantitative monetary objectives.[42] The report described the wide variety of existing practices. Richardson and Pöhl set out an overview of the monetary policy approach of their institutions, but Pöhl sounded especially skeptical about quantitative targets, to which he attributed a primarily psychological function; in his view, targets had importance in shaping the expectations of labor and employer bargainers, but not as an operational feature of monetary policy. While the Bundesbank had observed the monetary target framework "faithfully," it was not—as Pöhl put it—"obsessed" by monetary indicators, and knew that it should take account of a large number of other factors. Smaller countries were inevitably more concerned with the exchange rate than with indicators of monetary growth. Erik Hoffmeyer, governor of Danmarks Nationalbank, argued that the publication of a quantitative indicator would perhaps even be counterproductive, and Wim Duisenberg of the Nederlandsche Bank "admitted" that for the Netherlands "monetary objectives had never had a particular actuality." The representative of the EC Commission, Padoa-Schioppa, summed up the discussion by stating that "quantitative monetary indicators held a decreasing importance for central banks." The exchange rate was the critical instrument of policy. Lamfalussy agreed with this interpretation, but emphasized that the "problem of monetary credibility remained." The CoG chairman, de la Genière, also said that inflation still remained a problem, and that there was some need for "enlightened monetarism," even if the committee should pay "less attention to monetary objectives than in the past or in other milieux."[43] The issue of the use of monetary policy became highly politicized. The director of the Dutch treasury, Piet Korteweg, wrote a sternly worded note to his French equivalent (and chair of the EC Monetary Committee) in response to a big surge in interventions that seemed to indicate market expectations of a parity change in the French franc that were not justified by "fundamentals." The Dutch commented that "if fundamentals do not justify these exchange rate expectations the question poses itself whether monetary policy is sufficiently utilized to ensure the maintenance of the existing rates."[44]

At this time the Bank of England cast the European discussion in terms of the difference between a small- and a large-country approach, in which small countries took an exchange rate target and large countries needed to worry about monetary aggregates. Germany appeared to the British economists to be the only EMS country following a large-country monetary policy approach that did not rely on exchange rate objectives. For this reason Britain, which had a similar stance with a high priority on a domestic monetary target, could not join the EMS without coming into conflict with Germany. Indeed, British membership at this time appeared possible only if the pound sterling would "displace the [Deutsche Mark] as the standard currency within the EMS."[45]

The events that changed the EMS came from market attacks, and in particular from the increased vulnerability of the French franc. The Belgian devaluation of 1982 was the critical moment for small-country convergence in the new monetary framework, but March 1983—the crisis of a large country—became the structural break that turned the EMS into a model of how to achieve monetary stability.

A major speculative attack on the French franc began in March 1983, and on March 21 a much more dramatic and comprehensive revaluation occurred. The French franc and the lira were devalued by 2.5

percent, the Irish pound by 3.5 percent, and the Deutsche Mark was revalued by 5.5 percent, the Netherlands guilder by 3.5 percent, the Danish krone by 2.5 percent, and the Belgian franc by 1.5 percent. A general widening of bands had been briefly discussed, but the idea was then dropped.

In the wake of the general realignment, Pöhl made some fundamental and quite radical suggestions: that there might be frequent but small parity alterations, or that the bands should be widened. Lamfalussy commented that the transformation of the EMS into what Samuel Brittan had termed the "crawling peg" mechanism might not be seen as a failure, and that it would still represent a contribution to stability. The most vigorous defense of the older concept of the EMS came from de la Genière, who argued that the system might be "a brake on divergence and a useful constraint." This was clearly the role that he felt the exchange rate mechanism (ERM) had played in French politics. There had been a stark and obvious choice between continuing in the ERM and imposing budgetary austerity, the course advocated by Finance Minister Jacques Delors, and leaving the ERM to embark on a strategy of economic nationalism, as proposed above all by the minister of industry, Jean-Pierre Chevènement. On March 14, in bilateral negotiations with Germany, France had threatened that it might leave the EMS altogether. Some of these threats may have been nothing more than a negotiating ploy, but they were deeply destructive. De la Genière summed up the process as follows: "The threat of monetary adjustments, and the psychodramas that they represent, contribute to bringing a little more wisdom to the economic policy of the member countries." It was important to avoid the impression that the system would be softened.[46]

The French solution to the severe 1983 crisis became a model for a new vision of how central banks could operate politically in order to produce enhanced economic stability. That vision was especially important in the domestic political context of France and Italy. The idea underlying the French strategy of the *franc fort*, which began with the crisis of March 1983, was that it would constrain domestic policy. Mitterrand had to wrestle with a fractious range of coalition partners: with the Communists, whom he wanted to marginalize politically, but also with leftist Jacobin Socialists such as Chevènement, who wanted a national path of economic development, which in practice meant a boost to competitiveness through devaluation. Some of the most important industrial leaders, such as Jean Riboud, president of the large oil and gas development company Schlumberger, also pleaded for a national path in secret "night visits" to the Elysée presidential place.[47] At other moments the same coalition problems arose for center-right governments, with nationalist Gaullists looking for a more étatist solution while liberal Giscardiens sought more international accommodation. The attraction of an externally imposed monetary regime lay in the limits it imposed on coalition politics, and in consequence it could be interpreted as a mechanism for strengthening the executive. A strong central bank could thus make politics work more efficiently and more stably. Italy, with its own history of unstable coalitions, and tensions between the wings of the largest ruling party, the Christian Democrats, also looked to external discipline as a source of reform.

Politics operated in a rather different way in Germany, as well as in the smaller European countries. German governments, though also based on coalitions, offered a higher degree of political coherence, and correspondingly less of a need (or a willingness) to refer to outside restraints. Their restraint was also provided by the anti-inflationary tradition of the Bundesbank. As a result smaller countries simply regarded Germany as a pole of monetary stability: the Netherlands and Austria (though not a member of the EC) had embarked on this course since the 1970s; they were now joined by Belgium and Denmark. In consequence, German policymakers looked as if they preferred the more radical "corner solutions" of either exchange rate flexibility or a complete monetary union. The Bundesbank saw no need for changeable bands as a way of imposing discipline (it used monetary aggregates and not exchange rates to determine policy) and disliked the monetary consequences that flowed from interventions. Pöhl thus seemed often to be in the peculiar position of sometimes making arguments that implied a need for greater flexibility, and sometimes being sympathetic to the arguments for a complete and irreversible fixing of the sort advocated by Padoa-Schioppa. Both versions had the overwhelming merit of not requiring interventions by the Bundesbank.

Pöhl later added to his set of arguments on the exchange rate issue the observation that adjustable exchange rates offered a larger scope for differences in interest rates, and used as evidence the difference of over 5 points between German and U.S. rates. He added that such a difference would not be possible if the dollar were linked into the European currencies in an EMS type of system. The advocacy of flexibility inevitably conflicted with the French conception of the role of exchange rates in limiting domestic political possibilities. De la Genière again insisted on the "pedagogic virtue" of the EMS, a point reinforced by the lessons of March 1983. An enlargement of the fluctuation bands would simply be "a sign that governments are giving themselves additional possibilities."[48]

The alternates' report of July 1983 was indecisive. It included the suggestion that in particular the big countries were too hesitant in adjusting exchange rates, but then went on to argue that frequent parity alterations might encourage speculation and increase the magnitude of changes. Fundamentally the report warned against transforming the EMS into a system of gliding parities. The report also rejected the idea, occasionally advocated in Frankfurt, of widening margins.[49]

France had definitively embarked on a new course, in which the exchange rate was considered a desirable constraint. The U-turn of the Mitterrand government became the model of a Socialist acceptance of the market and its discipline, not only for France but also for other European countries. Finance Minister Jacques Delors had been the crucial figure in persuading Mitterrand to turn to Europe as a source of political discipline, and the lessons of the 1983 experience provided a foundation for his subsequent campaigns as Commission president in Brussels. There were two major lessons. First, a firm monetary framework was needed for any experiment in market economics to work. Second, some sort of fiscal rule was needed: the 3 percent of GDP limit on government deficits that emerged as a response to the French crisis would later (in the 1990s) provide the guideline for a European approach.

A key part of the French strategy lay in the engineering of disinflation. By December 1983 de la Genière was speaking of monetary growth having been reduced from 15 percent in previous years to 9 percent in 1983; and for 1984 he wanted to establish a target slightly above the forecast 7.5 percent nominal GDP growth.[50] The changing French approach emphasized use of the exchange rate as a tool against inflationary expectations, and took the strong franc (franc fort) as a policy basis.

On the international level, even the United States appeared briefly to be worried about the exchange rate. In July 1983 the United States proposed some concerted interventions, even though according to Pöhl these were carried out in a "feeble and overtimorous" manner. They were certainly ineffective. But they marked a break with the previous U.S. stance of nonintervention.[51] In 1984 the monetary attention of the world was focused more and more monothematically on the staggering rise of the U.S. dollar. After a brief interlude of dollar weakness in January, the greenback continued to rise. U.S. policy had two effects on the European debate: in the first place, European problems had always been easier to solve in periods of dollar appreciation because of the dollar/Deutsche Mark polarization effect; second, anti-inflation credibility became an international fashion in what was subsequently called "the Great Moderation." The adoption of such policy in Europe made for greater policy convergence and hence also for a much smoother functioning of the EMS.

By the time the EMS celebrated its fifth anniversary, a kind of calm had descended. The central bank governors were keen not to become involved in a debate with finance ministers about the system, as that might give rise to worries or speculations on the currency markets; and they avoided participating in the meeting of the European Council on March 12, 1984. There was a low-profile meeting at Rambouillet on May 12–13, with some discussion of very modest incremental adjustments to the working of the EMS so as to reinforce its operation in a "significant and equilibrated" fashion. In 1983 even the regular meetings of the CoG became more intermittent. The alternates described the system as becoming much "firmer." The way to deter speculation, they argued, was to avoid realignments as far as possible, and thus inflict losses on speculators who were betting on pushing currencies off their EMS peg. Lamfalussy explained the greater stability of the system in part as a result of the difficulties faced by speculators in concentrating on more than one currency, and in part as a result of the strength of the current accounts of Germany and the United Kingdom. Pöhl took the more global view that the system was most under strain in a period of dollar weakness, and that the EMS had been conceived in 1979 as a barrier against such weakness.[52]

In the meeting of finance ministers on March 12, 1984, France's finance minister, Jacques Delors, proposed a more general discussion of means to improve the functioning of the EMS, including ensuring that the divergence indicator played a part in the process of policy adjustment. The communiqué of the meeting described the EMS as "a precious inheritance." In July the Dalgaard group (the Danish central bank official Henning Dalgaard had taken over Heyvaert's chairmanship of the foreign exchange experts' group) produced a wide-ranging report. It contained a section on the advantages of sterling's participation in the EMS, and of the reduction of the Italian fluctuation bands; another section proposed the removal of the 50 percent acceptance level that might be settled in ECUs for obligations arising out of the VSTF (which had originated in a German demand to prevent the Bundesbank from being overwhelmed by ECUs).[53] In the September CoG meeting Pöhl stated that the most important improvement in the working of the EMS would be the membership of all EC countries; and the new governor of the Bank of England, Robin Leigh-Pemberton, stated that he hoped the United Kingdom would join the system and that he supported the reports of the Dalgaard group and of the alternates.[54] Such a stance demonstrated a considerable degree of autonomy from the British government, since Prime Minister Margaret Thatcher was stridently opposed to EMS membership.

The veteran EC finance and monetary affairs commissioner, François-Xavier Ortoli, said that the Commission was not "displaying extreme activism," but was interested in mechanisms that would tend to a greater acceptance and use of the ECU.[55] The proposed measures were the small steps that had already been debated for years to allow a greater use of EC currencies in interventions. There was substantial agreement in the CoG on a "modest packet" of reforms: moving the rate of remuneration on the ECU close to a market rate (by basing the rate on the money market rather than on central bank discount rates); increasing the mobilization facilities, in other words, allowing central banks to acquire dollars or other EC currencies against ECUs for two successive three-month periods; and extending third-party use of official ECUs by other central banks.[56] Many governors also suggested removing the 50 percent acceptance limit. Most analysts at the time and subsequently saw these reforms as essentially "dead end" steps, in that they did not attempt to enhance the private use of ECUs.[57] But even on such relatively minor issues, it was hard to build a consensus. Belgium, the only large net debtor at this time, argued strongly in favor of allowing a greater use of ECUs in voluntary or intramarginal interventions; while the Bundesbank feared being overwhelmed by a flood of ECUs.[58] The packet as a whole was delayed by Germany, and Pöhl placed a reserve on the decision. Pöhl also expressed resentment of the Commission's attempt to launch proposals at the ECOFIN on December 10, 1984.[59] In 1985 the new governor of the Banque de France, Michel Camdessus (who had come into office in November 1984), appealed to the governors to produce an agreement on these issues, as they were "the professionals, and they ran the risk that others would get involved."[60]

Meanwhile there was some evidence that a limited private market in ECUs was developing. Lamfalussy presented material showing that bank credits in ECUs had risen by 80 percent from December 1983 to June 1984.[61] The EEC and the two other European communities of the 1950s, Euratom and the European Coal and Steel Community, had all launched ECU bonds, as had the European Investment Bank. The ECU clearly at this point overtook the other international artificial currency, the SDR, where the extent of private use was restricted through the absence of any official support. At the end of December 1981 there was an estimated 300 million in ECU bank deposits, but by June 1985 there were 33.342 billion. Over the same period the volume of SDR bank deposits had contracted from an estimated 10–14 billion to 1.666 billion.[62]

The major shocks continued to be external, generated by the long-extended phase of dollar appreciation. In 1984 the dollar rose by 15 percent relative to EC currencies, with interventions of $19 billion in purchases and $26 billion in sales doing little to affect a movement driven fundamentally by interest-rate differentials.

At the beginning of 1985, as the dollar reached its high-water mark on the foreign exchange markets, the governors embarked on a new extended analysis of the way in which the EMS had affected relative competitive positions. France had suffered from increased costs at the outset of the EMS and had corrected them with three realignments; but since 1983 the external balance was progressively deteriorating once more, according to the presentation given by Lamfalussy. The Netherlands and Denmark by contrast had experienced relative productivity gains. Pöhl observed that a strong dollar was preferable to the weak dollar of the late 1970s and strains between Germany and the other EEC members were not so immediately apparent. Inflation was being generally reduced. The U.S. authorities should be persuaded to build up reserves that could be used in intervention. Ciampi agreed with this diagnosis, but added a warning that constituted one of the first discussions of the impact of liberalized capital movements on southern European countries: the strong dollar, he said, had forced European high-inflation countries to maintain a high-interest-rate regime, and had consequently attracted potentially unstable capital inflows.[63]

All the governors participated in an informal meeting with finance ministers and with the EC Commission at Palermo (April 13–15, 1985), at which the small packet of reform measures was agreed. The new president of the Commission, Jacques Delors, argued that it was necessary for the CoG and the Monetary Committee to pay more attention to what was happening on the "institutionalist" side, and was thinking of the reforms as part of a general package of measures, including capital account liberalization, which would form the core of the Single European Act.[64] The central bank reforms designed to strengthen the EMS were accepted by the European Council in October 1985, with the first use of the new extended EMCF mobilization credits coming at the end of the year.[65] It is important to note that at this stage there was little inclination to move to a more generalized or formal fixing of the system to ensure that parity changes became a rarity. That consensus emerged only later in the 1980s. At the first meeting of the CoG he attended, Delors supported the idea of "dedramatizing" parity alterations, and found a powerful ally in Pöhl. This was the beginning of a tension-filled but ultimately productive relationship that was a key to the future discussion of monetary union. Pöhl concurred with Delors, warned that a buildup of differentials would bring an increase in potential tensions, and suggested periodic 2 to 3 percent alterations. Pöhl's skeptical thoughts about the future of the ECU were supported by Leigh-Pemberton, who described a central money and a European central bank as "almost futurism."[66]

In May 1985, in the presence of Delors, the CoG started a new round of discussion of the long-term prospects of the EMS. Pöhl suggested, remarkably, that it was "time to detach ourselves from the conclusions of Bremen—a text that was a little bit the product of a chance confluence of ideas—and return to the Werner Plan, which is a much more profound study of economic and monetary union, and which has many elements that are still perfectly valuable." Camdessus complained that "in some countries it was not accepted that the EU was an essential piece of the monetary construction." This was a thinly camouflaged reference to the fact that from the perspective of Paris, Germany was almost as problematical as the United Kingdom. Leigh-Pemberton also provided a quite surprising and bold view: the EMCF should evolve toward the functions of a central bank and not constitute a little IMF, "even if that meant recasting the decisions taken in Bremen and Brussels." It might "become the banker of the community."[67]

Delors started by recalling the debates of the late 1960s and early 1970s, which had pitted "monetarists" against "economists"; he then promised to take no initiatives except "in tight harmonization with the CoG and the Monetary Committee." He took a highly "economist" position that seemed to line up with German preferences: "It was necessary to avoid treating the monetary question in an incorrect way, as some people imagine that by the use of money it might be possible to remove institutional obstacles that derive from fundamental differences about the amount of sovereignty that states are prepared to concede to a European union."[68] Delors's thinking fitted in well with Pöhl's concerns, especially in the link he established between monetary issues and the new issue of capital market liberalization, which represented a major part of the Commission's agenda for strengthening European integration. According to the president of the Bundesbank, the CoG should remind heads of state that the "EMS works satisfactorily and much better than other community mechanisms. . . . The real problems stem from the nonmembership of the United Kingdom and the incomplete liberalization of capital movements. . . . the maintenance of exchange restrictions is incompatible with a path toward monetary union."[69] The governors and the alternates should continue to work toward a European money that could compete with the dollar. This extraordinary rapprochement between the Bundesbank and the Commission set the stage for the beginning of the big reform discussions of the late 1980s.

An informal ECOFIN meeting in Luxembourg on September 21, 1985, agreed that Delors would invite the heads of the CoG and the Monetary Committee for talks. The October 22 meeting produced an agreement that on October 25–26 the German state secretary in the Finance Ministry, Hans Tietmeyer, would present a document on reform of the EMS. On October 28 a further ECOFIN meeting finally proposed to incorporate the EMS more formally in the EC institutional structure by setting in motion the mechanism for a revision of the Treaty of Rome (an amendment of Article 107 was required).

The CoG clarified its position on strengthening the EMS to the finance ministers on November 12, 1985, referring to the following principles:

(a) there should be equilibrium between progress in the monetary and the non-monetary sphere;

(b) the decision-making process should remain unchanged and the checks and balances existing in Member States between central banks and governments should be respected;

(c) the change in the Treaty should be placed in the context of Economic and Monetary Union as the ultimate objective, taking into account the experience gained in the EMS as the framework for monetary co-operation.[70]

The report was discussed by the ECOFIN on November 18, 1985, with Delors arguing that "progressive improvement of the EMS was possible, but it required the agreement of the central bank governors, and it could be achieved through a practical approach not covered by the treaty." The German finance minister, Gerhard Stoltenberg, again raised the central point of the Emminger letter, stating that "the Commission's proposals had been carefully examined in the Federal Republic, notably in view of the undertaking the German Government had given the Bundesbank in 1978, on the occasion of the establishment of the EMS, that it would not take political decisions without the agreement of the central bank." Chancellor of the Exchequer Nigel Lawson noted that "the UK authorities could not accept the introduction of a monetary dimension." To all this, French Finance Minister Pierre Bérégovoy riposted by complaining about the "blackmail of Germany and the UK."[71]

Exchange rate crises continued, as a consequence of inadequate convergence. After a widening current account and budget deficit, Italy asked for a realignment on July 18, 1985, a Thursday, with an 8 percent devaluation. The request was to be kept secret until the close of business on the Friday, and the Banca d'Italia decided to limit interventions without publicizing this move. But the large energy company ENI decided to buy $125 million on the foreign exchange market and set off a chaotic panic. The Banca d'Italia then advised the treasury minister to close the foreign exchange market altogether.[72] The episode seemed to indicate to many newspaper commentators that Italy was bouncing the other EC countries into a realignment, and at the same time allowing insiders to benefit. Italy's reform package included a modification, though not a complete abandonment, of the infamous wage indexation mechanism, the *scala mobile*. For similar reasons, an Irish devaluation, also of 8 percent, was announced in August 1986.

The largest of the mid-1980s movements involved the devaluation of the French franc by 6 percent on April 6, 1986 (a Sunday). It was fundamentally designed to close the gap in competitiveness with Germany that had opened up since the last big realignment in March 1983. But it had been conducted in a rather messy way, because the meeting of an informal ECOFIN had led to market rumors of an imminent change of parities. In consequence at the end of the afternoon of Thursday, April 3, the Banque de France announced that on Friday it would no longer defend the exchange rate limits, and the other EMS central banks agreed to act in a similar way. (There had been a similar process on March 21, 1983, as well as for the Italian case in July 1985.) But the fact that there was formally no EMS for one day, April 4, 1986, caused considerable difficulties for ordinary commercial transactions, and the Bundesbank continued to quote a Deutsche Mark/dollar rate.[73]

These were the last old-style realignments, responding to a long-term shift of fundamentals. The next crises were to be driven by speculative pressures, stemming from much larger capital movements, and would raise much more basic questions about the sustainability of the system and the appropriate management of Europe's money.

In general, the European framework seemed to be becoming more attractive. A new EC member, Greece, on October 11, 1985, announced a stabilization plan involving a 15 percent devaluation of the drachma, though it remained outside the EMS. European financial support was an easier alternative to IMF-imposed austerity, and in the end it could be bought as part of a political deal in which Greece accepted the Single European Act (which required unanimity). At the European Council meeting in Luxembourg on December 3–4, 1985, it became clear that the support of the Greek government for the new framework depended on a satisfactory financial assistance framework. The most important piece of legislation for the advancement of the European project was thus bought with European funding for Greece.

The Single European Act, which was negotiated in 1985 and signed in February 1986, marked the beginning of a new acceptance of market principles. It emphasized four "freedoms," of goods, services, capital, and labor, and made the introduction of measures necessary for the completion of the internal market by the end of 1992 possible through a qualified majority voting process, in which larger countries had a greater voting power. Europe was beginning to embark on a new kind of liberalization, which would also require a new approach to exchange rate issues. The most important conversion took place in France. In 1985 France abandoned the system of managed credit that had been at the center of postwar development policy.[74] This was possible, as the new governor of the Banque de France Michel Camdessus argued, because of the success of the disinflation process. France was accepting the liberal and open international economy, but that acceptance prompted a new thinking about the way in which such an economy could and should be regulated.

The question of how far the EMS was responsible for the new policy convergence is not easy to answer. Exchange rates had become more stable, and inflation differentials, which had been very high in the early 1980s, began quite slowly to converge. But there was also a worldwide move to disinflation. The most convincing argument is that the EMS could be used to enhance policy credibility, because it functioned as a mechanism for "tying hands" (in the phrase of Francesco Giavazzi and Marco Pagano).[75] The improved policy environment required more institutional steps—not just the timid small measures that had been the hallmark of European debates in the first half of the 1980s.

In the context of the very limited reform discussion of the mid-1980s, it became apparent that the bold move envisaged by Delors of a liberalization of capital movements might endanger the whole system. In an academic study for the Federal Reserve completed at this time, Kenneth Rogoff examined the causes of the conspicuous success in the reduction of volatility in intra-EMS exchange rates (while the dollar, yen, and pound rates in relation to the Deutsche Mark had all become more volatile). He concluded that the convergence of inflation rates had been slow, and that there were high levels of variation in conditional (unanticipated) real interest rates. For Rogoff, the lesson was clear: the system was held together primarily by capital controls.[76] What would happen when these were abolished?

The debate about the source of enhanced credibility in the EMS came in a politicized form. Were the French fears of 1978 about the "empire of the Mark" incorrect? By the 1980s there was a near consensus about the new character of monetary hegemony in Europe. According to Giavazzi and Alberto Giovannini, "Germany is the centre country and runs monetary policy for the whole system." Stanley Fischer described the EMS as "an arrangement by France and Italy to accept German leadership, imposing constraints on their domestic monetary and fiscal policies."[77] The discussion focused on the asymmetry of adjustment: as in other fixed-exchange-rate systems, notably the interwar gold standard, the deficit countries adjusted while the surplus countries did not. Paul Krugman commented in 1990 that

> since the FRG [Federal Republic of Germany] is the most credibly anti-inflationary of the major European economies, it is useful for other nations to follow the FRG's lead as a way of borrowing credibility—a bit of political slipstreaming that is helped by the lucky coincidence that the economy with the sternest managers is also the largest. What is particularly interesting is the way that this strongly asymmetric system is entirely implicit, a matter of latent rather than manifest function. . . . One of the main difficulties with a move to a common currency might be that the ability to cloak reality would be reduced.[78]

This conclusion was not confined to economists. The British chancellor of the Exchequer, Nigel Lawson, saw Bundesbank President Karl Otto Pöhl as having played a decisive role in provoking a bitter and fateful backlash against German monetary hegemony: "It was the way in which Pöhl openly revelled in his role, via the EMS, of the ruler of Europe's monetary affairs and arbiter of its destiny . . . that the French . . . found so intolerable that they were prepared to sacrifice their own national independence in order to see the Bundesbank abolished."[79]

The head of the Bundesbank's International Department, Wolfgang Rieke, also tried to explain the accidental character of hegemony, and asserted that the Bundesbank had not sought its pivotal role: "use of the DM as a preferred intervention currency and its role as 'anchor' of exchange rate stability was not an explicit component of the original design of the EMS, though it was perhaps unavoidable to begin with. The adoption of the 'parity grid' rather than an ECU-based intervention system must have strengthened the DM's claim to that role. It was certainly not a role sought or imposed on the system by its largest partner."[80]

The debates about German power and what could or should be done about it arose immediately whenever questions of institutional reform were considered. The narrative of misbehaving hegemons, whether they were in Washington or in Frankfurt, provoked in other countries a call for more clearly elaborated rules and processes to keep the hegemons under the closer control of a broader international community. Such a demand for the application of procedural innovations was thus at the heart of the reflections and conclusions of the Delors Committee in the late 1980s. Delors himself, however, drew a much more subtle conclusion. He noted the substantial similarities between his own critique of the EMS and Karl Otto Pöhl's intellectually coherent preference for the clarity of corner solutions, either more flexibility of exchange rates or a complete overhaul that would require a much more substantial application of monetary discipline.

7

The Delors Committee and
the Relaunching of Europe

The Delors Committee—on which all the EC central bank governors sat in a personal capacity—occupies a prominent place in the demonology of those looking for conspiracies in committees. It was the decisive group that prepared the blueprint for Europe's transition to monetary union. Between September 1988 and April 1989, it developed a stage mechanism for the implementation of a union. The meetings occurred before the collapse of Communism in eastern Europe and the disintegration of the German Democratic Republic. Those geopolitical events created a new fear in France and other European countries about the extent of the new German power, and led to a search for ways of controlling and circumscribing Germany. But the thinking about the road map to European monetary union was already in place before the dramatic political upheavals that followed from the end of the Cold War.

The impact of the Delors Committee was a surprise. One of its most powerful members, Bundesbank President Karl Otto Pöhl, was generally believed to be opposed to any project for enhanced monetary cooperation, and the Euroskeptic British government thought that the governor of the Bank of England could line up with Pöhl to block any scheme of Delors. Since the committee's report required unanimity in order to be convincing or effective, it seemed more or less certain at the outset that the project would not lead to the visionary result intended by Jacques Delors. So how did the committee reach such a stunning outcome—without raising any of the big political and geopolitical concerns that dominated the later stages of planning for a common European money? The central bankers who dominated the committee merely saw themselves as doing their traditional job. In particular, they believed that they were elaborating a logic of international monetary cooperation that had already been debated and tested on the global level. The paradox was that the Bundesbank appeared to be the institution most opposed to institutionalized European and global monetary cooperation, but the solution devised was to imitate or adopt as much of the Bundesbank model as possible.

In retrospect, the report of the Delors Committee appears to have laid out a clear and unambiguous blueprint for monetary unification that would eventually result in the creation of the European Central Bank and the single currency. But at the time, there were considerable doubts about the viability of the report, even (or especially) among the members and staff of the committee. Invited by the economist Peter Kenen to produce a pamphlet on the Delors Report for Princeton University's International Economics series, Tommaso Padoa-Schioppa declined on the grounds that he did not think the outcome would be very significant. Even later, Pöhl complained that the report was "a confused piece of work. There were some wild ideas in it."[1] Erik Hoffmeyer, the veteran Danish central banker and a prominent presence on the CoG, was also surprisingly critical in public. In private, the British governor, Robin Leigh-Pemberton, claimed that "most of us, when we signed the Report in May 1989, thought that we would not hear much about it. It would be rather like the Werner Report."[2] Monetary union was still defined in a way that stopped significantly short of a single currency. An irrevocable fixing of exchange rates and "a currency area in which policies are managed jointly with a view to attaining common macroeconomic objectives" did not clearly and unambiguously provide for a single monetary authority. In fact the outcome looked more like an extension of the principle of international monetary cooperation and coordination—which is exactly what it was.

There are at least four ways of thinking about the negotiation of the last steps to monetary unification: first, in a broad perspective, as an issue of identity politics; second, as the outgrowth of political entrepreneurship on the part of the EC Commission; third, as a power struggle between nation-states; and fourth, as the product of a global debate about rules and rule-setting in an era of increasingly apparent financial globalization in which markets seemed more and more to be driving the political process. These interpretations are not necessarily mutually exclusive, but they focus on rather different elements in the story of European development.

At a fundamental level, it may be that the process was driven by a feeling of Europeanness. Nothing ever happens without ideals, or in this case without a certain idea of Europe. Some interpreters go as far as to claim that the "support for EMU by the political elites in most member states cannot be defined on the basis of materially defined economic or foreign policy interest." As a consequence, the monetary discussion was driven by allegedly "hot" visions of European identity rather than by cold political calculation.[3]

The second, and most popular, tradition of analysis sees monetary union as the outcome of a series of initiatives launched by the EC Commission from Brussels. The criteria determining the "success" of a Commission presidency relate mostly to the quality of leadership in suggesting new modes and mechanisms of integration. Commission presidents are expected to be policy entrepreneurs, and Jacques Delors appears to have been strikingly active and also unusually successful in this regard. European integration has been filled with many initiatives, which usually fizzled out in a bureaucratic swamp. Delors's initiatives were distinguished by the care with which they were embedded in an overall vision. He was quite candid about the extent of his ambition. In a July 1988 speech to the European Parliament in Strasbourg he stated: "we are not going to manage to take all the decisions we need between now and 1995 unless we see the beginnings of European government in one form or another."[4] Delors is without question the most charismatic and successful Commission president the European Community/European Union has ever had.

It was an initiative by Delors that launched the committee that is always referred to by his name. From the beginning, he had detached monetary affairs from the economics commissariat in the Commission and kept these issues as part of what might be regarded as a presidential *domaine réservé*. Delors brilliantly inveigled the central bankers into his plan. Academic observers describe the process, using a French term, as *engrenage*, a socialization process in which central bankers and civil servants are included "in order to form a solid network of influence."[5] The eventual success of his plan invites a comparison of the effectiveness of different Commission presidents and initiators of policy: Marjolin's initiatives in the 1960s in the end disappointed him;

Jenkins in the late 1970s produced overbold proposals that in the end were held to be unrealistic and were sidelined by Giscard and Schmidt; and on the other hand in the mid-1970s Ortoli was too sober and pragmatic. Delors worked with just the right mixture of vision and practical sense: the vision of a bold move to realize the idea of "Union," and the pragmatic acknowledgment that only the central bankers could remove the obstacles (especially the political and institutional barriers that existed in Germany and in the particular position of the Bundesbank). Dismissing the bankers as fundamentally obstructive, as Jenkins and German Chancellor Helmut Schmidt had done in the late 1970s, would only create an institutional impasse. Binding them in opened the way to a process of innovation.

The Commission-centered view of the integration process makes sense in a bigger way, in that many people could see the move to a single currency as a logical extension of the Single European Act of 1986 and the establishment of a unified market area in which capital would freely flow by 1992. Indeed the Commission itself adopted this position when it set out the argument for further advances in the move to European Union. At the start of the process, in 1985, Delors had reached the conclusion that free capital movement was essential to the realization of the 1992 program, and it was equally apparent that the free circulation of capital would require a new approach to monetary policy.[6] A significant step was made in November 1986, when the Commission directed the transfer of a substantial group of categories of capital movement from the conditional list of 1960 to the unconditional list. In 1988 a final directive provided for a general liberalization of capital movements. Eventually the 1989 Madrid summit acknowledged the strength of the logical link between capital market developments and monetary union when it determined that Stage One of monetary union would begin in July 1990 with the final removal of capital controls.

The Bundesbank began to worry that the new wave of European integration was being driven unilaterally from the monetary side, without any economic convergence. The Single European Act contained no new initiatives in nonmonetary areas, but pushed the capital liberalization issue, and also included an odd subheading in Article 20 that referred explicitly (but without any follow-up in the text) to Economic and Monetary Union. The oddity of a subheading that stood on its own was attributed by some to the machinations of German Foreign Minister

Hans-Dietrich Genscher. Delors later proudly referred to this reference as a "little white pebble" that he had carefully and deliberately thrown on the ground, like Petit Poucet in the fairy story, in order to show a way out of the maze (in the Hansel and Gretel version of the same story, birds eat up the breadcrumbs left as markers).[7]

As part of his initiative Delors also proposed to integrate the EMS (whose legal status was merely an agreement between central banks) into the Treaty of Rome, an idea heavily criticized by some central bankers, notably Leigh-Pemberton and Pöhl. As a consequence of Delors's new vision, the EMS and the ECU were both built into the Single European Act, a measure that added to the feeling in the Bundesbank that the process of European integration was being shifted unilaterally to the monetary dimension.[8]

The issue of whether capital market liberalization required a monetary union provoked substantial debate. As Robert Mundell had pointed out in the 1960s, free capital movements and a fixed exchange rate ruled out independent monetary policy; and in the later 1980s Tommaso Padoa-Schioppa reformulated this proposition as the "inconsistent quartet" of policy objectives: free trade, capital mobility, fixed or managed exchange rates, and monetary policy independence.[9] This was obviously not an analysis that was simply restricted to the European setting. But given the centrality of the principle of free trade to the European integration process, the analysis had a particular relevance to a Europe facing the consequences of capital market integration. An April 1987 report prepared by Padoa-Schioppa for the European Commission made this point very clearly.[10] Louis Tsoukalis noted sharply: "Most of the analysis and the new ideas on monetary union came from the Italians, the political institutions from the French, both in Paris and Brussels, the technical support, the organization, and the follow-up from the Commission, while the real power continued to reside with the Germans."[11]

Third, the late 1980s can be interpreted as an era of struggle in power politics. There is a naïve version, as well as a much more sophisticated gloss, on this interpretation. Daniel Gros and Niels Thygesen rightly dismiss the "simplistic argument that EMU was simply a quid pro quo: French acceptance of German reunification in return for EMU." But the argument has some appeal, and if it is presented in a sophisticated way, and includes the way in which internal and international bargaining between interests is reflected in the formulation of national policy, it has a substantial analytical power. Scholars such as Robert Putnam, Andrew Moravcsik, and Barry Eichengreen and Jeffrey Frieden try to explain the origins of foreign strategies in terms of a complex domestic balance of interests.[12]

The late 1980s saw a renewal of the long-standing clash of interpretations of European integration between France and Germany, again in response to the emergence of a strong German surplus position. French policymakers, especially the president of the French Republic, pressed for a mechanism of asserting political control of the economy, or "economic governance," while Germans, especially in the independent-minded central bank, argued that any institutional arrangement must shield a future central banking system from political interference. The Germans still repeated the "coronation" theory that had played a key role in the debates of the early 1970s: a move to monetary union should take place only when there was a substantive economic convergence. In contrast, for France monetary union looked like a way of laying the basis for a new economic policy at the Community level. The debates of the 1970s between "monetarists" (who held the French vision) and "economists" (the Germans) were thus revived. At the same time, a conspiracy theory began to flourish around the notion that Germany was imposing a fixed and final exchange rate regime that would impose a cost disadvantage in the form of a creeping loss of competitiveness on its neighbors. To some extent, these clashes were played out around the Delors Committee, and in the official French response to the committee; but surprisingly, they were not fought out within the committee.

Finally, the debates of the late 1970s recurred not just in a European setting but on a global level. As in the later 1970s, when problems in the United States and the rapid depreciation of the dollar had summoned a European response, the most fundamental international problems did not exist on a simply European stage. Many of the problems in Europe followed from the dramatic exchange rate movements between the Deutsche Mark and the dollar, which resulted in large part from the combination of Paul Volcker's tight monetary policy and the large fiscal deficits of the Reagan presidency (especially during the first term). In fact the negotiations about European monetary union began as a discussion of the institutional setting in which international monetary cooperation could really be made to work.

International Tensions and European Responses

The international tensions of the mid-1980s produced the most coherent—but also the least effective—set of institutional responses at any time since the collapse of the par value system. The central mechanism was the G-5 finance ministers' meeting, which at this time became extended to a G-7. At their meetings in New York's Plaza Hotel and in the Louvre in Paris, the finance ministers took on the question of what exchange rates were appropriate; and central bankers, who were also represented in the meetings, appeared to be overruled. The Plaza meeting (September 22, 1985) agreed on coordinated intervention to drive down the dollar exchange rate. The Bundesbank had been intervening regularly in the dollar market as the dollar rose, but then stopped in the spring of 1985, with the last big sale of dollars on March 1, and no interventions at all after March 4. But after the Plaza the Bundesbank and the Bank of Japan came back into the market with heavy dollar sales (see Figure 7.1).

The Plaza meeting had been preceded by an ECOFIN meeting in Luxembourg on September 21–22, when the European governments accepted increased intervention in the exchange markets. European and international or global discussions were locked together, often with the same participants meeting in different contexts.

The strength of the dollar highlighted the issue of current account surpluses in the creditor countries, Japan and Germany. In 1987 a Commission document referred to the "unprecedentedly large external imbalances between countries and huge swings in real exchange rates."[13]

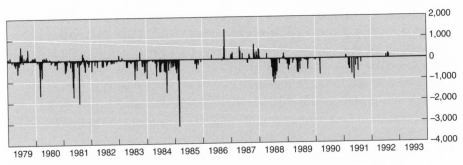

Figure 7.1. Deutsche Mark interventions in dollars, 1979–1993 (millions of DM).
Source: Federal Reserve Bank of Saint Louis.

Exchange interventions became highly politicized in the mid-1980s as a result of the increased liberalization of capital movements and the consequent change in policy instruments available to central banks. Control of credit, a traditional instrument of central bank policy in the 1960s and 1970s, in particular became ineffective in relation to cross-national capital flows. Moreover, intervention when not sterilized threatened the control of monetary policy. The Bundesbank continually worried about the monetary effects of buying foreign currency with Deutsche Marks. Finally, interventions could produce big effects on the balance sheets of central banks, leading to large and embarrassing losses, but also sometimes to gains that could be at least as difficult and embarrassing politically.

Interventions reached their highest level after the inception of the EMS in 1986–1987, at $192.9 billion gross (compared with $146.5 billion in 1983–1985); and a relatively large share of the interventions, about a fifth of the total, occurred in dollars.[14]

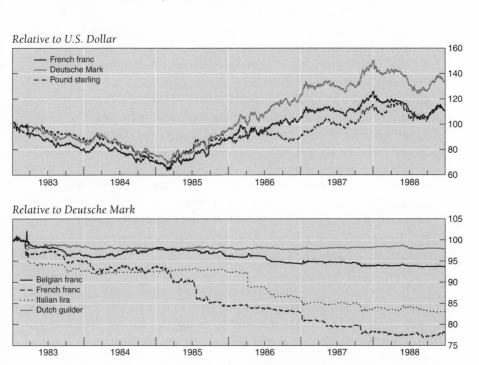

Figure 7.2. Exchange rates, 1982–1989. Beginning of period=100. *Source:* National data.

At the Plaza meeting there was no discussion of interest-rate policy or of monetary policy. Indeed, as Barry Eichengreen points out, "the web of interlocking agreements needed to lock in policy adjustments" was absent.[15] The Bundesbank was deeply suspicious of the whole exercise. Pöhl explained that it would be a mistake to fix exchange rate targets, as such targets would need to be defended through foreign exchange interventions.[16] The Bundesbank believed that Treasury Secretary James Baker had consulted too much with the German finance minister, Gerhard Stoltenberg, and with his state secretary, Hans Tietmeyer, and had ignored the legally guaranteed position of the German central bank. But Pöhl did agree to participate in the interventions to bring down the dollar, while insisting that other central banks take the lead in such interventions.

The mood worsened with the September 21, 1986, Gleneagles (Scotland) meeting of EC and U.S. finance ministers, where the Europeans resisted U.S. pressure for fiscal expansion, but apparently agreed that the Bundesbank would make more intramarginal interventions to support EMS parities. The meeting raised a problem that would be at the center of European and international tensions for the next five years: Was the Bundesbank really committed by the policy choices agreed by German ministers or government representatives in an international diplomatic negotiation? The Bundesbank almost reflexively resisted when it believed that it was being subjected to political pressure. At the Bundesbank Council meeting following Gleneagles, there was no rate change, and the United States started to attack German policymakers very directly. But the Bundesbank was really not strong enough to stand up to such an orchestration of demands, so it needed to cast around for allies. Some analysts have concluded that this was the moment at which a "pivotal shift" occurred in Europeanizing Germany's monetary policies. In particular, the Bundesbank needed to look more to a European mechanism for building support for its bargaining position in a German context.[17]

The same pressures that flowed very powerfully from Washington had occurred on the European level, though in a milder form. In July 1986 at the CoG, the Banque de France had set out proposals for increasing EMCF use of privately traded ECUs, and the Banca d'Italia—apparently in a coordinated attempt to put pressure on Germany—had prepared a proposal that official ECU holdings should be deposited in commercial banks, again with the aim of stimulating the use of the ECU.[18] From the Bundesbank's perspective, this looked like a way of developing a parallel currency that could then be used for interventions that might endanger German monetary control. Throughout this period the Frankfurt bank was worried that its domestic monetary target (with a corridor of 3.5–5.5 percent) was being exceeded and was leading to a risk of inflation. In September 1986 the director of the French treasury complained that Bundesbank resistance had been blocking progress on strengthening the EMS in the CoG and in the Monetary Committee.[19]

As in the past, the rapid decline of the dollar imposed enormous strains on the EMS. The Dalgaard group (on foreign exchange issues) asked whether more coordinated interventions might not have put a brake on the dollar fall, and thus also reduced the likelihood of a European crisis.[20] The fewer interventions there were, the more policy controversies centered on interest-rate differentials and hence on the issue of monetary policy.

The last parity alteration of the EMS before the debate on monetary union intensified took place on January 12, 1987, when the Deutsche Mark and the Dutch guilder were revalued by 3 percent and the Belgian franc by 2 percent. Even though the parity alterations were relatively small, this was one of the most traumatic incidents in the development of the EMS. The chair of the CoG formulated the point euphemistically as "excessive dramatization of the event before and during the realignment negotiations."[21] The parity changes had been predictable, and had been delayed for political reasons (Germany was facing a tightly fought election on January 25). Speculative pressure built up. This was the first of a new type of crisis, "prompted more by speculative unrest in currency markets, linked to the weakness of the dollar, than by macroeconomic divergence among the EMS participants."[22] But speculation and politics interacted. The high drama arose out of the heavy pressure from finance ministers upon the central banks. In November and December 1986 the Bundesbank had not lowered interest rates, despite pressure from the German government, which was responding to the international demands for greater expansion, fiscal or monetary. Because of the rate differentials, money flowed out of France, and the Banque de France engaged in massive interventions. On January 8, 1987, the Banque used over $2.5 billion in support operations for the franc; the Bundesbank too intervened, with over $1 billion on January 6 and 7 and $1.8 billion on January 8 (see Figure 7.1). France needed to take substantial amounts from the EMCF's Very-Short-Term Facility (4.935 billion ECU), while Germany built up an even larger surplus position in the EMCF (7.856 billion ECU in January 1987). As French market rates spiked, French policymakers attacked German interest-rate policy. German Finance Minister Gerhard Stoltenberg talked with the Bundesbank, then on January 9 consulted by telephone with his French counterpart, Edouard Balladur, and agreed to a small German revaluation of 3 percent. Only after that, on January 23, 1987, did the Bundesbank agree to lower the discount rate from 3.5 to 3 percent. In March 1987 Jacques Delors told the CoG that "December and January had been the worst phase since the creation of the EMS. The manner in which the system functioned had gravely hurt its credibility and that of Europe as a whole."[23] Even in the midst of the alignment negotiations, Balladur had asked the Monetary Committee and the CoG to consider "strengthening the EMS."[24] Immediately after the January devaluation, France demanded a new study on doing so in a way that would achieve "greater symmetry," more intramarginal intervention, and coordination of interest-rate policy. In other words, strengthening European monetary cooperation meant pressing Germany to lower interest rates. At the ECOFIN meeting on February 9, 1987, Balladur formalized this demand as a "move to a more advanced stage" of monetary cooperation, which would include reflection on the appropriate dollar and yen exchange rates.[25]

At the CoG in January 1987, Karl Otto Pöhl revived an idea that had been floated two years earlier of regularly conducting small (3 percent) parity changes in order to "dedramatize" the exchange rate issue and to deflect political heat from the Bundesbank. This was a proposal that many central bankers felt that they could endorse. The process of building alliances in Europe for the Bundesbank now began. Governor of the Banque de France Michel Camdessus also wondered whether the crisis had not shown that interest-rate changes alone were ineffective in preventing a speculative attack, and that a broader range of policy instruments might be needed. In particular, he endorsed Pöhl's bold suggestion that the CoG introduce a procedure for undertaking small-scale, regular, and nonpoliticized parity alterations. There might, he thought, be a distinction between "technical" parity alterations and "political" ones.[26]

There appeared to be a wide gulf between the extravagant anti-German rhetoric of politicians in Paris (as well as Washington) and the convergence in Basel of views on the best way of managing the EMS.

There had been an enormous amount of intervention, with a higher proportion of marginal than intramarginal intervention than had occurred in previous phases of the EMS. Such activity was a sure sign of a deep-rooted problem. From December 1986 until the devaluation, the EC central banks had sold 36 billion Deutsche Marks, with the Bundesbank itself being obliged to intervene in the final stages of the crisis as the exchange rate mechanism (ERM) margins were reached. The Bundesbank saw the consequent expansion of liquidity in Germany as inflationary. It feared that its monetary growth targets for 1987 would be viewed as unrealistic. Pöhl said that an abandonment of the monetary target—as had occurred in the United Kingdom—would have been seen as "laxity" and would have been criticized from the "monetarist" standpoint, which was still highly influential in Germany (but which he also repeatedly made clear he did not share).[27] He also expressed anger that these interventions had allowed speculators to profit while the central banks had to bear the losses.

The disputes were even more acute in the aftermath of the Louvre meeting (February 21–22, 1987), which had been preceded by intense Franco-American discussions, and at which the French finance minister, Edouard Balladur, had suddenly sprung on the other Europeans a target zone proposal for the whole international monetary system. He cosmetically renamed the target a "reference range" in order to placate opposition from those (especially well represented in the Bundesbank) who were committed to exchange rate flexibility. There was in fact no operational agreement, and the desired "ranges" were not made public. The idea to stabilize currencies "around current levels" had come in large part from U.S. worries about a continued dollar fall, but it corresponded perfectly to a French vision of what constituted monetary stability. Balladur later explained his reasoning at the G-6 summit as follows: "France must continue to show the same determination and tenacity in the reconstruction of the international monetary order as she shows in Europe for the monetary construction of Europe."[28] The principal rates agreed at the meeting were set at DM 1.825 and ¥153.50 against the U.S. dollar. The Bundesbank saw itself as a major victim. In 1985 Pöhl had described the notion of target zones, which was relentlessly advocated in

Washington by the Institute of International Economics and its frenetically active director Fred Bergsten, as "twenty years too late." Pöhl did not believe that there had been any agreement on target zones or pegging;[29] neither, interestingly enough, did Tietmeyer once he had become president of the Bundesbank in the 1990s, although he had negotiated this outcome at the Louvre meeting as state secretary in the German Finance Ministry.[30] From the German central bank perspective, there existed no concrete obligations to take monetary policy measures to ensure exchange rate stability.

In the March 1987 meeting of the CoG, after the Louvre meeting, Pöhl still could not contain his anger at the Americans, for exerting pressure for a revaluation of the Deutsche Mark, but also at the French policymakers, who had started to make a similar case. It was public comments from Washington and Paris that had, in his view, set off the January crisis.[31] As chair of the EC Monetary Committee, the influential German policymaker State Secretary Hans Tietmeyer made the point that the interventions that had followed the Louvre had been even higher than the U.S. current account deficit.[32]

In the turbulent discussions of early 1987, the Dutch central banker (and former finance minister) Wim Duisenberg emerged as the figure who could most effectively soothe the ruffled spirits of the central banking community—especially the powerfully explosive Germans, to whom he was intellectually close. He tried to put the drama of the January devaluation in the context of the nine preceding months of stability, and hoped that this thought might lower the level of political tension.[33]

Even before the events of January, the European Council had asked the Commission to report by the end of 1987 on developments in the EMS and on the consequences for the monetary system of the liberalization of capital markets.[34] Delors was completely convinced by the arguments that had been made, principally by Padoa-Schioppa, that the current mechanisms for exchange rate stability were incompatible with the 1992 liberalization program. The Commission duly put forward a new set of proposals on how to strengthen the EMS in the face of new capital movements and of "globalization" (one of the very early uses of the term in its modern meaning).[35]

The debate about the January realignment also started a parallel discussion at the CoG in February about "strengthening the operating mechanisms of the EMS," a process that produced a report on September 8, 1987. That document provided the basis for the so-called Basel-Nyborg Agreement, which at last formalized the practice of intra-marginal intervention. The proposals were accepted by the CoG at the September 8 meeting in Basel, and a few days later, on September 12, by the EC finance ministers meeting in Nyborg in Denmark.

The CoG report began with a reflection on the January experience: "Realignments have generally been carried out smoothly. In some cases they were nonetheless decided on under heavy pressure after being widely anticipated by the markets; the possibility of deciding upon a new set of central rates has sometimes tended to be linked to member states' domestic political calendars. Moreover, changes in central rates sometimes resulted in significant adjustments in market rates, thereby encouraging the belief that speculative activity prior to a realignment would be profitable." The agreement extended the duration of very-short-term financing by a month, taking the maximum to three and a half months, and the governors agreed to accept settlement in ECUs of outstanding VSTF claims as long as doing so did not produce an "un-balanced" reserve composition. The debtor quotas in the short-term monetary support facility were doubled. The acceptance limit for settle-ments in the official ECU was raised from 50 to 100 percent. Although there was "no automatic access" to financing for intramarginal interven-tions, such actions were possible, and there was a "presumption" that intramarginal interventions agreed to by the central bank issuing the intervention currency would qualify for support under the VSTF. These changes, it was hoped, would "strengthen" the system: in particular, more intramarginal intervention and more (and more unpredictable) movement within the bands would make one-way bets harder and raise the penalties for speculation (see Figure 7.3). Flexibility within the bands was thus a tool to be used against speculative pressures. Interventions were not sufficient on their own; and the hope was also expressed that better coordination of monetary policies would lead to greater stability. Such coordination would be an outcome of "joint monitoring of eco-nomic and monetary developments with the aim of arriving at common assessments of both the prevailing conjuncture and appropriate policy responses."[36] In practice, decisive progress toward monetary union could be achieved only when discussion between central bankers moved away from the exchange rate and toward the interest rate—in other words, from an external dimension of money to an internal one.

In a parallel paper, the EC Monetary Committee stated that it was desirable to "dedramatize realignments as far as possible." The MC also noted that the commitment to full capital market liberalization showed that the EMS authorities were "confident in the strength of the system."[37]

The Basel-Nyborg Agreement represented the end of a discussion that had dragged on since the early 1980s about institutional reform within the EMS. It was the first major institutional advance of the EMS; and at the same time, the monitoring provisions anticipated what would be needed in moving forward on the path to monetary integration. Basel-Nyborg also marked the end of a particular stretch of the road to monetary union. Since the creation of the EMS, discussions in the CoG had centered upon small incremental reforms intended to improve the functioning of the EMS. With Basel-Nyborg, the governors had done as much as could be done in this direction. Any further change would need a much larger and more political discussion, since it would require a treaty change. That in turn required an intergovernmental conference. In order to gain political momentum to act, governments would have to identify some major impediment to or malfunctioning of the system. Such irritations—the catalysts for change—in the 1980s derived primarily from global tensions surrounding the management of money.

In practice, however, the interpretation of Basel-Nyborg also produced constant controversies, with the result that participants began to demand more clarification or institutional rigor. Did the agreement suggest a large expansion of intramarginal intervention, and would a

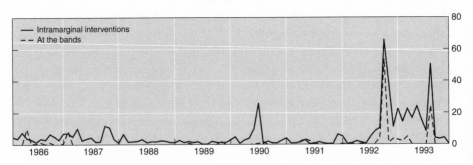

Figure 7.3. Marginal and intramarginal interventions, 1986–1993 (billions of $U.S.). *Source:* CoG files, ECB, Frankfurt am Main.

common statistical analysis automatically lead to policy adjustments? Germans repeatedly insisted on limitations, and correctly claimed that "according to the Basel-Nyborg Agreement, intramarginal interventions could be carried out only with the consent of the central bank issuing the intervention currency." The Bundesbank insisted on prior notice about such interventions. France, by contrast, demanded that the Germans apply Basel-Nyborg in a generously "prolonged and accentuated way."[38]

The European discussions of 1987—together with the interest in indicators at the G-7 finance ministers' level—led to intensification of the work of the expert groups. In November 1987 the Dalgaard group on foreign exchange policies, responding to the demands of the Basel-Nyborg Agreement, presented its report for the first time as an exercise in "surveillance," in effect replicating what was being done on the international level.[39] The extended report required the recruitment of a statistician to work on the surveillance exercise. But again there were hesitations, and different countries interpreted the agreement in distinctive ways. From the German perspective, surveillance became a dirty word. It meant the application of foreign pressure on German decisions, and especially the discussion of monetary policy issues in a variety of forums where the Bundesbank was either constrained (as in the G-7 framework) or not represented at all.[40]

Tensions within the German political and economic establishment, and also within the Bundesbank Council, increased in the late summer of 1987. The Deutsche Mark appreciated sharply against the dollar and against other European currencies in August and early September, reaching the top of its band. Other central banks and—to a very limited extent—the Bundesbank intervened, selling Deutsche Marks. In mid-September the Deutsche Mark fell back, and the other European banks now started Deutsche Mark purchases. At the IMF Interim Committee meeting of September 27, 1987, U.S. Treasury Secretary Baker enraged the Germans by calling for a stricter application of the "indicators approach" and in particular for "paths for monitoring indicators." "There is a broad recognition that the largest countries have a special responsibility to pursue sound and consistent policies." On Thursday, October 15, at a White House press briefing, Baker suggested that the dollar might be allowed to fall further in order to put pressure on Germany not to undertake new rises in interest rates. The language was incendiary:

he spoke of a policy directed by a "little clique of monetarists" in the Bundesbank.[41] The markets responded with a new Deutsche Mark appreciation, and European central banks intervened with around $900 million worth of Deutsche Mark sales: France alone sold some $600 million. Baker then flew to Frankfurt and held a surprise meeting with Stoltenberg and Pöhl. At the weekend, the American press reflected on how higher interest rates might affect a stock market that appeared to be overvalued. On Monday, October 19, a financial panic set in, and Wall Street stocks fell 22.6 percent, or 508 points.

For a few months it looked to a nervous world as if the spat in the G-7 might lead to a new 1929 and send the world into another Great Depression. The dollar continued to slide. The central banks embarked on large-scale coordinated intervention, and at the beginning of 1988 the three-year-long slide of the dollar came to an end. But the Bundesbank was also pressed to act on interest rates. Pressure on France intensified, and in November it needed to draw 3.4 billion ECU from the VSTF. The Bundesbank feared that Delors would use the German government's irritation with Frankfurt for not paying sufficient regard to international constraints as an opportunity to attack the German central bank's restrictive policy.[42] On October 22, 1987, President Pöhl told the Bundesbank Council that the government's urging of the Bundesbank to play a greater role in international cooperation was understandable and should be respected.[43] This wish translated directly into the formulation of policy on interest rates. Chancellor Kohl telephoned Pöhl to emphasize the political importance of easing rates. Pöhl explained to a tumultuous meeting of the Bundesbank Council on December 3 that a half-point cut on the eve of a European summit and the G-7 meeting would be a way of showing that Germany was cooperative, and he reminded the council that in addition to its legal obligation to defend the currency, the Bundesbank had a duty to support the government's economic policy. The council correspondingly cut the central policy interest rate (the discount rate) to 2.5 percent.[44] As Randall Henning has observed, "The dollar stabilization plus the easing of German monetary policy ended the U.S.-German currency conflict of the 1980s."[45] The move ended a great deal of the internal political tension in Germany, as the sharp appreciation of the real exchange rate that had occurred from 1985 to 1987 was unwound and partly reversed (see Figure 4.2, p.110).

A Relaunch

By comparison with the Americans, Europeans looked very docile and agreeable to the decisionmakers in Frankfurt. This lesson was reinforced by promptings from Bonn, with Finance Minister Stoltenberg telling the Bundesbank Council that while Germany should continue to work within the terms of the Louvre agreement, it was vital to increase cooperation with Germany's EMS partners, and especially with France.[46] As a result, some of the debate about international monetary cooperation shifted from the G-7 to the CoG. The Bundesbank started to take new initiatives, to the surprise of many observers. As Gros and Thygesen put it, "the most surprising element in the relaunching of EMU is that Germany nevertheless responded favourably and aggressively, rather than defensively as had been the pattern in earlier discussions in ECOFIN."[47] It was precisely the CoG that had been previously at the center of the defensive and blocking response from Germany.

At the Basel meetings, Pöhl was generally appreciative of the aftermath of Basel-Nyborg. There had been a new wave of dollar weakness after mid-August, but no European strain of the sort that in the past had almost always been associated with dollar jitters. In particular he praised the fact that the Banque de France had raised its rate by three-quarters of a point while other central banks, including the Bundesbank, were lowering theirs. He summed up the year's experience as follows: "Europe is not in a position to stabilize the dollar. Even large interventions do not work if the Federal Reserve does not participate and the U.S. does not follow appropriate policies. What matters is to preserve the EMS intact, and the Bundesbank will do all that it can to realize that objective." Delors joined him in speaking of "Europe's capacity to resist."[48]

But then the Germans were hit by a new series of unpleasant surprises. The early months of 1988 looked like a replay of the Louvre debacle, on a European rather than the global stage. Again, the drama was set in motion by a set of proposals from French Finance Minister Balladur. He had seen the January 1987 parity alteration as a humiliation imposed on the French government by the market and by the Germans. He intended to pay the Bundesbank back with the demand that the alignment be accompanied by an examination of ways to strengthen the EMS, and Basel-Nyborg was fundamentally the outcome of his initiative. But in the opinion of the French treasury, that agreement was not sufficiently wide-ranging to deal with all the issues that would arise from the creation of the integrated capital market. Balladur thought that Germany was primarily responsible for the financial crisis of October 1987, because of insufficient German economic stimulus, because of the Bundesbank increase of interest rates at the "wrong moment," and because of German toleration of an excessive weakening of the dollar. In a meeting with Stoltenberg at Karlsruhe on November 12, 1987, he pressed Germany to be more serious about the implementation of Basel-Nyborg, and agreed on the creation of a new Franco-German Economic Council, which France saw as a way of keeping up the international pressure on Germany.[49] A new French treasury memorandum of January 8, 1988, which was followed up by press articles and interviews, took up some of the older themes of the 1970s: in particular, the notion of symmetry, which had been at the center of the Fourcade proposals of the mid-1970s. Balladur argued that all member states should be brought into the narrow bands of the EMS, that asymmetries should be reduced (in other words, that Germany should undertake more adjustment), and that there should be a coordinated policy with respect to the dollar. The historian Éric Bussière correctly sees Balladur's campaign as a "continuation of debates that had started in the era of Georges Pompidou."[50] But the report also argued that the liberalization of capital markets logically required creating a zone with a single currency, managed by a common central bank and federal banks in all the member countries.[51] The new central bank would be given a "certain authority"; but such a scheme was unlikely to be realized until around 2000. Balladur then set out to push the case in a series of press interviews, in which he argued that the pound should be brought into the EMS, and also claimed that the Basel-Nyborg reforms, with the increased intervention obligations, had originated in French suggestions.[52]

The demand for an explicit mechanism to force greater German expansion was articulated even more dramatically by Italy. Finance Minister Giuliano Amato in a memorandum of January 1988 argued that there was a need for an institutional mechanism for the recycling of funds, and for the correction of external imbalances:

Indeed, there is a "fundamental problem" in the EMS, which can be attributed to the fact that there is no "engine of growth." Not only is the pivot currency of the system fundamentally undervalued, but the growth of domestic demand in Germany is lower than the average; the result is that the country has structural surpluses also vis-à-vis the rest of the EEC. These surpluses, both commercial and current, on the one hand induce tension within the exchange system, pushing up the D-mark, particularly when the dollar drops, and, on the other hand, they remove growth potential from the other nations. In the long run, the cohesion of the system could suffer.[53]

Again the German government reacted more enthusiastically to the foreign critique than the Bundesbank might have liked. On February 26, 1988, Foreign Minister Hans-Dietrich Genscher produced a "Memorandum for the Creation of a European Currency Area and a European Central Bank," in which he set out a proposal for monetary integration, although it also referred to the importance of the principles of independence and a commitment to price stability.[54] The Genscher memorandum may have been particularly irritating to the Bundesbank's leadership, and especially its harder-line members, as it had been prepared with the assistance of a relatively junior but dovish member of the Bundesbank staff, Peter-Wilhelm Schlüter.[55] But the Bundesbank also recognized that the suggestion contained in Genscher's proposal to create a committee of wise men who would after some time issue a report might be a way of restraining or moderating any impetus that might come from Jacques Delors.[56] In private, Pöhl was seething, arguing that Balladur was talking "verbiage" and that his "confused ideas" "made no sense." He felt that any discussion of further development of the EMS risked putting Germany in the position of the permanent naysayer.[57] In a press conference after the Bundesbank Council meeting, he explained carefully that European monetary union would be a failure if it were not accompanied by convergence in economic, financial, regional, and social policy; that the EMS needed to be more inclusive (in other words, the United Kingdom should join); that there should be a full liberalization of capital movements; that cooperation in the CoG should be intensified; and finally that a European central bank would need to be built on a federal basis with a firm commitment to price stability.[58]

In response to the Genscher memorandum the Bundesbank set out its views of the monetary integration discussion in a fifty-one-page and much more measured paper on "Further Development of the European Monetary System," which it sent to the German government. The paper presented a generally conciliatory approach that was more forthcoming than many in the Bundesbank would have liked, and began by pointing out that monetary stability was recognized as a common basis for policy on a national level and that within the European Monetary System the result had been greater exchange rate stability. "With that the fundamental preconditions for an economic union have been fulfilled." Germany would have to contribute constructively "in order to ensure that money and credit policy in an economically unified Europe are not less oriented toward stability than they are today in the Federal Republic." The paper also made the familiar point that monetary integration should not "hurry ahead" of a general economic convergence, as otherwise the "integration process would be burdened by considerable economic and social tensions." "Any step to fix currencies permanently in the Community and finally to replace them by a European currency would be doomed to failure unless a minimum of economic and fiscal consensus and decision-making occurs on the level of the Community." Monetary union would lead to more financial integration and an "intensification of competition." It would obviously reduce transaction costs. Finally, it would confer advantages in "dealings with third countries": "the Community would be less vulnerable to external shocks and would be able to represent its currency interests more effectively at the international level."[59]

The paper then examined the different options for monetary integration. It rejected the idea of a parallel currency as threatening stability. It also dealt with the issue that not all the member countries of the EC would be either able or willing to participate in the process. "The countries undertaking integration will not want to expose themselves to the risk of being partly dictated to by outsiders, and they expect that only countries that expose themselves to the same risk will participate."[60] Instead the Bundesbank document made the CoG crucial to the process, as the CoG offered the advantage of being institutionally outside the framework of the EEC treaties.

A parallel paper prepared by the CoG alternates reached a rather gloomy conclusion about the EMS in its current form. The EMS had not produced satisfactory outcomes in terms of economic growth, employment, or current account balances. There was a constant fear of a deflationary bias, and an asymmetry in the distribution of the adjustment and financing burdens; there was insufficient coordination of monetary policies; some countries did not participate; there was no adequate defense against external shocks; and the mechanism was not irreversibly oriented toward a unified currency area. The document suggested contemplating a shift away from the "absolute" priority of price stability—a demand that the Bundesbank found incendiary.[61]

In the CoG itself, at the April 1988 meeting the major topics were the inadequate growth of the European countries (which had—as in the late 1970s—led to U.S. but also French pressure on Germany to act as an international "locomotive"), and the issue of asymmetric adjustment: the issues that the Balladur and Amato papers had directly addressed and to which they had called for an institutional solution. The alternates' report presented the outcome of a substantive discussion. This preparatory meeting had discussed the mandate to review the working of the EMS, and improvements to deal with the asymmetry issue identified by Amato and others; but it also considered the modalities of a possible move to a single monetary zone and a European Central Bank. The alternates agreed that the idea of a central bank was premature, and they also expressed reluctance even to define criteria that might be used to judge at what point such a move might be appropriate. The Bundesbank in particular noted that there was no point in going further with EMS reform after the 1986–1987 debate; and President Pöhl even seemed to be going back on the Basel-Nyborg principles when in a press conference he denied the obligation of the Bundesbank to intervene intramarginally.[62]

At the April CoG meeting, in accordance with these doubts and hesitations, Pöhl tried to slow the pace of change, insisting that strict symmetry in adjustment policy would be impossible: "every effort should be made to maximize consensus and convergence with regard to broad economic objectives, including monetary objectives, and to harmonise economic and financial performances as far as possible. However, it was not desirable to aim for symmetry of exchange market interventions; the Deutsche Bundesbank remained opposed to the proposed diversification of monetary reserves within the EMS, but it had no objection to the Alternates being asked to consider the question of symmetry of objectives and policies as long as they did not confine themselves to intervention techniques and procedures." He also was skeptical about how rapidly progress would be made on these issues:

It was not certain that a decision would be taken on procedure at the European Council in Hanover at the end of June, even if the possibility of Mr. Genscher's ideas becoming German Government proposals could not be ruled out. Whatever the case, if it was decided to create an independent panel of wise men to study the question of the monetary structure of Europe, such a procedure would perhaps be acceptable as preparatory to the studies the Governors would be undertaking. Indeed, it was questionable whether the Governors ought to be the first to insist that they alone carry out an objective and full analysis of these questions.

Increased monetary coordination would be impossible without giving up autonomous national policies; and there were sharp limits to monetary policy as the sole supporting mechanism of the EMS. But the real force of Pöhl's intervention hit home at the end of the discussion, when he explained that the CoG had a very different status from that of the EC Monetary Committee, in that it was not a Community institution:

> Irrespective of the date of creation of the two Committees, the central banks were in any event senior to the Monetary Committee. There was an important fundamental issue at stake that went beyond this aspect of protocol, namely that these bodies, whatever they represented and even if there were legal grounds, should not deal with subjects that lay within the competence of the central banks. The EMS rested on an agreement between central banks and not between governments. This was a vital point for the Deutsche Bundesbank and meant that it would not participate in discussions in the Monetary Committee about, for example, official reserve diversification or the extension of the maturity of the swap operations for the creation of ECUs. The Monetary Committee could, of course, address institutional issues.[63]

Pöhl further developed the same point in print. "In a monetary union with irreversibly fixed exchange rates the weak would become ever weaker and the strong ever stronger. We would thus experience great tensions in the real economy of Europe. . . . In order to create a European currency, the governments and parliaments of Europe would have to be prepared to transfer sovereign rights to a supranational institution." As a beginning, Pöhl suggested—doubtless not entirely seriously (since it would have been a violation of the German convention)—that responsibility for exchange rate realignments should be transferred from governments and finance ministers to the CoG.[64]

The same hesitancy that characterized the CoG was also expressed in the Monetary Committee. In May 1988 the British chairman, Geoffrey Littler, concluded in a report to be presented to the EC ministers that the ERM worked well, that there was some modest improvement in coordination procedures, and that there was some problem with the ultimate objective of monetary union. "The question was raised as to how far towards these goals progress might be made without the prior or parallel assumption of a willingness on the part of Member States to submerge their fiscal and political autonomy." This report also made clear the centrality of the central banks to any reform discussion in recognizing "that the EMS was based on an agreement between central banks and that changes to it were the preserve of the Governors."[65]

The old issue of the EMCF revived when Italy suggested that the EMCF could become an instrument of deeper monetary cooperation. The Bundesbank and the CoG secretariat argued in reply that an enlarged role for the EMCF was impossible, since the EMCF was the "creation of the Council" and thus might be legally and politically bound by the economic priorities of the Council.[66]

On the eve of the June 1988 Hanover meeting of the European Council, Pöhl was in an explosive mood. He told the Bundesbank Council that the establishment of a Franco-German Economic Council had confirmed the Bundesbank's worst fears, and that the central bank governors were being demoted to the role of assistants to the finance ministers; he also complained of the "confused" ideas of the new French finance minister, Pierre Bérégovoy (a Socialist), who had announced on television that the central banks would reduce interest rates.[67] But Pöhl also reported on the discussions he had held on May 26 with the government in Bonn, in which he had pleaded with Chancellor Kohl not to make commitments in Hanover that would affect the activities of the central bank, while Genscher had pushed on with the idea of a committee of wise men. Pöhl had claimed to Kohl that Bérégovoy was not really interested in a European Central Bank, but rather in pressuring the Bundesbank in the current spat over monetary policy.[68] Immediately after the June 1 meeting of the Bundesbank Council, Pöhl wrote to Kohl to explain that too early an abandonment of the possibility of altering parities would require a considerable transfer of resources; that an economic and monetary union could develop only over a substantial period; and that a parallel currency developing out of the ECU would be a harmful initiative. He thought that the best option was for the European governments to call on the CoG to investigate a currency union as the endpoint of a process of economic integration. He also stated—once more—the importance of central bank independence and a commitment to price stability.[69]

In fact Pöhl achieved some victories. The Franco-German Economic Council was not a decision-making institution and had only consultative powers. Kohl also decided that the only way in which the Bundesbank could be brought along with the process initiated by Delors and Genscher was to include the central bankers in the committee of wise men that the Hanover Council meeting would appoint. Delors in particular had been a forceful advocate of giving the central banks the guiding hand in sketching out possible paths to monetary union.[70]

The Hanover meeting (June 27–28, 1988), which endorsed the idea of creating a committee of wise men, produced one big surprise: Delors himself would chair the committee. Kohl had personally insisted on the appointment, in part because of the high degree of trust established between the two men by their shared background in social Catholicism. The nomination infuriated the British government. Chancellor of the Exchequer Nigel Lawson later referred to the "disaster of having Jacques Delors as the committee's chairman, or even as one of its members," since the presence of the Commission president would carry an authority in the EC for the committee's eventual report that would not have existed if the report had simply come from the technocratic CoG.[71] At the time, Bank of England officials noted their alarm. Nevertheless, Margaret Thatcher concurred in the belief that the powerful presence of Pöhl would prevent the committee from reaching any dangerous conclusion on European monetary integration.

The members of the committee were the central bank governors, Demetrios J. Chalikias (Greece), Carlo Azeglio Ciampi (Italy), Maurice F. Doyle (Ireland), Wim Duisenberg (Netherlands), Baron Jean Godeaux (Belgium), Erik Hoffmeyer (Denmark), Pierre Jaans (Luxembourg), Jacques de Larosière (France), Robert Leigh-Pemberton (United Kingdom), Karl Otto Pöhl (Germany), Mariano Rubio (Spain), and José A. Tavares Moreira (Portugal). They were to act in a personal capacity rather than as representatives of their institutions, and would not be accompanied by any staff who might restrain them. For both the Banque de France and the Bundesbank this was an important decision, in that the governors of the two banks were highly forceful personalities who did not necessarily represent the institutional consensus of the bodies over which they presided. There were also three independent experts, including the general manager of the BIS, Alexandre Lamfalussy, the Danish economics professor Niels Thygesen, and the Spanish banker, economist, and former finance minister Miguel Boyer. Delors also insisted on including the EC commissioner in charge of agricultural policy, Frans Andriessen. There were also to be two staff positions, rapporteurs who would play a critical role in the constant process of drafting and redrafting position papers and the eventual report. Originally, in Delors's vision these two men were to have been closely aligned with Delors and the Commission: Tommaso Padoa-Schioppa, who was a past director-general of monetary affairs in the Commission, and was a key intellectual influence on Delors's thinking about the consequences of capital liberalization; and Jean-Paul Mingasson, who until 1989 was the head of the Commission's Monetary Affairs Directorate. The Bundesbank objected to the domination of the committee by the EC Commission, but Delors went ahead and briefed the press about the nomination of Padoa-Schioppa.[72] When de Larosière met Delors soon after Hanover, Delors argued that the "present formula" was "the least damaging one." He promised to be "flexible on methods of work" but raised the "basic question," which he said had not been addressed at Hanover, of the relation between the monetary and exchange rate systems and the institutional apparatus and political aims of the EEC. De Larosière made a plea for the BIS to "play an important logistical and intellectual role." Karl Otto Pöhl was also reassuring in discussions with de Larosière, emphasizing that "decisions can only be taken by us."[73]

Many people quickly drew the conclusion that Delors was flattering the central bankers. In reality, Pöhl was extremely irritated. He conducted an angry telephone call with Kohl in the middle of the Hanover Council meeting.[74] He claimed that the Monetary Committee would have been a more appropriate forum for the discussion of monetary union. In the presence of Finance Minister Stoltenberg on June 30, 1988, Pöhl told the Bundesbank Council that the choice of chairman and the character of the secretariat guaranteed that the EC Commission would dominate the work of the committee and that what he termed "Latin" monetary views would prevail at the expense of German commitment to the culture of stability.[75] It was extremely hard to pacify Pöhl. Chancellor Kohl himself felt obliged to make an appearance before the Bundesbank Council, where he underlined his strong political commitment to the independence of the Bundesbank. But the tone of the chancellor's remarks was much more critical than that of Helmut Schmidt in the celebrated November 1978 meeting. Kohl began by providing a striking and far-sighted account of the importance of the EC, explaining that it was likely that Austria and the Nordic countries would apply to join, and that there was also "great interest" in the EC in eastern Europe (a remarkable statement *before* November 1989). But above all, Kohl stressed the importance of Franco-German relations, which "went beyond the economic." The Bundesbank should not be so fussy. "It was not a question of principle whether the interests of the central bank were referred to in an additional clause of the ratifying law or in the preamble." In reply, Pöhl simply reminded the chancellor that international commitments, both in the G-7 and in Europe, were progressively limiting the independence of the central bank.[76]

On July 4, 1988, Pöhl called Leigh-Pemberton and other governors, starting by saying "how unhappy he was about the formation of the Committee and the fact that Delors was chairman," and stating that the appointment of Padoa-Schioppa would mean "that the report would immediately get a strong bias in the wrong direction." He proposed that there be three rapporteurs, with a German and a Briton to balance Padoa-Schioppa, and suggested that the best course would be to get the secretarial apparatus established in Basel under the eye of Lamfalussy.[77] The third, British, member of the secretariat for the committee was an addition that would presumably have slowed the committee's deliberations and made agreement harder.[78] Largely at the insistence of Pöhl and the Bundesbank, however, the balance of the committee was tilted back away from the Commission and toward the central bankers by the appointment (in place of Mingasson) of a BIS official and former German Finance Ministry and IMF employee, Gunter Baer, whose position would be much closer to that of the central banks. At an informal meeting of the governors in Basel on July 13, both Jaans and Pöhl expressed the fear that the CoG might become an "empty shell," in that it would be bypassed by Delors, but de Larosière and Leigh-Pemberton explained that the governors need not be isolated "if we were clever."[79]

The Meetings of the Delors Committee

The Delors Committee was given a clear brief: not to discuss the desirability of monetary union, but rather to focus on the institutional question of how it might be achieved. The report was crafted as a technical exploration of what was possible, and not as a political manifesto on integration. In fact some members expressed doubts about the extent of their governments' political commitment to monetary union. As the Irish governor Maurice Doyle put it, no one in Europe believed the European Council when it said it wanted economic and monetary union.[80] As a result, even skeptics in the committee could believe they were achieving their goals by just spelling out precisely what monetary union would involve (and thus precisely showing how difficult it would be).

The committee also clearly took its point of departure from the Single European Act, and, as Alexandre Lamfalussy and Padoa-Schioppa repeatedly emphasized, the single market required a more effective policy coordination process even if there was to be no economic and monetary union.

Given the divergent starting positions, with a combination of skeptics and enthusiasts, managing the work of the committee was a task of great difficulty, and required the finest levels of political sensitivity. There were seven meetings in all (September 13, October 10, November 8, and December 13, 1988; January 10, March 14, and April 11–12, 1989), amounting to some sixty-five hours of debate and discussion, as well as numerous informal bilateral meetings. Delors later said that he had strongly resolved simply to listen rather than attempt to guide the committee. Some members referred to him as a "remarkable manipulator." Others thought that he "led from the back," giving an impression that consensus was emerging out of the interactions of the committee. Pöhl was often deliberately difficult. Later he claimed that Delors had contributed little and that the substance of the report came from the governors. Delors realized quite well that Pöhl had political instructions to be cooperative, and that he could not block agreement. On the other hand, he also appreciated that Pohl would do anything that was needed to get a result that looked like a Bundesbank-type central bank. In that sense, the repeated emotional outbursts were what some participants later described as a "smokescreen."[81]

Delors also had some luck on his side. The three central bankers who came to play a dominant role in the committee all had very firm views, but two, Robin Leigh-Pemberton and Jacques de Larosière, were also men of extreme politeness and tact. From the outset it looked as if Leigh-Pemberton, whose government was firmly opposed to the whole project, might wreck the discussion. In fact the presence of the invariably polite and constructive Leigh-Pemberton helped to harness and constrain Pöhl. He had obviously worried from the start about the obstructive position of his government, but Margaret Thatcher had told him explicitly: "I have confidence in Karl Otto Pöhl. If he is proposing something, you can accept it."[82] Thatcher in fact had less insight into the political wiles of Pöhl than did Delors. De Larosière took his independence very seriously. He believed that the German concept of central bank independence would bring benefits for France as well; and in the course of the committee's meetings, he faced and withstood tremendous antagonism from the French Finance Ministry.

The members of the committee took different stances on the question of how much they should liaise with their national authorities. In particular, the most dominating personalities isolated themselves from their domestic political settings. Jacques de Larosière met the French president on December 1, 1988, but did not inform the Finance Ministry and had no regular contacts with it. He was supported by a small and loyal staff at the Banque de France. The British Treasury was gripped by fear that Robin Leigh-Pemberton was a loose cannon, but his staff at the Bank of England loyally defended the governor and ensured that the Treasury was not briefed until after the meetings of the Delors Committee and the information lag gave Leigh-Pemberton a substantial informational advantage. An EMU group was established in the U.K. Treasury under the chairmanship of Geoffrey Littler, and Leigh-Pemberton acknowledged that "there is no reason why I should not seek 'guidance' from the group"; but the senior Bank of England staff resisted such pressure. Anthony Loehnis, a director of the bank, complained that the Treasury's view was "over-influenced, I think, by fear of the Prime Minister's dislike of a common currency, a European Central Bank or (horror of horrors) a United States of Europe." Leigh-Pemberton doled out simple reassurances: after the first meeting of the committee he wrote to Chancellor of the Exchequer Nigel Lawson that all was going well, "the pragmatists were well to the fore and seemingly in a strong majority; the idealists relatively muted; and Delors himself neutral."[83] Lawson was fearful at the time and described the committee as "the Apotheosis of Central Banks."[84] He complained that the Dutch governor, Wim Duisenberg, systematically and extensively benefited from the expertise of the Nederlandsche Bank, whose support enabled him to play a very positive role in the last stages of the committee's work. By contrast, Pöhl avoided contacts with the German ministries and also with the Bundesbank staff, and thus was the loosest of the cannons on the deck of the Delors Committee. He boasted that he "played things by ear," but this approach may well have reduced his effectiveness on the committee.[85]

In response to the threat that the central bankers might really come up with a plan, Lawson formulated a distinct sabotage plan: "It was clear to us, too, that Robin [Leigh-Pemberton]'s tactics should be to assemble the widest possible opposition within the Committee both to any early treaty amendment required to achieve the full EMU objective espoused by Delors, and to anything that smacked of a recommendation to take any particular course of action." But he was frustrated in this hope, he believed, largely by the inconstancy of Pöhl, who "proved a broken reed [who] made a number of sceptical interventions in the Committee's deliberations, but he never really engaged himself."[86]

Pöhl's weaknesses strengthened the position of the committee's staff, in particular of the Italian rapporteur, who was intellectually and personally very close to Jacques Delors. An extensive memorandum, drafted by Tommaso Padoa-Schioppa, was circulated to the committee on September 1, 1988. It set out an agenda and raised the central issues that would appear in the report, but always in the form of questions. Padoa-Schioppa mapped out a philosophy of making progress by "steps": in other words, avoiding both the paralyzing incrementalism that had characterized discussions in the early 1980s, and also the idea of a revolutionary or big bang approach. He saw the process as a logical and legal development following from the Single European Act, in other words following the metaphor of Delors's "little white pebble." Finally, he emphasized that the process needed to have a political accountability. "The organizational structure and decision making process of the Monetary Authority will presumably have to reflect the plurinational character of the Community." The document made explicit the necessity of revising the Treaty of Rome: "Article 102 of the Single European Act states that 'further development in the field of economic and monetary policy necessitating institutional changes should be based on article 236 of the Treaty of Rome, which implies the accord of an intergovernmental conference and ratification by member states.'"[87]

Padoa-Schioppa also directly confronted the budgetary implications of monetary policy. "In nations with a federal structure, in which there is one currency and one central bank, no formal constraint is in general imposed by the federal authorities on the budgetary decisions of local governments."[88] What safeguards would be required to render the conduct of monetary policy in a monetary union independent of the pressure for "monetary expansion" that large public deficits and debts might generate?

The questions were put as follows: "Would the organizational structure be dependent on the chosen model of monetary integration?" Second, was there a possible parallel or prior process to the radical changes that required treaty revision? "Is there still room for 'noninstitutional' progress toward a monetary union, i.e., for progress based on the existing legal arrangements? In particular, can the monetary policy decisions of national authorities be bound by decisions taken by one of the existing Community organs (Monetary Committee, Council of Ministers, Committee of Governors . . .)?"[89]

Finally, the document made it clear that the independence of central banks would be a major focus of discussions:

> It is often stated that a European Monetary Authority should be independent. . . . What meaning should be given to the concept of independence? What institutional, legal, and organizational provisions would be necessary to ensure independence? If independence implies that the Monetary Authority is given the status of a "Community institution" (like the Council, the Commission, the European Parliament, and the Court of Justice), what should be the relationships between the Authority and other Community institutions? To whom should the Authority be accountable? What forms should this accountability take? Should there be provisions requiring the policy decisions of the Authority to be consistent with general economic policies formulated by the Community? Who would appoint the members of the decision-making bodies of the Authority?[90]

Jacques Delors ensured that the committee worked under rather unusual conditions. Each meeting was taped, and the tape was transcribed (almost all of these tapes have been preserved). No member was to quote other members, and the confidentiality of the entire process was emphasized again and again. This was designed above all as a protective device against political interference from the British government. Delors also tried to build consensus. At the opening of the first meeting, on September 16, 1988, he said: "Never are we going to give the impression that there is disagreement amongst us. We are a team, we do teamwork to serve our Masters and that is all. Were we a group of academics, doubt-lessly there might be differences of opinion, but we are not going to dra-matise them and we are not going to turn the meeting of this group into a series, like *Dynasty* or *Dallas*—and one that would be less attractive too."[91] The reference to "masters" was a clear reminder of the fundamen-tally political task that had been set at Hanover by democratically elected politicians. The task of the central bankers was the limited one of offer-ing a technical solution to the political challenge. The location of the meetings, at the BIS in Basel, and thus even outside the territory of the EC, irritated some members of the Commission, but Delors saw it as a key to success. He also regularly stayed on in Basel after the meetings to work with Baer and Padoa-Schioppa on the drafting of texts.

If the creation of EMU lay in a treaty, however, it clearly could not be accomplished without political consent. It is, after all, governments that negotiate and parliaments that ratify treaties, not central banks. How far did the central bankers consult the politicians about what was happening? The most difficult relationship was that in Paris. In December 1988 de Larosière met alone with President Mitterrand to ensure that there would be no extraneous political intervention, and explained that there could be no agreement without the complete independence of a future central bank and also of its constituent institutions. Mitterrand gave a complicated and ambiguous reply, but no straightforward refusal. De Larosière took the president's response as perhaps not a green light, but at least an amber "proceed with caution." He communicated this degree of French political acceptance to Delors, and also to some other political figures, notably the Dutch prime minister, but not to the French treasury.[92]

At the first meeting the British representative, Bank of England Gov-ernor Robin Leigh-Pemberton, began with a note of caution: "I don't say that I am against monetary integration, I am arguing about forcing the pace of it." At the end of that meeting, Karl Otto Pöhl spoke with a di-rect aggressiveness that he subsequently concealed more carefully, when he pleaded for more realism, and for forgetting about the utopian solutions of a hard currency union. "Maybe we can save a lot of time if we concentrate on that, but we should tell the Heads of State and gov-ernments that we are of the opinion and we have agreed that for the time being there is no realistic chance for monetary union in the sense of the Werner Report. We should be honest and we should say that and we should stop all this talk by people like Helmut Schmidt and Giscard, etc. If we are all of this opinion, if we all agree on that that would be a very strong statement, I would subscribe [to] it immediately." This intervention provoked Delors also to push in the direction of greater realism, and to start from the apparently harmless notion that the EMS was as important a model for subsequent development as the problematical Werner Plan. Later some economists complained that the Delors Report had "simply updated the Werner report and filled in the gaps with very little involvement of professional economists;"[93] but in fact the committee spent a great deal of time examining such issues as fiscal rules for a monetary union.

The discussion of Werner as a model at the first meeting was part of a carefully planned strategy on the part of Delors and his rapporteurs. In a briefing note circulated in advance, they had emphasized the importance of drawing lessons from Werner: "the ambitions of the Werner Report were not achieved partly because of (1) a failure to fully implement it and (2) a sharp change in the economic environment, but also because of intrinsic weaknesses." The four principal weaknesses had been "insufficient constraints on national policies; institutional ambiguities; inappropriate policy conception; lack of internal momentum."[94]

At the initial meeting, many of the speakers took up the Werner theme of parallelism. Monetary unification needed to be accompanied by a greater measure of fiscal control. Duisenberg stated: "The existing procedures of co-ordination are too free; we need more centralization there and the transfer of sovereignty." Only Thygesen tried to stand out against the concept of parallelism, on the grounds that it would make for a perpetual deadlock: "I think it would be worrisome if we were to draw the inference from the Werner Report that progress always has to be in parallel, has to wait for the area that is most difficult. At one time it was necessary to move ahead in the monetary area, even if economic integration was not progressing. I suggest that we have today a situation where economic integration has to a large extent caught up with the monetary cooperation that we have."[95]

The second meeting (October 10, 1988) focused much more on regional policy, and on whether monetary union would lead inexorably to an increase in inequality between regions (and hence demand the countervailing application of structural funds) as well as alterations of real wage rates. The Irish governor, Maurice Doyle, representing what was still one of the poorest countries in the European Community, and the major beneficiary of its structural funds, worried that growth in the Community was not sufficient to avoid increasing income disparities. As a consequence, he argued that the move to monetary union would require a higher level of transfers to promote infrastructure, education, and training in the outlying areas.

Alexandre Lamfalussy raised the central point, which would continue to the end of the working of the committee to be the major focus of debate: whether the necessary fiscal discipline would need to be imposed by a treaty or binding constraint, or whether market forces would be sufficient. He cited cases from the United States and Canada as well as from Europe where cities and states in a federation were insufficiently disciplined. De Larosière responded by arguing that Europe needed to create a new disciplinary mechanism at the community level. Delors raised the prospect of a two-speed Europe, in which one or two countries might need a "different kind of marriage contract."[96]

There was, however, remarkably little interest or enthusiasm in seeing the EMS as a simple basis for future monetary unification. Pöhl repeatedly reminded the committee that only five currencies were in the "real" EMS, as Italy still had the wider margins regime. The eventual report said little about the EMS, and in consequence needed to specify new mechanisms for cooperation and coordination. At the initiative of de Larosière, the report eventually stated that "the EMS has not fulfilled its full potential" (paragraph 5) and highlighted the absence of sufficient convergence of fiscal policies.

At this stage it was still possible to interpret the overall tone as hesitant. In response to an argument by Niels Thygesen, the only figure who consistently came across as an enthusiast for monetary unification, that the benefits of exchange rate flexibility were increasingly modest and shrinking, Leigh-Pemberton noted that few Governors agreed with this proposition.[97]

Pöhl started to argue that the CoG would be the "best avenue" for increased monetary cooperation. By the third meeting (November 8, 1988), he had developed a precise proposal for transforming or "upgrading" the CoG into a Bundesbank-like system: "Call it a European Central Bank Council, you have a chairman who would be elected not just for one year but for three years and who could attend the meetings in Brussels, could get a little more profile, etc., and then this Council could give recommendations, let us say on monetary policy in the respective member countries of the EC, on economic and fiscal policy even, if it affects the exchange rate stability, price stability in the EEC." He added: "That means, by definition, that gradualism is hardly conceivable." In particular, he thought that the CoG might even develop a competence in the setting of exchange rates: "We could suggest that at least we examine whether the exchange rate pattern is reasonable, appropriate. I think there is no better institution than the Council of Central Bank Governors to come to an objective judgment, and if we would come to such a conclusion that would be very rare of course and wouldn't happen very often, but let us assume we would say with these surpluses in Germany the best thing to do is to have a little realignment."[98] The Bundesbank model remained a constant point of reference. In particular, it was the experience of the Bundesbank Council, with representation of the German regional central banks (*Landeszentralbanken*) but no attempt to have weighted voting (in relation to population or economic size), that provided the strongest basis for arguing against a more political version of a European Central Bank.

At this point de Larosière felt strengthened to announce that he would in practice carry out a bid for greater independence from the French political authorities:

> what I am suggesting in my paper implies, I didn't put it that way but it does imply, a very profound modification of the relationship between the governing body of the Banque de France and the Ministry of Finance. In my view it is absolutely clear; I didn't stress it, but it is there. I would like that to happen, and I know there will be upheaval in the Treasury, but it is also something we have to see as the positive side. Don't you think Europe would be stronger with central banks that would be more independent, autonomous, in a structure like the one I described than not to change anything in the legal aspects and to sort of muddle through?[99]

De Larosière's stance indeed produced a major showdown with the French treasury.

There remained a sort of defense mechanism that de Larosière left in place to protect himself against the ferocious domestic criticism to which he was exposed for abandoning traditional French positions on economic governance. He asked the Banque de France to prepare a paper on the possible establishment of a European Reserve Fund, which would go beyond the EMS in providing for a pooling of reserve resources, and which took up some of the French proposals for how the EMS should have looked in 1978 and 1979. While Germany wanted to act fundamentally in line with the existing institutional framework, France preferred to institutionalize the earlier stages of monetary integration. De Larosière skillfully presented the new version of a reserve fund not as an economic government but rather as a sort of training ground for a future European Central Bank that could be established only after the changes that would require a treaty. The French suggestion also had the advantage of addressing the issue of variable speed, in that only some of the member countries would participate, and Great Britain could comfortably be left on one side. This paper was carefully, even ostentatiously, coordinated with the French treasury—in contrast with the bulk of de Larosière's contributions to the committee's proceedings. It remained in the final report as the only item on which the committee did not offer a unanimous stance (Section 53); and the report made clear that this was not an essential part of the process of establishing monetary union. The "training ground" and "symbol of the political will" arguments appeared as two of the three principal justifications; as a third element, it was simply stated that the "concerted management of exchange rates" would be facilitated by means of (with the important provision "possibly") "visible" intervention on the exchange markets.

After the third meeting, Padoa-Schioppa produced a note in which he laid out the three-step mechanism that would eventually be at the heart of the committee's report:

> after a first step based on the existing Treaty, a new Treaty would be stipulated on the basis of Article 236 of the Treaty of Rome, that would provide the legal basis for all the actions and developments that are necessary to reach the final stage of the economic and monetary union. Given the choice of a gradualistic approach, many clauses of the treaty will come into force only in later stages, this approach has been followed in the past by the community, and appears to be apt to establish the process on firm ground and to give it the necessary credibility.

The note also clearly specified the characteristic balance in Delors's vision between market dynamics and the mechanisms of an international treaty:

To the maximum possible extent adjustment should occur by way of market mechanisms. A first direction of policy, therefore, should aim at making such mechanisms more effective. In the business sector this may require a stronger competition policy. In the labour market this would require promoting flexibility of wages and differentiated trends in labour costs according to the differences in productivity of the various regions of the Community. However, even improved market mechanisms will not be sufficient to bring about adjustment and therefore a second direction of policies will be necessary to supplement them. Such policies require financial resources, but have also an important qualitative dimension that may, if properly designed, significantly enhance the effectiveness of any given amount of funds made available through the Community budget. The programme of doubling the resources of structural funds to 13 billion ECUs per year by 1992, coupled with the reorganization of the community structural policies, significantly improves the ability of the Community to deal with these problems. However, the Committee considers that in a more advanced stage of the process these mechanisms should be further extended and made more effective.[100]

On December 2 Baer and Padoa-Schioppa circulated what they termed a "skeleton report," in which they laid out possible mechanisms through which the ECU could evolve into a common currency. One was simply to extend the private use and market acceptance of the private ECU. But there was a more dramatic and radical path: "a second option would be to alter the present arrangements and to introduce the ECU as an additional currency, which would no longer represent a weighted average of Community currencies, but would be independently defined, have fixed but adjustable exchange rates vis-à-vis national currencies, and be managed under the responsibility of the European system of central banks."[101]

The document also talked about transfer payments as complementing market mechanisms in generating a single market. "Market forces would—at least in the short run—exacerbate rather than mitigate the differences between poorer and richer member countries and cause serious strains and frictions in the Community. In order to be able to address the problem of structural differences between member countries and concomitant disparities in levels of per capita income, the Community must possess a system of financial transfers." The skeleton report also spelled out the need for fiscal rules: "The first aim must be to establish arrangements that will effectively limit the scope for budget deficits that can be incurred by individual member countries of the Community. Safeguards in this respect will have to include (in accordance with the criteria laid down for a European system of central banks) strict ceilings on the maximum permissible access to monetary financing, as well as on borrowing in non-Community currencies. In addition, agreement must be reached on a system of binding rules which limits the maximum size of national budget deficits." What sort of rules? The skeleton report added some possibilities in parentheses: "in relation to GDP? confining deficits to investment spending?"[102]

The suggestion about fiscal limits was a response to a note addressed to Delors from Mingasson in the Commission, which referred to the "setting of rules relative to the size of budget deficits and their financing; adoption of medium-term guidelines for key financial targets and economic programs in the Member States; joint adoption of budgetary objectives when felt appropriate, as part of a budgetary and economic coordinated policy."[103]

In the Baer and Padoa-Schioppa plan, the limits would be coordinated through a new institution. In the first stage, there would be a process; in the second, a mechanism for economic governance:

Stage 1: replacement of the 1974 Council Decision on economic convergence by a new procedure for budgetary policy co-ordination. This would be based on quantitative guidelines [expressed as a percentage of GDP], aimed at assessing fiscal performances and, where such developments are judged inadequate, triggering consultations and performance clauses of the same kind as those applying to conditional Community credits. Stage 2: the Centre for economic policy decisions (CEPD) would start operating with a view to promoting convergence and co-ordination of economic policy in the Community. Following the programme set out in the new Treaty, legislative and executive measures would be taken, at the Community as well as the national level, leading to the creation of a European Fiscal System (EFS).[104]

Finally, the skeleton report set out an institutional schema for the new monetary regime:

The system should consist of a Federal European Monetary Institution (FEMI) and national central banks. At the final stage the FEMI would be responsible for the formulation of the thrust of monetary policy in the medium term, the execution of the Community's exchange rate policy vis-à-vis third currencies and the co-ordination of short-term action (such as the adjustment of interest rates and other policy instruments). The national central banks would be entrusted with the implementation of these policies in accordance with guidelines established for the FEMI.[105]

The Padoa-Schioppa note as well as the "skeleton report" laid the basis for a new discussion in December, when Pöhl and Duisenberg severely criticized the focus on institutional engineering, and the minutes of the meeting recorded: "It was generally felt that the skeleton went too far in considering the transition to a single currency as essential to a monetary union. A single monetary policy had to be considered more important than a common currency."[106]

Lamfalussy drew out the debate about whether market forces were enough to ensure fiscal convergence. The minutes of the December meeting of the committee record his suggestion that "the idea, not shared by him, that market discipline was sufficient to bring about fiscal convergence should be considered in the report." Pöhl said that "the report should be clear in stating that [monetary union] required a substantial increase in the resources devoted to transfers."[107]

Lamfalussy went on to develop his proposal for an alternative to market discipline into a suggestion for the creation of a center for macrofiscal coordination, which would allow Europe to make a significant contribution to global financial stability. The new institution would work on the following binding regulations:

1. Establishment of limits on national budgetary deficits and rules governing their financing; these binding limitations should be recognized by changes in national legislation in accordance with provisions agreed in the treaty.
2. A onetime consolidation of budgetary positions in those countries that lie outside the limits stipulated under (1).
3. Annual coordination of budgetary policies (within the framework of setting the Community's macroeconomic policy mix), leaving the possibility of temporarily waiving the limits stipulated under (1).
4. Harsh procedures aimed at exerting peer pressure on countries that in the course of executing their budgets deviate from the

agreed objectives; this would involve, for example, special meetings.[108]

In a memorandum written for the Delors Committee in response to a paper by Claudio Borio of the BIS on the fiscal arrangements of federal states, Lamfalussy noted:

> With widely divergent "propensities to run deficits" prevailing in the various European countries, I doubt whether we could count in the foreseeable future on a convergence within a European EMU similar to that observed in most contemporary federal systems. Nor do I believe that it would be wise to rely principally on the free functioning of financial markets to iron out the differences in fiscal behavior between member countries: (a) the interest premium to be paid by a high-deficit member country would be unlikely to be very large, since market participants would tend to act on the assumption that the EMU solidarity would prevent the "bankruptcy" of the deficit country; and (b) to the extent that there was a premium, I doubt whether it would be large enough to reduce significantly the deficit country's propensity to borrow. There is, therefore, a serious risk that, in the absence of constraining policy coordination, major differences in fiscal behavior would persist within a European EMU. This would be one contrast between most contemporary federal systems and a European EMU. . . . Such a situation would appear even less tolerable once the EMU was regarded as part and parcel of the world economy, with a clear obligation to cooperate with the United States and Japan in an attempt to preserve (or restore) an acceptable pattern of external balances and to achieve exchange rate stabilisation. To have the smallest chance of reaching these objectives, all cooperating partners need flexibility in the fiscal/monetary policy mix—as we have so often told the United States. In short, it would seem to me very strange if we did not insist on the need to make appropriate arrangements that would allow the gradual emergence, and the full operation once the EMU is completed, of a Community-wide macroeconomic fiscal policy which would be the natural complement to the common monetary policy of the Community.[109]

This clear statement that a monetary union also requires some measure of fiscal union seems apposite and intellectually compelling—and has indeed been borne out in the difficulties encountered in the Eurozone in 2009 and since.

The major conflicts so far during the committee's work had concerned timing. De Larosière wanted to establish working institutions more quickly, with a European Central Bank working from Stage Two. Pöhl, by contrast, argued for a slower institutionalization, in part because the changes he foresaw required the framework of a treaty, and in part because (in the tradition of German policy on integration that went back to Karl Schiller) he wanted convergence to be demonstrated before the institutional "coronation" occurred. In consequence, large parts of the final sessions were devoted to consideration of how many new commitments should be made in the initial stage of the monetary union—or, to put the point the other way round, just how "soft" Stage One should be.

At the fifth meeting, on January 10, 1989, there was significant opposition to de Larosière's plan for a European Reserve Fund. The minutes record:

> The main objections included:
> —doubts whether an ERF was really needed; most of the tasks assigned to the ERF could in principle be performed by a strengthened Committee of Governors, possibly supported by additional committees and a permanent research staff. These auxiliary committees could be set up within the existing institutional framework;
> —the objectives of the ERF gave the impression of overemphasis on exchange market interventions vis-à-vis third currencies as a means of improving the working of the EMS; monetary policy coordination was mentioned only as a second task, although it should be the main instrument for enhancing EMS cohesion;
> —the creation of the ERF constituted an institutional step which in accordance with Art. 102A implied a procedure prescribed in Art. 236, i.e., the conclusion of a Treaty; setting up the ERF on the basis of a Council resolution and, where necessary, changing national legislation was not considered to be an acceptable alternative;
> —some members were concerned that limiting the participation in the ERF to member countries observing margin obligations within the narrow band would institutionalize the separation of Community countries into two groups.[110]

Was there a model for how future European central banking institutions might look? In this context, Pöhl embarked on an extraordinary series of reflections about how the American model might be more suited to European needs than would be the example of the Bundesbank. "On the contrary . . . an ESCB [European System of Central Banks] should be constructed in my view very similarly to, let us say, the American system more than the German system. I would not advocate the German system as a model for many reasons which we can discuss when we come to that point. I am not convinced, frankly speaking, that the German system is the most optimal system, I think that the American system is much better than ours."[111] Perhaps he thought that the position of the Federal Reserve chairman was more eminent and dignified than that of the Bundesbank president, who was only *primus inter pares* on the central bank Council.

Pöhl's reflection on the charms of the Federal Reserve was really just a prelude to the real point of his statement, that institutions mattered less than the adoption of appropriate rules for shaping national policies within the European context:

> I don't think we need major institutional changes, for instance, in order to avoid a crisis in the EMS if it would happen. We don't need a Reserve Fund, for instance, which wouldn't help to get a crisis under control. The most important thing is that we should aim for, you called it a set of rules and I think that maybe we should call it a set of principles or a set of rules, but what is meant is that we are aiming for more convergence in economic performance. If we would recommend to the Council that all member states of the Community would commit themselves to a policy which would lead to inflation rates, let us say below 3% as an example, and to reduce their budget deficit to levels, let us say below 3% of GDP, very concrete steps which wouldn't need any institutional change but would be a very very major and substantial step in the direction of a monetary and economic union. These are the kind of recommendations we should not forget in our Report. Talking about the first step I think we have to mention at some occasion that as long as divergences exist to the extent that we have them, realignments and changes in exchange rates have to be a legitimate instrument for the adjustment process.[112]

This is the first mention of the 3 percent budget deficit figure, which was to form a crucial (and highly controversial) part of the Maastricht Treaty and of the Stability and Growth Pact that was intended to give a fiscal anchor to the single currency. Three percent in fact surprised most of the economists who had participated in the discussions of the late 1980s and had not been willing to give any precise figure as to what might be an appropriate fiscal stance.

The strongest insistence on controlling and supervising mechanisms to ensure a high degree of economic convergence in Stage Two came not from the Bundesbank but from de Larosière on February 14, 1989:

> I think that progressively one will have to move toward a global vision of the objectives of monetary policy for all the participants, in other words, one would have to have a clear idea as to what one wants to have in terms of the average price level, what one wants in terms of growth targets and exchange rate targets, and one must ensure that each participating country will move toward these overall targets and objectives, that there be true convergence and that this or that country do[es] not deviate. In order to ensure that there won't be deviations one will have to have controlling mechanisms, supervisory mechanisms in Stage 2 already.

He then suggested as a phrase for the final report: "economic and monetary union without a sufficient degree of convergence of budgetary policies would be unlikely to be durable." But at a later stage, when the final draft was being discussed, he pointed out that there was a problem with the concept of "binding constraints on the size and financing of budget deficits": "who," he asked, "is going to be judge of the enforceability . . . there is no police." Lamfalussy had suggested adding "and enforceable" to the demand for binding constraints, but the suggestion was not taken into the report.[113]

The strongest resistance to the idea of formal budgetary controls came from Delors, but he argued the case in a very peculiar way. Mingasson had drafted a note to the effect that the completion of the Single European Act would mean that there would be an effectively functioning market that corresponded to the ideas of the 1960s on an optimal currency area: "The European area will then constitute an 'optimum monetary area,' in which exchange rate stability will be in the interests of each of the parties."[114] In Delors's view, similarly, the greatest possibility of effective control came from a well-functioning market that enshrined the principle of competition:

> Economic union would rest on four main pillars: the rules of competition which prevent one country from exaggeratedly subsidising its economic activities. There are rules governing competition, we have

had them for a long time and they are becoming more and more effective as has become apparent during the last four years. Then an environment which will ensure that the market . . . will operate as well as
possible. We have quite a lot of texts on concentrations, takeover bids.
Then a Community policy which would concentrate on co-operation
and regional development. Fourthly, close co-operation between budget policy with a greater or lesser degree of constraint imposed.[115]

It is striking that in the course of this discussion Delors envisaged that
there would be a modest long-term increase in the size of the Community budget, from 1.2 percent of the GDP of the member countries in
1992 to 3 percent by the end of the century. In other words, a substantially enhanced central Community budget could act as a stabilizer for
market expectations.

In the same meeting there was also a little pinprick against the power
of finance ministers, when de Larosière insisted that the European
Council, and not the Council of Ministers (that is, the finance ministers), should nominate the four members of the central board of a European Central Bank. De Larosière explained: "Ministers of finance have
to be ridden over roughshod from time to time. They think that they
are the masters of everything, and from time to time they have to be
reminded that there are others."[116]

Some of the stormiest clashes were reserved for the penultimate round
of discussions, when a full draft report was discussed, on March 14,
1989. This was the moment when many observers believed that the discussion was "almost derailed."[117] Pöhl came with thirty pages of quite
radical amendments. As a consequence of the German stance, Hoffmeyer stated that he could not sign the report as currently drafted. The
Banque de France reported that Pöhl was putting in doubt "in a radical
style all the main points of agreement of the six previous meetings."[118]
The Bank of England recorded that Pöhl would not accept the ECU as a
future currency, was not prepared to recommend a treaty change, and
would not agree to a central bank.[119] The first stage of monetary union
seemed to be becoming ever softer. Lamfalussy stated:

the only major substantive recommendation in that first stage today is
to suggest that the Committee of Governors change their method of
work and shift toward ex ante policy recommendations, which are not
binding, of course, but which are explicit recommendations. That is a

major shift, and that is a major proposal; all the rest is interesting, but when you say the same thing about fiscal policies and budgetary policies you know perfectly well that there is no budgetary committee comparable to the governors and with independent sovereign states that doesn't mean much.[120]

Even this served as an irritant to Pöhl, who reminded the committee that he did not make the Bundesbank policy, and that he could not legally commit the Bundesbank Council.[121]

Pöhl also rejected any notion that the committee should make a political gesture in favor of monetary union. He was visibly chafing against the political masters:

> Who can give the political signal? The politicians, the governments. What can be the political signal? Of course, they could say that we decided today that we will start to negotiate a Treaty for EMU, but I will not propose that, because I think we fool ourselves. Firstly, we all know that several governments in Europe are not prepared to start such negotiations at this stage, that is for sure, neither the British Government and I think also the German Government. The German Government has said in its Annual Report they have made a warning against premature institutional changes, so I don't think they will accept that. So two governments at least, I don't know about Denmark, Holland, other countries, I don't know about France, I don't know whether governments in Europe are really prepared at this stage to negotiate a Treaty which would imply far-reaching transfers of sovereignty rights.

He continued his tirade by pointing out how few countries satisfied any notion of economic convergence:

> As long as almost half of the membership of the EEC is either not able or not willing to fulfil the rules which are already there—the EMS is there and it is clearly defined and it works—as long as 5 countries, if I am not mistaken, are either not able (in some cases) or not willing (in the case of Britain or in the case of Italy, which is also unfortunately after 10 years only half a member—and it seems to me, if I may say so as a footnote, a little bizarre that the Prime Ministers of Spain and Italy, I read, are the ones who ask for monetary union. Two countries which are obviously not in a position to fulfil the given rules). As long as that is the case I don't think it makes much sense to negotiate a Treaty.

Talking about negotiations for a treaty would thus be highly "unrealistic."[122]

Delors replied to this onslaught by stating that the central bankers were in fact there as "personal representatives of your governments" and that the whole process depended on a "transfer of sovereignty." In other words, he returned to his initial reminder that there were political masters. "Nobody doubts that a treaty will be needed, nobody contests this."[123] This was exactly also the view of de Larosière, who had written to Leigh-Pemberton to explain that the treaty arrangements were the central issue of the whole Delors process.[124]

De Larosière was conciliatory in tone toward Pöhl's objections, but he added that there could still be an overall goal of inclusiveness. "It is also necessary from a technical point of view to say—and here I think we would all agree—that if there are some lags in full participation in some transitional steps by some, there could be arrangements whereby the necessary technical things would have to be handled by those who are in full participation, pending the arrival of the others."[125]

Pöhl then went on to attack another aspect of the proposed report, namely the concentration on what was still termed the ECU. He suggested instead a phrasing that would weaken the role of the ECU.

> Firstly, the Committee was of the opinion that the monetary union does not necessarily require a single currency. However, political and psychological reasons suggest that a single currency would be a desirable feature of a monetary union. A declaration that the ecu, properly defined (not the basket ecu), should assume the role of the future single currency of the Community could be made at the outset, in order to ensure private agents that there would be no discontinuity between the present ecu and the single currency of the union, and that ecu obligations would be payable at face value in ecu if the transition to the single currency had been made at the time of the maturity of the contract. But it was also felt that such a declaration might better be left for a time considerably closer to the birth of the common currency.

Pöhl saw little evidence of any widespread private use of the ECU.[126]

At the end of this highly turbulent session, Wim Duisenberg, who was seen by the enthusiasts for EMU as a Bundesbank-like "non-believer," made a proposal under which the European Council should invite the Community bodies, the Monetary Committee and the CoG, to make concrete proposals on the basis of the Delors Report. In this way he was brought into the consensus.

The next and final round of meetings, on April 11–12, 1989, was curtailed by the leaking of central points of the new draft report to the *Financial Times*. The publicity generated a fear of increasing political pressure, in particular from Lawson and Margaret Thatcher, with the result that the members of the committee were reluctant to leave room for another series of discussions. In one decisive regard, the new draft seemed to meet one of the major thrusts of Pöhl's demands, by including "price stability" as the major objective of the new central banking system.

Pöhl started off by saying that the text was "much more agreeable than the last version," or, as he later put it, "very very cooperative." But some major issues remained. Pöhl managed to secure the deletion of a section that recommended weighted voting in the future ECB. There was also a revival of the older discussion on economic governance. De Larosière spoke of the desirability of establishing an ad hoc committee of the Council of Ministers, and warned against putting the Commission in charge of the implementation and supervision of member countries' policies: an initiative that was firmly blocked by Delors, who did not want to see an erosion of the Commission's powers by some new institution. Some other last-minute changes altered the balance of the report: thus in paragraph 17, where the draft suggested that there would be a pluralism that "would require a degree of autonomy in economic decision-making to remain with independent member countries," de Larosière pressed for the replacement of "independent" with "individual" member countries: they could not really be regarded as independent any more.[127]

But the greatest tensions concerned what sort of follow-up would be required. The committee still seemed to be completely split in its view of whether immediate preparations for a treaty were needed. In particular for de Larosière, the treaty was the heart of the project: "Indeed, I do consider that the time has now come to start the process of negotiating a Treaty and that part, of course, will comprise a preparatory subpart, but that is not an extreme position. . . . It is vital for me, and it is not the manifestation of an extreme position, that the softness of the first stage be in a way offset by the indication that now is the time to launch a process of negotiation." He was outraged by the presentation of a Duisenberg outline as a negotiated compromise that could not be further debated: it was a "diktat" which was "absolutely intolerable" and which "I cannot accept."[128] There was a related issue, namely whether the committee should see itself as providing simply a technical study of the hypothetical ways of arriving at monetary union, and leaving the "whether" and the "when" to politicians. But de Larosière, followed by Ciampi, Rubio, Thygesen, Andriessen, and Boyer, wanted to delete the word "whether."[129]

De Larosière continued to emphasize his preference for a more dramatic first stage that might include a pooling of reserves, and talked about the proposed solution for the first stage as "extremely soft." Ciampi supported de Larosière strongly. By contrast, Pöhl reemphasized what he thought of as modesty: "If we ask too much from the governments and parliaments in Europe, there is a very great risk that this Report will have the same fate as the Werner Report, because then the failure of the whole thing is already embedded, if we ask too much. We are all aware what the positions of the governments are in Europe." This point was very strongly supported by Leigh-Pemberton, who emphasized the hesitation of some governments—he meant, of course, chiefly his own: "Even if we wished to give or suggest a political signal in the shape of Treaty change, let me say quite frankly we are not going to get it. It requires the unanimous vote of the Heads of State and I can tell you that that vote will not be unanimous, certainly over a period of years which is probably commensurate with stage one."[130]

The hesitant governments clearly did not include the southern Europeans. Rubio presented Spain as eager to move quickly on the path of monetary unification and the correspondent convergence of inflation and interest rates—which the Spanish and Italian governments saw largely in terms of delivering budgetary savings on interest-rate expenditure. Thygesen tried to present the need for an immediate treaty change by pointing out the inadequacies of the EMS as currently constituted. "We have discovered in our discussion of the present EMS that the scope for intensifying coordination significantly beyond what exists today is very limited." Lamfalussy reiterated his understanding of what constituted the decisive change of Stage One, trying to argue that it was in one important regard a highly significant institutional innovation: "The only substantive point in stage one, as it stands today, is that the Committee of Governors would shift in its practice from ex post discussion of monetary policy events gradually towards an ex ante co-ordination effort of monetary policies. If you go through the text, this is the only thing that is in that stage one." But Pöhl almost immediately contradicted this interpretation, in that an ex ante coordination of monetary policies "is not in the text and I would not be able to deliver, because this would not be consistent with the existing laws in the Federal Republic of Germany which I have to obey. In the first place the laws would have to be changed in order to achieve that. We have an independent Central Bank Council which takes decisions and I am not even sure I can deliver all the things I propose, and that is why I wanted to introduce something like: 'we are acting in a personal capacity.'" De Larosière, increasingly convinced that Stage One contained no innovations, seconded this view:

> I think it is, indeed, soft without pejorative, I think it is soft, I think Alexandre [Lamfalussy] was wrong, there is no ex ante co-ordination— though it is not written in, the language is very careful..No, no, no. Look at page 31, it is very important to see what is said. It is said: "you can formulate opinions on the overall orientation of monetary and exchange rate policy," I think we can always do that and I actually believe that every month we do it, and then as well as on "measures taken by individual countries." So, we are kindly invited to formulate opinions on the overall orientations of what we gentlemen have decided as measures. I think this is no real advancement vis-à-vis what happens. Then this is the boldest thing: "in particular, the Committee would be consulted in advance of national decisions on the course of monetary policy." That is indeed the greatest advancement, but you see you are going to change it.[131]

Near the end of the discussion, Pöhl resumed his explosive assertiveness: "Mr. Chairman, I really don't know what the . . . is [going on] here in this group, I really can't understand that, because, firstly, I am not prepared to accept the argument that the external world is looking at us, that they expect us to give a signal and that we are losing credibility if we don't give the signal. We are not politicians, who are we, as Robin [Leigh-Pemberton] rightly said? We are not politicians who have to give signals and we are not losing our credibility. We are losing our credibility if we make proposals which are completely unrealistic."[132]

At the end of the discussion Leigh-Pemberton produced the definitive argument against deferring the final text for a new meeting and a new round of discussions. "If I show this damned thing to the Treasury they're going to be mad. Now I'm going to be under strong pressure to show this paper to the world. They're going to clamp down on me because of all this independence stuff. If they know that I have a week to reflect, they're going to ask me to make amendments and I'm going to be dead. . . . I'm protecting myself."[133] Thus in an instance of historical irony, Leigh-Pemberton, and the fear of Margaret Thatcher's rage, made the Delors Report happen.

A similar irony produced the detailed language of the report. The drafting was subject to a large number of interventions and suggestions, especially from de Larosière, Leigh-Pemberton, and Pöhl. Leigh-Pemberton in particular took great care to tone down the report and make the language more skeptical, and was greatly assisted by the staff of the Bank of England, in particular by John Arrowsmith. Indeed, the overwhelming majority of drafting suggestions came from Leigh-Pemberton, though Margaret Thatcher remained completely unaware of the extent to which the report was a product of what was still a government bank in Threadneedle Street. The Bank of England's alterations were primarily intended to reinforce the view that the report's main function was not prescriptive but rather to lay out the concrete implications of what would be entailed by a move to monetary integration. The primary responsibility would in this way be handed back to the politicians.[134] In a letter to Delors of March 21, 1989, Leigh-Pemberton insisted that "we should not seek to pretend that the path will be easy," adding, "I do not agree that we should rely on institutional progress as the most effective way forward." Pöhl too hammered away at the absence of convergence in the EMS and the large and persistent budget deficits in certain countries. This point proved crucial, and the Maastricht Treaty's convergence criteria derived from the importance of this discussion.[135]

The final report elaborated a clear path to monetary union, defined as "a currency area in which policies are managed jointly with a view to attaining common macroeconomic objectives." But the Delors Committee added the rider: "The adoption of a single currency, while not strictly necessary for the creation of a monetary union, might be seen for economic as well as psychological and political reasons as a natural and desirable further development of the monetary union. A single currency would clearly demonstrate the irreversibility of the move to monetary union, considerably facilitate the monetary management of the Community and avoid the transactions costs of converting currencies."[136]

In its initial stage, the path to monetary union would go through the central banks and through Basel. The major mechanism of the transitional, pretreaty, phase of integration was the CoG (Section 52):

Fourthly, the 1964 Council Decision defining the mandate of the Committee of Central Bank Governors would be replaced by a new Decision. According to this Decision the Committee of Central Bank Governors should:

—formulate opinions on the overall orientation of monetary and exchange rate policy, as well as on measures taken in these fields by individual countries. In particular, the Committee would normally be consulted in advance of national decisions on the course of monetary policy, such as the setting of annual domestic monetary and credit targets;

—express opinions to individual governments and the Council of Ministers on policies that could affect the internal and external monetary situation in the Community, especially the functioning of the EMS. The outcome of the Committee's deliberations could be made public by the Chairman of the Committee;

—submit an annual report on its activities and on the monetary situation of the Community to the European Parliament and the European Council;

The Committee could express majority opinions, although at this stage they would not be binding. In order to make its policy coordination function more effective, the Committee would set up three sub-committees, with a greater research and advisory role than those existing hitherto, and provide them with a permanent research staff:

—a monetary policy committee would define common surveillance indicators, propose harmonized objectives and instruments, and help to gradually bring about a change from ex post analysis to an ex ante approach to monetary policy cooperation;

—a foreign exchange policy committee would monitor and analyse exchange market developments and assist in the search for effective intervention strategies;

—an advisory committee would hold regular consultations on matters of common interest in the field of banking supervision policy.

The second and third stages were much more ambitious. In Stage Two the new European System of Central Banks would absorb both the EMCF and the CoG. It would manage the transition from the combination of monetary policies of national central banks to a common monetary policy. In the third stage, exchange rates would be locked finally and irrevocably. The ESCB would pool reserves and manage interventions with regard to third currencies. "With the establishment of the European System of Central Banks the Community would also have created an institution through which it could participate in all aspects of international monetary coordination" (Section 38). Delors emphasized that monetary integration would need to be accompanied by a consolidation of the single market and competition policy, as well as by an evaluation and adaptation of regional policies (Section 56).

The Bundesbank responded directly to the Delors Report. Internally, it welcomed the report as an "optimal" solution from its viewpoint, with a federal central banking system, a commitment to price stability, and a rejection of the idea of a parallel currency. Members of the Bundesbank Council recorded their surprise that "astonishingly all the committee members agreed with the German position."[137] Subsequently a major discussion developed about whether under the new mechanism the CoG could commit the Bundesbank to action, which would be a violation of the autonomy provisions of the central bank law. In a letter to Chancellor Kohl, the Bundesbank set out its institutional opinion very directly: "our views" were expressed, in the descriptive and analytical parts of the report, as well as in the fundamental recommendations. The letter then focused on paragraph 7, with its reference to the CoG, and the Council decision to define more extensively the competence and tasks of the CoG. "If in the course of time our capacity to act is reduced, this can only be accepted if the political commitment to an economic and currency union is at the same time affirmed and not set in doubt once again." An intergovernmental conference should be called only when the preliminary work had been satisfactorily accomplished. The current progress should not be endangered by a premature fixing of exchange rates. The Bundesbank also pointed out that a fixing of exchange rates would lead to greater pressures to make transfers via the structural funds of the EC budget.[138]

At the opposite end of the argumentative spectrum, the French treasury set out its view that the report had allowed the new institution to exist in the absence of any type of democratic accountability (a refrain that would recur continually in discussions of the proposals for and then the operation of the ECB). The French officials believed that the governors were confronting the British and French governments with an ultimatum.[139]

At a meeting of the EC finance ministers at the Hotel La Gavina at S'Agaro on the Spanish Costa Brava on May 19–20, 1989, there was considerable hostility to the central recommendation of the report in paragraph 39 ("the decision to enter upon the first stage should be a decision to embark on the entire process"). It was also unclear whether the United Kingdom was prepared to accept any discussion of a treaty revision. "Some might say Mr. Lawson has committed himself to phases two and three," commented Onno Ruding, the Dutch finance minister; "others might say he has not." Both the Dutch and the German ministers sounded rather cautious. German Finance Minister Theodor Waigel stated: "We favour an EC intergovernmental conference, but this needs preparation and a time cannot be fixed."[140]

At the Madrid summit of June 26–27, 1989, however, the heads of government accepted the Delors Report as "a sound basis for future work." In particular, Madrid accepted the Delors follow-up procedures (paragraphs 64–66), which entrusted more work to the ECOFIN as well as to the CoG, the Monetary Committee, and the EC Commission, to implement the first stage and to provide suggestions to serve as the basis for a revised treaty at an intergovernmental conference. Margaret Thatcher was furious; she had been outmaneuvered by Delors and felt betrayed by Robin Leigh-Pemberton, whom she never forgave and thenceforth treated as a weak-willed and overpolite representative of Britain's effete ruling elite. The British chancellor of the Exchequer, Nigel Lawson, had consistently argued that Stage One was desirable but that there was no need for a new treaty or for further stages. But Thatcher could not really disagree either with anything in the first stage, which had emerged as a result of the efforts of Pöhl but also especially of Leigh-Pemberton in the "softest" possible form. She merely emphasized that "there is nothing automatic about going beyond stage one."[141] Britain remained rather outside the process, even after the United Kingdom joined the EMS exchange rate mechanism in October 1990. Indeed, in November the Bank of England issued a statement to the other European central banks: "The Governor of the Bank of England records that the UK authorities do not accept the case for a single currency and monetary policy. He has nevertheless participated fully in the discussions of the Governors' Committee on this draft statute."[142]

The Madrid summit was followed by some more skeptical commentary from Frankfurt. In an interview with the *Financial Times*, Pöhl seemed to cast doubts on the later stages of the integration program and in particular on the need for "an EC bank." British journalists interpreted the interview as implying that "the West German government is underplaying the difficulties of establishing such an institution," and implied that Pöhl was "echoing the arguments of Mrs. Margaret Thatcher." In the interview, Pöhl argued that it would take "many years" before there was satisfactory economic convergence. "He believes the basic issue over the European central bank proposals—the transfer of monetary sovereignty away from the present national institutions—has been grasped by relatively few people, one of whom is Mrs. Thatcher. There is some doubt whether this has been understood by Chancellor Helmut Kohl." Then he added: "If the idea spread and the (German) population understood what it is about—namely that it centres on their money, and that decisions on it would be taken not by the Bundesbank but by a new institution—then I would imagine that considerable resistance might arise." He also stated that the issue of the site of a future central bank was of "absolute importance" but that the debate was "an indication of the political problems in setting up such an institution."[143]

A few days after the interview, Pöhl wrote to German Finance Minister Waigel, arguing against drawing the central bank governors formally into meetings of the ECOFIN. The Bundesbank case was that the EC treaty gave strong powers to the Commission, but not on the question of "currency political issues." Pöhl reminded Waigel about the phrase in the Single European Act about the "responsibility of central banks."[144]

The view of what had been achieved was much more positive at the Banque de France. There the main emphasis was on filling the institutional lacunae left by the report. A paper prepared by the Banque de France set out observations on the need to control the central banking system. It recommended the creation of a secretariat that would constitute the embryo of the future central bank: it would conduct visits of countries being discussed; engage in foreign exchange operations; report semiannually on the economic situation of the Community; and propose the orientation of monetary policy in the Community.[145]

At the CoG on July 11, 1989, Delors presented a report on the negotiations at Madrid, as well as on the previous day's ECOFIN meeting, at which a very tight deadline for the preparatory work for the first stage of monetary union had been set. For both de Larosière and Pöhl, the negotiations provided an opportunity to reemphasize the crucial theme of central bank independence. De Larosière took very seriously the dual obligations of the CoG and the Council, as specified in paragraph 65 of the Delors Report, which had been accepted at Madrid. First of all, he insisted that the CoG must be seen as a real committee, with a profile and an independence that made it a very serious partner; all the committee's actions should be guided by this principle. "If progress was to be made on both fronts—economic and monetary—it was necessary for the Council of Ministers to take care of the Community's macroeconomy and for the Committee of Governors to deal with monetary policy. The more these two bodies were strengthened, the better." Pöhl added that not much attention had been given in the political debates to what for him was the key issue of central bank independence. "This last aspect was also referred to in the report on EMU but had not been raised in the public discussions. And yet it was a very important point, as a more independent Committee of Governors, representing a kind of nucleus of the future European system of central banks, was not possible unless its members enjoyed sufficient independence in their own countries."[146] The relaunching of Europe was not possible, according to the view that was deeply held by both Delors and Pöhl, without a relaunching of the CoG.

The independence discussion was not just an abstract or theoretical concern. It became acutely political at exactly the moment that the Delors recommendations were being translated into a central bank statute and a treaty framework, because the massive economic and fiscal shock of German political reunification breathed new fire into the contentious debates over German monetary policy and its impact on the rest of the Community.

8

Designing a Central Bank

The 1990s saw the emergence of a new philosophy of central banking, in which independence of central banks from the political process became a core component of the culture of monetary stability. Europe played a pivotal role in the formulation of the new philosophy, largely because designing a new central bank outside the framework of the nation-state raised new conceptual issues. In every country, there was a continual and natural tension between governments' wish to control and manipulate monetary policy for the sake of short-term growth and short-term political advantage, and the logical prerequisites for long-term monetary stability. If stable money were to be an international rather than a merely national good, that conflict would take on an additional level of complexity. That was especially the case in the European context, where there were contrasting philosophies of monetary management, with on one side an entrenched German view of the importance of central bank autonomy, and on the other side a French emphasis on traditions of economic management and the primacy of politics.[1]

The CoG occupied a central role in this debate, offering as it did a sanctum where central bankers could commune in an environment largely free of immediate political pressure. It was chiefly responsible for drawing up the details of a new monetary constitution, and thus for leaving its intellectual imprint on Europe's future monetary institutions. In the aftermath of the Delors Report, the CoG began to transform itself from a committee or forum for the exchange of ideas and information into the skeleton apparatus of a central bank. The translation of the Delors Report into a potential basis for a new central bank depended on the extension of the existing, rather informal, group structure of the CoG. The governors, in their personal capacity, had constituted the core of the Delors Committee. The report provided the big vision, as it were, the poetry of monetary reform. The governors now hoped that they would be able to write the "prose version" of the treaty provisions that would govern any new institutional advance. There was an explicit acknowledgment that, far from being marginalized as the governors had feared at the outset of the negotiations about the new monetary order, the CoG was the "prefiguration" of new institutions.[2]

A political science distinction is helpful in considering the function of the central bankers in developing notions from the Delors Report into an institutional reality. The Delors Committee has sometimes been described as an "epistemic community" in that its success depended on its ability to project a shared vision. What distinguishes an epistemic community from a merely bureaucratic body is that whereas the bureaucracies "operate largely to preserve their missions and budgets," the epistemic community applies "consensual knowledge to a policy enterprise subject to their normative objectives."[3] Bureaucratic structures are much more limited, and cannot easily work in a transformative way, because they are protecting interests rather than promoting ideas. By contrast, the process described in this chapter is less one of bureaucratic capture than of the promotion of an idea or a vision.

Institutional Change

The most immediate outcome of the new prominence of central bankers was institutional. The CoG was given a higher profile by the ECOFIN decision of November 13, 1989. An obvious sign of the CoG's new importance was Bundesbank President Karl Otto Pöhl's altered view of the committee: previously he had declined to take the chair when it should have devolved on him by rotation and seniority, and he seemed to have a rather low view of the CoG's significance and relevance. By contrast, now he wanted to be chairman for a two- or three-year term, so that he could preside over the work of the committee while it was engaged in the fundamental task of drawing up the statutes for a future European Central Bank. There were other signs of institutional change. In an extensive list of proposals to other central bank governors, Pöhl suggested language about independence, the use of money stock as an intermediate target for policy, and innovations in institutional design, including an alteration of seating arrangements to restrict participation at the round table. The chairman would represent the committee to the ECO-FIN. Pöhl's initiative reflected more than simply personal proclivities. The major issue was the one that had been at the heart of every discussion of the Bundesbank, namely central bank independence. The idea of a well-designed central bank seemed to be fundamentally a question of taking over a German model that was already functioning well. The future ECB thus came to look more and more like an internationalized version of the Bundesbank. From the German standpoint, it was especially important that there be no joint meetings of the governors with the ECOFIN, as that might be held to diminish the committee's independence. The secretary-general would "receive his instructions from the chairman." There would be a research component to the work of the secretariat. The chairman of the Committee of Alternates, who would be elected by the CoG, would cooperate closely with the chairman of the EC Monetary Committee.[4]

In December 1989 the committee agreed to elect Pöhl for a three-year term and end the convention of an annually rotating chair.[5] The chairman was now responsible for representing the CoG vis-à-vis the ECO-FIN and the general public. Pöhl now saw himself as having the task of representing Europe's central banking fraternity. The secretariat would be enhanced, and a research division added. The chairman would propose the secretary-general and other members of the secretariat.

In addition, and in conformity with the recommendations of the Delors Report, three subcommittees were established to deal with monetary policy, foreign exchange policy, and banking supervisory issues. The first two of these corresponded more or less to the informal groups that had been known only by the names of their chairmen, Bastiaanse and Raymond (monetary policy) and Heyvaert and Dalgaard (foreign exchange policy). The last, which had already been informally established in March 1989, was a new departure that signaled a new level of interest in financial stability issues on the part of the European official community.[6] These subcommittees that emerged from existing groups of experts were in practice embryo divisions or departments of a new central bank—or at least an anticipation of the department structure of the European Monetary Institute.

Some central banks were inevitably suspicious of the new powers that were being developed by the CoG. The greatest reservations about a body that was building itself into an institution came from Paris. A

Banque de France memorandum worried that the chairman would give instructions to the secretary-general, and spoke of "excessive prerogatives" that were "difficult to accept" and would deprive the CoG of its previous "collegial character."[7] There was also some skepticism on the Bundesbank Council, with one member arguing that a return to the 1964 regime was preferable, in that it would be a violation of the 1957 Bundesbank Law if the German central bank were to be bound by decisions of a European committee of central bankers.[8] There was also a competition with EC agencies, including Eurostat, the European statistical agency, whose operation would be critical in monitoring compliance with convergence criteria. The governors wanted to be in control of such data as balance of payments and monetary statistics.[9]

The transformation of the CoG from a talking shop to a proto–central bank was also underlined by an alteration of the seating arrangements, again at the insistence of Pöhl. In January 1990 a reform was agreed, in accordance with the Pohl letter, under which only the governors, an invited member of the EC Commission, the chairman of the alternates, the secretary-general, and a rapporteur would sit at the main table.[10] The other representatives of central banks or of the Commission were consigned to back seats. The number of staff accompanying governors to the meetings was cut to two. The secretary of the EC Monetary Committee, who had previously attended CoG meetings, was no longer invited; and the MC retaliated by ending its practice of inviting a member of the CoG secretariat. The old-timers were shocked; the old collegiality and informality had been replaced by a new formality and officiousness. In this respect, the CoG really became more of an international institution and indeed an embryonic central bank.

Drawing Up a Statute

The framing of the new European monetary order occurred in several different contexts: the tensions following from German monetary policy, which created problems for French policymakers (and also for U.S. policymakers); the political suspicions following from the sudden German unification process in 1990; but also a longer-term debate about the desirability of central bank independence. A fundamental conflict broke out over the choice of the forum that should realize the proposals of the Delors Committee. The French and German finance ministers,

Pierre Bérégovoy and Theo Waigel, met on August 24–25, 1989, at Rottach-Egern on the south German Tegernsee, a meeting that proved to be the beginning of a period of very close German-French rapport on monetary arrangements. Both ministers agreed to push for the Monetary Committee and the CoG to be the central arenas for discussion. The central bank governors, Pöhl and Jacques de Larosière, as well as Jean-Claude Trichet, director of the French treasury, were also prominent participants in the Tegernsee meeting. The financial experts faced some competition: a study group under President Mitterrand's policy adviser Elisabeth Guigou believed that it was foreign ministers who should be responsible for a proposal that would lead to a new EC treaty, and wanted to exclude the technocrats. But the Guigou paper was largely ignored. The EC Monetary Committee then prepared a paper that was presented to an informal ECOFIN and CoG meeting in Ashford Castle (March 31–April 1, 1990) in Ireland, which in practice left the elaborations of the detailed draft to the CoG.[11]

When central bankers design a new central bank, they obviously draw lessons from their own experiences. In the 1960s the members of the CoG had emphatically asserted their independence from Community institutions, from the Commission and the Council; but in reality the majority were highly dependent on governments and finance ministers. The debate of the early years had thus focused heavily on the relations of national governments with European institutions. The general issue of central bank autonomy or independence, which had been a prominent concern in the 1920s, in the era of the fiercely proud Bank of England governor Montagu Norman, was not very widely discussed in the golden years of post-1945 economic growth. In part, monetary policy was not seen as a centrally important aspect of general economic policy-making; in part, the international fixed-exchange-rate system provided a simple monetary rule.

In the 1970s high levels of inflation and the end of the par value system ensured that there was more discussion not only of monetary policy (including at the CoG), but also of the circumstances in which an optimal monetary policy could begin to be implemented.

Two large issues emerged as crucial, the first concerning the status of a central bank, the second relating to the policy guidelines to be adopted. The two were clearly closely related in that a wrong institutional framework for central banking might be expected to lead to bad policy decisions. In both cases, there was a wide variety of practices among the national European central banks. Achieving some sort of reconciliation between the different modes of operating appeared to be an intractable issue, but during the 1990s both questions were resolved. The first was resolved by the treaty process. The issue of monetary policy formulation could not be dealt with in this way, and in fact it was eventually handled in the European Monetary Institute through the development of a new institutional mechanism.

Central Bank Independence

Three European central banks, those of Germany, the Netherlands, and Switzerland, as well as the Federal Reserve System after 1979, were frequently held up as models of good policy-making. These countries had quite independent central banks, with clearly defined mandates and competences. In addition, it was in Germany and Switzerland that central banks first adopted a clear monetary target. They had significantly lower inflation levels than central banks with lower degrees of political autonomy.

During the 1980s a substantial academic literature developed concerning the inflation performance as well as macroeconomic stability and growth. The new consensus suggested that in industrial countries, but also more generally, central bank independence was closely correlated not only with lower rates of inflation but also with better economic performance. It was already well known that monetary authorities were frequently subject to political pressures that produced higher levels of monetary growth.[12] The newer literature initially developed on the basis of an appreciation that establishing firm commitment mechanisms was an essential element in the establishment of policy credibility.[13] The approach emphasized the contractual element of the position of central banks, and consequently focused on the explicitly defined terms of contracts or laws establishing central banks.

The literature became so vast because of the problems of defining precisely what is meant by central bank independence. One deceptively simple approach takes the statutes of the central banks as a guide, and then measures legal independence. It tries to quantify variables concerning the appointment, dismissal, and term of office of the governor or chief executive; variables on conflicts between the executive branch and the central bank and the degree of participation of the central bank in the formulation of monetary policy and in the budgetary process; the objectives as stated in the charter of the central bank; and legal restrictions on the ability of the public sector to borrow from the central bank. But laws do not cover every eventuality, and there is often a substantial area in which power politics can intrude.

Second, it is possible to look simply at the rate of turnover of governors/chief executives. A high turnover and brief tenures are characteristics of many unstable political and monetary regimes in the second half of the twentieth century, especially outside Europe (though France in the 1930s had a very rapid rotation of central bank governors).

Third, the use of questionnaires may give some sense of perceptions of central bank independence in practice.[14] This approach rests on the notion that central bank independence is actually not easily measured by formal legal criteria, and that the actual practice of central bank operations is what is decisive.

All these approaches raise conceptual problems. The codings that are applied to establish legal independence are sometimes rather arbitrary, and scholars have for instance disagreed on the importance of whether a given central bank has a government representative on its board. Surprisingly often, academics discover that in the country that they know best, the laws do not fully describe the realities of central bank appointments and discussions within the central bank, while for more remote countries they are prepared to accept the letter of the banking laws. Thus the French economist Edmond Malinvaud found that Vittorio Grilli, Donato Masciandaro, and Guido Tabellini overstated the degree of French independence; the Italian economist Alberto Alesina criticized the approach of Robin Bade and Michael Parkin to the position of the Italian bank; and the Dutch Sylvester Eijffinger and Jakob de Haan thought that the Nederlandsche Bank was more independent than was represented in Alex Cukierman's survey.[15] In this way an apparently rigorous scientific exercise becomes very quickly and evidently random and arbitrary. In a letter to the *Financial Times* protesting against a ranking table produced by the journalist David Marsh showing the Italian institution as the least independent European central bank, the eminent Italian central banker Carlo Ciampi wrote that "a meaningful appraisal of central bank independence requires a thorough evaluation of the institutional setting and of the bank's modus operandi as developed over time and consolidated in practice."[16]

Turnover of central bankers need not necessarily be a measure of political interference; it could indeed be (as it was in the case of the nineteenth-century Bank of England, whose governorship rotated every two years) a way of combatting influence and clientilism. Finally, the survey approach is also problematic in that the perception of independence often follows from observing the demonstrated effects of independence (such as low inflation), and the approach thus generates a circularity when used to determine the nature of the link between central bank independence or autonomy and specific outcomes such as price stability or economic growth.

In the light of these problems, different analyses may be required that are not so simply quantifiable. A more subtle approach involves examining the political and social setting within which the central banks work. They reflect a particular culture; thus it is often persuasively argued that the German outcome in terms of the policy of the Bundesbank is a response to a high preference by German voters and politicians for monetary stability as a result of the experience of two severe inflations associated with the world wars, which led to the effective expropriation of middle-class Germans. Stability is thus not a simple chance feature of an arbitrary approach to central bank design, but rather the product of a deep social and political consensus. Such analysis raises the question of whether the design features can be simply and successfully appropriated or imitated when the consensus is absent.

Another approach to the problem thinks of central banks as exposed to very powerful domestic interests, and sees the existence of a powerful financial community as pressing for a stability-oriented policy. This account seems to offer some insights into the behavior of the Bank of England before 1945, when the central bank was a transmission mechanism for the interests of the City of London, and perhaps it applies also to the modern history of the Bundesbank.[17]

Some observers have noted what is sometimes called the Thomas Becket effect: that with strong central banks, even political appointments turn out quickly to adapt to the prevailing ethos of the central bank. King Henry II of England had appointed his good friend and reliable official, Thomas à Becket, archbishop of Canterbury at a time when the crown was locked in a bitter conflict with the church; but he then found that Becket was as loyal to his new office as to the old and in the end ordered the archbishop's assassination (or martyrdom). As applied to central banks, the effect can obviously be explained in institutional terms: Manfred Neumann, for instance, argues that "the conditions of contract and of office would have to be set such that the appointee free him- or herself from all former political ties or dependencies and accepts the central bank's objective of safeguarding the value of the currency as his or her professional leitmotif."[18] But this does not seem the best or most plausible type of explanation, in that it was not the fact that kings cannot sack archbishops that led Becket to change his stance, but rather a deep commitment to a set of values as embodied in a particular institution. To take a well-known recent central banking example, Helmut Schmidt hoped to tame a Bundesbank that he felt was obstructing his government's aims by appointing State Secretary Karl Otto Pöhl to the board of the Bundesbank; but Pöhl identified with the Bundesbank view even before he was appointed as president (which required the government's nomination, and thus might have been thought of as an incentive for Pöhl to toe a more politically compliant line). Another powerful example of the influence of unwritten rules and conventions is that of the postwar Nederlandsche Bank, whose governor, according to the banking law, could be dismissed by the government; in practice this never happened, and an ethos developed in which such a dismissal became unthinkable. The political environment and the climate of expectations mattered more than the formal text of the law.

With all its weaknesses, there is no doubt that the new academic literature had some effect on the climate of opinion. By the 1990s, central bank independence was often thought to be a prerequisite for sound policy, although it was not listed as one of the ten commandments for a good institutional governance and policy framework as portrayed in the original formulation by John Williamson of the so-called Washington consensus.[19] The academic literature as well as the practice of the highly regarded central banks (Germany and Switzerland came top in nearly all surveys of central bank independence) led to a widespread recognition that independence would bring improvements in the policy environment. Central banks became more willing to listen to academics, and academics consulted more freely with the central banking community. Thus Eijffinger's and Eric Schaling's influential discussion lists as helpful commentators on earlier drafts the major intellectual central bankers of the time, Mervyn King, Tommaso Padoa-Schioppa, Hans Tietmeyer, and Nout Wellink.[20]

The general political climate also mattered in the discussion of the legal position of central banks. In 1989–1990 the issue of institutional redesign suddenly seemed an urgent priority for some of the countries making the transition from the planned economy to the market. In the Czech Republic, Poland, and Hungary, central bank independence was a major part of the reform package designed to secure a stable macro-economic framework. At the same time, in 1989 the Bank of Japan's position relative to the government was strengthened, and New Zealand in 1990 dramatically increased the independence of the Reserve Bank.[21] These new developments gave impetus to a trend that was already well under way. The struggle for increased independence for Europe's central bank had already started before the intellectual revolution in economic thinking on the subject in the late 1980s, and before the political upheavals of 1989–1990 created a new framework for conceptualizing the relationship of political institutions and rules to political and social processes. In some notable cases, the debate was associated with the beginnings of the EMS: in particular, the Bundesbank and the Banca d'Italia had used the negotiations over Europeanized money in the late 1970s to increase their own political autonomy.

The deeper origins of the discussion about central bank autonomy lay in clashes in the high-inflation environment of the 1970s, when monetary policy was the subject of acute political controversies. The tension between the Bundesbank and the German government reached a highpoint in the aftermath of Chancellor Helmut Schmidt's EMS proposals. When Schmidt appeared before the Bundesbank Council in its meeting of November 1978 to appeal for its support in concluding the EMS agreement, he said: "The Bundesbank will play a decisive role also in decisions that are to be taken. It will be two or more likely three or four years before there is an international law dimension to this issue; an addition to the Treaty of Rome or a new treaty is not in my view an issue for this decade, and until then the question will be in essence an affair of central banks. For me the independent position of the German central bank stands outside any discussion."[22]

In Italy, the arrest of Governor Paolo Baffi in 1979 was a major shock to an institution that thought of itself as a central force for stability in the rather unstable world of Italian politics. In the wake of Baffi's vindication, in the so-called *divorzio* of 1981, the Banca d'Italia was no longer obliged to absorb the excess supply of short-term treasury bills. Thus after 1981 it regained control of monetary policy that had been lost in the interwar years. The reform measure had been widely discussed as a necessity following from Italy's membership in the wider-band version of the EMS. In its annual report for 1980, the Banca d'Italia had already called for an end to the practice of buying treasury bills. But such a move did not necessarily require any alteration of the statute of the bank (and thus does not show up on survey studies of comparative central banking laws). The notable improvement in the Banca d'Italia's independence as regards monetary policy was carried out simply by an exchange of letters between the governor and the treasury minister, with no new law required and no involvement of the legislature. It was justified explicitly by reference to the European context, and in terms of Italy's new membership in the EMS.[23]

While the Italian central bank was becoming more independent, strains between the French government and the Banque de France were increasing. In the radical left-wing phase of the first two years of the presidency of François Mitterrand, the bank was effectively consigned to the sidelines. In the winter of 1981–82 Governor Renaud de la Genière refused to agree to an increase in treasury advances, but the government simply devised a new form of treasury bond to meet its financing needs. De la Genière had been assured in 1979 by the center-right government that he would serve a five-year term without being dismissed; he was worried that the leftist government might not honor this pledge, but he did in fact serve out his term, and when it expired, in 1984, the French government had moved to the political center.[24]

The highly politicized clashes of the early 1980s gave an impetus to calls for legal changes to guarantee greater autonomy for the Banque de France and the reversal of the controls imposed in the 1930s. Two former governors pleaded for a stronger Banque. Olivier Wormser in 1984 stated that an independent bank was "an indisputable advantage for a country, whether large or small" and that the existing statute of the Banque de France was "insufficient." De la Genière in 1986 argued that since the Popular Front government of 1936 the central bank had been "too much in the hands of the government." He also prepared a detailed reform proposal.[25] Raymond Barre also argued for a reform, and in 1985 the right-wing politician Charles Pasqua introduced a bill that would have made dismissal of the governor more difficult.[26] When the right won the legislative elections in 1986 and formed a government under Jacques Chirac, the new prime minister promised a law that would establish the autonomy of the Banque, but in fact not much happened. Finance Minister (and subsequent prime minister) Edouard Balladur was skeptical about an independent central bank, perhaps as a result of his difficult relations with the Bundesbank. Edith Cresson, the French prime minister in 1991–1992, had in the past stated that the Bundesbank model of independence had been imposed on Germany by the United States, and that Europe should not be subject to such an external intervention.[27]

When Jacques de Larosière succeeded Michel Camdessus as governor in January 1987, he took some symbolic steps to emphasize his understanding of the importance of an independent central bank. Although he had a splendid official residence at the Banque de France, he retained his own Paris apartment so that he could easily resign if there were to be a policy disagreement with the government. In the Delors Committee, he fully supported the notion of central bank independence for a new European institution, and defended this notion articulately when he was accused of sacrificing France's national interests by Pierre Bérégovoy's treasury director, Jean-Claude Trichet, in a memorable and painful meeting on April 27, 1989, in the aftermath of the publication of the Delors Report. The position of the French government at this time still involved a belief that Bundesbank-style independence would be unconstitutional in that it ran counter to the conception of a government that "determines and conducts the policy of the nation." The redefinition of the role of the Banque de France did indeed eventually require a legal change to the French constitution. Trichet, who thought it his mission to spell out the legal implications of France's policy commitment, complained that the recommendation of the Delors Report was "too Germanic" and that de Larosière had subscribed to the strongest possible formulation of the doctrine of central bank independence. De Larosière then explained that independence was not only an essential precondition for a successful negotiation with Germany, but that it would also bring substantial benefits for France and for French fiscal policy.[28] The showdowns between Trichet and de Larosière inevitably did not occur in a purely French context; even more extraordinarily, the key German policymakers witnessed another such clash in the context of the bilateral Franco-German discussions.

French policy for a long time remained in denial. During the debate on the Maastricht referendum, President Mitterrand on television denied that the treaty involved a commitment to central bank independence. But in the end Mitterrand accepted greater independence for the Banque de France in accordance with the logic of the European integration process. The new bank law was passed in June 1992, and it was the assurance of a new independence that allowed the Bundesbank to give a unique support to France in the currency turbulence of 1992–1993 (discussed below). Some hints of the older French position still remained politically potent. In September 1992, Trichet's successor as treasury director (and later also his successor as governor of the Banque de France), Christian Noyer, was still stating that central bank independence was incompatible with France's republican traditions, in that the Republic was "one and indivisible." Centralized states such as France or Japan (which as he pointed out had an excellent record in fighting inflation) exercised a political control over central banks, while independent central banks were fundamentally suited to federal states such as Germany, Switzerland, or the United States (and hence also, presumably, although he did not point this out at the time, the European Community).[29]

In Britain, the 1979 Conservative Party election manifesto had alluded to the desirability of central bank independence, but after the Conservative victory, the new government of Margaret Thatcher lost interest in the subject. (Thatcher had also been critical of Labour Prime Minister James Callaghan for standing on the sidelines of the EMS and thus allowing Britain to become marginalized.) Ten years later, the issue of the position of the central bank became acute again. Chancellor of the Exchequer Nigel Lawson in September 1988 asked Treasury officials to draw up a plan for greater Bank of England independence, in which the bank would be given some statutory duties, including the preservation of the value of the currency.[30] The step seemed congruent with Lawson's wish to move into the EMS. But Prime Minister Thatcher was not sympathetic, and saw the political importance of interest rates in a country where a large part of the population (and especially potential Conservative voters in marginal constituencies) had variable-rate mortgages.

Central Bank Independence in Practice

Central bank independence was at the core of the discussions of the Delors Committee and of the recommendations of the Delors Report, as well as of the controversies that it provoked at the political level, especially in Paris. Without inclusion of this principle, the text would have been unacceptable to Germany. The result was reflected in the draft statute evolved by the alternates in 1990, whose first article seemed to echo the terms of the 1957 Bundesbank Law. But the key to independence was actually not to be found in the specific text of an article of the statute, but rather in the mechanism for putting the statute into force.

Three aspects of the new institutional arrangements were vital to German willingness to move to sacrifice the Bundesbank's role in monetary policy. First, a national law, even one such as the Bundesbank law that seemed to command a deep national political consensus, could always be altered by legislative process. On the other hand, altering an international treaty that created the European Union would require the unanimity of the signatories. Consequently, Bundesbankers who reflected on why their 1980s skepticism about EMU had later turned into support for the process always gave the answer that what mattered was central bank independence; and that while the Bundesbank was protected by a law, the ECB was backed by an international treaty. This operation seemed to echo one of the most successful operations in German monetary and economic history: the currency reform of 1948 and the new monetary institutions (the Bank Deutscher Länder, the forerunner of the Bundesbank) were not the creation of German law, but originated from an Allied military government. Many Germans quickly realized that in the long run this setting of monetary institutions outside a democratic framework made them better off, as it removed the institution from political controversy and from the temptation to politicians to make legal and institutional changes. The second vital aspect of the new arrangements lay in a mechanism for excluding the European Parliament from any influence on monetary policy-making. The Frankfurt central bankers saw the risk that transferring the business of central banking to a European level would involve a new array of political actors, including the EC Commission and the European Parliament.[31] Third, there was an awareness that law and practice do not always conform. The Bundesbank negotiators were particularly emphatic in their insistence that independence had to be a "lived reality."[32]

The most intensive debates about the philosophy of institutional design took place in the Monetary Committee, where both finance ministries and central bankers were represented. At the February 1990 meeting, Treasury Director Jean-Claude Trichet represented the older position of the French government when he criticized the paper prepared by the CoG secretariat on the grounds that it was "not acceptable" that in the case of a conflict between goals for the new institution the priority should be given to price stability. There was also, he believed, a need to consider "economic policy objectives," or in other words, growth. But Trichet also criticized the secretariat for limiting the role of the new institution as a lender of last resort, and he made clear his dislike for any arrangement that required the European Central Bank to report to the European Parliament. It was also clear that the Banque de France supported this position. The British Treasury representative, Nigel Wicks, agreed that the ECB should not be controlled, as did Hans Tietmeyer in the German Finance Ministry; but Wicks added the interesting suggestion that the ECB might be split up into functions, so as to allow full independence in monetary policy but not in other policy areas.[33] From Paris, Pierre Bérégovoy was still profoundly skeptical about the idea of central bank autonomy.

The Monetary Committee found two other aspects of the institutional architecture problematic. What would happen in Stage Two? Germany, supported by a broad grouping of Belgium, Luxembourg, Denmark, Ireland, and the Netherlands, saw no real need for Stage Two institutions at all, besides offering the kind of technical functions that the CoG in fact already provided. A separate stage was therefore redundant, and would only be an unnecessary and unwelcome invitation to increased politicization of central banking. By contrast, France and Italy, while recognizing that ultimate responsibility would remain with national authorities until Stage Three, thought that there would be a need for a "factory" to be established during Stage Two in order to create the basis for immediate policy effectiveness in the next stage.[34]

A further issue was raised by the prospect of the availability of new financial resources. Who should control them, and on the basis of what conditionality? The history of EC conditionality was a saga of softness and failure, and interestingly there was no distance between France and Germany on this issue. Discussing the deteriorating situation in Greece in late 1989, Trichet wondered whether a new conditionality mechanism should be applied to a new loan, but went on to comment that "the IMF was the better vehicle for conditionality." Tietmeyer agreed, on the grounds that EC discussions tended to be politicized and affected by interest linkage. "Country conditionality would be watered down by politics, including by interventions by the Commission and the Foreign Affairs Council."[35] The whole history of European integration was one of sharp limits on attempts to impose conditionality on member countries.

In seeking to avoid politically influenced monetary decisions, the Monetary Committee was writing itself out of the future of the European design and making central bankers the decisive part of the process. At the May 1990 meeting of the MC, there was a consensus to recommend guarantees of the institutional, operational, personal, and financial autonomy of the national central banks operating in the new system. The July 1990 report of the MC emphasized the single or unitary nature of EMU (in other words the linkage of economic and monetary union), but also talked about flexibility in participation and the need for economic convergence. The latter point reflected the long-standing German and Dutch idea that EMU might be a long-term goal, but that it should not involve members with a suspect convergence record (while Italy, partly supported by France and Belgium, had thought that a better course would be to create ambitious and early dates for institutional development, in effect rushing the fences to get integration quickly). In line with the German views, the Monetary Committee report also emphasized that the passage to Stage Two and Stage Three might not necessarily be made simultaneously by all member countries, and that measures should be taken to reinforce market discipline over budget deficits. The Monetary Committee's "orientations" for the Intergovernmental Conference (IGC), needed to prepare an amendment to the Treaty of Rome, provided for a procedure for monitoring and avoiding excessive deficits. It recognized that member states needed to remain "masters of the main aspects of budgetary policy," but at the same time stated that "a stability-oriented monetary policy can in the long run only be successful if supported by sound budgetary policy." That meant a prohibition on the monetary and compulsory financing of public deficits, and a no-bailout rule: "It must be clear that the Member States do not stand behind each other's debts." In the MC's view, the consequence of such a rule would be that financial markets would exert discipline by imposing differential interest rates and "ultimately by refusing to lend." A majority of the committee wanted to establish a mechanism for enforcing legally binding positions, perhaps through the European Court of Justice.[36]

A parallel EC Commission document also argued that a monetary union without an economic counterpart might see large divergences of economic outcome and "could lead to an excessive burdening of monetary policy. . . . The Community monetary institution would have an overdominant role. The questions of independence and accountability would be seen in a more extreme light."[37]

The CoG made a similar point. As Pöhl presented the governors' conclusions to an informal ECOFIN meeting in March 1990, the CoG "stressed the importance of budgetary discipline and its key role in the Economic Union, which must be realized in parallel with the Monetary Union. Sound budgetary policies are indispensable and complementary to stability-oriented monetary policies." Pöhl emphasized that "it is essential to avoid in the future the repetition of developments often observed both within and outside the Community, namely that budgetary laxness has been tolerated on the basis that monetary policy would compensate for any shortfall."[38]

The newly pronounced emphasis on central bank autonomy raised questions about the future role of the Monetary Committee. A strengthening of the central bank side of cooperation might logically imply that central banks should no longer be represented in the MC: such a stance was taken by the German government. Many finance ministers saw a strengthening of the Monetary Committee as a necessary counterweight to the central banks, and some suggested that as the national central bank governors and then the ECB acquired greater authority and autonomy in the monetary policy sphere there should be a clearer separation of powers with regard to monetary and fiscal policy.[39]

Meanwhile the CoG began to run with the ball on institutional design of the new central banking system. In April 1990 Pöhl made a proposal at the CoG for draft statutes on the objectives, organization, functions, instruments, and voting system of a new bank.[40] In May Delors distributed a note from the Commission about the institutional character of EMU. In particular, the Commission was concerned about three issues: voting within the ECB, democratic control, and external monetary policy. The Commission proposed a weighted voting system as in the EC, with the addition that the ECB board should be required to cast its vote as a bloc to avoid divisions. The "reconciling of Eurofed independence with democratic control" was quite problematical. The term preferred by the Commission to describe the future institution, Eurofed, captured some sense of the desirability of political control in its allusion to the American model; the CoG's favorite term, the European System of Central Banks, did not. But both versions saw some attraction in the U.S. example, in which the board or council had a permanent core. Delors reported that "the European Parliament wished to exercise such control but this seemed unacceptable and the Commission proposed that it should provide the 'scapegoat' or 'fuse' as it were; if the European Parliament disagreed with the policy being followed by Eurofed, it could table a motion censuring the Commission, as at present." Finally, the Commission wanted external monetary policy to be decided jointly by the finance ministers and the governors.[41]

The governors were resistant to any hint of political supervision, and believed that any measure of political control would in practice mean pressure to inflate. They also wanted to escape from any obligation to accept quantitative inflation targets—a view that was gaining acceptance among policy-oriented academic economists.[42] Pöhl stated emphatically: "A press communiqué should never contain normative price increases; this would give the impression that a certain rate of inflation was being aimed at, whereas the objective was in fact to reduce it. It was perhaps essentially a question of presentation. For example, when the Bundesbank published its monetary targets, it explained that they had been calculated taking account of the potential growth rate (or assumed real growth) and the unavoidable inflation rate."[43]

De Larosière seized the initiative and proposed that the CoG should concern itself fundamentally with the drafting of the ECB statute rather than with expressing views on the large range of issues that Pöhl wanted to consider (including the role of the national central banks and the issuing of ECUs). Central bank governors were after all not very well equipped to handle the political issues, quite apart from the fact that such demands coming from them would look either self-interested or like a surrender to German pressure for a Bundesbank model (and both of these accusations could obviously be made simultaneously). As a result, a great deal of the Bundesbank's campaign on the political aspects of institutional design was handled by the permanent representative of Germany at the Intergovernmental Conference, State Secretary

Horst Köhler. In the CoG, Pöhl took a more technical stance, and proposed that the ECB statute should be built around a number of principles:

- the fluctuation margins should eventually be abolished, i.e., parities should be irrevocably locked;
- there should be a single monetary policy, which would be implemented by the institution to be set up;
- the priority objective was price stability;
- the institution should be independent from both national governments and other Community bodies;
- the payment system should operate smoothly;
- a single currency should ultimately be created;
- there should be no monetary financing of public sector deficits;
- there should be no bailing out [of national states].[44]

Pöhl believed that "responsibility for monetary policy was indivisible—he had already said so at a conference in Paris—but some might not take that view and might propose other solutions." The preparation of the statute thus set off an intense political clash. The governor of the Bank of England began to worry about a "two-speed Europe" dominated by a "German bloc" with locked exchange rates.[45]

At its Dublin summit meeting on June 26–27, 1990, the European Council asked the CoG to undertake preparatory work for the forthcoming Intergovernmental Conference on monetary union, which would run in parallel with an IGC on political union. The CoG took as its guideline two principles: price stability as the primary objective of the central bank; and the indivisibility and centralization of monetary policy. This would not be "in contradiction with the principles of federalism and subsidiarity."[46] The model of the Bundesbank looked powerfully attractive as a guide for central banking practice, and many participants felt that the new institution was in fact designed to replicate the structure and philosophy of the Bundesbank. In the draft statute prepared by the CoG, there was a direct echo of the relationship of the German central bank to the government in Article 2, specifying the "objectives" of the system, and stating that the system of central banks would "support the general economic policy of the Community." Yet at this point the Community had no mechanism for defining a single economic policy to go alongside the single monetary policy of the new central bank, and the phrase was consequently altered by the government negotiators into the much less intellectually satisfactory obligation to "support the general economic policies in the Community."[47]

As a result of the dialogue between the European Council and the CoG, the alternates were assigned the responsibility of producing a draft statute on the basis of the principles that had been at the core of the governors' discussion in May 1990. The initial debates focused upon the name: should the new institution be called the European Central Bank, or should it have a "lower-profile" name, such as Authority or Agency? Should it be given the task "to support the stability of the financial system"? This phrase was placed in square brackets to indicate that it was controversial. What should the legal status of the institution be in the Community?[48]

A report to the alternates' committee by a group of legal experts in August 1990 set out the quadripartite institutional structure of the EC (Parliament, Council, Commission, Court of Justice) and pointed out that the European Investment Bank and the Center for Vocational Training were "Community organs." But a central bank was not analogous to these institutions, and the report recommended very strongly that the European System of Central Banks should *not* be classified as an EC institution.[49]

At the same time, the insistence on the independence of the central bank explicitly echoed the much older debate about the relationship of the Commission to national governments. The wording chosen in Article 7 on autonomy deliberately recalled the language of 1967 describing the role and position of the European Commission: "in the performance of their duties, they [Commissioners] shall neither seek nor take instructions from any Government or from any other body. . . . Each Member State undertakes to respect this principle and not to seek to influence the members of the Commission in the performance of their tasks."[50]

In July the CoG agreed on the "one man one vote" principle for the ECB Executive Board, which in case of a conflict would apparently mean that the effective power of the Bundesbank would be greatly reduced. There would be no rotation of voting equivalent to the arrangement that prevails in the Open Market Committee of the Federal Reserve banks, whereby only the New York bank (perhaps to be considered the American equivalent of Frankfurt as the site of the financial powerhouse) has a permanent vote.[51] The central bankers thus rejected the original plan of the EC Commission, which would have made the system much more political. The shift later attracted a great deal of criticism in Germany, which looked to be the loser if the institution was viewed in terms of a balance of power, with influence shifting to the numerous softer-currency and southern countries. But in fact the decision reflected the experience of successful consensus forming in the CoG, and indicated the extent to which the Bundesbank was now prepared to trust the stability-oriented monetary philosophies now emerging in other central banks. The exercise of consensus formation in practice, as events later materialized, combined with the avoidance of the formal votes that characterized the Federal Reserve's Open Market Committee, generally gave German interests a *greater* rather than a *lesser* voice in the ECB Council. But this design element was also probably predicated on the assumption that the accession criteria to the EMU would be set sufficiently strictly to stop the inclusion of very soft countries; the design would indeed eventually prove to be problematical with the expansion of membership in EMU.

By September 1990 there was substantial agreement on the major design features, including independence and the unitary monetary policy, but some disagreement remained about the division of responsibilities between the Council and the Executive Board of the ECB, and how operations might be decentralized without impairing unitary monetary policy and coherent exchange rate policies and operations. The options ranged from including all national central banks within the system to maintaining central banks with their own balance sheets, with specified contributions to a central institution.[52]

Pöhl presented this outcome to the ECOFIN on September 8, making clear the great importance that price stability would have for the new regime:

> Starting with the objective, we want to underline the unequivocal statement in the Delors Report that the primary objective of the system must be to preserve price stability. But, of course, giving primacy to this objective must not be misinterpreted as an invitation to act in a single-minded manner and without due regard to other economic policy objectives. There is full recognition that monetary policy is not conducted in a vacuum, and the new system shall, without prejudice to the objective of price stability, support the general economic policy

of the Community. This will be explicitly stated in the draft statute. However, there should be no misunderstanding: in the event of a conflict between price stability and other economic objectives, the governing bodies of the system will have no choice but to give priority to its primary objective. There can be no compromise in this respect.

This was the solution eventually adopted in the enumeration of ECB tasks in Article 2, and it seemed to strengthen the emphasis on price stability in comparison to the U.S. system, where the concept appeared only in 1977 and was qualified by a dual mandate that also referred to high employment. Pöhl also insisted that the ECB not be categorized as an EC institution:

> Our unanimous support of an independent system should not be interpreted as an attempt to escape from democratic accountability or as a claim of exclusive competence to conduct a stability-oriented monetary policy. But we are convinced, on the basis of actual experience in our countries, that success in pursuing a monetary policy in accordance with the primary objective hinges critically on having safeguards against political pressures. Even more than in some of our countries this is likely to be true in a large Community, given the different traditions and experiences with inflation.[53]

The Bundesbank's response to the remaining uncertainties was to press for all monetary policy-making to be concentrated in the ECB Executive Board.[54] Such an arrangement would be less political, less subject to a confrontation of divergent national interests on monetary policy, and would prevent the national central banks of smaller or softer countries from playing an excessive role. This pressure was completely in accordance with Pöhl's statement to the ECOFIN that "The preparation of the Council's work will lie with the Executive Board, as will the execution of the system's operations."[55] But this solution, in which decisions were left to the small board, attracted some opposition, as a board that was not directly linked to the national central banks might develop into a new and dangerous sort of supranational monetary government.

An analogous debate took place over the operational conduct of the new central banking system. In the September 1990 alternates' discussions, the Germans and Italians pressed for a centralized solution, with France and Britain wanting more decentralization of ECB operations, allowing greater room for specific monetary policy preferences, in particular in operations with government debt. The compromise eventually worked out included three elements: central execution of exchange market interventions; execution at a national level of domestic monetary policy, with directives from the center, but the means of execution (what kind of paper central banks might take, and in what volume) left to national central banks; and a pooling of profits with profit sharing in accordance with a key.[56] One major issue concerned the instruments available to the bank in making monetary policy. In the Anglo-American central banking tradition, the crucial tool of the central bank was open market operations. Denmark, Finland, and Norway as well as Portugal used sales and purchases of government securities. But the practice raised continental, especially German, worries that such an instrument of monetary policy could be overused and amount to a ready way of monetizing government debt. Although the Bundesbank had begun to use repos—repurchase agreements with central banks agreeing a short-term purchase of securities—as its major monetary instrument in the 1970s (it was the first continental central bank to do so), the Bundesbank had also depended much more on standing facilities, lending at below-market rates, as a way of regulating the supply of liquidity (as did the Netherlands and Finland, Norway, and Sweden). Germans consequently resisted abandoning discount operations until the set of instruments for the future ECB provided for a longer-term financing facility. In addition, Germany, along with Austria, Italy, and Portugal, relied on permanent reserve requirements for banks (unremunerated in the German and Austrian cases) as a monetary policy instrument. In the September governors' meeting, Robin Leigh-Pemberton tried to leave open the possibility that the central bank might influence the money market through credit and overdraft facilities to governments. This view was also reflected in the commentary, namely that "the ECB and the NCBs [national central banks] would not be prevented from purchasing government securities in the secondary market, but only in the context of monetary policy operations."[57]

The alternates' discussion occurred at the same time as positions at the political level had become harshly polarized. A dispute had flared up in the aftermath of the October 27 and 28, 1990, meeting of the European Council in Rome. At Rome, the discussions had been carefully channeled by Italian civil servants, notably by Tommaso Padoa-Schioppa.

Italian Prime Minister Giulio Andreotti had managed to push through an agreement to start Stage Two on January 1, 1994, largely by securing in advance the agreement of Chancellor Helmut Kohl. In its meeting, the European Council wanted to call the monetary institution created in Stage Two the European Central Bank, but the Dutch government quickly responded with a statement that also reflected the position of the Bundesbank. According to The Hague, the new institution was something different from an ECB. The main German and Dutch fear was that if there were to be a gradual institutional evolution of the ECB, the door would open to increasing political pressure on policy, as well as in regard to the potential membership of a monetary union.

The EC Rome meeting laid out plans for a market-based EMU, which would promote both price stability and growth. The Monetary Union involved a new independent monetary institution, responsible for single monetary policy based on a single currency, and with a primary goal of maintaining price stability. Stage Two was to begin on January 1, 1994, and, in advance of that date, EC member countries would be under an obligation to participate in the EMS exchange rate mechanism (ERM). In that stage, the monetary institution would reinforce the coordination of monetary policy, prepare a single monetary policy, and supervise the development of EMU. There was a "process" that would "ensure the independence of the new monetary institution at the latest when monetary powers have been transferred."[58]

The U.K. government fiercely objected to the outcome of Rome, because of the road map it laid down for monetary union, but London was isolated in its stance. Other governments accepted but noted the lack of clarity about whether Stage Two was conditional on fiscal improvement, and whether the monetary institution was the same as in Stage Three, namely the European Central Bank.[59] Tommaso Padoa-Schioppa and the Banca d'Italia believed that the institution created in 1994 would be the ECB. This was implied in the agreement reached at the Council, though not explicitly stated. The October 1990 Rome communiqué had stated: "At the start of the second phase, the new Community institution will be established."[60]

There were thus two parallel fault lines: one in which Britain looked isolated from all the other member countries, and a second running between France and Germany. In November 1990 the EC Monetary Committee was the scene of a bitter clash involving Trichet and the

British, when Trichet ridiculed the British proposal for a hard ECU (which in some ways looked similar to de Larosière's proposals in the Delors Committee, and to older French ideas of a parallel currency). Trichet saw this new proposal emanating from London as little more than a delaying tactic.

Meanwhile, the Bundesbank felt that the EC Commission was discredited by the increasingly obvious polarization in the Monetary Committee. The German state secretary in the Finance Ministry, Horst Köhler, also reached a devastating verdict, noting that the Commission was engaging in "shadow boxing," that it had no "clear line of analysis," and that it was "drawing inappropriate conclusions." Such debates left major uncertainties about the future of the economic and currency union.[61] On November 5, 1990, Andrew Crockett of the Bank of England presented the British proposal on the hard ECU to the alternates, who greeted it with considerable skepticism and saw it as a potential source of exchange rate turbulence.

The critical issue of central bank independence produced a whole series of auxiliary policy consequences: insistence on fiscal rules, on absence of direct accountability of the future monetary institution to European institutions, as well as on policy flexibility in the implementation of monetary policy. Throughout the debate between the CoG and the Council, as mediated by Delors, the governors maintained a unified stance as the central part of their vision for how integrated monetary management should function. On December 6, 1990, Pöhl wrote a sharply worded letter to Delors complaining that the EC Commission had prepared extensive documentation on the coordination of monetary policy targets (in which it called for credit targets as well as a targeting of monetary aggregates) and had thus intervened in an issue that belonged strictly in the domain of the central banks. Such an action in his view constituted a subversion of the March 12, 1990, Council decision.[62]

When the CoG discussed the draft statute in November 1990, the controversies focused on three major elements, and in each case the Bundesbank representatives were insistent on a solution that translated German answers onto the European level.[63]

1. *Exchange rate intervention.*   Exchange rates are obviously political, and attempts to fix global exchange rates had been negotiated not by

central banks but by governments, either through the IMF or later increasingly in the framework of G-7 finance ministers' meetings. Even in Germany, the Bundesbank was not responsible for foreign exchange policy according to the 1957 Bundesbank Law; and one of the most long-standing struggles of the Bundesbank involved the argument that the government should recognize that foreign exchange policy had consequences for monetary policy. In particular, the Bundesbank shied away from the possibility of intervention commitments that would require the use of Deutsche Marks with potentially inflationary consequences in Germany. From the French point of view, however, a great deal of the attraction of new institutional arrangements lay in the improved management of exchange rates. This was particularly a topic for discussion at the Monetary Committee meetings, where the French treasury pressed especially vigorously for the view that government should determine and define the external value of the currency. The Bundesbank's Hans Tietmeyer tried to counter that exchange rate policy was properly the business of the central bank (although, in reality as well as in German law, that responsibility fell to the government). A March 1990 interim report by the Monetary Committee included as the responsibility of the governments not only the adoption (and eventual abandonment) of central rates, but also the "setting and redefining of target zones." The reference to Balladur's old concept from the mid-1980s, which horrified the Germans, was dropped from the final version, which simply set out two contrasting views of how exchange rate policy should be managed. In October the Monetary Committee simply said that "the ECB shall be consulted with a view to reaching a consensus prior to any decision relating to the exchange rate regime of the Community."[64]

In the CoG discussions, Pöhl was skeptical about the desirability of including references to exchange rate intervention: "The exchange rate policies and operations of the system should never conflict with the priority of price stability. He therefore suggested deleting the sentence in square brackets and including an additional phrase to the effect that 'the commitment to exchange rate policies should not be in contradiction to the task of maintaining price stability.' He said that the system should not be obliged to intervene in the foreign exchange markets when such action would be incompatible or interfere with the monetary policy objectives of the system." De Larosière was less enthusiastic about this suggestion and instead proposed "adding a sentence to the article stating that the consultations aimed at reaching a consensus should be guided by the overriding principle of price stability. He felt that any further elaboration would be politically unacceptable."[65]

The Bundesbank and the Nederlandsche Bank suggested adding to Article 4 the requirement that the Community's exchange rate policy be subject to the consent of the ECB.[66] The result, which appeared as a formulation in the Maastricht Treaty, was seen by the Bundesbank as a European equivalent of the famous Emminger letter, a get-out clause that protected the central bank from really extreme consequences of foreign exchange commitments by governments.

At the March 12, 1991, IGC of personal representatives (the negotiators immediately below the ministerial level) and the March 18 ministerial-level meeting, German State Secretary Horst Köhler insisted that the principle of unanimity be applied to Council decisions on the exchange rate system, so that Germany would in practice hold a veto. Finally, at the IGC ministerial meeting of December 2–3, 1991, German Finance Minister Theo Waigel achieved what was thought to be a German victory with the formula that "general orientations" rather than "guidelines" would be given by EC governments on exchange rate policy. Article 109.2 of the Maastricht Treaty eventually stipulated: "These general orientations shall be without prejudice to the primary objective of the ESCB [European System of Central Banks] to maintain price stability."

2. *Lender-of-last-resort functions.* It would be reasonable to assume that the central bank issuing a new currency would take over the functions normally associated with existing national central banks. But assumptions about central banks' operations—and their willingness to state clearly what the objectives were—varied significantly from country to country. In particular, the Germans worried about the moral hazard implications of central bank regulation of the financial sector. Before the First World War, the German Reichsbank had been widely viewed as providing the ultimate support of the financial sector. Its origins lay in a response to the severe financial crisis of 1873, and the big German banks saw the central bank as a backstop. But the experience of hyperinflation in the 1920s led to a new approach, and a feeling that unlimited support for the financial system contained a danger to monetary

stability; and in consequence, the idea of a central bank as a lender of last resort had much less support in late-twentieth-century Germany than in the Anglo-Saxon world, where Walter Bagehot's 1867 treatise, *Lombard Street*, was still widely regarded as the basic text for modern central bank behavior.

There was thus considerable uncertainty about the wording of the statute on financial sector regulation. In the draft produced by the alternates, the "tasks" of the ECB included "to support the stability of the financial system"; and Article 25 on "Prudential Supervision" included the following tasks for the ECB, which were placed in square brackets to indicate that they were not yet consensual:

> 25.2. [The ECB may formulate, interpret and implement policies relating to the prudential supervision of credit and other financial institutions for which it is designated as competent supervisory authority.]
>
> 25.3. [The ECB shall be entitled to offer advice to Community bodies and national authorities on measures which it considers desirable for the purpose of maintaining the stability of the banking and financial systems.]
>
> 25.4. [The ECB may itself determine policies and take measures within its competence necessary for the purpose of maintaining the stability of the banking and financial systems.]

The Bundesbank wanted to avoid references to an explicit role for the ECB in supervising banks, "especially in the context of maintaining the stability of the banking and financial system and the delicate question of moral hazard. These two articles could be misinterpreted as a lender-of-last-resort function."[67] As a consequence, the items in square brackets were in the end excised from the CoG draft.

3. *Supervisory board.*   The Delors Report had recommended the appointment of a supervisory board, which would necessarily have provided a higher element of political involvement and control. The governors now abandoned any such proposition. Again, this step was in line with the preferences of the Bundesbank, which was confident that it provided a good institutional template for a future European monetary order, and that the directorate or bank council should bear sole responsibility for setting monetary policy.

After the CoG's meeting on December 11, 1990, the draft statute was sent on to the Rome IGC, with only two issues left unresolved: the distribution of income from central banking operations, and the mechanism for modifying ECB statutes (in particular in the likely case of a subsequent enlargement of the monetary union). Both of these matters were obviously very political, and the CoG was clearly not the appropriate forum for their resolution. A text on both issues was only included in the April 1991 draft statute.

When the European Council started the two parallel IGCs, one on political and the other on monetary union, a new round of controversy broke out, along the lines of the old divisions between a German view, which was now termed "fundamental" about the need for gradual policy convergence, and the Italian and French position, which was now given the sobriquet "telescopic." In the latter view, a sort of shock therapy would be applied in order to harness market forces to accelerate nominal convergence in goods markets as well as in financial markets. The German enthusiasm for monetary union seemed to have cooled.[68]

In December 1990, just as the CoG finalized its draft statute, Karl-Otto Pöhl told the House of Lords Select Committee on the European Communities: "I do not need a European Central Bank. The Bundesbank is good enough for me." By contrast, Jean-Claude Trichet, the director of the French treasury, told the same committee that convergence would be a consequence of monetary union and not a prerequisite.[69] At the Rome Council meeting, Delors had complained that "we might have to provoke a political crisis" if the attempts to deflect EMU were successful. "In all this euphoria," he said, "someone has to play Cassandra."[70]

Italy tried to refocus the discussion on the need for a quick establishment of the ECB. In December 1990 the Banca d'Italia circulated a memorandum in the CoG, "The Functions of the European Central Bank in the Second Phase of Economic and Monetary Union." It tried to distinguish between "qualitative" policy (the structural characteristics of policy instruments), which would be made by the new institution, and "quantitative" policy (interest rates and liquidity), which would remain with the central banks. At the end of the second phase, with a common approach to open market operations and minimum reserves, the ECB would also take over monetary policy. But already in the second phase there would be foreign exchange interventions conducted through the ECB. In addition, the ECU would be strengthened through a specification of conditions for foreign exchange interventions in private ECUs.[71]

The Italian initiative looked as if it corresponded quite precisely to a draft treaty presented on December 10, 1990, by the EC Commission, which referred to a "Eurofed" already instituted in Stage Two, a stage that would not be conditional on any policy convergence.

The discussion prompted by these initiatives polarized the CoG in the subsequent meeting (January 8, 1991). De Larosière echoed the Rome communiqué when he said that he wanted to set up "at the beginning of Stage Two an ECB and an ESCB as defined in the draft Statute." Stage Two would be of only limited duration and be concerned solely with the preparation of Stage Three. By contrast, Pöhl tried to downplay the consequences of the language used at Rome. The communiqué "should not be seen as a legal document but as a statement of political intent." Responsibility for monetary policy would "remain in the hands of national authorities until a decision concerning the passage to the third phase had been taken following an assessment which would take place three years after the start of Stage Two. It should be borne in mind that during this period exchange rates could be changed and therefore the situation might not be significantly different for a period of at least six to eight years." The new institution had nothing to do with either an ECB or an ESCB. He injected a skeptical note: "It also remained to be seen whether, at this stage, a treaty change—which would be necessary to create the proposed institution—would be acceptable to member states. Furthermore, the character of Stage Three had to be absolutely clear before the institutional arrangements were discussed in detail." Henning Christopherson, the EC Commissioner for Economic and Financial Affairs, thought that the second stage would include "an embryonic form of the ECB and ECSB."[72]

The clash between the Italian and French approach and that of the Germans and the Dutch was sidestepped as another front opened up in the conflict over institutional design. It concerned the way in which a new money should be established. Three governments (the United Kingdom, Spain, and France) put forward alternative visions to that of the CoG draft, in which the single currency was an evolution of the ERM's basket currency: the United Kingdom, wanting to signal its distance from the project, proposed a radically incompatible alternative based on the idea of a hard ECU.[73] There should be no basket currency, and no reliance on one national currency, but rather a link to the most stable currency at the time. In case of realignments, the hard ECU would thus never be devalued against any participating currency. The idea of the hard ECU had originated in 1989 in the private-sector City European Committee chaired by Michael Butler, but was taken up again in the immediate aftermath of the Delors Report by the U.K. Treasury as a way of watering down the Delors recommendations so as to get a common currency without any political appendages, with no fiscal dimension, no regional dimension, and above all no central bank. The concept was first officially articulated in June 1990, when Leigh-Pemberton circulated it to his colleagues with the request that "I should like to discuss these [ideas] with you at our next meeting of the EC Governors' Committee." The request went unmet. At that time, Leigh-Pemberton advertised the scheme's fundamental attraction as bringing "collective counter-inflationary pressure to bear throughout the Community, while leaving the ultimate responsibility for national monetary policy decisions in national hands."[74]

Spain identified in substance with major elements of the British proposal, and urged a hard basket, in which there would be a change in the basket composition of the ECU at each realignment, to ensure that the ECU would not be devalued against the strongest EMS currency, in other words the same feature as the British proposal for a stable European currency. But elsewhere there was a suspicion that the "hard ECU" was a wedge that was being deliberately and skillfully inserted by British negotiators in order to drive France and Germany apart.[75]

The most critical alternative proposal came from the French government, which saw in the CoG version too much of the hand of the Bundesbank, and pushed for a greater role for the ECU, as well as more political control of the ECB and a stronger role for the European Council. France also, like Italy, saw the EMS as part of the new treaty and consequently deduced a need for all member states to participate. French ministers advocated an idea of "economic governance" that should function at a political level in parallel to the new monetary institutions; and for a brief time Finance Minister Bérégovoy also took up the "hard ECU" plan. But then, in a dramatic meeting in the Elysée on January 26, 1991, President Mitterrand instructed him to desist; there should be "no reversal of alliances. The ally is Germany! The Brits are aligned with the United States!"[76]

Germany's draft treaty proposals looked very different from the French or British schemes. Germany emphasized "ground rules" that were designed to ensure a genuinely competitive market and rapid price adjustment: a commitment to price liberalization, freedom from uniform wage-setting, and a stipulation that price indexation would require the consent of the new central bank. Fiscal policy would be limited by a "golden rule" permitting deficits only to finance investment and not current expenditure. In Stage Two, there would be only a Council of Governors of the member states and no ECSB.[77]

These rules were at the outset a matter of simply bilateral Franco-German negotiations, and indeed the EC Commission complained that the twelve member countries had never engaged in the political discussion of convergence.[78] Delors reported to the CoG that "there was disagreement over the degree of stringency of rules in the economic area." In addition there were differences over the responsibility for external economic policy, and about democratic accountability. "At present there were tensions between member states as to the underlying philosophy of institutions. Positions had hardened dogmatically and doctrinally and considerable efforts would have to be made to resolve the problem." But he ended his statement with an emphatic call for further involvement by the CoG, which he saw as "an integral part of the Community structure." In the same CoG meeting, de Larosière firmly distanced himself from the French government paper, explaining that his dissent from the official Paris position provided "an insight into the intellectual independence of the Banque de France, which was not institutionally involved in the negotiations at the IGC."[79]

In the first part of 1991, under the Luxembourg presidency of the EC, the controversies in the preparation of the draft statute and a draft treaty focused on financial issues concerned with the operation of the ECB, and on the mechanisms for moving through Stages Two and Three. The Bundesbank worried that the central bank governors' documents were not treated as the basis for negotiations by the IGC personal representatives, but were merely viewed as one option among many.[80] The personal representatives drew up an informal nonbinding document (called in EC parlance a nonpaper) that gave a decisive role to the political authorities in any decisions by the ECB to increase capital, as well as in the allocations of profits from the ECB operations to a reserve fund.[81] The Luxembourg proposals also provided for sanctions in regard to excessive deficits, and wanted to leave the decision on the start of Stage Three to the European Council.

According to the Luxembourg proposals, the ECB Board of Governors, essentially an enlarged version of the CoG, would take the place of the European Monetary Cooperation Fund and assume the functions and powers of the CoG as early as Stage One, and its functions would then be transferred to the ESCB in 1996. Thus in effect Stage One would be subdivided into two substages. The ECSB would then take over responsibility for the operation of the clearing system.[82] That timetable was strenuously opposed by the EC Commission, and on June 10 at an ECOFIN meeting Belgian Finance Minister Philippe Maystadt proposed that a new institution, the European Monetary Institute, be established in January 1994, right at the beginning of Stage Two. In response to the Luxembourg nonpaper, the CoG alternates worked on reconciling the original draft of the statute with amendments proposed by the IGC. Both the Banking Supervisory Subcommittee and the alternates wanted to retain the draft statute's provision on banking regulation. All except one of the alternates wanted to keep the ECB Statute's Article 21.1 on avoiding monetary financing of the public sector.

At this stage, although there was a substantial consensus among the governors about the no-bailout formulation of Article 21.1, prohibiting central bank purchases of government securities on the primary but not on the secondary market, the CoG's staff was skeptical about the impact of such a restriction on future national fiscal policies in the monetary union. A CoG paper stated the point explicitly:

> Article 21.1 will *not suffice* to exert as much discipline as is needed to avoid excessive budget deficits, or to induce markets to correctly set interest rates on public debt. On the one hand, public entities may still enjoy a privileged access to financial markets as a result of national fiscal, banking, and prudential regulation. On the other, markets may expect that governments will ultimately be bailed out when encountering difficulties in refinancing their debt, and governments may expect the same. Finally . . . Article 21.1 would not prevent that budget deficits lead to pressure being exerted on the ECB to pursue a more accommodating monetary policy.[83]

The CoG sent a revised statute to the EC presidency on April 26, 1991, with a mechanism for allocating income based on relatively simple population and GDP criteria, adjusted every five years, with the same key being used to determine subscriptions to the new institution, the transfer of foreign reserve assets, and the determination of voting on financial matters. The issue of amending the system's operation was handled by a simplified amendment procedure.

There followed a shock to the central banking community, when on May 16, 1991, Karl Otto Pöhl abruptly announced his resignation as Bundesbank president for "personal reasons." It was easy for commentators to interpret the move as a political gesture, an outcome of a deteriorating personal relationship with Chancellor Helmut Kohl, and especially of Pöhl's frustrations about German fiscal policy in the wake of German unification.[84] But there were also differing visions of Europe in Frankfurt and Bonn; and Pöhl also sincerely felt that the security precautions that surrounded the head of the Bundesbank imposed a heavy burden on his young family. With surprising rapidity, the most charismatic and voluble—as well as volatile—European central banker stepped off the stage.

The Transitional Process

By the summer, when the alternates were discussing the institutional arrangements for Stage Two, it was clear that the ECB would not operate at that time—in line with the proposals of the Luxembourg presidency. The new Netherlands presidency of the ICG initially took over from its predecessor the suggestion that the transitional institution should be called the European Monetary Institute. There were now two draft statutes being discussed in parallel: one for the intermediate, Stage Two institution (the EMI; see Appendix A), and one for the final European Central Bank and ESCB of Stage Three (see Appendix B).

Stage Two of monetary union—the transitional phase—raised much greater political difficulties for the central bankers than Stage Three. First of all, some governors wanted the EMI to have a capital endowment of its own; others thought this unnecessary. As a compromise, Article 15 of the statute, though not establishing an initial endowment, allowed the EMI Council to call for a capital subscription. The Bundesbank did not want the EMI to engage in banking operations, as this "might be misinterpreted by markets that the new monetary Institution had a role in exchange rate policies."[85] Essentially, the Bundesbank saw the EMI as the logical continuation of the CoG. As the new Bundesbank president, Helmut Schlesinger, a veteran and eminently respected figure of the bank, explained to the Bank of England, the Committee of Governors would be "reformulated" as a "Governors' Council, which would discuss and agree on monetary policies to achieve the convergence necessary for stage 3," as well as playing a central role in the determination of exchange rate policy with regard to third countries. It should be independent at an early stage. As Schlesinger put it quite quaintly, "if we had to give independence to one's children it was better not to wait until they were twenty years old."[86] In addition, the convergence criteria in the treaty should be refined in order to reduce the danger that politicians would override the convergence mechanism.

The issue of the Stage Two institution was the subject of intense bilateral Franco-German diplomacy in the spring of 1991. The Germans thought that the preparatory work should be done as much as possible in what Kenneth Dyson and Kevin Featherstone call "the technical institutional venues," the Monetary Committee and the CoG.[87] Neither the German Finance Ministry nor the Bundesbank wanted an ECB in Stage Two. This position could be defended most effectively at the CoG. At the meeting of the CoG alternates on July 7–8, 1991, Hans Tietmeyer stated that he "rejects the idea of a progressive development of responsibilities of a supranational monetary institution during Stage Two. The institution should not have a Board of Directors. . . . He also rejects the name 'European Monetary Institute' proposed by the Dutch Presidency." The French position was diametrically opposed. Philippe Lagayette of the Banque de France noted "the usefulness of a central bank from the start of Stage Two if this stage is short. It should be the embryo of the final institution."[88]

In other areas too, major differences in national approaches came to the surface. The most contentious issues in the design of the EMI involved the extent of its competence and the management of reserves. Article 6.4 in the CoG's draft provided: "Subject to a [unanimous] decision by the Council of the EMI, the EMI may hold and manage foreign exchange reserves as an agent for and at the request of national central banks." The CoG's Foreign Exchange Committee was divided over whether the EMI should manage reserves: the British, Dutch, and German representatives were skeptical, while the French negotiators saw this capacity as central to the effective operation of a transition regime, with the risk that otherwise the EMI would be an "empty shell." Managing reserves would give the EMI the ability to "develop its clients."[89]

A similar clause was kept through the initial discussions but does not appear in the final version of the Maastricht Treaty. In practice, the EMI would not receive reserves from national central banks.

A further debate concerned the desirability of the EMI's engagement in the supervision of the financial sector. Article 5, which listed the advisory functions, included advice on prudential banking supervision:

> 5.3. In accordance with Article 109D(4) of the Treaty, the EMI shall be consulted regarding any proposed Community act in the monetary, prudential or financial field; it shall also be consulted by national authorities regarding draft legislative provisions within its field of competence, in particular with regard to Article 4.3.
>
> 5.4. The EMI shall be entitled to offer advice to and to be consulted by the Council, the Commission and the competent authorities of the Member States on the scope and implementation of Community legislation relating to the prudential supervision of credit institutions and to the stability of the financial system.

But the German alternate expressed a reservation regarding a consultative role for the EMI in the prudential and financial field, and this provision does not appear in the final Maastricht Treaty.

The alternates were divided on the critical issue of who would nominate the president of the new institution. They reflected a rift at the political level, where the personal representatives of France and Germany took sharply opposed positions, with Trichet advocating a president and vice-president appointed from outside the existing central banking fraternity, and Köhler calling for the governors to choose one of their own. In consequence, the corresponding article (9) appears in two variants in the CoG's draft. In one (preferred) version, the governors would appoint a president and a deputy president themselves from their own number; in the second, the president would be appointed by the European Council after consultation with the European Parliament and with the Committee of Governors. In the first variant, the option was left open of having a managing director, again with two alternative schemes, one an election by the CoG, and the other appointment by the European Council. In the governors' meeting on October 28, 1991, Wim Duisenberg, Hans Tietmeyer (representing Schlesinger), and Robin Leigh-Pemberton strongly opposed the inclusion of any externally elected member, while de Larosière and Ciampi strongly backed the managing director option.[90]

The move from Stage Two to Stage Three, and in particular the convergence criteria that would be a precondition for entering Stage Three, were likewise highly contentious. The debates also became more difficult because of the obvious hostility of the United Kingdom to any mechanism that would drive it into a monetary union. At an ECOFIN meeting on June 10, there had been an agreement that no member state could be obliged to participate in Stage Three, but that none should obstruct the progress of others. On the fringes of the subsequent European Council meeting on June 28–29, John Major, the British prime minister, made it clear that he would not sign an agreement at Maastricht that created a legal obligation to adopt the single money without an opt-out.[91]

On September 10, 1991, at the CoG Delors reported on the previous day's ministerial IGC meeting under the Dutch presidency. The finance ministers' meeting had been highly controversial, and the finance ministers had rejected the convergence criteria. Eleven delegations had approved January 1, 1994, as the beginning of Stage Two. Ten voted in favor of creating a European Monetary Institute, with two (the German and Netherlands representatives) opposed. Delors consequently presented the three principles that would govern the transition to Stage Three as "no veto, no lockout, no compulsion." There was no support for a transition period for countries unable to fulfill the convergence criteria. The EC Commission president finished with a warning: "his greatest worries concerned the overall effectiveness of the system; the ultimate compromise might produce a system in which the European Central Bank, with its total independence, would be able to act very quickly, while its economic counterpart might operate according to very slow procedures, and would therefore not be able to take the decisions which would make for balance between Economic Union on the one hand and Monetary Union on the other."[92]

At the subsequent Apeldoorn IGC meeting, the Italians argued that if a distinct body such as the EMI was to be created for Stage Two, it should be abolished at the outset of Stage Three. The Italian negotiators may have feared that they would be excluded from Stage Three, and saw the provisional institutional arrangement for the transition as a way of keeping Italy involved in the critical policy debates, since Stage Two created the "platform" of instruments for the eventual union. Meanwhile Trichet referred in private to the need to get to the bottom of "the abominable Italian problem."[93]

The Netherlands presidency successfully pushed for the acceptance of convergence criteria, which were adopted on October 28, and laid the basis for a successful outcome of the negotiation in Maastricht. These convergence criteria included debt levels under 60 percent of GDP; public deficits under 3 percent (the 3 percent figure was sometimes supposed to have come from the turbulent experiences of the Mitterrand regime in 1981–1983); inflation within 2 percent of the average of the best three performers, and interest rates within 2 percent of the lowest three in the European Union. The United Kingdom had consistently argued that in particular the 3 percent rule was too restrictive, and as late as November 25 a strange coalition of the Commission, Greece, Spain, and the United Kingdom opposed the imposition of fines and sanctions for violations.[94]

The Dutch presidency of the IGC proposed modifications of the CoG's draft of the ECB/ESCB statute (see Appendix B). The governors' draft statute had provided a supervisory role for the ESCB, including the possibility of designating the ECB as a competent supervisory authority. The new version proposed by the Dutch presidency limited the ECSB's involvement in prudential supervision, in that it was only supposed to "contribute to the smooth conduct" of such policies; and it limited supervision to credit institutions, whereas the governors had had a more extensive view of financial institutions. It also modified the ESCB's involvement in the harmonization of statistics. It deleted the governors' reference to making the volume and denomination of coins subject to approval by the ECB Board. Above all, it seemed to be more restrictive of the principle of central bank independence. It omitted the governors' proposal to be involved in the appointment of national central bank governors, and it rejected the idea of a renewed appointment to the eight-year term of membership on the Executive Board.[95]

There was also the sensitive issue of who was to run the national central banks in future. Would the establishment of a European institution imply that the appointment of central bankers should no longer be a purely national choice, given their impact on European decisions? On November 12, 1991, the chairman of the CoG wrote to the Council president, Dutch Prime Minister Wim Kok, that the CoG would suggest for Article 14 of the ECB statute—in regard to national central banks—a formulation that "the Governor of a national central bank is appointed by the national authorities of the Member State after consultation with the Governing Council of the ECB." In the end, such a requirement, which would have constituted a major breach in the powers of national governments, and could have appeared as a power grab on the part of the central bankers, never appeared in the treaty text. Another objection to the Dutch presidency's proposals involved the requirement that there be an ECB representative sitting in a newly constituted Economic and Social Committee, which would take the place of the EC Monetary Committee. The central bankers rejected this, as it seemed to compromise the autonomy of the central bank by drawing it into a discussion of policy at a governmental level.[96]

A new arena of controversy was also opening up around the issue of who would participate in Stage Three. It was clear both that at least one country (the United Kingdom) would not subscribe to the new arrangements, and that other EC members would not satisfy the criteria that would be established as a measurement of monetary convergence and hence of the appropriateness of adopting a single currency. Articles 47 and 48 of the ECB draft statute laid down the institutional framework for cooperation between the countries moving to Stage Three. Some central banks, notably the Banca d'Italia and the Central Bank of Ireland, but also the Institut Monétaire Luxembourgeois, wanted the banks of member countries with derogations or exemptions to participate, without voting rights on monetary policy. Others, including the Bank of England, which would clearly be destined to stand on the sideline, but also the Banco de Portugal as well as the Bundesbank and the Banque de France, thought that monetary cooperation should not take place within the ECB context, but should occur in a separate body that might be called the "Assembly." Even though it was clear that this "Assembly" was highly impractical, and although the most powerful central banks lined up behind the narrow concept of the ECB, the failure to reach consensus meant that the CoG simply sent the two alternatives for Article 47 to the IGC. In a note, Gunter Baer suggested that these options were political and that the final choice should be left to the European governments.[97] The chairman of the CoG then sent alternative text proposals for the transitional provisions of the ECB statute to the IGC.

According to the Netherlands draft of October 28, 1991, the EMI together with the European Union Commission would report by the end of 1996 on the progress made by member states in meeting their EMU obligations and in achieving "a high degree of convergence." But at the IGC meeting of ministers and officials on November 25–26, 1991, the Germans rejected the idea of giving the EMI strong responsibilities in monetary policy. Horst Köhler prepared to concede that the EMI could manage some reserves, but there was to be no compulsion to transfer reserves. Also in November 1991, on the eve of the final Maastricht conference, in a final and intense political negotiation, EMI decisions were not to be binding for the national central banks, and were subject to the consent of the ECB when the latter institution was established. At this point there was consensus on everything except the transition to the third stage, the exemptions for the United Kingdom, and a formulation of European policy on economic and social cohesion—the issues that were left to the Maastricht meeting of the European Council, which would produce the final treaty. In the final draft the EMI was a much softer version of the institutional transition than had been envisaged in the Delors Report. As Niels Thygesen pointed out acerbically, "As regards the EMI's role in policy coordination it is difficult to see any significant changes relative to the performance of the committee of central bank governors set up in Stage One. The council of the EMI may formulate, by qualified majority, opinions or recommendations on monetary and exchange rate policy in the member states and convey these views confidentially. It may publish unanimously adopted opinions and recommendations. This does not go beyond what can be done by the present committee of central bank governors and its president."[98]

Designing Policy

With the start of Stage One, within the CoG, the initially quite informal experts' groups that had been created in the 1970s emerged with enhanced importance as protodepartments of a central banking structure. The nomenclature changed; they were now referred to as subcommittees. The two long-lived groups had been concerned with exchange rate issues (including the technical mechanism of "concertation") and monetary policy. A third area was added to tackle what looked like an increasingly important concern in central banking, namely bank supervision. Both Jacques de Larosière and Karl Otto Pöhl had raised the issue of formalizing the groups during the debates of the Delors Committee. De Larosière proposed a Foreign Exchange Policy Subcommittee and a

Monetary Policy Subcommittee. At the January 1989 CoG meeting Pöhl added: "it has been said in Scenario A that there should be a Committee for banking supervision; this has to be clarified whether that is acceptable or not, but I would be prepared and ready to accept also that we would set up two other committees."[99] This would lead the CoG to create a third committee: the Banking Supervision Subcommittee.

Monetary Policy Coordination

The Delors Report stated in paragraph 24 that the "shift from national monetary policies to a single monetary policy is an inescapable consequence of monetary union and constitutes one of the principal institutional changes." De Larosière had tried unsuccessfully to replace the word "single" with "common," on the grounds that "single" implied a unique set of instruments, whereas in reality the various national central banks used a wide range of rather different instruments. The Maastricht Treaty establishing the ECB Statute defined a basic task as "to define and implement the monetary policy of the Community" (Article 3) and specified a primary objective of price stability. But there was no guidance on the strategy that should be adopted, and policy implementation was described only in very general terms. Articles 17–20 left open a wide range of possible monetary functions and operations (see Appendix B).

Since the 1970s the CoG had repeatedly considered, not just in committee meetings but also in the work of the experts' groups, the coordination of monetary policy instruments. Such coordination was clearly a prerequisite for EMU, but there was a host of national peculiarities. During the 1980s there had been a rapprochement of monetary policy-making in the EC, as there had also been on an international or global level; but no consensus existed about the policy instruments to be used, and in consequence no move to any real kind of harmonization occurred.

On July 28, 1989, the veteran Danish central banker Erik Hoffmeyer, then the chairman of the CoG, had sent a letter to the other governors recommending the establishment of a system of common monetary targets that would be "clearly visible and well understood by politicians and the general public."[100] But the suggestion raised immediate objections. In particular, as Pöhl pointed out, there was the long-standing issue of the differences among the policy frameworks of small and larger countries. Smaller countries, notably the Netherlands and Austria (then still a non-EC member), had used an exchange rate target and had effectively annexed themselves to the policies of the Bundesbank. Larger countries followed their own monetary policies, but without a consistency in approach that would be needed for an EC-wide formulation of policy. Pöhl prepared a letter to this effect for the chairman of the CoG, which he never sent, but whose contents he presented verbally in the course of a discussion in Basel. "As we all know, there is to date no money stock definition (monetary base, M1, M2, M3) which would be equally relevant to all EC countries. The individual monetary aggregates differ from country to country with respect to their longer-term stability properties (relation to GNP, to the price level etc.), their controllability, signaling effect vis-à-vis the general public etc. We therefore cannot be sure that a search for the best indicator for each country will lead to an aggregate defined in the same way; the opposite will probably be the case."[101] Hoffmeyer's solution was to suggest a general agreement on monetary policy monitoring. The central banks of England, France, Ireland, Italy, Spain, and Portugal supported this proposal.[102] Pöhl's response was to suggest a coordinated anti-inflation policy as an "essential prerequisite" to Stage One of monetary union: "The consistency of the national monetary targets must therefore be derived from the common stability objective."[103]

The CoG repeatedly emphasized the need to move to "commonly agreed and mutually consistent targets and indicators of monetary policy," but in practice such an evolution proved extremely difficult.[104] The coordination of monetary policy was a focus of discussion on May 14 and 15, 1990, both in the alternates' meeting and in the principal committee. There was a substantial amount of publicity, with press reports that there would be "commonly agreed money supply targets" for 1991.[105] But the discussion among the central bankers was much more sober. The Danish alternate, Richard Mikkelsen, and the Bundesbank alternate, Wolfgang Rieke, argued against normative targets for inflation, which would produce political controversy because many governments would use different inflation projections for budget calculations. Crockett also rejected the idea of an inflation target, on the grounds that inflation could not be controlled by central banks alone. He was also worried about the multiplicity of possible price indices.[106] By November

30, 1989, Pöhl was writing to the central bank governors that "a formal harmonization of the money stock definition should therefore not be attempted."[107]

The Monetary Policy Subcommittee was clearly of much greater importance as the work on increased coordination developed. There were disputes about the chairmanship in succession to the Banque de France official Robert Raymond, and Germany attempted to block an Italian candidate.[108] In the meantime, the scale of the task for Stage Two was gradually being cut back. Later, in February 1991, de Larosière argued: "There would be a need for the Governors to do some work on the instruments that would lead the Community to a global monetary policy, for example the creation of a single monetary aggregate for the Community."[109] But there were substantial technical problems. There were different definitions of money, different methodologies for measuring yields, and different policy instruments. The German tradition of rediscounting bills rather than undertaking repo transactions (selling securities with a repurchase agreement) went back to nineteenth-century banking, but it was sneered at by other central bankers as constituting "financial archaeology."[110]

During 1990 the CoG considered a report by a group, chaired by Raymond, working on the establishment of a common framework for monitoring monetary policy. This part of the preparatory work for EMU was less satisfactory: indeed, apart from a commitment to a general view of price stability ("Monetary policy had meaning only if it strangled inflation") it was hard to achieve any consensus.[111]

Raymond's group had presented two major conclusions:

1. The complex task of drawing the central banks closer together had to be accompanied by the periodic publication of simple illustrative points of reference, be they policy intentions, explicit targets or merely assumptions.
2. What was said and done should appear not as a political compromise but as the expression of a coherent strategy.[112]

The Bundesbank was emphatic about the undesirability of mentioning a specific inflation target in any communiqué. As Pöhl put it:

A press communiqué should never contain normative price increases; this would give the impression that a certain rate of inflation was being aimed at, whereas the objective was in fact to reduce it. It was perhaps essentially a question of presentation. For example, when the Bundesbank published its monetary targets, it explained that they had been calculated taking account of the potential growth rate (or assumed real growth) and the unavoidable inflation rate. This latter concept had been abandoned as being too defeatist, and reference was now made to real growth and nominal growth, which in effect implied a certain rate of inflation. The object of the exercise was in fact primarily to make monetary policies compatible, especially for the ERM countries. This could be said publicly, but without stating quantified targets.

De Larosière expressed his "disappointment" with Pöhl's skeptical reservations, which to some extent echoed those of Robin Leigh-Pemberton and the Bank of England.[113]

In August 1990 the Monetary Policy Subcommittee argued that the new system of central banks would be unlikely to be able to follow the U.S. example of 1979–1982 and work with the monetary base; and that the centralized execution of operations would be difficult because of different sources of high-powered money and different interest rates. As a consequence, a number of options were laid out, with central operations but a decentralized operation of the repo market or—alternatively—a central setting of limits for each national operation.[114] At the same time the subcommittee also commented that the draft proposal by the alternates for Chapter IV of the draft statute of the European Central Banking System was overambitious: instead of a task "to determine the supply of money and credit," a more modest objective, "to formulate and implement the monetary policy of the Community, in particular by influencing the quantity of money and credit," would be preferable.[115] In September 1990 a CoG paper recommended a first ex ante exercise in coordinating monetary policy in November 1990, in which governors would "assess" monetary policy objectives vis-à-vis Community policy. But the document also recognized that the "final goal" of inflation close to zero could not be reached in the time span of the exercise, and warned of two dangers: too much deflation would have a depressing effect on output and employment, and for currencies in the ERM a sharp tightening of monetary policy would produce capital flows that would lead to the opposite effect to that intended.[116]

A new attempt in the summer of 1991 did not produce much of an advance. Denmark, Greece, Spain, Ireland, Italy, Luxembourg, and Portugal expressed their willingness to introduce the proposed changes in official broad aggregates, but Germany and France were still reviewing the proposals. In addition, a number of problems simply could not be solved, and the variety of national monetary and banking practices seemed baffling. "No decision had been reached with regard to data collection and the treatment of mutual funds. . . . There was no general agreement as to whether treasury bills should be included in aggregates. A further pending issue had related to the treatment of residents' deposits held abroad."[117]

At the alternates' meeting in July 1991, there was a proposal to "generally encourage" attempts to harmonize broad monetary aggregates, but even this apparently inoffensive idea provoked some dissent. The Bank of England's representative, Andrew Crockett, expressed his "doubts whether further financial integration will allow monetary policy to be based on stable relationships between monetary aggregates and intermediary objectives."[118]

In May 1992 the CoG gave a special mandate to the Monetary Policy Subcommittee, asking for preliminary studies to "examine the possible concepts of the single monetary policy as well as the methods and organizational aspects of its execution, with due regard to the appropriate involvement of the national central banks." At the end of 1992 the CoG started a fact-finding review of current monetary instruments. At this stage the Bundesbank was still laying out its philosophy of monetary rule-based management founded on an "overarching guideline" of medium-term monetary targeting as the most appropriate future model for the ESCB. Looking forward, it thought that the bigger area of the monetary zone would reduce the likelihood of exchange rate shocks, and thus also the need for discretionary decision and intermediate targets. A minimum reserve requirement for banks was "unavoidable," and there should not be "too much emphasis" on open market policy with official securities. The Germans contemplated "preferential treatment" for private paper. This model was contrasted with a British approach, with frequent market interventions and no minimum reserves, which it held was appropriate only for a more centralized financial market.[119] In a decentralized market, there would be a large variety of securities with different prices, so that the ECB would in effect be compelled to perform constant arbitrage operations. The Bundesbank contrasted the German model, which had what it termed a "low operational frequency," in that policy rates were seldom changed, with the British model, which allowed rapid changes and sharp differentiations of price stimuli. The Germans also contemplated a third model, based on Danish experience, in which an interest-rate corridor would be set; but that option again demanded a great deal of arbitrage. There was clearly, at this late stage, no capacity to solve an issue that had been debated intensely ever since the breakdown of the par value system in the early 1970s.

It took a major crisis in the European exchange rate mechanism (discussed in Chapter 9) to shift the discussion finally to a realization that the older debates about symmetric or asymmetric adjustment were futile, and that the acceptance of a goal of price stability could offer a way out of the dilemma. It was price stability that identified the "right" monetary policy, and all countries had to behave consistently with this principle. That acceptance eventually gave exchange rate stability a firm basis and allowed a move to monetary union. An additional, also very important, consequence of agreeing on price stability as the overriding objective of monetary policy was that monetary policy was depoliticized. Another way of seeing the development was to reflect on the transformation of monetary policy from a discretionary policy activity into a technically discretionary one; in other words, the policy framework was no longer left to national authorities.[120] Before the agreement was reached, the issue was the political one of choosing the "optimal" point on a Phillips curve between unemployment and inflation. After the agreement was reached, the problem became the technical one of achieving price stability. The new agreement also underpinned central bank independence, because the ECB would not be called upon to make political choices, which must ultimately find a basis in popular will, but only technical ones, which could, indeed should, be attributed to technical bodies. The maturing of this agreement in the CoG was thus a fundamental component of the supersession of an exchange-rate-oriented cooperation mode by an interest-rate-oriented cooperation mode, which allowed movement to monetary union.

The postcrisis October 1993 report by the CoG on "The Single Monetary Policy of the ECSB: Strategic and Implementation Issues" was deliberately eclectic, giving "only preliminary or conditional answers," but it adopted many parts of the Bundesbank model. As general principles, the report emphasized accountability (through the formulation and announcement of targets), transparency (the targets should be "clear and understandable to the public"), effectiveness (the central bank should be able to control the development of the selected variables), continuity, and a medium-term orientation (to "provide the central bank with some discretion in response to short-term deviations from the target"). The report considered direct inflation targeting (which was just beginning to be widely discussed as a monetary policy goal) as being the clearest demonstration of the ESCB's commitment to price stability, but then rejected such a target as more appropriate to a small open economy. In its general overview, the report concluded that an intermediate monetary target in a medium-term framework provided the best policy setting, since the intermediate target would "provide the authorities with information on (future) inflation, which would otherwise be difficult to process" and would "play a signaling role, which can condition public expectation about the monetary policy stance and inflation." Since the intermediate target was "immediately observable and controllable by the central bank," it was thought to solve the time-inconsistency problem in which the monetary authority might be tempted to adopt inflation to cushion the effects of real shocks on unemployment. The appeal of the intermediate target lay in the inability of central banks to control price developments directly and promptly in response to other short-term influences. The report acknowledged that "the coexistence of two targets (an official inflation target in addition to the intermediate monetary target) could make monetary policy less transparent and could lead to confusion and uncertainty regarding the intentions of the ESCB." The report also argued that the German practices of reserve requirements and standing facilities "could be useful" in monetary management, and would have the additional merit of allowing a greater measure of operational decentralization.[121]

Behind the formulations of the report lay an increasing commitment to the idea that a known model, namely that of the Bundesbank, was the best way of removing uncertainty in the unforeseeable phase of the transition, when it was unclear how monetary aggregates would behave, as well as the optimal route to establish credibility for the new central bank. There would thus be a need to "gain credibility right from the start of Stage Three, for which a high degree of flexibility could be harmful." One of the most powerful arguments for the adoption of an intermediate target for the money supply was that "such a target is currently used by and large with success, including by the Deutsche Bundesbank (whose currency has acted as an anchor for the EMS)."[122]

The report shrank from major institutional innovations in the financial sector. A Europe-wide payment system was not feasible or necessary, since both the United States and Germany worked adequately with decentralized payments systems; all that was needed was a capacity for the cross-border transfer and same-day settlement of interbank funds.

In their retrospective survey, Gros and Thygesen reached a damning verdict on the inconclusive outcome of the monetary policy debate of the early 1990s: "An early illustration of the inherent weakness of stage I procedures was the inability of the Committee of Central Bank Governors to arrive at any announceable conclusion to their first effort at setting coordinated intermediate monetary targets."[123] In fact the discussions that followed the major exchange rate crises of 1992 and 1993 created the final consensus that was needed to solve the monetary policy conundrum.

The European Monetary Institute thus could offer effective solutions. The technical aspects of monetary harmonization were handled better in part simply because it had a bigger staff (200 by 1996) than did the CoG, even after the committee's scope expanded in the early 1990s. Article 8 of the EMI Statute made the organization's independence clear: the EMI could not seek or take advice from EU institutions or bodies, or from governments of member states. Article 109f of the Maastricht Treaty ("Transitional Provisions") allowed qualified majority formulation of opinions and recommendations on the conduct of monetary policy in member states.

The institutional availability of the EMI quickly solved the monetary policy problem that had been intractable under the regime of the CoG. In this respect, the EMI's ability to solve the monetary policy challenge seemed to validate the French institutionalist approach of rushing fences rather than waiting for convergence.

Foreign Exchange Rate Issues

During the meetings of the Delors Committee, there had been extensive and controversial discussion of whether exchange rate policy constituted a meaningful concept. Karl Otto Pöhl pointed out that in a floating regime there could be no exchange rate policy, and de Larosière retorted that there was never anything like complete free floating.[124] But there was an obvious problem with the German position, in that exchange rate policy for smaller economies has a direct and decisive impact on monetary policy and economic policy.[125] By 1990 this debate had become a major bone of contention at the level of high politics and in the Monetary Committee. A French target zone proposal was fiercely resisted by Tietmeyer and in the end was dropped. In the CoG, Pöhl objected to any drafting that referred to "exchange rate objectives" and succeeded in replacing it by "exchange rate policies." But by September 1990 he was demanding that this phrase be dropped altogether, and he was successful.[126]

"Concertation" in the systematized and regular exchange of information on exchange rate actions remained a primarily technical exercise. It was clear that officials could not handle the big political issues involved in the discussion of whether exchange rates were at the right level: but neither could the governors. This proved to be one of the major flaws of the governance structure of the European monetary order in the early 1990s (see Chapter 9).

Bank Supervision

The penultimate draft of the Delors Report specified in paragraph 32 that the "system would participate in the coordination of banking supervision policies of the national supervisory authorities." But in the final report, "national" was deleted, leaving the implication that the supervisory authorities would be European.

The question of how far the ECB should be engaged in bank supervision had been one of the contentious issues in drafting the statute, with governments pressing for the retention of supervision as a national prerogative, and central bankers seeing supervision as at least a potential task for the ECB.

Just before the establishment of the Delors Committee, a third group— or, as it was now known, subcommittee—was established to deal with bank supervision. This new subcommittee was chaired by Brian Quinn of the Bank of England.[127] The initiative had come from Huib Muller, of the Nederlandsche Bank, who was also chairman of the Basel Committee on Banking Supervision, and Tommaso Padio-Schioppa, of the Banca d'Italia, who was also chairman of the Banking Advisory Committee to the EC Commission (and would later follow Muller as chair of the Basel Committee). They argued that there was a satisfactory framework for drawing up legislative proposals on banking supervision in the EC, but no adequate way of drawing up policies on prudential supervision. Muller had written to the central bank governors to outline the basis of the proposal for vesting supervisory policy matters in a European monetary authority:

> However, there was agreement that the existing arrangements for the formulation of policy in the area of prudential supervision were not structured in such a way as to take full account of contemporaneous developments in the structure of the financial system in Community countries. In particular, the group noted the issues raised by the growing interdependence in recent years between the banking systems of different countries and between the banking system and other financial markets. These close links, assisted by product innovation and technical developments, are creating risks for banks and for the financial system which pose challenging questions for the central banks, which have special responsibilities for dealing with disturbances in financial markets. All EC central banks already have a direct or indirect involvement in the supervision of banks in their countries. The group agreed that progress toward economic and monetary union would be very likely to increase the degree of interdependence between national banking systems in the Community and would strengthen the need for central bank involvement in the prudential supervision of banks and other closely related financial Institutions. . . . Senior representatives of EC central banks therefore propose to meet regularly in the future to discuss such matters at the time of the meetings of the Banking Advisory Committee. If agreeable to the Committee of EC Governors, the group would take the form of a sub-committee of the Committee of EC Governors, who would receive reports of its deliberations.[128]

Muller's memorandum specifically identified the problem of the development of transnational banking groups with ownership located in more than one EC member country.

In the CoG, Duisenberg stated powerfully the view that banking supervision needed to occur at the European level.[129] Such a move would deal with a very powerful objection to global attempts by the Basel Committee to evolve what became the "Core Principles of Banking Supervision": Quinn, who was also a veteran member of the Basel Committee, repeatedly worried that global rules evolved by a committee of central bankers might lack "democratic legitimacy."[130] There was, however, considerable opposition to the CoG's developing a major competence in this field. The president of the German Credit Supervisory Office (Bundesaufsichtsamt für das Kreditwesen) wrote to Pöhl in early 1989 protesting attempts to Europeanize banking supervision, which he saw as parallel to the initiatives of the G-10 and of the Basel Committee on Banking Supervision (see Chapter 4) as potentially reducing the competitiveness of German banking. At the same time, Tietmeyer argued that banking supervision was a responsibility of finance ministers, and not of central banks, and that the German ministry should be represented in CoG discussions of this issue. Pöhl tried to respond to these domestic German critiques by pointing out that any decision would need to be taken by governments and parliaments, and that such a moment of choice lay in the distant future. There was similar opposition from France's banking commission, which urged the governor of the Banque de France to exercise "vigilance" because Brian Quinn was believed to favor the transfer of supervisory and regulatory authority to the ECB.[131]

In February 1990, at the EC Monetary Committee meeting in Brussels, there was complete agreement that the different national rules regarding bank regulation should be left in place.[132] Delors was unwilling to force the pace on this issue, and stated that the EC Commission approached the issue of banking supervision with an "open mind": the ESCB should simply "participate in the coordination of national policies but would not have a monopoly on those policies."[133]

On June 29, 1990, in the alternates' meeting, Andrew Crockett proposed that "a further objective of the ESCB will be to preserve the integrity of the financial system." Tietmeyer objected that this outcome should be considered a "task" rather than an "objective." At the governors' meeting to discuss such a goal, the wording was softened, mostly in response to the German position. It was agreed that "any suggestion that the System should undertake rescue operations in favour of individual banks should be avoided," though there might be a need to deal with (rather vaguely defined) "sudden developments" in financial markets. The wording changed, so that "preserve" became "support," and "integrity" became "stability." That phrasing seemed to preclude any responsibility to act as a classical central bank lender of last resort. In the end, the "tasks" of Article 3 were watered down to the much less far-reaching and less ambitious goal "to promote the smooth operation of the payment system."[134]

In October 1990, when the alternates discussed the CoG's Banking Supervision Subcommittee proposals on draft articles for the central bank statute, Hans Tietmeyer restated the skeptical position of the Bundesbank, which was consistently worried about the moral hazard implications of central bank involvement in supervision. If the central bank took on the responsibility of regulating, it would also deliver an implicit commitment to rescue banks should there be bad developments that it had overlooked. Tietmeyer provided a neat encapsulation of the German philosophy of regulation: "This did not mean from the view of the Board of the Deutsche Bundesbank that the ECB should not support the stability of the financial system, but that it should never be written down; this would be moral hazard."[135] The Luxembourg non-paper of May 10, 1991, spoke instead of the central bank participating in "the coordination and execution of policies relating to the prudential control and stability of the financial system."[136]

In June 1991 the IGC seemed possibly to exclude any financial sector supervisory role for the ESCB and the ECB, contrary to the governors' draft statute:

> The relevant provisions were introduced into the Statute with three considerations in mind: first, the System, even though operating strictly at the macroeconomic level, will have a broad oversight of developments in financial markets and institutions and therefore should possess a detailed working knowledge which would be of value to the exercise of supervisory functions. Secondly, there is a legitimate interest on the part of the system in the maintenance of sound and stable financial markets. Thirdly, legislative changes in regulatory provisions may have important technical consequences for the conduct of monetary policy. . . . However, the Statute recognizes the evolutionary character of financial markets and the concurrent need to adapt prudential supervision. For this reason Article 25.2 offers the possibility of designating the ECB as a competent supervisory authority, for example, if it were necessary and desirable to formulate and implement a Community-wide supervisory policy for pan-EC financial conglomerates. Such a task could be undertaken by the ECB only if it were designated as the competent supervisory authority through secondary Community legislation.[137]

There was an opportunity to discuss a concrete example of the problem in September 1991, after the collapse of the Bank of Credit and Commerce International (BCCI).[138] Before that, bank failures and their consequences looked like such a remote possibility that the highly sensitive issues involved had not been really discussed since the 1974 Herstatt case, when the failure of a small German bank had raised the problem of international counterparty risk. The director of the Institut Monétaire Luxembourgeois, Pierre Jaans, explained that the BCCI was legally based in Luxembourg and in the Cayman Islands, but had extensive operations in London, the Middle East, the Far East, and Africa. As a result the BCCI banking group could not be fitted into the philosophy of supervision on a consolidated basis that had been developed since the 1970s. Leigh-Pemberton asked whether a repetition of such a collapse was possible. It clearly was, although the systemic issues involved in large-scale banking crises only really became apparent in 2007–2008. For the moment, the BCCI looked idiosyncratically unique and banking in general reassuringly solid. Moreover, the BCCI affair also contributed to the erosion of any impetus to include a broader mandate for securing financial stability, because it brought considerable criticism of Brian Quinn, the Bank of England director who had taken over Huib Muller's international role of pushing for more international coordination of banking supervision and regulation. Thus far from strengthening the case for a sustained and coordinated European approach to the issues of a newly vigorous international banking system, the BCCI collapse actually weakened the demand for action.

Thus the governors' draft referred to the possibility that the ECB would take over banking supervision and regulation functions, but by the time this proposal was included in the Maastricht Treaty provisions on monetary policy (Article 105, Section 6) it was accompanied by so many provisos that it looked as if the hurdles to effective European banking supervision could not be set higher.[139] The intrusion of politics had thus resulted in a fundamental flaw in the new European monetary order.

Maastricht

In September 1991 the Dutch central banker André Szász wrote an unusually candid note on what had been achieved in the lead-up to the

Maastricht negotiation. He argued that the "tasks which are now vested in this committee [CoG] pursuant to a Council decision of 12 March 1990 but which have thus far remained in large measure a dead letter" should now be taken up once again: the coordination of monetary policy, the formulation of views on "the overall orientation of monetary and exchange rate policy," and finally, the responsibility of expressing "opinions to individual governments and the Council of Ministers on policies that might affect the internal and external monetary situation in the Community and, in particular, the functioning of the European Monetary System."[140] The functioning of the EMS had in fact become a very substantial threat to the negotiations on further European monetary integration.

The meeting of the European Council on December 9–10, 1991, in Maastricht finalized the draft of a treaty that had substantially been prepared in advance. In particular, the statutes of the European Monetary Institute and the European Central Bank deviated from the governors' draft legislation only with regard to banking supervision and some of the claims for central bank independence (see Appendixes A and B). The most controversial aspects that were settled only at a late stage were the discussion of the entry criteria for EMU (with the German and Dutch preference for tough criteria) and the question of a British opt-out, which was the subject of frantic last-moment direct negotiation with the British prime minister, John Major. Article 109e specified under the transitional arrangements:

> 4. In the second stage, Member States shall endeavour to avoid excessive government deficits.
> 5. During the second stage, each Member State shall, as appropriate, start the process leading to the independence of its central bank, in accordance with Article 108.

Article 109f(3) laid down the way in which the EMI would prepare the transition:

> At the latest by 31 December 1996, the EMI shall specify the regulatory, organisational and logistical framework necessary for the ESCB to perform its tasks in the third stage. This framework shall be submitted for decision to the ECB at the date of its establishment.

Finally, the crucial Article 109j set out the convergence criteria for

- the achievement of a high degree of price stability
- the sustainability of the government financial position
- the observance of the normal fluctuation margins provided for by the exchange rate mechanism of the European Monetary System, for at least two years, without devaluing against the currency of any other member state
- the durability of convergence achieved by the member state and of its participation in the exchange rate mechanism of the European Monetary System as reflected in the long-term interest-rate levels

Article 109j(4) set the timing of the transition to the third stage:

> If by the end of 1997 the date for the beginning of the third stage has not been set, the third stage shall start on 1 January 1999. Before 1 July 1998, the Council, meeting in the composition of Heads of State or of Government, after a repetition of the procedure provided for in paragraphs 1 and 2, with the exception of the second indent of paragraph 2, taking into account the reports referred to in paragraph 1 and the opinion of the European Parliament, shall, acting by a qualified majority and on the basis of the recommendations of the Council referred to in paragraph 2, confirm which Member States fulfil the necessary conditions for the adoption of a single currency.

The treaty was signed in Maastricht on February 7, 1992, though its subsequent ratification was surprisingly rocky and threatened to destroy the EMS (see Chapter 9). The problem was a political one in that the debate about monetary union became embroiled in a general discussion of the single market and of the competence of national governments in a period of quite severe recession. But there was also a technical problem in that the EMS and its operation were built into the treaty by the convergence provisions of Article 109j. Any major upset in the EMS would thus destroy the prescribed path to monetary union. An omen of the future difficulty came when the Bundesbank on December 19, 1991, just a few days after the conclusion of the Maastricht European Council meeting, voted to raise its interest rates.

Preparation for the Transition

It was the CoG secretariat that managed the preparatory work for the move to Stage Two of EMU, and also started work on Stage Three in those areas where the preparation was expected to be exceptionally time-consuming and thus could not await the establishment of the European Monetary Institute. In late 1992 a number of working groups began operating. A group on accounting issues prepared an inventory of the accounting methodologies used in EC central banks. A group under the chairmanship of Alex Jarvis, the Bank of England's general manager of the printing works, considered the printing and issuing of a European banknote. Its report of June 1993 laid out a broad range of options, from identical banknotes through common banknotes with discrete national symbols (on the lines of the Federal Reserve symbols on U.S. notes), through common notes with easily identifiable symbols (such as the Eiffel Tower for France), notes with one side national and one side European, national notes with European features, to national notes with a discrete Community symbol such as a flag. It recommended public opinion surveys to judge the acceptability of the different options, and also advocated a "neutral committee of renowned historians" to determine genuinely European subjects for the common options. The denomination of the future banknotes was also addressed: there was agreement that 1 ECU should be a coin, and disagreement whether the smallest note should be 2 or 5 ECU. The largest denomination was envisaged as 500, roughly in line with existing practice in the Netherlands and Germany, both of which had high-denomination notes (the 1,000-guilder note accounted for 40 percent of note circulation in the Netherlands, and the DM 1,000 and DM 500 notes for 41 percent of the German circulation).[141]

A statistics working group identified gaps in the availability of central bank statistics, and recommended that by Stage Three each country should provide a monthly report of the breakdown of banks' foreign positions into those with residents of countries participating in the monetary union and those with residents of non-EC and EC countries that were not in EMU. In addition, it pressed for more timely collection and transmission of central bank data by the end of 1994. Most member countries at this stage could not provide breakdowns of banks' foreign claims between the private and public sector, and some countries calculated only quarterly rather than monthly data.[142]

In May 1993 the Foreign Exchange Policy Subcommittee concluded an interim report on the operational functions and ECU-related tasks of the EMI. The chief operational issues concerned the taking over of the EMCF functions, as well as the holding and management of foreign exchange reserves for and at the request of national central banks. The function of reserve management was designed so as not to interfere with members' monetary policy in Stage Two.[143]

In April and July 1993 the CoG discussed the prohibition on extending central bank credit to public entities (Article 104 of the Maastricht Treaty). The EC Commission formulated a draft law on the basis of this recommendation, which was adopted as secondary legislation in December 1993 and—as the CoG noted—closely "mirrored" its own view.[144]

On October 29, 1993, in a meeting that was intended to celebrate the entry into effect of the Maastricht Treaty, the heads of state or government agreed that the EMI should be located in Frankfurt. At the same time they selected Alexandre Lamfalussy as its president. Initially the obvious candidate would have appeared to be the Dutch central banker, Wim Duisenberg, who had just taken over the chair of the CoG. But Duisenberg was unwilling to leave his position at the Nederlandsche Bank, as was widely supposed because he did not see much future in the European monetary union.[145] In an attempt to avoid a major diplomatic embarrassment, the Belgian prime minister, Jean-Luc Dehaene, pressed Lamfalussy into service. It was an elegant solution, not only in bringing a technically brilliant economist to the job, but also politically, in that the appointment did not prejudge the issue of who was to head the ECB (a decision left by the statute to the European governments, not to the central bankers, who would select the head of the EMI). Lamfalussy had explicitly declared that he did not want to be considered as a candidate for the first presidency of the ECB (this was also a consequence of his age: he was sixty-four).

Duisenberg's reserved stance was not unrealistic. There were few reasons to be optimistic. The EMS had been shaken by the 1992–1993 currency crises (examined in Chapter 9). By 1994 not one European state fulfilled all the convergence criteria, and the Italian foreign minister, Antonio Martino, brazenly suggested that the exercise should simply proceed without any convergence criteria.[146]

Work on the EMI thus looked like central bankers huddling on the deck in a typhoon. In the aftermath of the European Council decision, in November 1993, the CoG established a "preparatory group," consisting of the president-elect of the EMI, the chairman and secretary-general of the CoG, and the chairman of the CoG alternates' committee.

In practice, for an initial six-month transition period, the work of the new institution would take place in both Basel (where most of the staff came from) and Frankfurt. The final move to Frankfurt was delayed until November 15, 1994. The CoG secretariat's information system would provide the basis for that of the EMI. There was a clear sense that the new institution was the successor organization of the CoG. It perfectly embodied the CoG philosophy; the legal framework of Maastricht also ensured that this vision would be the guideline for the new monetary union. The people huddled on the deck would survive the typhoon.

The ECB statute represents the high-water mark of the idea of an independent central bank committed to the unique goal of price stability. The outcome of Maastricht was possible only because of the widespread consensus about central bank independence, which made it seem as if the astonishing act of European monetary integration could occur without any substantial transfer of sovereignty. Tommaso Padoa-Schioppa saw this emphasis on the independent central bank as part of a more general acceptance of "minimum government" that made a new stage of European integration possible.[147] As he implied, the discussion of central banking was part of a broader trend that prepared the way for what was later dismissively referred to as "market fundamentalism." But the consensus inevitably shone a new kind of spotlight on the central banks.

Had central bankers taken on too much of the burden of responsibility for providing a stable economic and social order? Had they insisted too much on the separation of central banking from politics? After the Maastricht discussion, European politics braced for a blame game in which central bankers played against politicians. A Euroskeptic Briton wrote about this phase: "Many central bankers are intelligent, courteous and affable: your typical central banker is quite a high class of person, much nicer, one imagines, than your average politician. But politicians have at some point to confront the consequences of their mistakes; their unaccountable central bankers do not." By contrast, a Europhobic American economist made the exactly opposite claim: "Central bankers are a tough, mean lot, but in the end the kind-hearted politicians will tell them what to do."[148] Had politicians abdicated too much? That was the question that was tested in 1992 and 1993, in the immediate aftermath of the Maastricht Treaty. An astonishing series of violent financial crises destroyed the credibility of governments that had wagered their reputations on the ability to maintain fixed exchange rates. Markets then blew up governments. The outcome left central bankers more powerful and more prestigious than ever before.

The EMS Crises

The road from the Delors Committee and the Maastricht Treaty to monetary union was quite rough. Five years of stability after 1987, when the last realignment had taken place and the EMS was apparently strengthened by the Basel-Nyborg Agreement, were followed by a dramatic shock. Suddenly everything seemed to fall apart. In 1992–1993 the European monetary order appeared fundamentally endangered by a series of dramatic exchange crises that began in peripheral countries, Italy and the United Kingdom, and then affected nonmembers of the EC in Scandinavia as well as new members of the EMS, Spain and Portugal. France, pursuing a policy of the strong franc (*franc fort*), had tied itself to Germany and initially seemed secure. But by the end of the process of contagion, France was also endangered: thus the central Franco-German relationship that had formed the core of the integration project was now vulnerable. In the end, the experience of crisis was good for Europe and for the European process, and a crisis summit produced a workable outcome that allowed more room for flexibility while keeping to the road to monetary union.

There were three elements of crisis that were interwoven in the early 1990s. First, there was a geopolitical discussion as a result of the surprise of German unification. The new increase in German power as a result of the addition of some 16 million new Germans prompted other countries to think of institutional ways of limiting the new German strength. Second, there was a technical crisis of the exchange rate system, which seemed to refute a widespread technocratic and academic but also market assumption that the EMS/ERM rates had reached a state of quasi-permanency. Third, there was the long-standing global issue of the role of the dollar and the problems it posed for the international financial order. The detailed narrative of how these elements interact shows some characteristic signs of the complex European system of bargaining between states, central banks, and a wide variety of institutionalized social and political factors. Problems were made worse by a long-running denial of the real problems, and the repeated enunciation of convictions that political will and the European dream could be a substitute for economic policy convergence. The advantage of secret meetings was that they could give central bankers an opportunity to diverge from the optimistic script and to air their concerns: but those discussions were also constrained by fears of leaks that might (and eventually did) produce explosive crises of confidence. At the very last moment, also in a standard scene of the European political drama, shaken by the real possibility of failure, countries reached an agreement that rescued the system by injecting a new element of flexibility.

Capital Flows between Core and Periphery

The 1992–1993 crisis is interesting as a milestone on the integration road, but also because it offers an anticipation of the events of 2010–2012. Fixed exchange rates and what appeared to be a very hard and tight currency commitment mechanism sparked capital flows to the fringe countries, where the capital inflows induced price and wage inflation and an increasing loss of competitiveness. The pattern that produced the crisis thus proved to be an accurate predictor of what the future monetary union would produce. Like the later crisis, the institutional and political framework also produced an intense discussion as to where the policy mistakes had been made: at the periphery or in the core?

The crises of 1992–1993 initially affected the periphery and then rippled back to the core; but what made the experience so devastating and dramatic was that the major cause of the crises seemed to lie in the center, in the anchor currency, the Deutsche Mark. The German problem could be analyzed in technical terms, as a mismatch between fiscal policy (which was highly expansionary as a result of the high costs of German unification) and monetary policy (which had a traditional anti-inflation orientation, and now needed to counteract the inflationary potential emanating from fiscal policy). The interaction between fiscal and monetary policies resulted in high interest rates that punished the countries whose economic fortunes were interlocked with that of Germany through exchange rate commitments in the EMS. But the German problem could also be analyzed in political terms, as a consequence of the unification of West and East Germany in October 1990. Consequently, every time German policymakers asserted their monetary preferences, the audience felt the resonance of the new German power potential. Inevitably, policy discussions led to the thought that the experience of monetary coordination involved both the extension of German power and the protection of German interests.

After 1987 the European exchange rate system seemed to have been frozen. The five years of exchange rate stability between 1987 and 1992 coincided with the intense discussion of the form of a future monetary union and the implementation of the blueprint of the Delors Report in the form of the Maastricht Treaty. Was the apparent locking of exchange rates a source of strength or a likely cause of profound destabilization? The first answer was given by those who were enthusiastic about the fundamentally political momentum in favor of monetary integration that had initially been generated by Delors (and then greatly reinforced by uncertainties about how Germany would deal with its profoundly altered geopolitical role). At the beginning of 1992 the CoG alternates discussed whether there should be a final realignment of exchange rates before the currency union entered into effect. The treaty clearly permitted this, but most of the alternates "pointed out that it would not be consistent with the achievement of a high degree of convergence or with the spirit of the treaty." They concluded that an alteration should not "be precluded, but it is very unlikely and not recommendable given the convergence that should have taken place before."[1] By April 1992 they had reached a consensus that there should be no final realignment.

In advancing the view that exchange rates had been in effect locked, the central bankers had not gone out on any extreme theoretical limb. They were sharing a consensus that had become widely established among both academics and policymakers, and for a long time was apparently held by market participants as well, namely that the extent of the political commitment was creating a virtuous cycle in which it would become easier for governments to meet their commitments and sustain their credibility. Lorenzo Bini Smaghi and Stefano Micossi, for instance, laid out the key to the mechanism when they argued that "Improved conditions of stability-oriented policies may help reduce the (real) cost of government borrowing and the external financing constraint, thanks to the expanded inflow of foreign capital."[2] Jeffrey Frankel, Steven Phillipps, and Menzie Chin, looking in 1993 at the statistical record of interest-rate convergence and exchange rate stability, applauded the wisdom of the Maastricht criteria and concluded that "investor faith in the exchange rate stability provided by the EMS seems to have improved particularly in 1990–91 relative to 1988–89."[3] Financial markets did not offer any indication of an impending crisis either, and interest-rate differentials between Germany and other members of the EMS fell in the course of 1992. The only important exception to the general consensus about exchange rate stability in the EMS came from the Bundesbank.

A perverse reaction followed the determination that the EMS could simply glide smoothly into monetary union. The expectations of locked exchange rates with only a very small chance of parity alteration set in motion a market mechanism that threatened the eventual policy outcome. The combination of credibly fixed exchange rates with continued interest-rate differentials made it possible for capital to move in a "convergence play": large amounts of capital flowed into the higher-inflation countries, which maintained higher interest rates as part of the counter-inflationary strategy. The investors making this speculative play believed that they would always be able to detect signs of an imminent crisis, and could move their money out again while the central banking systems mounted a last-ditch defense that would in effect pay out the speculators. One sign, which in retrospect was interpreted as worrying, was that in some of these cases, domestic holders of financial instruments, who did not believe that they could be so nimble, started to move assets out of the currencies subject to the speculative play.[4] The use of new statistical techniques to highlight incompatibilities or inconsistencies between the policies of different national governments added a new dimension to an old speculative game of betting against a government committed to an unsustainable policy. The central banks were trapped: if they reduced interest rates, they encouraged domestic borrowers into a wave of credit expansion. The main macrofinancial characteristic of the lead-up to an eventual crisis of the system lay in very substantial capital inflows to Italy, as well as to late entrants to the

EMS, Spain and the United Kingdom. The countries receiving these inflows often interpreted them as a sign of confidence stemming from long-term policy improvement, when the reality was that much of the calculation was simply driven by interest-rate differentials.

The dilemma gave rise to different explanations for the crises that almost destroyed the EMS in 1992 and 1993. A first line of analysis explained the problems in terms of the cost-competitiveness problems of the countries that attracted the large inflows, Italy and Spain, and then also the United Kingdom, as higher rates of inflation and real wage growth made for increasing lack of competitiveness and then also balance-of-payments problems. The Bundesbank labeled these countries as the "weaker members." But such an explanation could not account for the speculative attacks that eventually also engaged countries such as France and Denmark, where there was no evidence of any significant wage cost divergence from Germany.

A second interpretation in consequence saw the problems as lying fundamentally with the central or hegemonic country, with the shock of German reunification and the policy mix of loose fiscal policy with large transfers to eastern Germany (DM 139 billion in 1991, equivalent to 53 percent of German private savings, or 5 percent of GDP) and the tight anti-inflationary monetary policy of the Bundesbank.[5] The German policy combination placed a strain on other countries similar to that imposed by the mix of large budget deficits and an anti-inflationary stance in the United States in the early 1980s during the first Reagan administration.

Third, the crises could be thought of in terms of the models of exchange rate crises developed by Maurice Obstfeld in 1986, in which expectations of devaluation can push a country into devaluation.

Fourth, the crisis showed that in some countries there were political limitations on raising short-term interest rates, which made the defense of the exchange rate system ultimately impossible.

Finally, some analyses suggested that it was the prospect of EMU that promoted the breakdown, because the conditions of the Maastricht Treaty were interpreted as being too harsh, and thus politically unrealistic.[6]

The discussion of potential instability had begun already at the time of the Delors Report. In fact one of the most prescient analyses of the subsequent problems was given during the meetings of the Delors

Committee by Alexandre Lamfalussy, who saw the potential vulnerability of the EMS as a powerful argument for going ahead quickly with EMU—though this was inevitably an argument that could not really be presented in public, because it might undermine confidence in the existing European currency arrangements. On January 10, 1989, Lamfalussy said:

> I am extremely preoccupied by what might happen to the EMS, not in three years' time, but in one year and that is very much along the line of the argument because we have now gone very far in liberalising capital movements—I am happy with that and it is a fact. This liberalisation is happening in a world environment where expectations may run in all possible directions, where the speed of transmission of interest rate movements is extremely speedy, and because also I do see basic imbalances in terms of current accounts within the EMS. I think, this has to be said very bluntly. We do have these basic imbalances and therefore things may happen within the EMS that will need a very very careful handling, not excluding perhaps exchange rate changes, etc. but it has to be under control, it will have to be put under control so as not to waste really ten years of very very successful experience. It is for this reason that I would be in favour of a first stage which could be implemented as quickly as possible and not in a two or three-year distant future, but starting this autumn or at least at the end of this year.[7]

In a similar vein, the Bundesbank repeatedly emphasized the importance of increased flexibility on exchange rates. Even before the Delors Report and before the shock of German unification, Vice-President Helmut Schlesinger had publicly called for exchange rate flexibility as the appropriate adjustment tool for weaker EMS member states, and warned against the "overloading" of monetary policy.[8]

In the alternates' meeting on November 7, 1988, a notable difference in approaches surfaced during the discussion of how European central banks should react to movements of the dollar. The Bundesbank representative was in favor of responding to rises in the dollar rate with an increase in interest rates, and of foreign exchange interventions in case of a falling dollar; the Banque de France set out exactly the case for making the opposite response, with interventions against a rising dollar and interest-rate reductions in the case of a fall (see Figure 9.1).[9]

In August 1989 in the Bundesbank Council Pöhl warned that he considered the high valuation of the peseta and the lira to be unsustainable, and that if the situation continued Germany would be pushed into increasing its interest rates: the resistance by other countries to revaluations thus lay at the root of the Bundesbank's perception of a need to raise rates. Finance Minister Theo Waigel replied that realignment was difficult, because other EMS members were hostile, but that the German government did not "reject realignment categorically." In the same meeting, members of the council expressed fear that the alteration of the status of the CoG might threaten the autonomy of the Bundesbank in making decisions, and that this was becoming an institution that might put pressure on German rates.[10] Within the EC Monetary Committee, the Finance Ministry's state secretary, Hans Tietmeyer, warned of a "false discussion" and stated that the German government had told France that it was not looking for any realignment of the Deutsche Mark/franc rate, but that there was a need for "careful analysis" of the policy mix of the member countries. Tietmeyer also delivered a stern warning about the "self-satisfied character" of the discussion.[11]

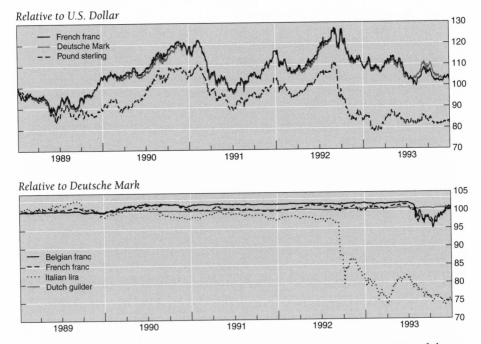

Relative to U.S. Dollar

French franc
Deutsche Mark
Pound sterling

Relative to Deutsche Mark

Belgian franc
French franc
Italian lira
Dutch guilder

Figure 9.1. Exchange rates, 1989–1993. Beginning of period = 100. *Source:* National data.

Within the CoG, the Dalgaard group (dealing with exchange rate issues) had already provided some warning signs before it was absolutely clear what would happen with regard to German unification. In May 1989 France had once again criticized German interest-rate moves.[12] In November 1989 Dalgaard contrasted two approaches to the exchange rate issue:

> An optimistic view had been that the exchange rate mechanism had handled the problems without too much difficulty, despite the advanced stage reached in the liberalisation of capital movements and the long interval of almost three years since the last realignment. Another view had held that recent experience had shown that the situation in the EMS might be precarious; even relatively vague rumours could trigger very large interventions. This highlighted the need to ensure that exchange rates were convincing at all times.[13]

In December 1989 Dalgaard reported to the CoG on the apparently long-lasting if not permanent move of the Deutsche Mark and the Dutch guilder to the top of the narrow band. In essence, the dynamic that would blow apart the EMS in the two major crises of 1992 and 1993 was already apparent then. Dalgaard stated the finding of his group:

> The polarisation had been due to two factors. The first was a clear loss of market confidence in the assertion that there would be "no realignment in the foreseeable future." The markets did not expect an imminent realignment, but there was increasing talk of such a possibility in view of the lack of progress in convergence, public statements regarding the usefulness of realignments and the expectation that the Italian authorities might adopt the narrow margin on the occasion of a realignment. The second factor had to do with developments in eastern Europe; while these had been seen at the beginning of November as an element of uncertainty likely to weaken the Deutsche Mark temporarily, they were now expected to benefit the German currency by stimulating growth in Germany, which in turn would lead to an increase in German interest rates.[14]

The German demand for greater exchange rate flexibility in the lead-up to the 1992 establishment of the single market became more problematical as a consequence of the major geopolitical changes of 1989–1990. The German case was no longer analytically so clear, because of the distortions emanating from German fiscal policy. German political union shocked both the European system and international monetary relations. As much criticism came from across the Atlantic as from other European countries. By 1991 the U.S. Treasury was angry that European central bankers would tighten their monetary policy in unison with the Bundesbank's response to German unification.[15] At the same time, Germany remained chronically uneasy about the modalities of operation of the system. In June 1990 the Bundesbank expressed irritation that the Banque de France had bought DM 5 billion without consulting the Bundesbank, in contravention of the EMS operating rules.[16]

The German central bank embarked on a series of interest-rate increases to deal with inflationary pressures arising from the massive fiscal transfers that followed in the aftermath of German unification. On November 2, 1990, it moved the Lombard rate from 8 to 8.5 percent, and through 1991 further increases occurred while U.S. rates were being cut and the dollar was weakening. On February 1, 1991, the German discount rate was raised from 6 to 6.5 percent, and the Lombard rate to 9 percent. On August 16 these rates were moved up to 7.5 and 9.25 percent, and on December 20 to 8 and 9.75 percent respectively. Finally, on July 17, 1992, the Bundesbank set the discount rate as 8.75 percent.

Within Germany there was even more explicit discussion of the need for parity changes, with intense debates in the Bundesbank Council about whether these could be negotiated even though the traditionally weak currencies were paradoxically at the top of their (wider) bands, because of the attractions of high interest rates. Germans feared that a reluctance among other EMS members to change parities would lead to a new wave of pressure on German interest-rate policy, even before the economic storm unleashed by German unification and its fiscal and monetary consequences.[17]

In the meantime the Bundesbank was waging its own war on the subject of German monetary unification. Debates about German domestic policy proved a major distraction from the concurrent steps to monetary integration on a European level, and produced much greater tensions between government and central bank than did the European issues. In 1990 the Bundesbank's advice on the appropriate conversion rate between eastern and western Deutsche Marks had been publicly and humiliatingly rejected by Chancellor Helmut Kohl. The CoG could be used as an additional forum in which the Frankfurt central bankers could put pressure on the German government. In December 1990, at the same meeting at which the statute of the future ECB was finally approved, the committee discussed the rise in German interest rates. The chairman of the alternates' committee, Jean-Jacques Rey, presented the case that there was only a very limited room for interest-rate cuts, and that it would be undesirable for the Bundesbank to "soften its non-accommodating policy stance." He stated:

> Although there was no simple way to avoid possible tensions, two important points had been made. Firstly, it was important to abstain from behaviour that would publicise conflicting priorities in the member states; after all, stability-oriented policies were to remain a common goal. Secondly, it was important to review the appropriateness of the policy mix, particularly in respect of fiscal policies, and it had been widely stressed that it was of the utmost importance for the new German Government to be seen to be taking steps towards reining back the budget deficit, thereby relieving monetary policy of an otherwise increased burden.

Leigh-Pemberton and de Larosière criticized the German interest-rate increases. But Pöhl responded very vigorously to such criticism by attacking the German government's fiscal policy, and added: "The primary reason for the rise in market short-term interest rates could be attributed to the banks' window-dressing of their end-year accounts, which had caused trouble and misunderstandings in previous years. However, there was also the influence of the Deutsche Bundesbank, which had no choice but to pursue a restrictive monetary policy."[18]

The major challenges followed from the extension of the EMS to include countries that were not really convergent with the old core. In particular, Spanish membership, on June 19, 1989, with wider (±6 percent) margins led to an expansion of capital movements in a convergence game. As a result of the fixed exchange rates and high interest levels, Spain began to attract very large capital inflows, and continued to have substantially higher inflation rates than other EMS countries. In 1989 the Bundesbank's increases in interest rates were followed by other central banks, but not by Italy and Spain, which continued to attract substantial inflows. Portuguese developments followed the same pattern after the country joined the EMS/ERM in a surprise move on April 6, 1992. The move itself produced a discussion as to whether the CoG should have a greater involvement in decisions on EMS membership. The governor of the Banco de Portugal had to deny that his bank had been opposed to the EMS membership.[19]

On January 5, 1990, Italy, which had been under the wider-bands regime since 1979, moved into the narrow bands, with a devaluation of 3.8 percent of the central rate (but with the margins of fluctuation remaining at the lower end of the old 6 percent band). As in Spain, the move to greater discipline was followed by an inflow of capital and the possibility of cutting rates, which the Banca d'Italia interpreted as a sign of new credibility in the markets.[20]

The United Kingdom and Membership of the EMS

The Spanish experience was repeated in even more dramatic form in the United Kingdom. On October 8, 1990, five days after German unification, the British pound joined the EMS/ERM. This move had long been opposed by the British prime minister, Margaret Thatcher, who had argued: "You can either target the money supply or the exchange rate, but not both. . . . The only effective way to control inflation is by using interest rates to control the money supply. If, on the contrary, you set interest rates in order to stick to a particular exchange rate, you are steering by a different and potentially more wayward star. . . . The result of plotting a course by this particular star is that you steer straight on to the reefs."[21] By contrast, Bank of England Governor Robin Leigh-Pemberton had made his opinion clear that ERM membership was a good way of establishing an external anchor to bring down persistently high British inflation levels. He had long argued this case, not only in meetings of the CoG but also in public. In a speech in 1989 he had stated: "ERM member-countries have dramatically improved their inflation performance in recent years. . . . the inflation gap with Germany has been much reduced in Italy and virtually eliminated in France."[22] Welcoming Britain's new exchange rate anchor, he told an audience in Tokyo in October 1990: "It's a great event in our economic life. It is something I have looked forward to for a very long time."[23] Other countries had also applied consistent pressure on the United Kingdom to join, although Karl Otto Pöhl had confessed in 1987 to his Dutch friends that he would not be pushing for British entry if he thought that there was any real chance that they actually would join the ERM.[24]

The rate at which sterling entered the EMS should have been, both legally and logically, the subject of negotiation in the EC Monetary Committee, as the other member countries were taking on an obligation to defend the British rate. But the United Kingdom short-circuited the negotiation by declaring its preference for a central rate of DM 2.95. In weekend talks in Brussels on October 6 and 7, Bundesbank officials used the large British current account deficit as evidence that 2.95 was too high, and Board member Tietmeyer argued for a rate of 2.90. Later Pöhl said that he had thought 2.60–2.65 would be more appropriate. On the other hand, French officials thought 2.95 was too low and would give British exporters an unfair advantage. The result was that there was no effective alternative to the rate proposed by London.[25] The Italian chair of the Monetary Committee, Mario Sarcinelli, suggested that there should be some change in the central rate just to teach the British the lesson that they "could not dictate to their new ERM partners." But that rather confrontational view was ignored.[26] The Monetary Committee's report to the EC ministers stated that "On balance, and given that a proposed rate had already been announced, the committee was led to recommend that rate." But it did add a warning, that the 6 percent wider fluctuation margins reflected the fact that "the convergence of the U.K. economy on best performance in the Community is not yet satisfactory."[27]

In Britain there was also dissension about whether the central rate (at DM 2.95) was appropriate. The Treasury held the view that it was impractical to do anything except to use the prevailing market rate. Other commentators took a much wider range of positions. Some suggested that sterling was undervalued. Most analysts, however, argued for a much lower rate: the investment house Phillips and Drew and the National Institute of Economic and Social Research argued for a rate below 2.70, while the U.S.-based British economist John Williamson found that sterling's equilibrium rate had been as low as 2.24 at the beginning of 1990. Within the Bank of England, some senior officials also believed that the proposed rate was unrealistic and would lay the ground for future speculative attacks. Andrew Crockett, the director responsible for international affairs, noted that there was a "significant danger" of locking in the British exchange rate at too high a level and subsequently discovering "that the domestic economy was weakening by more than we anticipated, and our external competitiveness was insufficient to permit exports to become the engine of renewed growth. If we did this, and subsequently kept the exchange rate unchanged, it could be a mistake of historic proportions."[28] Interpretation of the current account position was quite ambiguous. Chancellor of the Exchequer Nigel Lawson had argued frequently—and most prominently in his September 1988 speech at the IMF annual meetings—that if the deficit stemmed from the private rather than the public sector it was inherently sustainable, since it corresponded to private sector capital flows.

The political arguments in Britain relied on two inherently contradictory positions. First, the maintenance of the exchange rate was seen as a credibility-enhancing anti-inflationary tool. Second, EMS membership was expected to bring down interest rates as a consequence of a gain in anti-inflationary credibility, and would consequently bring a politically desirable and economically expansive growth of credit. In other words, it *would* produce inflation. Mrs. Thatcher saw this as the major part of the political appeal of EMS membership, and indeed insisted that the news of a cut of interest rates from 15 to 14 percent should be given priority over the ERM announcement.[29] A paper submitted to the chancellor of the Exchequer on June 1, and sent on to the prime minister on June 8, argued that "it would seem a reasonable starting point to suppose that entering the ERM at an effective rate some way above present levels would be desirable if other factors bearing upon the tightness of monetary conditions remained unchanged." A draft minute to the chancellor of October 3, 1990, argued that "to maintain the downward pressure on inflation it will be vital that there is no fall in the exchange rate."[30] In later papers the Treasury somewhat speciously argued that its officials had been so mesmerized by the political struggle with the prime minister over EMS membership that they had not been able properly to consider the technical aspects of membership. When the interest-rate part of the British calculation did not work out, it became highly attractive to place the blame on the German policy mix.

Thatcher's successor as prime minister, John Major, complained that "The Bundesbank is too formidable an institution not to grasp the effects of its decisions, but neither it nor the German government did more than express sympathy and understanding for the havoc its policy was causing elsewhere."[31]

Initially, however, there were no complaints about the participation of sterling in the EMS/ERM. On the contrary, the very first phase was quite difficult, as Britain could not implement the additional interest-rate cuts that had been eagerly anticipated by the politicians at the time of joining; but then the situation improved quite quickly. At the beginning of 1991 the CoG alternates reported that "the overall feeling had been one of broad satisfaction with the way in which [foreign exchange markets] had been handled, especially within the ERM. It had been noted that sterling had strengthened a little in recent weeks as the market had absorbed the message of the authorities that the exchange rate would be a focal point for monetary policy decisions in the United Kingdom."[32]

Nearly three years later, the British Treasury argued that "the experience of how the ERM worked in the 1980s did not seem to have provided very clear warnings of the difficulties that we and others were to experience in the 1990s."[33] But there had actually been plenty of danger signs; it was just that they were ignored. A consequence of the new optimism was that the warnings that had been included in a prescient paper by the CoG secretariat's economic unit in December 1990 on policy dilemmas that would arise in the operation of ERM were largely overlooked.[34] So too was the half-yearly CoG discussion of multilateral surveillance in July 1991, which concluded that "over the past two years, there has been a clear lack of progress toward the necessary degree of convergence and that the present level of convergence in a large number of member countries is clearly inadequate."[35] The other warnings came from Germany, where policymakers continued to indicate concern about inflation and its implications for German interest-rate policy. In May 1991, for instance, Tietmeyer in the alternates' meeting of the CoG pointed to "accelerating M3 [broad money] growth in Germany more recently and excluded any cut in interest rates. . . . He insisted that a further weakening of the Deutsche Mark could not be tolerated."[36] But the German origins of the warnings made them inherently suspect in London.

The events of 1991 seemed to support the optimistic outlook. At the beginning of the United Kingdom's ERM membership, there had admittedly been a moment of uncertainty when sterling fell on the exchange markets, and it was impossible to think about interest-rate cuts. From February 1991, however, a virtuous circle set in, with cuts in interest rates demonstrating to the markets that the ERM membership was a success. In the March CoG meeting in Basel, the alternates reported that the Bank of England had made it clear that "a further cut would be undertaken only when it was considered to be consistent with exchange rate stability within the ERM." But Bank of England Governor Robin Leigh-Pemberton also made explicit the double nature of British policy-making in that purely domestic considerations continued to play a major part in motivating decisions: "the possibility of further reductions in interest rates would be linked not only to the position of sterling within the ERM but also to domestic considerations."[37] At the alternates' meeting in May 1991, the Bank of England's representative, Andrew Crockett, "confirmed that the Bank of England was not yet sure enough about inflation to take a lead in the process toward lower interest rates."[38] However, the policy stance quickly changed.

British interest rates had been cut from 15 percent in October 1990 to 11 percent by July 1991. Inflation also fell over the same period, from 10.9 percent to 5.8 percent. Both business and the political opposition pressed for even faster and more dramatic cuts in interest rates. By the autumn of 1991, the interest-rate differential to Germany had largely disappeared: this was a faster convergence than U.K. policymakers had originally envisaged. This success story set the stage for a surprise election victory in April 1992 by John Major's Conservatives.

The Illusion of Stability

The period between the fall of 1991 and the summer of 1992 saw the high point of complacency about the system's stability. The CoG Monetary Policy Subcommittee in October 1991 was the setting for a strange discussion in which the United Kingdom, Italy, and Spain worried about the acceleration of inflation in Germany and suggested that the Deutsche Mark might no longer be able to provide a satisfactory anchor for the system and that perhaps a system of "co-anchorage" was required. At the end of the year, the CoG Foreign Exchange Subcommittee presented what even the Banque de France saw as an overly optimistic account of how credibility in the EMS was increasing.[39]

The Foreign Exchange Subcommittee had concluded that "there seems to be little doubt that credibility in the ERM parity grid has strengthened" as a consequence of increased economic convergence and a new policy framework in which a "hard currency" had become a generally shared priority. Its report noted that "the potential competitiveness gains from devaluation are likely to be small and short-lived because of the impact on the domestic inflation process." Any devaluation would damage the credibility of the hard currency approach. In addition, the relative weakening of the Deutsche Mark had reduced the perceived likelihood of realignment; further economic convergence could be expected in the course of the transition to monetary union; and external imbalances in the system were being reduced. The German current account surplus had fallen from 4.6 percent of GDP in 1989 to 2.9 percent in 1990, and a deficit was expected in 1991. The U.K. deficit, on the other hand, had fallen from 3.9 percent to 2.4 percent in 1990. The report did not discuss the fact that the Spanish and Italian positions were deteriorating, but it did warn that inflation tendencies in the high-inflation countries were strengthening. However, the warning was counterbalanced by a positive assessment of the consequences following from the lower long-term interest rates produced by increased convergence. The new credibility of the system meant that the lower cost of government borrowing countered a potential spiral of debt accumulation.[40]

In November 1991 the alternates reported that "in certain respects the members of the ERM were already in a de facto currency union. Although the greater credibility of exchange rate parities in itself was to be welcomed, it meant that interest rates had a tendency to converge and that interest rate policy could be constrained." They considered the possibility of dangerous rumors of a realignment, but considered them more likely to occur just before the final fixing of currencies than in the ratification of Maastricht. The new chairman of the CoG, Erik Hoffmeyer, who had taken over after Pöhl's abrupt departure from the Bundesbank, optimistically noted that "if sufficient convergence was achieved by the member states during Stage Two to enable the transition to Stage Three to be made, it would be difficult to imagine that there would be a need to discuss a realignment." Only the new Bundesbank President Helmut Schlesinger dissented from the view that the EMS had already become a currency union, and warned his colleagues that in setting monetary targets for 1992, the Bundesbank would have to take into account the very rapid monetary growth of the fourth quarter of 1991. In short, "he did not feel that it would be correct to describe the ERM as a de facto currency union, since exchange rate realignments could still take place in the future."[41]

Some of the technical reports in Basel presented a more somber picture than that reflected in the generally upbeat tone of the governors' discussions. A report on "Credibility in the ERM" in December 1991 brought renewed doubt. The alternates noted that "it was likely that monetary policy would remain overburdened in the pursuit of price stability."[42] And the Foreign Exchange Policy Subcommittee warned that

> the risk of speculative pressures in the expectation of a "last realignment" in the run-up to the final stage of EMU was potentially disruptive and should be considered by the Governors. It was considered doubtful whether public reaffirmation of the principles set out in the Basle/Nyborg Agreement would have a sufficiently stabilizing effect on the markets. Finally, sharp fluctuations of the U.S. dollar, which gave rise to disturbances in the ERM, should be addressed through concerted actions involving the U.S. authorities, although this presupposed that a common view could be reached on the appropriate level of the U.S. dollar exchange rate.[43]

Generally, the CoG did not respond favorably to such potentially politically explosive warnings about the stability of the system. Many governors indeed now believed that the old argument about the exchange rate mechanism forcing Germany's competitors to become more expensive no longer applied. De Larosière, for instance, commented on the shift of competitiveness, and wanted to generalize from the French experience: "in terms of unit labour costs, the Deutsche Mark had lost competitiveness over the period since 1986 whilst other currencies had fared similarly against a range of indicators. He did not feel that it was in the interests of the EMS to question the sustainability of the parity grid, so as not to complicate the task of those countries which had to make necessary adjustments."[44]

At the beginning of 1992, the greatest strains seemed to have passed. The Bundesbank had increased its central rates by 0.5 percent at the end of December 1991, with the discount rate now at 8.0 percent and the Lombard rate at 9.75 percent, and the hike produced a strong effect on the Deutsche Mark/dollar exchange rate, but not on European exchange rates. In January 1992, exchange market interventions had virtually ceased and short-term interest rates had declined in most EC countries from the high levels reached at the end of 1991. The width of the narrow band had effectively been reduced to a much smaller range than permitted under the EMS agreement, with exchange rates fluctuating by only about 2 percent, following a period in which the width had been extended to the maximum permissible limit, with interventions being required at the margin. The Foreign Exchange Policy Subcommittee reported that the markets had been surprised by a larger-than-expected increase in the Bundesbank's Lombard rate, but even that was not a great shock. The alternates expressed a general consensus that Bundesbank policy had been appropriate: "With some reservations regarding the size of the increase in the lombard rate, the Alternates had generally acknowledged that the decision had not been unexpected and that it had helped to strengthen the credibility of the Deutsche Bundesbank's policy stance."[45]

In fact there had been a very lively and controversial discussion at the alternates' meeting. In that setting, the chairman of the Foreign Exchange Policy Subcommittee, Fabrizio Saccomanni, had concluded that "tensions had abated, but the ERM remains vulnerable" not just to problems emanating from the U.S. dollar but also from "pressure on sterling as the United Kingdom did not follow interest-rate rises." He noted that there had been no prior consultation before the German increase in interest rates. Tietmeyer defended the Bundesbank's interest-rate policy, only to be sharply contradicted by Andrew Crockett from the Bank of England, who "insisted that the cyclical position of countries is normally different, requiring different monetary policies," and expressed disappointment that the German rate rise had been 0.5 percent rather than 0.25 percent.[46]

By contrast with the alternates, the governors' meeting was harmonious. The governors affirmed their commitment to an all-out maintenance of the system. De Larosière said that he "agreed that tensions within the EMS had decreased although there remained risks at the global level, particularly with respect to the U.S. dollar's volatility and its possible consequences for the functioning of the world financial system." Leigh-Pemberton also stated optimistically: "The UK Government had made it clear that it would raise interest rates if necessary rather than devalue or seek a realignment. Little intervention had however been required, despite the currency's position near the bottom of the wide ERM band." But he began his comments on a note of caution: "the United Kingdom had not followed the December interest-rate rises since to have done so would have been seen as a serious political failure for the UK Government." Schlesinger was worried about the likelihood of a last-minute political intervention in setting exchange rates: "when politicians were confronted with this problem, the tendency was to take political factors into consideration. Any room for maneouvre in this regard should be minimised."[47]

In February 1992 the discussion of monetary policy changes became more urgent as the Bundesbank's anti-inflation policies in response to German unification were increasingly blamed outside as well as inside Germany for a long recession. How could international cooperation be used to solve the policy dilemma of how to modify the German central bankers' stance? A strained deliberation occurred on the issue of whether countries (in practice, Germany) should consult in the committee and elsewhere before carrying out policy shifts. Schlesinger said that "he did not think that central banks could go further than the procedure they currently followed. Already in December of the past year, he had reported on some of the views which had been expressed within the Deutsche Bundesbank's Central Bank Council and had indicated the possibility of a decision without being able to say what that decision would be. A central bank could do no more than communicate to others the kind of information that it could give to its own Government before action was taken."[48]

At the G-10 meeting in January 1992, the general manager of the BIS, Alexandre Lamfalussy, presented the views of academic economists who had argued that a revaluation of the Deutsche Mark would have made sense a year and a half earlier, but would now be problematical and unleash new waves of speculative pressure.[49] In mid-June the CoG alternates noted that all members shared the view that "the credibility of the prevailing central parities in the ERM has grown significantly, and the system has become instrumental in promoting central bank cooperation and in coordinating monetary policies."[50]

In the meantime the EMS had become larger, and the fringe countries inevitably provided a source of instability. At a "tense and bad-tempered" meeting of the Monetary Committee in April 1992, Portugal was taken into the wider band system of the EMS/ERM at a middle rate of 178.735 Portuguese escudos to the ECU. The problem was that, like the United Kingdom, the Portuguese minister of finance had come to the meeting with a commitment to an already predetermined rate (180), and apparently had no room for negotiation because of the publicity given to the imminent ERM membership. The slight reduction in the valuation was intended to teach a lesson about the responsibility of the Monetary Committee as a forum for negotiation.[51]

There were five factors contributing to increased instability in the EMS. One was the increase in labor costs: in early 1992 a large gap started to open up between Germany and the United Kingdom, with U.K. costs rising at a rapid rate. Second, policy-making in the United Kingdom had been paralyzed by the prominence given to the interest-rate issue and by the perception that Britain was caught in a uniquely severe economic crisis. British interest rates were politically much more sensitive because of the prevalence of adjustable mortgage rates, which ensured that home-owners would be instantly hit by monetary tightening. In July 1992 the British National Savings issued a high-interest-rate bond, paying over 10 percent, but the Treasury was rapidly forced to withdraw it after protests from the building societies (the equivalent of American savings and loan institutions). This episode was read by the markets as a signal that there was no political possibility of defending the pound with the interest-rate tool. Third, inflation in Germany increased, and with it pressure on the Bundesbank to tighten interest rates. Fourth, there was a sharp episode of dollar weakness from April to August 1992, in which the dollar depreciated by 20 percent against the Deutsche Mark. Despite this, the Federal Reserve cut interest rates on July 2. The cover of *The Economist* on August 29, 1992, depicted the falling dollar as the world's main problem. Dollar weakness, then, as in the 1970s and 1980s, produced the effect of "dollar polarization" in which the Deutsche Mark strengthened relative to other European currencies.[52] Finally, new political uncertainty emerged about the sustainability of the Maastricht process and triggered speculative attacks that would not have occurred in the absence of such political bad news.

Schlesinger was increasingly nervous. The Bundesbank's conflicts with the Bonn government had been highlighted in the wake of Pöhl's resignation. Schlesinger's anxiety was compounded by a palace revolt in Frankfurt, where a politically diverse gang of four regional bank (*Landeszentralbank*) presidents on the board of the Bundesbank staged an open revolt against his leadership, in particular against his endorsement of the Maastricht Treaty. Such internal dissent, conducted with a publicity unprecedented in the history of the Bundesbank, seemed to indicate that Bundesbank meetings would be even more contentious, and that the upward pressure on German interest rates would continue.[53] Nevertheless, at the central bank council meeting on January 23, 1992, the Bundesbank issued a declaration to the effect that the institutional shape of the final stage of EMU was "largely in accordance with the recommendations of the Bundesbank." At the same time, the declaration stated that the issue of monetary union was fundamentally political and required a political decision.

These internal German debates may have sensitized Schlesinger to the fragile nature of the political negotiations and the possibility of dramatic market reactions. In the March meeting of the CoG, he asked to delete the paragraphs in the draft annual report that characterized amendments to the treaty as having been "generally well received by the markets."[54] In April he spoke openly about risks in the exchange markets that the central banks could not take on, and de Larosière underlined the importance of a convergence of economic policies.[55]

In May the Monetary Policy Subcommittee of the CoG added its warnings: "Narrow interest-rate differentials suggested that there was little room for maneuver by individual countries other than in the context of properly coordinated action. . . . If German inflation did not decline significantly and monetary growth continued to exceed its target, this might threaten price stability in the Community and generate strong tension in the ERM." The alternates added their concerns about "a situation in which the ERM allowed little room for maneuver with respect to interest rates and that the resilience of inflation resulted to some extent from different factors. Some of these factors would not respond to a tightening of monetary policy and it was important to encourage the elimination of structural rigidities wherever possible." Schlesinger hit another nail into the coffin with the statement: "Community countries were converging toward a higher rate of inflation; it would be inappropriate if monetary policy in Member States, with the exception of Germany, concentrated on reducing interest rates without tackling the resultant inflationary pressures. It would be unsatisfactory if the inflation criterion in the Treaty on European Union could be met whilst inflation rose in the best performing countries."[56]

In May the one-year-forward exchange rate of the Italian lira against the Deutsche Mark, which was already just below the lower level of the fluctuation band, fell sharply. The U.K. forward rate also started to fall, although it remained well within its EMS bands.

The Maastricht Debate

Then came a final source of instability: doubt about the direction of the whole process of monetary integration. On June 2, 1992, the Danish electorate unexpectedly and by a narrow margin voted against the Maastricht Treaty, with 50.7 percent against and 49.3 percent in favor. This rejection was widely interpreted as a beginning of a general revolt by the European populace (or rather by profoundly nationally conscious and different peoples) against the technocratic (Eurocratic) elite that had run far ahead of the popular will. The consequence was that there were now grave doubts about the Maastricht Treaty, which inevitably shocked the foreign exchange markets. At an informal meeting of the CoG on June 15, Hoffmeyer started by saying that he had contemplated resigning as chairman but had concluded that such an act would give "the wrong impression." De Larosière immediately thought of the consequences for France, where he believed that voters were "sound" on Maastricht but worried by complications resulting from the Single European Act.[57]

At a breakfast meeting of the CoG alternates, Philippe Lagayette of the Banque de France stated that "speculation about the possibility of realignment had become rather more open," and specifically tried to warn the United Kingdom against moving to the narrower band. The mood worsened when the Greek representative stated that his country—even more peripheral and fiscally irresponsible than Portugal—was contemplating EMS membership, and the Dutch and German representatives immediately retorted that "membership should not be considered automatic." The chairman of the CoG Foreign Exchange Policy Subcommittee, Fabrizio Saccomanni, explained that exchange risk perception had increased generally. There were now specific Italian and French debates.[58]

Italy's early elections on April 5, 1992, had produced a meltdown for the old parties, underlined the weakness of the Italian economy, and heightened uncertainty about the exchange rate strategy.[59] The Banca d'Italia calculated in 1991 that there had been a 5 percent loss of competitiveness since the last exchange rate realignment, and argued that this could easily be compensated through rationalization measures and required no realignment.[60] By contrast, industrial interests took a much more gloomy line, and the major business lobbies complained about the worsening competitiveness of the Italian economy. The industrial federation Confindustria in its June 1992 annual meeting attacked the "exchange rate straitjacket." The prominent Milanese steel manufacturer Alberto Falck denounced the "foolish attitude" of the government on the exchange rate. In responding to the clash of interpretations between the Banca d'Italia and the business world, the Italian press liked to amplify external criticisms of the parity regime. On June 19, for instance, *La Stampa* quoted Bundesbank President Helmut Schlesinger as saying: "The EMS is not a fixed exchange rate system. It has become like that because some governments refuse to devalue."[61]

During the summer an anti-European revolt developed, first in Denmark, whose electors rejected the Maastricht Treaty, and then in France. President Mitterrand announced that a referendum on Maastricht would be held on September 20, and approval of the treaty looked increasingly precarious.

The political upheaval went along with heightened nervousness in foreign exchange markets. In July at the CoG, Erik Hoffmeyer reported on the ECOFIN meeting that had taken place on July 13, when he had relayed the governors' view that "convergence was not proceeding at a satisfactory rate."

> The Committee [CoG] was concerned about Germany's anchor role and, finally, fiscal policy in many countries was inappropriate. The Committee was concerned that unrest in the exchange markets had reappeared which had led to the conclusion that the credibility of the ERM was not as unconditional as it had been previously. The Dutch Minister subsequently stressed that any measures which were taken in Germany for internal reasons had repercussions throughout the EMS which were not wholly satisfactory. The German representative reacted sharply and pointed out that there were so many tensions in the German economic system, such as the growth of money supply, credit expansion and the difficulties with the Eastern *Länder* [states], that he could not exclude a tightening of monetary policy.[62]

Schlesinger suggested publishing the reports of the Monetary Policy Subcommittee, "particularly that relating to public finances; support from the committee with regard to the various member states' convergence programs would help to obtain greater backing from public opinion." This was a potentially subversive step, in that public opinion was moving against the costs that were believed to be resulting from the EMS. De Larosière was unsurprisingly critical of the German stance. He began by noting "that the ex-post report concluded that the monetary policies of the Community countries were on the whole appropriate, although this assessment would have to be reviewed if the following risks appeared: inflationary prospects in Germany; the possibility of a weaker-than-expected economic recovery; the persistence of the wrong type of policy mix in Community countries; or the remaining uncertainties surrounding the ratification of the EMU Treaty. He said these risks were to some extent materialising." He then remarked that he "welcomed Mr. Schlesinger's comments that he was aware of the consequences of any decision to be taken by the Deutsche Bundesbank on its EC partners; it would be a problem for some countries to have to tighten their monetary policies in order to avoid exchange rate difficulties. . . . the strains in some countries that could be created by certain anti-inflationary policies in Germany should not be underestimated."[63]

In March, Leigh-Pemberton had talked about "considerable pressure for an interest-rate cut."[64] In July he was ostentatiously mild. He began by saying that "the situation in the United Kingdom was currently difficult." But he "welcomed Mr. Schlesinger's understanding approach to the difficulties of Germany's ERM partners, although the situation was made more difficult when the media reported on statements which appeared to have been made by the Deutsche Bundesbank concerning a realignment of the ERM currencies."[65]

Only two days after the governors' gathering, on July 16, the Bundesbank Council, in what was regarded as a "historic meeting," raised the German discount rate from 8 to 8.75 percent.[66] The vote was preceded by a fierce discussion. Some members of the council argued that interest-rate rises would not put any brake on the explosive growth of M3, which might even be fueled by speculative anticipation of parity changes; there were even suggestions that interest-rate reductions might lower the pace of monetary expansion. Another very obvious, and very familiar, reason for exercising restraint in interest-rate policy was the international situation, in that it was quite possible to imagine that a new conflict would destroy not just the EMS but also the Maastricht process. Economics Minister Jürgen Möllemann attended the meeting, and begged the central bankers to consider the effect of their actions on East Germany and on Europe. But Möllemann was not a heavyweight figure, even though he had just been appointed as Genscher's successor to the position of deputy chancellor. He was a showman, who had worked as an elementary-school teacher before turning to politics, initially as a Christian Democrat and then as a Liberal. Within a year he would be forced to resign in the aftermath of a corruption scandal. Möllemann provided a perfect target for the Bundesbank to demonstrate that it would not receive instructions from politicians. The Frankfurt bankers ignored him, and may indeed have believed that a demonstration of monetary discipline was necessary precisely for the sake of the future of the European monetary order.[67] Indeed, in a previous meeting at the Bundesbank Council in June, Finance Minister Theo Waigel had said that the Bundesbank "must not be taken over by its partners."[68]

The British complained about a "whispering campaign" from Germany pushing for realignment. Three days before the crucial Bundesbank meeting, the *Financial Times* had quoted a "senior official" of the Bundesbank as saying that "countries which thought they were suffering from Germany's monetary policies could take the initiative by seeking realignment within the European Monetary System. . . . We are not in a fixed exchange rate system yet."[69] The British Foreign Office instructed the Bonn embassy to protest to the president of the Bundesbank against "a particularly unhelpful follow-up to the Chancellor's major speech on Friday evening in which he gave a robust defence of the ERM and the UK's determination to maintain its present parities."[70] On July 29 the pound fell to its lower limit against the Portuguese escudo, and—at a very modest level—obligatory interventions began. From August 7, on the same principle, there were also sales of Spanish pesetas for sterling. But most importantly, on August 5 sales of Deutsche Marks to support sterling began.

A more efficient way of reducing the strains on the EMS might lie in intervention on a global level to stop the rise of the Deutsche Mark against the dollar. The Europeans pressed the U.S. Treasury to this effect. On August 21, 1992, eighteen central banks intervened in the foreign exchange market buying dollars, but the action had no major effect on the dollar/Deutsche Mark rate. The Federal Reserve, which had been skeptical about this intervention, then pleaded to stop the interventions. One of the reasons Federal Reserve officials later gave for their opposition to intervention was that the Bundesbank was against it, on the grounds that the crisis was an opportunity to fundamentally change the EMS. The president of the New York Fed, William Mc-Donough, later reported:

> The Federal Reserve had only two choices: either to have the desk intervene for the Treasury alone, as we had once earlier this year, or to participate in the intervention. If we did not join the Treasury, we believed that it would be even worse than an ill-advised intervention. It would become public sooner or later, that the American monetary authorities were split at a time when the dollar was weak and the European monetary system was showing ever greater signs of stress. We made the decision, approved by the Chairman, that the wiser choice was to join the Treasury. Together we bought $300 million against German marks. . . . After a brief lift, the dollar dropped further and set a new low of DM 1.4255 later that day. The following Monday, we had a repeat. Against very strong advice from the Federal Reserve, the Treasury again instructed the desk to organize a coordinated intervention. Faced with the same choice, the Federal Reserve chose to keep the American authorities united and joined in the intervention. . . . We had authorization to buy up to $300 million. Even during the intervention, the dollar continued to fall and I stopped our intervention, with the later agreement of the Treasury, rather than risk further damage from a counterproductive effort.

But as the postmortem discussion of the coordinated intervention developed in the Open Market Committee, McDonough referred to the position of the Frankfurt bankers:

> all during September we were very much in the mode of not wishing to intervene because of the likely counterproductive effect on [our] domestic markets, especially the bond market. Therefore, in fact, I didn't have any discussions of "What if . . . ?" or "What do you think we should do?" with them. At that time the main thing that would have inhibited any desire by the Germans to do an intervention operation with us is that they very much wanted the ERM to come apart in order to stop having the monetary policy problems they had and to establish what they think is the single most important principle of the mechanism, i.e., that it be flexible. So, I think the main concern they had was purely internally European.[71]

Before August 21 there had been little intervention in dollars. There were interventions amounting to DM 9.7 billion in the EMS, mostly

(DM 6.5 billion) in intramarginal support for the Banca d'Italia. But it was clear to many central bankers as well as almost all the market participants who took bigger and bigger bets against them that intervention and foreign borrowing could not really do the job (see Figure 9.2). In a memorandum for the U.K. Treasury on August 12, the Bank of England had set out the views of its European and Markets divisions that "the fundamental defence of sterling had to lie in a willingness to raise interest rates." On August 17 the bank was so alarmed by sterling weakness that it noted: "Given the present market sentiment towards both the dollar and sterling, it must be questionable whether we can carry on even until 20 September with our current operational stance, without getting sufficiently close to limit down against the DM for official intervention to defend the parity to be completely on the line." But significantly in this memorandum, the recommended strategies were to step up intramarginal intervention, to move to an internationally shared intervention strategy, and to conclude a big foreign loan (£5 billion). The paper no longer talked about an interest-rate rise.[72] The market consensus at this time was that such an increase would run into insurmountable political resistance.

On August 24 Michel Sapin, the new French finance minister of the Socialist government headed by Pierre Bérégovoy, invited his British, German, and Italian colleagues as well as the respective central bank governors to the gleaming new and ultramodern Finance Ministry building in Bercy. They focused on the European situation rather than on global dynamics. The British minister, Norman Lamont, began with

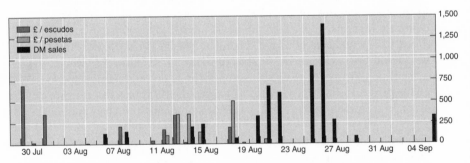

Figure 9.2. Operations to defend the British pound, July–September 1992 (millions of DM). *Source:* Bundesbank memorandum, September 8, 1992, B330/31627, Historisches Archiv, Deutsche Bundesbank, Frankfurt am Main.

an appeal for coordinated interest-rate reductions in Europe and an "activation" of the Basel-Nyborg arrangements for intramarginal interventions. France and Italy also pressed for German rate cuts. German Finance Minister Theo Waigel reemphasized the German insistence on the priority of stability, and from the Bundesbank perspective Hans Tietmeyer came out with the shocking suggestion that the summer would be a propitious moment for a realignment. He was also prepared specifically to suggest a German revaluation. Waigel did not explicitly challenge this proposal, but it was clear that Italy and the United Kingdom had already considered and rejected a parity change, and that France would regard an abandonment of the *franc fort* as a political humiliation.[73]

The meeting was followed by new attempts to produce a way out. Italian Prime Minister Giuliano Amato made a secret trip to Paris on Sunday, August 31, to try to persuade the French that there should be a general EMS evaluation, but Bérégovoy was clear that he could not help, because any change in parity would be courting a defeat in the Maastricht referendum on September 20, and Amato believed that Italy could not hold on until then. In another move, John Major wrote to Chancellor Kohl to ask the Bundesbank to reduce rates; Kohl did not reply.[74] At a meeting in the Bonn Chancellery on September 2, Schlesinger and Tietmeyer, supported by Waigel, convinced Kohl that such a reduction would not be appropriate. *The Economist* commented: "The dollar has plunged, and no American seems to give a hang. Yet Europeans are grimly determined to keep their place in the exchange-rate mechanism, regarding devaluation as a disgrace."[75]

The Bank of England's covert intervention increased as sterling slipped across the 75 percent divergence threshold of the ERM to close at DM 2.7923, with over £1 billion being spent. The financial press did not pick up this action, and indeed the *Financial Times* reported that "the Bank of England narrowly avoided the need to support the currency through intervention."[76]

In early September the Bank of England became slightly more optimistic and took the view that Britain might survive the speculative pressure at least until the referendum date of September 20, when tensions might be reduced by a positive outcome or when the whole system might blow up (with the responsibility falling squarely on French shoulders). On September 4 the Bank of England announced a 10 billion

ECU credit from the Bundesbank, of which half would be used immediately in exchange intervention; and drew 1.104 billion ECU from the European Monetary Cooperation Fund's Very-Short-Term Facility (VSTF). The large credit was a desperate act of commitment to the parity and appeared to rule out any change, since the repayment would in that case be a heavy loss for the Bank of England. Italy, whose leaders recognized the logic created by the British move, immediately raised interest rates.

The September 1992 Crisis

The situation deteriorated quickly after an informal ECOFIN meeting in Bath on September 4–5: the British chancellor of the Exchequer, Norman Lamont, chaired the meeting, and repeatedly pressed the increasingly angry Bundesbank president to cut rates. The Italian finance minister, Piero Barucci, tried to start a discussion about a general exchange rate realignment. He complained that despite strong Italian exchange rate interventions, the lira exchange rate was lower and interest rates higher. The initiative was blocked by France but also by Lamont. The German presentations focused on how the major problems stemmed from Washington rather than from the mismatch between German fiscal and monetary policy. Finance Minister Theo Waigel complained that "in the markets it was clear that no one in the United States was prepared to support their own currency." On the subject of German interest rates, Waigel claimed that both Schlesinger and Tietmeyer had said that German rates had peaked. When Schlesinger spoke he also took up the American theme: "The origins of tensions in the markets were the movement of the dollar and the behaviour of the U.S. authorities." As for German rates, there was no room for maneuver through an immediate reduction in rates, but also "no need for rates to increase." Lamont then took up the topic of interest rates and stated that "there was a specifically European dimension resulting from the position of Germany. We needed European action on the European part of the problem."[77] After the meeting, Lamont and his advisers briefed the press about a German "promise" not to raise rates: "It's the first time this has been said openly and publicly. Growth in the EC has been slowing, and prospects are not brilliant. Many people would like to see lower interest rates." Lamont had mischaracterized the actual German commitment reflected in the agreed statement, which said simply: "the Bundesbank in present circumstances has no intention to increase rates and is watching closely the further development of the economy."[78]

The apparent promise of German help at first led the markets to concentrate their speculative attacks on currencies with no formal defense mechanisms. Finland was forced to let the markka depreciate on September 8, and the Swedish Riksbank raised its marginal lending rate to 75 percent. Within the EU, Italy looked like the most vulnerable target for market pressure.

The interest-rate moves were not successful in stemming speculative attacks. One reason was that there were widespread doubts about whether such a policy regime could be maintained for more than a short time: this was a classic problem of credibility that had affected central banks in nineteenth-century and interwar crises. The technology of foreign exchange trading made for additional vulnerability in the early 1990s: the new algorithms that were used by some of the most influential and dynamic market participants made the defense moves of the central banks fundamentally unsustainable. "Dynamic hedging" based on the models of Fischer Black and Myron Scholes depended on a price relationship between the market value of the securities traded (in this case a foreign currency) and the price of the underlying security. But an active defense of the exchange rate through interest-rate rises increased the measure of "delta," or the hedge ratio, and the formula automatically indicated that positions should be made shorter still. In this case the Black-Scholes calculation was simply replicating an older trading assumption that central banks could be pushed by very volatile markets. Institutionally magnified through large leveraged positions, such bets by powerfully leveraged financial institutions made central banks virtually powerless.

By the next meeting of the CoG on September 8, the sense of imminent crisis was acute. The alternates had prepared a benign press statement to the effect that the committee was "confident that the available means and instruments are fully adequate to preserve exchange market stability."[79] The discussion focused initially on the Italian position: coincidentally it was a Banca d'Italia official, Fabrizio Saccomanni, who as chairman of the Foreign Exchange Policy Subcommittee began the briefing. In late August poor U.S. economic data and strong growth of German monetary aggregates had put the dollar into a sharp decline, and opinion-poll predictions about the French referendum intensified the strain. The subcommittee made some concrete proposals: first, intervention in support of the dollar; second, that "an increase of differentials between weak and strong currencies in the ERM was likely to have a stabilising effect provided that any such increase was seen to be the result of mutually supporting actions"; and third, more coordinated interventions in selling Deutsche Marks. But Schlesinger was quite firm and much more oriented toward economic fundamentals:

> He stressed that the Deutsche Bundesbank had not supported the statement which had been made on 28th August by EC Finance Ministers on behalf of their governments. On the question of whether to take symbolic monetary policy measures, he pointed out that he had already said to the press following the Deutsche Bundesbank Council's meeting on the previous Thursday that in present circumstances there was no room to lower German interest rates, nor any reason to increase them. He would reiterate this to journalists following the current meeting. The interpretation placed by the German press on President Mitterrand's recent statement in reply to a question about the status of a future European central bank had made the situation even more difficult; gathering support for the ratification of the Maastricht Treaty in Germany would not be made easier. Given the various factors, it would be impossible for the Deutsche Bundesbank to lower money market interest rates in Germany at this time.

Leigh-Pemberton simply said that the briefing paper "laid too much stress on the difficulties that were being experienced on account of the German/U.S. interest-rate differential and too little on the future of EMU in the context of the French referendum." He added, however, that there was a clear threat to Britain's ability to stay within the EMS/ERM, referring to the generally held market belief that increases in interest rates were a political impossibility: "it would be undesirable on domestic grounds if ERM developments forced U.K. interest rates to be raised; that would not only worsen the recession, but would also erode domestic political support for ERM and the Community more generally, and make it harder to maintain sterling's position in the wide ERM band." The governor of the Banco de España, Luis Angel Rojo, said that "the central banks should cooperate as much as possible in order to prevent a realignment that, under present circumstances, would increase tension and have negative consequences for the future of the EMS."[80]

Schlesinger's final contribution was defiantly realistic: "With reference to the sentence in the draft statement prepared by the alternates that the Committee of Governors was confident that the available means and instruments were fully adequate to preserve exchange market stability, he said that he did not share this confidence. There was a strong disequilibrium as far as real rates of exchange were concerned; he could not subscribe to the view that a statement along those lines would secure exchange rate stability."[81] He noted that the dramatic pace of the DM 9.5 billion liquidity increase had been exceeded in only two previous instances: in 1973, when the Bundesbank had finally abandoned Bretton Woods and had moved to floating; and in the traumatic EMS realignment of 1987. In retrospect, analyses by the IMF and the Bundesbank concluded that the inflows into the Deutsche Mark in September 1992 were substantially below the Bundesbank's sterilization capacities, and thus that the inflows need not have led to a surge in German monetary growth.[82]

On September 10 Lamont prepared a draft letter to Schlesinger, which the Bank of England successfully deterred him from sending, which emphasized his disturbance at learning "that sources at the Bundesbank were reported as saying that a devaluation of sterling was inevitable."[83]

Knowledge about the attitude of the Frankfurt bankers was quite widespread. In Washington, the Federal Reserve had the clear impression that the Bundesbank wanted a fundamental alteration of the EMS and was discouraging the Americans from contemplating any foreign exchange intervention that might push the dollar up and thus incidentally relieve the pressures on the weaker European currencies.

The European question was whether there would simply be an Italian change of parity or a general realignment. The Bundesbank view was that the former would not be effective, and that a general debate in the EC Monetary Committee was needed. This interpretation is supported by later academic research, which has demonstrated how much less costly an early general realignment would have been: such an action would have signaled a high degree of political commitment to the integration process, while an individual action, taken by one country alone (namely Italy) was a signal to markets of discord and incoherence in policy-making, and of the absence of political will.[84] On Friday, September 11, 1992, obligatory interventions to support the lira amounted to DM 8.5 billion, and there was a new crisis negotiation in Germany.

In a meeting with Kohl and Waigel in the guesthouse of the Bundes-bank in Frankfurt, the German government agreed to initiate negotia-tions for a revaluation, and the Bundesbank representatives agreed that such a step would provide a justification for a cut in German interest rates. Waigel phoned Barucci to say that the Bundesbank could not con-tinue interventions in support of the lira, and that a realignment, pref-erably a general one, was needed. This message was conveyed to the governor of the Banca d'Italia, Carlo Ciampi, while he was in a meeting with the prime minister. He was so shocked by the German revelation about the Emminger letter of 1978 (when Chancellor Schmidt had promised to release the Bundesbank from intervention obligations) and its implications for Bundesbank operations in the EMS that his face drained of its color.

Germany sent Finance Ministry State Secretary Horst Köhler as well as Tietmeyer to Paris and Rome to discuss the realignment. But there was no discussion at the highest political level, and Kohl never tried to speak with Amato or with the British prime minister during this phase when the crisis was intensifying. Major felt that Kohl was simply un-comfortable with any economic or financial discussion.[85] Ciampi made it clear that he thought a general realignment of the EMS rates was de-sirable.[86] But the French chairman of the EC Monetary Committee, Jean-Claude Trichet, was reluctant to call a physical meeting on Satur-day, September 12, and the EMS governments and central banks were consulted by telephone, bilaterally. In the course of these discussions Trichet came to the conclusion that only Italy wanted a realignment vis-à-vis the Deutsche Mark, and that a physical meeting was thus unnecessary. It was certainly correct that the British government was at the highest level opposed to any such maneuver. The United Kingdom held the chair of the ECOFIN and did not propose any discussion of realignment at the ministerial level. But the German central bankers and their Dutch allies were keen to see a more general alteration of ex-change rates, and Italy also did not want to face the spotlight alone. The Dutch central bank representative on the EC Monetary Committee ex-pressed his willingness to attend a meeting with the goal of negotiating a realignment.[87] Other sound-money countries were more reluctant: when the British chancellor of the Exchequer asked the Danish finance minister in July 1992 about the possibility of realignment, he was told that Denmark wanted to stay with the Deutsche Mark. French Finance

Minister Michel Sapin was especially reluctant to undertake any dramatic move before the September 20 referendum. The French position was that a real meeting might be interpreted as signaling a general realignment, but that such a move was not really justified by the fundamentals. In that way, the French and the British were held together by the belief that a meeting would be a very dangerous signal. A devaluation of the franc against the Deutsche Mark had been ruled out by the French government, and Prime Minister Bérégovoy insisted firmly on this position. Even a depreciation of the franc in the context of a general realignment would have been perceived as a painful humiliation for France, and would be punished by the voters. On Sunday, September 13, a last Italian attempt to secure a general realignment occurred. Saccomanni spoke with the Bank of England, while Italian Prime Minister Giuliano Amato spoke to his British counterpart, John Major, who was staying at the Queen's residence in Balmoral, Scotland. He explained Italy's impossible situation, and that there would need to be a change of parities before the markets opened on Monday. Germany would respond to this move with a small reduction in interest rates (0.25 percent in the Lombard rate). Amato suggested as directly as he could that Britain might do well to follow this move, but Major was still convinced of the essential strength of the pound and perhaps even remembered his foolhardy claim that sterling would soon replace the Deutsche Mark as the strong currency of Europe. At the end of the conversation, Amato simply stated that he would have to go on his own with a new parity. When Major said, "Good luck, Giuliano," he replied ominously, "I should say good luck, John."[88]

Instead of the solution initially favored by the Germans, in which there would be a 3.5 percent devaluation of the lira and a 3.5 percent revaluation of the Deutsche Mark, the Italian devaluation was eventually accompanied by a revaluation of *all* the other EMS currencies by 3.5 percent. France and Britain were completely opposed to any move of their currencies against the Deutsche Mark. Thus, in effect, only the Italian rate moved, and the drama of the weekend produced no general realignment.

The British chancellor of the Exchequer, Norman Lamont, had for some time been intrigued by the possibility of a general realignment, and the issue was raised in a minute of August 6, 1991, and again in a discussion at 11 Downing Street in December 1991. But Treasury officials rejected these suggestions on the grounds that it was not clear that such a move would have an impact on German interest rates; but above all that the whole issue depended on the position of France. "If the French had not themselves come to the conclusion that a realignment was desirable, we would not be able to persuade them."[89] That this view was entirely accurate was confirmed by Trichet's unwillingness to call a physical meeting of the EC Monetary Committee on September 12. A great deal in French politics depended both on the maintenance of the hard franc and on support for Italy. France believed that EMU needed Italy for political reasons, but worried about the technical practicalities of the Italian exchange rate. In the summer, Major and Lamont had in fact unsuccessfully hinted to their French counterparts that a change in the franc rate might be needed, but they spent most of their energies in their campaign to persuade the Bundesbank to lower rates. They were clearly profoundly worried by the severity of the British economic downturn. The gross domestic product fell 4 percent over two years, and unemployment rose to over 10 percent, making this the worst U.K. recession in the second half of the twentieth century.

In public Lamont had committed himself very firmly to maintaining the pound's parity within the ERM, and in a speech on July 10, 1992, to the European Policy Forum had stated that a unilateral devaluation "could only put interest rates up, not down." Leaving the ERM would be a "cut and run" operation and would produce a "fall in the pound probably unprecedented in the last forty years."[90] As late as September 14, Treasury and Bank of England officials were sent to explain to a skeptical Bundesbank that the DM 2.95 rate was consistent with the relative economic performance of the two countries.

In fact the markets were not calmed by the Italian move. On Monday, September 14, the Banca d'Italia had briefly intervened to stop the lira from rising too quickly, buying Deutsche Marks (but selling sterling and pesetas).[91] But already the next day there was a renewed need for Deutsche Mark sales to support the lira, and a total of DM 13.5 billion was sold by the European central banks, 9.5 billion of this to support the Swedish krona. A final push to the vulnerable pound was given by the publication of an unauthorized quotation from Helmut Schlesinger in the German newspaper *Handelsblatt* on September 16, in which he reportedly said that "further devaluations cannot be excluded." On

September 16, DM 43 billion were sold to buy British pounds, and another DM 10 billion to buy lire, including DM 3.3. billion in obligatory intervention at the bottom of the lira's new range. Britain sold £28 billion in reserves on this day alone. Critically, however, the Bundesbank decided to stop its own interventions. The Netherlands and Belgium reduced their interest rates in a vain bid to take some of the heat out of the crisis. Three rounds of European concertation took place on Wednesday, September 16. In the first, Britain announced interest-rate increases, and the governor of the Bank of England raised the possibility of a temporary suspension of Britain's EMS/ERM participation. At 11:00 A.M. U.K. time, however, the rise in the interest rate from 10 to 12 percent failed to move the pound from its ERM floor of 2.7780. At 2:15 P.M. a second increase, to 15 percent, also had no effect. In the second concertation, Britain talked about realignment, but other countries were skeptical and suggested that the double-digit alterations of parity required to stabilize market expectations could not be agreed on overnight, and that in any case there was no guarantee that the operation would be a success. In the third and final round, Britain announced the suspension of its EMS/ERM membership and asked for the calling of a special meeting of the Monetary Committee. Italy, Spain, and Portugal asked to be released from their intervention obligations, but France resisted this suggestion on the ground that it would have meant the complete end of the EMS. In a nighttime meeting of the EC Monetary Committee (September 16–17), Italy made the demand again, but it was rejected. The Italian representatives talked about their uniquely difficult political situation and then announced the temporary suspension of EMS membership.

At the end of the affair, the governor of the Bank of England wrote a stinging personal letter to Schlesinger, protesting against Schlesinger's attempt to justify in a conversation with *Financial Times* journalists the actions of the Bundesbank by referring to its agreement to a large U.K. credit tranche and its willingness to do intramarginal interventions. "As you will be aware, the Bundesbank bought sterling only for our own account, and we were given the very clear signal that you were not willing to do so for your own account."[92]

The EMS looked profoundly weakened. But the challenge involved more than the British and Italian currencies. One of the great successes of increased monetary cooperation in Europe was generally thought to be the increased private use of the ECU, which could be read as a measure of market acceptance of the idea of monetary union. Euronotes and commercial paper denominated in ECU had been expanding steadily since the mid-1980s, with a 50 percent increase in the twelve months before September 1991. But the crisis in 1992 produced a contraction, with a 20 percent fall in holdings of these securities, to 8.6 billion ECU in September. In the intense period of the crisis, an interest-rate premium developed in the short-term market, reaching 200 basis points on the worst days, as the idea of a synthetic currency came to be regarded as suspicious in the context of a market panic.[93]

The major losses in the attempts to support the lira and the pound were borne by the Banca d'Italia and the Bank of England. But the Bundesbank incurred substantial losses as well, a fact that helped to intensify that institution's skepticism about the functioning of the ERM. A calculation in November showed a loss on the interventions of DM 1.566 billion, although this was in part compensated by profits from the sales of dollar securities ceded by the Banca d'Italia and the Bank of England. Bundesbank officials also noted rather sourly that the Banque de France had made a substantial profit, which they estimated at DM 500 million, from its action in the crisis, in particular from the successful operation to defend the French franc.[94]

The Banque de France aroused some hostility in Italy because of its opposition to attempts to discuss the possibility of Italian reentry into the EMS mechanism. In fact the Paris central bankers were right to be worried. The next stage of the crisis, the attack on the French franc, was the most puzzling and disturbing element in the 1992 drama. Whereas it was clear that there was some issue of competitiveness in the Italian and the British cases, this was not true for France. Some commentators had even reached the conclusion that French fundamentals were stronger than those of Germany. In consequence, any financial attack appeared to be paradoxical. It could be driven only by concerns about the outcome of the French referendum on the Maastricht Treaty. Markets were looking in this situation for a demonstration of political will—and that was, in the end, what they got.

Large intramarginal interventions by the Bundesbank were needed to support the French franc. The outcome of the referendum on September 20, with 51 percent of French voters approving the Maastricht Treaty, was too narrow to reassure markets. In a series of dramatic meetings in

Washington during the annual meeting of the IMF, France first agreed on September 21 to bear the eventual cost of such intramarginal interventions by the Bundesbank; the next day, after Kohl had called from Washington to speak with Waigel and Schlesinger, Schlesinger agreed to extend more credit, but hesitated about issuing a joint Franco-German declaration in support of existing rates. Trichet put a great deal of pressure on his German counterparts not to "abandon" France, and as a result they contacted Chancellor Kohl, who confirmed "the exclusively political decision" to continue to support the French franc. Trichet spoke privately with the German state secretary, Horst Köhler, as he later reported in a detailed account of the negotiations prepared for President Mitterrand: "I told him with brutality that the Bundesbank (and Germany) were making a mistake if they thought they could treat us in the same way that England and Italy had been treated quantitatively and qualitatively. We were not comparable, neither economically nor politically nor strategically."[95] Undoubtedly in response to the heavy and direct political pressure applied by Chancellor Kohl (Mitterrand as well as John Major believed that Kohl had given "instructions," which would have been contrary to the Bundesbank Law), the Bundesbank raised the amount of Deutsche Marks it was willing to use in interventions. The EMS interventions of September 1992 in consequence beat all records, with 65.971 billion ECU in intramarginal interventions and 53.644 billion ECU at the bands. On September 23 France and Germany issued a joint declaration that the existing central rates accurately reflected the underlying economic conditions; but on the same day, Spain, Portugal, and Ireland introduced temporary capital controls.

The appearance that the Franco-German rate was treated differently from any other EMS parity alienated some EMS members. When the Foreign Exchange Policy Subcommittee met at the end of October, there were tensions because the members believed that the French franc had been rescued by the extent of intramarginal intervention, using the Bundesbank swap line that was not available to all EMS members. The Italians complained that they had exhausted their reserves in intramarginal intervention, and were dependent on the EMCF.[96] There were now varying notions of what policy measures were effective. France, Ireland, and the Netherlands argued that interest-rate increases were an appropriate policy tool; the United Kingdom claimed that they were not. Denmark, Italy, and the EC Commission argued that the multilateral mechanisms of the EMS had become "ineffective or obsolete." Italy underlined that it was almost impossible to undertake precautionary realignments. There was a general consensus that interventions at the margin were ineffective, as they seemed to be a prelude to parity alterations.[97]

Drawing Lessons from Crisis

By the time the CoG met again in November, the world had changed, and the EMS seemed to be contracting back into the Snake format, with two of the major European currencies now outside the mechanism. At the alternates' meeting, Tietmeyer noted that interest-rate moves could not be "symmetrical" if the internal stability of the system was to be preserved. It was up to the weaker currencies to increase their rates, but they had been unwilling to take decisions that would be politically costly. Philippe Lagayette of the Banque de France noted that the principle of unlimited intervention at the margin, in other words the obligation that fell heavily on the Bundesbank, was crucial for the defense of the system. Andrew Crockett from the Bank of England stated that "a policy of early realignments could be difficult to implement in practice." Especially in the case of real shocks, such as that of German reunification, inflation differentials offered "a poor guide to whether changes in real exchange rates were needed." The debate seemed to have become paralyzed. The most interesting suggestion, not taken up by any other speaker, was that of Tietmeyer: that wider fluctuation margins in the system should be adopted.[98]

At the CoG meeting, the representatives of the two "victims" of the crisis were the first to speak. Ciampi began the governors' discussions by saying that

> the events in September had severely injured the EMS and that the prestige and credibility of the central banks had also been diminished. For years, the Committee had been proud of the progress that had been made towards convergence, which to a large extent had been due to the proper functioning of the EMS and which, for a long time had been credible to the markets. The natural weaknesses of the system had been revealed: first, that implicit in the inconsistency, in the present period of transition, of full freedom of movement of goods and capital with monetary policy still in the hands of national authorities;

second, a degree of cohesion among Member countries lower than expected.

Leigh-Pemberton added that "it was very disappointing that sterling was once again outside of the ERM. However, it was the U.K. government's intention to reenter the ERM as soon as possible. He believed that the body of political opinion in the United Kingdom against reentry could be overcome if a convincing case could be made about the appropriate parity and the United Kingdom's counter-inflationary performance."[99] This announcement was already quite at odds with the government, as Chancellor of the Exchequer Lamont was increasingly attempting to present the exit from the ERM as a major success.

Schlesinger was predictably much more frank in drawing lessons from the crisis. He presented the collapse as the inevitable outcome of a test of strength between politicians and markets:

> Politicians should be made to understand that one could not just wait until certain political events, such as the French referendum, had occurred before taking action, since the markets acted more quickly on expectations. It was not enough to say that fundamentally the EMS was a good thing; if a realignment was necessary, it had to be negotiated by all relevant parties, including the politicians, in person rather than over the telephone. He added that tension in the EMS could not be alleviated by requiring a country, the currency of which was strong in the exchange markets but which has inflationary problems at home, to cut its interest rates; that might lead to a further rise in its price level. The priority of price stability was essential according to the EMS rules as well as to the Maastricht Treaty.[100]

The criticism of governments that had attempted to avoid meetings was aimed less at Britain (with whose government Schlesinger was engaged in a very public row about responsibility for the ignominious British departure from the EMS) than at France, whose government had not been willing to call a meeting of the Monetary Committee in the crisis weekend before the exit of sterling from the EMS on "Black Wednesday" (September 16, 1992).

De Larosière tried to sound a more optimistic note by looking at the improved global outlook. In particular, he drew attention to the waning of the threat that had been posed by a falling dollar:

the falling differential between U.S. and European interest rates, mainly the result of a reduction in German interest rates, was favorable to a more stable exchange rate situation in Europe. Furthermore, long-term interest rates in the US had edged up owing to uncertainties about fiscal policy under the Clinton administration, whilst those in Europe had been declining. As a consequence, the dollar had risen to a more comfortable level although he agreed that it should not rise to the extent that it produced inflationary difficulties for European countries.

He then added a note on France: "nothing would have been possible had the economic fundamentals been wrong and had the French franc been at an uncompetitive level. Furthermore, the Deutsche Bundesbank's statement that there was no fundamental problem in the Deutsche Mark/French franc parity, and the significant lines of credit that the Deutsche Bundesbank had extended to the Banque de France, had been underpinned by the credibility of the fundamentals."[101]

The nervousness on the exchange markets continued. On November 19 the Swedish Riksbank raised its marginal lending rate to 20 percent, but the defense was unsuccessful, the speculative attack continued, and the krona was floated and the interest rate reduced to 12.5 percent. The Scandinavian drama had an immediate impact on the weaker ERM currencies. On November 22 there was an additional 6 percent realignment of the Spanish and Portuguese currencies, but markets remained nervous, and continued to expect other adjustments. The speculation now shifted to the Irish pound, the Danish krone, and also the French franc. In its December meeting the CoG noted that "uncertainties had arisen as the policy of the 'franc fort' had been questioned by some politicians in the debates taking place ahead of next March's legislative elections." The report of the Monetary Policy Subcommittee provoked substantial disagreement. It called for a much greater measure of flexibility in altering exchange rates. The report concluded: "When realignments become unavoidable, they should be undertaken as early as possible although frequent realignments had drawbacks. Moreover, realignments would be ineffective and even counterproductive if they were not accompanied by adequate measures to restore stability." Schlesinger wholeheartedly supported this report and its implications; de Larosière by contrast retorted that "he wished that Mr. Borges' report had shown a little more understanding of the economic reality in some countries in which greater unemployment was being observed and would be experienced in 1993." He concluded: "The French authorities had not hesitated to use the interest-rate weapon during the tension in September, and there had been no hesitation in increasing interest rates, particularly at the shorter maturities, when the French franc had come under renewed attack. At his forthcoming annual press conference on monetary policy, he would stress that monetary policy in France was aimed at reducing the rate of inflation but that it would endeavor to encourage economic growth." At the end of the meeting, he added that "while he had not stated it publicly, the task of keeping inflation as low as possible would be facilitated by some decline in German interest rates."[102] It was clear that profound disagreement prevailed as to whether earlier exchange rate alterations would have been desirable. The CoG was never able to make a clear statement about such a policy lesson from the crisis.

Carlo Ciampi even saw some positive result from the long period of exchange rate stability before the outbreak of the crisis, in that it had allowed employers and unions to finally abandon the wage indexation (*scala mobile*) that had been at the heart of controversy about Italian competitiveness since the 1970s. But he was worried about the system as a whole: "against the background of the three recent realignments, he was concerned that a further realignment might cause the system to collapse; everything must be done to ensure this would not happen. Once the parities in the system were felt to be appropriate, it was the responsibility of all of the members of the system to defend them. Better cohesion would reduce the need for intervention."[103]

In December the CoG alternates produced a report on the lessons to be drawn from the exchange rate crises. The EMS should not become either a crawling-peg regime or a quasi-currency union. Wider bands (as had been suggested by Tietmeyer) were also not an appropriate policy response; neither were emergency restrictions on capital movements. Instead, the report focused on policy credibility: "credibility of national policies was an indispensable complement to the analysis of indicators."[104] This was a typically cautious but also unfortunately typically inadequate central bank response, analyzing a fundamental problem but without casting around for a really satisfactory solution.

That the alternates' report needed to be a compromise, and that the governors' own report would be even more watered down, was clear from the varied responses produced by the different central banks. On the one hand, there were the banks that felt vulnerable to speculative attacks, and thus wanted to extend the financing of interventions. The Central Bank of Ireland was worried that the ERM might be viewed as the main anti-inflationary instrument used in many member countries, and that there might consequently not be "a readiness to acquiesce in a realignment, where this is not justified by fundamental economic considerations." The Irish bank also pointed out that the narrowing of the fluctuation band led to destabilizing market perceptions that a currency moving within the full range of the band might be vulnerable. It called for mechanisms by which the burdens of defending the exchange rate would be shared. Irish policymakers knew that they were standing next in line for a speculative attack. The Banque de France in its document even more strongly defended the principle of unlimited obligatory interventions, on technical grounds because a limit would become known and would invite the markets to test it, on historical grounds in that solidarity had required such operations, and on the legal grounds that this was the basis of the December 5, 1978, agreement establishing the EMS. The National Bank of Belgium also emphasized the importance of intramarginal interventions; and the Banco de España stated specifically its sympathy for exploring ways of widening the financing of intramarginal interventions.[105]

Italy, which had already been forced out of the EMS, was more pessimistic about the possibility of rescuing interventions. The Banca d'Italia's document emphasized that the Basel-Nyborg principles had created a "prescription" that "realignments should in future be infrequent and as small as possible." But it warned that the practice of discussing realignments bilaterally in telephone conversations instead of in a meeting of the Monetary Committee was "dangerously inadequate," and that the monitoring process had become increasingly "perfunctory." The amounts available through the VSTF amounted to only 17.5 billion ECU, while the daily foreign exchange market transactions were $1 trillion and the overall size of the EC bond market was $4.5 trillion.[106]

By contrast with France or Spain, German central bankers did not believe that more intervention could rescue an unstable system. The Bundesbank's emphasis was predictably different, emphasizing that the Basel-Nyborg Agreement "expressly affirmed" "the need to adjust central rates in good time." It worried about the ability of individual debtor banks to repay unlimited borrowings on time, as well as about the effects of the monetary policy consequences of unlimited intervention on the creditor central banks (that is, the Bundesbank). The German document called instead for an "internal agreement" on a ceiling for the financing of interventions through the central bank VSTF. It also worried about the potential losses to creditor central banks arising out of devaluations.[107]

Philippe Lagayette of the Banque de France responded directly to German suggestions for a possible suspension of interventions by arguing that such a move would destroy the credibility of the EMS, and that the precedent of July 1985 (when interventions supporting the lira had been suspended) represented an "isolated incident rather than a collective decision."[108] He also wanted to ensure a greater use of the ECU.

A new draft of the alternates' report, dated February 23, 1993, was much more critical and reflected some of the German concerns. First, there should be "no implicit or explicit interest-rate ceilings preventing an effective defense of the currency against speculative attacks." This point ignored the fact that a major part of the origins of the crisis lay in the markets' assumption that there were inevitably political considerations that limited interest-rate increases and made an interest-rate defense ineffective. Second, intervention alone "may have a limited effectiveness in containing tensions and may even exacerbate them." As a consequence, there was no support from most alternates for a formal mechanism for coordinating intramarginal interventions, and it would not be advisable to lay down precise rules on the implementation of Basel-Nyborg. Finally, the monitoring of exchange rates by the CoG that had been introduced in 1987 had clearly failed, and there was no adequate early warning system. "Had a procedure of periodic assessments of parities been current practice in recent years, it would probably be fair to say that authorities would not have been taken so strongly by surprise by the crisis in the exchange market."[109] This was a statement of profound institutional failure. Andrew Crockett from the Bank of England had put the point even more bluntly in a note: "If Governors will be unable to reach a judgment on whether or not parities are sustainable, I submit we will be very far from a basis for strengthening the system. I do hope that we can agree on a more positive conclusion!"[110]

In the first months of 1993, the hope expressed by Ciampi of enhanced cohesion and effective collective action continued to be at the center of debate. Could the whole construction of European integration survive a repetition of the shock of September 1992? At the Monetary Committee in December 1992, Trichet said that "losing faith in the ERM was equivalent to losing faith in Europe." The Germans and the Dutch criticized the politicization of exchange rates that in their view had undermined the system's credibility; they also raised the issue of the losses on VSTF debts for creditor countries following a devaluation, and urged a more constructive intervention system.[111] In the January 1993 CoG meeting Ciampi reverted to the debate about the dangers of speculation: "the attacks against the French franc had to be rebuffed if the system was to survive. However, this implied that other currencies that came under pressure should enjoy a similar defense when their economic fundamentals were considered to be sound." It had become increasingly clear that the relationship at the heart of the European story was the intricate Franco-German dance. De Larosière stated:

> The German-French declaration on the appropriateness of the parity of the French franc vis-à-vis the Deutsche Mark was not to be interpreted in the sense that the parities of the Danish krone and the Irish pound were not appropriate. However, the maintenance of the parity between the German and French currencies was crucial to the survival of the EMS. He thanked the Deutsche Bundesbank for its support and added that the resolve of the French authorities had been demonstrated by raising interest rates at a time when the French economy was performing below capacity and without any inflationary tensions.[112]

The whole issue became highly political, with conspiracy theories about currency attacks circulating widely. Some advisers in the German Chancellor's Office, for instance, believed that the British prime minister was making references to the yen and the dollar in an act of revenge, intended to stoke speculation against the franc "by casting doubt on ERM in order to destroy it."[113]

Saccomanni's subcommittee was riven by tensions, and the chairman staked out two extreme positions: blaming inadequate domestic adjustment, or "blaming the system for its failure to elicit from all members an effective co-operative response to the tension."[114]

The chairman of the alternates, Jean-Jacques Rey, produced a paper arguing that intervention alone could not deal with system crises, and recommending new mechanisms to monitor divergences. Some later academic research indeed claimed to show that publicly announced interventions, as most of the large EMS interventions had been, were even likely to increase the probability of speculative attacks.[115] The CoG started to think about mechanisms for deterring short-term speculative movements. The Irish governor, Maurice Doyle, reported that "a new component had developed in the past week when over fifty banks throughout Europe had taken, virtually simultaneously, short positions in the Irish currency unrelated to investment or trade transactions. He felt that the possibilities for curbing such speculative activity should be studied."[116] The CoG discussion reflected an intense public scrutiny of financial operations in the wake of the EMS crises. French Finance Minister Michel Sapin compared currency speculators to the *agioteurs* (speculators) who had been guillotined during the French Revolution, and in January 1993 warned that they would "pay for their mistakes" if they persisted.[117] In internal papers, the Banque de France however argued that a Dutch plan for penalizing speculators by letting exchange rates fall sharply to the lower band limit and then suddenly intervening to produce a sharp appreciation might be dangerous and that making the punishment of speculators a "primary objective" of exchange rate policy would endanger stability.[118]

De Larosière repeated his by now quite forthright criticism of German policy:

> On the question of sharing responsibilities, the defense of a currency whose economic fundamentals were regarded as sound should be undertaken with the solidarity of the members of the system who should act in a coordinated manner. Solidarity demonstrated by the anchor currency country in the support of the currencies of other Community countries which were pursuing policies of monetary stability and whose fundamentals were sound would reinforce the stability of the system as a whole without calling into question the soundness of the anchor country's currency. For its part, the anchor currency could only fulfil its role properly if that country had a well-balanced policy mix. From the French perspective, the current imperfect policy mix in Germany had a destabilising influence on French monetary policy; the more that the latter had to be tightened in order to preserve the parity of the French franc vis-à-vis the Deutsche Mark, the greater became the market's view that the monetary policy stance in France could not be maintained.[119]

Schlesinger, by contrast, argued that the size of compulsory interventions needed to be limited. "On the question of defining symmetry, it could not be said to be symmetrical if a currency was forced to discontinue its fight against inflation and take steps that would encourage it." He emphasized that "It had never been concluded that parities could not be adjusted during Stages One and Two of EMU, and that should be plainly stated."[120]

The speculative attacks did indeed knock the Irish pound off its parity, with a 10 percent reduction in the central rate at the end of January 1993. Denmark had engaged in substantial intervention in support of the krone, and pressure had been reduced once German interest rates came down. Schlesinger explained that this move had not been influenced in any way by concern about the Danish krone. Ciampi concluded that "the continuous attacks against various currencies confirmed that a mistake had been made in September when the central banks had not faced up to the problems posed for the parity grid."[121]

De Larosière now concluded that "the recent ERM crisis had originated not in the ERM mechanisms but in the fact that the fundamental principle according to which exchange rates should be stable but adjustable had not been respected. Realignments that had become necessary because of changes in relative competitiveness had not been made promptly enough."[122] De Larosière insisted that policy improvements in France had strengthened competitiveness. He noted that he had not received complaints or suggestions from French businessmen indicat-

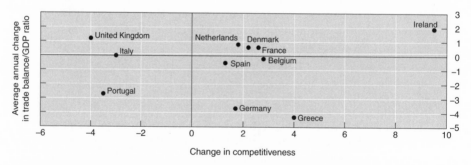

Figure 9.3. Competitiveness and overall trade balance, 1990–1992. *Source:* CoG, December 30, 1992, paper: "Competitiveness, Cyclical Perfomance, and Trade Balances in the European Community," CoG files, ECB, Frankfurt am Main.

ing that the franc was overvalued or uncompetitive—while in the 1980s this had been a continual theme for lament (see Figure 9.3).

Maurice Doyle also complained that "a collective view had not been taken in September 1992."[123] The critique accorded with the view that had been at the heart of Lamfalussy's presentations in the 1980s, which placed great emphasis on relative competitive positions. But it was too harmless an account of the dynamics that were involved in the exchange rate crisis of 1992. De Larosière's analysis of the problems of competitiveness did not really address the issues that would blow up in 1993. There was little divergence in terms of competitiveness between France and Germany, but this fact did not necessarily mean that there could be no speculative attack. The analysis of the CoG secretariat's economic unit even suggested that French (along with Danish and Belgian and especially Irish) competitiveness was increasing relative to that of Germany, while Italian, British, and Portuguese competitiveness had clearly deteriorated.

There is an additional irony in that the same argument that was presented by de Larosière, that French competitiveness was improving relative to that of Germany, was made in a spectacular and public way by George Soros, the man who was widely credited with bringing down the pound in September 1992. In June 1993 he wrote in an open letter to the London *Times:* "France is gaining in competitiveness against Germany. It has a significantly lower inflation rate and its industry has been more adept at adjusting its cost structure than German counterparts. The Bundesbank has kept interest rates too high, too long. It could have lowered short-term rates gradually without endangering its reputation, but it missed the boat. Germany is now in a worse recession than France, and has a large and growing budget deficit."[124] Martin Wolf in the *Financial Times* also wrote about the "dethronement of the D-Mark."[125]

The competitiveness approach was empirically difficult to implement. As Daniel Gros and Niels Thygesen point out in their analysis, officials "were confronted by a confusing array of indicators and other information out of which they had to filter the relevant message. . . . Italian officials, in particular at the Banca d'Italia, were apparently looking at the figures on ULC [unit labor costs] relative to Germany and decided that the lira was not greatly overvalued, since on the ULC basis it had only returned to the 1980 level and compared to the average of the 1970s it had actually depreciated."[126]

An alternative track was simply to blame capital flows and speculation. The complaint that foreigners and foreign banks were largely responsible for speculation was repeated by the Danish governor, Erik Hoffmeyer, in March. A great deal of attention had been given in the press to the role of Soros in the British crisis, in which he had made a gain of some £1 billion by betting against the Bank of England.

In the face of such massive pressure, central banks and governments appeared helpless. Their only defense against speculation lay in rhetorical emphasis on governments' determination not to abandon a fixed exchange rate commitment. Strong language was supposed to demonstrate political will and determination. But the British case of September 1992 had indicated that political will was not enough if it went against a deep current of public opinion. In the March discussion, de Larosière cited opinion polls showing that 72 percent of French people were against devaluation and only 11 percent in favor. But Doyle added that at the end of 1992, Irish opinion polls had also shown 70 percent support for maintaining the parity, but that at the beginning of the next year this support faded as the unemployment consequences of maintaining parity began to be widely discussed.[127]

The alternates initiated a discussion of whether central banks might temporarily suspend intervention obligations (there was a precedent: this had been done unilaterally by the Bundesbank on July 18, 1985). However, such a step would need the involvement of finance ministers, and the possibility of such action might lead to new waves of market panic.

In the discussion of the alternates' report, Schlesinger worried about the capacity of the CoG to reach a consensus on which exchange rates were sustainable. "He queried how the Committee could recommend that a consensus had to be reached on assessments which would have a wide margin of uncertainty and important political implications." When it came to the discussion of interest rates, he said that "he could not accept any proposal which would prevent a country from pursuing its stability-oriented monetary policy or which would undermine it." He also made it clear that the Bundesbank in September 1992 had had no choice except to suspend its interventions, after it had committed DM 60 billion in obligatory interventions in support of the lira and the pound. "The Bundesbank had considered from the start of the EMS that there could be situations in which it would have to ask the German government to free it from its intervention obligations. Any solution to this issue should not be publicized, but he wondered what was meant by 'when substantial and prolonged compulsory interventions were taking place, the issue could be discussed in the Committee, if necessary, on short notice,' since the decisions ultimately rested with the political authorities."[128] These were exactly the circumstances in which Helmut Schmidt in 1978 at the commencement of the EMS had promised to protect the Bundesbank from its exchange intervention obligations.

In a restricted session (without advisers) following the regular March meeting, Schlesinger and de Larosière expressed strong support for an Italian return to the EMS in a wider band, but Schlesinger added "that a new parity was difficult to determine under present circumstances and that it might be wise to postpone the reentry into the ERM until there had been a period of stable floating without intervention but guided by monetary policy."[129]

In March, parliamentary elections in France produced a shift to the right, with a new government under Edouard Balladur as prime minister and Edmond Alphandéry as finance minister. In the last days before the election, President Mitterrand had tried to call for an emergency G-7 summit to promote economic growth, in other words, to force Germany to expand. Balladur's explicit commitment to the hard franc (*franc fort*) strategy calmed markets, and by April the tensions in the system seemed to have been reduced. But for Balladur, the maintenance of the EMS depended on a compromise: according to the *Financial Times*,

> the new government would like some public show of monetary co-operation from Germany. Narrowing the franc/D-Mark fluctuation bands in the EMS is mentioned in Paris, but the Bundesbank might object that such a move would make its intervention in support of the franc more predictable, and therefore harder to wrong-foot speculators. But it seems likely that Paris will expect some early gesture from Germany to reciprocate its promise to create an identikit Bundesbank by giving the Banque de France autonomy in monetary policy-setting.[130]

In fact just a few months earlier Balladur had published a book in which he had attacked the "preordained technocratic plans" of the Maastricht Treaty.[131]

The CoG report on "Implications and Lessons to Be Drawn from the Recent Exchange Rate Crisis" was sent to the EU Council and the

Commission on April 26, 1993. It stated boldly that there should be no interest-rate ceilings stopping an effective defense of a currency, and called for enhanced surveillance in regard to the sustainability of central rates or the desirability of a timely realignment. But it also implicitly acknowledged that there was a limit to possible interventions, and in this way indirectly confirmed the centrality of the Bundesbank's view and of the 1978 Emminger letter: "there cannot be an automatic and mechanistic response to market tensions, involving symmetrical action on the part of the authorities with weak and strong currencies."[132]

The markets seemed to have become calmer, but political tensions remained. In Schlesinger's view the lowering of French interest rates "reflected the reduction of the hitherto high-risk premium on the French franc as the consequence of the continuance of the 'franc fort policy'; France's experience had shown that if a country managed its currency correctly, it was able to reduce the level of its interest rates toward or even below those prevailing in Germany." At the same time as he expressed approval of French policy, Schlesinger attacked the Commission and asked Jacques Delors to explain "the apparent contradiction between the report in that morning's *Financial Times* that the Commission had called for a two-percentage-point cut in short-term interest rates in the Community and had urged an easing of German monetary policy to stimulate economic recovery, and comments made by the German minister of finance in the *Frankfurter Allgemeine Zeitung* denying that the Bundesbank had been asked to cut the German discount rate in order to stimulate growth."[133] Delors responded by saying that, at his request, the growth initiative submitted to EU finance ministers had included no reference to interest rates. In this way, he bowed to the dominance of the Bundesbank.

De Larosière criticized the reference in the alternates' draft oral report (for presentation to the ECOFIN) to a suspension of interventions, as this would destroy the whole conceptual framework of the EMS. "Introducing the possibility of suspending interventions during the course of the day would amount to eliminating the foundation of the system and, thereby, its credibility."[134] But such an acceptance of an emergency let-out clause was in fact the basis of Bundesbank policy ever since the Emmminger letter.

The alternates also suggested a mechanism whereby an examination of the sustainability of parities would be transmitted in the strictest confidence by each governor to the respective finance minister.[135] But the governors realized that an assessment could not always be expected to produce a formal conclusion that a particular central exchange rate had become unsustainable.[136]

In May the CoG discussed the improving situation in France (largely the consequence of a new major DM 10 billion swap line concluded between the Bundesbank and the Banque de France), as well as the heightened vulnerability of the Spanish peseta, which had required concerted intervention on April 23. The question of how to respond to the possibility of a new crisis was deeply polarizing within the CoG, and as a result this question was basically sidestepped. More countries were beginning to demand that they be treated by Germany in the same way that France was, and looked enviously at what they termed a "sweetheart deal."[137] Italy, the United Kingdom, Spain, Portugal, Ireland, Denmark, all had received no support from Frankfurt, while the Bundesbank knew the extent of the political imperative behind solidarity with Paris. The governors were on much stronger ground talking about fiscal rather than monetary policy. Much more consensus existed on the persistence of threats to fiscal stability, and on the danger that the Maastricht criteria would not be met by 1996.[138]

After an attempt at an unorthodox defense, in which the Banco de España sold put options in the peseta at well below the ERM floor in a sign of its determination to defend the rate at any price, the peseta was devalued by 8 percent on May 16. This was the third Spanish devaluation of the crisis, taken two weeks before a general election that seemed likely to bring a change in the Spanish government. A 6.5 percent devaluation of the Portuguese escudo followed quickly.

Germany lowered interest rates gradually in the face of weak domestic demand, with the discount rate falling from January to July from 8.25 percent to 6.75 percent. But other countries, facing the same macroeconomic situation but with fewer concerns about possible inflation, lowered rates more aggressively. France moved from 9.10 percent to 6.75 percent, and Belgian rates were substantially below German rates, falling from 7.50 percent to 6.00 percent. The absence of any interest-rate premium on French or Belgian francs, with a very small risk of devaluation, prompted large inflows into the Deutsche Mark.[139] The markets looked calm. The IMF's annual report, written over the summer but published in September, sounded optimistic about the EMS.

The Final EMS Crisis

Tensions started to rise again in early July after another public Franco-German spat. Finance Minister Alphandéry had announced on a radio program, when asked about the high level of interest rates, that he would "on his own initiative" call a meeting to undertake a "concerted reduction in French and German rates"; the Germans promptly responded by canceling the regular bilateral meeting scheduled for July 3.[140] Tempers flared, and some French politicians told the German parliament that "Maastricht is dead."[141] On July 22 the Banque de France used DM 22 billion for intramarginal interventions within the space of a few hours and raised its overnight borrowing rates from 7.75 to 10 percent; and in an emergency Franco-German nighttime meeting in Munich, Schlesinger and Tietmeyer refused to commit the Bundesbank to any interest-rate response (see Figure 9.4). At this time Tietmeyer suggested that a longer-term solution to the problems of the EMS would require the widening of margins. Alphandéry nevertheless announced that "those who have cast doubt in people's minds about our determination to defend the franc will end up paying for it."[142]

A final crisis did in fact lead to the widening of the ERM fluctuation bands to 15 percent on August 2, 1993. On July 29 the Bundesbank Council had not cut the discount rate, though the Lombard rate was taken down by 0.5 percent. On July 30 (a Friday) a German delegation traveled to Paris, where they were confronted by French demands for a cut in the *Wertpapierpensionssatz* (a subsidiary interest rate, which had

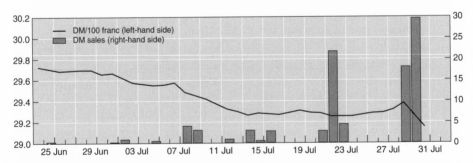

Figure 9.4. Interventions in French franc crisis, June 25–July 31, 1993 (billions of DM). *Source:* Calculated from B330/32834, Historisches Archiv, Deutsche Bundesbank, Frankfurt am Main.

a signaling function but did not require a Bundesbank Council decision) and continuing unlimited franc purchases by the Bundesbank. In the first two hours of morning trading, the Banque de France used DM 5.5 billion in intramarginal intervention in support of the franc. Alphandéry threatened to let the franc drop to its lower margin in order to compel the Bundesbank to undertake additional (and theoretically unlimited) interventions. The Germans and Dutch briefly contemplated suspending interventions, and then, when the French negotiators did not secure these objectives, the Banque de France itself decided to suspend the intramarginal interventions (at 11:00 A.M.), allowing the franc to fall to the lower intervention point. There then occurred some discussion of a temporary German departure from the EMS, followed by a German suggestion of a temporary widening of the exchange bands to 6 percent or more. Tietmeyer asked Duisenberg as chairman of the CoG to start negotiations with the other central bankers on exchange rates. Meanwhile, in Paris, Banque de France officials, though willing (unlike the treasury) to contemplate a French devaluation, were thought to be "livid" about the Bundesbank's failure to drop rates on July 29.[143]

In the end, none of these suggestions was accepted by the French negotiators. They spoke with Prime Minister Balladur and agreed that the attack was against the EMS as a whole rather than on the French franc in particular. The result of the French insistence was that massive obligatory interventions continued through the day: DM 7.5 billion had been sold in Paris and 1.2 billion in Frankfurt by 1:00 P.M. By the end of trading at 5:00, a total of DM 19.9 billion in Paris and 4.2 billion in Frankfurt had been used. The French perception that this was not just a crisis of the French franc was fundamentally correct. Substantial Deutsche Mark interventions were needed to support the Belgian franc and the Danish krone, and Spain was also using Deutsche Marks in currency support operations (DM 765 million on July 28, 4.04 billion on July 29, and 31 billion on July 30); on July 30 Portugal also sold DM 500 million to support its currency.[144] The situation could obviously not simply be resolved by a unilateral French devaluation. But neither would a simple German revaluation work. The problem lay in the determination of Belgium and the Netherlands to continue their close link with the Deutsche Mark.

On a German initiative, the EC Monetary Committee was summoned for a crisis meeting in Brussels. Over the weekend of July 31–August 1,

1993, there were long meetings of the Monetary Committee and then of governors and finance ministers in different groupings. The initial negotiating positions were widely divergent. At the beginning of the Monetary Committee meeting, Trichet presented three French "demands": for a cut in German interest rates, for unlimited intervention, and that the Bundesbank take French francs into its reserve portfolio (a suggestion that Balladur had already made in 1986). Tietmeyer interrupted, savagely asking, "Haven't you forgotten a fourth demand?" and then breaking the grim silence with the lugubrious statement that "the fourth demand, Monsieur le Président, is that Germany immediately renounce its monetary sovereignty."[145] Many participants feared that the EMS would split into two, with the Benelux countries and Denmark following Germany into a new version of the small Snake of the 1970s, and the other countries going with the French franc. The Netherlands refused to participate in an EMS that did not include Germany. Probably a decisive moment occurred at the ministerial meeting when the British chancellor of the Exchequer, Kenneth Clarke, an unusual Europhile in John Major's cabinet who saw himself as an "honest broker" in the EMS/ERM, made a passionate appeal to avoid the complete breakdown of the EMS.[146] De Larosière then made a decisive suggestion, after telephoning with Balladur, and in the face of passivity from a shell-shocked and exhausted Alphandéry: that the bands should be widened, not just to the 6 or 8 percent that had been suggested by Tietmeyer, but to 20 percent. On the Monday night the wider bands—of 15 percent—were agreed. Tietmeyer thought that the Brussels agreement "merely swept away the illusions of the EMS," and in that sense welcomed the clarity that the system's final crisis had brought.[147]

Overall, DM 31.2 billion had been spent on interventions in support of the French franc on July 30, 1993, alone (with DM 45.9 billion having been used in intramarginal interventions since June 25, with the addition of DM 25.7 billion in obligatory interventions on July 20). France had drawn 16.2 billion ECU from the EMCF's VSTF. According to a Bundesbank calculation, if the interventions had been halted at 1:00 P.M. on the Friday, the exercise would have cost only DM 8.7 billion. In addition, DM 3.2 billion was used for the defense of the Belgian franc (mostly in intramarginal interventions by the National Bank of Belgium, with a small amount of DM 5 million in obligatory interventions by the Bundesbank and DM 410 million by the Nederlandsche Bank). DM 3.8

billion were used to support the Danish krone, mostly in Copenhagen and Amsterdam.

The financial fallout from the crisis was easier to resolve than the institutional questions. It had always been part of the Bundesbank's defense of its wish to limit engagement that it could not face large balance-sheet losses. In the course of mounting defenses of the old parities, however, central banks had built up huge positions. By November 15, 1993, the Banque de France had repaid the large swap lines that had been agreed with the Bundesbank, though it continued to hold a DM 50 billion line with the BIS. The Bundesbank calculated that it had realized a relatively small loss of DM 139 million, not on its interventions to support the French and the Danish currencies (which were compensated by the partner central banks), but on its ECU holdings.[148]

The intellectual legacy of the July crisis was harder to deal with. The chairman of the CoG alternates, Jean-Jacques Rey, drew the conclusion that the collapse had stemmed from "the failure of the system to deliver, in a timely and orderly fashion, the nominal exchange rate changes which had been warranted by underlying fundamentals, and a growing perception of conflict between internal and external monetary policy objectives in a situation in which the credibility of the system as a whole had been undermined." But the softening of the exchange rate commitment raised the challenge of providing some alternative guide. One alternate argued for an explicit inflation target as a policy anchor. The alternates were also worried about the reliance on the EMI as "an institutional answer," as this might create false expectations. They concluded that "the convergence process had to be broadened so as to encompass structural problems which could not be solved by increased exchange rate flexibility and monetary policy."[149]

The Bundesbank was relatively optimistic about the future, and argued that "the process of monetary integration in Europe need not be disrupted by the temporary widening of margins of fluctuations."[150] Other commentators sounded a much bleaker note. Helmut Schmidt reached a devastating verdict on the "Vanity Fair in particular in Frankfurt and Bonn, but not just there": four governments "through naïve national prestige considerations (in Rome, Paris, London, Bonn) practically destroyed the EMS that Giscard and I called to life in the late 1970s on the basis of Monnet's ideas. . . . Governments believed they could create something much better with their Maastricht Treaty."[151]

In drawing lessons from the crisis for monetary policy, the CoG in its April 1993 document had concluded not only that more "timely" realignments were needed, but that "there cannot be an automatic and mechanistic response to market tensions, involving symmetrical action on the part of authorities of countries with weak and strong currencies." As Peter Kenen pointed out, this was a veiled allusion to the message of the October 1978 Emminger letter, in which the Bundesbank had sought relief through government action from its international commitments and obligations. But it was also a clear rejection of the idea that the EMS was based on a symmetry of response.[152]

It needed a dramatic crisis to finalize the decisive intellectual shift that had lain at the heart of many CoG discussions in the 1980s. This basic understanding had coalesced around the Bundesbank view that monetary policy should have price stability as its dominant objective. Eventually there was an understanding that the discussions about symmetric or asymmetric adjustment responsibilities between "strong" and "weak" currencies—which had been a persistent feature of European debates since the 1970s—were futile so long as there was no definition of the central point around which symmetry or asymmetry should develop. The (mostly French) supporters of symmetry could not justify why a strong-currency country should adjust around some mechanical average of exchange rate behavior that had no welfare optimality and thus put price stability at risk in that country. The supporters of asymmetry in Frankfurt could not, on their side, explain why the entire burden should be on the weak-currency countries. The issue was solved only once it was recognized that there was one criterion (price stability) that identified the "right" monetary policy and that all countries had to behave consistently with this principle. This eventually gave exchange rate stability a firm basis and in time allowed the move to monetary union. The result was paradoxical: a severe crisis that shook nerves, destroyed confidence, and was generally supposed to have made the realization of the Maastricht Treaty impossible, produced the real foundation for monetary union.

The fundamental dilemma of the CoG throughout its history had been that it could not really address adequately the fundamental issue of exchange rates. That was too political a matter. As a consequence, the only way of making monetary cooperation work necessarily involved the abolition of exchange rates. The Maastricht Treaty was better and more coherent as an intellectual construct, but it was an experiment, and its outcome much more uncertain. The fundamental problem was that exactly the same combination of structural imbalances and large capital flows that could be suddenly reversed could in fact continue to exist after the introduction of the single currency ended the availability of the exchange rate tool. Such a reversal was thus capable of producing a crisis even more politically hard to manage than the drama of 1992–1993 had been.

The immediate consequence of the 1992–1993 exchange rate trauma made many of the participants accept that the idea of crisis could play a useful role by shaking up deeply entrenched positions. If only the crisis were big enough, some solution would inevitably be found: the necessity stemmed from the enormous investment of political capital already sunk into the European project. In this particular instance, it was clear that Germany (and especially the Bundesbank) since the original debates of 1978 was unwilling to undertake an unlimited commitment in support of the exchange rate mechanism, even in the politically vital case of the French franc. So it was necessary to find a way of making that support redundant. The consequence of this positive outcome was an excessive degree of optimism about crisis solubility. European monetary union was built on a foundation of a devastating crisis, but that fact made both Europe's technocrats and its political leaders overconfident about the stability of the order they were creating.

Conclusion

The Euro and the Legacy of the Committee of Governors

In 1999 the Euro came into existence after the irrevocable locking of exchange rates among eleven currencies. In January 2002, with great rapidity, new notes and coins replaced the old national currencies. At the least, these steps represent an amazing logistical achievement. The new money was also stable in respect of inflation and inflation expectations.

But questions remained. The fundamental problem of European Monetary Union lies in its incompleteness or lopsidedness. There was a much better preparation for the monetary side of monetary union than for the fiscal concomitants that should have underpinned its stability (and prevented the threat of large-scale monetization of fiscal debt burdens). No adequate provision on a European basis existed for banking supervision and regulation, which, like fiscal policy, was left to diverse national authorities. An explosion of banking activity occurred simultaneously with the transition to monetary union and may well have been stimulated by the new single money. A "banking glut" led to a new challenge to monetary policy-making. Neither of these problems, fiscal or banking, was a uniquely European one, but the complexity of interaction between different levels of authority and different interests produced a coordination problem that was uniquely difficult to deal with in the European context. To use an engineering analogy, the monetary union without a well-established base in a fiscal regime and without a stable financial system had a very high center of gravity that made for vulnerability and instability.

The incompleteness of a monetary union without the broader framework of political institutional innovation stems from a lack of clarity

382

masked by the inspiring language in the 1957 Treaty of Rome. It was not just the treaty preamble's goal of ever closer union that posed a challenge. An even deeper problem lies in the character of the endeavor itself, in the establishment of a common market. What is a common market? What degree of standardization and regulation is required? Does a common market need a common money? Not necessarily, so long as money is relatively stable and people can use it as a reliable measure of value and as a basis for calculation about the future. At the same time, there is a great deal of historical evidence that monetary instability can destroy or undermine the operation of markets. When there is a real threat to money, with large differences in price behavior and in expectations about inflation—as there was in Europe in the 1970s and 1980s—a common market might thus indeed require a common monetary framework. So international or global problems such as the end of the par value system fundamentally required some sort of coordinated European response. The basis for such action was carefully laid out in the founding document of the EEC, the Treaty of Rome. Article 235 gave wide-ranging power to the Council of Ministers to institute "appropriate provisions" to ensure the functioning of the common market, and Article 236 provided a process of treaty amendment that would be needed to create the institutional framework for monetary union.

Monetary coordination worked so much better than other mechanisms for supranational cooperation in Europe because it was well accepted as part of an international bargaining process. There were well-institutionalized committees that could be the fora or loci for such discussions. Discussions of and preparations for closer monetary coordination took place first at a global level—from Bretton Woods in 1944 to the Smithsonian conference in 1971 to the Plaza finance ministers' meeting in 1985. When there were flaws and imperfections in the global plans, and international tensions rose, it made sense to Europeans to try to find a European solution, such as the European Monetary System in 1978 or the plans for monetary union developed in the Delors Committee in 1988–1989. The Committee of Central Bank Governors established in 1964 with five European members was simply at the outset a European pendant to similarly functioning international committees, notably the G-10 governors' meetings, which also began in 1964 and also took place in Basel. Of the ten states that were held to be the largest industrial countries of the western world at the time, eight were

European (Belgium, France, Germany, Italy, the Netherlands, Sweden, Switzerland, and the United Kingdom), and five were members of the European Economic Community.

Outside the narrow monetary sphere in which central bankers operated, there were innumerable coordination problems between governments (twenty-eight EU member states after the 2012 enlargement, of which seventeen were in the Eurozone in 2011) and a wide range of domestic interests and lobby groups, unions, employers, and political parties, and then EU institutions (the Commission, the ECOFIN, the Eurogroup, the ECB) with very divergent concepts of how monetary policy should respond to economic shocks. Coordinating responses to a crisis inevitably strained these relations, and attention focused once more in a simplified way on the relations between big governments—especially the relations between Berlin and Paris. In a memorable turn of phrase in May 2010, German Chancellor Angela Merkel told the German Bundestag: "the rules must not be oriented toward the weak, but toward the strong. That is a hard message. But it is an economic necessity. That must have consequences for the European Union."[1]

Precedents

In the recent financial turmoil in Europe, increasing attention is being devoted to the U.S. precedent. In the early years of the republic, the United States was only weakly federalized. But in 1790 Alexander Hamilton successfully argued—against James Madison and Thomas Jefferson—that the war debt accumulated by the states in the War of Independence should be assumed by the federation. One of his most appealing arguments was that this was an exercise in providing greater security and thus reducing interest rates, from the 6 percent at which the states funded their debt to 4 percent. The same argument about lower borrowing costs was a major motivator for southern European countries to look for the discipline of monetary union in the 1990s.

The U.S. historical case on how to promote more stable public finance also looks like an attractive precedent for Europeans today. Hamilton emphasized the importance of a commitment to sound finance:

> For when the credit of a country is in any degree questionable, it never fails to give an extravagant premium, in one shape or another, upon

all the loans it has occasion to make. Nor does the evil end here; the same disadvantage must be sustained upon whatever is to be bought on terms of future payment. From this constant necessity of *borrowing* and *buying dear,* it is easy to conceive how immensely the expences of a nation, in a course of time, will be augmented by an unsound state of the public credit.

He also provided a stronger reason for following good principles of fiscal discipline than merely the pursuit of expediency:

> While the observance of that good faith, which is the basis of public credit, is recommended by the strongest inducements of political expediency, it is enforced by considerations of still greater authority. There are arguments for it, which rest on the immutable principles of moral obligation. And in proportion as the mind is disposed to contemplate, in the order of Providence, an intimate connection between public virtue and public happiness, will be its repugnancy to a violation of those principles.

It was those principles that made the fiscal union what he called "the powerful cement of our union."[2]

The condition for success was that the Union raise its own revenue, initially mostly through federally administered customs houses. That is also a logic that applies in modern Europe, where a reformed fiscal system might include a common administration of value-added tax, or a Hamiltonian customs system.

In the American case, the Union was bought at a price. The potential exposure to the common liability of Virginia, the most politically powerful state in the Union, was limited with a ceiling. Only this inducement moved Madison to drop his opposition and agree to the proposal for debt assumption. (This compromise, which also led to the capital's being moved to the new site of Washington, on the border of Virginia and Maryland, may be a precedent for limiting German liabilities in the case of the creation of a common European bond or Eurobond.) But there are other reasons for thinking that the experiment in federalized finance was not immediately successful. Two important parts of Hamilton's financial architecture were not realized, or realized only imperfectly. First, he proposed a model of joint stock banking on a national scale, which ran into immediate opposition, and which curiously was much more influential in Canada than in the United States. Second, the proposal for a national central bank was eventually blocked by political opposition. The charter of the First Bank of the United States was allowed to lapse in 1811; and one generation later the charter of the Second Bank of the United States was successfully opposed by Andrew Jackson in 1836.

Neither did the Hamiltonian scheme of federal finance guarantee a peaceful commonwealth. In fact the fiscal union proved to be explosive rather than cohesive. The country was torn by civil war in the 1860s, as a result of what was in large part a dispute about states' rights and the distribution of financial burdens. Until the 1860s, it was customary to refer to the United States in the plural rather than in the singular ("the United States are . . ."). In attempting to end the immoral practice of slavery, Abraham Lincoln originally proposed that slaveowners should be compensated by the public purse for the loss of their property. But such a step would have been unacceptably expensive. So in the end, the Virginians (and the rest of the South) were expropriated by the Union— at least that is the way they saw things.

The Work of the Committee of Governors

The U.S. historical precedent of building a union is full of problems and traps that might augment worries about transfers from one state or region to another. The European path was however never laid out with such clarity. The problem of the logic of integration, in which one part of the process requires action in other areas, is evident in the story of the discussion of the monetary issue that remained the major focus, even the obsession, of those who pursued more integration. Everything else seemed to be built on a monetary base. The central bank governors' committee was established to deal with a specific challenge of European exchange rate policy, and then evolved as a mechanism for tackling a rather broader range of other problems as well. Those problems facing the CoG included:

1. *Exchange rate policy.* The German and Dutch revaluations of 1961 had taken place without consultation with other EEC members. As a consequence it became clear that it was desirable to set up an institutional framework that would allow for a frank discussion of exchange rate issues. The experience of the fixed exchange rate regime such as Bretton Woods (or later the EMS) is that exchange rates become highly

politically charged. Consequently, even in a confidential and secure setting, these issues can in practice rarely be discussed, at least not ex ante. The IMF was unable to provide such a forum in the Bretton Woods regime or subsequently; the CoG also failed in this regard. Nevertheless, in Europe the existence of some mechanism for currency coordination in the EMS created the possibility of establishing a stable exchange rate area in the 1980s that allowed new measures of economic and even political integration that would have been impossible or very difficult in an environment in which exchange rates moved completely freely. Without the 1978 exchange rate agreement, the 1986 Single European Act would have been inconceivable; and the Single European Act in turn gave an impulse to the creation of a monetary union.

2. *Global coordination.* From the beginning to the end of the work of the CoG, and indeed beyond, the problems of European monetary relations increased during episodes of dollar weakness, when there were substantial hot money inflows into the Deutsche Mark. Addressing the dollar problem thus became much more crucial, and above all more easily manageable, than thinking about internal disparities among European currencies. As a result, the major driving force of the need to integrate more on the European level was concern about the position of the dollar in the international monetary system. The greatest impulses for European action were thus also moments of international difficulties: the early 1970s, the crisis of the Bretton Woods regime, the sharp phase of dollar weakness in 1978, and the dollar decline in the late 1980s. A new European money would possibly be a replacement for the dollar, and thus might also make for a more robust international monetary system. There were also parallels in thinking about how an international currency could operate between attempts to redesign or reform the IMF's Special Drawing Right (SDR) on the one hand and ideas of making the European Currency Unit (ECU) into a currency on the other.

3. *The management of support operations for member countries facing temporary balance-of-payments difficulties.* In 1964 Italy negotiated with the United States and the International Monetary Fund rather than with other EEC members. The CoG subsequently discussed support operations for problem countries such as France and the United Kingdom, and in the 1970s the European Monetary Cooperation Fund evolved as a way of administering short-term and very-short-term facilities. The

discussions of 1978 on a European Monetary System, and in 1988–1989 of the Delors Committee on monetary union, were also concerned with the elaboration of support and transfer systems. Reform initiatives had to deal with the problem that a support system could produce wrong incentive structures. Thus in the early and mid-1970s Italy felt that it had become a much more powerful player in the EC by not observing the rules than it had been in the 1960s, when it was more disciplined. It was clear that creditors' fears of losing their money locked them into a dependence on the debtor country. In general, the support operations that took place in the framework of central bank cooperation were handled quite well, but only because they were completely depoliticized and managed through a mechanism that relied on automaticity. The European Monetary Cooperation Fund established in 1973 was never a forum for serious debate or for any application of policy conditionality, and managed only a rather small and insignificant part of Europe's monetary reserves. In short, it never became a European Monetary Fund. The 1978 negotiations that created the EMS also provided for a European Monetary Fund, but it was never realized, largely because of the opposition of the German Bundesbank (see Chapter 6).[3] During the Delors Committee negotiations, a consensus gradually emerged that a future European Central Bank should in no circumstances act like a European Monetary Fund. In practice, something like an EMF was created only in 2010–2011 after a new round of potentially destructive crises. Even then the European Financial Stability Facility and its planned successor, the European Stability Mechanism, were initially too small to contend with dangerously destabilizing speculative attacks. In retrospect, it is clear that this issue should have been addressed and solved at a much earlier stage. A solution would have required a much more effective approach to the coordination of fiscal policies than European countries were prepared to concede in the 1990s.

4. *Monetary policy coordination.* From the early 1970s, once the policy rule imposed by the par value system disappeared, the CoG discussed mechanisms for the coordination of monetary policies in the member countries. Harmonization increasingly became the focus of its activity, and lay at the heart of the process of intellectual convergence within the CoG. But that convergence was fitful and eventually very incomplete. Attempts to have a debate about the ex ante coordination of monetary policy—which were pushed very vigorously in the early 1970s by the

EC Commission and especially by Raymond Barre—failed to have any real effect on the practice of policy. The obvious objection was brought up again and again, especially by the Bundesbank, that the president of the Bundesbank was simply one member of the Central Bank Council and could not commit it in advance to any particular course. There was also, despite substantial technical work, never any agreement on which instruments or which measures of monetary policy should be used. The vast differences between national approaches to the operating conditions of monetary policy could not be effectively dealt with until a single monetary policy was actually implemented with the introduction of the single currency.

5. *Financial stability.* From the early 1970s, the CoG was also from time to time concerned with the repercussions of financial-sector problems on monetary policy. But since international structures emerged at the same time to discuss financial stability issues (the Basel Committee on Banking Supervision; see Chapter 4), and since the Bundesbank model of central banking did not include considerations of lender-of-last-resort activity, this part of the CoG's work became ever less important. The statutes as framed by the Maastricht Treaty did not refer to financial stability and severely restricted the circumstances in which the ECB could enter into banking supervision and regulation.

6. *Independent central banking.* The CoG also evolved into an advocate of the idea of central bank independence, even though such a goal had not figured at all prominently in the original discussions of the 1950s and 1960s. Advocacy of central bank independence in the CoG was quite effective, in large part because the practice of the Bundesbank coincided with a broad and general intellectual shift that emphasized the desirability of such independence for the formation of good— and, in particular, a time-consistent—monetary policy.

Exchange rates were always at the core of policymakers' concern. The CoG provided an essential forum for negotiating the details of the European Monetary System (which was legally an agreement between central banks) and elaborating them in the September 1987 Basel-Nyborg Agreement, and it subsequently played a central role in the process of thinking through European Monetary Union in the Delors Committee.

The issues of the exchange rate and of monetary policy were solved very quickly and effectively in the 1990s. The result completely transformed the character of the European project. Monetary union—through the creation of a nonstate money—was an amazing and unprecedented achievement. Some of the most intractable problems of European cooperation—exchange rate and monetary policy issues—were solved as it were by the waving of a wand. Most obviously, the controversies inherent in the exchange rate issue—at least those relating to exchange rates between member countries—could simply be abolished by the establishment of monetary union. The European Monetary Institute successfully formulated the basis for a common monetary approach. The support issue seemed to be irrelevant because it was hard to imagine that balance-of-payments problems would arise in a monetary union. The involvement of monetary authorities in government finance was ruled out by the stipulations of the Maastricht Treaty forbidding the ECB to purchase government bonds, and the absence of support was a vital part of the "no-bailout" philosophy woven into the treaty (Article 104.1 of the Maastricht Treaty, Article 21 of the ECB statute, and Article 104.1 of the Lisbon Treaty). The banking and financial-sector stability issue had been taken off the agenda in the early 1990s, with no immediately bad effects; but the neglect brought major and deleterious repercussions after 2007.

The CoG's historical importance lies chiefly in the fact that in the late 1980s, after twenty-five years of discussion, an intellectual consensus emerged that had not previously existed. The Delors Committee could not have done its work, and laid out the blueprint for Maastricht and for monetary union, if it had not been preeminently a committee of central bankers. The statutes of the EMI and the ECB could not have been productively hammered out by anyone other than central bankers. Twenty-five years of discussion also highlighted the exchange rate issue and that of monetary policy as essential to the proper functioning of European politics: if neglected, they had tremendous political force, enough to shatter the fragile framework of cooperation.

The focus of the ECB was medium-term monetary and price stability, originally defined as "a year-on-year increase in the harmonized index of consumer prices for the euro area of below 2 percent." Initially the policy was radically anti-inflationary, but in early 2001 the ECB ceased to claim that it was aiming at a rate "safely below 2 percent."[4] In May 2003 stability was officially redefined as "inflation rates below but close to 2 percent over the medium term." In pursuit of that goal, from the beginning it used two analytical "pillars": the analysis of real activity and financial conditions in the economy (economic analysis), and monetary analysis (but with no monetary targets).[5]

A Transformative Event?

Most assessments of EMU at its fifth anniversary concluded that the single currency had done well as an anti-inflation mechanism, but that it had been a disappointment in terms of output and productivity growth. Some at that time hoped for an employment miracle.[6] But in vain. The tenth anniversary did not look that different. As a European Commission document put it: "While the euro is a clear success, so far it has fallen short of some initial expectations. Output and particularly productivity growth have been below those of other developed economies."[7] The verdict reflects some of the exaggerated hopes that had originally been vested in the innovation of the Euro. It was inevitable that the introduction of a single measure of value was expected to produce some efficiency gains, and that the common capital market was believed to be a good way of allocating capital to where it was most needed. In the early 2000s some econometric analysis claimed that the integration of EU bond and equity markets would bring 1 percentage point of additional GDP growth over a ten-year period.[8] But a surge in Europe's growth rate, which had been consistently below that of the United States or of Asia since the 1980s, would have required something more. Money alone could not do it. Some other spur to growth was needed. In 2000 the EU Lisbon summit launched the "Lisbon process," intended to build a new knowledge-based economy and make the European Union the most competitive economy in the world by 2010. Some countries did indeed experience a dramatic surge of growth in the 2000s, but for rather old-fashioned reasons such as an increase in public investment or a real estate boom. Diagnoses of the technical and educational failures of Europe in 2010 did not differ that much from those made a decade earlier. Most commentators concerned with long-term prospects still saw the United States and especially the very dynamic emerging markets as likely to remain the world engines of growth in the twenty-first century.[9] The financial crisis that erupted after 2007 only inclined many to greater pessimism about the United States, without providing any grounds at all to be more optimistic about Europe.[10]

The excessive initial hopes in the transformative power of a currency reform laid the basis for the potential for a dramatic reversal of sentiment about the benefits of a single currency. The turning of sentiment is linked with the broader phenomenon of a backlash against globalization. In many parts of Europe, globalization is widely seen as a major threat to the social order, and the resentments are exploited by politicians eager to establish a higher political profile. Workers, especially in manufacturing, are faced with a threat of job losses or radical reductions in income as a consequence of low-wage competition from Asia and from eastern Europe. Workers in manufacturing and in services are worried about the effects of immigration on income levels. Politically, the backlash against globalization is associated with the extremes of left and right, which often take their themes and rhetorical engagement from each other. But since the conventional right and the conventional left compete against each other and need to mobilize as many votes as possible, they are also likely to borrow some of the antiglobalization language in order to maximize their support and prevent a slippage of voters to the extremes. Politicians then periodically succumb to pressure to transform this antiglobalization rhetoric into policy.

The antiglobalization movement however finds it hard to identify concrete targets against which to direct the widespread malaise. Protests directed against American fast-food restaurants do not really seem adequately to confront the issues raised by globalization. Some more general symbol is required for a mobilization of protest. In consequence, the single currency has long been a popular whipping boy for antiglobalization sentiment.

When the Euro was launched as a physical currency, some prices changed quite visibly. Though price increases were not really observed in consumer price indices (the impact of the changeover to the new money is estimated at only 0.2 percent), the fact that prices for some very common daily items of consumption seemed to increase dramatically spurred a wave of unrest. In Italy the price of national food icons jumped, coffee by 30 percent and pizza by 16 percent.[11] In Germany, popular newspapers launched campaigns detailing the effects of the "Teuro" (expensive Euro; *teuer* = expensive). The immediate wave of dissatisfaction surrounding the introduction of the Euro quickly ebbed, and public-opinion surveys conducted by Eurobarometer have shown increasing support for the single currency (2000: 53 percent; 2004: 62 percent; 2005: 65 percent).[12]

The early wave of dissatisfaction holds an instructive lesson: price rises following the introduction of the Euro were instrumentalized by governments, and Europe's politicians took at least some part in the mobilization of critical opinion in order to pursue electoral advantage.

In the mid-2000s, German Finance Minister Hans Eichel endorsed the view that the Euro had led to price increases, and Consumer Affairs Minister Renate Künast created an office to marshal complaints from customers. The Greek Socialist government under Costas Simitis encouraged a one-day boycott of shops as a protest against the new prices.

The first ten years of the Euro's existence were overshadowed by two long-running sagas, both of which attracted a great deal of public attention and seemed to define the struggle over the currency: struggles over the character of monetary policy and who made it, and struggles over competitiveness. The debates deflected attention from the main issues, the unsustainability of Europe's (and the world's) approach to banking and the effects of the financialization explosion on public credit.

The first was a political saga. There was a long-standing public spat particularly involving French and Italian politicians who criticized the allegedly severe monetary austerity of the ECB and its effect on competitiveness. Competitiveness had become a critical concept for people and politicians, who saw themselves as living in a world of global competition, which they then translated into primarily national terms, in other words, competition between national economies. In the 1990s French President Jacques Chirac tried to distance himself from the *franc fort* policy of the Banque de France, which had been a crucial part of the lead-up to monetary union. Nicolas Sarkozy as finance minister in 2004 attacked the ECB's inflation target of "below but close to 2 percent" as excessively restrictive.[13] This critique became especially vigorous as the external exchange rate of the Euro soared. High interest rates were blamed for an uncompetitive currency and for France's industrial malaise. Sarkozy went on to make such criticism a central point of his successful presidential campaign in 2007, and called for an aggressive cheap money policy that would lower the exchange rate. As he put it, "We accept monetary dumping by other countries; why should we be the only economic zone in the world that can't put currency at the service of employment?"[14] Italian Prime Minister Silvio Berlusconi said he did not think it wise to "place new constraints on the economy" when growth was threatened and drew an analogy to the policies of Herbert Hoover during the Great Depression.[15] The criticism was both highly personalized and politicized. Nationalities as a consequence seemed to be reflections or personifications of a particular monetary culture.

The pressure on monetary policy was consistently resisted by the ECB, and also attracted stern rebukes from other politicians, especially in Germany. The first ECB president, Wim Duisenberg, responding to a call from Belgian Finance Minister Didier Reynders to cut interest rates, stated in 2001: "I hear, but I do not listen."[16] The second president of the ECB, Jean-Claude Trichet, repeatedly insisted on the importance of central bank independence. Trichet's hard position was especially intriguing given that when President Chirac had nominated him as the first ECB president there had been substantial German-Dutch opposition to him on the grounds that he would be too compliant with political authorities. Once in the ECB, he was completely firm, and began to be seen as more German than the Germans.

The German finance minister, Peer Steinbrück, built a reputation as a hard financier by standing up to Sarkozy. "I don't think," he said, "that the ECB can be taken, or should be taken, on a leash."[17] After a meeting of Eurogroup finance ministers in July 2007, when Sarkozy took the place of his finance minister in order to present France's position, Steinbrück commented: "I do not know why he rattles at the cage like this—it is completely idiotic."[18]

The reappearance of a Franco-German discord after the 2008 financial crisis made it easy to revive geopolitical interpretations of the Euro's problems. Such interpretations seemed more plausible because of an increasingly apparent divergence within the Eurozone.

The second saga is economic. From 2005 to 2009 the relative competitiveness of many southern European countries continued to deteriorate. The development was often graphically depicted as a scissors widening to the detriment of the South. During the same period the German coalition government under Gerhard Schröder embarked on a series of labor market reforms that made the German economy more flexible, and set off an export boom and a rising level of current account surpluses. From 2005 to 2009, Germany was the world's largest exporter.

In May 2008 a retrospective survey in the ECB's *Monthly Bulletin* interpreted the discrepancy between northern and southern wage costs as part of a process of catch-up. Some of the language could be interpreted as a warning: "If induced by structural inefficiencies or misaligned national policies (including wage-setting policies), such differentials may be worrisome. As national monetary and exchange rate policies are no longer available options within the euro area, it is important to ensure that the remaining mechanisms of adjustment to shocks function properly."[19] At the outset of monetary union, many had assumed that the fact of currency union simply abolished current account problems and had "put an end to Europe as an area of monetary tensions, exchange rate crises, and macroeconomic imbalances." But such a view became increasingly untenable. As *The Economist* put it in 2010, "we are moving beyond short-term fiscal deficit issues . . . towards problems like competitiveness, and what was previously a taboo subject—the issue of Eurozone imbalances."[20]

It is not easy to determine the cause of these developments, which contributed to an increased tension in Europe that was already evident before the U.S. subprime crisis started to affect Europe. According to one interpretation, southern European countries had institutional dynamics, in particular a highly protected labor market, that meant that inflationary behavior by unions and employer negotiators continued even in a low-inflation regime, a phenomenon generally referred to as "inflation persistence."[21]

Other explanations claim that there is no need to invoke such deep-seated institutional mechanisms, and that the inflationary developments simply reflect the strength of the capital inflows generated by the advent of the single currency. Since investment decisions are made on the basis of the real interest rate, in other words, allowing for price developments, rather than the nominal rate, a surge of capital at the same nominal rate as prevailed elsewhere amounted to a reduction in the real rate.[22] Spanish or Greek real interest rates were substantially below the German levels, so that investment in Germany was choked off and investment in the south was boosted. Far from there being a corrective built into the system—as existed in the classical gold standard—this modern version of an international economy without exchange rates turned out to be a mechanism to intensify imbalances.

The southern countries were experiencing substantial capital inflows. Lower interest rates sparked private-sector construction booms, which were especially dramatic in Spain and Ireland. In other countries, notably Greece and Portugal, more of the expansion occurred in the public sector. The fiscal position of Ireland and Spain appeared to be strong, in large part because government revenues were swollen by taxes paid in the real estate boom. The result was that, even in the apparently fiscally solid capital-importing countries, the private-sector bubble concealed what was in retrospect an unsustainable fiscal position.

The difference in the operation of the monetary union from that of the classical gold standard was a consequence of a new degree of financialization, with capital flows channeled through financial institutions rather than into widely dispersed bond markets. The Eurozone capital market became extensively integrated. Cross-border lending now surged. Large financial institutions operated in this single capital market across national boundaries even though some countries retained substantial and largely unwritten barriers to cross-national financial ownership. Big mergers, such as those between Santander and Abbey National in 2004 and Unicredit and Hypovereinsbank (which had previously acquired a dominant share in the Austrian banking industry) in 2005, began to create Europe-wide superbanks. The phenomenon of the expansion of the banking system in the aftermath of a relaxation of financial constraints was sometimes termed "excess elasticity."[23]

There was no adequate institutionalized response to the problems raised by financialization, despite the increasing popularity of a so-called macroprudential approach, championed in particular at the BIS. Even while finance became internationalized, each country preserved its own idiosyncratic system of financial supervision and regulation. Though there was extensive discussion about the possibility of shifting supervision to the European level, there were major practical obstacles to making such a shift—apart from built-in bureaucratic resistance from existing regulators.[24] In particular, regulation was often linked to implicit or explicit lender-of-last-resort functions. But such activity had a significant fiscal cost, which could not be assumed at a European level in the absence of a sustained EU fiscal capacity, but would need to remain an issue for national governments and national parliaments. As a result, much of the literature has concentrated on how bailouts and rescues should be paid for after a financial crisis, when national authorities (and their taxpayers) are reluctant to bear the financial burden of bailing out depositors or creditors in other states.[25] The institutional framework of the 1990s unambiguously limited socially beneficial postcrisis resolution. But it also severely restricted the capacity to provide efficient preventative or precrisis prudential supervision.

Beginning in 1999 the ESCB's Banking Supervison Committee performed regular macroprudential analyses of the EU banking sector. From 2003 on, its findings were published in an annual report titled "EU Banking Sector Stability." An EU memorandum of understanding set out a basis for flows of information and for identifying the appropriate authority to take the lead in the event of a crisis. There was some recognition that this was a rather weak halfway house between national regulators and a truly European mechanism. In 2008 the ECB stated: "the Eurosystem's framework for monitoring and assessing financial stability requires further improvements. An important challenge in this regard—not only for the Eurosystem but also for central banks and supervisory authorities worldwide—relates to the development of enhanced quantitative approaches to identifying financial stability risks and to assessing the potential impact of the materialisation of these risks."[26]

Governments as well as private borrowers increasingly financed themselves from abroad—but from within the Eurozone. In the wake of the transition to monetary union, debt holding became internationalized. This is what distinguishes the European experience from that of another economy that has also built up a high debt burden. Japan, despite a horrendously high proportion of debt to GDP, is usually thought to be very stable because the lenders (debt holders) are overwhelmingly domestic. They are also aging, and thus need to hold investments to pay for their retirement. In consequence, there is an overwhelming home bias. Until the late 1990s and the advent of monetary union most EU government debt was domestically held: in 1998 the overall ratio of foreign-held debt was only 1:5. That ratio climbed rapidly in the aftermath of the introduction of the Euro. In 2008, on the eve of the financial crisis, three-quarters of Portuguese debt, half of Spanish and Greek debt, and over two-fifths of Italian debt was held by foreigners. A significant proportion, especially in the case of Greece, Portugal, and Italy, was held by banks.

Was the deterioration of fiscal positions merely a European phenomenon, driven by a relaxation of market discipline on fiscal policies that followed from the apparent logic of monetary union? The same trajectory occurred in the United States, from fiscal responsibility in the 1990s (under President Clinton) to persistent high deficits in the 2000s under Bush. So other explanations are that the United States also provided a bad example, or (more plausibly) that the markets were apparently willing to finance almost limitless amounts of government debt, because they perceived the debt of industrial countries as an entirely risk-free asset. Bank regulators, pushed by governments desperate for cheap financing, then embedded this conventional wisdom in their regulatory codes.

As long as markets were (erroneously) confident that there was some implicit guarantee that followed from membership in the Eurozone, cheap financing looked sustainable, even at high debt levels. But then the dramatic revelation of the deterioration of the Greek financial situation in October 2009 led to a progressively fraught debate on how losses should be distributed among debtors, creditor banks, and creditor governments. The weaker European countries now looked like a chain of dominos. Though Greece was only a small country, with some 2.5 percent of the GDP of the Eurozone, the handling of the Greek crisis had obvious implications for other European debtors and set off a flight to quality. By July 2011 the consequences caught up with one of the largest European economies, Italy, when Finance Minister Giulio Tremonti set out a fiscal stabilization plan and Prime Minister Silvio Berlusconi rejected it, because, as he explained, he needed to win elections. In Italy as in Greece, market sustainability was now pitted against political or democratic sustainability. Reform came with governments that looked more technocratic—under the premiership of former EU Commissioner Mario Monti in Italy and former ECB Vice-President Lucas Papademos in Greece.

Initially in the financial crisis that broke out in 2007, the ECB's crisis actions were both innovative and uncontroversial. There was no criticism, because it was generally assumed that the fundamental problem was one of liquidity, and that no threat to bank solvency existed. The quick and massive provision of central bank liquidity in August 2007, in the aftermath of difficulties in the IKB Deutsche Industriebank, and then again after the September 2008 collapse of Lehman Brothers, looked like a well-judged application of the classic nineteenth-century lessons of Walter Bagehot on central banking: provide liquidity in large quantities when needed (albeit, in this case, not at the penalty rates that Bagehot also recommended).

The questioning of the sustainability of the financing of states and thus of country solvency represented a fundamental threat to the whole regulatory approach to banking stability. Regulators had built into their calculations of capital adequacy the assumption that the debt of industrial countries was completely secure. With the collapse of that assumption, banks became vulnerable. The interbank market started to freeze, and the collapse of normal banking operations posed an acute deflationary threat (with parallels to the twentieth-century Great Depression). Central bank action in these circumstances was necessary, but also posed risks that are not inherent in classic liquidity operations. What if central bank purchases of securities resulted in future losses, since there was no agreement on how in the long term the liabilities would be met?

What was the ECB doing? Prohibited by the Maastricht Treaty from the direct purchase of government bonds, it is explicitly allowed to purchase security in the context of normal monetary policy operations. But the bond purchases were clearly a stopgap measure. A permanent solution would require some mechanism at the other end of the central bank bridge, sanctioned by voters and taxpayers. Technocratic interventions seemed to have reached their limit. Two key German policymakers on the ECB Council resigned in 2011: Bundesbank President Axel Weber and Chief Economist and Board member Jürgen Stark. Former Bundesbank President Helmut Schlesinger considered the decision to buy peripheral government bonds as "crossing the Rubicon."[27]

The aftermath of the financial crisis has been an enduring paralysis of the banking system. The interbank market has collapsed. Banks no longer trust each other enough to lend even on an overnight basis. As a consequence, the ECB has become a preferred depository of overnight funds. In circumstances that were never foreseen by the founders, the ECB has become a central element in the functioning of Europe's banking system.

Tackling a twin crisis requires action on both fronts: the problem of unsustainable public finances, and that of zombie banks. Both tasks are harder in a low-growth context. But conventional macro policies are not enough to solve the problem. Europe needs to continue with microeconomic reforms designed to produce a return to growth—in short, to resume the ambitions of the 2000 Lisbon program.

The incompleteness of the Treaty of Rome still poses a problem. The interaction of technocrats in committees (in Eurospeak this is "comitology") can coordinate the varied national policies in some areas, but their work can never be completely successful. In particular, committees cannot be an adequate substitute for a political mechanism that generates a legitimate and general political will. In the 1990s, critics often pointed out that monetary unions were fragile without some measure of fiscal union.[28] In the aftermath of the post-2007 Great Recession, this lesson has become brutally apparent. It is striking that in the discussions of the Delors Committee, Jacques Delors assumed that the European Union budget would rise to some 3 percent of GDP before monetary union was achieved. In 2012 it stood at no more than 1.1 percent of EU GDP. Most of the innovative solutions—as opposed to short-term palliative fixes—to address current weaknesses involve some measure of fiscal federalization. The answer might be a common fund created by bank levies in order to assure resources for deposit insurance of the many cross-border financial institutions and to provide a capacity for the fiscal resolution of banking problems; or some measure of common unemployment or social insurance provision, to cushion the impact of unanticipated shocks. It would be a mistake to believe that 1999, the completion of monetary union, could be a simple and satisfying end to Europe's long struggle over money. It isn't.

Maastricht Treaty Text and Committee of Governors' Draft of the Statute of the European Monetary Institute

PROTOCOL (NO. 19) TO THE
STATUTE OF THE EUROPEAN
MONETARY INSTITUTE

(Maastricht Treaty)

The High Contracting Parties,
desiring to lay down the Statute of
the European Monetary Institute,
Have Agreed upon the following
provisions, which shall be annexed
to the Treaty establishing the
European Community:

Article 1—Constitution and name

1.1. The European Monetary Institute
(EMI) shall be established in accordance
with Article 109f of this Treaty; it shall
perform its functions and carry out
its activities in accordance with the
provisions of this Treaty and of this
Statute.

1.2. The members of the EMI shall be
the central banks of the Member States
('national central banks'). For the
purposes of this Statute, the Institut

DRAFT STATUTE OF
THE EUROPEAN
MONETARY INSTITUTE

28 OCTOBER 1991

Article 1—Constitution and name

1.1 The European Monetary Institute
established pursuant to Article 109D
of the Treaty (hereinafter called "the
EMI") shall perform its functions and
carry out its activities in accordance
with the provisions of the Treaty and
of this Statute.

1.2 The members of the EMI shall be
the central banks of the Member States
of the Community (hereinafter referred
to as "the national central banks"). For

403

monétaire luxembourgeois shall be regarded as the central bank of Luxembourg.

1.3. Pursuant to Article 109f of this Treaty, both the Committee of Governors and the European Monetary Cooperation Fund (EMCF) shall be dissolved. All assets and liabilities of the EMCF shall pass automatically to the EMI.

the purpose of this Statute, the Institut Monétaire Luxembourgeois shall be regarded as a national central bank.

1.3 Pursuant to Article 109D of the Treaty, the Committee of Governors shall be dissolved and the European Monetary Co-operation Fund (hereinafter called "the EMCF") shall cease to exist. All assets and liabilities of the EMCF shall pass on automatically and in their entirety to the EMI.

Article 2—Objectives

The EMI shall contribute to the realisation of the conditions necessary for the transition to the third stage of Economic and Monetary Union, in particular by:
—strengthening the coordination of monetary policies with a view to ensuring price stability;
—making the preparations required for the establishment of the European System of Central Banks (ESCB), and for the conduct of a single monetary policy and the creation of a single currency in the third stage;
—overseeing the development of the ECU.

Article 2—Objectives

The EMI shall contribute to the realization of the conditions necessary for the move to the final stage of Economic and Monetary Union (called hereafter "EMU"), in particular by:
—strengthening the co-ordination of monetary policies with a view to ensuring price stability;
—making the preparations required for the conduct of a single monetary policy in the final stage and for the creation of the European System of Central Banks (hereinafter called "the ESCB") and of the single currency;
—overseeing the development of the ecu.

Article 3—General principles

3.1. The EMI shall carry out the tasks and functions conferred upon it by this Treaty and this Statute without prejudice to the responsibility of the competent authorities for the conduct of the monetary policy within the respective Member States.

Article 3—General principles

3.1 The EMI shall carry out the tasks and functions conferred upon it by the Treaty and this Statute without prejudice to the responsibility of the national authorities for the conduct of the monetary policy within their respective Member States.

3.2. The EMI shall act in accordance with the objectives and principles stated in Article 2 of the Statute of the ESCB.

3.2 The EMI shall act consistently with the objectives and principles stated in Article 2 of the Statute of the ESCB and of the European Central Bank (hereinafter called "the ECB").

Article 4—Primary tasks

Article 4—Primary tasks

4.1. In accordance with Article 109f(2) of this Treaty, the EMI shall:
—strengthen cooperation between the national central banks;
—strengthen the coordination of the monetary policies of the Member States with the aim of ensuring price stability;
—monitor the functioning of the European Monetary System (EMS);
—hold consultations concerning issues falling within the competence of the national central banks and affecting the stability of financial institutions and markets;
—take over the tasks of the EMCF; in particular it shall perform the functions referred to in Articles 6.1, 6.2 and 6.3;
—facilitate the use of the ECU and oversee its development, including the smooth functioning of the ECU clearing system.
The EMI shall also:
—hold regular consultations concerning the course of monetary policies and the use of monetary policy instruments;
—normally be consulted by the national monetary authorities before they take decisions on the course of monetary policy in the context of the common framework for ex ante coordination.

4.1 The EMI shall strengthen the co-operation between the national central banks and shall promote the co-ordination of the monetary policies of the national central banks with the aim of achieving price stability. It shall hold regular consultations concerning the course of monetary policies and the use of monetary policy instruments. The EMI shall normally be consulted before national monetary authorities take decisions which may alter the course of monetary policy as established in the context of the common framework for ex ante co-ordination.
4.2 The EMI shall oversee the functioning of the European Monetary System (called hereafter "the EMS"). In this context, it shall perform the functions referred to in Articles 6.1 to 6.3.
4.3 The EMI shall prepare the conditions necessary for the ESCB to perform its functions in the final stage of EMU, respecting the principles of free and competitive markets. It shall in particular:
—prepare the instruments and the procedures necessary for carrying out the single monetary policy in the final stage of EMU;

4.2. At the latest by 31 December 1996, the EMI shall specify the regulatory, organizational and logistical framework necessary for the ESCB to perform its tasks in the third stage, in accordance with the principle of an open market economy with free competition. This framework shall be submitted by the Council of the EMI for decision to the ECB at the date of its establishment. In accordance with Article 109f(3) of this Treaty, the EMI shall in particular:
—prepare the instruments and the procedures necessary for carrying out a single monetary policy in the third stage;
—promote the harmonization, where necessary, of the rules and practices governing the collection, compilation and distribution of statistics in the areas within its field of competence;
—prepare the rules for operations to be undertaken by the national central banks in the framework of the ESCB;
—promote the efficiency of cross-border payments;
—supervise the technical preparation of ECU bank notes.

—prepare the rules for standardising the accounting and reporting of operations to be undertaken by the national central banks in the framework of the ESCB;
—promote the harmonisation, where necessary, of the conditions governing the collection, compilation and distribution of statistics in the areas within its field of competence;
—promote the efficiency of cross-border payments consistent with the requirements of the final stage;
—oversee the technical preparation of ecu bank-notes and be consulted on the preparation of the issue of ecu coins.
4.4 The EMI shall oversee [and promote] the development of the ecu, including the smooth functioning of the ecu clearing system.
4.5 The EMI shall hold consultations on issues falling within the competence of the central banks and affecting the stability of credit institutions and financial markets.

Article 5—Advisory functions

5.1. In accordance with Article 109f(4) of this Treaty, the Council of the EMI may formulate opinions or recommendations on the overall orientation of monetary policy and exchange rate policy as well as on related measures introduced in each Member State. The EMI may submit opinions or recommendations to

Article 5—Advisory functions

5.1 The EMI may formulate opinions on the overall orientation of monetary policy and exchange rate policy as well as the respective measures introduced in a Member State. It may also formulate opinions when consulted in accordance with Article 4.1. The EMI may express opinions to governments and the Council on policies which might governments and to the Council on policies which might affect the internal or external monetary situation in the Community and, in particular, the functioning of the EMS.

5.2. The Council of the EMI may also make recommendations to the monetary authorities of the Member States concerning the conduct of their monetary policy.

5.3. In accordance with Article 109f(6) of this Treaty, the EMI shall be consulted by the Council regarding any proposed Community act within its field of competence. Within the limits and under the conditions set out by the Council acting by a qualified majority on a proposal from the Commission and after consulting the European Parliament and the EMI, the EMI shall be consulted by the authorities of the Member States on any draft legislative provision within its field of competence, in particular with regard to Article 4.2.

5.4. In accordance with Article 109f(5) of this Treaty, the EMI may decide to publish its opinions and its recommendations.

affect the internal and external monetary situation in the Community and, in particular, the functioning of the EMS.

5.2 The EMI may make recommendations to the national central banks concerning the conduct of their monetary policy.

5.3 In accordance with Article 109D(4) of the Treaty, the EMI shall be consulted regarding any proposed Community act in the monetary, prudential or financial field; it shall also be consulted by national authorities regarding draft legislative provisions within its field of competence, in particular with regard to Article 4.3.

5.4 The EMI shall be entitled to offer advice to and to be consulted by the Council, the Commission and the competent authorities of the Member States on the scope and implementation of Community legislation relating to the prudential supervision of credit institutions and to the stability of the financial system.

5.5 The EMI may publish its opinions and its recommendations.

Comments

1. While, as confirmed in Article 14.2, opinions and recommendations have no binding force in a legal sense, they differ in their connotation. A recommendation may be more specific than an opinion, and need not be in response to an action or proposal by the party to whom the recommendation is addressed. Opinions provide an assessment of issues, whereas recommendations present an invitation to take some action.

2. Whereas under Article 5.3 the EM1 would be consulted in the context of the adoption of legislation, under Article 5.4 (which mirrors Article 25.1 of the Statute of the ECB) the EMI would play an advisory role in the application of such legislation.

Article 6—Operational and technical functions

6.1. The EMI shall:
—provide for the multilateralization of positions resulting from interventions by the national central banks in Community currencies and the multilateralization of intra-Community settlements;
—administer the very short-term financing mechanism provided for by the Agreement of 13 March 1979 between the central banks of the Member States of the European Economic Community laying down the operating procedures for the European Monetary System (hereinafter referred to as 'EMS Agreement') and the short-term monetary support mechanism provided for in the Agreement between the central banks of the Member States of the European Economic Community of 9 February 1970, as amended;
—perform the functions referred to in Article 11 of Council Regulation (EEC) No 1969/88 of 24 June 1988 establishing a single facility providing medium-term financial assistance for Member States' balances of payments.

Article 6—Operational and technical functions

6.1 The EMI shall:
—provide for the multilateralisation of positions resulting from interventions by the national central banks in Community currencies and the multilateralisation of intra-Community settlements;
—administer the very short-term financing mechanism provided for by the Agreement between the central banks of the Community of 13th March 1979 laying down the operating procedures for the European Monetary System (hereinafter called "the EMS Agreement") and the short-term monetary support mechanism provided for in the Agreement between the central banks of the Community of 9th February 1970, as amended;
—perform the functions referred to in Article 11 of Council Regulation (EEC) No. 1969/88 of 24th June 1988 establishing a single facility providing medium-term financial assistance for Member States' balances of payments.
6.2 The EMI may receive monetary reserves from the national central banks and issue ecus against such

6.2. The EMI may receive monetary reserves from the national central banks and issue ECUs against such assets for the purpose of implementing the EMS Agreement. These ECUs may be used by the EMI and the national central banks as a means of settlement and for transactions between them and the EMI. The EMI shall take the necessary administrative measures for the implementation of this paragraph.

6.3. The EMI may grant to the monetary authorities of third countries and to international monetary institutions the status of 'Other Holders' of ECUs and fix the terms and conditions under which such ECUs may be acquired, held or used by Other Holders.

6.4. The EMI shall be entitled to hold and manage foreign exchange reserves as an agent for and at the request of national central banks. Profits and losses regarding these reserves shall be for the account of the national central bank depositing the reserves. The EMI shall perform this function on the basis of bilateral contracts in accordance with rules laid down in a decision of the EMI. These rules shall ensure that transactions with these reserves shall not interfere with the monetary policy and exchange rate policy of the competent monetary authority of any Member State and shall be consistent with the objectives of the EMI and the proper functioning of the Exchange Rate Mechanism of the EMS.

assets for the purpose of implementing the EMS Agreement. These ecus may be used by the EMI and the national central banks as a means of settlement and for transactions between them and the EMI. The EMI shall take the necessary administrative measures for the implementation of this paragraph.

6.3 The EMI may grant to the monetary authorities of third countries and to international monetary institutions the status of "Other Holders" of ecus and fix the terms and conditions under which such ecus may be acquired, held and used by Other Holders.

6.4 Subject to a [unanimous] decision by the Council of the EMI, the EMI may hold and manage foreign exchange reserves as an agent for and at the request of national central banks.

Article 7—Other tasks

7.1 Once a year the EMI shall address a report to the Council on the state of the preparations for the third stage. These reports shall include an assessment of the progress towards convergence in the Community, and cover in particular the adaptation of monetary policy instruments and the preparation of the procedures necessary for carrying out a single monetary policy in the third stage, as well as the statutory requirements to be fulfilled for national central banks to become an integral part of the ESCB.

7.2 The EMI may perform additional tasks conferred upon it by the Council, acting unanimously on a proposal from the Commission and following consultation with the EMI and in co-operation with the European Parliament. The Council decision shall be in accordance with Articles 2 and 3.

Article 8—Independence

The members of the Council of the EMI who are the representatives of their institutions shall, with respect to their activities, act according to their own responsibilities. In exercising the powers and performing the tasks and duties conferred upon them by this Treaty and this Statute, the Council of the EMI may not seek or take any instructions from Community institutions or bodies or governments of Member States. The

Article 7—Other tasks

7.1 Once a year the EMI shall transmit a report to the Council on the state of the preparations for the final stage of EMU. This report shall cover in particular the adaptation of monetary policy instruments and the preparation of the procedures necessary for carrying out the single monetary policy in the final stage as well as the statutory requirements to be fulfilled for central banks to become an integral part of the ESCB. This report shall also include an assessment of the progress towards convergence in the Community.

7.2 The EMI may perform additional tasks conferred upon it by the Council, acting unanimously on a proposal from the Commission and following consultation with the EMI and in co-operation with the European Parliament. The Council decision shall be in accordance with Articles 2 and 3.

Article 8—Independence

The members of the Council of the EMI who are the representatives of their institutions shall act, with respect to their activities, according to their own responsibilities. In exercising the powers and performing the tasks and duties conferred upon them by the Treaty and this Statute, neither the EMI nor any member of its Council may seek or take any instructions from Community institutions or bodies or governments of Member States. The

Community institutions and bodies as well as the governments of the Member States undertake to respect this principle and not to seek to influence the Council of the EMI in the performance of its tasks.

Community institutions and bodies as well as the governments of the Member States undertake to respect this principle and not to seek to influence the members of the Council of the EMI in the performance of their tasks.

Article 9—Administration

Article 9—Administration

9.1. In accordance with Article 109f(1) of this Treaty, the EMI shall be directed and managed by the Council of the EMI.
9.2. The Council of the EMI shall consist of a President and the Governors of the national central banks, one of whom shall be Vice-President. If a Governor is prevented from attending a meeting, he may nominate another representative of his institution.
9.3. The President shall be appointed by common accord of the governments of the Member States at the level of Heads of State or of Government, on a recommendation from, as the case may be, the Committee of Governors or the Council of the EMI, and after consulting the European Parliament and the Council. The President shall be selected from among persons of recognized standing and professional experience in monetary or banking matters. Only nationals of Member States may be President of the EMI. The Council of the EMI shall appoint the Vice-President. The President and Vice-President shall be appointed for a period of three years.
9.4. The President shall perform his duties on a full-time basis. He shall not engage in any occupation, whether

ALTERNATIVE A
9.1 The EMI shall be directed and managed by the Council of the EMI.
9.2 The Council of the EMI shall comprise the Governors of the national central banks. If a Governor is unable to attend a meeting, he/she may nominate another representative of his/her institution.
9.3 The Council of the EMI shall appoint a President and a Vice President from among its members for a period of three years. Should the President or Vice President not complete his/her term, the Council shall choose a new President or Vice President, as the case may be, for the remainder of the term.
9.4 The President, or, in his/her absence the Vice President, shall chair the meetings of the Council of the EMI and, without prejudice to Article 21, present the view of the EMI externally.
9.5 The Rules of Procedure of the EMI shall be adopted by the Council of the EMI.

ALTERNATIVE B
9.1 The EMI shall be directed and managed by the Council of the EMI.
9.2 The Council of the EMI shall comprise the President, Vice President,

gainful or not, unless exemption is exceptionally granted by the Council of the EMI.

9.5. The President shall:

—prepare and chair the meetings of the Council of the EMI;

—without prejudice to Article 22, present the views of the EMI externally;

—be responsible for the day-to-day management of the EMI. In the absence of the President, his duties shall be performed by the Vice-President.

9.6. The terms and conditions of employment of the President, in particular his salary, pension and other social security benefits, shall be the subject of a contract with the EMI and shall be fixed by the Council of the EMI on a proposal from a Committee comprising three members appointed by the Committee of Governors or the Council of the EMI, as the case may be, and three members appointed by the Council. The President shall not have the right to vote on matters referred to in this paragraph.

9.7 If the President no longer fulfils the conditions required for the performance of his duties or if he has been guilty of serious misconduct, the Court of Justice may, on application by the Council of the EMI, compulsorily retire him.

9.8. The Rules of Procedure of the EMI shall be adopted by the Council of the EMI.

and the Governors of the national central banks. If a Governor is unable to attend a meeting he/she may nominate another representative of his/her institution, The President and the Vice President shall not have the right to vote.

9.3 The President and the Vice President shall be appointed President for a period of three years, by the European Council after consultation with the European Parliament Council and, as the case may be, the Committee of Governors or the Council of the EMI. The President and the Vice President shall be selected among persons of recognised standing and professional experience in monetary or banking matters.

9.4 The President and the Vice President shall perform their duties on a full-time basis. Without approval of the Council of the EMI they shall not occupy any other office or employment, whether remunerated or not, except as a nominee of the EMI.

9.5 The President shall prepare and chair the meetings of the Council of the EMI, present, without prejudice to Article 21, the views of the EMI externally, be responsible for the day-to-day management of the EMI, and be the Chief of Staff of the EMI. In the absence of the President, his/her duties shall be performed by the Vice President.

9.6 The terms and conditions of employment of the President and the Vice President shall be the subject of contracts with the EMI and shall be fixed by the Council of the EMI on the proposal of a Committee comprising three members appointed by the Council of the EMI and three members appointed by the Council. 9.7 If the President or the Vice President no longer fulfils the conditions required for the performance of his/her duties or if he/she has been guilty of serious misconduct, the Court of Justice may, on application by the Council of the EMI, compulsorily retire him/her. 9.8 The Rules of Procedure of the EMI shall be adopted by the Council of the EMI.

Comments

1. Article 9.4 in Alternative A and Article 9.5 in Alternative B: While accepting the President should present the views of the EMI externally, this would not preclude other Governors on the EM1 Council from expressing their views publicly.

2. A majority of Governors favours Alternative A. Failing the adoption of this Alternative, a majority of Governors would accept a compromise according to which Alternative A would be combined with the appointment of a "Managing Director". However, views differ with respect to:

—the appointment procedure, i.e., whether the Managing Director should be appointed by the EMI Council or the Council of Ministers upon proposal from the EMI Council;

—the position of the Managing Director in the EMI Council, i.e., whether he/she would preside over the EMI Council or simply have a seat in the EMI Council; either way the Managing Director would have no vote.

Article 10—Meetings of the Council of the EMI and voting procedures

10.1. The Council of the EMI shall meet at least ten times a year. The proceedings of Council meetings shall be confidential. The Council of the EMI may, acting unanimously, decide to make the outcome of its deliberations public.
10.2. Each member of the Council of the EMI or his nominee shall have one vote.
10.3. Save as otherwise provided for in this Statute, the Council of the EMI shall act by a simple majority of its members.
10.4. Decisions to be taken in the context of Articles 4.2, 5.4, 6.2 and 6.3 shall require unanimity of the members of the Council of the EMI. The adoption of opinions and recommendations under Articles 5.1 and 5.2, the adoption of decisions under Articles 6.4, 16 and 23.6 and the adoption of guidelines under Article 15.3 shall require a qualified majority of two thirds of the members of the Council of the EMI.

Article 10—Meetings of the Council of the EMI and voting procedures

10.1 The Council of the EMI shall meet at least ten times a year. The proceedings of the meeting shall be confidential. The Council of the EMI may decide to make the outcome of its deliberations public.
10.2 Subject to Article 10.5 each Governor or his/her nominee shall have one vote.
10.3 Save as otherwise provided for in the present Statute, the Council of the EMI shall act by simple majority of the Governors.
10.4 Decisions to be taken in the context of Articles 4.3, 5.5, 6.2, and 6.3 shall require unanimity among the Governors. The adoption of recommendations in the context of Article 5.2 and of decisions on guidelines as referred to in Article 14.3 shall require a qualified majority of two-thirds of the Governors.
10.5 For any decision to be taken under Articles 15.3, 15.5, 15.7, and 16, the votes in the Council of the EMI shall be weighted according to the key adopted pursuant to Article 15.1. A decision by a qualified majority shall be approved if the votes cast in favour represent at least {70%} of the total.

Comments
1. The definition of guidelines referred to in Article 10.4 is given in Article 14.4.
2. In accordance with Article 10.5, all decisions on financial matters will be subject to weighted voting. The weights

will be determined in accordance with Article 15.1 by a decision of the Council of the EMI.

Article 11—Interinstitutional cooperation and reporting requirements

11.1. The President of the Council and a member of the Commission may participate, without having the right to vote, in meetings of the Council of the EMI.

11.2. The President of the EMI shall be invited to participate in Council meetings when the Council is discussing matters relating to the objectives and tasks of the EMI.

11.3. At a date to be established in the Rules of Procedure, the EMI shall prepare an annual report on its activities and on monetary and financial conditions in the Community. The annual report, together with the annual accounts of the EMI, shall be addressed to the European Parliament, the Council and the Commission and also to the European Council.

The President of the EMI may, at the request of the European Parliament or on his own initiative, be heard by the competent Committees of the European Parliament.

11.4. Reports published by the EMI shall be made available to interested parties free of charge.

Article 11—Inter-institutional co-operation and reporting requirements

11.1 A member of the Commission may take part in the proceedings of the Council of the EMI but not in the voting.

11.2 The President of the EMI shall be invited to participate in meetings of the Council whenever it deals with matters relating to the tasks and functions of the EMI.

11.3 At a date to be established in the Rules of Procedure, the EMI shall prepare an annual report on its activities and on the monetary and financial conditions in the Community. The annual report, together with the annual accounts of the EMI, shall be transmitted to the European Council, the Council, the European Parliament and the Commission. The President of the EMI may be invited to appear before the European Parliament on this occasion and also before the competent Committees of the European Parliament where the circumstances so justify.

11.4 Reports published by the EMI shall be made available to interested parties free of charge.

Article 12—Currency denomination

The operations of the EMI shall be expressed in ECUs.

Article 13—Seat

Before the end of 1992, the decision as to where the seat of the EMI will be established shall be taken by common accord of the governments of the Member States at the level of Heads of State or of Government.

Article 14—Legal capacity

The EMI, which in accordance with Article 109f(1) of this Treaty shall have legal personality, shall enjoy in each of the Member States the most extensive legal capacity accorded to legal persons under their law; it may, in particular, acquire or dispose of movable or immovable property and may be a party to legal proceedings.

Article 15—Legal acts

15.1. In the performance of its tasks, and under the conditions laid down in this Statute, the EMI shall:

Article 12—Currency denomination

The operations of the EMI shall be expressed in ecu.

Article 13—Legal capacity

13.1 Pursuant to Article 109D of the Treaty, the EMI is endowed with legal personality.
13.2 In each of the Member States the EMI shall enjoy the most extensive legal capacity accorded to legal persons under their laws. It may in particular acquire or dispose of movable or immovable property, recruit personnel and may be a party to legal proceedings.
13.3 Disputes between the EMI, on the one hand, and its creditors, debtors or any other person, on the other, shall fall within the jurisdiction of the competent national courts, save where jurisdiction has been conferred upon the Court of Justice.

Article 14—Legal acts

14.1 In the performance of its tasks, the EMI shall deliver opinions and, under the conditions laid down in this Statute,

—deliver opinions;
—make recommendations;
—adopt guidelines, and take decisions, which shall be addressed to the national central banks.
15.2. Opinions and recommendations of the EMI shall have no binding force.
15.3. The Council of the EMI may adopt guidelines laying down the methods for the implementation of the conditions necessary for the ESCB to perform its functions in the third stage. EMI guidelines shall have no binding force; they shall be submitted for decision to the ECB.
15.4. Without prejudice to Article 3.1, a decision of the EMI shall be binding in its entirety upon those to whom it is addressed. Articles 190 and 191 of this Treaty shall apply to these decisions.

make recommendations, take decisions and adopt guidelines which shall be addressed to the national central banks.
14.2 Opinions and recommendations shall have no binding force.
14.3 The Council of the EMI may adopt guidelines laying down the methods for the implementation of the technical conditions necessary for the ESCB to perform its functions in the final stage of EMU. These guidelines shall have no binding force; they shall be submitted for decision to the ECB.
14.4 Without prejudice to Article 3.1, a decision shall be binding in its entirety upon those to whom it is addressed. Articles 190 and 191 of the Treaty shall apply in all respects to decisions taken by the EMI.

Article 16—Financial resources

16.1. The EMI shall be endowed with its own resources. The size of the resources of the EMI shall be determined by the Council of the EMI with a view to ensuring the income deemed necessary to cover the administrative expenditure incurred in the performance of the tasks and functions of the EMI.
16.2. The resources of the EMI determined in accordance with Article 16.1 shall be provided out of contributions by the national central banks in accordance with the key referred to in Article 29.1 of the Statute of the ESCB and be paid up at the establishment of the EMI. For this purpose, the statistical data to be used for the determination of the key shall be provided by the Commission, in

Article 15—Financial resources

15.1 The Council of the EMI, acting [unanimously] [by a qualified majority of two-thirds of the Governors] shall determine the key which assigns a weight to each national central bank.
15.2 Save for a decision by the Council of the EMI in accordance with Article 15.3, expenditure incurred in the performance of the tasks and functions of the EMI shall be covered by contributions to be made by the national central banks in accordance with the key referred to in Article 15.1.
15.3 The Council of the EMI, acting [unanimously] [by a qualified majority] may decide to endow the EMI with its own capital. The amount of capital of the EMI shall be determined by the Council of the EMI, acting by a qualified

accordance with the rules adopted by the Council, acting by a qualified majority on a proposal from the Commission and after consulting the European Parliament, the Committee of Governors and the Committee referred to in Article 109c of this Treaty.

majority, with a view to ensuring an income deemed necessary to cover the [administrative] expenditure incurred in the performance of the tasks and functions of the EMI.

15.4 The capital of the EMI determined in accordance with Article 15.3 shall be subscribed by the national central banks in accordance with the key referred to in Article 15.1.

15.5 The Council of the EMI, acting by a qualified majority, shall determine the form in which capital shall be paid up.

15.6 The shares of the national central banks in the subscribed capital of the EMI may not be transferred, pledged or attached.

15.7 The Council of the EMI shall take all other measures necessary for the application of this Article.

Comments
Unless there is a decision by the Council of the EMI under Article 15.3, the EMI would be financed by contributions in accordance with Article 15.2. The majority of Governors saw no need to make the decision on the endowment of the EMI with capital subject to the requirement of unanimity. This view received even wider support if expenditure was defined as "administrative" in Article 15.3, which would imply that the capital of the EMI could remain small.

Article 17—Annual accounts and auditing

Article 16—Annual accounts and auditing

17.1. The financial year of the EMI shall begin on the first day of

16.1 The financial year shall be the calendar year.

January and end on the last day of December.

17.2. The Council of the EMI shall adopt an annual budget before the beginning of each financial year.

17.3. The annual accounts shall be drawn up in accordance with the principles established by the Council of the EMI. The annual accounts shall be approved by the Council of the EMI and shall thereafter be published.

17.4. The annual accounts shall be audited by independent external auditors approved by the Council of the EMI. The auditors shall have full power to examine all books and accounts of the EMI and to obtain full information about its transactions. The provisions of Article 188c of this Treaty shall only apply to an examination of the operational efficiency of the management of the EMI.

17.5. Any surplus of the EMI shall be transferred in the following order:

(a) an amount to be determined by the Council of the EMI shall be transferred to the general reserve fund of the EMI;

(b) any remaining surplus shall be distributed to the national central banks in accordance with the key referred to in Article 16.2.

17.6. In the event of a loss incurred by the EMI, the shortfall shall be offset against the general reserve fund of the EMI. Any remaining shortfall shall be made good by contributions from the national central banks, in accordance with the key as referred to in Article 16.2.

16.2 The Council of the EMI shall adopt an annual budget before the beginning of each financial year.

16.3 The annual accounts shall be drawn up in accordance with the principles established by the Council of the EMI. The annual accounts shall be approved by the Council of the EMI.

16.4 The annual accounts shall be audited by an independent external auditor appointed by the Council of the EMI. The provisions of Articles 203 and 206a of the Treaty shall not apply to the EMI.

16.5 A surplus of the EMI shall be transferred in the following order:

(a) an amount to be determined by the Council of the EMI shall be transferred to the general reserve fund of the EMI;

(b) the remaining surplus shall be distributed to the shareholders of the EMI in proportion to their subscribed shares.

16.6 In the event of a loss incurred by the EMI, the shortfall shall be offset against the general reserve fund of the EMI. A remaining shortfall shall be made good, by contributions from the national central banks, in proportion to their subscribed shares.

Comments

Articles 16.5 and 16.6 will only be applicable if a decision is taken pursuant to Article 15.3 to endow the EMl with its own capital.

Article 18—Staff

18.1. The Council of the EMI shall lay down the conditions of employment of the staff of the EMI.

18.2. The Court of Justice shall have jurisdiction in any dispute between the EMI and its servants within the limits and under the conditions laid down in the conditions of employment.

Article 19—Judicial control and related matters

19.1. The acts or omissions of the EMI shall be open to review or interpretation by the Court of Justice in the cases and under the conditions laid down in this Treaty. The EMI may institute proceedings in the cases and under the conditions laid down in this Treaty.

19.2. Disputes between the EMI, on the one hand, and its creditors, debtors or any other person, on the other, shall fall within the jurisdiction of the competent national courts, save where jurisdiction has been conferred upon the Court of Justice.

19.3. The EMI shall be subject to the liability regime provided for in Article 215 of this Treaty.

19.4. The Court of Justice shall have jurisdiction to give judgment pursuant to any arbitration clause contained in a contract concluded by or on behalf of the EMI, whether that contract be governed by public or private law.

Article 17—Staff

17.1 The Council of the EMI shall lay down the conditions of employment of the staff of the EMI.

17.2 Disputes between the EMI and its staff may be brought before the Court of First Instance provided for in Article 168A of the Treaty which shall have jurisdiction.

Article 18—Judicial control and related matters

18.1 The acts of the EMI shall be open to review and interpretation by the Court of Justice under the conditions laid down for the legal control of the acts of Community institutions. The EMI may institute proceedings under the same conditions as Community institutions. Articles 173 to 178, 183 and 184 of the Treaty shall be applicable accordingly.

18.2 In the case of non-contractual liability, the provisions of Article 215 of the Treaty shall apply to damage or loss caused by the EMI or by its staff in the performance of their duties.

Comments

Article 18 mirrors the corresponding paragraphs of Article 35 of the draft Statute of the ESCB. Given the transitory nature of the EMI and the limited obligations of national central banks in Stage Two, it is not felt necessary to make provision for a situation in which a national central bank fails to fulfill its obligations under the Statute of the EMI.

19.5. A decision of the EMI to bring an action before the Court of Justice shall be taken by the Council of the EMI.

Article 20—Professional secrecy	*Article 19—Professional secrecy*

20.1. Members of the Council of the EMI and the staff of the EMI shall be required, even after their duties have ceased, not to disclose information of the kind covered by the obligation of professional secrecy.
20.2. Persons having access to data covered by Community legislation imposing an obligation of secrecy shall be subject to such legislation.

19.1 Members of the Council of the EMI and the staff of the EMI shall be required, even after their duties have ceased, not to disclose information of the kind covered by the obligation of professional secrecy.
19.2 Persons having access to data covered by specific secrecy Community legislation shall be subject to such legislation.

Article 21—Privileges and immunities	*Article 20—Privileges and immunities*

The EMI shall enjoy in the territories of the Member States such privileges and immunities as are necessary for the performance of its tasks, under the conditions laid down in the Protocol on the Privileges and Immunities of the European Communities annexed to the Treaty establishing a Single Council and a Single Commission of the European Communities.

The Protocol on the privileges and immunities of the European Community shall apply to the EMI, the members of its Council and its staff to the extent necessary for the performance of the tasks of the EMI.

Article 22—Signatories	*Article 21—Signatories*

The EMI shall be legally committed to third parties by the President or the Vice-President or by the signatures of two members of the staff of the EMI who have been duly authorized by the President to sign on behalf of the EMI.

The EMI shall be legally committed vis-à-vis third parties by the signature of the President or the Vice President or by the signature of two members of the staff of the EMI who have been duly authorised by the President to sign on behalf of the EMI.

Article 23—Liquidation of the EMI

23.1. In accordance with Article 109l of this Treaty, the EMI shall go into liquidation on the establishment of the ECB. All assets and liabilities of the EMI shall then pass automatically to the ECB. The latter shall liquidate the EMI according to the provisions of this Article. The liquidation shall be completed by the beginning of the third stage.

23.2. The mechanism for the creation of ECUs against gold and US dollars as provided for by Article 17 of the EMS Agreement shall be unwound by the first day of the third stage in accordance with Article 20 of the said Agreement.

23.3. All claims and liabilities arising from the very short-term financing mechanism and the short-term monetary support mechanism, under the Agreements referred to in Article 6.1, shall be settled by the first day of the third stage.

23.4. All remaining assets of the EMI shall be disposed of and all remaining liabilities of the EMI shall be settled.

23.5. The proceeds of the liquidation described in Article 23.4 shall be distributed to the national central banks in accordance with the key referred to in Article 16.2.

23.6. The Council of the EMI may take the measures necessary for the application of Articles 23.4 and 23.5.

23.7. Upon the establishment of the ECB, the President of the EMI shall relinquish his office.

Article 22—Liquidation of the EMI

22.1 Pursuant to Article 109G of the Treaty, the EMI shall go into liquidation on the establishment of the ECB. The liquidation shall be terminated by the beginning of the final stage of EMU.

22.2 The mechanism for the creation of ecus against gold and US dollars as provided for by Article 17 of the EMS Agreement shall be unwound by the first day of Stage Three of EMU in accordance with the provisions of Article 20 of the said Agreement.

22.3 All claims and liabilities arising from the very short-term financing mechanism and the short-term monetary support mechanism, as provided for by the Agreements referred to in Article 6.1, shall be settled by the first day of Stage Three of EMU.

22.4 All remaining assets of the EMI shall be disposed of and all remaining liabilities of the EMI shall be settled.

22.5 The proceeds of the liquidation in accordance with Article 22.4 shall be distributed to the national central banks in accordance with the key adopted under Article 15.1.

22.6 The Council of the EMI shall take the measures necessary for the application of Articles 22.4 and 22.5.

22.7 Upon the establishment of the ECB, the President and the Vice President of the EMI shall relinquish their office, [without prejudice to their contractual rights.]

Comments

1. Articles 22.2 to 22.6 deal with the rules and procedures for the liquidation of the EMI which has to be terminated before the beginning of the final stage of EMU. The unwinding of the mechanism for the creation of ecus (Article 22.2) is necessary to enable the national central banks whose countries have entered into Stage Three of EMU to fulfill their obligations under Article 30 of the draft Statute of the ESCB. The unwinding of outstanding transactions under the very short-term financing and the short-term monetary support mechanisms does not preclude a refinancing under the revised EMS Agreement in Stage Three (see transitional provisions of the draft Statute of the ESCB).

2. The wording between brackets in Article 22.7 would be necessary only if Alternative B in Article 9 were chosen.

Maastricht Treaty Text and Committee of Governors' Draft of the Statute of the European Central Bank

PROTOCOL ON THE STATUTE OF
THE EUROPEAN SYSTEM OF
CENTRAL BANKS AND OF THE
EUROPEAN CENTRAL BANK

9 DECEMBER 1991

(Maastricht Treaty)

DRAFT STATUTE OF THE
EUROPEAN SYSTEM OF CENTRAL
BANKS AND OF THE
EUROPEAN CENTRAL BANK

26 APRIL 1991

CHAPTER I—
CONSTITUTION OF THE ESCB

CHAPTER I—
CONSTITUTION OF THE SYSTEM

*Article 1—The European System
of Central Banks*

Article 1—The System

1.1. The European System of Central Banks (ESCB) and the European Central Bank (ECB) shall be established in accordance with Article 4a of this Treaty; they shall perform their tasks and carry on their activities in accordance with the provisions of this Treaty and of this Statute.
1.2. In accordance with Article 106(1) of this Treaty, the ESCB shall be composed of the ECB and of the central banks of the Member States ('national central

Pursuant to Article . . . of the EEC Treaty, a system, consisting of a central institution to be known as "The European Central Bank" (hereinafter "the ECB") and of the participating central banks of the Member States of the Community (hereinafter "national central banks"), is hereby established and shall be known as the "European System of Central Banks" (hereinafter the "System").

banks'). The Institut monétaire luxembourgeois will be the central bank of Luxembourg.

CHAPTER II—OBJECTIVES AND TASKS OF THE ESCB	CHAPTER II—OBJECTIVES AND TASKS OF THE SYSTEM

Article 2—Objectives	*Article 2—Objectives*
In accordance with Article 105(1) of this Treaty, the primary objective of the ESCB shall be to maintain price stability. Without prejudice to the objective of price stability, it shall support the general economic policies in the Community with a view to contributing to the achievement of the objectives of the Community as laid down in Article 2 of this Treaty. The ESCB shall act in accordance with the principle of an open market economy with free competition, favouring an efficient allocation of resources, and in compliance with the principles set out in Article 3a of this Treaty.	2.1 The primary objective of the System shall be to maintain price stability. 2.2 Without prejudice to the objective of price stability, the System shall support the general economic policy of the Community. 2.3 The System shall act consistently with the principles of free and competitive markets.

Article 3—Tasks	*Article 3—Tasks*
3.1. In accordance with Article 105(2) of this Treaty, the basic tasks to be carried out through the ESCB shall be: —to define and implement the monetary policy of the Community; —to conduct foreign exchange operations consistent with the provisions of Article 109 of this Treaty; —to hold and manage the official foreign reserves of the Member States;	The basic tasks to be carried out through the System shall be: — to formulate and implement the monetary policy of the Community; —to conduct foreign exchange operations in accordance with the prevailing exchange rate regime of the Community as referred to in Article 4.3; —to hold and manage [the] official foreign reserves of the participating countries;

—to promote the smooth operation of payment systems.

3.2. In accordance with Article 105(3) of this Treaty, the third indent of Article 3.1 shall be without prejudice to the holding and management by the governments of Member States of foreign exchange working balances.

3.3. In accordance with Article 105(5) of this Treaty, the ESCB shall contribute to the smooth conduct of policies pursued by the competent authorities relating to the prudential supervision of credit institutions and the stability of the financial system.

—to ensure the smooth operation of payment systems;

—to participate as necessary in the formulation, co-ordination and execution of policies relating to prudential supervision and the stability of the financial system.

Article 4—Advisory functions

In accordance with Article 105(4) of this Treaty:

(a) the ECB shall be consulted:

—on any proposed Community act in its fields of competence;

—by national authorities regarding any draft legislative provision in its fields of competence, but within the limits and under the conditions set out by the Council in accordance with the procedure laid down in Article 42;

(b) the ECB may submit opinions to the appropriate Community institutions or bodies or to national authorities on matters in its fields of competence.

Article 4—Advisory functions

4.1 The ECB shall be consulted regarding any draft Community legislation and any envisaged international agreements in the monetary, prudential, banking or financial field. In accordance with Community legislation, the ECB shall be consulted by national authorities regarding any draft legislation within its field of competence.

4.2 The ECB may give opinions to any Community or national authority on matters within its field of competence.

4.3 The ECB shall be consulted with a view to reaching consensus, consistent with the objective of price stability, prior to any decision relating to the exchange rate regime of the Community, including, in particular, the adoption, abandonment or change in central rates [or exchange rate policies] vis-à-vis third currencies.

4.4 The ECB may publish its opinions.

Article 5—Collection of statistical information

5.1. In order to undertake the tasks of the ESCB, the ECB, assisted by the national central banks, shall collect the necessary statistical information either from the competent national authorities or directly from economic agents. For these purposes it shall cooperate with the Community institutions or bodies and with the competent authorities of the Member States or third countries and with international organizations.

5.2. The national central banks shall carry out, to the extent possible, the tasks described in Article 5.1.

5.3. The ECB shall contribute to the harmonization, where necessary, of the rules and practices governing the collection, compilation and distribution of statistics in the areas within its fields of competence.

5.4. The Council, in accordance with the procedure laid down in Article 42, shall define the natural and legal persons subject to reporting requirements, the confidentiality regime and the appropriate provisions for enforcement.

Article 6—International cooperation

6.1. In the field of international cooperation involving the tasks entrusted to the ESCB, the ECB shall decide how the ESCB shall be represented.

6.2. The ECB and, subject to its approval, the national central banks

Article 5—Collection of statistical information

5.1 In order to undertake the tasks of the System, the ECB, assisted by the national central banks, shall collect the necessary statistical information either from the competent national authorities or directly from economic agents. For these purposes, it shall co-operate with the competent authorities of the Community, the Member States or third countries and with international organisations.

5.2 The national central banks shall carry out, to the extent possible, the tasks described in Article 5.1.

5.3 The ECB shall promote the harmonisation, where necessary, of the conditions governing the collection, compilation and distribution of statistics in the areas within its field of competence. Community legislation shall define the natural and legal persons subject to reporting requirements, the confidentiality regime and the appropriate provisions for enforcement.

Article 6—International co-operation

6.1 In the field of international co-operation involving the tasks entrusted to the System, the ECB shall decide whether the System shall be represented by the ECB and/or the national central banks.

may participate in international monetary institutions.

6.3. Articles 6.1 and 6.2 shall be without prejudice to Article 109(4) of this Treaty.

6.2 The ECB and, subject to its approval, the national central banks may participate in international monetary institutions.

CHAPTER III—
ORGANIZATION OF THE ESCB

CHAPTER III—
ORGANISATION OF THE SYSTEM

Article 7—Independence

Article 7—Independence

In accordance with Article 107 of this Treaty, when exercising the powers and carrying out the tasks and duties conferred upon them by this Treaty and this Statute, neither the ECB, nor a national central bank, nor any member of their decision-making bodies shall seek or take instructions from Community institutions or bodies, from any government of a Member State or from any other body. The Community institutions and bodies and the governments of the Member States undertake to respect this principle and not to seek to influence the members of the decision-making bodies of the ECB or of the national central banks in the performance of their tasks.

In exercising the powers and performing the tasks and duties conferred upon them by the Treaty and this Statute, neither the ECB nor a national central bank nor any member of their decision-making bodies may seek or take any instructions from Community institutions, governments of Member States or any other body. The Community and each Member State undertake to respect this principle and not to seek to influence the ECB, the national central banks and the members of their decision-making bodies in the performance of their tasks.

Article 8—General principle

Article 8—General principle

The ESCB shall be governed by the decision-making bodies of the ECB.

The System shall be governed by the decision-making bodies of the ECB.

Article 9—The European
Central Bank

9.1. The ECB which, in accordance with Article 106(2) of this Treaty, shall have legal personality, shall enjoy in each of the Member States the most extensive legal capacity accorded to legal persons under its law; it may, in particular, acquire or dispose of movable and immovable property and may be a party to legal proceedings.
9.2. The ECB shall ensure that the tasks conferred upon the ESCB under Article 105(2), (3) and (5) of this Treaty are implemented either by its own activities pursuant to this Statute or through the national central banks pursuant to Articles 12.1 and 14.
9.3. In accordance with Article 106(3) of this Treaty, the decision-making bodies of the ECB shall be the Governing Council and the Executive Board.

Article 9—The European
Central Bank

9.1 The ECB is hereby established and shall have legal personality.
9.2 In each of the Member States the ECB shall enjoy the most extensive legal capacity accorded to legal persons under their laws; it may, in particular, acquire or dispose of movable and immovable property and may be a party to legal proceedings.
9.3 The property of the ECB shall be exempt from all forms of requisition or expropriation. Disputes between the ECB, on the one hand, and its creditors, debtors or any other person, on the other, shall be decided by the competent national courts, save where jurisdiction has been conferred on the Court of Justice.
9.4 The function of the ECB shall be to ensure that the tasks conferred upon the System under Article 3 shall be implemented either by the ECB's activities pursuant to this Statute or through the national central banks pursuant to Article 14.
9.5 The decision-making bodies of the ECB shall be the Council of the ECB and the Executive Board.

Article 10—The Governing Council

10.1. In accordance with Article 109a(1) of this Treaty, the Governing Council shall comprise the members of the Executive Board of the ECB and the Governors of the national central banks.

Article 10—The Council of the ECB

10.1 The Council of the ECB shall comprise the President, the Vice President, the other members of the Executive Board and the Governors of the national central banks.

10.2. Subject to Article 10.3, only members of the Governing Council present in person shall have the right to vote. By way of derogation from this rule, the Rules of Procedure referred to in Article 12.3 may lay down that members of the Governing Council may cast their vote by means of tele-conferencing. These rules shall also provide that a member of the Governing Council who is prevented from voting for a prolonged period may appoint an alternate as a member of the Governing Council.

Subject to Articles 10.3 and 11.3, each member of the Governing Council shall have one vote. Save as otherwise provided for in this Statute, the Governing Council shall act by a simple majority. In the event of a tie, the President shall have the casting vote. In order for the Governing Council to vote, there shall be a quorum of two-thirds of the members. If the quorum is not met, the President may convene an extraordinary meeting at which decisions may be taken without regard to the quorum.

10.3. For any decisions to be taken under Articles 28, 29, 30, 32, 33 and 51, the votes in the Governing Council shall be weighted according to the national central banks' shares in the subscribed capital of the ECB. The weights of the votes of the members of the Executive Board shall be zero. A decision requiring a qualified majority shall be adopted if the votes cast in favour represent at least two thirds of the subscribed capital of the ECB and represent at least half of the shareholders. If a Governor is unable to

10.2 Subject to Article 10.3, only members of the Council of the ECB present in person shall have the right to vote. Each member shall have one vote. The Rules of Procedure referred to in Article 12.3 shall provide that a member of the Council of the ECB who is prevented from voting for a prolonged period may appoint an alternate as a member of the Council of the ECB. Save as otherwise provided for in the Statute, the Council of the ECB shall act by a simple majority. In the event of a tie, the President shall have the casting vote. In order for the Council of the ECB to vote, there shall be a quorum of two-thirds of the members. If the quorum is not met, the President may convoke an extraordinary meeting at which decisions may be taken without regard to the quorum referred to above.

10.3 For any decisions to be taken under Articles 28, 29, 30, 32 and 33, the votes in the Council of the ECB shall be weighted according to the national central banks' shares in the subscribed capital of the ECB. A decision by a qualified majority shall be approved if the votes cast in favour represent at least [. . . X] of the subscribed capital of the ECB. If a Governor is unable to be present, he may nominate an alternate to cast his weighted vote.

10.4 The proceedings of the meetings shall be confidential. The Council of the ECB may decide to make the outcome of its deliberations public.

10.5 The Council of the ECB shall meet at least ten times a year.

be present, he may nominate an alternate to cast his weighted vote.

10.4. The proceedings of the meetings shall be confidential. The Governing Council may decide to make the outcome of its deliberations public.

10.5. The Governing Council shall meet at least ten times a year.

Article 11—The Executive Board

11.1. In accordance with Article 109a(2)(a) of this Treaty, the Executive Board shall comprise the President, the Vice-President and four other members. The members shall perform their duties on a full-time basis. No member shall engage in any occupation, whether gainful or not, unless exemption is exceptionally granted by the Governing Council.

11.2. In accordance with Article 109a(2)(b) of this Treaty, the President, the Vice-President and the other Members of the Executive Board shall be appointed from among persons of recognized standing and professional experience in monetary or banking matters by common accord of the governments of the Member States at the level of the Heads of State or of Government, on a recommendation from the Council after it has consulted the European Parliament and the Governing Council.

Their term of office shall be 8 years and shall not be renewable.

Only nationals of Member States may be members of the Executive Board.

Article 11—The Executive Board

11.1 The Executive Board shall comprise the President, the Vice President and four other members. The members of the Executive Board shall be selected among persons of recognised standing and professional experience in monetary or banking matters.

The members shall perform their duties on a full-time basis. No member shall, without approval of the Council of the ECB, receive a salary or other form of compensation from any source other than the ECB or occupy any other office or employment, whether remunerated or not, except as a nominee of the ECB.

11.2 The President and the Vice President shall be appointed for a period of eight years by the European Council, after the Council of the ECB has given its opinion, and after consultation with the European Parliament.

11.3 The other members of the Executive Board shall be appointed, for a period of eight years, by the European Council after the Council of the ECB has given its opinion.

11.3. The terms and conditions of employment of the members of the Executive Board, in particular their salaries, pensions and other social security benefits shall be the subject of contracts with the ECB and shall be fixed by the Governing Council on a proposal from a Committee comprising three members appointed by the Governing Council and three members appointed by the Council. The members of the Executive Board shall not have the right to vote on matters referred to in this paragraph.

11.4. If a member of the Executive Board no longer fulfils the conditions required for the performance of his duties or if he has been guilty of serious misconduct, the Court of Justice may, on application by the Governing Council or the Executive Board, compulsorily retire him.

11.5. Each member of the Executive Board present in person shall have the right to vote and shall have, for that purpose, one vote. Save as otherwise provided, the Executive Board shall act by a simple majority of the votes cast. In the event of a tie, the President shall have the casting vote. The voting arrangements shall be specified in the Rules of Procedure referred to in Article 12.3.

11.6. The Executive Board shall be responsible for the current business of the ECB.

11.7. Any vacancy on the Executive Board shall be filled by the appointment of a new member in accordance with Article 11.2.

11.4 The terms and conditions of employment of the members of the Executive Board, in particular their salaries, pensions and other social security benefits shall be laid down in contracts with the ECB and shall be fixed by the Council of the ECB on the proposal of a Committee comprising three members appointed by the Council of the ECB and three members appointed by the Council of the European Communities. The members of the Executive Board shall not have the right to vote on matters referred to in this paragraph.

11.5 If a member of the Executive Board no longer fulfils the conditions required for the performance of his duties or if he has been guilty of serious misconduct, the Court of Justice may, on application by the Council of the ECB or the Executive Board, compulsorily retire him.

11.6 Each member of the Executive Board present in person shall have the right to vote and shall have, for that purpose, one vote. Save as otherwise provided, the Executive Board shall act by a simple majority of the votes cast. In the event of a tie, the President shall have the casting vote. The voting arrangements will be specified in the Rules of Procedure referred to in Article 12.3.

11.7 The Executive Board shall administer the ECB.

Article 12—Responsibilities of the decision-making bodies

12.1. The Governing Council shall adopt the guidelines and take the decisions necessary to ensure the performance of the tasks entrusted to the ESCB under this Treaty and this Statute. The Governing Council shall formulate the monetary policy of the Community including, as appropriate, decisions relating to intermediate monetary objectives, key interest rates and the supply of reserves in the ESCB, and shall establish the necessary guidelines for their implementation. The Executive Board shall implement monetary policy in accordance with the guidelines and decisions laid down by the Governing Council. In doing so the Executive Board shall give the necessary instructions to national central banks. In addition the Executive Board may have certain powers delegated to it where the Governing Council so decides.
To the extent deemed possible and appropriate and without prejudice to the provisions of this Article, the ECB shall have recourse to the national central banks to carry out operations which form part of the tasks of the ESCB.
12.2. The Executive Board shall have responsibility for the preparation of meetings of the Governing Council.
12.3. The Governing Council shall adopt Rules of Procedure which determine the internal organization of the ECB and its decision-making bodies.

Article 12—Responsibilities of the decision-making bodies

12.1 The Council of the ECB shall take the decisions necessary to ensure the performance of tasks entrusted to the System under the present Statute. The Council of the ECB shall formulate the monetary policy of the Community including, as appropriate, decisions relating to intermediate monetary objectives, key interest rates and the supply of reserves in the System, and shall establish the necessary guidelines for their implementation. [The Council of the ECB shall delegate to the Executive Board such necessary operational powers as it thinks fit for implementing the monetary policy decisions and guidelines. The Council of the ECB may delegate other powers as it may specify to the Executive Board.] [The Executive Board shall implement monetary policy in accordance with the decisions and guidelines laid down by the Council of the ECB.]
12.2 When implementing monetary policy in accordance with the decisions and guidelines established by the Council of the ECB, the Executive Board shall give the necessary instructions to national central banks. The Executive Board shall have responsibility for the preparation of Council of the ECB meetings.
12.3 The Council of the ECB shall adopt Rules of Procedure which determine the internal organisation of the ECB and its decision-making bodies.

12.4. The Governing Council shall exercise the advisory functions referred to in Article 4.
12.5. The Governing Council shall take the decisions referred to in Article 6.

12.4 The Council of the ECB shall exercise the advisory functions referred to in Article 4.
12.5 The Council of the ECB shall take the decisions referred to in Article 6.

Article 13—The President

13.1. The President or, in his absence, the Vice-President shall chair the Governing Council and the Executive Board of the ECB.
13.2. Without prejudice to Article 39, the President or his nominee shall represent the ECB externally.

Article 13—The President

13.1 The President, or, in his absence, the Vice President shall chair the Council of the ECB and the Executive Board of the ECB.
13.2 Without prejudice to Article 39, the President or his nominee shall present the views of the ECB externally.

Article 14—National central banks

14.1. In accordance with Article 108 of this Treaty, each Member State shall ensure, at the latest at the date of the establishment of the ESCB, that its national legislation, including the statutes of its national central bank, is compatible with this Treaty and this Statute.
14.2. The statutes of the national central banks shall, in particular, provide that the term of office of a Governor of a national central bank shall be no less than 5 years. A Governor may be relieved from office only if he no longer fulfils the conditions required for the performance of his duties or if he has been guilty of serious misconduct. A decision to this effect may be referred to the Court of Justice by the Governor concerned or the Governing Council on grounds of infringement of this Treaty or of any

Article 14—National central banks

14.1 The Member States shall ensure that their national legislation including the statutes of the national central banks is compatible with this Statute and the EEC Treaty.
14.2 The statutes of the national central banks shall in particular provide that the Governor of a national central bank is appointed by the national authorities of the Member State after consultation with the Council of the ECB. The term of office shall be no less than 5 years. The Governor may be relieved from office only for serious cause resting in his person. A decision to this effect may be referred to the Court of Justice by the Governor concerned or the Council of the ECB.
14.3 Subject to Article 14.5, the national central banks are an integral part of the System and shall act in

rule of law relating to its application. Such proceedings shall be instituted within two months of the publication of the decision or of its notification to the plaintiff or, in the absence thereof, of the day on which it came to the knowledge of the latter, as the case may be.

14.3. The national central banks are an integral part of the ESCB and shall act in accordance with the guidelines and instructions of the ECB. The Governing Council shall take the necessary steps to ensure compliance with the guidelines and instructions of the ECB, and shall require that any necessary information be given to it.

14.4. National central banks may perform functions other than those specified in this Statute unless the Governing Council finds, by a majority of two thirds of the votes cast, that these interfere with the objectives and tasks of the ESCB. Such functions shall be performed on the responsibility and liability of national central banks and shall not be regarded as being part of the functions of the ESCB.

accordance with the guidelines and instructions of the ECB. The Council of the ECB shall take the necessary steps to ensure compliance with the guidelines and instructions of the ECB, and shall require that any necessary information be given to it.

14.4 [To the full extent possible in the judgement of the Council of the ECB, the national central banks shall execute the operations arising out of the System's tasks.] [The Executive Board shall, to the extent possible and appropriate, make use of the national central banks in the execution of the operations arising out of the System's tasks.]

14.5 National central banks may perform on their responsibility and liability functions other than those specified in this Statute unless the Council of the ECB finds, by a qualified majority of two-thirds of the votes cast, that these interfere with the objectives and tasks of the System. Such functions shall not be regarded as being part of the System.

14.6 For the purpose of this Statute, the Institut Monetaire Luxembourgeois shall be regarded as a national central bank.

Article 15—Reporting commitments

15.1. The ECB shall draw up and publish reports on the activities of the ESCB at least quarterly.

15.2. A consolidated financial statement of the ESCB shall be published each week.

Article 15—Inter-institutional co-operation and reporting commitments

15.1 The President of the Council of the European Communities and a Member of the Commission may attend meetings of the Council of the ECB. They may take part in the Council of the ECB's deliberations but not in the voting.

15.3. In accordance with Article 109b(3) of this Treaty, the ECB shall address an annual report on the activities of the ESCB and on the monetary policy of both the previous and the current year to the European Parliament, the Council and the Commission, and also to the European Council.

15.4. The reports and statements referred to in this Article shall be made available to interested parties free of charge.

15.2 The President of the ECB shall be invited to participate in meetings of the European Council and Council of the European Communities when matters relating to the System's objectives and tasks are discussed.

15.3 The ECB shall draw up an annual report on the activities of the System and on the monetary policy of both the previous and current year at a date to be established in the Rules of Procedure. The President shall present the annual report to the European Council, the Council of the European Communities and the European Parliament. The President and members of the Executive Board may attend meetings of the European Parliament's specialised committees, if circumstances justify.

15.4 The ECB shall draw up and publish reports on the activities of the System at regular intervals.

15.5 A consolidated financial statement of the System shall be published each week.

15.6 The reports and statements referred to above shall be made available to interested parties free of charge.

CHAPTER IV—
MONETARY FUNCTIONS AND
OPERATIONS OF THE SYSTEM

Article 16—Bank notes

In accordance with Article 105a(1) of this Treaty, the Governing Council shall have the exclusive right to authorize the issue of bank notes

Article 16—Notes and coins

16.1 The Council of the ECB shall have the exclusive right to authorise the issue of notes within the Community. The notes issued by the ECB and the within the Community. The ECB and the national central banks may issue such notes. The bank notes issued by the ECB and the national central banks shall be the only such notes to have the status of legal tender within the Community. The ECB shall respect as far as possible existing practices regarding the issue and design of bank notes.

national central banks shall be the only notes to have legal tender status.
16.2 Provisions concerning the legal tender status of Community currencies shall be established according to the Community legislation. The Council of the ECB shall make the necessary arrangements for the exchange of notes denominated in Community currencies by the national central banks at par value.
16.3 The volume and denomination of coins issued within the Community shall be subject to approval of the Council of the ECB. The coins shall be put into circulation by the ECB and/or the national central banks.

CHAPTER IV—
MONETARY FUNCTIONS AND
OPERATIONS OF THE ESCB

*Article 17—Accounts with the ECB
and the national central banks*

In order to conduct their operations, the ECB and the national central banks may open accounts for credit institutions, public entities and other market participants and accept assets, including book-entry securities, as collateral.

*Article 18—Open market
and credit operations*

18.1. In order to achieve the objectives of the ESCB and to carry out its tasks, the ECB and the national central banks may:

*Article 17—Accounts with the ECB
and the national central banks*

In order to conduct their operations, the ECB and the national central banks may open accounts for credit institutions, public entities and other market participants and accept assets including book-entry securities as collateral.

*Article 18—Open market
and credit operations*

18.1 In order to achieve the objectives of the System and to carry out its tasks, the ECB and the national central banks shall be entitled:

—operate in the financial markets by buying and selling outright (spot and forward) or under repurchase agreement and by lending or borrowing claims and marketable instruments, whether in Community or in non-Community currencies, as well as precious metals;
—conduct credit operations with credit institutions and other market participants, with lending being based on adequate collateral.
18.2. The ECB shall establish general principles for open market and credit operations carried out by itself or the national central banks, including for the announcement of conditions under which they stand ready to enter into such transactions.

—to operate in the financial markets by buying and selling outright (spot and forward) or under repurchase agreement claims and marketable instruments, whether in Community or in foreign currencies, as well as precious metals;
—to conduct credit operations with credit institutions and other market participants [, with lending being based on adequate collateral].
18.2 The ECB shall establish general principles for open market and credit operations carried out by itself or the national central banks including the announcement of conditions under which they stand ready to enter into such transactions.

Article 19—Minimum reserves

Article 19—Minimum reserves

19.1. Subject to Article 2, the ECB may require credit institutions established in Member States to hold minimum reserves on accounts with the ECB and national central banks in pursuance of monetary policy objectives. Regulations concerning the calculation and determination of the required minimum reserves may be established by the Governing Council. In cases of non-compliance the ECB shall be entitled to levy penalty interest and to impose other sanctions with comparable effect.
19.2. For the application of this Article, the Council shall, in accordance with the procedure laid down in Article 42, define the basis for minimum reserves and the maximum permissible ratios

The ECB shall be entitled to require credit institutions to hold minimum reserves on accounts with the ECB and national central banks. Regulations concerning the calculation and determination of the required minimum reserves shall be established by the Council of the ECB. In cases of non-compliance the ECB shall be entitled to levy penalty interest and to take steps to pursue the matter in the supervisory sphere.

between those reserves and their basis, as well as the appropriate sanctions in cases of non-compliance.

<table>
<tr>
<td>

Article 20—Other instruments of monetary control

The Governing Council may, by a majority of two thirds of the votes cast, decide upon the use of such other operational methods of monetary control as it sees fit, respecting Article 2. The Council shall, in accordance with the procedure laid down in Article 42, define the scope of such methods if they impose obligations on third parties.

Article 21—Operations with public entities

21.1. In accordance with Article 104 of this Treaty, overdrafts or any other type of credit facility with the ECB or with the national central banks in favour of Community institutions or bodies, central governments, regional, local or other public authorities, other bodies governed by public law, or public undertakings of Member States shall be prohibited, as shall the purchase directly from them by the ECB or national central banks of debt instruments.
21.2. The ECB and national central banks may act as fiscal agents for the entities referred to in Article 21.1.
21.3. The provisions of this Article shall not apply to publicly-owned credit institutions which, in the context of the supply of reserves by central banks,

</td>
<td>

Article 20—Other instruments

The Council of the ECB may decide, by a qualified majority of two-thirds of the votes cast, upon the use of such other operational methods of monetary control as it sees fit.

Article 21—Operations with public entities

21.1 The ECB and national central banks shall not grant overdrafts or any other type of credit facility to the Community, Member States and other public entities of the Member States, nor purchase debt instruments directly from them.
21.2 The ECB and national central banks may act as fiscal agents for the entities referred to in Article 21.1.
21.3 The function of fiscal agent shall comprise all banking transactions except those referred to in Article 21.1 above.
21.4 The entities for which the ECB and national central banks act as fiscal agents in accordance with Articles 21.2 and 21.3 shall issue debt instruments either through the System or in consultation with it.

</td>
</tr>
</table>

shall be given the same treatment by national central banks and the ECB as private credit institutions.

Article 22—Clearing and payment systems

The ECB and national central banks may provide facilities, and the ECB may make regulations, to ensure efficient and sound clearing and payment systems within the Community and with other countries.

Article 23—External operations

The ECB and national central banks may:
—establish relations with central banks and financial institutions in other countries and, where appropriate, with international organizations;
—acquire and sell spot and forward all types of foreign exchange assets and precious metals; the term 'foreign exchange asset' shall include securities and all other assets in the currency of any country or units of account and in whatever form held;
—hold and manage the assets referred to in this Article;
—conduct all types of banking transactions in relations with third countries and international organizations, including borrowing and lending operations.

21.5 The provisions under this Article shall not apply to publicly-owned credit institutions.

Article 22—Clearing and payment systems

The ECB and national central banks may provide facilities, and the ECB may issue regulations to ensure efficient and sound clearing and payment systems inside the Community and with third countries.

Article 23—External operations

The ECB and the national central banks shall be entitled:
—to establish relations with central banks and financial institutions in third countries and, where appropriate, with international and supranational organisations;
—to acquire and sell spot and forward all types of foreign exchange assets and precious metals. The term "foreign exchange asset" shall include securities and all other assets in currency of any country or units of account and in whatever form held;
—to hold and manage the assets defined above;
—to conduct all types of banking transactions in relation to third countries and international and supranational organisations, including borrowing and lending operations.

Article 24—Other operations

In addition to operations arising from their tasks, the ECB and national central banks may enter into operations for their administrative purposes or for their staff.

Article 24—Other operations

In addition to operations arising from their tasks, the ECB and the national central banks may enter into operations that serve their administrative purposes or for their staff.

CHAPTER V—
PRUDENTIAL SUPERVISION

CHAPTER V—
PRUDENTIAL SUPERVISION

Article 25—Prudential supervision

Article 25—Supervisory tasks

25.1. The ECB may offer advice to and be consulted by the Council, the Commission and the competent authorities of the Member States on the scope and implementation of Community legislation relating to the prudential supervision of credit institutions and to the stability of the financial system.
25.2. In accordance with any decision of the Council under Article 105(6) of this Treaty, the ECB may perform specific tasks concerning policies relating to the prudential supervision of credit institutions and other financial institutions with the exception of insurance undertakings.

25.1 The ECB shall be entitled to offer advice and to be consulted on the interpretation and implementation of Community legislation relating to the prudential supervision of credit and other financial institutions and financial markets.
25.2 The ECB may formulate, interpret and implement policies relating to the prudential supervision of credit and other financial institutions for which it is designated as competent supervisory authority.

CHAPTER VI—FINANCIAL
PROVISIONS OF THE ESCB

CHAPTER VI—FINANCIAL
PROVISIONS OF THE SYSTEM

Article 26—Financial accounts

Article 26—Financial accounts

26.1. The financial year of the ECB and national central banks shall begin on

26.1 The financial year of the ECB and the national central banks shall begin the first day of January and end on the last day of December.

26.2. The annual accounts of the ECB shall be drawn up by the Executive Board, in accordance with the principles established by the Governing Council. The accounts shall be approved by the Governing Council and shall thereafter be published.

26.3. For analytical and operational purposes, the Executive Board shall draw up a consolidated balance sheet of the ESCB, comprising those assets and liabilities of the national central banks that fall within the ESCB.

26.4. For the application of this Article, the Governing Council shall establish the necessary rules for standardizing the accounting and reporting of operations undertaken by the national central banks.

on the first day of January and end on the last day of December.

26.2 The annual accounts of the ECB shall be drawn up by the Executive Board in accordance with the principles established by the Council of the ECB, The accounts shall be approved by the Council of the ECB and shall thereafter be published.

26.3 For analytical and operational purposes, the Executive Board shall draw up a consolidated balance sheet of the System, comprising the assets and liabilities of the ECB and those assets and liabilities of the national central banks that fall within the System.

26.4 For the application of this Article, the Council of the ECB shall establish the necessary rules for standardising the accounting and reporting of operations undertaken by the national central banks.

Article 27—Auditing

27.1. The accounts of the ECB and national central banks shall be audited by independent external auditors recommended by the Governing Council and approved by the Council. The auditors shall have full power to examine all books and accounts of the ECB and national central banks and obtain full information about their transactions.

27.2. The provisions of Article 188c of this Treaty shall only apply to an examination of the operational efficiency of the management of the ECB.

Article 27—Auditing

27.1 The accounts of the ECB and the national central banks shall be audited by independent external auditors recommended by the Council of the ECB and approved by the Council of the European Communities. The auditors shall have full power to examine all books and accounts of the ECB and national central banks, and to be fully informed about their transactions.

27.2 The provisions of Articles 203 and 206a of the Treaty shall not apply to the ECB or to the national central banks.

Article 28—Capital of the ECB

28.1. The capital of the ECB, which shall become operational upon its establishment, shall be ECU 5000 million. The capital may be increased by such amounts as may be decided by the Governing Council acting by the qualified majority provided for in Article 10.3, within the limits and under the conditions set by the Council under the procedure laid down in Article 42.

28.2. The national central banks shall be the sole subscribers to and holders of the capital of the ECB. The subscription of capital shall be according to the key established in accordance with Article 29.

28.3. The Governing Council, acting by the qualified majority provided for in Article 10.3, shall determine the extent to which and the form in which the capital shall be paid up.

28.4. Subject to Article 28.5, the shares of the national central banks in the subscribed capital of the ECB may not be transferred, pledged or attached.

28.5. If the key referred to in Article 29 is adjusted, the national central banks shall transfer among themselves capital shares to the extent necessary to ensure that the distribution of capital shares corresponds to the adjusted key. The Governing Council shall determine the terms and conditions of such transfers.

Article 28—Capital of the ECB

28.1 The capital of the ECB shall, upon its establishment, be ecu [. . . X] million. The capital may be increased from time to time by such amounts as may be decided by the Council of the ECB acting by a qualified majority.

28.2 The national central banks shall be the sole subscribers to and holders of the capital of the ECB. The subscription of capital shall be according to the key established pursuant to Article 29.

28.3 The Council of the ECB, acting by a qualified majority, shall determine the extent to which and the form in which capital shall be paid up.

28.4 The shares of the national central banks in the subscribed capital of the ECB may not be transferred, pledged or attached other than in accordance with a decision taken by the Council of the ECB.

28.5 If the key referred to in Article 29 is adjusted, the national central banks shall transfer among themselves capital shares to the extent necessary to ensure that the distribution of capital shares corresponds to the adjusted key. The Council of the ECB shall determine the terms and conditions of such transfers.

Article 29—Key for capital subscription

29.1. When in accordance with the procedure referred to in Article 109l(1) of this Treaty the ESCB and the ECB have been established, the key for subscription of the ECB's capital shall be established. Each national central bank shall be assigned a weighting in this key which shall be equal to the sum of:

—50% of the share of its respective Member State in the population of the Community in the penultimate year preceding the establishment of the ESCB;

—50% of the share of its respective Member State in the gross domestic product at market prices of the Community as recorded in the last five years preceding the penultimate year before the establishment of the ESCB;

—The percentages shall be rounded up to the nearest multiple of 0.05 percentage points.

29.2. The statistical data to be used for the application of this Article shall be provided by the Commission in accordance with the rules adopted by the Council under the procedure provided for in Article 42.

29.3. The weightings assigned to the national central banks shall be adjusted every five years after the establishment of the ESCB by analogy with the provisions laid down in Article 29.1. The adjusted key shall apply with effect from the first day of the following year.

29.4. The Governing Council shall take all other measures necessary for the application of this Article.

Article 29—Key for capital subscription

29.1 At the entry into force of this Statute, the key for subscription of the ECB's capital shall be established. Each national central bank shall be assigned a weight in this key which shall be equal to the sum of:

— [. . . X] of the share of its respective country in the population of the Community in the penultimate year preceding the entry into force of the Statute;

— [. . . X] of the share of its respective country in the gross domestic product at market prices of the Community as recorded in the last five years preceding the penultimate year before the entry into force of the Statute.

29.2 The statistical data to be used for the application of this Article shall be calculated by the Statistical Office of the European Communities in accordance with Community legislation.

29.3 The weights assigned to the national central banks shall be adjusted every five years after the entry into force of this Statute in analogy to the provisions laid down in Article 29.1. The adjusted key shall apply with effect from the first day of the following year.

29.4 The Council of the ECB shall take all other measures necessary for the application of this Article.

Article 30—Transfer of foreign
reserve assets to the ECB

Article 30—Transfer of foreign
reserve assets to the ECB

30.1. Without prejudice to Article 28, the ECB shall be provided by the national central banks with foreign reserve assets, other than Member States' currencies, ECUs, IMF reserve positions and SDRs, up to an amount equivalent to ECU 50 000 million. The Governing Council shall decide upon the proportion to be called up by the ECB following its establishment and the amounts called up at later dates. The ECB shall have the full right to hold and manage the foreign reserves that are transferred to it and to use them for the purposes set out in this Statute.

30.2. The contributions of each national central bank shall be fixed in proportion to its share in the subscribed capital of the ECB.

30.3. Each national central bank shall be credited by the ECB with a claim equivalent to its contribution. The Governing Council shall determine the denomination and remuneration of such claims.

30.4. Further calls of foreign reserve assets beyond the limit set in Article 30.1 may be effected by the ECB, in accordance with Article 30.2, within the limits and under the conditions set by the Council in accordance with the procedure laid down in Article 42.

30.5. The ECB may hold and manage IMF reserve positions and SDRs and provide for the pooling of such assets.

30.6. The Governing Council shall take all other measures necessary for the application of this Article.

30.1 Without prejudice to the provisions of Article 28, the ECB shall be endowed by the national central banks with foreign reserve assets, other than Community currencies and ecus, up to an amount equivalent to ecu [. . . X]. The Council of the ECB shall decide upon the proportion to be called up by the ECB at the entry into force of this Statute and the amounts called up at later dates.

30.2 The contributions of each national central bank shall be fixed in accordance with its share in the subscribed capital of the ECB.

30.3 Each national central bank shall be credited by the ECB with a claim equivalent to its contribution, The Council of the ECB shall determine the denomination and remuneration of such claims.

30.4 Further calls of foreign reserve assets beyond the limit set in Article 30.1 may be effected by the ECB in accordance with Community legislation.

30.5 The ECB shall be authorised to accept the pooling of IMF reserve positions and SDRs.

30.6 The Council of the ECB shall determine all other conditions required for the application of this Article.

Article 31—Foreign reserve assets held by national central banks

31.1. The national central banks shall be allowed to perform transactions in fulfilment of their obligations towards international organizations in accordance with Article 23.

31.2. All other operations in foreign reserve assets remaining with the national central banks after the transfers referred to in Article 30, and Member States' transactions with their foreign exchange working balances shall, above a certain limit to be established within the framework of Article 31.3, be subject to approval by the ECB in order to ensure consistency with the exchange rate and monetary policies of the Community.

31.3. The Governing Council shall issue guidelines with a view to facilitating such operations.

Article 32—Allocation of monetary income of national central banks

32.1. The income accruing to the national central banks in the performance of the ESCB's monetary policy function (hereinafter referred to as 'monetary income') shall be allocated at the end of each financial year in accordance with the provisions of this Article.

32.2. Subject to Article 32.3, the amount of each national central bank's monetary income shall be equal to its annual income derived from its assets held against notes in circulation and

Article 31—Foreign reserve assets held by national central banks

31.1 The national central banks shall be allowed to perform transactions in fulfilment of the obligations towards international organisations in accordance with Article 23.

31.2 All other operations in foreign reserve assets remaining with the national central banks after the transfers referred to in Article 30 shall be subject to approval by the ECB in order to ensure consistency with the exchange rate and monetary policies of the Community.

31.3 The Council of the ECB shall issue guidelines with a view to facilitating such operations.

Article 32—Allocation of monetary income of national central banks

32.1 The income accruing to the national central banks in the performance of the System's monetary policy function (called hereafter "monetary income") shall be allocated at the end of each financial year in accordance with the provisions hereafter.

32.2 Subject to Article 32.3 the amount of each national central bank's monetary income shall be equal to its annual income derived from its assets held against notes in circulation and deposit liabilities vis-à-vis credit institutions.

deposit liabilities to credit institutions. These assets shall be earmarked by national central banks in accordance with guidelines to be established by the Governing Council.

32.3. If, after the start of the third stage, the balance sheet structures of the national central banks do not, in the judgment of the Governing Council, permit the application of Article 32.2, the Governing Council, acting by a qualified majority, may decide that, by way of derogation from Article 32.2, monetary income shall be measured according to an alternative method for a period of not more than five years.

32.4. The amount of each national central bank's monetary income shall be reduced by an amount equivalent to any interest paid by that central bank on its deposit liabilities to credit institutions in accordance with Article 19.

The Governing Council may decide that national central banks shall be indemnified against costs incurred in connection with the issue of bank notes or in exceptional circumstances for specific losses arising from monetary policy operations undertaken for the ESCB. Indemnification shall be in a form deemed appropriate in the judgment of the Governing Council; these amounts may be offset against the national central banks' monetary income.

32.5. The sum of the national central banks' monetary income shall be allocated to the national central banks in proportion to their paid-up shares in the capital of the ECB, subject to any decision taken by the Governing Council pursuant to Article 33.2.

These assets shall be earmarked by national central banks in accordance with guidelines to be established by the Council of the ECB.

32.3 If at the entry into force of this Statute, in the judgement of the Council of the ECB, the balance sheet structures of the national central banks do not permit the application of Article 32.2, the Council of the ECB, acting by a qualified majority, may decide that, by way of derogation to Article 32.2, the monetary income shall be measured according to an alternative method for a period of not more than five years.

32.4 The amount of each national central bank's monetary income shall be reduced by an amount equivalent to any interest paid by that central bank on its deposit liabilities vis-à-vis credit institutions in accordance with Article 19.

The Council of the ECB may decide that national central banks shall be indemnified for cost incurred in connection with the issuance of bank notes or in exceptional circumstances for specific losses arising from monetary policy operations undertaken for the System. The indemnification shall be in the form deemed appropriate in the judgment of the Council of the ECB; these amounts may be offset against the national central banks' monetary income.

32.5 The sum of the national central banks' monetary income shall be allocated to the national central banks in proportion to their subscribed shares in the capital of the ECB, subject

32.6. The clearing and settlement of the balances arising from the allocation of monetary income shall be carried out by the ECB in accordance with guidelines established by the Governing Council.

32.7. The Governing Council shall take all other measures necessary for the application of this Article.

Article 33—Allocation of net profits and losses of the ECB

33.1. The net profit of the ECB shall be transferred in the following order:

(a) an amount to be determined by the Governing Council, which may not exceed 20% of the net profit, shall be transferred to the general reserve fund subject to a limit equal to 100% of the capital;

(b) the remaining net profit shall be distributed to the shareholders of the ECB in proportion to their paid-up shares.

33.2. In the event of a loss incurred by the ECB, the shortfall may be offset against the general reserve fund of the ECB and, if necessary, following a decision by the Governing Council, against the monetary income of the relevant financial year in proportion and up to the amounts allocated to the national central banks in accordance with Article 32.5.

to any decision taken by the Council of the ECB pursuant to Article 33.2.

32.6 The clearing and settlement of the balances arising from the allocation of monetary income shall be carried out by the ECB in accordance with the guidelines established by the Council of the ECB.

32.7 The Council of the ECB shall determine all other conditions required for the application of this Article.

Article 33—Allocation of net profits and losses of the ECB

33.1 The net profit of the ECB shall be transferred in the following order:

(a) an amount to be determined by the Council of the ECB shall be transferred to the general reserve fund;

(b) the remaining net profit shall be distributed to the shareholders of the ECB in proportion to their subscribed shares.

33.2 In the event of a loss incurred by the ECB, the shortfall may be offset against the own funds of the ECB or, following a decision by the Council of the ECB, against contributions from national central banks, in proportion to their subscribed shares.

CHAPTER VII—
GENERAL PROVISIONS

Article 34—Legal acts

34.1. In accordance with Article 108a of this Treaty, the ECB shall:
—make regulations to the extent necessary to implement the tasks defined in Article 3.1, first indent, Articles 19.1, 22 or 25.2 and in cases which shall be laid down in the acts of the Council referred to in Article 42;
—take decisions necessary for carrying out the tasks entrusted to the ESCB under this Treaty and this Statute;
—make recommendations and deliver opinions.
34.2. A regulation shall have general application. It shall be binding in its entirety and directly applicable in all Member States.

Recommendations and opinions shall have no binding force.

A decision shall be binding in its entirety upon those to whom it is addressed.

Articles 190 to 192 of this Treaty shall apply to regulations and decisions adopted by the ECB.

The ECB may decide to publish its decisions, recommendations and opinions.
34.3. Within the limits and under the conditions adopted by the Council under the procedure laid down in Article 42, the ECB shall be entitled to impose fines or periodic penalty payments on undertakings for failure to comply with obligations under its regulations and decisions.

CHAPTER VII—
GENERAL PROVISIONS

Article 34—Regulatory power

34.1 The ECB shall make the regulations and take the decisions, necessary for the performance of tasks entrusted to the System under the present Statute.
34.2 A regulation shall have general application. It shall be binding in its entirety and directly applicable. A decision shall be binding in its entirety upon those to whom it is addressed. Articles 191 and 192 of the Treaty establishing the EEC are applicable in all respects to the regulations made and decisions taken by the ECB.
34.3 According to Community legislation, the ECB and national central banks shall be entitled to impose sanctions on market participants and other economic agents which fail to comply with their obligations vis-à-vis regulations and decisions referred to in this Article.

Article 35—*Judicial control and related matters*

35.1. The acts or omissions of the ECB shall be open to review or interpretation by the Court of Justice in the cases and under the conditions laid down in this Treaty. The ECB may institute proceedings in the cases and under the conditions laid down in this Treaty.

35.2. Disputes between the ECB, on the one hand, and its creditors, debtors or any other person, on the other, shall be decided by the competent national courts, save where jurisdiction has been conferred upon the Court of Justice.

35.3. The ECB shall be subject to the liability regime provided for in Article 215 of this Treaty. The national central banks shall be liable according to their respective national laws.

35.4. The Court of Justice shall have jurisdiction to give judgment pursuant to any arbitration clause contained in a contract concluded by or on behalf of the ECB, whether that contract be governed by public or private law.

35.5. A decision of the ECB to bring an action before the Court of Justice shall be taken by the Governing Council.

35.6. The Court of Justice shall have jurisdiction in disputes concerning the fulfilment by a national central bank of obligations under this Statute. If the ECB considers that a national central bank has failed to fulfil an obligation under this Statute, it shall deliver a reasoned opinion on the matter after giving the national central bank concerned the opportunity to submit its observations. If the national central

Article 35—*Judicial control and related matters*

35.1 The acts of the ECB shall be open to review and interpretation by the Court of Justice under the conditions laid down for the legal control of the acts of Community institutions. The ECB may institute proceedings under the same conditions as Community institutions. Articles 173 to 178, 183 and 184 of the EEC Treaty shall be applicable accordingly.

35.2 The ECB shall be subject to the liability regime as provided for in Article 215 of the EEC Treaty.

35.3 The Court of Justice shall have jurisdiction to give judgement pursuant to any arbitration clause contained in a contract concluded by or on behalf of the ECB, whether that contract be governed by public or private law.

35.4 The decision of the ECB to bring an action before the Court of Justice shall be taken by the Council of the ECB.

35.5 The national central banks shall be liable according to their respective national laws.

35.6 The Court of Justice shall have jurisdiction in disputes concerning the fulfilment by a national central bank of obligations under this Statute. If the ECB considers that a national central bank has failed to fulfil an obligation under this Statute, it may bring the matter before the Court of Justice.

bank concerned does not comply with
the opinion within the period laid
down by the ECB, the latter may bring
the matter before the Court of Justice.

Article 36—Staff

36.1. The Governing Council, on a
proposal from the Executive Board,
shall lay down the conditions of
employment of the staff of the ECB.
36.2. The Court of Justice shall have
jurisdiction in any dispute between the
ECB and its servants within the limits
and under the conditions laid down in
the conditions of employment.

Article 37—Seat

Before the end of 1992, the decision as
to where the seat of the ECB will be
established shall be taken by common
accord of the governments of the
Member States at the level of Heads of
State or of Government.

Article 38—Professional secrecy

38.1. Members of the governing bodies
and the staff of the ECB and the
national central banks shall be
required, even after their duties have
ceased, not to disclose information of
the kind covered by the obligation of
professional secrecy.
38.2. Persons having access to data
covered by Community legislation
imposing an obligation of secrecy shall
be subject to such legislation.

Article 36—Staff

36.1 The Council of the ECB, on a
proposal from the Executive Board,
shall lay down the conditions of
employment of the staff of the ECB.
36.2 Disputes between the ECB and
its staff may be brought before the
Court of Justice which shall have
jurisdiction.

Article 37—Seat

The seat of the ECB shall be
established at [. . . X].

Article 38—Professional secrecy

38.1 Members of the governing bodies
and the staff of the ECB and the
national central banks shall be
required, even after their duties have
ceased, not to disclose information of
the kind covered by the obligation of
professional secrecy.
38.2 Persons having access to data
covered by specific secrecy Community
legislation shall be subject to such
legislation.

Article 39—Signatories

The ECB shall be legally committed to third parties by the President or by two members of the Executive Board or by the signatures of two members of the staff of the ECB who have been duly authorized by the President to sign on behalf of the ECB.

Article 40—Privileges and immunities

The ECB shall enjoy in the territories of the Member States such privileges and immunities as are necessary for the performance of its tasks, under the conditions laid down in the Protocol on the Privileges and Immunities of the European Communities annexed to the Treaty establishing a Single Council and a Single Commission of the European Communities.

CHAPTER VIII—AMENDMENT OF THE STATUTE AND COMPLEMENTARY LEGISLATION

Article 41—Simplified amendment procedure

41.1. In accordance with Article 106(5) of this Treaty, Articles 5.1, 5.2, 5.3, 17, 18, 19.1, 22, 23, 24, 26, 32.2, 32.3, 32.4, 32.6, 33.1(a) and 36 of this Statute may be amended by the Council, acting either by a qualified majority on a recommendation from the ECB and

Article 39—Signatories

The ECB shall be legally committed vis-à-vis third parties by the signature of the President or by the signatures of two members of the Executive Board or by those of two members of the staff of the ECB who have been duly authorised by the President to sign on behalf of the ECB.

Article 40—Privileges and immunities

The Protocol on the privileges and immunities of the European Community shall apply to the ECB, the members of its decision-making bodies and its staff to the extent necessary for the performance of the ECB's tasks.

CHAPTER VIII—AMENDMENT OF THE STATUTE AND COMPLEMENTARY LEGISLATION

Article 41—Simplified amendment procedure

41.1 By way of derogation to Article 236 of the EEC Treaty, Articles 5, 17, 18, 19, 21.2, 21.3, 21.4, 21.5, 22, 23, 24, 26, 32 and 36 may be amended by the Council of the European Communities, at the request of the ECB and after consulting the European Parliament

after consulting the Commission, or unanimously on a proposal from the Commission and after consulting the ECB. In either case the assent of the European Parliament shall be required.

41.2. A recommendation made by the ECB under this Article shall require a unanimous decision by the Governing Council.

and the Commission. The approval of the ECB's request for amendment requires a decision of the Council of the European Communities acting by a qualified majority.

41.2 Article 3 may be amended by the Council of the European Communities in accordance with the procedure referred to in Article 41.1 to the extent necessary to confer upon the System additional tasks which are not at variance with the System's objectives stated in Article 2 and do not impinge on the System's basic tasks defined in Article 3.

41.3 A request made by the ECB under this Article shall require a unanimous decision by the Council of the ECB.

Article 42—
Complementary legislation

Article 42—
Complementary legislation

In accordance with Article 106(6) of this Treaty, immediately after the decision on the date for the beginning of the third stage, the Council, acting by a qualified majority either on a proposal from the Commission and after consulting the European Parliament and the ECB or on a recommendation from the ECB and after consulting the European Parliament and the Commission, shall adopt the provisions referred to in Articles 4, 5.4, 19.2, 20, 28.1, 29.2, 30.4 and 34.3 of this Statute.

The Council of the European Communities, acting by a qualified majority on a proposal from the Commission and after consulting the ECB and the European Parliament, shall enact the legislation necessary for the application of Articles 4.1, 5.3, 16.2, 25.2, 29.2, 30.4 and 34.3.

CHAPTER IX—TRANSITIONAL AND OTHER PROVISIONS FOR THE ESCB

Article 43—General provisions

43.1. A derogation as referred to in Article 109k(1) of this Treaty shall entail that the following Articles of this Statute shall not confer any rights or impose any obligations on the Member State concerned: 3, 6, 9.2, 12.1, 14.3, 16, 18, 19, 20, 22, 23, 26.2, 27, 30, 31, 32, 33, 34, 50 and 52.

43.2. The central banks of Member States with a derogation as specified in Article 109k(1) of this Treaty shall retain their powers in the field of monetary policy according to national law.

43.3. In accordance with Article 109k(4) of this Treaty, 'Member States' shall be read as 'Member States without a derogation' in the following Articles of this Statute: 3, 11.2, 19, 34.2 and 50.

43.4. 'National central banks' shall be read as 'central banks of Member States without a derogation' in the following Articles of this Statute: 9.2, 10.1, 10.3, 12.1, 16, 17, 18, 22, 23, 27, 30, 31, 32, 33.2 and 52.

43.5. 'Shareholders' shall be read as 'central banks of Member States without a derogation' in Articles 10.3 and 33.1.

43.6. 'Subscribed capital of the ECB' shall be read as 'capital of the ECB subscribed by the central banks of Member States without a derogation' in Articles 10.3 and 30.2.

CHAPTER IX—TRANSITIONAL PROVISIONS FOR THE SYSTEM

[No transitional provisions were specified in the draft.]

Article 44—Transitional tasks
of the ECB

The ECB shall take over those tasks of the EMI which, because of the derogations of one or more Member States, still have to be performed in the third stage.

The ECB shall give advice in the preparations for the abrogation of the derogations specified in Article 109k of this Treaty.

Article 45—The General Council
of the ECB

45.1. Without prejudice to Article 106(3) of this Treaty, the General Council shall be constituted as a third decision-making body of the ECB.
45.2. The General Council shall comprise the President and Vice-President of the ECB and the Governors of the national central banks. The other members of the Executive Board may participate, without having the right to vote, in meetings of the General Council.
45.3. The responsibilities of the General Council are listed in full in Article 47 of this Statute.

Article 46—Rules of procedure
of the General Council

46.1. The President or, in his absence, the Vice-President of the ECB shall chair the General Council of the ECB.

46.2. The President of the Council and a member of the Commission may participate, without having the right to vote, in meetings of the General Council.

46.3. The President shall prepare the meetings of the General Council.

46.4. By way of derogation from Article 12.3, the General Council shall adopt its Rules of Procedure.

46.5. The Secretariat of the General Council shall be provided by the ECB.

Article 47—Responsibilities of the General Council

47.1. The General Council shall:
—perform the tasks referred to in Article 44;
—contribute to the advisory functions referred to in Articles 4 and 25.1.

47.2. The General Council shall contribute to:
—the collection of statistical information as referred to in Article 5;
—the reporting activities of the ECB as referred to in Article 15;
—the establishment of the necessary rules for the application of Article 26 as referred to in Article 26.4;
—the taking of all other measures necessary for the application of Article 29 as referred to in Article 29.4;
—the laying down of the conditions of employment of the staff of the ECB as referred to in Article 36.

47.3. The General Council shall contribute to the necessary preparations for irrevocably fixing the exchange rates of the currencies of Member States with a derogation

against the currencies, or the single
currency, of the Member States
without a derogation, as referred to in
Article 109l(5) of this Treaty.
47.4. The General Council shall be
informed by the President of the ECB
of decisions of the Governing Council.

Article 48—Transitional provisions for the capital of the ECB

In accordance with Article 29.1 each
national central bank shall be assigned a
weighting in the key for subscription of
the ECB's capital. By way of derogation
from Article 28.3, central banks of
Member States with a derogation shall
not pay up their subscribed capital
unless the General Council, acting by a
majority representing at least two thirds
of the subscribed capital of the ECB and
at least half of the shareholders, decides
that a minimal percentage has to be paid
up as a contribution to the operational
costs of the ECB.

Article 49—Deferred payment of capital, reserves and provisions of the ECB

49.1. The central bank of a Member State
whose derogation has been abrogated
shall pay up its subscribed share of the
capital of the ECB to the same extent as
the central banks of other Member
States without a derogation, and shall
transfer to the ECB foreign reserve
assets in accordance with Article 30.1.
The sum to be transferred shall be
determined by multiplying the ECU

value at current exchange rates of the
foreign reserve assets which have
already been transferred to the ECB in
accordance with Article 30.1, by the
ratio between the number of shares
subscribed by the national central bank
concerned and the number of shares
already paid up by the other national
central banks.

49.2. In addition to the payment to be
made in accordance with Article 49.1,
the central bank concerned shall
contribute to the reserves of the ECB,
to those provisions equivalent to
reserves, and to the amount still to
be appropriated to the reserves and
provisions corresponding to the
balance of the profit and loss account
as at 31 December of the year prior
to the abrogation of the derogation.
The sum to be contributed shall be
determined by multiplying the amount
of the reserves, as defined above and
as stated in the approved balance sheet
of the ECB, by the ratio between the
number of shares subscribed by the
central bank concerned and the
number of shares already paid up by
the other central banks.

Article 50—Initial appointment of the members of the Executive Board

When the Executive Board of the ECB
is being established, the President, the
Vice-President and the other members
of the Executive Board shall be
appointed by common accord of the
governments of the Member States at
the level of Heads of State or of

Government, on a recommendation from the Council and after consulting the European Parliament and the Council of the EMI. The President of the Executive Board shall be appointed for 8 years. By way of derogation from Article 11.2, the Vice-President shall be appointed for 4 years and the other members of the Executive Board for terms of office of between 5 and 8 years. No term of office shall be renewable. The number of members of the Executive Board may be smaller than provided for in Article 11.1, but in no circumstance shall it be less than four.

Article 51—Derogation from Article 32

51.1. If, after the start of the third stage, the Governing Council decides that the application of Article 32 results in significant changes in national central banks' relative income positions, the amount of income to be allocated pursuant to Article 32 shall be reduced by a uniform percentage which shall not exceed 60% in the first financial year after the start of the third stage and which shall decrease by at least 12 percentage points in each subsequent financial year.
51.2. Article 51.1 shall be applicable for not more than five financial years after the start of the third stage.

Article 52—Exchange of bank notes in Community currencies

Following the irrevocable fixing of exchange rates, the Governing Council shall take the necessary measures to ensure that bank notes denominated in currencies with irrevocably fixed exchange rates are exchanged by the national central banks at their respective par values.

Article 53—Applicability of the transitional provisions

If and as long as there are Member States with a derogation Articles 43 to 48 shall be applicable.

Appendix C

Dramatis Personae

Alphandéry, Edmond (1943–) Union pour la Démocratie Française (center-right) politician; French Minister of Economy and Finance under Prime Minister Balladur 1993–95.

Amato, Giuliano (1938–) Socialist politician; Undersecretary of State to the Italian Prime Minister's Office 1983–87; Deputy Prime Minister 1987–88; Minister of the Treasury 1987–89 and 1999–2000; Italian Prime Minister 1992–93 and 2000–01; Minister of the Interior 2006–08.

Andreotti, Giulio (1919–) Christian Democrat politician; Italian Prime Minister 1972–73, 1976–79, and 1989–92; Minister of the Interior 1954 and 1978; Foreign Minister 1983–89.

Andriessen, Frans (1929–) Catholic politician; Dutch Minister of Finance 1977–80; European Commissioner for Trade, Competition, and Agriculture 1981–93.

Ansiaux, Hubert (1908–87) President of the European Payments Committee 1947–55; member of Managing Board of the European Payments Union 1950–55; National Bank of Belgium, Director 1941–54, Deputy Governor 1954–57, Governor 1957–71; BIS Board, alternate member 1944–55, member 1957–82; Chairman of the CoG 1967–71.

Arsenis, Gerasimos D. (1931–) Governor of the Bank of Greece 1981–84; Minister of National Economy 1982–85; Minister of Finance 1984–85; member of Hellenic Parliament 1985–2004 and 2006–08; member of the CoG 1981–83.

Baer, Gunter (1941–) Economist at the IMF, the German Ministry of Finance, and the BIS; joint rapporteur to the Delors Committee for the Study of Economic and Monetary Union 1988–89; Secretary General of the BIS 1994–2004; Secretary General of the CoG 1990–93.

Baffi, Paolo (1911–89) Banca d'Italia 1936, Head of Research Department 1944–56, Economic Adviser 1956–60, Director General 1960–75, Governor 1975–79;

463

external consultant for the BIS Annual Report 1956–60; BIS Board, alternate member 1960–75, member 1975–89, Vice-Chairman 1988–89.

Baker, James Addison III (1930–) Republican Party politician; White House Chief of Staff 1981–85 and 1992–93; Secretary of the Treasury 1985–88; Secretary of State 1989–92.

Balladur, Edouard (1929–) Gaullist politician; technical adviser in the office of Prime Minister Pompidou 1966–68; Presidency of the Republic, Under-Secretary General 1969–73, Secretary General 1973–74; Minister of Economy and Finances 1986–88; French Prime Minister 1993–95; President of Committee on Foreign Affairs, National Assembly, 2002–07.

Barber, Anthony (1920–2005) Conservative Party politician, United Kingdom; Chancellor of the Exchequer 1970–74.

Barre, Raymond (1924–2007) Gaullist politician; EEC Commissioner for Economic and Financial Affairs 1967–73; Minister of Foreign Trade 1976; Minister for the Economy 1976–78; French Prime Minister 1976–81.

Bascoul, André Gérard (1934–) Banque de France, economist in Domestic Economy Division 1956–65; BIS, economist and assistant to the Secretary General of the CoG 1965–90; head of BIS Secretariat for Eastern European Countries and International Organizations 1990–99.

Bastiaanse, Adriaan (1921–) De Nederlandsche Bank 1948, assistant to director for economic affairs 1969–74, substitute for the vice-director 1973–79, Vice-Director 1979–84; Chair of the CoG Monetary Policy Harmonization Group (Groupe d'experts sur l'harmonisation des instruments de la politique monétaire) 1974–80.

Bérégovoy, Pierre (1925–93) Socialist politician; French Minister of Economy and Finance 1984–86; Minister of Budget 1984–86; Minister of the Economy, Finance, and Privatization 1988–92; French Prime Minister 1992–93.

Blessing, Karl (1900–1971) German Reichsbank 1920–31, Director 1937–39; BIS 1931–34, member of Board 1958–69; adviser, Ministry of Economic Affairs, 1934–37; President of the Deutsche Bundesbank 1958–69.

Boutos, Ioannis (1925–) New Democrat (center-right) politician; Greek Minister of Finance 1977–78; Governor of the Bank of Greece 1993–94; member of the CoG 1993.

Boyer, Miguel (1939–) Socialist politician; Spanish Minister of Economy, Finance, and Trade 1982–85; member of the Delors Committee for the Study of Economic and Monetary Union 1988–89.

Brandt, Willy (1913–92) Socialist politician; German Foreign Minister 1966–69; German Chancellor 1969–74; member of the European Parliament 1979–83.

Brunet, Jacques (1901–90) Chairman and Managing Director of Crédit National 1949–60; Governor of the Banque de France 1960–69; member of the BIS Board 1960–69.

Callaghan, James (1912–2005) Labour Party politician; Chancellor of the Exchequer 1964–67; Home Secretary 1967–70; Secretary of State for Foreign and Commonwealth Affairs 1974–76; Prime Minister of the United Kingdom 1976–79.

Camdessus, Michel (1933–) French Ministry of Treasury 1960, Assistant Director 1971–74, Deputy Director 1974–82, Director 1982–84; Banque de France, Deputy Governor 1984, Governor 1984–87; Managing Director of the IMF 1987–2000; member of the BIS Board 1984–87; Chairman of the Paris Club 1978–84; Chairman of the Monetary Committee of the EEC 1982–84; member of the CoG 1984–86.

Carli, Guido (1914–93) Member of the Board of Directors of the IMF 1947; Chairman of the Managing Board of the European Payments Union 1950–52; Italian Minister for Foreign Trade 1957–58; Governor of the Banca d'Italia 1960–75; BIS Board, alternate member 1959–60, member 1960–75; Chairman of the CoG 1971–72.

Chalikias, Demetrios J. (1925–) Greek Ministry of Coordination 1951–54; Bank of Greece, Economic Research Division 1957–74, Economic Adviser 1974–81, Deputy Governor 1981–84, Chairman of Committee on Monetary and Credit Policy 1982–92, Governor 1984–92; CoG, member 1984–92, Chairman 1989.

Chirac, Jacques (1932–) Gaullist politician; Secretary of State for Economy and Finance 1968–71; French Prime Minister 1974–76 and 1986–88; President of France 1995–2007.

Christodoulou, Efthymios (1932–) Bank of Greece, Economic Adviser and Director 1959–74, Director General 1974–79, Governor 1979–81 and 1992–93; member of the European Parliament 1984–90 and 1994–99; Alternate Minister of Foreign Affairs 1990; Minister of National Economy 1990–92; member of the CoG 1992–93.

Ciampi, Carlo Azeglio (1920–) Banca d'Italia 1946, head of Research Department 1970–73, Secretary General 1973–75, Deputy Director General 1976–77, Director General 1978, Governor 1979–93; Italian Prime Minister 1993–94; BIS Board, member 1979–93, Vice-Chairman 1994–96; President of the EU Competitiveness Advisory Group 1995–96; Italian Minister of Treasury, Budget, and Economic Planning 1996–99; President of the IMF Interim Committee 1998–99; President of the Italian Republic 1999–2006; Permanent member of Italian Senate 2006–; CoG, member 1979–81, 1983–87, and 1988–93, Chairman 1982 and 1987.

Clappier, Bernard (1913–99) Director of foreign economic relations at French Ministry of Economic Affairs 1951–63; Banque de France, Second Deputy Governor 1963, First Deputy Governor 1966–72, Governor 1974–79; BIS Board, alternate member 1964–73, member 1974–94, Vice-Chairman 1983–85 and 1989–91; CoG, member 1974–79, Chairman 1979.

Clarke, Kenneth (1940–) Conservative Party politician, United Kingdom; Chancellor of the Exchequer 1993–97.

Connally, John (1917–93) Democratic, later Republican Party politician; U.S. Treasury Secretary 1971–72.

Constâncio, Vitor Manuel Ribeiro (1943–) Portuguese economist and politician; Secretary of State for Planning 1974–75; Minister of Finance 1978; Banco de Portugal, head of Research Department 1975, Deputy Governor 1979 and 1981–84, Governor 1985–86 and 2000–09; Vice-President of the Executive Board of the ECB, 2010–; member of the CoG 1985–86.

Couzens, Ken (1925–2004) Joint Second Permanent Secretary at the U.K. Treasury (overseas finance) 1977–83.

Crockett, Andrew D. (1943–) IMF staff 1972–89; Executive Director of the Bank of England 1989–93; member of the Monetary Committee of the EU 1989–93; Alternate Governor of the IMF for the United Kingdom 1989–93; member (subsequently chairman) of OECD Working Party 3 1989–93; General Manager of the BIS 1994–2003.

Dagassan, Jean-Claude André (1933–) BIS, employee in various departments (loans, banking, new building) 1957–78, EMS agent 1978–88, Assistant Manager and then head of the Private ECU Clearing section 1988–96.

Dalgaard, Henning (1930–) Danmarks Nationalbank, head of International Department 1972–78, head of Foreign Department 1979–86, Assistant Governor 1986–90; Chair of the CoG foreign exchange policy experts' group 1983–90.

D'Aroma, Antonio (1912–2002) Banca d'Italia 1936–61; Office of the President of the Italian Republic 1948–55, personal assistant to President Einaudi 1949–55; BIS, Secretary General 1962–74, Assistant General Manager 1975–77; Secretary General of the CoG 1964–77.

De Gaulle, Charles (1890–1970) French President 1959–1969.

De La Genière, Renaud (1925–90) French Director of the Budget, 1967–74; Governor of the Banque de France 1979–84; member of the BIS Board 1979–84; CoG, member 1979–82 and 1984, Chairman 1983.

De Larosière De Champfeu, Jacques (1929–) French Finance Ministry 1960–63; Ministry of the Treasury 1965–67, Deputy Director 1967–71, Director 1974–78; OECD 1967–71; Cabinet Director at the Presidency of the Republic 1974; Managing Director of the IMF 1978–87; Governor of the Banque de France 1987–93; member of the BIS Board 1987–93; President of the Governors of the Central Banks of the G-10 Countries 1990.

Delors, Jacques (1925–) Socialist politician; French Minister of Economy and Finance 1981–83; Economics, Finance, and Budget Minister 1983–84; President of the European Commission 1985–95; Chairman of the Committee for the Study of Economic and Monetary Union (Delors Committee), 1988–89.

De Strycker, Cecil (1915–2004) National Bank of Belgium, Director 1958–71, Deputy Governor 1971–75, Governor 1975–82; BIS Board, alternate member 1956–71, member 1975–89; CoG, member 1975–82, Chairman 1978–79.

Dini, Lamberto (1931–) IMF Executive Director for Italy, Greece, Portugal, and Malta 1976–79; Italian Treasury Minister 1994; Italian Prime Minister 1995–96; Minister of Justice 1995–96; Minister of Foreign Affairs 1996–2001.

Dondelinger, Albert Marie Joseph Nicolas (1934–) Alternate Governor for Luxembourg International Bank for Reconstruction and Development (World Bank) 1967–76; member of the EC Monetary Committee 1971–76; associate member of the IMF Interim Committee 1972–76; member of the EMCF Board 1973–76; Luxembourg Banking Control Commission 1959–76; Chairman of Luxembourg Bankers Association 1977–78; member of the CoG 1974–76.

Doyle, Maurice F. (1932–2009) Irish Department of Finance 1953, Second Secretary 1977–81, Secretary 1981–87; Central Bank of Ireland, Director 1981–87, Governor 1987–94; Vice-President of the EMI Council 1994; member of the CoG 1987–93.

Duisenberg, Willem Frederik ("Wim") (1935–2005) IMF staff 1965–69; De Nederlandsche Bank, adviser to Governing Board 1969–70, Executive Director 1981–82, President 1982–97; professor of macroeconomics at University of Amsterdam 1970–73; Dutch Minister of Finance 1973–77; member of Parliament 1977–78; EMI, member of the Council 1994–97, President 1997–98; President of the ECB 1998–2003; BIS, Board member 1982–88 and 1990–94, President and Chairman of the Board 1988–90 and 1994–97; CoG, member 1982–84 and 1986–92, Chairman 1985 and 1993.

Einaudi, Luigi (1874–1961) Professor of public finance at University of Turin 1902–49 and 1955; member of Senate, Kingdom of Italy, 1919–45; Governor of the Banca d'Italia 1945–48; member of the BIS Board 1945–48; Constituent Assembly 1946–48; Senate of the Italian Republic April–May 1948 and 1955–61; Minister of the Budget and Vice–Prime Minister 1947–48; President of the Italian Republic 1948–55.

Emminger, Otmar (1911–86) Bank deutscher Länder (from 1957 the Deutsche Bundesbank), member of the Board of Governors 1953; Central Bank Council, member 1958, Vice-President and Vice-Chairman 1970; Executive Board of the IMF 1953–59; Chairman of Group of Ten Deputies 1964–67; BIS Board, alternate member 1969–77, member 1977–79; President of the Deutsche Bundesbank 1977–79.

Fazio, Antonio (1936–) Governor of the Banca d'Italia 1993–2005; Chairman of the Italian Exchange Office 1993–2005; member of the BIS Board 1993–2005; member of the CoG 1993.

Ferras, Gabriel (1913–70) Banque de France 1938; Alternate Representative for France in the European Payments Union 1953–63; IMF, Alternate Executive Director of the Managing Board 1953, Deputy Director of Exchange Restrictions Department 1953–56, Director of European Department 1956–63; General Manager of the BIS 1963–70.

Fourcade, Jean-Pierre (1929–) Center-right politician; French Minister of Economy and Finance 1974–76.

Fowler, Henry (1908–2000) Democratic Party politician; Secretary of the U.S. Treasury 1965–68.

Genscher, Hans-Dietrich (1927–) Liberal (FDP = Freie Demokratische Partei) politician; German Federal Minister of the Interior 1969–74; Federal Minister for Foreign Affairs and Deputy Federal Chancellor 1974–92.

George, Edward ("Eddie") (1938–2009) Bank of England, Executive Director 1982–90, Deputy Governor 1990–93, Governor 1993–2003; BIS, economist 1966–69, member of the Board 1993–2009; Personal Assistant to the Chairman of Deputies of IMF's Committee on International Monetary Reform 1972–74; Chairman of the G-10 Governors 1999; member of the CoG 1993.

Giscard d'Estaing, Valéry (1926–) Center-right politician; French Secretary of State for Finances 1959–62; Minister of Finance and Economic Affairs 1962–66; Minister of the Economy and Finance 1969–74; President of the French Republic 1974–1981.

Godeaux, Jean (1922–2009) Member of the Belgian delegation at the IMF 1949–55; President of the Belgian Banking Commission 1974–79; member of the EC's Banking Advisory Committee 1979–82; Governor of the National Bank of Belgium 1982–90; BIS, member of the Board 1982–90, President and Chairman of the Board 1985–87; President of the EMCF 1988–89; CoG, member 1982–87 and 1989, Chairman 1988.

Healey, Denis (1917–) Labour Party politician, United Kingdom; Chancellor of the Exchequer 1974–79.

Heyvaert, François (1922–2008) National Bank of Belgium 1941, Head of Foreign Department 1979–80; Chair of the CoG foreign exchange policy experts' group 1974–82.

Hoffmeyer, Erik (1924–) Professor of economics at University of Copenhagen 1959–64; Danmarks Nationalbank Economics Counselor 1959–62; Chairman of the Board of Governors 1965–94; CoG, member 1973–93, Chairman 1975–76, 1979–81, and 1991–92.

Holtrop, Marius Wilhelm (1902–88) President of De Nederlandsche Bank 1946–67; BIS, member of the Board 1946–58, President and Chairman of the Board 1958–67; IMF, Alternate Governor 1947–52, Governor 1952–57; Chairman of the CoG 1964–67.

Jaans, Pierre (1936–) Deutsche Bundesbank, Research Department, 1962–72; OECD, Financial and Fiscal Affairs Department, 1972–74; Luxembourg Banking Supervision Authority 1975; Banking Commissioner 1976–83; Director General of the Luxembourg Monetary Institute 1983–98; Vice-Chairman of the Board of Foreign Exchange Institute for Belgium and Luxembourg; member of the CoG 1990–93.

Janson, Georges (1921–) National Bank of Belgium 1946, Director 1971–88; BIS, director in Banking Department 1962–71, alternate member of the Board 1971–88; alternate member of the CoG, 1978–79 and 1988.

Jenkins, Roy (1920–2003) Labour Party politician, United Kingdom; Chancellor of the Exchequer 1967–70; Home Secretary 1974–76; President of the European Commission 1977–81.

Klasen, Karl (1909–1991) President of the Deutsche Bundesbank 1970–77; Member of the BIS Board 1970–77; CoG, member 1970–1973 and 1974–1977, Chairman 1973–74.

Kohl, Helmut (1930–) Christian Democrat politician; German Chancellor 1982–1998.

Köhler, Horst (1943–) State Secretary in German Finance Ministry 1990–93; Managing Director of the IMF 2000–04; President of the Federal Republic of Germany 2004–10.

Lagayette, Philippe (1943–) Vice-Governor of the Banque de France 1984–92; alternate member of the CoG.

Lahnstein, Manfred (1937–) German Permanent Undersecretary of Finance 1977–80; Chief of Staff to Chancellor Helmut Schmidt 1980–82; Federal Minister of Finance 1982; Federal Minister of Economic Affairs 1982.

Lamfalussy, Alexandre (1929–) Belgian economist, banker, and civil servant; Executive Director and Chairman of the Executive Board, Banque de Bruxelles, 1965–75; BIS, economic adviser and head of the Monetary and Economic Department 1976–85, Assistant General Manager 1981–85, General Manager 1985–93; President of the EMI 1994–97.

Lamont, Norman (1942–) Conservative Party politician, United Kingdom; Chancellor of the Exchequer 1990–93.

Larre, René (1915–99) French civil servant; Inspector of Finances 1945; Minister Plenipotentiary responsible for financial matters at the French Embassy in Washington, D.C., 1961–67; French Executive Director of the IMF 1964–67; Head of the Treasury Department, Ministry of Economic and Financial Affairs, 1967–71; General Manager of the BIS 1971–81.

Lawson, Nigel (1932–) Conservative politician, United Kingdom; Chancellor of the Exchequer 1983–89.

Leigh-Pemberton, Robert ("Robin"), Baron Kingsdown (1927–) Governor of the Bank of England 1983–93; Vice-Chairman of the BIS Board 1996–2003; CoG, member 1983–85 and 1987–93, Chairman 1986–87.

Littler, Geoffrey (1930–2010) Chairman of the EC Monetary Committee 1987–88; Second Permanent Secretary at the U.K. Treasury.

Major, John (1943–) Conservative Party politician, United Kingdom; Secretary of State for Foreign and Commonwealth Affairs 1989; Chancellor of the Exchequer 1989–90; British Prime Minister 1990–97.

Marjolin, Robert (1911–86) European Commission, commissioner responsible for economics and finance 1958–62.

Martin, William McChesney (1906–81) Chairman of Board of Governors of the U.S. Federal Reserve 1951–70.

Matthöfer, Hans (1925–2009) Socialist politician; German Finance Minister 1978–82.

Mauroy, Pierre (1928–) Socialist politician; French Prime Minister 1981–84.

McDonough, William Joseph (1934–) President of the Federal Reserve Bank of New York 1993–2003.

Mingasson, Jean-Paul (1941–) Civil servant at the French Ministry of Economy and Finance 1968–1980; European Commission, Director then Deputy Director-General at the Directorate General for Economic and Financial Affairs (responsible for monetary affairs) 1982–89; Director-General of the Directorate General for Budget 1989–2002 and of the Directorate General for Enterprise and Industry 2002–04.

Mitterrand, François (1916–96) Socialist politician; President of the French Republic 1981–95.

Monnet, Jean (1888–1979) President of the High Authority of the European Coal and Steel Community 1952–55.

Morelli, Giampietro (1929–) Banca d'Italia, representative for Latin America 1962–63; Economic Commission for Africa, Regional Adviser 1964–66; EC Commission, Head of the Financial Institutions and Capital Markets Division 1966–69; Director of the Secretariat of the Monetary Committee 1969–78; BIS, Secretary General 1978–94.

Mosca, Ugo (1914–87) Civil servant and diplomat at Italian Ministry for Foreign Affairs 1939–67; European Commission, Director General of the Directorate General for Economic and Financial Affairs, 1967–79.

Muller, Huib (1936–91) Chairman of the EEC Banking Advisory Committee 1982–1985; Chairman of the Basel Committee on Banking Supervision 1988–91.

Mundell, Robert (1932–) IMF staff 1961–66; professor of economics at University of Chicago 1966–71; professor of international economics at Graduate Institute of International Studies in Geneva, Switzerland, 1965–75; professor of economics at Columbia University 1974–; adviser to international organizations including the United Nations, the IMF, the World Bank, the European Commission (consultant to the Monetary Committee in 1970, and a member of its Study Group on Economic and Monetary Union in Europe in 1972–73), several governments, the Federal Reserve Board, the U.S. Treasury; member of the Bellagio-Princeton Study Group on International Monetary Reform 1964–78; Chairman of the Santa Colomba Conferences on International Monetary Reform 1971–87.

Murray, Charles Henry (1917–) Irish Department of Finance, Assistant Secretary 1961, Secretary 1969–76; Central Bank of Ireland, Director 1969–76, Governor 1976–81; CoG, member 1976–77 and 1978–81, Chairman 1977–78.

Noyer, Christian (1950–) Head of the French Treasury 1993–95; Vice-President of the ECB 1998–2002; Governor of the Banque de France 2003–; BIS, member of the Board 2003–, Chairman of the Board 2010–.

O'Brien, Leslie Kenneth (1908–95) Bank of England 1927, Deputy Chief Cashier 1951–55, Chief Cashier 1955–62, Executive Director 1962–64, Deputy Governor 1964–66, Governor 1966–73; BIS Board, member 1966–73 and 1974–83, Vice-Chairman 1979–83; member of the CoG 1973.

Ó Cofaigh, Tomás F. (1921–) Secretary General at Irish Department of Finance 1977–81; Central Bank of Ireland, Director 1977–81, Governor 1981–87; CoG, member 1981–83 and 1985–87, Chairman 1984.

Ortoli, François-Xavier (1925–2007) Gaullist politician; French Minister of Economy and Finance 1968–69; President of the European Commission 1973–77.

Ossola, Rinaldo (1913–90) Banca d'Italia, Economic Research Department 1938, head of International Economics Division 1964–67, economic adviser 1967–69, Deputy Director General 1969–75, Director General 1975–76; member of Italian delegation to the Organization for European Economic Cooperation 1947–49; member of Italian delegation at the IMF and World Bank 1950s; Chairman of the G-10 Deputies Group 1967–76; member of the EC Monetary Committee, the Economic Policy Committee, and OECD Working Party 3 1969–75; member of the Committee of Twenty 1972–74; Italian Minister of Foreign Trade 1976–79.

Padoa-Schioppa, Tommaso (1940–2010) Banca d'Italia, Economic Research Department 1970–79, head of Money Market Department 1973–79, Director of Economic Research Department 1983–84, Deputy Director General 1984–97; economic adviser to the Italian Treasury 1978–79; EC Commission, Director General of Economic and Financial Affairs 1979–83, Chairman of the Banking Advisory Committee, 1988–91; member of Group of Thirty 1980–2010; joint rapporteur to the Delors Committee for the Study of Economic and Monetary Union 1988–89; Chairman of Basel Committee on Banking Supervision 1993–97; member of the ECB Executive Board 1998–2005; Italian Minister of Economy and Finance 2006–08; Chairman of the IMF International Monetary and Financial Committee 2007–08.

Pizarro Beleza, Luís Miguel Couceiro (1950–) Professor of economics at Universidade Nova de Lisboa 1987–90; Portuguese Minister of Finance 1990–91; economist at the IMF 1984–87; Banco de Portugal, member of the Board 1987–90, Governor 1992–94; member of the CoG 1992–93.

Pöhl, Karl Otto (1929–) Head of department at German Economics Research Institute Ifo (Information und Forschung) 1955–60; Manager at the Federal Association of German Banks 1968–69; various governmental positions 1970–77; Deutsche Bundesbank, Vice-President 1977–80, President 1980–91; West Germany's Governor at the IMF 1980–91; Chairman of the G-10 Group of Central Bank Governors 1983–89; COG, member 1980–89, Chairman 1990–91.

Pompidou, Georges (1911–74) Gaullist politician; French Prime Minister 1962–68; President of the French Republic 1969–74.

Prodi, Romano (1939–) Italian economist and politician; Minister of Industry, Commerce, and Craftsmanship 1978–79; President of the Institute for Industrial Reconstruction 1982–89 and 1993–94; Italian Prime Minister 1996–98 and 2006–08; President of the European Commission 1999–2004.

Quinn, Brian (1936–) Economist at the IMF 1964–70; Bank of England, Executive Director 1988, Acting Deputy Governor 1995.

Raymond, Robert (1933–) Banque de France, International Department 1964–75, Research Department 1975–90, Credit Department 1990–94; General Director of the EMI 1994–98; ECB representative in Washington, D.C., and at the IMF 1999; Chair of the CoG monetary policy experts' group 1981–91.

Rey, Jean-Jacques (1937–) National Bank of Belgium, head of the Foreign Department 1982–88, Executive Director 1988–2000; alternate member of the BIS Board of Directors 1988–2000; Chairman of the EMI Monetary Policy Subcommittee 1995–98; Chairman of the G-10 Working Party on the Resolution of Sovereign Liquidity Crises 1995–96; Chairman of Committee of Alternates of the CoG 1990–94.

Richardson, Gordon (1915–2010) Governor of the Bank of England 1973–83; BIS Board, member 1973–85 and 1988–91, Vice-Chairman 1985–88 and 1991–93; CoG, member 1973–76, 1977–81, and 1982–83, Chairman 1976–77 and 1981.

Rieke, Wolfgang (1929–98) German civil servant; Director of International Currency Department of Bundesbank, 1978–94.

Rojo, Luis Angel (1934–) Professor of economics at Complutense University of Madrid 1966–71; Banco de España, head of Research Department 1971–88, Deputy Governor 1988–92, Governor 1992–2000; Vice-President of the EMI Council 1994–98; Member of the CoG 1992–93.

Rubio Jimenez, Mariano (1931–99) Banco de España, Vice-Director of Research Department 1965, Vice-Governor 1977–84, Governor 1984–92; Director General at the Treasury Ministry 1970–72; Member of the CoG 1986–92.

Saccomanni, Fabrizio (1942–) Banca d'Italia, head of the Foreign Department 1984–97, Managing Director for International Affairs 1997, Director General, 2006–; Chairman of the EMI Foreign Exchange Policy Subcommittee 1991–97.

Sapin, Michel (1952–) Socialist politician; French Finance Minister 1992–93.

Sarcinelli, Mario (1934–) Banca d'Italia 1958, Vice-Director-General 1976–82; Director General of the Treasury 1982–91; President of EC Monetary Committee 1989–90; Vice-President of the European Bank for Reconstruction and Development, 1991–94.

Schiller, Karl (1911–94) Socialist politician; German Minister of Economic Affairs 1966–72; Minister of Finance 1971–72.

Schleiminger, Günther (1921–2008) Alternate member of the Managing Board of the European Payments Union for Germany and Chairman of the EPU Group of

Alternates 1952–58; Head of the division for European monetary questions at the Deutsche Bundesbank 1958–68; Executive Director for Germany at the IMF 1968–74; BIS, Secretary General 1975–78, Assistant General Manager 1978–81, General Manager 1981–85.

Schlesinger, Helmut (1924–) Bank deutscher Länder (from 1957 Deutsche Bundesbank) 1952, Head of Economics and Statistics Department 1964–80, member of the Executive Board and Central Bank Council 1972–80, Deputy President 1980–91, President 1991–93; Member of the CoG 1991–93.

Schmidt, Helmut (1918–) Socialist politician; German Minister of Economics 1972; Minister of Finance 1972–74; Chancellor of the German Federal Republic 1974–82.

Schulmann, Horst (1939–94) German Ministry of Finance, head of Fiscal Affairs Department 1977–78; Federal Chancellery, head of Finance Section 1978; State Secretary of German Ministry of Finance 1981–82; Chairman of the EC Monetary Committee 1982.

Schweitzer, Pierre-Paul (1912–94) Director of the French Treasury 1953–60; Managing director of the IMF 1963–73.

Snoy et d'Oppuers, Jean-Charles (1907–91) Secretary-General of the Belgian Ministry of Economic Affairs 1944–59; Head of the Belgian delegation to the Intergovernmental Conference on the Common Market and Euratom 1956–57; Belgian Minister of Finance 1968–72; President of the European League for Economic Cooperation 1982–84.

Stoltenberg, Gerhard (1928–2001) Christian Democrat politician; German Minister of Finance 1982–89.

Szász, André (1932–) De Nederlandsche Bank, economist 1960, member of the Executive Board responsible for international affairs 1973–94; alternate member of the Managing Board of the European Monetary Agreement; member of the Ansiaux Group dealing with monetary matters on behalf of the Werner Committee 1970; member of the EC Monetary Committee 1973–94; member of the G-10 Deputies Group and of Working Party 3 of the OECD; alternate member of the CoG 1973–94.

Tavares Moreira, José Alberto (1944–) Secretary of State of the Portuguese Treasury 1980–81; Secretary of State of the Ministry of Finance 1985–86; Banco de Portugal, Governor 1986–92, member of the Advisory Board 1992–; member of the CoG 1986–92.

Thatcher, Margaret (1925–) Conservative Party politician; British Prime Minister 1979–90.

Théron, Marcel (1915–1993) Banque de France 1939, deputy representative for France at the IMF 1958–59, Director General for external affairs 1967–74, Second Deputy Governor 1974–79, First Deputy Governor 1979–80; Chair of the CoG foreign exchange policy experts' group, 1972–74.

Thygesen, Niels (1934–) Danish Ministry of Economic Affairs 1961–64; Professor of economics at University of Copenhagen 1971–2004; Head of Monetary Division and Studies, OECD, Paris 1971–73; adviser to the Governor of the Danmarks Nationalbank 1973–83; Chairman of the Danish Economic Council 1983–85; member of the Swedish government's Advisory Group on Economic Crisis 1992–93.

Tietmeyer, Hans (1931–) Deutsche Bundesbank, member of the Board 1990–91, Vice-President 1991–93, President 1993–99; BIS Board, member 1993–2003, Vice-Chairman 2003–2010; member of the CoG 1993.

Trichet, Jean-Claude (1942–) French Ministry of Finance 1971–75; adviser to the President of the Republic 1978–81; head of International Affairs at the Treasury and Chairman of the Paris Club 1985–93; Head of Treasury, Deputy Governor of the IMF and World Bank 1987; Chairman of the EC Monetary Committee 1992–93; member of the EMI Board 1994–98; Governor of the Banque de France 1993–2003; President of the ECB 2003–11; member of the BIS Board 1993–2003 and 2006–11; member of the CoG 1993.

Triffin, Robert (1911–93) Belgian-American economist; Chief of Latin American Section, Board of Governors of the Federal Reserve System, 1942–46; IMF, Director of Exchange Control Division, Washington, 1946–48, head representative in Europe and observer at OEEC Payments Commission, Paris, 1948–49; alternate U.S. representative on Managing Board of the European Payments Union 1949–51; consultant with United Nations Economic Commissions for Europe, Africa, Asia, and the Far East, as well as international organizations, national ministries of finance, and central banks, 1951–93.

Vandeputte, Robert (1908–97) Professor of economics at the Catholic University of Leuven 1933–78; National Bank of Belgium, Acting Director 1943–44, Regent 1954–71, Governor 1971–75; member of the BIS Board 1971–75; Belgian Minister of Finance 1981; CoG, member 1971–75, Chairman 1974–75.

Van Ypersele de Strihou, Jacques (1936–) Inspector General of the Belgian Treasury 1976–78; consultant to the Belgian Ministers of Finance De Clercq, Geens, and Vandeputte 1973–81; President of the EC Monetary Committee 1978–79.

Verplaetse, Alfons (1930–) National Bank of Belgium, Director 1985–88, Vice-Governor 1988–89, Governor 1989–99; head of Economic Office in Prime Minister's Office 1982–88; member of the EMI Board of Governors 1994–98; BIS, member of the Board 1989–2009, President and Chairman of the Board 1997–99; member of the ECB Governing Council 1998–99; member of the CoG 1989–93.

Volcker, Paul (1927–) U.S. Treasury Under-Secretary for International Monetary Affairs 1969–74; President of the Federal Reserve Bank of New York 1975–79; Chairman of the Federal Reserve Board 1979–87.

Waigel, Theodor (1939–) Christian Democratic politician; German Minister of Finance 1989–98.

Werner, Pierre (1913–2002) Luxembourg Commissioner for Banking Control and government adviser 1945–49; Minister of Finance and Minister of Defense

1953–59; Prime Minister and Minister of Finance 1959–64; Prime Minister, Minister of Foreign Affairs, Minister of the Treasury, and Minister of Justice 1964–69; Prime Minister and Minister of Finance 1969–74; chair of the 1970 group studying the prospects for European economic and monetary union, which produced the Werner Plan, 1970–71.

Whitaker, Thomas Kenneth (1916–) Ireland, Department of Finance, Principal 1947–56, Secretary 1956–69; Governor of the Central Bank of Ireland 1969–76; member of the CoG 1973–76.

Wormser, Olivier (1913–85) Governor of the Banque de France 1969–74; member of the BIS Board 1969–74; Ambassador to the Federal Republic of Germany 1974–77; CoG, member 1969–74, Chairman 1972–73.

Zijlstra, Jelle (1918–2001) Christian Democratic politician; professor of theoretical economics at Free University, Amsterdam, 1948; Dutch Minister of Economic Affairs 1952–59; Minister of Finance 1959–63; Prime Minister of the Netherlands 1966–67; President of De Nederlandsche Bank 1967–81; President of the BIS and Chairman of the Board 1967–81; member of the CoG 1967–81.

Zolotas, Xenophon Euthymiou (1904–2004) Professor of economics at Athens University 1928–68; Governor of the Bank of Greece 1944–49, 1955–67, and 1974–81; Prime Minister of Greece 1989–90; member of the CoG 1981.

Members of the Committee of Governors

Bank/Name of governor	Served as member (attended meetings) from/to
National Bank of Belgium	
Hubert Ansiaux	July 1964–January 1971
Robert Vandeputte	February 1971–February 1975
Cecil de Strycker	March 1975–February 1982
Jean Godeaux	March 1982–June 1989
Alfons Verplaetse	July 1989–December 31, 1993
Danmarks National bank	
Erik Hoffmeyer	(March 1972) January 1973–December 31, 1993
Banque de France	
Jacques Brunet	July 1964–April 1969
Olivier Wormser	May 1969–June 1974
Bernard Clappier	July 1974–October 1979
Renaud de la Genière	November 1979–November 1984
Michel Camdessus	December 1984–December 1986
Jacques de Larosière	January 1987–August 1993
Jean-Claude Trichet	September–December 31, 1993
Deutsche Bundesbank	
Karl Blessing	July 1964–February 1970
Karl Klasen	March 1970–May 1977
Otmar Emminger	June 1977–December 1979
Karl Otto Pöhl	January 1980–June 1991
Helmut Schlesinger	July 1991–September 1993
Hans Tietmeyer	October–December 31, 1993

Bank of Greece

Zenophon Zolotas	November 1980–September 1981
Gerasimos D. Arsenis	October 1981–December 1983
Demetrios J. Chalikias	January 1984–January 1992
Euthemios Christodoulou	February 1992–October 1993
Ioanni Boutos	November–December 31, 1993

Central Bank of Ireland

Thomas Kenneth Whitaker	March 1972–February 1976
Charles Henry Murray	March 1976–October 1981
Tomàs F. Ó Cofaigh	November 1981–March 1987
Maurice F. Doyle	April 1987–December 31, 1993

Banca d'Italia

Guido Carli	July 1964–August 1975
Paolo Baffi	September 1975–September 1979
Carlo A. Ciampi	October 1979–May 1993
Antonio Fazio	June–December 31, 1993

Commissariat au contrôle des banques/Institut monétaire luxembourgeois

Albert Dondelinger	January 1974–October 1976
Pierre Jaans	November 1976–December 31, 1993

De Nederlandsche Bank

Marius Wilhelm Holtrop	July 1964–April 1967
Jelle Zijlstra	May 1967–December 1981
Willem Frederik Duisenberg	January 1982–December 31, 1993

Banco de Portugal

Vitor Manuel Ribeiro Constâncio	September 1985–May 1986
José Alberto Tavares Moreira	June 1986–April 1992
Luis Miguel Couceiro Pizarro Beleza	May 1992–December 31, 1993

Banco de España

Mariano Rubio	September 1985–June 1992
Luis Angel Rojo	July 1992–December 31, 1993

Bank of England

Leslie O'Brien of Lothbury	December 1971–June 1973
Gordon Richardson of Duntisbourne	July 1973–June 1983
Robin Leigh-Pemberton	July 1983–June 1993
Eddie George	July–December 31, 1993

Chairs of the Committee of Governors
Marius W. Holtrop 1964–1967
Hubert Ansiaux 1967–1971
Guido Carli 1971–1972
Oliver Wormser 1972–1973
Karl Klasen 1973–1974
Robert Vandeputte 1974–1975
Erik Hoffmeyer 1975–1976
Gordon Richardson 1976–1977
Charles Henry Murray 1977–1978
Cecil de Strycker 1978–1979
Bernard Clappier 1979
Erik Hoffmeyer 1979–1981
Gordon Richardson 1981
Carlo Ciampi 1982
Renaud de la Genière 1983
Tomás F. Ó Cofaigh 1984
Wim Duisenberg 1985
Robin Leigh-Pemberton 1986–1987
Carlo A. Ciampi 1987
Jean Godeaux 1988
Demetrios J. Chalikias 1989
Karl Otto Pöhl (elected for a three-year term) 1990–1991
Erik Hoffmeyer 1991–1992
Wim Duisenberg 1993

Chairs of Groups/Subcommittees
Foreign Exchange Policy
Marcel Théron 1972–1974
Pierre Barre 1974
François Heyvaert 1974–1982

Henning Dalgaard 1983–1990
Fabrizio Saccomanni 1991–1993

Monetary Policy
Adraan Bastiaanse 1974–1980
Robert Raymond 1981–1991
Antonio Borges 1991–1993
Lucas Papademos 1993

Banking Supervision
Brian Quinn 1990–1993

Appendix E

Committee for the Study of Economic and Monetary Union (Delors Committee), 1988–1989

Members

Jacques Delors (President)
Frans Andriessen
Miguel Boyer
Demetrius J. Chalikias
Carlo Azeglio Ciampi
Jacques de Larosière
Maurice F. Doyle
Willem F. Duisenberg
Jean Godeaux
Erik Hoffmeyer
Pierre Jaans
Alexandre Lamfalussy
Robert Leigh-Pemberton
Karl Otto Pöhl
Mariano Rubio
José Alberto Tavares Moreira
Niels Thygesen

Rapporteurs

Gunter Baer
Tommaso Padoa-Schioppa

481

Chairmen of the Monetary Committee of the European Community, 1958–1998

Emile van Lennep	June 1958–September 1969
Bernard Clappier	October 1969–December 1973
Conrad J Oort	January 1974–December 1975
Karl Otto Pöhl	January 1976–December 1977
Jacques van Ypersele de Strihou	January 1978–December 1979
Jean-Yves Haberer	January 1980–December 1981
Horst Schulmann	January 1982–November 1982
Michel Camdessus	November 1982–December 1984
Hans Tietmeyer	January 1985–September 1987
Sir Geoffrey Littler	September 1987–December 1988
Mario Sarcinelli	January 1989–December 1990
Cees Maas	January 1991–June 1992
Jean-Claude Trichet	June 1992–October 1993
Sir Nigel Wicks	October 1993–December 1998

European Commission Presidents and Commissioners for Economics and Finance, 1958–

Commission presidency			Commissioner responsible for economics and finance (monetary issues)		
Name	Country	Dates	Name	Country	Dates
Walter Hallstein	West Germany	1958–1967	Robert Marjolin	France	1958–1967
Jean Rey	Belgium	1967–1970	Raymond Barre	France	1967–1973
Franco Maria Malfatti	Italy	1970–1972			
Sicco Mansholt	Netherlands	1972–1973			
François-Xavier Ortoli	France	1973–1977	Wilhelm Haferkamp	West Germany	1973–1977
Roy Jenkins	United Kingdom	1977–1981	François-Xavier Ortoli	France	1977–1985
Gaston Thorn	Luxembourg	1981–1985			
Jacques Delors	France	1985–1994	Henning Christophersen	Denmark	1985–1994
Jacques Santer	Luxembourg	1994–1999	Yves-Thibault de Silguy	France	1994–1999
Manuel Marín	Spain	1999			
Romano Prodi	Italy	1999–2004	Pedro Solbes	Spain	1999–2004
José Manuel Barroso	Portugal	2004–	Joaquín Almunia	Spain	2004–2010
			Olli Rehn	Finland	2010–

Chronology

1950

July 1   European Payments Union in operation

1952

July 25   Beginning of European Coal and Steel Community

1957

March 25   Signing of Treaty of Rome establishing the European Economic
                Community

Aug. 1   Establishment of Deutsche Bundesbank

1958

Jan. 1   Treaty of Rome in effect

July 3–11   Stresa conference launches Common Agricultural Policy

1959

May   First meeting of ECOFIN (Council of Ministers of European
                Economic Community; economics and finance ministers)

1961

March 4   Revaluation of Deutsche Mark

March 6   Revaluation of Netherlands guilder

Dec. 18   IMF launches General Arrangements to Borrow (GAB)

Dec. 19–20   EEC agrees principles of Common Agricultural Policy (CAP)

1962

Oct. 29   EEC Commission submits Action Programme for the Second
                Phase of the EEC, envisaging monetary union as an objective
                of a further stage of the EEC's development

1964

March 12–13	Speculative attack against Italian lira
March 14	Italian Governor Guido Carli negotiates lira support arrangement in Washington
May 8	EEC Council of Ministers decision to create CoG
July 6	First meeting of CoG at the BIS in Basel

1965

June 30	France withdraws from intergovernmental EC negotiations ("empty chair crisis")

1967

Jan. 29	"Luxembourg compromise" requiring unanimity on key EC Council decisions ends the empty chair crisis
Nov. 18	Devaluation of British pound by 14.3 percent

1968

Nov. 20	G-10 summit in Bonn discusses balance-of-payments support for France

1969

Feb. 12	EEC Commission memorandum on policy coordination, including possibility of short-term monetary support and medium-term financial assistance
April 28	Resignation of General de Gaulle as French president
Aug. 8	Devaluation of French franc by 11.1 percent
Oct. 24	Revaluation of Deutsche Mark by 9.3 percent
Nov. 6	German Foreign Minister Walter Scheel declaration on economic and monetary union
Dec. 1–2	EEC summit in The Hague confirms intention to achieve economic and monetary union by stages

1970

Feb. 9	Agreement setting up a system of short-term monetary support among EEC central banks
Feb. 12	German proposals for four-stage move to economic and monetary union
March 5	Commission publishes plan in stages for EMU
March 6	Creation of Werner Committee
Oct. 7	Presentation of Werner Report, proposing to create EMU in three stages
Oct. 30	EEC Commission plan on economic and monetary union by stages submitted to the Council of Ministers
Nov. 23	Council of Ministers discusses and criticizes Werner Report

1971

Feb. 8–9	Council of Ministers approves plan in stages for EMU
May 9–10	Germany and Netherlands float currencies
Aug. 15	President Nixon suspends gold convertibility of dollar ("closing the gold window")
Dec. 18	G-10 Smithsonian agreement on new structure of exchange rates

1972

Jan. 22	Denmark, Ireland, Norway, and United Kingdom sign treaties of accession to EEC
April 10	Basel Accord: EEC Six limits fluctuation margin to 2.25 percent either side of central parity (the "Snake")
April 27	Commission Vice-President Raymond Barre proposes European Fund for Monetary Cooperation
May 1	Denmark, Ireland, and United Kingdom join Snake
May 23	Norway becomes associate member of Snake
June 23	United Kingdom and Ireland leave Snake
June 27	Denmark leaves Snake
Sept. 25	Norwegian referendum rejects accession to EEC
Oct. 10	Denmark rejoins Snake
Oct. 19–20	EEC summit in Paris agrees to create European Monetary Cooperation Fund and to make transition to Stage Two of economic and monetary union in 1974

1973

Jan. 1	Denmark, Ireland, and United Kingdom join the EEC
Feb. 12	Devaluation of the U.S. dollar by 10 percent
Feb. 13	Italy leaves Snake
March 2	Currency markets closed
March 11–12	EEC Council of Ministers reaffirms 2.25 percent fluctuation margins but ends fluctuation margins with dollar
March 12	CoG report on currency valuation
March 14	Norway and Sweden become associate members of Snake
March 19	Currency markets reopen
June 29	Snake realignment: revaluation of Deutsche Mark by 5.5 percent
Sept. 17	Snake realignment: revaluation of Netherlands guilder by 5 percent
Oct. 16	Arab oil embargo: first oil shock
Nov. 19	Revaluation of Norwegian krone by 5 percent

1974

Jan. 19	France leaves Snake
March 4	Harold Wilson (Labour) forms government in United Kingdom
March 18	Italy uses short-term monetary support
June 26	Failure of Herstatt Bank
Sept. 16	Fourcade plan for new exchange rate system presented to EC Council of Ministers
December	G-10 Basel Committee on Banking Regulations and Supervisory Practices created

1975

March 8	Marjolin report: "Europe is no nearer to economic and monetary union than in 1969."
March 10–11	First meeting of reformed European Council (heads of state or government with ministers of foreign affairs)
April 21	Introduction of European Unit of Account (EUA) as basket of nine currencies
May 9	France returns to Snake de facto (formally on 10 July)
Nov. 1	All Saints' Day Manifesto published in *Economist*

1976

January	Italy starts negotiations for IMF standby arrangement
March 15	France leaves Snake
July 26	Netherlands Finance Minister Wim Duisenberg proposes target zones for non-Snake members
Oct. 18	Snake realignment: revaluation of Deutsche Mark against Netherlands guilder and Belgian franc by 2 percent; devaluation of Swedish krona and Norwegian krone by 1 percent and of Danish krone by 4 percent

1977

Jan. 3	United Kingdom obtains two-year standby credit of SDR 3,360 million from IMF
April 4	Snake realignment: devaluation of Swedish krona by 6 percent, and of Norwegian krone and Danish krone by 3 percent
Aug. 28	Sweden suspends association agreement with Snake; central rates of Norwegian krone and Danish krone reduced by 5 percent
Oct. 27	EC Commission President Roy Jenkins speech in Florence on monetary union as goal of European Community

1978

Feb. 13	Snake realignment: devaluation of Norwegian krone by 8 percent
April 7–8	European Council summit in Copenhagen with "fireside chat" on monetary coordination

May 12	First meeting of British, French, and German representatives about European Monetary System (EMS)
July 6–7	European Council summit in Bremen with proposals by French President Giscard d'Estaing and German Chancellor Schmidt for "zone of monetary stability in Europe"
July 16–17	G-7 summit in Bonn presses Germany and Japan to undertake expansionary policies
Sept. 18	Council of Ministers agrees that the ECU will be at the center of the EMS
Oct. 16	Snake realignment: revaluation of Deutsche Mark by 4 percent against Danish krone and Norwegian krone, and by 2 percent against Netherlands guilder and Belgian franc
Nov. 1	German Chancellor Schmidt and Italian Prime Minister Giulio Andreotti meet in Siena
Nov. 20	ECOFIN meeting finalizes details of EMS
Nov. 30	Chancellor Schmidt explains the EMS at a Bundesbank Council meeting
Dec. 4–5	European Council meeting in Brussels agrees establishment of EMS
Dec. 12	CoG accepts "Agreement between the Central Banks of the Member States of the European Economic Community Laying Down the Operating Procedures for the European Monetary System"
Dec. 12	Norway leaves Snake

1979

Jan. 1	EUA replaced by ECU (European Currency Unit)
March 13	EMS in effect
May 3	Electoral victory of British Conservative Party led by Margaret Thatcher
June 7–10	First direct elections to European Parliament
Sept. 24	First EMS realignment: revaluation of Deutsche Mark by 2 percent, and devaluation of Danish krone by 3 percent
Nov. 30	EMS realignment: devaluation of Danish krone by 5 percent

1980

Nov. 17	EC Council of Ministers postpones transition to "consolidated EMS"

1981

Jan. 1	Greece joins the EC
March 23	EMS realignment: devaluation of Italian lira by 6 percent
May 10	Election of François Mitterrand as president of French Republic

Oct. 5   EMS realignment: revaluation of Deutsche Mark and Nether-
                         lands guilder by 5.5 percent against Belgian, Danish, and Irish
                         currencies, and devaluation of French franc and Italian lira
                         by 3 percent against Belgian, Danish, and Irish currencies

1982

Feb. 22   EMS realignment: devaluation of Danish krone by 3 percent
                         and of Belgian franc by 8.5 percent
June 4–6   G-7 summit at Versailles
June 14   EMS realignment: revaluation of Deutsche Mark and Nether-
                         lands guilder by 4.25 percent; devaluation of French franc by
                         5.75 percent, and of Italian lira by 2.75 percent
Aug. 12   Mexico applies for IMF support; start of Latin American debt
                         crisis
Sept. 17   In Germany, Helmut Schmidt's government replaced by
                         center-right coalition under Helmut Kohl

1983

March 21   EMS realignment: revaluations of Deutsche Mark (+5.5 percent),
                         Netherlands guilder (+3.5 percent), Danish krone (+2.5 percent),
                         and Belgian franc (+1.5 percent); devaluations of French franc
                         and Italian lira (–2.5 percent) and Irish pound (–3.5 percent)
May 20   Luxembourg Monetary Institute established as Luxembourg
                         central bank
May 28–30   G-7 summit in Williamsburg, Virginia, overshadowed by
                         monetary disputes

1985

Jan. 7   Jacques Delors becomes president of EC Commission
April 13–15   Informal ECOFIN meeting in Palermo approves CoG agreement
                         on strengthening the EMS
June 14   Commission White Paper on the completion of the internal
                         market; Schengen open-border agreement signed by Benelux
                         countries, France, and Germany
July 1   Greece joins EMS
July 22   EMS realignment: devaluation of Italian lira by 8 percent; Greek
                         drachma devalued, and Greece granted 1.75 billion ECU
                         Community loan
Sept. 22   G-5 finance ministers' meeting in New York produces agreement
                         on orderly depreciation of dollar
Dec. 2   European Council agrees to complete internal European market
                         by 1992

Dec. 16–17	Agreement on Single European Act (signed February 17 and 28, 1986)

1986

Jan. 1	Portugal and Spain join the EC
April 6–7	EMS realignment: devaluation of French franc by 3 percent; revaluations of Deutsche Mark and Netherlands guilder by 3 percent, and of Belgian franc and Danish krone by 1 percent
Aug. 4	EMS realignment: Irish pound devalued by 8 percent
Sept. 6	Meeting of U.S. and EC finance ministers at Gleneagles, Scotland

1987

Jan. 12	EMS realignment: revaluations of Deutsche Mark and Netherlands guilder by 3 percent and of Belgian franc by 2 percent
Feb. 21–22	Meeting of G-7 finance ministers in Paris produces Louvre accord and discussion of (global) target zones
May 13	Spain joins EMS
July 1	Single European Act in force
Sept. 8	Basel-Nyborg Agreement: CoG accepts "strengthening the operating mechanisms of the EMS"
Sept. 12	Informal ECOFIN meeting in Nyborg, Denmark, approves CoG agreement
Oct. 19	Stock market collapse on Wall Street
Nov. 10	Portugal joins EMS

1988

Jan. 8	French treasury memorandum proposes common central bank
Feb. 26	Genscher memorandum on "Creation of a European Currency Area and a European Central Bank"
June 27–28	European Council in Hanover agrees to form committee on EMU (Delors Committee)
Sept. 13	First meeting of Delors Committee at the BIS in Basel

1989

April 12–13	Final meeting of Delors Committee
May 19–20	Discussion of Delors Report by ECOFIN at S'Agaro, Spain
June 19	Spain joins exchange rate mechanism (ERM) with wider (6 percent) bands
June 26–27	European Council summit in Madrid accepts Delors follow-up proposals
Sept. 21	Spanish peseta and Portuguese escudo included in ECU basket
Nov. 9	Fall of Berlin Wall

Nov. 13	ECOFIN agrees on proposals to strengthen economic and monetary cooperation under the first stage of EMU; Council decision of May 8, 1964, amended to increase profile and role of CoG

1990

Jan. 5	EMS realignment: devaluation of Italian lira by 3.7 percent; Italy returns to 2.25 percent fluctuation margin in EMS
April 19	French President Mitterrand and German Chancellor Kohl suggest political union at beginning of 1993
April 28	European Council meeting in Dublin agrees to consideration of political union
June 11	Bundesbank President Pöhl proposes two-speed process for moving to monetary union based on small core of low-inflation countries
June 26–27	European Council meeting in Dublin asks CoG to undertake preliminary work for Intergovernmental Conference on European monetary union
July 1	Monetary union between Federal Republic of Germany and German Democratic Republic
July 1	Beginning of Stage One of EMU
Oct. 3	German unification
Oct. 8	British pound joins EMS/ERM with 6 percent fluctuation margins
Oct. 27–28	European Council meeting in Rome (Rome I): all member states except United Kingdom agree to start EMU Stage Two on January 1, 1994
Dec. 15–16	European Council meeting in Rome (Rome II) and first meeting of Intergovernmental Conference

1991

Jan. 8	British presentation of hard ECU proposal
Feb. 25	Third meeting of Intergovermental Conference on EMU agrees on budgetary rules, with British dissent
April 9	CoG approves draft statute of ECB
June 28–29	European Council meeting in Luxembourg
Dec. 9–10	European Council meeting in Maastricht agrees to draft treaty on European Union

1992

Feb. 7	Signing of Treaty on European Union at Maastricht, the Netherlands

April 6	Portugal joins ERM with 6 percent fluctuation bands
June 2	Danish referendum rejects EU Treaty
June 3	President Mitterrand announces French referendum on Maastricht
July 17	Bundesbank increases discount rate to 8.75 percent
Sept. 4–5	Informal ECOFIN meeting in Bath, United Kingdom
Sept. 8	CoG meeting discusses exchange market crisis
Sept. 14	EMS realignment: devaluation of Italian lira by 3.5 percent; revaluation of ten other currencies by 3.5 percent
Sept. 16	British pound leaves EMS
Sept. 17	Italian lira leaves ERM; devaluation of Spanish peseta by 5 percent
Sept. 20	French referendum narrowly supports the Maastricht Treaty
Oct. 16	European Council meeting in Birmingham, England, stresses need for greater economic convergence
Nov. 19	Swedish krona floats
Nov. 22	EMS realignments: devaluation of Spanish peseta and Portuguese escudo by 6 percent
Dec. 10	Norwegian krone floats

1993

Jan. 1	Single European Market in force
Feb. 1	EMS realignment: devaluation of Irish pound by 10 percent
May 14	EMS realignments: devaluation of Spanish peseta by 8 percent and of Portuguese escudo by 6.5 percent
Aug. 2	ERM bands raised from 2.25 or 6 percent to 15 percent
Nov. 1	Treaty on the European Union in effect

1994

Jan. 1	Stage Two of EMU in effect; EMI established with Alexandre Lamfalussy as president; CoG ceases to exist
Nov. 1	EMI completes move from Basel to Frankfurt am Main

1995

Jan. 1	Austria, Finland, and Sweden join EU
Jan. 9	Austrian schilling joins ERM
March 6	Devaluations of Spanish peseta by 7 percent and of Portuguese escudo by 3.5 percent
April 9	ECOFIN abandons 1997 as starting date for EMU
Dec. 15–16	European Council meeting in Madrid agrees on starting Stage Three in 1999 and on naming of single currency as the Euro

1996

May 15	Nederlandsche Bank Governor Wim Duisenberg nominated by EMI Council as president from July 1, 1997
Oct. 14	Finnish markka joins ERM
Nov. 25	After turbulent meeting of Monetary Committee, Italian lira rejoins ERM
Dec. 13–14	EU Council meeting in Dublin specifies principles for exchange rate mechanism in EMU Stage Three and the main elements of the stability pact

1997

May 12	EU Council of Ministers warns Italy that measures on public finances are not adequate to allow Italy to join EMU in 1999
June 1	Victory of French left in second round of parliamentary elections
June 16–17	EU Council meeting in Amsterdam reaches agreement on Stability and Growth Pact
Oct. 13	Four German professors take case on postponement of introduction of Euro to German Constitutional Court
Oct. 13	Duisenberg states that "ten or eleven" states could start EMU in 1999
Nov. 4	France proposes Governor Jean-Claude Trichet of the Banque de France as the first president of ECB
Dec. 13–14	European Council meeting in Luxembourg agrees to establish Euro X Council for ten countries adopting Euro in 1999

1998

March 14	Devaluation of Greek drachma by 13.8 percent; Greece joins ERM
March 25	Convergence reports of EU Commission indicate that eleven countries qualify to join Euro: Austria, Belgium, France, Finland, Germany, Ireland, Italy, Luxembourg, Netherlands, Portugal, and Spain. Denmark, Sweden, and United Kingdom would also qualify, but do not wish to be founding EMU members.
March 27	In a recommendation to the German government, Bundesbank approves eleven-country membership
April 3	German Constitutional Court rules introduction of Euro constitutional
May 1–2	European Council summit in Brussels reaches compromise on appointment of Duisenberg as first president of ECB; he states that he will retire "totally voluntarily" before the end of his first term

| June 1 | ECB established and EMI abolished |
| Dec. 31 | Euro created by "irrevocable locking" of exchange rates of eleven countries |

1999

| Jan. 1 | ERM II launched with Danish krone and Greek drachma |
| Feb. 20–21 | G-7 meeting in Bonn agrees on creating Financial Stability Forum, chaired by BIS General Manager Andrew Crockett, to promote international financial stability |

2002

| Jan. 1 | Physical circulation of Euro notes and coins |

Interest Rates and Fiscal Balance

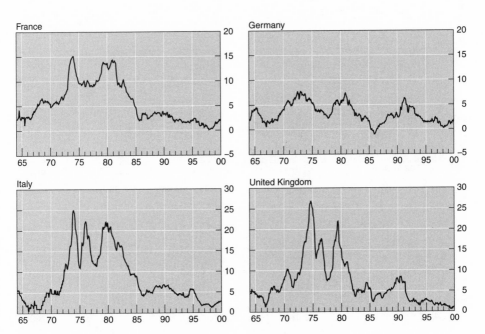

Figure AI.1. Inflation, 1965–2000: year-on-year percentage changes in consumer price index. *Note:* For Germany, figures are for West Germany before January 1991 and for unified Germany afterward. *Sources:* IMF, *IFS*; BIS; national sources.

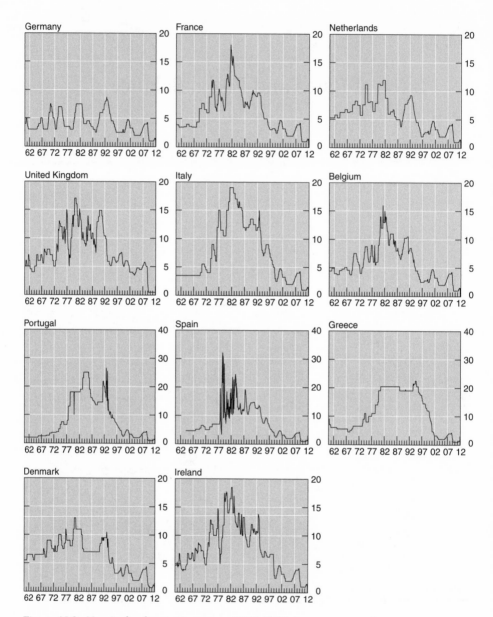

Figure AI.2. Nominal policy interest rates, 1960–2012, in percentages. *Sources:* Datastream; national data.

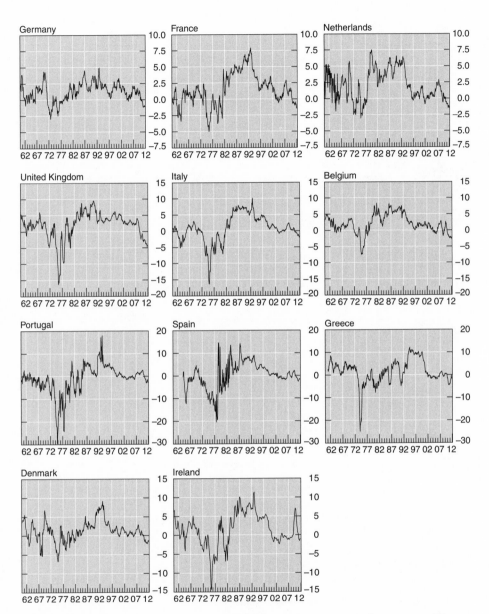

Figure AI.3. Real policy interest rates, 1960–2012, in percentages. Real rate = nominal policy rate minus 12-month change in consumer price index. *Sources:* Datastream; IMF, *IFS;* national data.

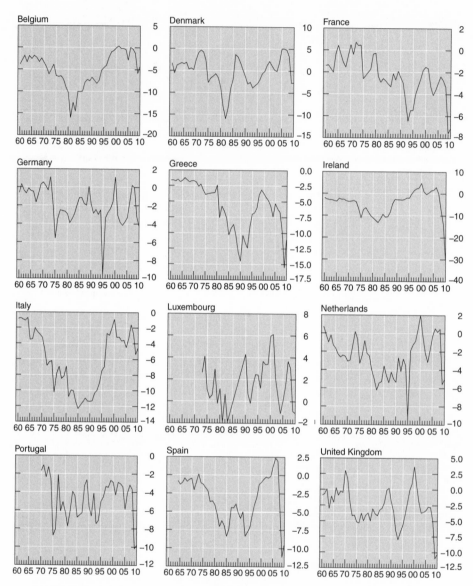

Figure AI.4. General government budget balances, 1960–2010, as a percentage of GDP. Budget balance = general government revenues minus total expenditure; a positive (negative) number indicates surplus (deficit). *Sources:* IMF World Economic Outlook database; OECD database.

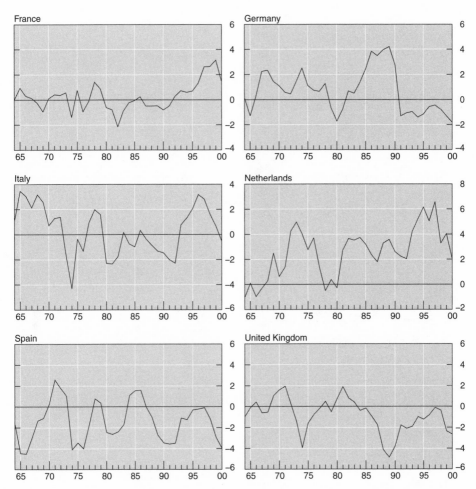

Figure AI.5. Current account balances, 1965–2000, as a percentage of GDP. A positive (negative) number indicates account surplus (deficit). *Note:* For Germany, from 1991 the balance-of-payments statistics include the external transactions of the former German Democratic Republic. *Sources:* OECD, *Economic Outlook;* European Commission, Annual Macro Economic database.

Notes

The following archival abbreviations are used in the notes.

AN	Archives Nationales, Paris
BdF	Banque de France archive, Paris
BIS	Bank for International Settlements archive, Basel
BoE	Bank of England archive, London
CAC	European Commission, central archives, Brussels
CMA	European Community, Council of Ministers Archive, Brussels
CoG	Committee of Governors files, European Central Bank, Frankfurt am Main
ECA	European Commission Archive
HADB	Historisches Archiv, Deutsche Bundesbank, Frankfurt am Main
IMF	International Monetary Fund archive, Washington, D.C.
NA	National Archive, London

Introduction

1. Milton Friedman, "Why Europe Can't Afford the Euro," *The Times,* November 19, 1997. The theme of political motivation also appears in Martin Feldstein, "The Failure of the Euro: The Little Currency That Couldn't," *Foreign Affairs,* January/February 2012, 105–116.
2. Jean Monnet, *Memoirs,* trans. Richard Mayne (London: Collins, 1978), p. 320.
3. http://www.telegraph.co.uk/finance/financialcrisis/8932640/Jacques-Delors-interview-Euro-would-still-be-strong-if-it-had-been-built-to-my-plan.html (accessed December 2, 2011).
4. Interview of October 27, 2011, in *Bild am Sonntag.* See http://www.bis.org/review/r111102c.pdf (accessed May 22, 2012).
5. Karl Griewank, *Gneisenau: Ein Leben in Briefen* (Leipzig: Koehler und Amelang, 1939), p. 175.
6. A. W. Phillips, "The Relationship between Unemployment and the Rate of Change of Money Wages in the United Kingdom 1861–1957," *Economica*

25 (1958), 283–299; Milton Friedman, "The Role of Monetary Policy," *American Economic Review* 68/1 (1968), 1–17.

7. See Appendix B.

8. A number of these have Internet identities—http://www.g10.org; http://www .g20.org—that also describe their historical development. A very large selection of documents produced by the CoG is available on the website of the European Central Bank: www.ecb.europa.eu.

9. Robert O. Keohane and Joseph S. Nye, *Power and Interdependence* (Boston: Little, Brown, 1977), p. 152.

10. Anne-Marie Slaughter, *A New World Order* (Princeton: Princeton University Press, 2005).

11. Georg Friedrich Knapp, *Staatliche Theorie des Geldes* (Leipzig: Duncker & Humblot, 1905).

12. Aristotle, *Nicomachean Ethics* 5.5, trans. W. D. Ross: "money has become by convention a sort of representative of demand; and this is why it has the name 'money' [*nomisma*]—because it exists not by nature but by law [*nomos*] and it is in our power to change it and make it useless"; http://classics .mit.edu/Aristotle/nicomachean.5.v.html (accessed December 1, 2011).

13. Matthew 22:21.

14. Eric Helleiner, *The Making of National Money: Territorial Currencies in Historical Perspective* (Ithaca: Cornell University Press, 2003).

15. Henry B. Russell, *International Monetary Conferences, Their Purposes, Character, and Results, with a Study of the Conditions of Currency and Finance in Europe and America during Intervening Periods, and in Their Relations to International Action* (New York: Harper & Brothers, 1898), p. 35; John Stuart Mill, *Principles of Political Economy with Some of Their Applications to Social Philosophy* (London: Parker Son and Bourn, 1862), pp. 371–372.

16. See Michael D. Bordo and Lars Jonung, eds., *Lessons for EMU from the History of Monetary Unions* (London: Institute of Economic Affairs, 2000).

17. Otmar Issing, "Currency Competition and European Monetary Union," Institute of Economic Affairs Occasional Paper 111, 2000, p. 31.

18. Niels Thygesen, "Perspectives on Europe's Monetary Unification," University of Copenhagen, Economic Policy Research Unit Analysis No. 23 (2004), p. 4.

19. Robert Skidelsky, *John Maynard Keynes: Fighting for Freedom, 1937–1946* (New York: Viking, 2000), p. 221.

20. Luigi Einaudi, *La guerra e l'Unità Europea* (Milan: Edizioni di Comunita, 1948), pp. 39–40; see also Pier Luigi Porta, "Libertà, mercato, giustizia sociale," in *Luigi Einaudi: Libertà economica e coesione sociale*, ed. Alfredo Gigliobianco (Rome: Laterza, 2010), p. 39.

21. See Benn Steil and Manuel Hinds, *Money, Markets, and Sovereignty* (New Haven: Yale University Press, 2009).

22. Aristotle, *Politics* 1.9. See also Curzio Gianninni, *The Age of Central Banks* (London: Edward Elgar, 2011); Carl Menger, *Grundsätze der volkswirthschaftslehre* (Vienna: W. Braumüller, 1871).

23. J. Peter Burgess and Bo Stråth, "Money and Political Economy: from the Werner Plan to the Delors Committee and Beyond," in *From the Werner Plan to the EMU: In Search of a Political Economy for Europe*, ed. Lars Magnusson and Bo Stråth (Brussels: Peter Lang, 2001), p. 128.

24. Tommaso Padoa-Schioppa, *Explaining the Euro to a Washington Audience* (Washington, D.C.: Group of Thirty, 2001), p. 13.

25. "Italian Debt Soars on EU Bail-out Fears," *Daily Telegraph*, October 18, 2011.

26. Robert A. Mundell, "A Theory of Optimum Currency Areas," *American Economic Review* 51 (1961), 509–517; Ronald I. McKinnon, "Optimum Currency Areas," *American Economic Review* 53 (1963), 717–725: Peter B. Kenen, "The Theory of Optimum Currency Areas: An Eclectic View," in *Monetary Problems of the International Economy*, ed. Robert Mundell and Alexandre Swoboda (Chicago: University of Chicago Press, 1969), pp. 41–60. See also Barry Eichengreen and Tamin Bayoumi, "Shocking Aspects of European Monetary Unification," in *Growth and Adjustment in the European Monetary Union*, ed. Francisco S. Torres and Francesco Giavazzi (Cambridge: Cambridge University Press, 1993), pp. 193–229.

27. Xavier Sala-i-Martin and Jeffrey Sachs, "Fiscal Federalism and Optimum Currency Areas: Evidence for Europe from the United States," in *Establishing a Central Bank: Issues in Europe and Lessons from the United States*, ed. Matthew B. Canzonieri, Vittorio Grilli, and Paul R. Masson (Cambridge: Cambridge University Press, 1992), pp. 195–219; and Tamim Bayoumi and Paul R. Masson, "Fiscal Flows in the United States and Canada: Lessons for Monetary Union in Europe," *European Economic Review* 39 (1995), 253–274. For a counterargument, see Jürgen von Hagen, "Fiscal Arrangements in a Monetary Union—Some Evidence from the U.S.," in *Fiscal Policy, Taxes, and the Financial System in an Increasingly Integrated Europe*, ed. Don Fair and Christian de Boissieux (Deventer: Kluwer, 1992).

28. Harold James, "The Historical Development of the Principle of Surveillance," *IMF Staff Papers* 42/4 (1995), 762–791; also James, *International Monetary Cooperation since Bretton Woods* (New York and Washington, D.C.: Oxford University Press and International Monetary Fund, 1996).

29. Philippe Jurgensen, *Ecu: Naissance d'une monnaie* (Paris: J. C. Lattès, 1991), p. 145.

30. Martin Feldstein, "EMU and International Conflict," *Foreign Affairs,* November/December 1997, 60–73; Milton Friedman, "Auf Kosten Dritter," *Capital,* July 11, 2001.

31. CoG, Fourth meeting of Delors Committee, December 13, 1988, transcript.

32. Quoted in Andreas Wilkens, "Der Werner-Plan: Währung, Politik und Europa 1968–1971," in *Aufbruch zum Europa der zweiten Generation: Die europäische Einigung 1969–1974,* ed. Franz Knipping and Matthias Schönwald (Trier: Wissenschaftlicher Verlag Trier, 2005), p. 231.

33. "Euro Rules 'Stupid' Says Prodi," *Financial Times,* October 18, 2002.

34. Council Regulations of June 27, 2005, 1055/2005 and 1056/2005.

35. See Hyun Song Shin, "Global Banking Glut and Loan Risk Premium," IMF Annual Research Conference Mundell-Fleming Lecture, November 10–11, 2011; also Shin, "Global Savings Glut or Global Banking Glut," VoxEU, December 20, 2011, http://www.voxeu.org/index.php?q=node/7446 (accessed December 28, 2011); Markus Brunnermeier, "European Debt Crisis," lecture at Princeton University, October 27, 2011.

36. For instance, G. Edward Griffin, *The Creature from Jekyll Island: A Second Look at the Federal Reserve* (Appleton, Wis.: American Opinion Publishing, 1994); Ron Paul, *End the Fed* (New York: Grand Central Publishing, 2009).

37. David M. Andrews, "Building Capacity: The Institutional Foundations of EMU," European Union Center Scripps College, Working Paper 2000, at http://eucenter.scrippscollege.edu/docs/wp/00andrews-buil.pdf (accessed December 1, 2011).

38. See Peter M. Haas, "Introduction: Epistemic Communities and International Policy Coordination," *International Organization* 46/1 (Winter 1992), 1–35. The concept was developed, on the basis of Michel Foucault's use of the episteme as a dominant way of looking at social reality, by John Ruggie, "International Responses to Technology: Concepts and Trends," *International Organization* 29 (Summer 1975), 569–570. See also G. John Ikenberry, "A World Economy Restored: Expert Consensus and the Anglo-American Postwar Settlement," *International Organization* 46/1 (Winter 1992), 289–321.

39. Anthony R. Zito, "Epistemic Communities, Collective Entrepreneurship and European Integration," *Journal of European Public Policy* 8/4 (2001), 590.

40. Horst Ungerer, *A Concise History of European Monetary Integration: From EPU to EMU* (Westport, Conn.: Quorum, 1997), p. 61.

41. HADB, ZBR 325 meeting, November 4, 1970.

42. July 5 meeting, in *Akten zur Auswärtigen Politik der Bundesrepublik Deutschland, 1971,* vol. 2 (Munich: Oldenbourg, 2002), doc. 228, pp. 1062–64.

43. Gianni Toniolo with the assistance of Piet Clement, *Central Bank Cooperation at the Bank for International Settlements, 1930–1973* (New York: Cambridge University Press, 2005), p. 443.

44. Ibid.

45. Gunter D. Baer, "The Committee of Governors as a Forum for European Central Bank Cooperation," in *Monetary Stability through International Cooperation: Essays in Honour of André Szász,* ed. Age Bakker (Dordrecht: Kluwer, 1994), pp. 154–155. See also David M. Andrews, "The Committee of Central Bank Governors as a Source of Rules," *Journal of European Public Policy* 10/6 (2003), 956–973.

46. Alain Peyrefitte, *C'était de Gaulle* (Paris: Gallimard, 2002), pp. 603, 663.

47. Quoted in Jonathan Story, "The Launching of the EMS: An Analysis of Change in Foreign Economic Policy," *Political Studies* 36 (1988), 397.

48. NA, PREM 16/1615, Couzens note for Wicks, March 31, 1978; PREM 16/1641, Prime Minister's conversation with Mr. Roy Jenkins, March 31, 1978.

1. A Napoleonic Prelude

1. See Luca Einaudi, *Money and Politics: European Monetary Unification and the International Gold Standard (1865–1873)* (Oxford: Oxford University Press, 2001).

2. Walter Bagehot, *A Practical Plan for Assimilating the English and American Money as a Step towards a Universal Money* (1869; reprint, London: Longmans Green, 1889), pp. vii–viii.

3. Ibid., p. 53.

4. Karl Helfferich, *Das Geld* (Leipzig: C. L. Hirschfeld, 1903), pp. 528, 530.

5. "Some Notes on Spain's Document on the ECU and the ESCB during Stage Two," Ministerio de Economia y Hacienda, February 15, 1991, http://ec.europa.eu/economy_finance/emu_history/index_en.htm (accessed December 1, 2011); quotes from Bagehot, *Universal Money,* p. 22.

6. Stresemann speech of September 9, 1929; "Société des Nations," *Journal Officiel,* spec. suppl. 75 (1929), 70.

7. John Hicks, *Critical Essays in Monetary Theory* (Oxford: Oxford University Press, 1967), p. 172.

8. Lars Jonung and Eoin Drea, "The Euro: It Can't Happen, It's a Bad Idea, It Won't Last: U.S. Economists on the EMU, 1989–2002," European Economy—Economic Papers 395, Directorate General Economic and

Monetary Affairs, European Commission, 2009, available at http://ec.europa
.eu/economy_finance/publications/publication16345_en.pdf (accessed December 1, 2011).

9. For example, the approach of Andrew Moravcsik, *The Choice for Europe: Social Purpose and State Power from Messina to Maastricht* (Ithaca: Cornell University Press, 1998). Moravcsik was criticized as Panglossian by Perry Anderson, *The New Old World* (London: Verso, 2009), p. 103.

2. The Origins of the Committee of Governors

1. See Ferenc Janossy, *The End of the Economic Miracle* (White Plains, N.Y.: International Arts and Sciences Press, 1971).

2. Harold James, *The End of Globalization: Lessons from the Great Depression* (Cambridge Mass.: Harvard University Press, 2001).

3. Jean-Jacques Servan-Schreiber, *Le défi américain* (Paris: Denoël, 1967).

4. Andrew Moravcsik, "De Gaulle between Grain and Grandeur: The Political Economy of French EC Policy, 1958–1970," *Journal of Cold War Studies* 2/2 (2000), 11.

5. Robert Triffin, *Gold and the Dollar Crisis: The Future of Convertibility* (New Haven: Yale University Press, 1960).

6. Tommaso Padoa-Schioppa, "The European Monetary System: A Long-Term View," in *The European Monetary System,* ed. Francesco Giavazzi, Stefano Micossi, and Marcus Miller (Cambridge: Cambridge University Press, 1988).

7. See Erin E. Jacobsson, *A Life for Sound Money: Per Jacobsson, His Biography* (Oxford: Oxford University Press, 1979), especially pp. 242–243; Alec Cairncross, *Years of Recovery: British Economic Policy, 1945–51* (London: Methuen, 1985); Christoph Buchheim, *Die Wiedereingliederung Westdeutschlands in die Weltwirtschaft, 1945–1958* (Munich: R. Oldenbourg, 1990); Barry Eichengreen, ed., *Europe's Post-War Recovery* (Cambridge: Cambridge University Press, 1995); Gianni Toniolo with the assistance of Piet Clement, *Central Bank Cooperation at the Bank for International Settlements, 1930–1973* (New York: Cambridge University Press, 2005), pp. 327–349. The authoritative history of the EPU is Jacob J. Kaplan and Günther Schleiminger, *The European Payments Union: Financial Diplomacy in the 1950s* (Oxford: Clarendon Press, 1989).

8. Barry Eichengreen, *The European Economy since 1945: Coordinated Capitalism and Beyond* (Princeton: Princeton University Press, 2007), pp. 84–85.

9. Paul Valéry, "Notes sur la grandeur et la décadence de l'Europe," in *Regards sur le monde actuel* (Paris: Stock, Delamani et Boutelleau, 1931),

p. 51. For the later use of Valéry's thought, see Michel Jobert's February 14, 1974, press conference, Aurelie Gfeller, "Re-Envisioning Europe: France, America and the Arab World, 1973–1974" (Ph.D. diss., Princeton University, 2008), p. 173.

10. Marius W. Holtrop, "Is a Common Central Bank Policy Necessary within a United Europe?" *De Economist* 105 (1957), 642–661; see also Willem F. V. Vanthoor, "Een oog op Holtrop: Grondlegger van de Nederlanse monetaire analyse" (Ph.D. diss., Amsterdam University, 1991).

11. BdF, 1489200205/46, November 10, 1957, Holtrop: Aide-Mémoire sur la collaboration entre banques centrales des pays du Marché Commun; January 13, 1958, Memorandum: Collaboration entre Banques Centrales des Pays du Marché Commun.

12. HADB, Direktorium meetings, November 4 and November 11, 1958.

13. HADB, B330/272, Holtrop to E. M. Bernstein (commenting on an article that Bernstein had published in the *Wall Street Journal*), January 24, 1961.

14. EEC, Mémorandum de la Commission sur le programme d'action de la Communauté pendant la deuxième étape, October 24, 1962, Brussels, p. 76.

15. Ibid., p. 80. See also EEC Commission, *Seventh General Report on the Activities of the Community (1 April 1963–31 March 1964)*, June 1964.

16. "Rumore," *Corriere della sera,* October 1, 1960, 1, reproduced in translation in *Luigi Einaudi: Selected Economic Essays,* ed. Luca Einaudi, Riccardo Faucci, and Roberto Marchionatti (Basingstoke: Palgrave Macmillan, 2006), 182–186.

17. BdF, 1489200205/46, Note, December 10, 1962.

18. BdF, 1489200205/46, minutes of Matignon meeting (November 9): Comité interministériel pour les questions de coopération Européenne, November 13, 1962.

19. BdF, 1489200205/46, December 5, 1962, Guindey (BIS) to Brunet.

20. BdF, 1489200205/46, December 7, 1962, Brunet to Holtrop; December 12, 1962, Note pour le Gouverneur.

21. Deutsche Bundesbank, *Auszug aus Presseartikeln* 9/63 (January 27, 1963), 1–3. See also Hubert Zimmermann, "The Fall of Bretton Woods and the Emergence of the Werner Plan," in *From the Werner Plan to the EMU: In Search of a Political Economy for Europe,* ed. Lars Magnusson and Bo Stråth (Brussels: Peter Lang, 2001), p. 58.

22. *Agence Europe,* no. 1590, July 1, 1963.

23. Banca d'Italia, Carli papers, 71/7/6, Italian-American Discussions of March 10–12 [1964]. See also Memorandum of conversation, March 11, 1964, in *Foreign Relations of the United States, 1964–1968,* ed. James E. Miller and David S. Patterson, vol. 12 (Washington, D.C.: Department of

State, 2001), doc. 93, pp. 180–183; Giorgio Fodor, "I prestiti internazionali all'Italia del 1964," in *Ricerche per la storia della Banca d'Italia,* vol. VII-1: *Stabilità e sviluppo negli anni Cinquanta. L'Italia nel contesto internazionale,* ed. F. Cotula (Laterza: Collana Storica della Banca d'Italia, 2001).

24. *Keesings Contemporary Archives,* 1964, 20281A.
25. Toniolo, *Central Bank Cooperation,* p. 385.
26. CAC, BAC 565/1995/206, Bericht über die 58. Tagung des Währungs-ausschusses, April 2, 1964.
27. Robert Triffin, "The Return to Convertibility, 1926–1931 and 1958–? Or Convertibility and the Morning After," *Quarterly Review, Banca Nazionale del Lavoro* 48 (March 1959), 3–57; and Triffin, *Gold and the Dollar Crisis.*
28 64/300/EEC, OJ P 77, May 21, 1964, p. 1206.
29. For instance, HADB, B330/18436 Schlüter memorandum: Betr. Tagung des Gouverneursausschusses am 11. Juli 1989, B330/018436, July 5, 1989.
30. Robert Marjolin, *Le travail d'une vie* (Paris: Robert Laffont, 1986), p. 305.
31. See Gunter D. Baer, "The Committee of Governors as a Forum for European Central Bank Cooperation," in *Monetary Stability through International Cooperation: Essays in Honour of André Szász,* ed. Age Bakker (Dordrecht: Kluwer, 1994); David M. Andrews, "Building Capacity: The Institutional Foundations of EMU," European Union Center Scripps College, Working Paper 2000, at http://eucenter.scrippscollege.edu/docs/wp/00andrews-buil.pdf (accessed December 1, 2011).
32. See David M. Andrews, "The Committee of Central Bank Governors as a Source of Rules," *Journal of European Public Policy* 10/6 (2003), 961–962.
33. CoG, Meeting 1, July 6, 1964, Basel. Up to Meeting 223, the minutes were in French; the texts quoted have been translated by the author.
34. CoG, Meeting 1, July 6, 1964.
35. CoG, Meeting 2, October 12, 1964, Basel.
36. CoG, Meeting 7, July 12, 1965, Basel.
37. See Charles A. Coombs, *The Arena of International Finance* (New York: John Wiley, 1976), pp. 53–57; Kristen Howell, "The Role of the Bank for International Settlements in Central Bank Cooperation," *Journal of European Economic History* 22/2 (1993), 377–378; Toniolo, *Central Bank Cooperation,* pp. 384–386.
38. See Catherine Schenk, *The Decline of Sterling: Managing the Retreat of an International Currency, 1945–1992* (Cambridge: Cambridge University Press, 2010).
39. See also Forrest Capie, *The Bank of England, 1950s to 1979* (Cambridge: Cambridge University Press, 2010).
40. CoG, Meeting 8, September 13, 1965, Brussels.
41. Capie, *Bank of England,* p. 217.

42. CoG, Meeting 12, May 9, 1966, Basel.
43. CoG, Meeting 13, July 11, 1966, Basel.
44. See Harold James, *International Monetary Cooperation since Bretton Woods* (New York and Washington, D.C.: Oxford University Press and International Monetary Fund, 1996), pp. 170–171; Alain Prate, *Les batailles économiques du Général de Gaulle* (Paris: Plon, 1978).
45. CoG, Meeting 18, May 8, 1967, Basel.
46. CoG, Meeting 20, September 11, 1967, Basel.
47. CoG, Meeting 19, July 11, 1966, Basel.
48. CoG, Meeting 25, July 8, 1968, Basel.
49. HADB, ZBR 269 meeting, July 18, 1968.
50. CoG, Meeting 26, September 10, 1968, Rotterdam.
51. "Raymond Barre, 83, Former French Premier, Dies," *New York Times*, August 27, 2007.
52. CoG, Meeting 29, March 10, 1969, Basel.

3. The Response to Global Monetary Turbulence

1. Amy Verdun, "The Political Economy of the Werner and Delors Reports: Continuity amidst Change or Change amidst Continuity," in *From the Werner Plan to the EMU: In Search of a Political Economy for Europe*, ed. Lars Magnusson and Bo Stråth (Brussels: Peter Lang, 2001), pp. 73–96.
2. *Report to the Council and the Commission on the Realization by Stages of Economic and Monetary Union in the Community*, October 8, 1970, http://ec .europa.eu/economy_finance/emu_history/documentation/chapter5 /19701008en72realisationbystage.pdf (accessed December 1, 2011); also *Bulletin of the European Communities* 11, suppl. (1970).
3. Hubert Zimmermann, "The Fall of Bretton Woods and the Emergence of the Werner Plan," in Magnusson and Stråth, *From the Werner Plan to the EMU*, p. 67.
4. Hubert Zimmermann, *Money and Security: Troops, Monetary Policy, and West Germany's Relations with the United States and Britain, 1950–1971* (Cambridge: Cambridge University Press, 2002), pp. 226–227.
5. *Community Topics 34, Economic and Monetary Union* (Brussels: EEC, 1972), p. 16.
6. Horst Ungerer, *A Concise History of European Monetary Integration: From EPU to EMU* (Westport, Conn.: Quorum, 1997), p. 61.
7. CoG, Meeting 27, December 9, 1968, Basel.
8. CoG, Meeting 29, March 10, 1969, Basel.
9. European Commission, Memorandum to the Council on the co-ordination of economic policies and monetary co-operation within the Community,

February 12, 1969, http://ec.europa.eu/economy_finance/emu_history/documentation/chapter2/19690212en015coordineconpoli.pdf (accessed December 1, 2011).

10. HADB, B330/7050, March 1, 1969, Emminger: Betr. "Monetärer Mechanismus" (Devisenbeistand).

11. CoG, Meeting 29, March 10, 1969.

12. CoG, Meeting 33, September 8, 1969, Basel; Meeting 34, November 17, 1969, Basel; Meeting 25, December 8, 1969, Basel.

13. HADB, ZBR 303 meeting, December 4, 1969.

14. CoG, June 23, 1969, Zijlstra to Ansiaux and Wormser to Ansiaux.

15. Zimmermann, "Fall of Bretton Woods," pp. 68–69. Willy Brandt, *Begegnungen und Einsichten 1960–1975* (Hamburg: Hoffmann und Campe, 1976), p. 322; Andreas Wilkens, "Der Werner-Plan: Währung, Politik und Europa 1968–1971," in *Aufbruch zum Europa der zweiten Generation: Die europäische Einigung 1969–1974,* ed. Franz Knipping and Matthias Schönwald (Trier: Wissenschaftlicher Verlag Trier, 2005), pp. 221–222; Andreas Wilkens, ed., *Interessen verbinden: Jean Monnet und die europäische Integration der Bundesrepublik Deutschland* (Bonn: Bouvier, 1999), pp. 409–412; Gérard Bossuat, "Drei Wege nach dem Gipfel von Den Haag. Monnet, Brandt, Pompidou und das Europa der 70er Jahre," in Wilkens, *Interessen verbinden,* p. 260.

16. Wilkens, "Der Werner-Plan," pp. 226–227; also see Hans Tietmeyer, *Währungsstabilität für Europa: Beiträge, Reden und Dokumente zur europäischen Währungsunion aus vier Jahrzehnten* (Baden-Baden: Deutsche Bundesbank, 1996), pp. 88–94.

17. Zimmermann, "Fall of Bretton Woods," p. 66.

18. Ivo Maes, "Projets d'intégration monétaire à la Commission européenne au tournant des années 1970," in *Milieux économiques et intégration européenne au XXe siècle: Les crises d'année 1970,* ed. Eric Bussière, Michel Dumoulin, and Sylvain Schirmann (Brussels: Peter Lang, 2006), p. 44.

19. *Bulletin of the European Communities* 1 (1970), 11–16, quote on 15.

20. Matthias Kaelberer, *Money and Power in Europe: The Political Economy of European Monetary Cooperation* (Albany: State University of New York Press, 2001), p. 118, quoting *Handelsblatt,* November 28/29, 1969.

21. February 12, 1970, Memorandum: Grundlinien eines Stufenplanes zur Verwirklichung der Wirtschafts- und Währungsunion in der EWG http://ec.europa.eu/economy_finance/emu_history/documentation/chapter4/19700212memorandumgrundlinieneines.pdf.

22. HADB, N2/153, April 2, 1970, Vermerk: Besprechung im Bundeswirtschaftsministerium am 26. März 1970; N2/155, April 15, 1970, Schöllhorn Aufzeichnung: Wirtschafts- und Währungsunion.

23. Bossuat, "Drei Wege," p. 372.
24. CoG, Meeting 37, March 9, 1970, Basel.
25. July 4, 1968, Robert Triffin: "Mémorandum relative aux questions moné-taires." See also Bossuat, "Drei Wege," p. 356.
26. IMF, April 7, 1970, SM/70/69, "The Mechanism of Exchange Rate Adjust-ment: Proposals with Respect to Exchange Rate Flexibility."
27. Bossuat, "Drei Wege," p. 358.
28. CoG, Meeting 37, March 9, 1970.
29. Ibid.
30. Banca d'Italia, Studi 629, August 1, 1972, Carli to Wormser.
31. CoG, Meeting 38, April 13, 1970, Basel.
32. HADB, N2/155, April 2, 1970, Vermerk Betr. Besprechung im Bundeswirtschaftsministerium am 26. März 1970.
33. CoG, Meeting 38, April 13, 1970.
34. CoG, Meeting 39, May 11, 1970, Basel.
35. CoG, Meeting 40, May 29, 1970, Venice.
36. Wilkens, "Der Werner-Plan," p. 231; HADB, N2/156, June 1, 1970, Jen-nemann Vermerk (on May 29–30, 1970, finance ministers' meeting); N2/156, Wortlaut der Erklärung von Wirtschaftsminister Prof. Schiller; HADB, ZBR 314 meeting, May 13, 1970, and 315 meeting, June 3, 1970.
37. HADB, N2/156, September 21, 1970, Jenneman and Dörner Vermerk.
38. HADB, N2/156, June 8, 1970, Emminger to Schöllhorn.
39. *Report to the Council and the Commission on the Realization by Stages of Economic and Monetary Union in the Community.*
40. Ibid., p. 8.
41. Ibid., pp. 11–12.
42. Ibid., pp. 17–18.
43. Ibid., p. 25.
44. Ibid., p. 26.
45. Ibid., p. 27.
46. CoG, letter of June 12, 1970; see Meeting 42, July 6, 1970, Basel.
47. CoG, Meeting 43, September 12, 1970, Basel.
48. CoG, Meeting 47, March 6, 1971, Basel.
49. John Williamson, "How Werner's Plan Could Help the British," *The Times,* January 19, 1971.
50. CoG, Meeting 43, September 12, 1970.
51. CoG, Meeting 44, November 8, 1970, Basel.
52. CoG, Meeting 45, March 6, 1971, Basel.
53. HADB, 325 meeting of ZBR, November 4, 1970.
54. HADB, N2/153, November 12, 1970, Betr. Ressortbesprechung am 11. November 1970: Werner-Bericht.

516 Notes to Pages 82–90

55. HADB, N2/K26(4), December 30, 1970, Emminger to Alwin Münchmeyer; December 23, 1970, Emminger to Schöllhorn.
56. HADB, ZBR 325 meeting, November 4, 1970.
57. Wilkens, "Der Werner-Plan," p. 239; Bossuat, "Drei Wege," p. 374.
58. Eric Roll, "Why the Common Market Is Still Incomplete," *The Times*, November 16, 1970.
59. *Journal official des Communautés Européennes*, 1970, C-140/20–26, October 30, 1970.
60. CoG, Meeting 44, November 8, 1970.
61. HADB, N2/K44(1), Emminger: Vermerk, Werner-Bericht und Vorschläge der Europäischen Kommission.
62. CoG, Meeting 45, December 12, 1970.
63. "Pompidou-Brandt Gespräch," January 25, 1971, in *Akten zur Auswärtigen Politik der Bundesrepublik Deutschland, 1971,* 2 vols. (Munich: Oldenbourg, 2002), doc. 27, 1:118–119.
64. Report of Poensgen on Council meeting of February 8–9, February 10, 1971, ibid., doc. 59, 1:294–296.
65. HADB, B330/7050, March 4, 1971, Betr. Aufzeichnung über die Sitzung des EWG-Währungsausschusses am 3.März 1971.
66. IMF, CF C/Germany/810, May 3, 1971, memorandum: April 30, 1971 meeting.
67. HADB, B330/7050, May 7, 1971; Betr. Sitzung des EWG-Währungsausschusses am 6.Mai 1971.
68. CoG, Meeting 50, June 12, 1971, Basel.
69. HADB, B330/7050, May 27, 1971, Vermerk: Sitzung des EWG-Währungsausschusses am 26.5.1971.
70. July 5 meeting, in *Akten zur Auswärtigen Politik der Bundesrepublik Deutschland, 1971,* doc. 228, 2:1062–64; also Brandt, *Begegnungen,* p. 342.
71. July 5 meeting, in *Akten zur Auswärtigen Politik der Bundesrepublik Deutschland, 1971,* doc. 229, 2:1065.
72. CoG, Meeting 51, July 11, 1971, Basel.
73. Zimmermann, "Fall of Bretton Woods," p. 62.
74. CoG, Meeting 53, November 8, 1971, Basel.

4. The Snake and Other Animals

1. Conrad J. Oort, *Steps to International Monetary Order* (Washington, D.C.: Per Jacobsson Foundation, 1974), p. 48; HADB, N2/K26 (2), Oort speech of May 11, 1976; also in Banca d'Italia, Studi 619.
2. Review of Giovanni Magnifico, *European Monetary Unification* (London: Macmillan, 1973), in CoG, 1158.

3. For an elaboration of this theme, see Harold James, *Europe Reborn: A History, 1914–2000* (Harlow, U.K.: Pearson Longman, 2003).

4. Robert Marjolin, "Report of the Study Group 'Economic and Monetary Union 1980,'" March 1975, p. 1; available at http://aei.pitt.edu/1009/1/monetary_study_group_1980.pdf (accessed December 1, 2011).

5. See Amy Verdun, "The Political Economy of the Werner and Delors Reports: Continuity amidst Change or Change amidst Continuity," in *From the Werner Plan to the EMU: In Search of a Political Economy for Europe,* ed. Lars Magnusson and Bo Stråth (Brussels: Peter Lang, 2001), pp. 73–96.

6. HADB, N2/K51(1), May 5, 1974, EEC Commission: Note concernant les taches du Comité des Gouverneurs des Banques Centrales.

7. Douglas C. Kruse, *Monetary Integration in Western Europe: EMU, EMS and Beyond* (London: Butterworth, 1980), p. 73.

8. *Bulletin of the European Communities* 9 (1973), 91. See also Jérôme Wilson, "De la création d'un marché international des capitaux à l'unification monétaire de l'Europe: Une initiative belge et privée," in *Milieux économiques et intégration européenne au XXe siècle: Les crises d'année 1970,* ed. Eric Bussière, Michel Dumoulin, and Sylvain Schirmann (Brussels: Peter Lang, 2006), pp. 69–85.

9. François-Xavier Ortoli, "The Personality of Europe and Economic and Monetary Union," speech, New York, September 26, 1974.

10. CoG, Meeting 60, June 10, 1972, Basel.

11. Ministerialdirigent Bömcke on EEC Council meeting of August 19, August 20, 1971, in *Akten zur Auswärtigen Politik der Bundesrepublik Deutschland, 1971,* 2 vols. (Munich: Oldenbourg, 2002), doc. 276, 2:1250–56.

12. CAC, BAC 565/1995/313, Monetary Committee, September 2, 1971.

13. "Un front commun européen," *Le Monde,* September 25, 1971.

14. BIS, March 6, 1972, RL (Larre) memorandum: Chronologie relative à la création éventuelle d'un Sécretariat Permanent du Comité des Gouverneurs de la C.E.E.

15. BIS, March 6, 1972, RL: Possibility of setting up a permanent secretariat for the Committee of Governors of EEC Central Banks; see also Banca d'Italia, Studi 628, March 2, 1972; BIS, March 6, 1972, RL (Larre) memorandum.

16. CoG, Meeting 56, February 14, 1972, Basel.

17. Banca d'Italia, Studi 628, February 18, 1972, O'Brien to Carli.

18. French Economics Ministry, Archives ME B12533, May 13, 1972, Pierre-Brossolette, Note sur la réforme du système monétaire international.

19. CoG, Théron Pre-report, January 8, 1972.

20. ECOFIN, March 21, 1972.

21. Patrick Halbeisen, "Cool Lover? Switzerland and the Road to European Monetary Union," in *European Central Banks and Monetary Cooperation after 1945*, ed. Piet Clement and Juan Carlos Martinez Oliva (Frankfurt am Main: Adelmann, 2006), pp. 99–117.

22. CoG, Meeting 58, April 10, 1972, Basel.

23. Ibid.

24. CoG, October 15, 1973, Preliminary Opinion to the Council on the Report of the Commission on the Adjustment of Short-Term Monetary Support Arrangements and the Conditions for the Progressive Pooling of Reserves.

25. CoG, June 21, 1973, Carli to Klasen (chairman of CoG).

26. CoG, Committee of Alternates, October 31, 1977: Report to the Committee of Governors on the Belgian Proposals for Improving Mutual Assistance Arrangements within the Community.

27. 71/143/EEC, March 22, 1971, Decision Setting up Machinery for Medium-Term Financial Assistance.

28. CoG, August 1, 1972, Carli to Wormser.

29. CoG, Meeting 64, November 11–13, 1972, Basel.

30. BoE, 6A/103/2, J.L.S., September 9, 1972: An Assessment of Our Experience in the Narrower Margins Scheme.

31. See CoG, Théron Group, Report No. 17, January 2, 1974.

32. BoE, 6A/103/2, August 16, 1972: I.E.T. note.

33. CoG, Meeting 61, July 10, 1972, Basel.

34. HADB, B330/7542 II, March 12, 1973: Stellungnahme der Praesidenten der EWG-Zentralbanken zur Frage des Wertmassstabes.

35. Harold James, *International Monetary Cooperation since Bretton Woods* (New York and Washington, D.C.: Oxford University Press and International Monetary Fund, 1996), p. 242.

36. HADB, B330/7051, Flandorffer: Bericht über die Sitzung des Währungsausschusses am 14. Februar 1973.

37. See CoG, Théron Group, Report No. 17, January 2, 1974.

38. Kruse, *Monetary Integration*, pp. 131–132.

39. See Otmar Emminger, "Deutsche Geld- und Währungspolitik im Spannungsfeld zwischem innerem und äusserem Gleichgewicht (1948–1975)," in *Währung und Wirtschaft in Deutschland 1876–1975*, ed. Deutsche Bundesbank (Frankfurt am Main: Fritz Knapp, 1976), p. 536.

40. CoG, Théron Group, Report No. 17, January 2, 1974.

41. HADB, B330/7051, January 22, 1974, Betr. Aussprache im EWG-Währungsausschuss am 21.1.1974.

42. CoG, Théron Group, Report No. 17, January 2, 1974.

43. CoG, Meeting 65, December 11, 1973, Basel.

44. CoG, May 17, 1974: Resolution of the Committee of Governors Concerning a Strengthening of Co-Ordination of the Central Banks' Monetary and Credit Policies.

45. See Charles Goodhart, *The Basel Committee on Banking Supervision: A History of the Early Years, 1974–1997* (Cambridge: Cambridge University Press, 2011), pp. 12–15.

46. "A World Banking Crisis?" *The Economist,* August 3, 1974.

47. See Goodhart, *Basel Committee.*

48. Ibid., p. 39.

49. HADB, B330/7052, February 7, 1975, Résumé de la discussion du Comité Monétaire.

50. CAC, BAC 565/1995/336, May 17, 1973, Monetary Committee: Reserve Assets and Convertibility.

51. CoG, Meeting 64, November 11–13, 1972.

52. BdF, 1430200701/5, April 26, 1972: Utilité d'un Fond dans la mise en oeuvre du régime de change spécifique à la Communauté.

53. BdF, 1430200701/5, April 29, 1972: Organisation et Statut d'un Fond Européen de Coopération Monétaire.

54. CoG, Meeting 60, June 10, 1972. See also report, June 1, 1972: Fonds Européen de Coopération Monétaire.

55. CoG, Meeting 61, July 10, 1972.

56. BoE, 6A/103/3, December 1972 Treasury Note: European Monetary Cooperation Fund.

57. Gérard Bossuat, "Drei Wege nach dem Gipfel von Den Haag. Monnet, Brandt, Pompidou und das Europa der 70er Jahre," in *Interessen verbinden: Jean Monnet und die europäische Integration der Bundesrepublik Deutschland,* ed. Andreas Wilkens (Bonn: Bouvier, 1999), p. 383.

58. CoG, Meeting 65, December 11, 1972.

59. CoG, Meeting 66, January 8, 1973, Basel; BoE, 6A/103/3, December 1972 Treasury Note: European Monetary Cooperation Fund.

60. HADB, N2/K44(1), January 9, 1973, Emminger to Pöhl; N2/K42(3), February 23, 1973, Bundesministerium der Finanzen: Betr. Europäischer Fonds für währungspolitische Zusammenarbeit.

61. CoG, Meeting 71, June 17, 1973, Basel.

62. CoG, Théron Group, Report No. 10, March 5, 1973.

63. CoG, Meeting 68, March 12, 1973, Basel, discussion of Théron Group, Report No. 10.

64. CoG, Meeting 64, November 11, 1972. For a concise summary of the "link" discussion, see John Williamson, *Understanding Special Drawing Rights (SDRs)* (Washington, D.C.: Peterson Institute for International Economics, 2009), p. 2.

65. Banca d'Italia, Studi 632, March 1, 1974, Hoffmeyer to Clasen.
66. CoG, Meeting 66, January 8, 1973.
67. EC Réglement 907/73.
68. BoE, 7A3/7, March 3, 1974: March 12, 1974, meeting.
69. CoG, Meeting 69, April 9, 1974, Basel.
70. Banca d'Italia, Studi 633, October 21, 1974, Avis du Comité des Gouverneurs au Conseil.
71. BoE, 7A3/7, March 5, 1974: March 12, 1974, meeting.
72. BoE, 7A3/7, February 13, 1974, M.J.B.: Meeting at Luxembourg, February 12.
73. HADB, N2/K44(1), January 9, 1973, Emminger to Pöhl.
74. CoG, January 8, 1975: Eléments de réflexions pour l'échange de vues du Comité des Gouverneurs sur les mandats donnés par le Conseil.
75. EC Réglement 397/75, February 17, 1975.
76. Banca d'Italia, Studi 658, October 10, 1975, Apunto; Studi 618, November 21, 1975, Draft Report to the Monetary Committee of the Ad Hoc Group United Kingdom.
77. CoG, Meeting 89, March 11, 1975, Basel; European Parliament, February 18, 1975, *Official Journal of the European Communities: Debates of the European Parliament*, no. 186 (1975), 93–94, quotation of Haferkamp on 97; and *avis* of February 18, 1975.
78. John B. Goodman, *Monetary Sovereignty: The Politics of Central Banking in Western Europe* (Ithaca: Cornell University Press, 1992), p. 154.
79. CoG, Meeting 101, May 11, 1976, Basel.
80. CoG, Meeting 103, July 13, 1976, Basel.
81. CoG, Meeting 106, December 6, 1976, Basel.
82. Marcello de Cecco, "Italy's Payments Crisis: International Responsibilities," *International Affairs* 51/1 (January 1975), 10.
83. IMF, CF C/Italy/810, December 23, 1976, L. A. Whittome note.
84. IMF, CF C/Italy/810, January 12, 1977, D. W. Green note.
85. CoG, Meeting 114, September 13, 1977, Basel.
86. Banca D'Italia, Studi 639, October 18, 1977, Jennemann to Magnifico.
87. BoE, 7A3/4, October 19, 1972: Meeting of Monetary Committee of EEC, October 16–17.
88. BoE, 7A3/4, October 12, 1972, Cassell: EEC Monetary Committee.
89. CoG, Meeting 63, October 18, 1972, Paris.
90. Ibid.
91. HADB, N2/K78(8), November 1, 1972, cable of German Permanent Representative in EEC: EC-Ratstagung vom 30/31 Oktober 1972 in Luxemburg.

92. HADB, Central Bank Council meeting 426, December 5, 1974.

93. BoE, 7A3/7, February 13, 1974, M.J.B. Meeting at Luxembourg, February 12, 1974.

94. CoG, Meeting 80, May 14, 1974, Basel.

95. BoE, 7A3/13, A.J.G.W., July 6 1976: EEC Governors' Meeting, Item 4.

96. BoE, 7A3/12, June 23, 1976: EEC Central Bank Governors.

97. HADB, N2/K26(8), March 21, 1976: Vermerk: Zur Frage der Existenz-berechtigung der von Herrn Bastiaanse geleiteten Arbeitsgruppen.

98. CoG, Meeting 80, May 14, 1974; Meeting 83, September 10, 1974, Basel.

99. BoE, 7A3/10, May 13, 1975, P. Gray Note: EEC Working Group on Harmonisation of Monetary Policy Instruments, Meeting of February 25–26.

100. CoG, Meeting 98, February 10, 1976, Basel.

101. HADB, N2/K78(8), May 25, 1978, Jennemann: Betr. Festlegung der Geldmengenziele in der EWG.

102. CoG, Meeting 108, February 8, 1977, Basel. See also BoE, 7A3/14, March 2, 1977, note on Meeting of EEC Governors, February 8.

103. BoE, 6A50/23, October 13, 1977: Publication of SUERF [Société Universitaire Européenne des Recherches Financières] Paper.

104. CoG, Meeting 104, September 14, 1976, Basel.

105. CoG, Meeting 103, July 12, 1977.

106. HADB, N2/K26(10), February 11, 1977, Vermerk Betr. 4. Programm (Dörner). Also EC Commission decision COM 77/620.

107. HADB, N2/K42(8), June 8, 1977, Betr.: Periodische Prüfungen (Jennemann).

108. CoG, Meeting 119, March 14, 1978, Basel.

109. CoG, Meeting 118, February 12, 1978, Basel.

110. CoG, March 14, 1978, Report on Improving the Co-ordination of National Economic Policies.

111. CoG, Meeting 116, December 13, 1977, Basel.

112. Ibid.

113. AN, 5AG3/2697, Note pour le Ministre August 29, 1974, (Jacques de Larosière); see also Emmanuel Mourlon-Druol, *A Europe Made of Money: The Emergence of the European Monetary System* (Ithaca: Cornell University Press, 2012), pp. 36–37.

114. AN, DAEF Carton 971 bis, La relance monétaire européen, September 16, 1974; also Mourlon-Druol, *Europe Made of Money*, pp. 37–38.

115. CoG, September 24, 1974, Boyer de la Giroday to Pierre Barre and André Bascoul (CoG).

116. HADB, N2/K51(5), September 16, 1974, Communication du Président du Conseil.

522 Notes to Pages 134–137

117. See J. J. Polak, "The SDR as a Basket of Currencies," *IMF Staff Papers* 26/4 (1974), 627–653; Polly Reynolds Allen, "Artificial Currencies: SDRs and ECUs," *Open Economies Review* 4/1 (1993), 97–110.

118. CoG, July 26, 1974, European Community OR II/430/74-F, Rapport du Groupe "Emprunts Communautaires."

119. See Margaret Garritsen de Vries, *The International Monetary Fund, 1972–1978: Cooperation on Trial* (Washington, D.C: IMF, 1985), p. 286.

120. CoG, Meeting 84, September 30, 1974, Washington, D.C.

121. Jacques van Ypersele, *The European Monetary System: Origins, Operation and Outlook* (Brussels: Commission of the European Communities, 1984), p. 44.

122. HADB, N2/K51(5), September 26, 1974, Betr. Sitzung des Ausschusses der EWG-Notenbankgouveneure am 30.9.1974 in Washington. Also see Banca d'Italia, Studi 633, September 25, 1974, note on Barre's oral report to the CoG.

123. See Amaury de Saint-Périer, "La France et la sauvegarde du système communautaire de change de 1974 à 1977," in Bussière, Dumoulin, and Schirmann, *Milieux économiques et intégration euopéenne*, p. 54.

124. CoG, December 4, 1974, Report of the Monetary Committee on Joint Floating.

125. CoG, Meeting 88, February 11, 1975, Basel.

126. CoG, Meeting 86, December 10, 1974, Basel; also HADB, N2/K44(2), December 12, 1974, Emminger to Pöhl; B330/7052, December 5, 1974, Jennemann Betr.: Stellungnahme des Währungsausschusses am 4.12.1974.

127. CoG, Meeting 88, February 11, 1975.

128. CoG, March 7, 1975, Heyvaert: Mise en oeuvre d'une politique commune de change: Compte rendu secret; Banca d'Italia, Studi 634, meeting of March 3–4, 1975.

129. CoG, Meeting 89, March 11, 1975.

130. Banca d'Italia, Studi 618, June 16, 1975, Summary of Snake Ministers' and Governors' Discussion. BdF, 1489200205/57, November 16, 1979, EEC Note.

131. Marjolin, "Report of the Study Group 'Economic and Monetary Union 1980,'" p. 1.

132. AN, CAEF, B0050484, Note pour le ministre de Jacques de Larosière, April 18, 1975: Réflexions sur une rentrée éventuelle du franc dans le "Serpent." See in general Mourlon-Druol, *Europe Made of Money*, p. 53.

133. CoG, Meeting 90, April 8, 1975, Basel.

134. CoG, Heyvaert Report No. 30; discussion in Meeting 89, March 11, 1975.

135. HADB, B330/7053, June 10, 1975, memorandum on June 9, 1975, Monetary Committee meeting.

136. The European Unit of Account was defined as the sum of the following monetary amounts: Deutsche Mark 0.828; British pound 0.0885; French franc 1.15; Italian lire 109; Netherlands guilder 0.286; Belgian franc 3.66; Luxembourg franc 0.14; Danish krone 0.217; Irish pound 0.00759.

137. CoG, Banque de France, Note sur les problèmes techniques soulévés par le mécanisme européen de retrécissement des marges; Committee of Alternates, June 8, 1975, Report on the French suggestions for adaptation of the Community Exchange Rate System.

138. HADB, B330/7053, August 13, 1975, Betr. Protokoll der Sitzung des EG-Währungsausschuss am 11. August.

139. CoG, Committee of Alternates, June 8, 1975, Report on the French Suggestions for Adaptation of the Community Exchange Rate System.

140. CAC, BAC 565/1995/367, July 10, 1975, Council Meeting.

141. HADB, ZBR 413, May 22, 1974.

142. CoG, Meeting 96, November 11, 1975, Basel; BoE, 7A3/11, GPS Note of November 13, 1975, Meeting of EEC Governors, November 11.

143. CoG, Meeting 96, November 11, 1975, Basel.

144. CAC, BAC 565/1995/368, August 27, 1975, Projet de Compte Rendu de la 47e Conférence des Ministres de Finance tenue à Venise le 24 août 1975.

145. CMA, CM2 1974 44, press release, October 21, 1974, following 310th meeting of ECOFIN; Mourlon-Druol, *Europe Made of Money*, p. 60.

146. *Bulletin of the European Communities: Commission Report on European Union,* June 25, 1975, doc. COM(75)400.

147. CAC, 19900568, Compte-rendu résumé, Conseil européen de Luxembourg, April 6, 1976; see Mourlon-Druol, *Europe Made of Money*, p. 82.

148. AN, 5AG3 911, Compte-rendu résumé, Conseil européen de La Haye, December 6, 1976; Mourlon-Druol, *Europe Made of Money*, p. 108.

149. Daniela Preda and Daniele Pasquinucci, *The Road Europe Travelled Along: The Evolution of the EEC/EU Institutions and Policies* (Brussels: Peter Lang, 2010), pp. 35–36.

150. CoG, Meeting 105, November 9, 1976, Basel.

151. NA, T384/1, July 6, 1976, Duisenberg to Finance Ministers of EEC members, letter from Duisenberg to Healey; also in HADB, N2/K26(2).

152. BdF, 1489200205/203, 220 meeting of Monetary Committee, September 10, 1976. See Mourlon-Druol, *Europe Made of Money*.

153. Giorgio Basevi et al., "The All Saints' Day Manifesto: Manifesto for European Monetary Union," *The Economist*, November 1, 1975.

154. See Giorgio Basevi et al., *Optica Report '75: Towards Economic Equilibrium and Monetary Unification in Europe* (Brussels: EEC Commission, 1976); Basevi et al., *Optica Report '76: Inflation and Exchange Rates: Evidence and*

Policy Guidelines for the European Communities (Brussels: EEC Commission, 1977).

155. CoG, January 12, 1977: A system of target zones for exchange rates in the Community (note from the Dutch alternates).

156. CoG, Meeting 109, March 8, 1977, Basel; Zijlstra and Clappier's views as reported by Bank of England, BoE, 7A3/14, March 10, 1977, "Meeting of EEC Governors, 8 March"; CoG, March 8, 1977, Rapport au Conseil et à la Commission sur les possibilités de mettre en oeuvre les propositions néerlandaises en matière de zones-cibles.

157. CoG, March 14, 1978, Report on Improving the Co-ordination of National Economic Policies.

158. Banca d'Italia, Studi 620, May 27, 1977, Monetary Committee memorandum: Exchange Rate Policy and the Adjustment Process: Note by the Members Nominated by the Commission.

159. IMF, International Financial Statistics database.

160. CoG, Meeting 110, April 19, 1977, Basel.

161. See Niels Thygesen, *Exchange Rate Experiences and Policies of Small Countries: Some European Examples in the 1970s,* Princeton Essays in International Finance, No. 136, December 1979, especially p. 19.

162. CoG, Meeting 115, November 8, 1977, Basel.

5. Negotiating the European Monetary System

1. CoG, July 18, 1977, statement by Gaston Geens at the Council Meeting on Economics and Finance; August 11, 1977, Janson to Bernard Breen (Central Bank of Ireland), enclosing proposal of Belgian minister Gaston Geens, Propositions d'amélioration des mécanismes de concours mutuel au sein de la Communauté. For more details on these plans and their implications in the EMS negotiations, see Emmanuel Mourlon-Druol, *A Europe Made of Money: The Emergence of the European Monetary System* (Ithaca: Cornell University Press, 2012).

2. HADB, N2/269, December 1, 1978, Emminger to Schmidt, with verbal protocol of central bank council meeting.

3. Roy Jenkins, "Europe's Present Challenge and Future Opportunity," speech at the European University Institute, Florence, October 27, 1977, available at http://aei.pitt.edu/4404 (accessed December 1, 2011).

4. BoE, 7A 3/14, January 14, 1977, W.P.C. Note.

5. CAC, Jenkins, Memorandum for the European Council, Copenhagen, April 7–8, 1978.

6. CoG, Meeting 121, May 9, 1978, Basel.

7. NA, PREM 16/1615, Couzens note for Wicks, March 31, 1978; PREM 16/1641, Prime Minister's conversation with Mr. Roy Jenkins on March 31, 1978.

8. CoG, Meeting 117, January 10, 1978, Basel.

9. CoG, Meeting 118, February 14, 1978, Basel.

10. CoG, Meeting 119, March 14, 1978, Basel.

11. Hans Roeper, "Der tolle Blumenthal," *Frankfurter Allgemeine Zeitung*, July 22, 1977; Klaus Wiegrefe, *Das Zerwürfnis: Helmut Schmidt, Jimmy Carter und die Krise der deutsch-amerikanische Beziehungen* (Berlin: Propyläen, 2005), pp. 212–213, 217–218.

12. Francesco Giavazzi and Alberto Giovannini, *Limiting Exchange Rate Flexibility: The European Monetary System* (Cambridge, Mass.: MIT Press, 1989).

13. BoE, 6A/218/6, September 20, 1978, FCO: Community attitudes to British participation in an EMS.

14. HADB, N2/264, Pöhl to Schmidt, March 21, 1978.

15. HADB, N2/264, Emminger to Schmidt, March 30, 1978, Betr.: Währungspolitische Fortschritte in Europa.

16. Johannes von Karczewski, *"Weltwirtschaft ist unser Schicksal": Helmut Schmidt und die Schaffung der Weltwirtschaftsgipfel* (Bonn: Dietz, 2008), p. 356; Wilfried Loth, "Deutsche Europapolitik von Helmut Schmidt bis Helmut Kohl," in *Aufbruch zum Europa der zweiten Generation: Die europäische Einigung, 1969–1984*, ed. Franz Knipping and Matthias Schönwald (Trier: Wissenschaftlicher Verlag Trier, 2004), p. 477.

17. Von Karczewski, *Weltwirtschaft*, p. 425.

18. NA, PREM 16/1615, Note for the record: Prime Minister's meeting with Chancellor Schmidt at the Bundeskanzlei, Bonn, on Sunday 12 March 1978.

19. Quoted in Jonathan Story, "The Launching of the EMS: An Analysis of Change in Foreign Economic Policy," *Political Studies* 36 (1988), 397.

20. Peter Ludlow, *The Making of the European Monetary System: A Case Study of the Politics of the European Community* (London: Butterworth, 1982), pp. 90–92.

21. NA, PREM 16/1615, Schmidt note on remarks at Copenhagen summit.

22. NA, PREM 16/1615, Note of Couzens, April 11, 1978, Prime Minister's discussion on 8 April with Chancellor Schmidt and President Giscard.

23. U.S. freedom of information release 248745, Prime Minister's Telephone Conversation with President Carter, 17 April 1978 at 20:30, available at http://www.margaretthatcher.org/document/111481 (accessed December 1, 2011).

24. NA, PREM 16.1615, John Hunt: Chancellor Schmidt, the Snake and Pooling Reserves, April 6, 1978.

25. NA, PREM 16/1634, June 22, 1978 DWH: European Currency Arrangements.
26. Philip Stephens, *Politics and the Pound: The Conservatives' Struggle with Sterling* (London: Macmillan, 1996), p. 6; Denis Healey, *The Time of My Life* (London: M. Joseph, 1989), pp. 438–439.
27. Henri Froment-Meurice, *Vu du Quai: Mémoires, 1945–1983* (Paris: Fayard, 1998), p. 474.
28. Ludlow, *European Monetary System*, p. 95.
29. Mourlon-Druol, *Europe Made of Money*, pp. 204–205.
30. NA, PREM 16/1616, May 30, 1978, Couzens to Stowe: Chancellor Schmidt's proposal for a European currency reform, Record of discussion with M. Clappier and Herr Schulmann over dinner at the Hay-Adams Hotel, Washington, on 26 May 1978.
31. NA, PREM 16/1634, June 19, 1978, Couzens to Stowe, European Monetary Co-operation, Discussions in Paris on 14 and 15 June 1978, Annex B: Herr Schulmann's draft for an agreement at Bremen.
32. Although he drew up a long and ambitious alternative plan: see Mourlon-Druol, *Europe Made of Money*, pp. 194, 209; NA, T 381/108, Couzens to Stowe, Possible UK counterdraft, June 29, 1978.
33. NA, PREM 16/1616, April 21 1978, Couzens Note for the Record.
34. See HADB, N2/264, April 3, 1978, Betr.: Van Ypersele Plan.
35. HADB, N2/K45(1), April 5, 1978, Betr. Aufzeichnung von Gouverneur de Strycker zur Wechselkurspolitik (Schlüter).
36. HADB, N2/K26(13), April 14, 1978, Karl Otto Pöhl to members of Central Bank Council, with memorandum by Peter Christian Schlüter.
37. CoG, Meeting 120, April 11, 1978, Basel.
38. IMF, International Financial Statistics database, consumer prices.
39. CoG, Meeting 120, April 11, 1978, Basel.
40. CoG, Meeting 121, May 9, 1978, Basel.
41. BdF, 1489200205/203, Note au Ministre de l'Économie et des Finances, 240ème session du Comité Monétaire, 11 et 12 mai 1978.
42. BdF, 1489200205/203, Note au Ministre de l'Économie et des Finances: 241ème session du Comité Monétaire, 5 et 6 juin 1978.
43. CMA, Intermédiaire 9688, June 9, 1978, Report of the Monetary Committee to the Council and the Commission.
44. CoG, Committee of Alternates, May 29, 1978: Efforts to Ensure Greater Exchange Rate Stability among EEC Member Countries' Currencies.
45. CoG, Meeting 122, June 11, 1978, Basel.
46. HADB, B330/17637, June 12, 1978, CoG, Efforts to Ensure Greater Exchange Rate Stability among EEC Member Countries' Currencies (Report to the Council).

47. Ibid.

48. CMA, Intermédiaire 9688, June 27, 1978, Monetary Committee, Conclusions of the Council's debate of 19 June, on possibilities of bringing about greater exchange rate stability in the Community.

49. *Bulletin of the European Communities* 6 (1978), 20–21, available at http://aei.pitt.edu/1454/1/Bremen_July_1978.pdf (accessed December 1, 2011).

50. Guido Thiemeyer, "Helmut Schmidt und die Gründung des Europäischen Währungssystems 1973–1979," in Knipping and Schönwald, *Aufbruch zum Europa*, p. 257.

51. NA, PREM 16/1634, Discussion by heads of government and the president of the Commission during the evening of 6 July 1978 in the Rathaus.

52. See HADB, Central Bank Council meeting 506, April 20, 1978.

53. Robert D. Putnam and C. Randall Henning, "The Bonn Summit of 1978: A Case Study in Coordination," in *Can Nations Agree? Issues in International Economic Cooperation*, ed. Richard N. Cooper et al. (Washington, D.C.: Brookings Institution), 1989, pp. 12–140.

54. Harold James, *International Monetary Cooperation since Bretton Woods* (New York: Oxford University Press, 1996), p. 299.

55. CoG, Meeting 123, July 11, 1978, Basel.

56. HADB, B330/14740, 512 meeting of ZBR, July 13, 1978.

57. Bundesarchiv Koblenz, B126/70442, July 14, 1978, Vermerk von Schlüter and Weber, Betr.: Schlussfolgerungen aus dem Bremer EG-Gipfel vom 6./7. Juli 1978 im Währungsbereich; Mourlon-Druol, *Europe Made of Money*, p. 207.

58. BdF, 1489200205/282, drafts of July 20, July 24, August 8, and August 23, 1978.

59. HADB, B330/14740, Stellungnahme des Zentralbankrats der Deutschen Bundesbank (Ergebnis der Beratungen in der ZBR-Sitzung am 07.09.1978).

60. Thus Wertz in the Bundesbank Central Bank Council Meeting of November 30, 1978 (HADB, B330/14740).

61. CoG, July 26, 1978, Note of a discussion in the Council of Ministers for Economic and Financial Affairs on the Future European Monetary System (July 24 meeting).

62. CoG, Heyvaert Group, Report No. 39, Interim Report on the European Monetary System, August 21, 1978.

63. Ibid.

64. Ibid.

65. HADB, ZBR 515, September 7, 1978: Stellungnahme des Zentralbankrats der Deutschen Bundesbank zu den Vorschlägen für ein europäisches Währungssystem.

528 Notes to Pages 168–173

66. *House of Commons Debates,* July 10, 1978, vol. 953, col. 1025, available at http://hansard.millbanksystems.com/commons/1978/jul/10/european -community-council-bremen-meeting (accessed December 1, 2011).
67. BoE, 1A/68/1, October 2, 1978, Couzens: The EMS: An Interim Assessment.
68. NA, FCO 30/4014, August 29, 1978, EMS concurrent studies: possible devices for increasing U.K. net receipts from the Community budget, excluding the Common Agricultural Policy.
69. Thiemeyer, "Helmut Schmidt," pp. 260–262.
70. NA, FCO 30/4029, November 5, 1978, Telegram no. 996, EMS.
71. See John B. Goodman, *Monetary Sovereignty: The Politics of Central Banking in Western Europe* (Ithaca: Cornell University Press, 1992), p. 168. See also CoG, Meeting 134, May 8, 1979, Basel.
72. CoG, Meeting 124, Basel, September 12, 1978, Basel.
73. Ibid.
74. Politisches Archiv des Auswärtigen Amtes, Berlin, September 12, 1978, Zwischenarchiv 122325, Vermerk von Kliesow, Gespräch des Bundeskanzlers mit Präsident Giscard am Dienstag, dem 12. September 1978, 16.20–16.30 Uhr (Anruf von Präsident Giscard), quoted in Mourlon-Druol, *Europe Made of Money,* p. 216.
75 Mourlon-Druol, *Europe Made of Money,* p. 217; French Foreign Ministry archive, B0050424, Confidential, September 15, 1978, Memorandum of understanding, Aachen. See also Politisches Archiv des Auswärtigen Amtes, Zwischenarchiv 122325, September 19, 1978, Vermerk von Brockdorff, Betr.: Europäisches Währungssystem, hier: Deutsch-französischer Gipfel in Aachen. On the bilateralization, see Ludlow, *European Monetary System,* pp. 217–225.
76. Roy Jenkins, entry for October 16, 1978, *European Diary, 1977–1981* (London: Collins, 1989), p. 325.
77. Mourlon-Druol, *Europe Made of Money,* p. 230; NA, FCO 30/4027, October 30, 1978, Michell to Jordan-Moss; Monetary Committee Alternates: 27 October 1978 meeting.
78. Mourlon-Druol, *Europe Made of Money,* p. 233; French Foreign Ministry archive, 1553, October 17, 1978, Telegram no. 4476-4500, Conseil ECOFIN.
79. Ludlow, *European Monetary System;* CoG, Meeting 125, October 9, 1978, Basel.
80. CoG, Meeting 127, November 14, 1978, Basel.
81. CoG, Meeting 126, October 30, 1978, Brussels.
82. Ibid.

83. CoG, November 1, 1978, Draft Report of the Committee of Governors to the Council on the European Monetary System.

84. Mourlon-Druol, *Europe Made of Money,* p. 237; NA, FCO 30/4021, October 12, 1978, Telegram no. 390, European Monetary System: Finance Council, October 16, 1978, meeting.

85. Mourlon-Druol, *Europe Made of Money,* p. 238; Historical Archives of European Union, Florence (hereafter HAEU), EN 1148, November 15, 1978, Note by Tickell of a call by the President of the European Commission on the British Prime Minister, 3 November 1978.

86. HADB, N2/269, December 1, 1978, Emminger to Schmidt, with verbal protocol of central bank council meeting. It has been translated into English by the Margaret Thatcher Foundation: www.margaretthatcher.org/document/111554 (accessed December 1, 2011).

87. HADB, B330/26258, November 16, 1978, Emminger to Schmidt, Betr. Stellungnahme des Zentralbankrats zum künftigen EWS.

88. HADB, B330/26258; translation by Margaret Thatcher Foundation.

89. Ibid.

90. Ibid.

91. Ibid.

92. HADB, N2/264, April 4, 1979, Matthöfer to Emminger.

93. BoE, 1A/61/2, November 15, 1978, visit of Lahnstein to Healey.

94. See Dimitri Grygowski, *Les États-Unis et l'unification monétaire de l'Europe* (Brussels: Peter Lang, 2009), pp. 286–287.

95. HAEU, EN 1148, December 11, 1978, Note of Tickell, Note of conversation between Chancellor Schmidt and the President of the European Commission at one of the intervals in the European Council, Brussels, 5 December 1978.

96. Jenkins, *European Diary,* p. 351; HAEU, EN 1148, December 8, 1978, Note of Tickell to Jenkins, European Council, 4 and 5 December 1978.

97. EC Réglement 3181/78, December 18, 1978, relating to the European Monetary System.

98. Agreement of March 13, 1979, EC *Compendium of Community Monetary Texts, 1979* (Brussels: European Communities, 1979), p. 55.

99. CoG, Meeting 128, December 12, 1978, Basel.

100. "L'Empire du Mark," *Le Monde,* December 6, 1978, p. 2.

101. NA, FCO 30/4029, Telegram no. 504, German-Italian talks in Siena on 1–2 November, EMS, November 2, 1978.

102. CoG, April 5, 1987, Report by Chairman of EC Monetary Committee to Knokke, ECOFIN.

6. The Malaise of the 1980s

1. Samuel Brittan, *Financial Times,* March 24, 1983.
2. See Curzio Giannini, *The Age of Central Banks* (London: Edward Elgar, 2011).
3. CoG, Meeting 162, January 12, 1982, Basel, quoting December 14, 1981, Note verbale du Comité des Gouverneurs au Conseil ECOFIN du 14 décembre 1981 sur l'avenir du SME.
4. CoG, Meeting 162.
5. Ibid.
6. HADB, ZBR 545 meeting, November 29, 1979: declaration by Matthöfer.
7. CoG, June 17, 1983, Dalgaard Report, No. 49, Report on Certain Aspects of the Working of the EMS; Cristina Mastropasqua, Stefano Micossi, and Roberto Rinaldi, "Interventions, Sterilisation and Monetary Policy in European Monetary System Countries, 1979–87," in *The European Monetary System,* ed. Francesco Giavazzi, Stefano Micossi, and Marcus Miller (London: CEPR, 1988), p. 256, gives the proportions for all interventions: 11.2 percent in 1979–1982, 10.5 percent in 1983–1985, and 15.2 percent in 1986–1987.
8. I am grateful to Helge Fosgaard, formerly of the Danmarks Nationalbank, for sifting through and evaluating Danish and other data for a few months from the 1980s that were not preserved in the BIS archives.
9. HADB, B330/22271, October 19, 1979, note: Währungsausschuss am 17. Oktober 1979.
10. HADB, September 27, 1979, Koordinierung der Wechselkurspolitiken gegenüber dritte Länder.
11. CoG, Meeting 141, January 8, 1980, Basel.
12. BdF, 1489200205/57, EC Commission, November 16, 1979: Politique communautaire de change vis-à-vis du dollar U.S.
13. BdF, 1489200205/57, December 5, 1979: Politique commune vis-à-vis du Dollar: Réunion du Groupe Heyvaert à Bâle les 3 et 4 décembre 1979.
14. BdF, 1489200205/58, January 25, 1980: FME: Projet de rapport préliminaire du Comité des Gouverneurs; HADB, N2/K55(8), April 10, 1980, note (Weber): Betr. Ausschuss der EG-Notenbankgouveneure 15. April 1980.
15. CoG, Meeting 141, January 8, 1980.
16. HADB, ZBR of January 17, 1980.
17. CoG, Meeting 142, February 12, 1980, Basel.
18. HADB, B330/26941, July 1, 1981, Pöhl to Tommaso Padoa-Schioppa.
19. CoG, Meeting 144, April 15, 1980, Basel.
20. CoG, Heyvaert report No. 48, January 27, 1982: Examination of the Operating Procedures of the ERM of the EMS and Proposed Amendments to the Agreement of 13th March 1979.

21. CoG, Meeting 149, November 11, 1980, Basel.

22. CoG, Meeting 152, February 10, 1981, Basel.

23. CoG, Meeting 153, March 10, 1981.

24. CoG, Meeting 159, October 30, 1981, London.

25. CoG, November 11, 1981, Compte rendu: October 31, 1981, Informal meeting of Ministers and Governors.

26. HADB, ZBR 588 meeting, September 21, 1981.

27. CoG, Meeting 159, October 30, 1981.

28. Yves Mamou, *Une machine de pouvoir: La Direction du Trésor* (Paris: La Découverte, 1987), p. 126.

29. HADB, B330/26942, February 23, 1982, Tommaso Padoa-Schioppa to members of EC Monetary Committee, "EMS Non-Paper."

30. HADB, B330/14554, December 4 1980: Betr. Fortsetzung der EWS-Diskussion; December 1, 1980, Commission papers: Fundamental Questions in Connection with the Institutional Phases of the EMS.

31. HADB, ZBR 592, November 5, 1981.

32. HADB, N4/51, March 9, 1982, Pöhl to Schmidt.

33. HADB, B330/26941, May 2, 1981, Tommaso Padoa-Schioppa to Pöhl.

34. HADB, 600 meeting, March 4, 1982; Peter B. Kenen, *Economic and Monetary Union in Europe: Moving beyond Maastricht* (Cambridge: Cambridge University Press, 1995), p. 163, gets the direction of the German pressure wrong.

35. CoG, Meeting 164, March 9, 1982, Basel.

36. HADB, ZBR 600 meeting, March 4, 1982.

37. CoG, March 8, 1982, Report of the Chairman of the Committee of Alternates.

38. CoG, Note verbale au Conseil ECOFIN du 15 mars 1982.

39. Robert Putnam and Nicholas Bayne, *Hanging Together: Cooperation and Conflict in the Seven Power Summits* (London: Sage, 1987), p. 135; Thierry Pfister, *La vie quotidienne à Matignon au temps de l'Union de la gauche* (Paris: Hachette, 1985); Philippe Jurgensen, *Ecu: Naissance d'une monnaie* (Paris: J. C. Lattès, 1991), p. 67.

40. Guido Carli, "International Financial Policies," in *International Economic Cooperation,* ed. Martin Feldstein (Chicago: University of Chicago Press, 1988), p. 139.

41. CoG, Meeting 170, November 9, 1982, Basel.

42. CoG, Meeting 174, March 8, 1983, Basel, annex to minutes, February 1983, Rapport spécial sur les pratiques actuelles concernant les objectifs monétaires intermédiaires quantitatifs dans les pays de la CEE.

43. CoG, Meeting 173, February 8, 1983, Basel.

44. CoG, Piet Korteweg to Michel Camdessus, January 31, 1983.

45. BoE, 6A/177/3, December 2, 1981, R. D. Clews note.

46. CoG, Meeting 175, April 12, 1983, Basel.

47. Georges Saunier, "Le gouvernement français et les enjeux économiques européens à l'heure de la rigeur 1981–1984," in *Milieux économiques et intégration européenne au XXe siècle: La relance des années quatre-vingt (1979–1992),* ed. Eric Bussière, Michel Dumoulin, and Sylvain Schirmann (Paris: Comité pour l'histoire économique et financière de la France, 2007), p. 127.

48. CoG, Meeting 178, July 12, 1983, Basel.

49. CoG, July 12, 1983: Rapport Oral du Président sur certains aspects du fonctionnement du SME.

50. CoG, Meeting 181, December 13, 1983, Basel.

51. CoG, Meeting 179, September 13, 1983, Basel.

52. CoG, Meeting 184, March 13, 1983, Basel.

53. CoG, Meeting 188, July 10, 1984, Basel (Report No. 52).

54. CoG, Meeting 189, September 11, 1984, Basel.

55. CoG, Meeting 188, July 10, 1984.

56. CoG, November 5, 1984, Dalgaard Report, No. 54, "Proposals for Strengthening the EMS."

57. Daniel Gros and Niels Thygesen, *European Monetary Integration* (London: Longman, 1992), p. 86.

58. See also HADB, B330/28139, November 6, 1984, Betr. Weiterentwicklung des EWS (a discussion of Dalgaard Report, No. 54).

59. CoG, Meeting 191, December 11, 1984, Basel.

60. CoG, Meeting 194, March 12, 1985, Basel.

61. CoG, Meeting 190, November 13, 1984, Basel. See also Jérôme Wilson, "De la création d'un marché international des capitaux á l'unification monétaire de l'Europe: Une initiative belge et privée," in *Milieux économiques et intégration européenne au XXe siècle: La crise des années 1970,* ed. Eric Bussière, Michel Dumoulin, and Sylvain Schirmann (Brussels: Peter Lang, 2006), pp. 69–85; David Lomax, "New Products and Instruments in Financial Services," in *Europe and the Future of Financial Services,* ed. Ugur Muldur and Olivier Pastré (London: Lafferty, 1987), p. 209.

62. Juanita Roushdy, *The Role of the SDR in the International Monetary System,* IMF Occasional Paper No. 51 (Washington, D.C., 1987), p. 36.

63. CoG, Meeting 193, February 12, 1985, Basel.

64. CoG, April 22, 1985, Compte rendu succinct de la discussion sur le SME à l'ECOFIN informel du 13 avril 1985.

65. October 28, 1985, decision 3066/85, *Official Journal of the European Communities,* November 1, 1985.

66. CoG, Meeting 195, April 15, 1985, Basel.

67. CoG, Meeting 196, May 14, 1985, Basel.

68. Ibid.

69. CoG, Meeting 199, September 10, 1985, Basel.

70. CoG, November 12, 1985, Opinion of the Committee of Governors Concerning the Monetary Provisions Proposed by the Commission Relating to Article 107 of the Treaty.

71. CoG, November 21, 1985, Summary Report of the Discussion by the ECOFIN Council on 18 November 1985 of the Monetary Provisions Proposed by the Commission.

72. HADB, B330/22681, August 2, 1985, Saccomanni to members of concertation group.

73. See CoG, April 28, 1986: Summary of the Alternates' Discussion of the Realignment on April 7, 1986.

74. CoG, Meeting 200, November 12, 1985, Basel.

75. Francesco Giavazzi and Marco Pagano, "The Advantage of Tying One's Hands: EMS Discipline and Central Bank Credibility," *European Economic Review* 32 (1988), 1055–82.

76. Kenneth Rogoff, "Can Exchange Rate Predictability Be Achieved without Monetary Convergence: Evidence from the EMS," *European Economic Review* 28 (1985), 93–115.

77. Francesco Giavazzi and Alberto Giovannini, "Models of the EMS: Is Europe a Greater Deutschemark Area?" in *Global Macroeconomics,* ed. Ralph C. Bryant and Richard Portes (New York: St. Martin's Press, 1987), p. 37; Stanley Fischer, "International Macroeconomic Policy Coordination," National Bureau of Economic Research Working Paper 2244, 1987, p. 41.

78. Paul Krugman, "Policy Problems of a Monetary Union," in *The European Monetary System in the 1990s,* ed. Paul de Grauwe and Lucas Papademos (London: Longman, 1990), p. 57.

79. Nigel Lawson, *The View from No. 11: Memoirs of a Tory Radical* (London: Bantam, 1992), pp. 662–663.

80. Wolfgang Rieke, "Alternative Views on the EMS in the 1990s," in *The European Monetary System in the 1990s,* ed. Paul de Grauwe and Lucas Papademos (London: Longman, 1990), p. 30.

7. The Delors Committee and the Relaunching of Europe

1. David Marsh, *The Euro: The Politics of the New Global Currency* (New Haven: Yale University Press, 2009), p. 123.

2. Alasdair Blair, *Dealing with Europe: Britain and the Negotiation of the Maastricht Treaty* (Aldershot: Ashgate, 1999), p. 151.

3. Daniela Engelmann, Hans-Joachim Knopf, Klaus Roscher, and Thomas Risse, "Identity Politics in the European Union: The Case of Economic and Monetary Union (EMU)," in *The Politics of Economic and Monetary Union,* ed. Petri Minkinnen and Heikki Paromäki (Boston: Kluwer, 1997), pp. 105–132, quotation on 105.

4. Delors speech of July 6, 1988, *Official Journal of the European Communities: Debates of the European Parliament,* no. 367 (1988), 140, Also see Wayne Sandholtz, "Choosing Union: Monetary Politics and Maastricht," *International Organization* 47/1 (1993), 1–39.

5. Jacques Delors, *Mémoires* (Paris: Plon, 2004), p. 193; Colette Mezzucelli, *France and Germany at Maastricht: Politics and Negotiations to Create the European Union* (New York: Garland, 1997), p. 22.

6. See Rawi Abdelal, *Capital Rules: The Construction of Global Finance* (Cambridge, Mass.: Harvard University Press, 2007), pp. 66–69.

7. Delors, *Mémoires,* p. 221; Charles Grant, *Delors: Inside the House That Jacques Built* (London: Nicholas Brealey, 1994), p. 74.

8. HADB, B3301/14552, November 15, 1985, Rieke to Tietmeyer; ZBR 691 meeting, December 5, 1985.

9. Robert A. Mundell, "Capital Mobility and Stabilization Policy under Fixed and Flexible Exchange Rates," *Canadian Journal of Economic and Political Science* 29/4 (1963), 475–485; Tommaso Padoa-Schioppa, "The European Monetary System: A Long-Term View," in *The European Monetary System,* ed. Francesco Giavazzi, Stefano Micossi, and Marcus Miller (Cambridge: Cambridge University Press, 1988), pp. 373–376.

10. Tommaso Padoa-Schioppa, *Efficiency, Stability and Equity: A Strategy for the Evolution of the Economic System of the European Community* (Oxford: Oxford University Press, 1987) (originally EC Report II/49/87); see also Grant, *Delors,* pp. 116–117.

11. Louis Tsoukalis, *The New European Economy: The Politics and Economics of Integration* (Oxford: Oxford University Press, 1991), p. 189.

12. Daniel Gros and Niels Thygesen, *European Monetary Integration,* 2d ed. (Harlow, U.K.: Longman, 1998), p. 411; Robert Putnam, "Diplomacy and Domestic Politics: The Logic of Two-Level Games," *International Organization* 10/42 (1988), 427–460; Andrew Moravcsik, *The Choice for Europe: Social Purpose and State Power from Messina to Maastricht* (Ithaca: Cornell University Press, 1998); Barry Eichengreen and Jeffry Frieden, eds., *Forging an Integrated Europe* (Ann Arbor: University of Michigan Press, 1998).

13. CoG, EC Commission, July 30, 1987: The Complete Liberalisation of Capital Movements and Strengthening the EMS.

14. See Lorenzo Bini Smaghi and Stefano Micossi, "Monetary and Exchange Rate Policy in the EMS with Free Capital Mobility," in *The European Mon-*

etary System in the 1990s, ed. Paul De Grauwe and Lucas Papademos (London: Longman, 1990), pp. 124–125.

15. Barry Eichengreen, *Globalizing Capital: A History of the International Monetary System* (Princeton: Princeton University Press, 1996), p. 151.

16. HADB, ZBR 686, September 26, 1985.

17. Peter Henning Loedel, *Deutsche Mark Politics: Germany in the European Monetary System* (Boulder: Lynne Rieder, 1999), p. 76.

18. CoG, Meeting 207, July 8, 1986, Basel.

19. See Eric Bussière, "Le ministère des finances et les enjeux économiques européens à l'époque de la cohabitation 1986–1988," in *Milieux économiques et intégration européenne au XXe siècle: La relance des années quatre-vingt (1979–1992),* ed. Eric Bussière, Michel Dumoulin, and Sylvain Schirmann (Paris: Comité pour l'histoire économique et financière de la France, 2007), p. 153.

20. CoG, Meeting 211, January 13, 1987, Basel.

21. CoG, March 23, 1987, Preliminary Report by the Chairman of the Committee of Governors on the Strengthening of the Operating Mechanisms of the EMS.

22. Gros and Thygesen, *European Monetary Integration,* p. 83.

23. CoG, Meeting 213, March 10, 1987, Basel.

24. Hans Tietmeyer, *Herausforderung Euro: Wie es zum Euro kam und was er für Deutschlands Zukunft bedeutet* (Munich: Hanser, 2005), p. 107.

25. Bussière, "Le ministère des finances," p. 155.

26. CoG, Meeting 211, January 13, 1987, Basel.

27. Ibid.

28. Bussière, "Le ministère des finances," p. 157.

29. HADB, ZBR 737, November 5, 1987. Pöhl: "The interpretation of the agreements, especially in the United States and in Great Britain, that target zones were agreed does not correspond to the result of the negotiation."

30. Author's conversation with Tietmeyer, March 1995.

31. CoG, Meeting 213, March 10, 1987, Basel.

32. CoG, June 15, 1987, Statement of Tietmeyer to ECOFIN.

33. CoG, Meeting 213, March 10, 1987.

34. The request was made at the European Council meeting of December 2–3, 1986; see HADB, B330/22702, Report of October 19, 1987, EC Commission: Creation of a European Financial Area.

35. HADB, B330/16564, August 20, 1987: Betr. Vertrauliche Kommissions-Aufzeichnung zur vollständigen Liberalisierung des Kapitalverkehrs und Stärkung des EWS.

36. CoG, September 8, 1987, Strengthening the Operating Mechanisms of the EMS.

37. CoG, September 12, 1987, Strengthening the EMS: Report by Chairman of Monetary Committee to Informal Meeting of Finance Ministers at Nyborg on 12 September 1987.

38. CoG, Meeting 239, November 14, 1989, Basel, for the Bundesbank position; Bussière, "Le ministère des finances," p. 160, for the French demand in November 12, 1987, bilateral talks; HADB, B330/16564, August 31, 1987: Betr. Änderungen im EWS.

39. CoG, Meeting 219, November 10, 1987, Basel.

40. HADB, ZBR 735, October 8, 1987.

41. "Helmut Schlesinger: Bank Chief Makes His Mark," *Los Angeles Times,* September 22, 1992.

42. HADB, B330/22702, November 6, 1987, Betr.: Weiterentwicklung des EWS.

43. HADB, ZBR, October 22, 1987.

44. HADB, ZBR 739 meeting, December 3, 1987.

45. C. Randall Henning, *Currencies and Politics in the United States, Germany and Japan* (Washington, D.C.: Institute for International Economics, 1994), p. 208.

46. HADB, ZBR 737 meeting, November 5, 1987.

47. Gros and Thygesen, *European Monetary Integration,* p. 397.

48. CoG, Meeting 219, November 10, 1987.

49. Bussière, "Le ministère des finances," p. 160.

50. Ibid., p. 163.

51. Kenneth Dyson and Kevin Featherstone, *The Road to Maastricht: Negotiating Economic and Monetary Union* (New York: Oxford University Press, 1999), pp. 164–166.

52. Interview with Balladur, *Le Figaro,* January 14, 1988.

53. HADB, B330/22706, n.d. [January 1988], Minister Amato's Memorandum on EMS: On "European Monetary Construction" (1): The Italian Position.

54. HADB, B330/18911, Hans-Dietrich Genscher memorandum: Memorandum für die Schaffung eines europäischen Währungsrames und einer europäischen Zentralbank, February 26, 1988.

55. Dyson and Featherstone, *The Road to Maastricht,* p. 331.

56. HADB, B330/18423, April 18, 1988, Dörner: Diskussion über die verschiedenen Vorschläge zur Weiterentwicklung des EWS.

57. HADB, B330/17837, May 1, 1988, transcript of Bundesbank Council meeting.

58. "Zeit noch nicht reif für europäische Notenbank," *Frankfurter Allgemeine Zeitung,* May 6, 1988; "Poehl Doubts European Unit Is Likely Soon," *Wall Street Journal Europe,* May 6, 1988.

59. HADB, B330/17837, Deutsche Bundesbank, 25. Mai 1988, "Weiterent-wicklung des Europäischen Währungssystems."

60. Ibid.

61. CoG, March 24, 1988, Working Document by the Office of the Chairman of the Alternates.

62. BoE, 8A/249/1, May 6, 1988, M. R. Lewis, Committee of EC Governors 10 May.

63. CoG, Meeting 224, April 12, 1988, Basel. See also HADB, B330/28901, May 4, 1988, Vorläufiger Bericht der Gouverneure.

64. *BIS Review,* May 13, 1988.

65. BoE, 8A/249/1, May 3, 1988, Monetary Committee.

66. See HADB, B330/18423, May 6, 1988, Dörner: Betr. Die Stellung des EFWZ.

67. HADB, ZBR 751, June 1, 1988, minutes; HADB, B330/17837, transcript of meeting.

68. HADB, N4/49, June 1, 1988, Bitterlich to Pöhl with transcript of May 26, 1988, Ministergespräch.

69. HADB, N4/51, June 1, 1988, Pöhl to Kohl.

70. Delors, *Mémoires,* pp. 332–333.

71. Nigel Lawson, *The View from No. 11: Memoirs of a Tory Radical* (London: Bantam, 1992), pp. 902–903.

72. David Buchan, "Delors to Brief Ministers on Monetary Study," *Financial Times,* July 11, 1988, p. 2.

73. BdF, 1489200205/88, July 11, 1988, De Larosière notes.

74. See Delors, *Mémoires,* p. 334.

75. HADB, ZBR 753, June 30, 1988.

76. HADB, ZBR 754, July 14, 1988.

77. BoE, 8A/250/1, July 4, 1988, J. R. E. Footman: Delors Committee.

78. HADB, B330/22710, July 4, 1988, Rieke: Betr. Weiterentwicklung der währungspolitischen Zusammenarbeit in der EG.

79. BoE, 8A/250/1, July 13, 1988, R. L.-P.: Private meeting of EC Governors in Basel.

80. CoG, First meeting of Delors Committee, September 13, 1988, transcript.

81. Personal interviews.

82. Personal interview with Alexandre Lamfalussy.

83. BoE, 8A/249/2, September 12, 1988, J. A. A. Arrowsmith note: Whitehall access to Delors Committee papers; 8A/250/1, September 14, 1988, Leigh-Pemberton to Lawson.

84. BoE, 8A/250/1, October 7, 1988, J. R. E. Footman: Delors Committee: Pöhl papers.

85. Personal interviews.

86. Lawson, *The View from No. 11,* p. 908.
87. CoG, Memorandum, September 1, 1988.
88. Ibid.
89. Ibid.
90. Ibid.
91. CoG, First meeting of Delors Committee, September 13, 1988, transcript.
92. Personal interview with Jacques de Larosière. See also Carel C. A. van den Berg, *The Making of the Statute of the European System of Central Banks: An Application of Checks and Balances* (Amsterdam: Dutch University Press, 2004), p. 100.
93. Charles Wyplosz, "European Monetary Union: The Dark Sides of a Major Success," *Economic Policy* 21/46 (2006), 209–210.
94. CoG, September 6, 1988, Baer to Padoa-Schioppa.
95. CoG, First meeting of Delors Committee, September 13, 1988, transcript.
96. CoG, Second meeting of Delors Committee, October 10, 1988, transcript.
97. BoE, 8A/250/1, October 17, 1988, Leigh-Pemberton notes.
98. CoG, Third meeting of Delors Committee, November 8, 1998, transcript.
99. Ibid.
100. CoG, November 17, 1988, Padoa-Schioppa: Note "Proceeding by Steps."
101. CoG, December 2, 1988, Gunter Baer and Tommaso Padoa-Schioppa, Skeleton Report.
102. Ibid.
103. CoG, December 1, 1988, J.-P. Mingasson, Economic Content of the Three Stages towards EMU.
104. CoG, December 2, 1988, Baer and Padoa-Schioppa, Skeleton Report.
105. Ibid.
106. CoG, Fourth meeting of Delors Committee, December 13, 1998, minutes.
107. Ibid.
108. CoG, January 4, 1989, Macrofiscal functions performed by the Center for Economic Policy Coordination.
109. CoG, January 31, 1989, Lamfalussy note.
110. CoG, Fifth meeting of Delors Committee, January 10, 1989, minutes.
111. Ibid., transcript.
112. Ibid.
113. CoG, April 11, 1989, meeting of Delors Committee, tape.
114. CoG, February 10, 1989, Mingasson note.
115. CoG, April 11, 1989, meeting, tape.
116. CoG, February 14, 1989, Sixth meeting of Delors Committee, transcript.
117. Van den Berg, *Making of Statute of European System of Central Banks,* p. 64.

118. BdF, Direction des changes, Compte rendu de la session de 14 mars du Comité Delors, quoted in Olivier Feiertag, "La conversion de la Banque de France à l'unification monétaire européenne: Le tournant du comité Delors (1987–1992)," in *Les banques centrales à l'échelle du monde du 20ᵉ au 21ᵉ siècle/Central Banks at World's Scale from the 20th to the 21st Century*, ed. Olivier Feiertag and Michel Margairaz (Paris: Presses de Sciences Po, 2012).

119. BoE, 8A/215/3, March 20, 1989, Arrowsmith note.

120. CoG, Sixth meeting of Delors Committee, March 14, 1989, transcript.

121. Ibid.

122. Ibid.

123. Ibid.

124. De Larosière to Leigh-Pemberton, February 2, 1989, quoted in Feiertag, "La conversion de la Banque de France."

125. CoG, Sixth meeting of Delors Committee, March 14, 1989, transcript.

126. Ibid.

127. CoG, Seventh meeting of Delors Committee, April 11–12, 1989, transcript.

128. Ibid., tape.

129. Feiertag, "La conversion de la Banque de France."

130. CoG, Seventh meeting of Delors Committee, April 11–12, 1989, transcript.

131. Ibid.

132. Ibid.

133. Ibid., tape.

134. Philip Stephens, *Politics and the Pound: The Conservatives' Struggle with Sterling* (London: Macmillan, 1996), p. 112.

135. CoG, March 21, 1989, Leigh-Pemberton to Delors; Pöhl in Delors Committee meeting, March 14, 1989.

136. The following quotations come from the Delors Report: Committee for the Study of Economic and Monetary Union, *Report on Economic and Monetary Union in the European Community. Presented April 17, 1989,* EU Commission Working Document, available at http://aei.pitt.edu/1007/1/monetary_delors.pdf (accessed December 1, 2011).

137. HADB, ZBR 772, April 20, 1989.

138. HADB, B330/22720, Bundesbank (Pöhl and Gleske) to Chancellor Kohl, June 16, 1989.

139. CoG, March 9, 1989, Note of Samuel Lajeunesse for Trichet.

140. "Finance Ministers Agree to Start Work on Delors Report," *Financial Times,* May 22, 1989.

141. "EC Moves on Monetary Union," *Financial Times,* June 28, 1989.

142. HADB, B330/24118, November 12, 1990, Statement of Governor of Bank of England.

143. David Marsh and Andrew Fisher, "Pöhl Doubts Need for EC Bank," *Financial Times*, July 1–2, 1989.
144. HADB, B330/22720, Pöhl to Waigel, July 6, 1989.
145. CoG, July 4, 1989, Banque de France paper.
146. CoG, Meeting 237, July 11, 1989, Basel; see also HADB, B330/18436, July 5, 1989, Betr. Tagung des Gouverneursausschusses am 11. Juli 1989.

8. Designing a Central Bank

1. See Nicolas Jabko, "The Hidden Face of the Euro," *Journal of European Public Policy* 17/3 (2010), 318–334.
2. Personal interviews; and HADB, B330/18436, July 5, 1989, Betr. Tagung des Gouverneursausschusss am 11. Juli 1989; also BdF, 1489200205/11, n.d. [1992], À l'intention de M. Lagayette: Commentaires sur la lettre de M. Van Wijk à Gunter Baer.
3. Amy Verdun, "The Role of the Delors Committee in the Creation of EMU: An Epistemic Community?" *Journal of European Public Policy* 6 (1999), 308–328; Peter M. Haas, "Introduction: Epistemic Communities and International Policy Coordination," *International Organization* 46/1 (Winter 1992), 19.
4. CoG, November 30, 1989, letter from Pöhl to central bank governors; see also HADB, ZBR 778, July 13, 1989, meeting; CoG, August 29, 1989: Role and Function of the Secretariat of the Committee of Governors.
5. CoG, Meeting 240, December 12, 1989, Basel.
6. HADB, B330/18903, May 11, 1990, Weber: Vermerk.
7. CoG, Banque de France memorandum, December 8, 1989.
8. HADB, ZBR meeting, August 24, 1989.
9. BdF, 1489200205/11, n.d. [1992], À l'intention de M. Lagayette: Commentaires sur la lettre de M. Van Wijk à Gunter Baer (5 February 1992).
10. CoG, Meeting 241, January 9, 1990, Basel.
11. See Colette Mazzucelli, *France and Germany at Maastricht: Politics and Negotiations to Create the European Union* (New York: Garland, 1997), pp. 65–66.
12. James Buchanan and Robert Wagner, *Democracy in Deficit* (Amsterdam: Academic Press, 1977).
13. Especially Finn E. Kydland and Edward C. Prescott, "Rules Rather than Discretion: The Inconsistency of Optimal Plans," *Journal of Political Economy* 85/3 (1977), 473–491; Robert J. Barro and David B. Gordon, "Rules, Discretion and Reputation in a Model of Monetary Policy," *Journal of Monetary Economics* 12 (1983), 101–121.

14. See Alex Cukierman, *Central Bank Strategy, Credibility, and Independence: Theory and Evidence* (Cambridge, Mass.: MIT Press, 1992); also Alex Cukierman, Steven B. Webb, and Bilin Neyapti, "Measuring the Independence of Central Banks and Its Effect on Policy Outcomes," *World Bank Economic Review* 6/3 (1992), 353–398.

15. See Robin Bade and Michael Parkin, "Central Bank Laws and Monetary Policy" (mimeograph, Department of Economics, University of Western Ontario, 1988); Alberto Alesina, "Macroeconomics and Politics," in *NBER Macroeconomics Annual,* ed. Stanley Fischer (Cambridge, Mass.: MIT Press, 1988), pp. 17–52; Alesina, "Politics and Business Cycles in Industrial Democracies," *Economic Policy* 8 (Spring 1989), 58–98; Alesina and Vittorio Grilli, "The European Central Bank: Reshaping Monetary Policy in Europe," in *Establishing a Central Bank: Issues in Europe and Lessons from the United States,* ed. Matthew Canzoneri, Vittorio Grilli, and Paul Masson (Cambridge: Cambridge University Press and CEPR, 1992), pp. 49–77; Vittorio Grilli, Donato Masciandaro, and Guido Tabellini, "Political and Monetary Institutions and Public Finance Policies in the Industrial Countries," *Economic Policy* 13 (October 1991), 341–376; Edmond Malinvaud, "Comment," *Economic Policy* 13 (October 1991), 376–379; Sylvester Eijffinger and Eric Schaling, "Central Bank Independence in Twelve Industrial Countries," *Banca Nazionale del Lavoro Quarterly Review,* no. 184 (March 1993), 49–89; Sylvester C. W. Eijffinger and Jakob de Haan, *The Political Economy of Central-Bank Independence,* Princeton Studies in International Economics 19 (Princeton: International Economics Section, Department of Economics, Princeton University, 1996).

16. Carlo Ciampi, letters, *Financial Times,* March 13, 1992.

17. Adam Posen, "Central Bank Independence and Disinflationary Credibility: A Missing Link?" *Oxford Economic Papers* 50 (1998), 335–359.

18. Manfred J. M. Neumann, "Precommitment by Central Bank Independence," *Open Economies Review* 2 (1991), 103.

19. John Williamson, "What Washington Means by Policy Reform," in *Latin American Readjustment: How Much Has Happened,* ed. Williamson (Washington, D.C.: Institute for International Economics, 1989).

20. Eijffinger and Schaling, "Central Bank Independence."

21. See EC Commission, February 5, 1990, The European Central Bank: National Systems Compared and Possible Options.

22. HADB, N2/269, December 1, 1978, Emminger to Schmidt, with verbal protocol of central bank council meeting, November 30, 1978.

23. Guido Tabellini, "Monetary and Fiscal Policy Coordination with a High Public Debt," in *High Public Debt: The Italian Experience* (Cambridge:

Cambridge University Press, 1988), pp. 90–126; Leila Talani, *Betting for and against EMU: Who Wins and Who Loses in Italy and in the UK from the Process of European Monetary Integration* (Aldershot: Ashgate, 2000), p. 43; Lucia Quaglia, *Central Banking Governance in the European Union: A Comparative Analysis* (Abingdon: Routledge, 2008), p. 77.

24. Robert Elgie and Helen Thompson, *The Politics of Central Banks* (London: Routledge, 1998), p. 120.

25. Yves Mamou, *Une machine de pouvoir: La direction du Trésor* (Paris: La Découverte, 1987), p. 123.

26. Elgie and Thompson, *Politics of Central Banks,* pp. 121–122.

27. Ibid., p. 124. André Szász, *The Road to Monetary Union* (Basingstoke: Macmillan, 1999), p. 149; *Le Nouvel Économiste,* August 5, 1988, p. 50.

28. See Kenneth Dyson and Kevin Featherstone, *The Road to Maastricht: Negotiating Economic and Monetary Union* (New York: Oxford University Press, 1999), pp. 186–187; and above all David Marsh, *The Euro: The Politics of the New Global Currency* (New Haven: Yale University Press, 2009).

29. Christian Noyer, "À propos du statut et de l'indépendance des banques centrales," *Revue d'économie financière* 22 (September 1992), 13–18; David Howarth, *The French Road to Monetary Union* (London: Palgrave, 2001), p. 131.

30. Nigel Lawson, *The View from No. 11: Memoirs of a Tory Radical* (London: Bantam, 1992), pp. 867–868, 1059–61; also Elgie and Thompson, *Politics of Central Banks,* p. 69.

31. CoG, alternates discussion, January 8, 1990.

32. Interview with Helmut Schlesinger.

33. HADB, B330/24112, Bericht über die Sitzung des Währungsausschusses, 22. February 1990.

34. BoE, 8A/225/2, April 24, 1990, Monetary Committee meeting.

35. BoE, 8A/225/1, October 21, 1989, Monetary Committee bureau.

36. CoG, March 26, 1990, Monetary Committee: Economic and Monetary Union beyond Stage 1: Orientations for the preparation of the intergovernmental conference.

37. CoG, EC Commission, March 23, 1990, Economic and Monetary Union.

38. CoG, Report by Chairman to Informal ECOFIN, March 26, 1990.

39. BoE, 8A/225/3, February 6, 1991, J. A. A. Arrowsmith, Future Role and Composition of Monetary Committee.

40. See also Carel C. A. van den Berg, *The Making of the Statute of the European System of Central Banks: An Application of Checks and Balances* (Amsterdam: Dutch University Press, 2004), p. 6.

41. CoG, Meeting 245, May 15, 1990, Basel.

42. Ben S. Bernanke et al., *Inflation Targeting: Lessons from the International Experience* (Princeton: Princeton University Press, 1999).
43. CoG, Meeting 245, May 15, 1990, Basel.
44. Ibid.
45. BoE, 4A39/11 EEC, June 18, 1990, note.
46. CoG, September 18, 1990, Introductory Report to the Draft Statute of the European System of Central Banks. Subsidiarity is the principle that decisions should be made at the lowest level of authority practicable: national rather than European, and provincial/state rather than national.
47. See Appendix B.
48. CoG, Committee of Alternates, July 24, 1990, Draft Statute.
49. CoG, August 31, 1990, Meetings of Legal Experts on certain aspects relating to the draft Statute of the "System."
50. Van den Berg, *Making of the Statute of European System of Central Banks,* p. 104.
51. CoG, Meeting 247, July 10, 1990, Basel.
52. CoG, September 5, 1990, Secretariat Note: Draft Statute.
53. CoG, September 8, 1990, Statement by President Pöhl on the Statute of the System.
54. CoG, September 9, 1990, Stellungnahme zum Draft Statute.
55. CoG, September 8, 1990, Statement by President Pöhl on the Statute of the System.
56. CoG, Committee of Alternates, September 9–10, 1990.
57. CoG, November 27, 1990, commentary.
58. European Council in Rome, October 27–28, 1990, Conclusions of the Presidency, available at http://www.europarl.europa.eu/summits/rome1/default_en.htm (accessed December 1, 2011).
59. Alexander Italiener, "Mastering Maastricht: EMU issues and How They Were Settled," in *Economic and Monetary Union: Implications for National Policy-makers,* ed. Klaus Gretschmann (Dordrecht: M. Nijhoff, 1993), p. 64.
60. European Council in Rome, October 27–28, 1990, Conclusions of the Presidency.
61. HADB, 230/24119, November 16, 1990, memorandum on November 14, 1990, meeting of Monetary Committee.
62. HADB, B330/24119, Pöhl to Delors, December 6, 1990.
63. CoG, Meeting 249, November 13, 1990, Basel.
64. Van den Berg, *Making of Statute of European System of Central Banks,* pp. 190–192.
65. CoG, Meeting 249, November 13, 1990, Basel.
66. CoG, November 21, 1990, Draft Statute Commentary.

67. CoG, Meeting 249, November 13, 1990.

68. "Rome Summit," *Financial Times,* December 17, 1990. See also Daniel Gros and Niels Thygesen, *European Monetary Integration: From the European Monetary System to Economic and Monetary Union* (Harlow, U.K.: Longman, 1998), pp. 407–409.

69. Martin Wolf, "Champions Enter the Lists for EMU," *Financial Times,* December 12, 1990.

70. "The Rome Summit," *Financial Times,* December 17, 1990.

71. BdF, 1489200205/90, December 24, 1990, Banca d'Italia: The Functions of the European Central Bank in the Second Phase of Economic and Monetary Union. See also Dyson and Featherstone, *The Road to Maastricht,* p. 520.

72. CoG, Meeting 251, January 8, 1991, Basel.

73. U.K. Treasury, *Economic and Monetary Union beyond Stage One: Possible Treaty Provisions and a Statute for a European Monetary Fund,* January 8, 1991.

74. BoE, 8A/222/1, July 14, 1989, S. D. H. Sargent, Alternative Models of Economic and Monetary Union; BoE, U.K. Treasury, An Evolutionary Approach to European Monetary Union, 1989; CoG, June 10, 1990, Leigh-Pemberton note.

75. See Rolf H. Hasse and Thomas Koch, "The Hard ECU—A Substitute for the D-Mark or a Trojan Horse?" *Intereconomics* 26/4 (July–August 1991), 159–166.

76. Dyson and Featherstone, *The Road to Maastricht,* pp. 35, 227–228, 678; Jean Quatremer and Thomas Klau, *Ces hommes qui ont fait l'Euro: Querelles et ambitions européennes* (Paris: Plon, 1999), pp. 202–203.

77. Dyson and Featherstone, *The Road to Maastricht,* pp. 411–412.

78. Quatremer and Klau, *Ces hommes qui ont fait l'Euro,* p. 191, quoting François Lamoureux.

79. CoG, Meeting 252, February 12, 1991, Basel.

80. HADB, ZBR meeting 817, February 28, 1991.

81. CoG, Meeting 256, June 10, 1991, Basel, report of Gunter Baer.

82. CoG, UEM 41/91, 43/91, Drafting of articles 109d and 109e; also May 3, 1991, The Presidency's Proposals for Stage Two of EMU.

83. CoG, Economic Unit, June 19, 1991, Monetary Financing of Budget Deficits in Stage Three.

84. See David Marsh, *The Most Powerful Bank: Inside Germany's Bundesbank* (New York: Times Books, 1992), pp. 26–31.

85. CoG, Meeting 259, October 28, 1991, Basel.

86. BoE, 9A/376/2, June 21, 1991, C. B. Briault, Discussions with Dr. Schlesinger, June 20, 1991.

87. See Dyson and Featherstone, *The Road to Maastricht,* p. 395.

88. CoG, Committee of Alternates, July 7–8, 1991.

89. BdF, 1489200205/118, May 6 1993, Services Étrangers to Governor: Les fonctions opérationelles de l'IME et sa mission concernant l'ECU.

90. CoG, Meeting 259, October 28, 1991.

91. See Alasdair Blair, *Dealing with Europe: Britain and the Negotiation of the Maastricht Treaty* (Aldershot: Ashgate, 1999), p. 179.

92. CoG, Meeting 258, September 10, 1991, Basel.

93. Quatremer and Klau, *Ces hommes qui ont fait l'Euro,* p. 193.

94. Blair, *Dealing with Europe,* p. 186.

95. Conference of the Representatives of the Governments of the Member States—Economic and Monetary Union, October 18, 1991, Draft Treaty Text Concerning the Transitional Chapter; Treaty Principles, October 18, 1991; CoG, November 1, 1991, Differences between the President's and the Committee of Governors' Versions of the Statutes of the ESCB and the ECB.

96. CoG, November 21, 1991, Hoffmeyer to Wim Kok (President of the Council of the European Communities).

97. CoG, October 25, 1991, Baer note.

98. Niels Thygesen, "Critical Notes on the Maastricht Treaty Revisions," in *Adjustment and Growth in the European Monetary Union,* ed. Francisco Torres and Francesco Giavazzi (Cambridge: Cambridge University Press, 1993), p. 13.

99. CoG, Fifth meeting of Delors Committee, January 10, 1989, transcript.

100. CoG, July 28, 1989, letter from Hoffmeyer to central bank governors.

101. HADB, B330/18899, Pöhl to Hoffmeyer, August 21, 1989, "Brief ist nicht abgegangen. Herr Pöhl hat den Inhalt Herrn Hoffmeyer in Basel mündlich vorgetragen."

102. HADB, B330/18899, Koch-Reuscher note, October 3, 1989, Betr. Vorschlag Hoffmeyers zur Einführung eines "monetary policy monitoring."

103. HADB, B330/24110, Pöhl to members of CoG, November 30, 1989.

104. CoG, March 26, 1990, Report by Chairman to Informal ECOFIN.

105. "EC Plan Would Link Monetary Targets," *International Herald Tribune,* May 4, 1990.

106. HADB, B330/28901, May 25, 1990, Rieke note, Gemeinsamer Rahmen für eine abgestimmte Preispolitik.

107. CoG, November 30, 1989, Pöhl to central bank governors.

108. HADB, B330/18903, May 11, 1990, Weber/Müller: "Vorsitz und Mandat."

109. CoG, Meeting 252, February 12, 1991.

110. Personal interview.

111. CoG, Meeting 245, May 15, 1990.

112. Ibid.
113. Ibid.
114. CoG, Monetary Policy Subcommittee, August 17, 1990: Special Report on the Operations of a European Central Banking System.
115. CoG, August 14, 1990, Monetary Policy Subcommittee: Comments on Chapter IV of Draft Statute of a European Central Banking system.
116. CoG Secretariat, September 18, 1990, Assessing the Mutual Compatibility of National Monetary Policies.
117. CoG, Meeting 257, July 9, 1991, Basel.
118. CoG, Committee of Alternates, July 2–3, 1991.
119. BoE, 9A/376/2, August 24, 1992, Deutsche Bundesbank: Monetary policy strategies for the European central Bank and their implementation.
120. This is a formulation of Tommaso Padoa-Schioppa. See Padoa-Schioppa, "Monetary Union and Competition: Notes for a Debate," *Politica Economica* 3/90 (1990); and Padoa-Schioppa, *The Euro and Its Central Bank: Getting United after the Union* (Cambridge, Mass.: MIT Press, 2004).
121. CoG, October 1993, Monetary Policy Subcommittee, The Single Monetary Policy of the ECSB: Strategic and Implementation Issues.
122. Ibid.
123. Gros and Thygesen, *European Monetary Integration,* p. 424.
124. CoG, April 11, 1989, meeting of Delors Committee, tape.
125. See Italiener, "Mastering Maastricht," p. 89.
126. Van den Berg, *Making of Statute of European System of Central Banks,* pp. 190–191.
127. CoG Secretariat, February 9, 1990, Note for the Attention of President Pöhl; also HADB, B330/24111.
128. Huib Muller, December 7, 1988: Note for EC-Governors, Prudential Supervision of Banks in the European Community.
129. CoG, Meeting 243, March 13, 1990, Basel.
130. Charles Goodhart, *The Basel Committee on Banking Supervision: A History of the Early Years, 1974–1997* (Cambridge: Cambridge University Press, 2011), p. 551.
131. HADB, B330/018436, January 26, 1989, Wolfgang Kuntze to Pöhl; February 20, 1989, Tietmeyer to Pöhl; February 23, 1989, Pöhl to Kuntze; BdF, 1489200205/118, May 5, 1992, Commission bancaire: Note pour le Gouverneur.
132. HADB, B330/24112, February 22, 1990, Report on Monetary Policy Committee.
133. CoG, Meeting 243, March 13, 1990.
134. CoG, Committee of Alternates, June 29, 1990; See also van den Berg, *Making of Statute of European System of Central Banks,* p. 67.

135. CoG, Committee of Alternates, October 16, 1990.

136. CoG, May 10, 1991, Nonpaper of IGC Presidency.

137. CoG, June 28, 1991, Banco de España, Comparison between the Governors' and the Presidency's Non-Paper. Draft Statutes of the ESCB; July 16, 1991, Explanatory Note.

138. See Goodhart, *Basel Committee*, pp. 392–395.

139. Peter B. Kenen, *Economic and Monetary Union in Europe: Moving beyond Maastricht* (Cambridge: Cambridge University Press, 1995), p. 33.

140. CoG, September 20, 1991, Szász note, "The Position of the Central Banks during Stage Two."

141. CoG, June 30, 1993, Interim Report: Printing and Issuing a European Banknote.

142. CoG, September 1993, Working Group on Statistics: Breakdowns, Frequency and Timeliness of Available Country Data.

143. CoG, June 14, 1993, The Status of Preparatory Work for the Move to Stages Two and Three of EMU.

144. CoG, December 7, 1993, The Status of Preparatory Work for the Move to Stages Two and Three of EMU.

145. Quatremer and Klau, *Ces hommes qui ont fait l'Euro,* p. 33.

146. See Pierre DuBois, "Euro qui comme Ulysse: L'unification monétaire dans l'Europe de 1992 à 1999," *Relations internationales* 100 (1999), 393–407.

147. Tommaso Padoa-Schioppa, *The Road to Monetary Union in Europe: The Emperor, the Kings, and the Genies* (Oxford: Oxford University Press, 2000), p. 186.

148. Bernard Connolly, *The Rotten Heart of Europe: The Dirty War for Europe's Money* (London: Faber and Faber, 1995); p. 277; Martin Feldstein, quoted in "From Bundesbank, a Clue to EC's Future Approach," *New York Times,* September 16, 1992.

9. The EMS Crises

1. CoG, Committee of Alternates, January 13, 1992; CoG, Meeting 262, January 14, 1992, Basel.

2. Lorenzo Bini Smaghi and Stefano Micossi, "Monetary and Exchange Rate Policy in the EMS with Free Capital Mobility," in *The European Monetary System in the 1990s,* ed. Paul de Grauwe and Lucas Papademos (London: Longman, 1990), p. 145.

3. Jeffrey Frankel, Steven Phillipps, and Menzie Chin, "Financial and Currency Integration in the European Monetary System: The Statistical Record," in *Adjustment and Growth in the European Monetary Union,* ed.

Francisco Torres and Francesco Giavazzi (Cambridge: Cambridge University Press, 1993), pp. 270–306.

4. See Guido Tabellini, "European Exchange Rate Credibility before the Fall: Comments," *European Economic Review* 38/6 (June 1994), 1221–23.

5. See Hans-Werner Sinn and Gerlinde Sinn, *Jumpstart: The Economic Unification of Germany,* trans. Juli Irving-Lessmann (Cambridge, Mass.: MIT Press, 1992).

6. Peter B. Kenen, Francesco Papadia, and Fabrizio Saccomanni, "Introduction," in Kenen, Papadia, and Saccomanni, *The International Monetary System* (Cambridge: Cambridge University Press, 1994), pp. 6–7; also Thomas D. Willett, "Some Often Neglected Aspects of the Political Economy of European Monetary Integration," in *The Challenge of European Integration,* ed. Berhanu Abegaz (Boulder: Westview Press, 1994), pp. 205–218.

7. CoG, Fifth meeting of Delors Committee, January 10, 1989, transcript.

8. Peter Norman and Simon Holberton, "Delors Team Opts for Economic Unity," *Financial Times,* December 10, 1988, p. 1; also Helmut Schlesinger, November 11, 1988, speech to Verband öffentlicher Banken, Munich: "Zur weiteren Entwicklung der währungspolitischen Kooperation auf internationaler und europäischer Ebene."

9. CoG, November 7, 1988, JPM (Mingasson), Note pour le président Delors.

10. HADB, Bundesbank ZBR 780, August 24, 1989.

11. HADB, B330/18899, October 20, 1989, EC Monetary Committee.

12. HADB, Bundesbank ZBR 774, May 18, 1989.

13. CoG, Meeting 239, November 14, 1989, Basel.

14. CoG, Meeting 240, December 12, 1989, Basel.

15. C. Randall Henning and Pier Carlo Padoan, *Transatlantic Perspectives on the Euro* (Pittsburgh: European Community Studies Association; Washington, D.C.: Brookings Institution Press, 2000), p. 13.

16. HADB, B330/25115, June 8, 1990, Note.

17. HADB, Bundesbank ZBR 780, August 24, 1989.

18. CoG, Meeting 250, December 11, 1990, Basel.

19. CoG, Meeting 265, April 14, 1992, Basel.

20. Luigi Spaventa, "Quegli straordinaria anni Novanta," in *Il cammino della Lira da Bretton Woods all'Euro,* ed. Andrea Santorelli (Milan: Atic Forex, 2007), p. 84.

21. Margaret Thatcher, *The Downing Street Years* (London: HarperCollins, 1993), p. 690.

22. Robin Leigh-Pemberton, *The Future of Monetary Agreements in Europe,* Special Lecture at the Queen Elizabeth II Conference Center (London: Institute of Economic Affairs, 1989), p. 22.

23. Quoted in Philip Stephens, *Politics and the Pound: The Conservatives' Struggle with Sterling* (London: Macmillan, 1996), p. 178.
24. André Szász, *The Road to European Monetary Union* (New York: St. Martin's Press, 1999), p. 175.
25. Stephens, *Politics and the Pound*, p. 174.
26. Kenneth Dyson and Kevin Featherstone, *The Road to Maastricht: Negotiating Economic and Monetary Union* (New York: Oxford University Press, 1999), p. 555.
27. CoG, October 8, 1990, Monetary Committee Report to Ministers.
28. BoE, 4A/39/11/EEC ERM, December 19, 1990, A. D. Crockett: Short-term Economic Prospects.
29. Stephens, *Politics and the Pound*, p. 168.
30. Quoted in U.K. Treasury, ERM Project Paper, December 21, 1993.
31. John Major, *John Major: The Autobiography* (London: HarperCollins, 1999), p. 314.
32. CoG, Meeting 251, January 8, 1991, Basel.
33. U.K. Treasury, ERM Project Paper, December 21, 1993.
34. CoG Secretariat, December 20, 1990, Policy dilemmas in the exchange rate mechanism in 1991.
35. CoG, EC Council, July 18, 1991. Also A. Szász, note of September 20, 1991.
36. CoG, Committee of Alternates May 13, 1991.
37. CoG, Meeting 253, March 12, 1991, Basel.
38. CoG, Committee of Alternates, May 13, 1991.
39. BdF, 1489200205/115, October 31, 1991, Principaux points discutés lors de la réunion du Sous-Comité de politique monétaire; 1489200205/117, Sous-comité politique de change.
40. CoG, FXP/91/03, December 1991, Annual Review of Developments in the European Monetary System.
41. CoG, Meeting 260, November 12, 1991, Basel.
42. CoG, Meeting 261, December 10, 1991, Basel.
43. CoG, FXP/91/03, December 1991, Annual Review.
44. CoG, Meeting 261, December 10, 1991.
45. CoG, Meeting 262, January 14, 1992, Basel.
46. CoG, Committee of Alternates, January 13, 1992.
47. CoG, Meeting 262, January 14, 1992.
48. CoG, Meeting 263, February 11, 1992, Basel.
49. HADB, B330/25877, January 15, 1992, Tietmeyer to Köhler.
50. CoG, Committee of Alternates, June 15, 1992; see also June 25, 1992: Prior Consultation among EC Central Banks in the Event of a Currency's Entry into the ERM or Its Move to the Narrow Band.

51. See Bernard Connolly, *The Rotten Heart of Europe: The Dirty War for Europe's Money* (London: Faber and Faber, 1995), pp. 126–127; also BoE, 4A/39/11/EEC ERM, April 6, 1992, Crockett: Monetary Committee.
52. See Francesco Giavazzi and Alberto Giovannini, *Limiting Exchange Rate Flexibility: The European Monetary System* (Cambridge, Mass.: MIT press, 1989).
53. See "Krach auf dem Olymp," *Die Zeit,* February 7, 1992.
54. CoG, Meeting 264, March 10, 1992, Basel.
55. CoG, Meeting 265, April 14, 1992, Basel.
56. CoG, Meeting 266, May 12, 1992, Basel.
57. BoE, 9A/351/2, June 16, 1992: Informal Meeting of EC Governors, June 15, 1992.
58. BoE, 9A/351/2, July 15, 1992, A. D. Crockett note of July 14, 1992, breakfast meeting.
59. CoG, Meeting 266, May 12, 1992, Basel.
60. Banca d'Italia, *Economic Bulletin* 15 (October 1992).
61. *Corriere delle Sera,* July 20, 1992; Leila Simona Talani, *Betting for and against EMU: Who Wins and Who Loses in Italy and in the UK from the Process of European Monetary Integration* (Aldershot: Ashgate, 2000), pp. 177–178, 182.
62. CoG, Meeting 268, July 14, 1992, Basel.
63. Ibid.
64. CoG, Meeting 264, March 10, 1992.
65. CoG, Meeting 268, July 14, 1992.
66. Hans Tietmeyer, *Herausforderung Euro: Wie es zum Euro kam und was es für Deutschlands Zukunft bedeutet* (Munich: Hanser, 2005), p. 178.
67. HADB, Bundesbank ZBR 850, July 16, 1992.
68. Tietmeyer, *Herausforderung Euro,* p. 178.
69. *Financial Times,* July 13, 1992.
70. BoE, 9A/376/2, July 14, 1992, FCO to Bonn embassy.
71. Federal Reserve Open Market Committee, October 6, 1992, transcript, available at http://www.federalreserve.gov/monetarypolicy/files/FOMC 19921006meeting.pdf (accessed December 1, 2011).
72. Quoted in U.K. Treasury, ERM Project Paper, December 21, 1993.
73. Tietmeyer, *Herausforderung Euro,* p. 180.
74. Major, *John Major,* p. 324.
75. "What a Week," *The Economist,* August 29, 1992.
76. *Financial Times,* August 25, 1992.
77. BoE, 4A/39/11/EEC ERM, September 4, 1992, informal round table.
78. "Pound Gets Help from Germans," *Independent,* September 6, 1992; "The ERM and Maastricht," *Financial Times,* September 7, 1992.

79. CoG, September 7, 1992, Committee of Alternates draft: Common Position of the Committee of Governors for Oral Presentation to the Press.

80. CoG, Meeting 269, September 8, 1992, Basel.

81. Ibid.

82. IMF, *International Capital Markets I: Exchange Rate Management and International Capital Flows* (Washington, D.C., April 1993), p. 56; Deutsche Bundesbank, "The Impact of External Transactions on Bank Liquidity, the Money Stock and Bank Lending," *Monthly Report,* January 1993.

83. BoE, 9A/376/2, draft letter.

84. William H. Buiter, Giancarlo Corsetti, and Paolo A. Pesenti, *Financial Markets and European Monetary Integration: The Lessons of the 1992–1993 Exchange Rate Mechanism Crisis* (Cambridge: Cambridge University Press, 1998).

85. Major, *John Major,* p. 315.

86. Tietmeyer, *Herausforderung Euro,* p. 184.

87. Szász, *Road to European Monetary Union,* p. 174.

88. Interview with Giuliano Amato, September 9, 1994.

89. U.K. Treasury, ERM Project Paper, December 21, 1993.

90. Quoted in Stephens, *Politics and the Pound,* p. 213.

91. Fabrizio Saccomanni, "1990–1999: Dialogo alla fine del millennium (fra banca central e cambisti)," in Santorelli, *Il cammino della Lira,* p. 117.

92. BoE, 4A/39/11 EEC-ERM, September 30, 1992, letter.

93. CoG, FXP/93/01, March 1993, Recent Developments in the Use of the Private ECU: A Review of the Issues.

94. HADB, B330/32836, November 24, 1992, Kloft memorandum for Tietmeyer.

95. Jacques Delors, *Mémoires* (Paris: Plon, 2004), p. 410; Tietmeyer, *Herausforderung Euro,* pp. 189–191. Marsh gives the most detailed account: David Marsh, *The Euro: The Politics of the New Global Currency* (New Haven: Yale University Press, 2009), pp. 164–168.

96. BdF, 1489200205/117, November 6, 1992: Crise du SME: Réunion du Sous-Comité de politique de change (29–30/10/1992).

97. CoG, October 29/30, 1992, Exchange Rate Sub-Committee.

98. CoG, Committee of Alternates, November 8, 1992.

99. CoG, Meeting 270, November 10, 1992, Basel.

100. Ibid.

101. Ibid.

102. CoG, Meeting 271, December 8, 1992, Basel.

103. Ibid.

104. CoG, Alternates' Report, December 8, 1992, draft.

105. CoG, Central Bank of Ireland, n.d. [January 1993], Views on need to reinforce the institutional and technical aspects of the EMS; BdF, January 27, 1993, La crise du SME et ses implications; National Bank of Belgium, January 26, 1993, Implications and lessons to be drawn from the recent exchange rate crisis: the views of the National Bank of Belgium; Banco de España, January 27, 1993, Note on the review of institutional and technical arrangements in the EMS.

106. Banca d'Italia, November 5, 1992, The functioning of the EMS in the light of the events of September 1992.

107. CoG, Bundesbank, January 30, 1993: Institutional and technical arrangements governing central bank cooperation in the framework of the EMS.

108. CoG, February 23, 1993, Lagayette: Proposition d'amendements au projet de rapport.

109. CoG, February 23, 1993, alternates' draft report.

110. CoG, Crockett to Baer, February 19, 1993.

111. BoE, 9A/351/2, December 1, 1992, Monetary Committee.

112. CoG, Meeting 272, January 12, 1993, Basel.

113. BoE, 9A/376/2, January 14, 1993, cable from Bonn embassy to FCO.

114. CoG, Meeting 272, January 12, 1993.

115. Helmut Stix, "Does Central Bank Intervention Influence the Possibility of a Speculative Attack? Evidence from the EMS," Österreichische Nationalbank Working Paper 80, November 4, 2002.

116. CoG, Meeting 272, January 12, 1993, Basel.

117. Alexander Macleod, "After Currency Swings, Europe Seeks Order," *Christian Science Monitor*, September 30, 1992; "Paris Warns Speculators," *New York Times*, January 5, 1993.

118. BdF, 1489200205/119, March 5, 1993, Sous-comité de politique de change: Enhancing the Two-Way Risk in the ERM.

119. CoG, Meeting 272, January 12, 1993, Basel.

120. Ibid.

121. CoG, Meeting 273, February 9, 1993, Basel.

122. Ibid.

123. Ibid.

124. "Down with the Mark," *The Times*, June 9, 1993.

125. Martin Wolf, "Dethronement of the D-Mark," *Financial Times*, March 27, 1993.

126. Daniel Gros and Niels Thygesen, *European Monetary Integration: From the European Monetary System to Economic and Monetary Union*, 2d ed. (Harlow, U.K.: Longman, 1998), p. 216.

127. CoG, Meeting 274, March 9, 1993, Basel.

128. Ibid.

129. Ibid.

130. "French Elections: Defence of Franc to Dictate Policy," *Financial Times*, March 29, 1993, p. 2.

131. Edouard Balladur, *Dictionnaire de la réforme* (Paris: Fayard, 1992), p. 191.

132. CoG, April 26, 1993, Implications and Lessons to Be Drawn from the Recent Exchange Rate Crisis. See also Peter B. Kenen, *Economic and Monetary Union in Europe: Moving beyond Maastricht* (Cambridge: Cambridge University Press, 1995), p. 163.

133. CoG, Meeting 275, April 20, 1993, Basel.

134. Ibid.

135. Ibid.

136. CoG, April 22, 1993, draft oral report for informal meeting of ECOFIN, May 22–23, 1993.

137. HADB, Bundesbank ZBR 870, May 7, 1993.

138. CoG, Meeting 276, May 11, 1993, Basel.

139. See Deutsche Bundesbank, *Monthly Report*, August 1993, pp. 19–27.

140. "Waigel Cancels French Talks after Paris Urges Rate Cuts," *Financial Times*, June 25, 1993, p. 3.

141. "Shocking Words Upset EC's Oldest Family," *Financial Times*, July 1, 1993, p. 2.

142. "France Lifts Rates to Defend Franc," *Financial Times*, July 24, 1993, p. 2.

143. BoE, 9A/376/4, August 11, 1993: ERM Crisis: Views at the Banque de France.

144. Statistical material from HADB B330/39193.

145. Jean Quatremer and Thomas Klau, *Ces hommes qui ont fait l'Euro: Querelles et ambitions européennes* (Paris: Plon, 1999), pp. 202–203.

146. BoE, 4A/39/11 EEC-ERM, August 3, 1993, Jeremy Heywood to John Trundle.

147. Tietmeyer, *Herausforderung Euro*, p. 211.

148. HADB, B330/32834, December 9, 1993, Neuenkirch: Kursverlust der Bundesbank aus der ECU Position.

149. CoG, Meeting 279, September 14, 1993, Basel.

150. Deutsche Bundesbank, *Monthly Report*, August 1993, p. 27.

151. Helmut Schmidt, "Jean Monnet und das neue Gesicht Europas nach dem Zweiten Weltkrieg," in *Interessen verbinden: Jean Monnet und die europäische Integration der Bundesrepublik Deutschland*, ed. Andreas Wilkens (Bonn: Bouvier, 1999), p. 16.

152. CoG, April 26, 1993, Implications and Lessons to Be Drawn from the Recent Exchange Rate Crisis; Kenen, *Economic and Monetary Union in Europe*, p. 163.

Conclusion

1. Angela Merkel, speech to German Bundestag, May 19, 2010, http://www
   .bundesregierung.de/Content/DE/Regierungserklaerung/2010/2010-05
   -19-merkel-erklaerung-eu-stabilisierungsmassnahmen.html.
2. Alexander Hamilton, "Report on the Public Credit," January 9, 1790,
   available at http://www.gwu.edu/~ffcp/exhibit/p13/p13_3.html (accessed
   December 1, 2011).
3. CoG, Meeting 141, January 8, 1980, Basel.
4. Tommaso Padoa-Schioppa, *The Euro and Its Central Bank: Getting United
   after the Union* (Cambridge, Mass.: MIT Press, 2004), p. 79.
5. See Hans-Peter Scheller, *The European Central Bank—History, Role and
   Functions* (Frankfurt am Main: ECB, 2006); Otmar Issing, *The Birth of the
   Euro,* trans. Nigel Hulbert (Cambridge: Cambridge University Press, 2008).
6. For instance, Adam S. Posen, ed., *The Euro at Five: Ready for a Global
   Role?* (Washington, D.C.: Institute for International Economics, 2005).
7. European Commission, "EMU@10: Successes and Challenges of 10 Years
   of EMU," *European Economy* 2 (2008), 3, available at http://ec/europa.eu/
   economy_finance/publications/publication12682_en.pdf (accessed December 1, 2011). See also Jean Pisani-Ferry, *Coming of Age: Report on the
   Euro Area* (Brussels: Breugel, 2008).
8. London Economics, "Quantification of the Macroeconomic Impact of Integration of EU Financial Markets," Report to the European Commission,
   2002; see also http://www.bis.org/review/r070927b.pdf (accessed December 1, 2011).
9. See for instance Robert W. Fogel, "Capitalism and Democracy in 2040:
   Forecasts and Speculations," NBER Working Paper 13184, 2007.
10. See for instance Tyler Cowen, *The Great Stagnation: How America Ate All
    the Low-Hanging Fruit of Modern History, Got Sick, and Will (Eventually)
    Feel Better* (New York: Dutton, 2011).
11. BBC, "Italy Rows over Rising Euro Prices," January 3, 2002. For an aca-
    demic treatment see Eugenio Gaiotti and Francesco Lippi, "Pricing Be-
    havior and the Introduction of the Euro: Evidence from a Panel of Restau-
    rants," CEPR Discussion Paper No. 4893, February 2005, available at
    http://ssrn.com/abstract=730525.
12. http://www.gesis.org/en/data_service/eurobarometer/standard_eb_trend
    /trend/currency.htm.
13. "French Minister Attacks ECB on Inflation," *Financial Times,* June 10,
    2004.
14. "Sarkozy Warns EU to Revise Fiscal Policy or Lose Popular Support," *Fi-
    nancial Times,* April 3, 2007.

15. "How Europe's Stability Pact Buckled under Slowing Growth and Political Resistance to Budget Discipline," *Financial Times*, September 25, 2002.

16. "Blunt Central Banker Who Likes to Defy Convention," *Financial Times*, February 8, 2002.

17. "Sarkozy Told to Lay Off ECB," *Financial Times*, May 9, 2007.

18. Quoted in David Marsh, *The Euro: The Battle for the New Global Currency* (New Haven: Yale University Press, 2011), p. 231.

19. ECB, *Monthly Bulletin*, May 2008, p. 84.

20. Tommaso Padoa-Schioppa, "Building on the Euro's Success," in Posen, *Euro at Five*, p. 172; "Not a Bang but a Whimper: The Threat Facing the Eurozone," *The Economist*, January 25, 2010.

21. Olivier Blanchard and Jordi Gali, "Real Wage Rigidities and the New Keynesian Model," NBER Working Paper 11806, 2005; Luca Benati, "Investigating Inflation Persistence across Monetary Regimes," *Quarterly Journal of Economics* 123/3 (2008), 1005–60.

22. Claudi Borio and Piti Disyatat, "Global Imbalances and the Financial Crisis: Link or No Link?" BIS Working Paper 346, 2011, available at http://www.bis.org/publ/work346.pdf (accessed January 30, 2012); Hyun Song Shin, "Global Banking Glut and Loan Risk Premium," IMF Mundell-Fleming Lecture, Washington, D.C., November 7, 2011, available at http://www.imf.org/external/np/res/seminars/2011/arc/pdf/hss.pdf (accessed May 18, 2012).

23. Borio and Disyatat, "Global Imbalances," pp. 24–26; Shin, "Global Banking Glut."

24. Alessandro Prati and Garry J. Schinasi, *Financial Stability in European Economic and Monetary Union*, Princeton Studies in International Finance No. 86 (Princeton: International Finance Section, Department of Economics, Princeton University, 1999).

25. Charles Goodhart and D. Schoenmaker, "Burden Sharing in a Banking Crisis in Europe," *Sveriges Riksbank Economic Review* 2 (2006), 34–57.

26. ECB, *Monthly Bulletin*, May 2008, p. 122.

27. Marsh, *The Euro: Battle for the New Global Currency*, p. 253.

28. Michael D. Bordo and Lars Jonung, "The Future of EMU: What Does the History of Monetary Unions Tell Us?" NBER Working Paper 7365, 1999; Lars Jonung and Eoin Drea, "The Euro: It Can't Happen, It's a Bad Idea, It Won't Last: U.S. Economists on the EMU, 1989–2002," European Economy—Economic Papers 395, Directorate General Economic and Monetary Affairs, European Commission, 2009, available at http://ec.europa.eu/economy_finance/publications/publication16345_en.pdf (accessed December 1, 2011).

Acknowledgments

From the beginning to the end of the work on this project, I have been magnificently supported and assisted by the head of information and collaboration at the Bank for International Settlements, Piet Clement. While I was in Basel I had inspiring conversations with Claudio Borio, Stephen Cecchetti, and Philip Turner. Also in the BIS, Maria Friesen worked with enormous determination in piecing together data on interventions and on financing through the European Monetary Cooperation Fund, as well as on the list of dramatis personae. Michela Scatigna and Lillie Lam helped greatly in producing the graphs.

The archives of the Committee of Governors are now located at the European Central Bank in Frankfurt, and are looked after by the expertly managed archive division headed by Emily Witt and Stuart Orr. Matthias Weber and, in particular, Jan Lohman guided me through the documents at the very time that they were being reclassified (and also in part being made publicly available) with consistent goodwill and imagination.

This work would have been impossible without the support of the archivists at the Deutsche Bundesbank, in particular Rolf Herget and Gerd-Christian Wannovius, both of whom are animated by the best spirit of the Bundesbank. I also benefited very substantially from the help of Sarah Millard and Michael Anson at the Bank of England, Fabrice Reuze at the Banque de France, and Alfredo Gigliobianco and the historical section of the Banca d'Italia, as well as Luisa Palla at the European Commission archives in Brussels.

In the course of this project I spoke with a substantial number of participants in and observers of the work of the Committee of Governors, including Bill Allen, Giuliano Amato, John Arrowsmith, Gunter Baer, André Bascoul, Jacques de Larosière, Leonhard Gleske, Alexandre Lamfalussy, Tommaso Padoa-Schioppa, Lionel Price, Fabrizio Saccomanni, Hanspeter Scheller, Helmut Schlesinger, Peter-Wilhelm Schlüter, Hans Tietmeyer, Jean-Claude Trichet, and Klaus Weber. In 2010 a number of the participants convened at a seminar in Basel, where they reflected on their now historical experiences: Gunter Baer, Forrest Capie, Andrew Crockett, Henning Dalgaard, Erik Hoffmeyer, Alexandre Lamfalussy, Robert Raymond,

Jean-Jacques Rey, Fabrizio Saccomanni, Hanspeter Scheller, Helmut Schlesinger, André Szász, and Hans Tietmeyer.

The organizational side of the work was aided by a steering committee of the BIS and the European Central Bank, composed of Yogesh Anand, Piet Clement, Jim Etherington, Alan Mortby, and Philip Turner from the BIS and Gabriel Fagan, Gilles Noblet, Stuart Orr, Roman Schremser, and Michel Stubbe from the ECB. In November 2011 a group of academic commentators—Barry Eichengreen, Marc Flandreau, Jürgen von Hagen, Gert Jan Hogeweg, Hanspeter Scheller, Niels Thygesen, and Gianni Toniolo—provided some very helpful comments and responses to the manuscript. So too did Meg Jacobs of MIT and the Wylie Agency, and my old friend from previous literary ventures, a truly inspiring editor, Michael Aronson of Harvard University Press.

While working on the book I was based in part in Princeton and in part at the European University Institute in Florence. I should like to thank in particular Josepp Borrell, Miguel Maduro, Yves Mény, and Tony Molho for guidance and inspiration, and to record my gratitude to Nicky Koniordos for exceptional administrative assistance and imaginative support. In addition, I attended many illuminating discussions of current central banking issues organized by Governor Marek Belka, Øyvind Eitrheim, David Marsh, Pawel Kowalewski, and Marc Uzan. Emmanuel Mourlon-Druol of the EUI and now at the University of Glasgow shared with me his important work on the origins of the European Monetary System, which is being published in 2012; some of his research is reflected in Chapters 4 and 5.

Finally, I need to thank my children, for putting up with repeated absences to collect historical material, and Marzenna James, who accompanied the manuscript from beginning to end with insight, imagination, and love.

Index

11-12

C61

EMMA S. CLARK MEMORIAL LIBRARY

SETAUKET, NEW YORK 11733

To view your account,

renew or request an item,

visit www.emmaclark.org